AFRO-AMERICAN RELIGIOUS STUDIES:

A Comprehensive Bibliography with
Locations in American Libraries

compiled by

ETHEL L. WILLIAMS
School of Religion Library, Howard University

and

CLIFTON L. BROWN
Department of History, Howard University

The Scarecrow Press, Inc.
Metuchen, N.J.   1972

Preface

This present volume is the outgrowth of the recognition on the part of the compilers, both as librarians and writers in the field, that there is a pressing need for a comprehensive bibliographical guide for sources in the area of African and Afro-American religious studies. Though the present work is comprehensive, we acknowledge that in no way can it be considered definitive. Particularly in the in the areas of Islam and indigenous religions in Africa, denominational records of Black churches, personal papers of Black clergymen and laymen, and denominational publications, much work remains to be done.

The compilers are grateful to all who have assisted in making this volume possible, particularly to Dean Samuel L. Gandy and the officials of Howard University for various forms of assistance provided during the entire project. Gratitude is also extended to Esme Bhan, Linda Bowles, Elizabeth Davis, Harriette Harris, Lawrence Howard Jr., Brenda Johnson, Jacqueline Matthews, Henry Osborne, Macie O. Tillman, and Roland Timity who typed the manuscript and assisted with the research. Grateful acknowledgment is extended to Mr. Reginald Biddle, Assistant Librarian, School of Religion Library, who has been most helpful in the completion of the project.

Ethel L. Williams

Clifton F. Brown

Howard University

Washington, D. C.

January, 1971

iii

Introduction: The Use of the Volume

All entries are listed topically under five general headings. These general headings are divided and sub-divided into particular topics relating to the general area. Individual entries are alphabetically arranged by authors under these particular topics. Therefore, in order for the bibliography to be of maximum benefit, it is suggested that the user first consult the topics as outlined in the Table of Contents. An index is provided, listing authors alphabetically, with entries indicated by topical code numbers.

A service provided for the user (by this bibliography) is that all entries note at least one location from which an item can be obtained (see Key to Location Symbols). Also, in those instances where a title does not suggest the subject of the entry, a brief annotation is included.

At the conclusion of the volume, three appendices are provided. Appendix I lists periodicals and serials which relate in their general scope to African and/or Afro-American religious studies. Appendix II lists relevant manuscript collections. Appendix III lists sources consulted in the compiling of this bibliography.

Key to Location Symbols

A&M	Florida Agricultural & Mechanical University, Tallahassee, Fla.
CLU	University of California, Los Angeles, Calif.
CtY	Yale University, New Haven, Conn.
CtY-D	_____ Divinity School
DAU	American University Library, Wash., D.C.
DAU/W	_____ Wesley Theological Seminary
DCU	Catholic University, Wash., D.C.
DFO	Folger Shakespeare Library, Washington, D.C.
DGU	Georgetown University Library, Wash., D.C.
DGW	George Washington University Library, Wash., D.C.
DHU	Howard University, Wash., D.C.
DHU/L	_____ Law School Library
DHU/MO	_____ Moorland-Spingarn Collection

DHU/R	_____ School of Religion Library
DLC	U. S. Library of Congress, Wash. , D. C.
FSU	Florida State University, Tallahassee, Fla.
GAU	Atlanta University & Interdenominational Theological Seminary, Atlanta, Ga.
GEU-T	Candler School of Theology, Atlanta, Ga.
GU	University of Georgia, Athens, Ga.
ICMcC	McCormick Theological Seminary, Chicago, Ill.
ICRL	Center for Research Libraries, Chicago, Ill.
ICU	University of Chicago, Ill.
IEG	Garrett Theological Seminary, Evanston, Ill.
INRE	Earlham College, Richmond, Ind.
INU	Indiana University, Bloomington, Ind.
KyBB	Berea College, Berea, Ky.
KyLxCB	Lexington Theological Seminary, Lexington, Ky.
KyU	University of Kentucky, Lexington, Ky.
MBU	Boston University, Boston, Mass.
MH	Harvard University, Cambridge, Mass.
NcD	Duke University, Durham, N. C.
NcMjHi	Methodist Historical Society, Lake Junaluska, N. C.
NcSalL	Livingston College, Salisbury, N. C.
NIC	Cornell University, Ithaca, N. Y.
NjMD	Drew University, Madison, N. J.
NjPT	Princeton Theological Seminary, Princeton, N. J.
NN	New York Public Library, New York City
NNC	Columbia University, New York City
NN/Sch	New York Public Library-Schomburg Collection, New York City
NNUT	Union Theological Seminary, New York City
OClWHi	Western Reserve Historical Society, Cleveland, Ohio
OO	Oberlin College, Oberlin, Ohio
OOxM	Miami University, Oxford, Ohio
OrU	Oregon University, Eugene, Oregon
OWibfU	Wilberforce University, Wilberforce, Ohio
OWoC	College of Wooster, Wooster, Ohio
PFL	Friends Library, Philadelphia, Pa.
PHC	Haverford College, Haverford, Pa.
PHi	Historical Society of Pa. ; Philadelphia, Pa.
PLU	Lincoln University, Oxford, Pa.
PPPrHi	Presbyterian Historical Society, Philadelphia, Pa.
PSW	Swarthmore College, Swarthmore, Pa.
RPB	Brown University, Providence, R. I.
RPCJB	John Carter Brown Library, Providence, R. I.
SCBHC	Samuel Colgate Baptist Historical Collection, Colgate Rochester Divinity School, Rochester, New York

v

ScU	University of South Carolina, Columbia, S. C.
TNF	Fisk University, Nashville, Tenn.
TNMph	Methodist Publishing House, Nashville, Tenn.
TxD	Perkins School of Theology, Dallas, Tex
Vi	Virginia State Library, Richmond, Va.

Table of Contents

(Entries Are by Following Classification)

			Page
I.	African Heritage		11-68
	A.	Ancient Egypt	11
	B.	Coptic Church--Ethiopia and Egypt	11-12
	C.	Africa: Indigenous Religions--Islam and Christianity	12-23
	D.	Early Missionary Activities (to 1800)	23
	E.	Christian Chruch and Africa	23-68
		1. Later Missionary Activities (since 1800)	23-59
		a. Ghana (Gold Coast)	23-24
		b. Nigeria	24-26
		c. South Africa	26-31
		d. Kenya	31-32
		e. Sudan	32
		f. Tanzania (Tanganyika)	33
		g. Chad	33
		h. Gabon	33
		i. Dahomey	33-34
		j. Congo--Uganda (Belgian Congo)	34-38
		k. Ethiopia (see also I-B)	38-39
		l. Rhodesia--Northern and Southern, Zambia, Zimbabwe	39-40
		m. Cameroon	40
		n. Sierra Leone	40-41
		o. Liberia	41-43
		p. Guinea	43
		q. Portuguese Africa	43-44
		r. General	44-55
		s. Other areas	55-59
		t. Malawi (Nyasaland)	59
		2. Independent Churches and Movements	59-61
		3. Recent Status	61-68
		a. West Africa	61-62
		b. East Africa	62
		c. South Africa	62-65
		d. Central Africa	65
		e. General	65-68
II.	Christianity and Slavery in the New World		69-166
	A.	Slavery in the West Indies and South America	69-71
	B.	Religious Instruction of the Slaves	71-76
	C.	Slavery and Biblical Interpretation	76-89
	D.	Slavery, Negroes, and the Church	89-148

	1.	General	89-114
	2.	Roman Catholic	114-116
	3.	Congregational (United Church of Christ)	116-121
	4.	Disciples of Christ (Christian Churches)	121
	5.	Friends--Quakers	122-129
	6.	Methodist Episcopal (United Methodist)	129-135
	7.	Presbyterian	135-141
	8.	Protestant Episcopal and Anglican	141-143
	9.	Lutheran	143
	10.	Unitarian Universalist Association	143-146
	11.	Seventh Day Adventist	146
	12.	Baptist	146-148
	13.	Reformed Church	148
	14.	Moravian	148
E.	Slave Revolts	148
F.	Abolition, Abolitionists, and Colonization	149-158
G.	The Freedman--Reconstruction	158-160
H.	Spirituals, Gospel Songs, Music, Poetry	160-166

III. The American Negro and the American Religious Life
     [for contemporary status, see Section V] — 167-320

A. Religious Development of the Negro — 167-265
   1. The Negro Church — 167-201
      a. Denominations
         i.   African Methodist Episcopal — 167-177
         ii.   African Methodist Episcopal Zion — 177-180
         iii. Christian Methodist Episcopal — 180-182
         iv.   National Baptist — 182
         v.   Progressive National Baptist Convention — 182
         vi.   National Baptist Convention, U.S.A. Inc.--Negro Baptist in general — 182-188
         vii. National Baptist Convention of America — 188-190
         viii. General Negro Churches--Negro Church-related Colleges--Methodist Historical Society — 190-198
      b. Storefront Churches and Sects — 198-205
         i.   Churches of God — 198
         ii. Holiness Church — 198
         iii. Daddy Grace--House of Prayer — 198
         iv. Cults and Sects, General — 198-200
         v.   Storefront Churches — 200-201
   2. Negroes--Religion — 201-205
      a. Black Jews — 201
      b. Black Muslims — 201-205
      c. Migrations--Effect on Religion — 205
   3. Evaluation and Aspects of Negro Religion and Church — 205-227
   4. Negro Ministers, Priests, and Laity--Writings — 228-254
   5. Negroes in White Denominations — 255-265
B. Foreign Missions--the Americas (excl. U.S.) — 265-267

C. Church and National Religious Organizations-- Race
    Relations (including home missions)   267-290
    1. Churches
        a. General   267-277
        b. Roman Catholic   271-276
        c. Congregational (United Church of Christ)   276
        d. Disciples of Christ (Christian Churches)   276-277
        e. Friends--Quakers   277
        f. Methodist Episcopal (United Methodist)   277-282
        g. Presbyterian   282-284
        h. Protestant Episcopal   284-286
        i. Lutheran   286
        j. Seventh Day Adventist   286-287
        k. Baptist   287-289
        l. Judaism   289-290
        m. Eastern Orthodox   290-300
    2. Organizations   290-300
        a. General   290-295
        b. Federal Council of Churches   295-296
        c. National Council of Churches of Christ
            in the U.S.A.   296-297
        d. World Council of Churches   297-298
        e. United Nations and Agencies   298
        f. American Missionary Association   298-300
D. Prejudice and Segregation in Religion and Higher
    Education   300-318
E. Bible and Race Relations   318-320

IV. The Civil Rights Movement, c1954-1967   321-359
     A. The Church, Synagogue and Integration   321-345
         1. General   321-330
         2. Roman Catholic   331-335
         3. Congregational (United Church of Christ)   335
         4. Disciples of Christ (Christian Churches)   336
         5. Friends--Quakers   336-337
         6. Methodist Episcopal (United Methodist)   337-340
         7. Presbyterian   341
         8. Protestant Episcopal   342
         9. Lutheran   342
         10. Seventh Day Adventist   342-343
         11. Baptist   343
         12. Judaism   343-344
         13. Church of the Brethren   344
         14. Unitarian Universalist Association   344-345
     B. Southern Christian Leadership Conference and
         Martin Luther King, Jr.   345-354
     C. Social Action--General   354-358
     D. Organizations   358-359

V. The Contemporary Religious Scene   360-392
    A. Church and the Urban Crisis   360-367
    B. Black Separatism   367-382
        1. Black Theology, Black Power, and Black
            Religion   367-377

ix

	2.	Black Caucuses	377-378
	3.	Reparations	378-381
	4.	National Committee of Black Churchmen--	
		Local Groups	381-382
C.		The Jew and the Negro	382-383
D.		General	383-385
E.		Racism and Contemporary Church	386-392

Appendix I   393-400
Appendix II   401-403
Appendix III   404-409

Index   411-454

I. African Heritage

A. ANCIENT EGYPT

Adams, W. Y. "Post Pharaonic
Nubia in the Light of Archae-
ology I, II, III." Journal of
Egyptian Archaeology 50, 51,
52 (1964, 65, 66), pp. 102-
120, 147-62, 160-178.
DCU/SE
Dunham, Dows. The Royal
Cemeteries of Kush. Cam-
Bridge, Mass.: Published for
the Museum, Harvard Univer-
sity of Fine Arts, 1950-58,
vols. I-IV. DLC
Hawks, Francis Lister. The
Monuments of Egypt; or,
Egypt, a Witness for the Bible.
New York: G. P. Putnam,
1854. DHU/MO
Mercer, Samuel Alfred Broune.
The Religion of Ancient Egypt.
London: Luzac & Co., 1949.
DHU/MO
Moret, Alexandre. Kings and
Gods of Egypt. New York:
G. P. Putnam's Sons, 1911.
DHU/MO
Petrie, Sir William Matthew
Flinders. Personal Religion in
Egypt before Christianity. New
York: Harper & Brothers,
1909. NN/Sch
Pirenne, Jacques. La Religion
et la Morale Dans l'Egypte

Antique. Neuchâtel: La Bacon-
nière, 1965. NN/Sch
Price, Ira Maurice. The Monu-
ments and the Old Testament;
Evidence from Ancient Records
... Chicago: The Christian
Culture Press, 1907. Chapter
9, "Israel Under the Glow of
Egypt." DHU/MO
Pritchard, James B. (ed.). An-
cient New Eastern Texts Relat-
ing to the Old Testament.
Princeton, N. J.: Princeton Uni-
versity Press, 1954. DHU/R
Includes practice of religion
in Egypt.
Russell, Michael. ... Nubia and
Abyssinia Comprehending their
Civil History ... Illustrated by
a Map, and Several Engravings.
New York: J. & J. Harper,
1833. DHU/MO
Velde, H. T. Seth, God of Confu-
sion. A Study of His Role in
Egyptian Mythology and Religion.
Leiden: E. J. Brill, 1967.
DHU/R
Yahuda, Abraham S. The Lan-
guage of the Pentateuch in its
Relation to Egypt ... London:
Oxford University Press, 1933.
DHU/MO

B. COPTIC CHURCH--ETHIOPIA AND EGYPT

Amero, Constant. Le Négus
Menelik et L'Abyssinie Nou-
velle ... Paris: J. Lefort,
1897. NN/Sch
Apostolical Constitutions. Ethi-

opic Version. The Ethiopic
Didascalia; or, the Ethiopic Version of the Apostolical Constitutions, Received in the Church
of Abyssinia. With an English

(Apostolical Constitutions, cont.)
Translation. Edited and Trans-
lated by Thomas Pell Platt.
London: Published for the
Oriental Translation Fund of
Great Britain and Ireland by
R. Bently, 1834.   NN/Sch
Arce, Laurent d'. ... L'Abys-
sinie, Étude D'Actualité
(1922-1924). Avignon: Li-
brairie Aubanel Frères, 1925.
                          NN/Sch
Baeteman, Joseph. Etiopia:
Tradusione di Giulio Barsotti.
Parma: Istituto Missioni
Estere, 1935.   NN;NB
Bible N. T. Coptic. London:
British School of Archaeology
in Egypt. n. p., 1924.
                         DHU/MO
-- John. Coptic. ... The Gospel
of St. John According to the
Earliest Coptic Manuscript.
Edited with Translation, by
Sir Herbert Thompson, London:
British School of Archaeology
in Egypt, 1924.   DHU/MO
"The Coptic Church in Egypt."
Christian Union (5:12, Dec.,
1854), pp. 555-59.   DHU/R
Dixon, D. M. "The Origin of the
Kingdom of Kush (Napata-
Meroe)." Journal of Egyp-
tian Archaeology (50; 1964),
pp. 121-32.   DCU/SE
Ethiopian Orthodox Church.
Ebony (15; Aug., 1960), pp.
125+.   DHU/MO
Geddes, Michael. The Church
History of Ethiopia. London:
Printed for R. Chiswell,
1696.   DHU/MO
Hansberry, William Leo.
"Sources for the Study of
Ethiopian History." Howard

University Studies in History. "
no. 11, Nov., 1930.
                         DHU/MO
Isaac, Ephraim. The Ethiopian
Church with a Chapter on the
Traditional Art of Ethiopia
by Marjorie LeMay. Boston:
Henry N. Sawyer Co., 1968.
                         DHU/R
Mett, John Raleigh. Strategic
Points in the World's Con-
quest; the Universities and
Colleges as Related to the
Progress of Christianity.
Chicago: Fleming H. Revell
Company, 1897.   NN/Sch
Moore, Dale H. "Christianity in
Ethiopia." Church History
(5:3, Sept., 1936), pp. 271-
84.   DHU/R
Noshy, Ibrahim. The Coptic
Church. Washington: Ruth
Sloan Associates, 1955.
                         DHU/MO
Quinton, G. G. H. Ethiopia and
the Evangel. London: Mar-
shall, Morgan, and Scott,
1949.   DHU/MO
Rees, A. Herbert. "Ethiopia
and Her Church." East and
West Review (2; 1936), pp.
22-29.   DHU/R
Riley, Willard D. Wisdom in
Ethiopia. New York: Vant-
age Press, 1959.
                         DLC; NN/Sch
Snowden, Frank M. Blacks in
Antiquity. Ethiopians in the
Greco-Roman Experience.
Cambridge, Mass.: The Bel-
knap Press of Harvard Univer-
sity Press, 1970.   DHU/R
Chapter IX, Early Christian
attitude toward Ethiopians:
Creed and conversion.

C. AFRICA: INDIGENOUS RELIGIONS--ISLAM AND CHRISTIANITY

Abdul, M. O. A. "Yoruba Divina-
tion and Islam." Orita, The
African Journal of Religious
Studies. (4:1, Je., 1970), pp.

17-25.   DHU/R
Abrahams, Willie. The Mind of
Africa. Chicago: University
of Chicago Press, 1963. DHU/R

Addison, James T. "Ancestor Worship in Africa." Harvard Theological Review (17:2, 1924), pp. 155-71. DHU/R

Alexandre, Pierre. "A West African Islamic Movement: Hamallism in French West Africa." Robert I. Rotberg and Ali A. Mazrui (eds.). Protest and Power in Black Africa. (New York: Oxford University Press, 1970), pp. 497-512. DHU/R

Allen, Roland. "Islam and Christianity in the Sudan," International Review of Missions. (9; Oct., 1920), pp. 31-48. DHU/R

Anderson, J. N. D. Islamic Law in Africa. London: H. M. S. O., 1954. DHU/MO

Atterbury, Anson Phelps. Islam in Africa. New York: G. P. Putnam's Sons, 1899. DHU/R

Ayandele, E. A. "A Legitimate Branch of the Church Universal-A Review Article." Orita, The African Journal of Religious Studies. (4:1, Je., 1970), pp. 44-61. DHU/R Native Churches in Africa.

Azikiwe, Ben N. "Fragments of Onitsha History." Journal of Negro History (15:4, Oct., 1930), pp. 474-97. DHU

Bacta, C. G. Christianity in Tropical Africa. London: Oxford University Press, 1968. DHU/R

Balandier, George. "Messianism and Nationalism in Black Africa," Pierre L. Van den Berghe, Africa, Social Problems of Change and Conflict. San Francisco: Chandler Pub. Co., 1965. pp. 443-48; 457-58. DLC

Barrett, David B. "Analytical Methods of Studying Religious Expansion in Africa." Journal of Religion in Africa (III:1, 1970), pp. 22-44. DHU/R

Basden, George Thomas. "After

Paganism-What?" East and Review (5:1, Ja., 1939), pp. 22-34. DHU/R

Bender, C. ...Religious and Ethical Beliefs of African Negroes, Duala and Wakweliland. Girard, Kan. : Haldeman-Julius Co., 1925. NN/Sch

Ben-Jochannan, Yosef. African Origins of the Major "Western Religions." New York: Alkebu-Lan Books, 1970. DHU/R African roots of contemporary black religion in America.

Berger, Morroe. Islam in Egypt Today. Social and Political Aspects of Popular Religion. Cambridge: Cambridge University Press, 1970. DHU/R Current religious organization in Egypt.

Bible, N. T. Matthew. Matthew's Gospel Translated into the Grebo Language. West Africa: Cape Palmas, 1836. DHU/MO

Birinda. (Prince). La Bible Secrete Des Noirs Selon Le Bouity, Doctrine Initiatique de l'Afrique Equatoriale. Illustrations par la Comtesse S. de Villermont et R. Kempf d'après l'auteur. Commentaires de Jean-Rene Legrand. Paris: Omnium Litteraire, 1952. DLC

Bleeker, Sonia. The Ibo of Biafra. New York: William Morrow & Co., 1969. DHU Chapter 5, "Religion and the Arts."

Blyden, Edward Wilmot. The Arabic Bible on the Soudan; an Idea for Transliteration. London: C. M. Phillips, 1910. DHU/MO Negro author.

--Christianity, Islam and the Negro Race. Edinburgh: University Press, 1967. DHU/R; FSU Reprint of 1888 ed.

-- Islam in Western Sudan,"

(Blyden, E. W. cont.)
Journal of the African Society.
(2; Oct. , 1902), pp. 11-37.
CtY; DLC; NN
-- "The Koran in Africa."
Journal of the African Society.
(4; Ja. , 1905), pp. 157-77.
CtY; DLC; NN
--"Mohammedanism and the Ne-
gro." Fraser's Magazine (96;
1875), pp. 598+.   DLC;OO
--"Mohammedanism and the Negro
Race." Methodist Quarterly
Review (59:1, Ja. , 1877), pp.
100-127.   DHU/R
Butler, Alfred J. Ancient Cop-
tic Churches of Egypt. Ox-
ford: Clarendon Press, 1970.
DHU/R
Reprint of 1884 edition.
Calloway, Henry. The Religious
System of the Amazulu. Lon-
don: Trubner and Co. , 1868-
70.   NN/Sch; DHU/MO
Charles-Picard, Gilbert. Les
Religions de l'Afrique Antique.
Avec 11 gravures hors texte,
21 gravures et une carte dans
le texte... Paris: Plon, 1954.
NN/Sch
Cobern, Camden McCormick.
The New Archeological Discov-
eries and their Bearing upon
the New Testament and upon
the Life and Times of the
Primitive Church... Introduc-
tion by Edward Naville... New
York and London: Funk &
Wagnalls Co. , 1917. DHU/MO
Cooper, Joseph
Un Continent Perdu, ou l'es-
clavage et la Traite en Af-
rique (1875) Avec Quelques
Observations Sur la Manière
dont ils se Pratiquent en Asie
et Dans d'autres Contrées
Sous le nom de Système Con-
tractuel de la Main-d'oeuvre.
Ouvrage Traduit del'anglais et
Contenant une Pref. de M. Ed.
Laboulaye. Paris: Hachette,
1876.   CtY-D
Courlander, Harold. "Gods of

the Haitian Mountains." Jour-
nal of Negro History (29:3, Jl. ,
1944), pp. 339-72.   DHU
Danquah, Joseph Boakye. The
Akan Doctrine of God. Lon-
don: Lutterworth Press, 1944.
DHU/MO
-- Ancestors, Negroes and God;
the Principles of Akan-Ashanti
Ancestor-Worship. Gold Coast:
George Boakye Pub. Co. ,
1938.   DHU/MO
Deschamps, Hubert Jules. ...Les
Religions de L'Afrique Noire.
Paris: Presses Universi-
taires de France, 1954.
NN/Sch
Dickson Kuvesi and Paul Elling-
worth. Biblical Revelation and
African Beliefs. Maryknoll,
N. Y. : Orbis Books, 1970.
DHU/R
Dobbins, Frank Stockton. Error's
Chains: How Forged and
Broken. A Complete Graphic
and Comparative History of the
Many Strange Beliefs, Supersti-
tious Practices, Domestic Pe-
culiarities, Sacred Writings,
Systems of Philosophy, Legends
and Traditions, Customs and
Habits of Mankind Throughout
the World, Ancient and Modern.
New York: Standard Publishing
House, 1883.   DHU/MO
Driberg, Jack Herbert. "The
Secular Aspect of Ancestor-
Worship in Africa." Journal of
the Royal African Society (35;
Ja. , 1936), p. 21. DHU/MO
Dubois, William Edward B. The
Negro... London: Oxford Uni-
versity Press, 1970. DHU/R
Repr. of 1915 ed. Chapt. IV,
The Niger and Islam. "
Dye, William McEntyre. Moslem
Egypt and Christian Abyssinia.
New York: Atkin & Prout
Printers, 1880.   DHU/MO
Eby, Omar. The Sons of Adam.
Scottsdale, Pa. : Herald Press,
1970.   DHU/R
Brief accounts of Americans

in Africa and their experiences of Muslim-Christian and Afro-American encounters.

Entwistle, Mary. The Call Drum. New York: Friendship Press, 1928.   DHU/MO

Epega, David Onadele. The Mystery of Yoruba Gods. Lagos: The Hope Rising Press, 1931.   MH

Evans, Luther. The Book of Thoth. New York: Comet Press Books, 1960. DHU/MO Egyptian God of time.

Evans-Pritchard, Edward E. Nuer Religion. Oxford: Oxford University Press, 1956.   DHU/R

--Theories of Primitive Religion. Oxford: Clarendon Press, 1965.   DHU/MO

--Witchcraft, Oracles, and Magic Among the Azanale. Oxford: Oxford University Press, 1937.   DHU/R

Farrow, S. S. Faith Fancies and Fetish, or Yoruba Paganism. New York: Macmillan Company, 1926.   DHU/R

Ferguson, John. "Aspects of Early Christianity in North America." L. A. Thompson and J. Ferguson. Africa in Classical Antiquity... Nigeria: Ibadan Univ. Press, 1969.   DHU/R

Fernandez, James W. "The Affirmation of Things Past: Alar Ayong and the Bwiti as Movements of Protest in Central and Northern Giaban." Robert I. Rotberg and Ali A. Mazrui (eds.). Protest and Power in Black Africa (New York: Oxford University Press, 1970), pp. 427-57. DHU/R

--"African Religious Movements, Types and Dynamics." Journal of Modern African Studies (2; 1964), pp. 531+. DHU/MO

--Microcosmogency and Modernization in African Religious

Movements. Quebec: Center for Developing-Asia Studies, McGill University, 1969. DLC

Fitzgerald, M. L. "Crusade and Jihad." Dini Na Mila (5:1, Mr., 1971), pp. 5-8. DHU/R Religious character of Jihad and Crusade.

Fortes, Meyer. Oepidus and Job in West African Religion. New York: Cambridge University Press, 1959. DHU/MO;DHU/R

France, H. "Worship of the Thunder God Among the Awuna." Journal of African Society (8; Oct., 1908), pp. 78-81.
                                      CtY;DLC; NN

Franklin, John Hope. From Slavery to Freedom. New York: Alfred A. Knopf, 1967.
                                      DHU/R
Negro author.
African ideas of religion, pp. 31-34.

Frazer, James George. The Fear of the Dead in Primitive Religion; Lectures Delivered on the William Wyse Foundation at Trinity College, Cambridge. London: Macmillan & Co., 1933-36. DHU/MO

--The Golden Bough. A Study in Magic and Religion. London: Macmillan & Co., 1913-15. 12 vols. DHU/R; DHU

Frease, E. F. "Islam in North Africa." Missionary Review (38; Je., 1915), pp. 408-15.
                                      DHU/R

Gaba, C. R. "The Idea of a Supreme Being Among the Anlo People of Ghana." Journal of Religion in Africa (2:1, 1969), pp. 64-79. DHU/R

Gairdner, G. D. A. "Mohammedanism in South Africa." South African Quarterly (1; Dec., 1914; Feb., 1915), pp. 53+.
                                      IU; NN; NNC

Gairdner, W. H. "Islam in Africa: The Sequel to a Challenge." International Review of Missions. (13; Ja., 1924), pp. 3-

(Gairdner, W. H. cont.)
25.   DAU/W
Gartlan, Jean. "The Christen-
ing of Pagan Customs in
Ghana." Catholic World (190:
1, 136, Nov. , 1959), pp. 101-
106.   DHU/R
Gouilly, Alphonse. L'Islam dans
L'Afrique Occidentale Fran-
çaise. Paris: Larose, 1925.
                       DHU/MO
Graham, Lorenz B. How God
'Fix' Jonah... New York: Rey-
nal & Hitchcock, 1946.
                       DHU/MO
"Stories on Verses from
the Bible ... in the idiom of
the West African native."
Greenberg, Joseph. The Influ-
ence of Islam on a Sudanese
Religion. New York: J. J.
Augustin, 1947.   DHU/MO
Griffith, Francis Llewellyn.
Christian Documents from Nu-
bia. London: H. Milford, 1928.
                       NN/Sch
Hadfield, Percival. Traits of
Divine Kingship in Africa.
London: Watts, 1949.
                       DHU/MO
Haitz, Linn. Juju Gods of West
Africa. Saint Louis: Concord-
ia Pub. House, 1961. DHU/R
Hansberry, William Leo. "Af-
rica and the Western World."
Midwest Journal (7:2, Summer,
1955), pp. 129-55. DHU/MO
"The African and the Chris-
tian West," pp. 147-48.
--"Indigenous African Religions."
In Africa Seen by American
Negroes. Paris: Presence
Africaine, 1958.   DHU/MO
Hartland, F. S. "Problems of
Early Religion in the Light of
African Folklore." Man (1:2,
1901).   CtY;DLC;OO
Hartmann, M. "Islam and Cul-
ture in Africa." Moslem
World (1; 1911), pp. 373-80.
                       DHU/R
Herskovits, Melville J. The Hu-
man Factor in Changing Af-

rica. New York: Alfred A.
Knopf, 1962.   DHU/R
Chapter 13, Religion and
the Arts.
--The Myth of the Negro Past.
Boston: Beacon, 1958.
                       DHU/R; INU
Chapter 7, The Contempo-
rary Scene: Africanisms in
religious life.
-- and Frances S. An Outline
of Dahomean Religious Beliefs.
Menasha, Wisc. : George Banta
Co. , 1933.   DHU/MO
Hetherwick, Alexander. "Islam
and Christianity in Nyasaland."
Moslem World (17; Apr. , 1927),
pp. 184-186.   DHU
Hewson, Leslie A. An Introduc-
tion to South African Method-
ists. Cape Town: Printed by
the Standard Press, 1951?
                       NN/Sch
Hodgson, E. Out of the Darkness;
the Story of an Indigenous
Church in the Belgian Congo.
London: Victory Press, 1946.
                       NN/Sch
Hofmeyr, Jan Hendrik. Christian
Principles and Race Problems.
Johannesburg: S.A. Institute
of Race Relations, 1945.
                       DHU/MO
-- Hoernlé Memorial Lectures
for 1945--1946--1947. Jo-
hannesburg: S. A. Institute of
Race Relations, 1948.
                       NN/Sch
Church and race relations.
Holway, James D. "The Quran
in Swahili," Muslim World
(61:2, Apr. , 1971), pp. 102-
110.   DHU/R
Huddleston, Trevor. "The Christian Churches in Independent
Africa." African Affairs (68:
270, Jan. , 1969), pp. 42-48.
                       DHU/MO
Idowu, E. Bolaji. "The Challenge
of Witchcraft." Orita, The African Journal of Religious
Studies. (4:1, Je. , 1970), pp.
3-16.   DHU/R

--God in Yoruba Belief. London:
Longmans, 1962. DHU/MO
Irstam, Tor. The King of Ganda, Studies in the Institutions
of Sacral Kingship in Africa.
Sweden: Hakan Ohlssons
Boktryskeri, 1944. DHU/MO
International African Seminar.
5th Zaria, Nigeria, 1964. Is-
lam in Tropical Africa; Stud-
ies Presented and Discussed
at the Fifth International Afri-
can Seminar, Ahmadu Bello
University Zaria, January
1964. Edited by I. M. Lewis...
London: Oxford University
Press, 1966. A&M; DHU/MO
Iwarsson, J. "Moslem Mass
Movement Toward Christianity
in Abyssinia." Moslem World
(14; Jl., 1924), pp. 286-9.
DHU
Johnson, William Henry. Afri-
cans and the Church. To the
Afro-American of the United
States this Pamphlet is Af-
fectionately Dedicated by the
Compiler, Dr. William Henry
Johnson, Who is Declining in
His Years Has Found in the
bosom of the Catholic Church
that Peace which Passeth All
Understanding, and Hopes that
Others of His Race will Study
Her Beautiful Doctrines and
Her Claim to Their Spiritual
Allegiance. Albany, N. Y. :
Catholic Chronicle Press, 1916.
NN/Sch
Negro author.
Junod, Henri A. "Moral Sense
Among the Bantu." Interna-
tional Review of Missions (16;
Ja., 1927), pp. 85-90.
DHU/R
Kanyua, Jesse Ndwiga. "The
Traditional Religion of the Em-
bu People." Dini Na Mila (5:
1, Mr., 1971), pp. 1-58.
DHU/R
Describes the religious as-
pects of this tribe of Kenya
before the British came.

Kidder, B. F. "Some Supersti-
tions of North Africa and
Egypt." John Henry Barrows
(ed.). The World's Parliament
of Religions. Vol. II (Chicago:
Parliament Publishing Co.,
1893), p. 1362. DHU/R
Kilson, Marion. "Taxonomy and
Form in Ga Ritual." Journal
of Religion in Africa (III:1,
1970), pp. 45-66. DHU/R
King, Noel Q. The Religions of
Africa. New York: Harper &
Row, 1970. DHU/R
Knappert, Jan. "Swahili Re-
ligious Terms." Journal of
Religion in Africa (III:1, 1970),
pp. 67-80. DHU/R
Kritzeck, James (ed.). Islam in
Africa... New York: Van Nos-
trand-Reinhold Co., 1969.
DHU/R
Laing, George E. F. A King for
Africa. London: United So-
ciety for Christian Literature,
1945. DHU/MO
Negro author.
Includes discussion of Afri-
can religion.
Leeuwen, Arend Theodoor Van.
Christianity in World History.
The Meeting of the Faiths of
East and West. New York:
Charles Scribner's Sons, 1964.
DHU/R
Part V. The Challenge of
Islam.
Levtzion, Nehemia. Muslims and
Chiefs in West Africa. A
Study of Islam in the Middle
Volta Basin in the Pre-Colonial
Period. Oxford: Clarendon
Press, 1968. DLC
Lewis, Archibald R. (ed.). The
Islamic World and the West,
A. D. 622-1492. New York:
John Wiley & Sons, Inc., 1970.
DHU/R
Chapter I, Selections from
the Koran concerning Jesus
and Christianity.
Lewis, I. M. (ed.). Islam in
Tropical Africa. Oxford: Ox-

(Lewis, I. M. cont.)
ford University Press, 1966.
                                    DHU/R
Lienhardt, G. Divinity and Ex-
perience; the Religion of the
Dinka. Oxford: Clarendon
Press, 1961.   DHU/MO
Lighton, George. "The Numeri-
cal Strength of Islam in the
Sudan." Moslem World (26;
1936), pp. 253-73.   DHU/R
Loewen, Jacob A. "The Func-
tion of Myth in Society."
Practical Anthropology (16:4,
Jl.-Ag., 1969), pp. 159-70.
                                    DHU/R
-- "Myth Analysis." Practical
Anthropology (16:4, Jl.-Ag.,
1969), pp. 178-85.   DHU/R
--"Myth and Mission: Should A
Missionary Study Tribal
Myths?" Practical Anthro-
pology (16:4, Jl.-Ag., 1969),
pp. 147-50.   DHU/R
-- "The Structure and Content of
Myths." Practical Anthropol-
ogy (16:4, Jl.-Ag., 1969),
pp. 150-59.   DHU/R
Long, Charles H. "Primitive
Religion." Charles J. Adams
(ed.). A Reader's Guide to
the Great Religions. (New
York: The Free Press, 1965),
pp. 1-30.   DHU/R
    Negro author.
Loram, Charles T. "The Separatist Church Movement."
International Review of Missions (15; 1926), pp. 476-82.
                                    DHU/R
Lucas, J. Olumide. The Religion
of the Yoruba. Lagos, Ni-
geria: C. M. S. Bookshop, 1948.
                                    DHU/MO
    Also: Robert O. Collins
    (ed.). Problems in African
    History (Englewood Cliffs,
    N. J.: Prentice-Hall, 1968),
    pp. 29-35.   DHU/MO
Lugira, A. M. "African Traditional Religion vis-à-vis
Christianity." Dini Na Mila
(4:2, My., 1970), pp. 23-

34.   DHU/R
Macdonald, James. "Manners,
Customs, Superstitions, and
Religions of South African
Tribes." Journal of the Anthropological Institute (19;
pp. 264-96) DLC; CtY; CU
Malcolm, L. W. D. "Islam in
the Cameroons." Journal of
the African Society (21; 1921),
pp. 35-46.   CtY; DLC; NN
Mathews, Basil Joseph. "Islam
and Western Civilization.
The Influence of Western Na-
tions and Western Science,
Commerce and Thought on the
Mohammedan World." Mis-
sionary Review of the World.
(49; Dec., 1926), pp. 937-
44.   DHU/R
Mazrui, Ali A. On Heroes and
Uhuru-Worship Essays on Independent Africa. London:
Longman Group Limited, 1967.
                                    DHU/R
    Chapter 11, Islam, Politi-
cal Leadership and Economic
Radicalism in Africa.
Mbiti, John S. African Religions
& Philosophy. New York:
Frederick A. Praeger, 1969.
                                    DHU/R
    Native Kenyan theologician
surveys the religion of Africa.
--Concepts of God in Africa.
New York: Praeger Publish-
ers, 1970.   DHU/R
McCall, Daniel F. (ed.). West-
ern African Religion. New
York: Frederick A. Praeger,
1969.   DHU
    "Boston University Papers
on Africa, vol. 4." Chapters
on Islam, Christianity and trib-
al religions."
Memoirs of Naimbanna, a Young
African Prince. Philadelphia:
Printed for Thomas Dobson, at
the Stone-House, no. 41,
South Second Street, 1799.
                                    NN/Sch
Mendelsohn, Jack. God Allah
and Ju Ju; Religion in Afri-

ca Today. New York: Thomas Nelson & Sons, 1962. DHU/R

Migeod, Frederick William Hugh. "The Basis of African Religion." Journal of the African Society (19; Oct., 1919), pp. 20-34. CtY; NN; DLC

Mileham, Geoffrey S. Churches in Lower Nubia. Philadelphia: The University Museum, 1910. DHU/MO

Miller, Walter Richard Samuel. For Africans Only. London: Lutterworth Press, 1950. NN/Sch

-- "Islam in Africa." International Review of Missions (15; 1926), pp. 556-68. DHU/R

Milligan, Robert H. The Fetish Folk of West Africa. Chicago: Fleming H. Revell Co., 1912. NN/Sch

"Missionaries and Moslems in Africa." Missionary Review of the World (26; Je., 1903), p. 461. DHU/R

Mitchell, Richard P. The Society of the Muslim Brothers. London: Oxford University, 1969. DHU/R
Chapter 9, Discusses the spiritual solution of problems in Egypt.

Mutwa, Credo Vusa'mazula. My People, My Africa. New York: The John Day Co., 1969. DHU/R
Written by a Bantu of South Africa whose thesis is that Christianity will never be completely understood and accepted by the Bantu.

Mveng, Engelbert. L'art d'Afrique Noire; Liturgic Cosmique et Langage Religieux. Tours: Mame, 1964. NcD

Nadel, Siegfried Frederick. A Black Byzantium. London: Oxford University Press, 1942. DHU/MO
Effect of Mohammedanism on Nupe culture in Nigeria.

Nassau, Robert Hamill. Fetichism in West Africa. New York: Charles Scribner's Sons, 1904. DHU/MO

Nelson, J. Robert. "No Myopia in Ethiopia." Christian Century (88:6, Feb. 10, 1971), pp. 180-82. DHU/R

Nina Rodrigues, Raymundo. ...O Animismo Fetichista Dos Negros Bahianos; Prefacio e Notas de Arthur Ramos... Rio de Janeiro, Civilizacao Drasioleira, s.a., 1935. NcD

-- ...Os Africanos no Brasil; Revisão e Prefacio de Homero Pires. Sao Paulo, Companhia editora Nacional, 1932. NcD

Nketia, J. H. Funeral Dirges of the Akan People. Achimota: James Townsend & Sons, 1955. DHU/MO

Northcott, C. "Ecumenical Reaches Africa." Christian Century (75; Dec. 17, 1958), pp. 1454-5. DHU

Northcott, William Cecil. Christianity in Africa. London: Westminster Press, 1963. NN/Sch; DLC; DLC; A&M

Oosthuizen, Gerhardus Cornelis. The Theology of a South African Messiah: An Analysis of the Hymnal of "The Church of the Nazarites." Leiden: E. J. Brill, 1967. DHU/R

Osir, Clerah. "An Analysis of the Religious and Philosophical Contents of the Names of God from the Luo of Kenya." Dini Na Mila (5:1, Mr., 1971), pp. 1-7. DHU/R

Parrinder, Edward Geoffrey. African Traditional Religion. London: Hutchinson's Univ. Library, 1954. DHU/MO

-- West African Religion, Illustrated from the Beliefs and Practices of the Yoruba, Ewe, Akan, and Kindred Peoples. With a Foreword by Edwin Smith. London: Epworth Press, 1949. DHU/R; DHU/MO; OWibfU

Parsons, Robert T. Religion in
an African Society. A study
of the religion of the Kono
People of Sierra Leone in its
social environment, with spe-
cial reference to the function
of religion in that society.
Leiden: E. J. Brill, 1964.
                        NN/Sch
Patton, Cornelius Howard. The
Lure of Africa. New York:
Missionary Education Move-
ment of the United States and
Canada, 1917.   NN/Sch
Mohammedanism in Africa.
Pauw, Berthold B. A. Religion
in a Tswanca Chiefdom. Ox-
ford: Oxford University Press,
1960.   DHU/R
Peel, John D. Y. Aladura: A
Religious Movement Among
the Yoruba. London: Oxford
University Press, 1968.
                        DHU/R
Phillips, J. E. Tracy. "Obser-
vation on Some Aspects of
Religion Among the Azande
'Niam-Niam' of Equatorial
Africa." Journal of the Anthro-
pological Institute (56; 1926),
pp. 178-88.   CtY; DLC
Radin, Paul (ed.). and Elenor
Marvel. African Folktales and
Sculpture. New York: Pan-
theon Books, 1966.   DHU/R
(Bollingen series. vol. 32.)
"Special nature of African folk
literature."
-- ... Primitive Religion: its Na-
ture and Origin. New York:
The Viking Press, 1937.
                        DHU/MO
African tribal religions.
Rattray, Robert Sutherland.
Ashanti. Oxford: Clarendon
Press, 1923.   DHU/R
Traditional religion in
Ghana, by the Antropological
Department in Ashanti, West
Africa.
-- Religion and Art in Ashanti.
Oxford: The Clarendon
Press, 1927.   DHU/MO

Reynolds, Barries. Magic, Divi-
nation and Witchcraft Among
the Barotse of Northern Rhodesia. Berkeley: University
of California Press, 1963.
                        DHU/R
Roome, William John Waterman.
"The Dead Weight of Islam in
Equatorial and Southern Afri-
ca." Moslem World (4; 1914),
pp. 273-91.   DHU
Roscoe, John. The Baganda;
an Account of Their Native
Customs and Beliefs. London:
Macmillan and Co., 1911.
                        DHU/MO
Ross, Brownlee John. "The Re-
ligion of the Bantu, and that of
Early Israel." South African
Outlook. (56; Jl., 1, 1926),
pp. 156-8.   OO; CtY
Rusillon, Henry. "Islam in
Madagascar," Moslem World
(12; 1922), pp. 286-9.   DHU
Shannon, Alexander Harvey.
"Christian Slavery in North
Africa." Methodist Review
(Quarterly) (72:2, Apr., 1923),
pp. 288-96.   DHU/R
Smith, Edwin William. African
Beliefs and Christian Faith.
An introduction to theology for
African students, evangelists
and pastors. London: The
United Society for Christian
Literature, 1937.   DHU/R
-- (ed.). African Ideas of God.
London: Edinburgh House
Press, 1950.   DLC
Sourey, J. Ch. Sorciers Noirs
et Sorcier Blanc: la Magie,
la Sorcellerie et Ses Drames
en Afrique. Bruxelles, Lib.:
Encyclopédique, 1952.
                        DHU/MO
Sowande, Fela. Black Experi-
ence of Religion. Mim.
Speech given at Conference
on Continuities and Disconti-
nuities in Afro-American Societies and Cultures. April 2-
4, 1970. Sponsored by Committee on Afro-American So-

cieties and Cultures. Social
Science Research Council.
Pam. File; DHU/R
Speel, C. J. "The Disappearance
of Christianity from North Af-
rica in the Wake of the Rise
of Islam." Church History (29:
4, Dec. 1960), pp. 379-97.
DHU/R
Stow, N. "The Religious Con-
ceptions of Some Tribes of
Buganda in British Equatorial
Africa." Anthropos (3; 1909),
pp. 213-18.
DCU/AN; CtY; DLC
--"The Religious Conceptions of
the Kanironda." Anthropos (5;
1910), pp. 359-62.
DCU/AN; DLC; CtY
Sundkler, Bengt G. M. Bantu
Prophets in South Africa. Lon-
don: Oxford University Press,
1961. DHU/MO
--The Christian Ministry in Af-
rica. Uppsala: Swedish Insti-
tute of Missionary Research,
1960. OWibfU; DLC
Taylor, John Vernon. Processes
of Growth in an African
Church. London: SCM Press,
1958. OWibfU; DLC
--The Primal Vision. Christian
Presence Amid African Re-
ligion. Philadelphia: Fortress
Press, 1963. DHU/R
Tegnaeus, Harry. Le Héros
Civilisateur; Contribution à
L'Étude Ethnologique de la Re-
ligion et de la Sociologie Afri-
caines. Stockholm, 1950.
DHU/MO
Tempels, Placide. Bantu Phi-
losophy. New York: Univer-
sity Place Book Shop, 1959.
DHU/R
Terry-Thompson, Arthur C.
The History of the African
Orthodox Church. New York:
n. p., 1956. DLC
Thompson, W. "Moslem and
Pagan in Cameroon," Asia
(24; Oct. , 1924), pp. 764-7.
DLC; MH; CtY; DCU

Trimingham, John Spencer. The
Christian Church and Islam in
West-Africa. London: SCMP,
1956. DHU/MO
--Islam in Ethiopia. London:
Frank Cass & Co. , 1965.
DHU/R
Turner, Henry McNeal (bp.).
"The American Negro and His
Fatherland." J. W. E. Bowen
(ed.). Africa and the American
Negro: Address and Proceed-
ings of the Congress on Africa.
(Miami, Fla. : Mnemosyne Pub.
Inc. , 1969), pp. 195-98.
DHU/R
Negro author.
Tyms, James Daniel. "African
Contributions to World Religion."
Roucek, J. S. and Kiernan
(eds.). The Negro Impact on
Western Civilization. (New
York: Philosophical Library,
1970,) pp. 109-37. DHU/R
Negro author.
Ullendorff, Edward. Ethiopia
and the Bible. New York: Ox-
ford University Press, 1968.
DHU/MO
Umunna, V.N. "Nigerian Pagan-
ism as a Preparation for the
Gospel." East and West Re-
view (5:2, Apr. , 1939), pp.
139-45. DHU/R
Usher, Roland G. "Primitive Law
and the Negro." Journal of
Negro History (4:1, Ja. , 1919),
pp. 1-6. DHU
Verger, Pierre. ...Dieux d'Af-
rique; Culte des Orishas et
Vodouns a l'ancienne Cote des
Enslaves en Afrique et à Bahia,
la Baie de Tous les Saints au
Brésil. Paris: P. Hartmann,
1954. NcD
Walker, Andre R. Rites et
Croyances des Peuples du Ga-
bon; Essai sur les Pratiques
Religieuses d'Autrefois et d'-
Aujourd' hui... Paris: Pres-
ence Africaine, 1962. NN/Sch
Warmelo, N. J. Contributions To-
ward Venda History, Religion

(Warmelo, N. J. cont.)
and Tribal Ritual. Pretoria:
The Government Printer,
1932.   DHU/MO
Watson, A. "Islam in Egypt and
Sudan," Missionary Review of
the World. (30; My., 1907),
pp. 351-8.   DHU/R
Webster, Hutton. Primitive Secret Societies. A Study in
Early Politics and Religion.
New York: Macmillan Co.,
1908.   DHU/R
"Development of tribal societies."
Weeks, John H. Among the
Primitive Bakongo. A record
of thirty years' close inter-
course with the Bakongo and
other tribes of equatorial Af-
rica, with a description of
their habits, customs, and re-
ligious beliefs. London:
Seeley, Service and Co., 1914.
                          DHU/MO
Welch, F. G. "Christian Educa-
tion and African Culture."
Learning for Living (10:5,
My., 1971), pp. 19-21.
                          DHU/R
Welch, Galbraith. Africa Before They Came. The Continent North, South, East, and
West, Preceding the Colonial
Powers. New York: William
Morrow & Co., 1965.   DHU
"Islam in Africa" and "Big
God and Little Gods."
Welch, James. Religious Studies
in an African University. Iba-
dan: University Press, 1950.
                          DHU/MO
An inaugural lecture deliv-
ered on the Foundation Day
ceremonies at the Ibadan Uni-
versity College, Nigeria. Lec-
ture covers Islam, West Af-
rican indigenous religion,
Christian theology, and Graeco-
Christian theology.
Welton, Michael R. "Themes in
African Traditional Belief and
Ritual." Practical Anthropol-

ogy (18:1, Ja.-Feb., 1971),
pp. 1-18.   DHU/R
Westermann, Diedrich. The Africa and Christianity. Lon-
don: Oxford University Press,
1937.   DHU/R; NN/Sch; OU;
                    NcD; NjPT
--"Islam in the Eastern Sudan."
International Review of Mis-
sions (2; Mr., 1913), pp.
454-85. (1; Apr., 1912), pp.
618-58.   DAU/W
Williams, Joseph John. Africa's
God... Chestnut Hill, Mass.:
Boston College Press, 1936-
38.   DHU/MO
Williams, W. B. "Fighting the
Devil in Africa." Missionary
Review (39; Ag., 1916), pp.
597-601.   DHU/R
Willoughby, William Charles.
Nature-Worship and Taboo.
Hartford, Conn.: Hartford
Seminary Press, 1932.
                          DHU/R
Willoughby, William Charles.
Race Problems in the New
Africa. A study of the rela-
tion of Bantu and Britons in
those parts of Bantu Africa
which are under British con-
trol. Oxford: Clarendon
Press, 1923.   DHU/MO
Contrast between Muslims
and Christians, pp. 256-9.
--The Soul of the Bantu. Garden
City, N.Y.: Doubleday, Dor-
an & Co., Inc., 1928. DHU/R
Wilson, Monica. Communal Rit-
uals of the Nyakyusa. London:
Oxford Univ. Press, 1959.
                          DHU/R
Tribe in East Africa that
occupies the northern end of
Lake Nyasa.
Wipper, Audrey. "The Gush
Rebels." Robert I. Rotberg
and Ali A. Mazrui (eds.).
Protest and Power in Black
Africa. (New York: Oxford
University Press, 1970), pp.
377-426.   DHU/R
Wordsworth, J. "Islam and

Christianity in Africa." Missionary Review of the World.
(32; Sept. , 1909), pp. 691-5.
                          DHU/R
Zwemer, Samuel Marinus. "Is-

lam at Cape Town." Moslem
World (15; Oct. , 1925), pp.
327-33.   DHU
--"Islam in Africa." Moslem
World (15; Jl. , 1925), pp. 217-
22.   DHU

D. EARLY MISSIONARY ACTIVITIES (TO 1800).

Conference of Missionary Socie-
ties in Great Britain and Ire-
land. Bibliography of African
Christian Literature. Com-
piled by Rev. Canon F. Row-
ling... and Rev. C. E. Wilson
... London: Conference on
Missionary Societies of Great
Britain and Ireland, 1933.
                     CtY-D; DLC
Edwards, Bryan. History of the
British Colonies in the West
Indies. London: Stockdale,
1793-1801. Book 4, Chapters
3, 4 and 5. Religion of the
First Slaves. DHU/MO; NN/Sch
Hair, P. E. H. "Guides to the
Records of Early West Afri-
can Missions." Journal of
Religion in Africa (1:2, 1967),
pp. 129-37.   DHU/R
--"Protestants as Pirates,
Slavers, and Proto-Mission-
aries: Sierra Leone 1568 and
1582." Journal of Ecclesi-
astical History (21:3, Jl. ,
1970), pp. 203-24.   DHU/R

Halsey, Abram W. "Can Africa
be Christianized?" Missionary
Review (33; Je. , 1910), pp.
433-9.   DHU/R
Hilford, M. R. "Solving the African Problem." Missionary Review (39; Je. , 1916), pp. 408-
18.   DHU/R
Laurent de Lucques, Father. Relations sur le Congo du Père
Laurent de Lucques (1700-
1717) Traduits et Annotées
par Mgr. J. Cuvelier.
Bruxelles: n. p. , 1953.
                     NN/Sch
Mackenzie, J. "Spiritual Clinic
in Africa." Missionary Review (41; My. , 1918), pp.339-
42.   DHU/R
St. John, B. "Missionary Occupation of Africa." Missionary
Review (40; Nov. , 1917), pp.
811-14.   DHU/R
Society for Promoting Christian
Knowledge... Publication for
East and Central Africa. London: n. p. , 1928.   NNAB

E. CHRISTIAN CHURCH AND AFRICA

1. Later Missionary Activities (since 1800)

a. Ghana (Gold Coast)
Alleyne, Cameron Chesterfield
(bp.). Gold Coast at a
Glance. New York: The Hunt
Printing Co. , 1931.
          DHU/MO;NN/Sch; DLC
Alston, Leonard. The White
Man's Work in Asia and Afri-
ca. A Discussion of the Main
Difficulties of the Colour Ques-

tion. London: Longmans,
Green and Co. , 1907. DHU/R
    See Chapter II, "Christian
Ethics & Philosophy in Rela-
tion to the Lower Races."
Barnes, Roswell P. "The Ghana
Assembly in the Evolution of
Missions." Religion in Life
(27:1, Spr. , 1958), p. 362.
                    DHU/R

Bartels, Francis Lodowic. The
Roots of Ghana Methodism.
Cambridge: University Press
in Association with Methodist
Book Depot, Ghana, 1965.
                         NN/Sch
Cox, Melville Beveridge. Re-
mains of Melville B. Cox,
Late Missionary to Liberia.
With a memoir. Boston:
Light & Horton, 1835. NN/Sch
Edited by Gershom F. Cox.
Edward, (Brother). "Plenty how-
do" from Africa; Letters and
Stories from the Liberian
Bush. West Park, N.Y.:
Holy Cross Press, 1941.
                         NN/Sch
Ellis, Alfred B. The Tshi-
Speaking People of the Gold
Coast of West Africa. Their
Religion, Manners, Customs,
Laws, Language, etc. Lon-
don: Chapman & Hall, 1894.
                         DHU/MO
Howell, E. Milford. "Nigerian
Baptist Leaders and Their
Contributions." Doctoral dis-
sertation. Southwestern Bap-
tist Theological Seminary,
1956.
Kemp, Dennis. Nine Years at
the Gold Coast. London: Mac-
millan, 1898.   NN/Sch
Mobley, Harris. The Ghanian's
Image of the Missionary.
Leiden: E.J. Brill, 1970.
                         DHU/R
O'Rorke, M. "Religion in the
Gold Coast." Hibbert Journal
(22; Oct., 1924), pp. 773-81.
                         DHU/R
Parsons, Robert T. The
Churches and Ghana Society,
1918-1955. A survey of the
work of the Protestant Mission
Societies and the African
churches which they established
in their assistance to Society
development. Leiden: E.J.
Brill, Inc.,   DHU/MO; NN/Sch
The Churches and Ghana
Society, 1918-1955.

Ramseyer, Friedrich August.
Four Years in Ashantee by
the Missionaries Ramseyer
and Kuhne. Ed. by Mrs.
Weitbrecht; with Introduction
by Rev. Dr. Gundert and
Preface by Prof. Christleib.
New York: R. Carter, Brothers, 1875.
                  DHU/MO; NN/Sch
Reyburn, William D. "Polygamy, Economy and Chris-
tianity in the Eastern Camer-
oun." Practical Anthropology
(6:1, Ja.-Feb., 1959), pp.
1-19.   DHU/R
Smith, Noel. The Presbyterian
Church of Ghana, 1835-1960;
A Younger Church in a Chang-
ing Society. London: University of Oxford Press, 1967.
                         DLC
Southon, Arthur Eustace.
Methodist Book Depot; Lon-
don: The Cargate Press,
1934.   NN/Sch
Wiltgen, Ralph M. Gold Coast
Mission History, 1471-1880.
Techny, Ill.: Divine Word
Publications, 1956.
                  DHU/MO; NN/Sch

b. Nigeria
Ajayi, J. Christian Missions in
Nigeria, 1841-1891; the Mak-
of a New Elite. Evanston,
Ill.: Northwestern Univ.
Press, 1965.
                  DHU/MO;NN/Sch
Anderson, Susan. "So This is
Africa" (to the Missionary
Minded). Nashville, Tenn.:
Broadman Press, 1943.
                  DHU/MO; NN/Sch
Andre, Marie. Les Martyrs
Noirs de L'Ouganda. Paris:
Bloudeet Gay, 1936. NN/Sch
Ayandele, E.A. The Missionary
Impact on Modern Nigeria
1842-1914. London: Long-
mans, 1966.   DHU/MO
Barber, Mary Ann Serrett.

Oshielle: or, Village Life in the Yoruba Country; from the Journals and Letters of a Catechist There, Describing the Rise of a Christian Church in an African Village. London: J. Nisbet and Co., 1857. NN/Sch

Basden, George Thomas. Edith Warner of the Niger; the Story of Thirty-three Years of Zealous and Courageous Work Amongst Ibo Girls and Women. London: Seeley, 1927. NN/Sch

Broadbent, T. David S. The World Before Them; Stories of Northern Nigeria. London: Edinburgh House, 1949. NN/Sch

Bulifant, Josephine Christiana. Forty Years in the African Bush. Grand Rapids, Mich.: Zondervan, 1950. NN/Sch

Christian Council of Nigeria. Building for Tomorrow; a Pictorial History of the Protestant Church in Nigeria. Lagos: Christian Council of Nigeria, 1960. DHU/MO

Church Missionary Society. Nigeria the Unknown: a Missionary Study Text-Book on Nigeria... London: 1921. NN/Sch

Cooksey, Joseph James. Religion and Civilization in West Africa. London: World Dominion Press, 1931. DHU/MO;NN/Sch

--A Serious Aspect of the Abyssinian Situation... London: New Midway Press, 1935. NN/Sch

Delano, Isaac O. The Singing Minister of Nigeria; the Life of the Rev. Canon J. J. Ransome-Kuti. London: United Society for Christian Literature, 1942. NN/Sch Negro author.

Dodds, Fred W. (ed.). Nigerian Studies, by Nigerian Missionaries. London: Holborn Press, 1920? NN/Sch

Green, Charles Sylvester. New Nigeria; Southern Baptists at Work in Africa. Richmond, Va.: Foreign Mission Board, Southern Baptist Convention, 1936. NN/Sch

Helser, Albert David. In Sunny Nigeria, Experiences Among a Primitive People in the Interior of North Central Africa; Introduction by Otho Winger... New York: F. H. Revell, 1926. NN/Sch

Jordan, John P. Bishop Shanahan of Southern Nigeria; With an Introduction by His Grace, Most Rev. David Mathew, and a Note by His Excellency Rt. Rev. Charles Heerey. Dublin: Clonmore & Reynolds, 1949. NN/Sch

Livingstone, William Pringle. Dr. Hitchcock of Uburu: an Episode in Pioneer Medical Missionary Service in Nigeria. Edinburgh: Foreign Mission Committee of the United Free Church of Scotland, 1920. NN/Sch

Maddry, Charles E. Day Dawn in Yoruba Land. Nashville: Broadman Press, 1939. NN/Sch

M'Keown, Robert L. Twenty-five Years in Qua Iboe; the Story of a Missionary Effort. London: Morgan & Scott, 1912. NN/Sch

Miller, Walter Richard Samuel. Reflections of a Pioneer. London: Church Missionary Society, 1936. NN/Sch

Nadel, Siegfried Frederick. Nupe Religion. London: Routledge & Paul, 1954. DHU/MO

Nau, Henry. We Move Into Africa; the Story of the Planting of the Lutheran Church in Southeastern Nigeria. St. Louis, Mo.: Concordia Pub. House, 1945. NN/Sch

Okon, Gabriel. "The Role of the
Catholic Mission in the Devel-
oping of Education in Eastern
Nigeria, 1902-1960." Mas-
ters thesis, Howard Univer-
sity, 1968.
Page, Jesse. The Black Bishop,
Samuel Adjai Crowther. Lon-
don: Simpkin, Marshall, Ham-
ilton, Kent & Co., 1910.
                    DHU/MO; NN/Sch
--Samuel Crowther, the Slave
Boy Who Became Bishop of
the Niger. London: S.W.
Partridge & Co., 1889.
                            NN/Sch
Parrinder, Edward Geoffrey.
Religion in an African City.
London: Oxford University
Press, 1953.
    Missions - Nigeria, pp. 86-
106.
Percy, Douglas Cecil. Doctor
to Africa; the Story of Stir-
rett of the Sudan. New York:
Sudan Interior Mission, 1948.
                            NN/Sch
Sadler, George W. A Century
in Nigeria. Nashville:
Broadman Press, 1950.
                            NN/Sch
Schauffler, A. F. "White 'Ma'
of Calabar; a Review of the
Life of Mary Slessor, of Cal-
abar." Missionary Review
(39; Oct., 1916), pp. 767-72.
                            DHU/R
Shaw, Trever. Through Ebony
Eyes; Evangelism Through
Journalism in West Africa.
London: United Society for
Christian Literature, Lutter-
worth Press, 1956. NN/Sch
Tucker, Sarah. Abbeokuta; or,
Sunrise Within the Tropics:
an Outline of the Origin and
Progress of the Yoruba Mis-
sion. New York: R. Carter
& Brothers, 1854.
              NN/Sch; CtY-D
Uchendu, Victor C. "Missionary
Problems in Nigerian Society."
Practical Anthropology (11:3,

My.-Je., 1964), pp. 105-17.
                            DHU/R
Veenstra, Johanna. Black Dia-
monds. Grand Rapids, Mich.:
Meyer-Book Co., 1929.
                            NN/Sch
Waddell, Hope Masterton.
Twenty-Nine Years in the
West Indies and Central Africa:
A Review of Missionary Work
and Adventure, 1829-1858.
New York: T. Nelson and
Sons, 1863.   NN/Sch
Walker, Frank Deaville. A
Hundred Years in Nigeria, the
Story of the Methodist Mission
in the Western Nigeria Dis-
trict, 1842-1942. London:
The Cargate Press, 1942.
                            NN/Sch
--The Romance of the Black
River; the Story of the C.M.S.
Nigeria Mission. London:
Church Missionary Society,
1938.   NN/Sch
Ward, William J. ...In and
Around the Oron Country; or,
The Story of Primitive Meth-
odism in S. Nigeria. By
Rev. W. J. Ward. London:
W. A. Hammond, 190-?
                            NN/Sch
Webster, James Bertin. The
African Churches Among the
Yoruba, 1888-1922. Oxford:
Clarendon Press, 1964.
              DHU/R; DHU/MO
Weeks, Annie Florence. Build-
ers of a New Africa, a Com-
pilation. Nashville, Tenn.:
Broadman Press, 1944.
                            NN/Sch
Young-O'Brien, Albert Hayward.
...She had a Magic; the Story
of Mary Slessor. London:
J. Cape, 1958.   NN/Sch
    Author's pseud., Brian
O'Brien, at head of title.

c. South Africa
"Archbishop Approves Apartheid."
Christian Century (81; Mar.

11, 1964), p. 325. DHU/R
Badertscher, Jean. La Ségré-
gation Raciale en Afrique du
Sud. Lausanne: Editions du
Soc, 1962. DLC
Bedwell H. Kenneth. Black
Gold; the Story of the Inter-
national Holiness Mission in
South Africa which United
with the Church of the Naza-
rene, Nov. 29, 1952. Acorn-
hoek, Transvaai, Union of
South Africa. Kansas City,
Mo.: Beacon Hill Press,
1953. NN/Sch
Benham, Marian S. Henry
Callaway, M.D., D.D. First
Bishop for Kaffraria, his life
History and Work. London:
Macmillan, 1896. NN/Sch
"Boers and Christianity in South
Africa." Missionary Review
of the World (23; Je., 1900),
pp. 462-7. DHU/R
Bokwe, John Knox. Ntsikana.
Lovedale, So. Africa: Printed
at the Mission Press, 1914.
DHU/MO
Bridgman, Frederick B. "The
Ethiopian Movements in South
Africa." Missionary Review of
the World (27; Oct., 1904),
pp. 434-45. DHU/R
British Council of Churches. In-
ternational Dept. The Future
of South Africa. A study by
British Christians. Pub-
lished for the British Council
of Churches. London: SCM
Press, 1965. DLC
Brown, William Eric. The Cath-
olic Church in South Africa:
From its Origins to the Pres-
ent Day. Edited by Michael
Derrick. New York: P. J.
Kenedy, 1960. NN/Sch
Brownlee, Margaret. The Lives
and Work of South African
Missionaries. Cape Town:
University of Cape Town,
School of Librarianship, 1952.
DHU/MO
Butterfield, Kenyon Leech.

...Report of Dr. Kenyon L.
Butterfield on Rural Conditions
and Sociological Problems in
South Africa. New York:
n.p., 1929. NN/Sch
Callaway Godfrey. Mxamli, the
Feaster; a Pondomisi Tale of
the Diocese of St. John's, So.
Africa. New York: Macmillan
Co., 1919. NN/Sch
--The Pilgrim Path; a Story of
an African Childhood; with an
introduction by the Rt. Rev.,
the Lord Bishop of St. John's.
London: Society for the Propa-
gation of the Gospel in Foreign
Parts, 1933. NN/Sch
--The Soul of An African Padre.
...With a preface by the Most
Rev. W. M. Carter... Mil-
waukee: Morehouse Pub. Co.,
1932. NN/Sch
Campbell, Belle McPherson.
Madagascar. Chicago: Wom-
an's Presbyterian Board of
Missions of the Northwest,
1889. NN/Sch
Campbell, John. Africaner; or,
Missionary Trials. Philadel-
phia: Presbyterian Board of
Publication, 1840. NN/Sch
--The Life of Africaner: a
Namacqua chief of South Af-
rica. Prepared for publica-
tion by the editors. New
York: G. Lane & P. P. Sand-
ford for the Sunday School
Union of the Methodist Episco-
pal Church, 1841. NN/Sch
--Travels in South Africa, Under-
taken at the Request of the
London Missionary Society;
being a Narrative of a Second
Journey in the Interior of that
Country. London: F. West-
ley, 1822. NN/Sch
Carstens, Kenneth. "The
Churches on Trial." George
M. Daniels. Southern Africa:
A Time for Change. (New
York: Friendship Press, 1969),
pp. 71-5. DHU

"Catalogue of South African Missions." Missionary Review of the World (23; Apr., 1900), p. 318.   DHU/R
Chalmers, John A. Tiyo Soga; a Page of South African Mission Work. Edinburgh: Andrew Elliott, 1877. NN/Sch
Chamberlin, David. Moffat of Kuruman. London: Sheldon Press, 1931.   NN/Sch
Chapman, Louise Robinson. Africa, O Africa. Kansas City: Beacon Hill Press, 1945.   DHU/MO
    The author tells of her twenty years as a missionary under the Church of the Nazarene in Swaziland, southern Africa.
The Christian Handbook of South Africa. Die Suid-Afrikaanse Kristen-Handboek... Lovedale, So. Africa. Published by the Lovedale Press on behalf of the Christian Council of South Africa, 1938.
                             NN/Sch
Christianity and the Natives of South Africa. A Year-book of South African Missions. v. 1, 1929.   NN/Sch
    Published under the auspices of the General Missionary Conference of South Africa. Lovedale, C. P. South Africa. Printed by the Lovedale Institution Press. Rev. J. Dexter Taylor.
Christofersen, Arthur Fridjof. Adventuring With God: The Story of the American Board Mission in South Africa. Durban: Inanda Seminary, 1967.
                                 DLC
Coan, Josephus R. "The Expansion of the Mission of the African Methodist Episcopal Church in South Africa." Doctoral dissertation, Hartford Seminary Foundation, 1961.
             CtY-D (Film)
Coppin, Levi Jenkins (bp.).

Letters from South Africa. Philadelphia: A. M. E. Book Concern, 1902.   NN/Sch
    Negro author.
--Observations of Persons and Things in South Africa, 1900-1904. n. p., 1905.
             NN/Sch; NcD
    Part second (210p.) has special t.-p.: Letters from So. Africa, by Bishop L. J. Coppin. Philadelphia.
Cousins, Henry Thomas. From Kafir Kraal to Pulpit; the Story of Tiyo Soga, First Ordained Preacher of the Kafir Race. London: S. W. Partridge, 1899.   NN/Sch
Crowther, E. "Church's Task in South Africa." Christian Century (83:30, Jl. 27, 1966), pp. 933-5.   DHU/R
Cushman, Mary Floyd. Missionary Doctor, the Story of Twenty Years in Africa. New York: Harper & Bros., 1944.
                              NN/Sch
Davies, Horton, (ed.). South African Missions, 1800-1950. An anthology compiled by Horton Davies and R. H. W. Shepherd. London: Nelson, 1954.   DHU/MO; NN/Sch
Dubé, J. L. "Native View of Christianity in South Africa." Missionary Review of the World (24; Je., 1901), pp. 421-6.   DHU/R
DuPlessis, Johannes. The Evangel in South Africa. Cape Town: Cape Times, Ltd., Printers, 1912.   NN/Sch
--A History of Christian Missions in South Africa. New York: Long Green & Co., 1911. DHU/MO; NN/Sch
Du Toit, Stefanus. Die Heilige Skrif en Rasseverhoudinge, met Besondere Toepassing op Suid-Afrikaanse Toestande. Potchefstroom: Pro Reg-Pers, 1959.   DLC
Favre, Edouard. ...Les Vingt-

Cinq Ans de Coillard au Les-
souto. Paris: Société des
Missions Evangéliques, 1931.
NN/Sch
Frame, George. Blood Brother
of the Swazis; the Life Story
of David Hind. Kansas City,
Mo.: Beacon Hill Press,
1952.   NN/Sch
Fuller, J. Latimer. South Afri-
can Native Missions; Some
Considerations. Leed: R.
Jackson, 1907.   NN/Sch
Hance, Gertrude Rachel. The
Zulu Yesterday and Today;
Twenty-Nine Years in South
Africa. New York: Fleming
H. Revell Co., 1916. NN/Sch
Helander, Gunnar. Must We In-
troduce Monogamy? A study
of Polygamy as a mission
problem in South Africa.
Pietermaritzburg: Shuter &
Shooter, 1958.   NN/Sch
Hubbard, Ethel Daniels. The
Moffats. New York: Mis-
sionary Education Movement of
the United States and Canada,
1917.   NN/Sch
Humphreys, Nicholas. Mission-
ary in South Africa. With a
Foreword by the Rt. Rev.
Bishop Count David O'Leary.
London: Blackfriars Publica-
tions, 1953.   NN/Sch
Hutchinson, Bertram. "Some
Social Consequences of Mis-
sionary Activity Among South
African Bantu." Practical
Anthropology (6:2, Mr.-Apr.,
1959), pp. 67-76.   DHU/R
"Is Prayer Enough? Apartheid in
South Africa." Newsweek (55;
Apr. 25, 1960), p. 100. DHU
Jalla, Adolphe. Pionniers Parmi
les Ma-Rotse, par le Mission-
naire Adolphe Jalla. Avec de
Nombreuses Gravures.
Florence: Imprimerie Claudi-
enne, 1903.   NN/Sch
Kicherer, Johannes Jacobus. An
Extract from the Rev. Mr.
Kicherer's Narrative of his

Mission in South Africa; To-
gether With a Sketch of the
Public Conference with the
Hottentots in London, Nov. 21,
1803. Wiscasset: Printed by
Babson & Rust, 1805. NN/Sch
--"The Rev. Mr. Kicherer's
Narrative of his Mission to
the Hottentots." (In London
Missionary Society. Transac-
tions of the Missionary Society
...London, 1804, v. 2, no. 1,
p. 1-48. illus., ports.)
NN/Sch
Jones, (Mrs.) David Benjamin.
David Jones, Ambassador to
the Africans. Kansas City,
Mo.: Beacon Hill Press,
1955.   NN/Sch
A Life's Labours in South Africa;
The story of the Life-Work of
Robert Moffat, Apostle to the
Bechuana Tribes... London:
J. Snow, 1871.   NN/Sch
Livingstone, David. Missionary
Travels and Researches in
South Africa. New York:
Longmans, Green & Co., 1917.
DHU/MO; NN/Sch
MacKenzie, William Douglas.
John MacKenzie, South Afri-
can Missionary and Statesman.
London: Hodder & Stoughton,
1902.   NN/Sch
Mackintosh, Catharine Winkworth.
Coillard of Zambesi; the Lives
of François and Christina
Coillard, of the Paris Mission-
ary Society, in South and Cen-
tral Africa (1858-1904). New
York: American Tract Society,
1907.   NN/Sch
Main, John K. Africa Looks
Ahead. New Advance in Af-
rica. London: Livingstone
Press, 1947.   NN/Sch
Mears, William. The Church
and the Bantu. Cape Town:
Methodist Book Depot and Pub.
House, 1933.   NN/Sch
Moffat, Robert. Missionary
Labours and Scenes in South
Africa... New York and Pitts-

(Moffat, Robert cont.)
burgh: Robert Carter, 1845.
DHU/MO; NN/Sch
Olinton, Desmond Kenilworth.
The South African Melting
Pot: A Vindication of Missionary Policy 1799-1836.
London: Longman-Green,
1937.   NN/Sch
Orchard, Ronald Kenneth. To-
morrow's Men in Africa.
London: Livingstone Press,
1948.   NN/Sch
Paton, David MacDonald, (ed.).
Church and Race in South Af-
rica. Papers from South Af-
rica, 1952-57, illustrating the
Churches' search for the Will
of God. London: SCM Press,
1958. DHU/MO; NN/Sch
Pederson, Pernie C. Mission
in South Africa; Studies in
the Beginning and Development
of the Indigenous Lutheran
Church in the Union of South
Africa. Minneapolis, Minn. :
Augsburg Pub. House, 1957.
NN/Sch
"Political Strangulation for South
African Churches?" Chris-
tian Century (71:45, Nov. 10,
1954), pp. 1355+.   DHU
Puaux, Frank. Les Bassoutos;
une mission Française au
Sud l'Afrique. Paris: Li-
brairie G. Fischbacher, 1881.
NN/Sch
"Racial Good Will Wins a Round
in South Africa." Christian
Century (83; Nov. 16, 1966),
p. 1401.   DHU
Ross, Brownlee John. Brown-
lee J. Ross, His Ancestry and
Some Writings. Lovedale:
C. P. , So. Africa, Lovedale
Press, 1948.   NN/Sch
Sales, Richard, (ed.). Christo-
fersen, Arthur Fridjof, Ad-
venturing With God: The Story
of the American Board Mis-
sion in South Africa. Durban:
Inanda Seminary, 1967.   DLC
Scenes and Services in South

Africa. The story of Robert
Moffat's half-century of Mis-
sionary Labours... London:
J. Snow, 1876.   NN/Sch
Scott, Anna M. Day Dawn in
Africa; or, Progress of the
Protestant Episcopal Mission
at Cape Palmas, West Africa.
New York: Prot. Episc. Soc.
for the Promotion of Evangel-
ical Knowledge, 1858.
DHU/MO; NN/Sch
Shaw, William. The Story of
My Mission Among Native
Tribes of South Africa. Lon-
don: Wesleyan Mission House,
1872.   NN/Sch
Shepherd, Robert Henry Wishart.
Bantu Literature and Life.
South Africa: Lovedale Press,
1955.   NN/Sch
--Where Aloes Flames; South
African Missionary Vignettes.
London: Lutterworth Press,
1948.   NN/Sch
Smit, M. T. R. African Great-
heart; the Story of Cornelius
Sejosing. London: Lutter-
worth Press, 1945.   NN/Sch
Smith, Edwin William. The
Blessed Missionaries, Being
the Phelps-Stokes Lectures
Delivered in Cape Town in
1949. Cape Town: Oxford
University Press, 1950.
NN/Sch
--The Life and Times of Daniel
Lindley (1808-80). Missionary
to the Zulus. New York:
Literary Publishers, 1952.
NN/Sch; DHU/MO
--The Religion of Lower Races,
as Illustrated by the African
Bantu. New York: Macmillan
Co. , 1923.   NN/Sch
Smith, J. Allister. A Zulu
Apostle, Joel Mbambo Matun-
fwa. London: Salvationist
Pub. and Supplies, 1953.
NN/Sch
Snell, C. D. "Missions and Prob-
lems in South Africa." Church
Missionary Review (63; Jl. ,

1912), pp. 420-26.   DHU/R
South African Churches Asked to
Consultation.   Interchurch
News (1; Jl., 1960), p. 1.
                                    DLC
Student Christian Association.
Christian Students and Modern
South Africa.   A Report of
the Bantu-European Student
Christian Conference.   Fort
Hare, June 27-July 3, 1930.
Fort Hare: Alice C. P. 1930.
                                  DHU/MO
Taylor, William (bp.).   Christian
Adventures in South Africa...
New York: Nelson & Phil-
lips, 1877.   NN/Sch
"Voice of the Shepherds; Pro-
testing of Apartheid Measures
in South Africa."   America
(101; My., 30, 1959), p. 384.
                                    DHU
White, Amos Jerome.   Dawn in
Bantuland; an African Experi-
ment; or, An Account of Mis-
sionary Experiences and Ob-
servations in South Africa.
Boston: Christopher Pub.
House, 1953.
    Negro author.
Whyte, Quintin.   Behind the Ra-
cial Tensions in South Africa.
Johannesburg: South African
Institute of Race Relations,
1953.   NN/Sch
Wilder, George Albert.   The
White African; the Story of
Mafavuke "Who Dies and Lives
Again."   Told by himself, at
the request of his relatives
and friends...   Bloomfield,
N. J.:   Morse Press, 1933.
                                  NN/Sch
World Council of Churches.   Re-
port on the World Council of
Churches' Mission in South Af-
rica, April-December 1960.
Prepared by the WCC Delega-
tion to the Fry, Chairman and
others.   Geneva: n. p., 1961.
                                 NcD; DLC
Wright, Charlotte.   Beneath the
Southern Cross; the Story of

an American Bishop's Wife in
South Africa.   New York:
Exposition Press, 1955.
    OWibfU; DHU/MO; NN/Sch;
                    DLC; TNF; CtY-D

d. Kenya
Bewes, Thomas Francis Cecil.
Kikuyu Conflict.   Mau Mau
and the Christian Witness.
London: Highway Press, 1954.
                                  NN/Sch
Blakeslee, Helen Virginia.   Be-
yond the Kikuyu Curtain.   Chi-
cago: Moody Press, 1958.
                                  NN/Sch
Carey, Walter.   Crisis in Kenya.
London: A. R.   Mowbray & Co.,
1953.   DHU/MO
Collister, Peter.   Pioneers of
East Africa.   By P. Collister
and E. Vere-Hodge.   Nairobi:
Eagle Press, 1956.
Gogarty, Henry Aloysius, (bp.).
Kilima-njaro; an East-African
Vicariate.   New York: Socie-
ty for the Propagation of the
Faith, 1927.   NN/Sch
Hobley, Charles William.   Bantu
Beliefs and Magic with Par-
ticular Reference to the Ki-
kuya and Kamba Tribes of
Kenya Colony.   London: H. F.
and G. Witherby, 1922.
                                  DHU/MO
    East Africa after the war,
    pp. 286-302.
Ludwig, Charles.   Witch Doc-
tor's Holiday.   Anderson, Ind.:
The Warner Press, 1945.
                                  NN/Sch
Perlo, Filippo.   ...Karoli, il
Costantine Magno del Kenya.
Torino: Instituto Missioni
Consolata.   NN/Sch
Sangree, Walter H.   Age, Prayer
and Politics in Tiriki, Kenya.
Oxford: Oxford University
Press, 1966.   DHU/R
Stowe, David M. "A Marriage in
Nairobi." The New Missionary
Herald, United Church Board

(Stowe, D. M. cont.)
for World Ministries (12:2,
Fall, 1970), pp. 10-11.
Pam File; DHU/R
Welbourn, Frederick Burkewood.
Religion and Politics in Ugan-
da, 1952-1962. Nairobi:
East African Publishing House,
1965.   NN/Sch

e. Sudan
Bingham, Rowland V. Seven
Sevens of Years and a Jubi-
lee. The Story of the Sudan
Interior Mission. New York:
Evangelical Publishers, 1943.
                             NN/Sch
Brownlee, Charles. Reminis-
cences of Kaffir Life and His-
tory, and Other Papers by the
Late Hon. Charles Brownlee;
with a Brief Memoir by Mrs.
Brownlee. Lovedale, So.
Africa: Lovedale Mission
Press, 1896.   NN/Sch
Chapman, William. A Pathfind-
er in South Central Africa.
A story of pioneer missionary
work and adventure. London:
W. A. Hammond, 1910.
                             NN/Sch
Davidson, Hannah Frances.
South and South Central Af-
rica; a Record of Fifteen
Years' Missionary Labors
among Primitive Peoples.
Elgin, Ill. : Printed for the
author by Brethren Pub. House,
1915.   NN/Sch
Geyer, Franz Xaver, (bp.).
Durch Sand, Sumpf und Wald;
Missionsreisen in Zentral-Af-
rika; mit 395 Bildern und 9
Karten. Neue Ausgabe. Frei-
burg im Breisgau: Herdersch
Verlagshandlung, 1914.
                             NN/Sch
Giffen, John Kelly. The Egyp-
tian Sudan. New York: F. H.
Revell, 1905.   NN/Sch
Gowan, Richard. "The Religious
Imperative: Gordon in the

Sudan." Perspective (11; Wint.,
1970), pp. 319-32.   DHU/R
Gwynne, L. H. "Missionary Work
in the Sudan," Church Missionary Review of the World
(72; Sept., 1926), pp. 245-
50.   DHU/R
Hinderer, Anna (Martin). Seven-
teen Years in the Yoruba
Country. Memorials of Anna
Hinderer, gathered from her
journals and letters; with an
introduction by Richard B.
Hone... London: Seeley, Jackson and Halliday, 1872.
                             NN/Sch
Kumm, K. "Sudan an Unevangel-
ized Land." Missionary Review of the World (27; Mr.,
1904), pp. 212-6.   DHU/R
Milligan, Robert H. The Jungle
Folk of Africa... New York:
F. H. Revell Co., 1908.
                             NN/Sch
Moor, Vincent de. La Croisière
Bleue et les Missions d'Af-
rique. Paris: Desclée, De
Brouwer & cie, 1932.
                             NN/Sch
Rothberg, Robert I. Christian
Missionaries and the Creation
of Northern Rhodesia, 1880-
1924. Princeton, N. J.:
Princeton University Press,
1965.   NN/Sch; A&M
"South African Bishops." Com-
monweal (79; Mar. 13, 1964),
pp. 704-5.   DHU
Sudan United Mission. Execu-
tive Committee. Annual Re-
port and Review. 190-
                             NN/Sch
Trimingham, John Spencer. The
Christian Approach to Islam
in the Sudan. London: New
Oxford Univ. Press, 1948.
                             NN/Sch
"Two Views on Race: Archbishop W. P. Whelan and South
African Bishops' Conference."
America (110; Mar. 14, 1964),
p. 328.   DHU

f. Tanzania (Tanganyika)
Briggs, J. In the East African
War Zone. London: Church
Missionary Society, 1918.
NN/Sch
Cole, Henry. Children of the
Dark Continent. Foreword by
the Rev. Canon Copner. Lon-
don: F. Griffiths, 1933. NN/Sch
Hore, Edward Goode. Tanga-
nyika; Eleven Years in Central
Africa. London: Stanford,
1892. NN/Sch
Jacques, Oliver. Africa Called
Us. Washington, D. C.: Re-
view and Herald Pub. Assoc.,
1952. NN/Sch
Kootz-Kretschmer, Elise. Si-
chyajunga; ein Leben Unruhe.
Herrnhut: Missions-Buchhand-
lung, 1938. CtY-D
Rugambwa, Laurian. "Bishop of
Tanganyika: Made a Cardinal
by Pope John XXIII." Negro
History Bulletin (24; Jan.,
1961), pp. 94-5. DHU/MO
Smith, Herbert Maynard. Frank
Bishop of Zanzibar; the Life
of Frank Weston, D. D., 1871-
1924. London: Society for
Promoting Christian Knowledge. New York: Macmillan,
1926. NN/Sch
Stirling, Leader. Bush Doctor;
Being Letters from Dr.
Leader Stirling, Tanganyika
Territory. Westminster, Lon-
don: Published by Parrett &
Neves for the Universities'
Mission to Central Africa,
1947. NN/Sch
Stuart-Watt, Eva. Africa's Dome
of Mystery. Comprising the
first descriptive history of the
Wachagga people of Kiliman-
jaro, their Evangelization,
and a girl pioneer climb to
the crater of their 19,000 ft.
snow shrine. London: Mar-
shall, Morgan & Scott, 1930.
NN/Sch
White, Paul Hamilton Hume.

...Doctor of Tanganyika. Illustrated by thirty-four original photographs taken by the
author. London: Paternoster
Press, 1952. NN/Sch
-- ...Jungle Doctor's Enemies.
With thirty-two illustrations
by Harry Swain and Boothroyd.
London: Paternoster Press,
1951. NN/Sch

g. Chad
Addison, James Thayer. Fran-
çois Coillard. Hartford,
Conn.: Pub. for the National
Council of the Protestant Epis-
copal Church by Church Mis-
sions Publishing Co., 1929.
NN/Sch
Anderson, August Magnus.
Ukanya; Life Story of an Afri-
can Girl. Anderson, Ind.:
The Warner Press, 1931.
NN/Sch

h. Gabon
Grebert, F. ...Au Gabon (Af-
rique Equatoriale Française).
Paris: Société des Missions
Evangeliques de Paris, 1948.
NN/Sch
Ireland, William B. Historical
Sketch of the Zulu Mission in
South Africa. Boston: Amer-
ican Board of Commissioners
for Foreign Missions, 1864.
NN/Sch; DHU/MO
Myers, John Brown. The Congo
for Christ; the Story of the
Congo Mission. London: S.
W. Partridge, 1911. NN/Sch
Nassau, Robert Hamill. Corisco
Days; the first Thirty Years
of the West Africa Mission.
Philadelphia: Allen, Lane &
Scott, 1910. NN/Sch

i. Dahomy
Endicott, Mary Austin. Spot-
light on Africa. Illustrations

(Endicott, M.A. cont.)
by courtesy of Methodist
Prints--New York, D. G. Ri-
dout--Toronto. Toronto: Com-
mittee on Missionary Educa-
tion, Literature Dept., Wom-
an's Missionary Society,
United Church of Canada,
1945.   NN/Sch
Guilcher, Rene François. ...
Au Dahomey Avec le Père
Dorgère. L'Activité Pacifi-
catrice d'un Missionaire.
Lyon: Procure des Missions
Africaines, 1939.   NN/Sch
Laffitte, J. Le Pays des Negres,
et la Cote des Esclaves, par
M. L'Abbe Laffitte. Tours:
A. Mame, 1878.   NN/Sch
Lawyer, Zelma Wood. I Mar-
ried a Missionary. Abilene,
Tex.: Abilene Christian Col-
lege Press, 1943.   NN/Sch

j. Congo--Uganda (Belgian Congo)
Anet, Henri. Message of the
Congo Jubilee and West Africa
Conference, Leopoldville,
Congo Belge, Africa, Sept. 15,
to 23, 1928. Leopoldville,
Congo Belge: Conseil Protes-
tant du Congo, 1929. NN/Sch
Arnot, Frederick Stanley. Bihé
and Garenganze; or, Four
Years' Further Work and
Travel in Central Africa...
London: J. E. Hawkins, 1893.
                         NN/Sch
--Gareganze; or, Seven Years'
Pioneer Mission Work in Cen-
tral Africa. London: J. E.
Hawkins, 1890.   NN/Sch
--Missionary Travels in Central
Africa. London: A. Holness,
1914.   NN/Sch
Baptist Missionary Society. Rise
and Progress of the Work on
the Congo River. By the
Treasurer. 2d ed. London:
Alexander & Sheppard, 1885.
                            GAU
Bedinger, Robert Dabney. Tri-

umphs of the Gospel in the
Belgian Congo. Richmond:
Presbyterian Committee of
Publication, 1920. DHU/MO
Bell, John. A Miracle of Afri-
can Missions; the Story of Ma-
tula, a Congo Convert. New
York: London: F. H. Revell
Co., 1903.   NN/Sch
Bentley, H. Margo. W. Holman
Bentley... the Life and Labours
of a Congo Pioneer, by his
widow, H. M. Bentley. London:
Religious Tract Society, 1907.
                         NN/Sch
Beslier, Genevieve G. ... L'-
apotre du Congo, Mgr. Aug-
ouard; Avant-Propos de S. G.
Mgr. Le Roy... Paris: Edi-
tions de La Vraie France,
1926.   NN/Sch
Boone, Clinton C. Congo as I
Saw It. New York: Ives,
1927.   NN/Sch
     Negro author.
--Liberia as I Know It. Rich-
mond, Va.: n. p., 1929.
                         NN/Sch
Burton, William F. Congo
Sketches; Illustrated by the
author. London: Victory
Press, 1950.   NN/Sch
--Missionary Pioneering in Con-
go Forests. A narrative of
the labours of William F. P.
Burton and his companions in
the native village of Luba-
Land. Compiled from letters,
diaries and articles by Max
W. Moorhead... Preston,
Eng.: R. Seed & Sons, print-
ers, 1922.   DHU/MO
-- When God Changes a Man. A
true story of this great change
in the life of a slave-raider.
London: Victory Press, 1929.
                         NN/Sch
Buxton, T. F. V. "Uganda: A
Retrospect and an Inquiry."
The East and the West (3; Jl.,
1905), pp. 248-61. DHU/R
     Discussion of Christianity
in Uganda.

Conseil Protestant du Congo. Findings of Conferences Held Under the Leadership of Dr. John R. Mott ... at Leopoldville, Mutoto and Elisabethville, Congo Belge, 1934... Leopoldville-Quest, Congo Belge, Conseil Protestant du Congo. New York: International Missionary Council, 1934.

Constance Marie, Sister. ... Essai d'Adaptation... preface du Reverend Père P. Charles, S. J. Namur, Edition Grands lacs: Anvers, En Vente Chez les Soeurs Missionaries de Notre Dame d'Afrique, 1947.
NN/Sch

Corey, Stephen Jared. Among Central African Tribes: Journal of a Visit to the Congo Mission. Cincinnati: Foreign Christian Missionary Society, 1912.   NN/Sch

Crawford, John R. Protestant Missions in Congo, 1878-1969. Kinshasa, Democratic Republic of Congo: Librairie Evangelique du Congo, n. d.
DHU/R

Cultrera, Samuele. ... Eroismo ed Avventure di Missionari al Congo nel Secolo XVII. Torino: Societa Editrice Internationale, 1926.   NN/Sch

Cuvelier, Jean (bp.). L'ancien Congo d'après les Archives Romaines (1518-1640) par Mgr. J. Cuvelier et L'Abbe L. Jadin... Bruxelles: 1954.
NN/Sch

-- (ed.). Documents sur une Mission Française au Kakongo, 1766-1776. Bruxelles: 1953.   NN/Sch

Davis, William Ellsworth. Ten Years in the Congo. New York: Sheed & Ward, 1951.
NN/Sch
Negro author.

Denis, Leopold. ... Les Jésuites Belges au Kwango, 1893-1943.

Monographie sur la Mission du Kwango, Devenue Actuellement les Vicariats apostoliques du Kwango et de Kisantu. Bruxelles: L'Edition Universelle, 1943.   NN/Sch
(Museum Lessianum. Section missiologique. no. 27.)
NN/Sch

Doering, Alma E. Leopard Spots or God's Masterpiece, Which? ... Attempting the Answer After 18 Years of Missionary Service among Races of Three Colors, White, Black, and Copper. Chicago: Evangel Pub. House, 1916.
NN/Sch

Dieu, Léon. ... Dans la Brousse Congolaise. (Les Origines des Missions de Scheut au Congo), Liège: Maréchial, 1946.   NN/Sch

Dreves, Francis M. The African Chronicles of Brother Giles. London: Sands & Co., 1929.   NN/Sch
Story of the work accomplished in Uganda by the first missionary to set forth from England. cf. Author's note.

Duncan, Sylvia. Bonganga; Experiences of a Missionary Doctor. London: Odhama Press, 1958.   NN/Sch

Dye, Royal J. (Mrs.) Bolenge: A Story of Gospel Triumphs on the Congo. Cincinnati, O. : Foreign Christian Missionary Society, 1909.
DHU/MO; NN/Sch

Ellis, James J. Dan Crawford of Luanza; or, 37 Years' Missionary Work in Darkest Africa. London: Hulbert, 1927.   NN/Sch

L'Eglise au Congo et au Ruanda-Urundi. Bruxelles: Oeuvres Pontificales Missionaries, 1950.   NN/Sch

Fahs, Sophia Blanche. ... Uganda's White Man of Work; a Story of Alexander M.

(Fahs, S. B. cont.)
   Mackay. New York: Young
   People's Missionary Move-
   ment, 1907.   NN/Sch
Frank, Louis. ... Le Congo
   Belge... Bruxelles: La Ren-
   aissance du Livre, 1930.
                      NN/Sch
Fullerton, William Young. The
   Christ of the Congo River.
   London: Carey Press, 1929.
                      NN/Sch
Gale, Hubert P. Uganda and
   the Mill Hill Fathers. Lon-
   don: Macmillan, 1959.
                      NN/Sch
Garlick, Phyllis L. Uganda
   Contrasts. London: Church
   Missionary Society, 1927.
Geronimo da Montesarchio (Fr.)
   ...Jérome de Montesarchió,
   Apotre du Vieux Congo.
   Couverture d'A. de Vinck...
   Namur: Grands Lacs, 1951.
                      NN/Sch
   (Collection Lavigerie.(no.
39))
Graham, Robert Haldane Carson.
   Under Seven Congo Kings, by
   R. H. Carson Graham, for
   thirty-seven years a mission-
   ary in Portuguese Congo.
   London: Carey Press, 1931.
                      NN/Sch
Grubb, Norman Percy. Christ
   in Congo Forests; the Story
   of the Heart of Africa Mis-
   sion. London: Lutterworth
   Press, 1945.   NN/Sch
Guebels, Léon. ... Les Anciens
   Rois de Congo... Namur:
   1948.   NN/Sch
Harford, Charles Forbes. Pilk-
   ington of Uganda. Chicago:
   Fleming H. Revell Co., 1890.
                      NN/Sch
Harrison, Alexina (Mackay).
   A. M. Mackay, Pioneer Mis-
   sionary of the Church Mis-
   sionary Society to Uganda.
   New York: A. C. Armstrong
   and Son, 1890.   DHU/MO
Hattersley, Charles W. The

Baganda at Home: With One
   Hundred Pictures of Life and
   Work in Uganda. London:
   The Religious Tract Society,
   1908.   NN/Sch
Hemmens, Harry Lathey. Congo
   Journey. London: Carey
   Press, 1939.   NN/Sch
Hemptinne, Jean Felix de. La
   Politique des Missions Protes-
   tantes au Congo. Examen du
   Rapport de la Conference Gén-
   érale Tenue a Leopoldville,
   Septembre 1928. Par Men-
   seigneur de de Hemptinne.
   Elisabethville: Editions de
   l'Essor du Congo, 1929.
                      NN/Sch
Hensey, Andrew Fitch. My
   Children of the Forest...
   With an Introduction by Pres-
   ident Charles T. Paul. New
   York: George H. Doran Co.,
   1924.   NN/Sch
Hulme, Kathryn Cavarly. The
   Nun's Story... Boston: Little
   Brown, 1956.   NN/Sch
Industrial, Self-Supporting Mis-
   sionaries. A Practical Scheme
   Inaugurated by the Congo
   Training Institute, Colwyn
   Bay, North Wales. Colwyn
   Bay: Printed by E. R. Jones,
   1892?   NN/Sch
Johnson, T. Broadwood. Tramps
   Round the Mountains of the
   Moon, and the Back Gate of
   the Congo State. Boston:
   D. Estes, 1909.   NN/Sch
Jones, Herbert Gresford.
   Uganda in Transformation,
   1876-1926. London: Church
   Missionary Society, 1926.
                      NN/Sch
Jump, Chester Jackson. Congo
   Diary, by Chester and Mar-
   garet Jump. New York: Amer-
   ican Baptist Foreign Mission
   Society, 1951.   NN/Sch
Kellersberger, Julia Lake (Skinner).
   Congo Crosses; a Study of
   Congo Womanhood. Boston:
   The Central Committee on the

United Study of Foreign Missions, 1936. NN/Sch
--God's Ravens. New York: Fleming H. Revell Co., 1941. NN/Sch
-- A Life for the Congo; the Story of Althea Brown Edmiston. New York: London: Fleming H. Revell Co., 1947. NN/Sch
Kitching, Arthur Leonard. On the Backwaters of the Nile; Studies of Some Child Races of Central Africa. New York: C. Scribner's Sons, 1912. NN/Sch
Kittler, Glenn D. The White Fathers; Introduction by Bishop Laurian Rugambwa. New York: Harper, 1957. NN/Sch
Lerrigo, Peter Hugh James. Omwa? Are You Awake? New York: Fleming H. Revell Co., 1936. NN/Sch
--Rock Breakers; Kingdom Building in Kongo Land. Edited by the Department of Missionary Education, Board of Education of the Northern Baptist Convention... Philadelphia: The Judson Press, 1922. NN/Sch
Lillingston, Kathleen M. E. Glimpses of Uganda. London: Church Missionary Society, 1939. NN/Sch
Lloyd, Albert Bushnell. Apolo the Pathfinder; Who Follows? London: Church Missionary Society, 1934. NN/Sch
--Uganda to Khartoum; Life and Adventure on the Upper Nile. London: T. F. Unwin, 1906. NN/Sch
Lory, Maris Joseph. ... Face à l'Avenir; L'Eglise au Congo Belge et au Ruanda-Urundi. Tournai: Casterman, 1958. NN/Sch
Mabie, Catharine Louise Roe. Congo Cameos. Philadelphia: Judson Press, 1952. NN/Sch

MacDonnell, John de Courey. King Leopold II, His Rule in Belgium and the Congo. New York: Cassell & Co., 1905. NN/Sch
Mackay, Alexander Murdoch. A. M. Mackay, Pioneer Missionary of the Church Missionary Society of Uganda. By his Sister. New York: A. C. Armstrong, 1890. NN/Sch
Nelson, Robert Gilbert. Congo Crisis and Christian Mission. St. Louis, Bethany Press, 1861. NN/Sch
Oldham, Joseph Houldsworth. Florence Allshorn and the Story of St. Julian's. New York: Harper, 1950. NN/Sch
Paul, Austin. Trumpet Notes in Congo; Foreword by Howard W. Ferrin. Brooklyn: Africa Inland Mission, 1949. NN/Sch
Pearce, Gordon James Martin. Congo Background. London: Carey Kingsgate Press, 1954. NN/Sch
Peeters, Paul. Henry Beck de la Compagnie de Jésus, Missionaire au Congo Belges. Lillo: Desolée De Brouwer, 1898. NN/Sch
Pierpont, Ivan de. Au Congo et aux Indes: Les Jesuites Belges aux Missions. Kwango, par Ivan de Pierpong; Ceylan, par Victor Le Cocq; Bengale Occidental. Bruxelles: C. Bulens, 1906. NN/Sch
Purvis, John Bremner. Through Uganda to Mount Elgon. New York: American Tract Society, 1909. NN/Sch
Rombauts, Hugo. ... Les Soirées de Saint-Broussebourg... Namur, Grands Lacs; Scheut-Bruxelles: Editions de Scheut, 1948. NN/Sch
Roome, William John Waterman. Apolo, the Apostle to the Pygmies. London: Marshall, Morgan & Scott, 1935. NN/Sch

(Roome, W. J. W. cont.)
--Through the Lands of Nyanza,
Central Africa. London: Mar-
shall, Morgan & Scott, 1920.
                    NN/Sch
Salotti, Carlo (Cardinal). ... La
Rancon de l'Uganda... Namur:
Grands Lacs, 1939. NN/Sch
Scholler, Clement. Contrasts
... Evolutions... Bruxelles:
C. Bulens, 1941.   NN/Sch
Shepherd, William Henry. Pres-
byterian Pioneers in Congo.
Presbyterian Committee of
Publication, 1917.   NN/Sch
Negro author.
Smith, H. Sutton. "Yakusu" the
Very Heart of Africa, Being
Some Account of the Protes-
tant Mission at Stanley Falls,
Upper Congo. London: Mar-
shall, n. d.   DHU/MO
Springer, John McKendree.
Christian Conquests in the
Congo. New York: Methodist
Book Concern, 1927. NN/Sch
--Pioneering in the Congo. New
York: The Katanga Press,
1916.   NN/Sch
Springes, Helen Emily (Chap-
man).   Camp Fires in the
Congo. Boston: Mass. Cen-
tral Committee on the United
Study of Foreign Missions,
1936.   NN/Sch
Stinetorf, Louise A. Beyond the
Hungry Country. Philadelphia:
Lippincott, 1954.   NN/Sch
-- White Witch Doctor. Phila-
delphia: Westminster Press,
1950.   NN/Sch
Stock, Sarah Geraldina. The
Story of Uganda and the Vic-
toria Nyanza Mission. New
York: Fleming H. Revell,
n. d.   NN/Sch; DHU/R
Streicher, Henri. Les Bienheur-
eux Martyrs de l'Ouganda.
Alger: Maison-Carrée, 1920.
                    NN/Sch
Taylor, John Vernon. The
Growth of the Church in Bu-
ganda. London: SCM Press,

1958. DHU/R; OWilbfU
Thoonen, J.P.   Black Martyrs.
London: Sheed & Ward, 1941.
         DHU/MO; NN/Sch
Tilsley, George Edwin. Dan
Crawford, Missionary and Pio-
neer in Central Africa. New
York: Revell, 1929. NN/Sch
Warburton, Mabel C. "Uganda,
1877-1927, 'Go Forward' The
Jubilee of the Mission."
Church Missionary Review (73:
859, Sept. , 1927), pp. 220-
29.   DHU/R
Weeks, John H. A Congo Path-
finder: W. Holman Bentley
Among African Savages. Lon-
don: Religious Tract Society,
1910.   NN/Sch
Wells, Goldie Ruth. Sila, Son
of Congo. St. Louis, Mo. :
Bethany Press, 1945. NN/Sch
Willis, John Jamieson. An Afri-
can Church in Building. Lon-
don: Church Missionary So-
ciety, 1925.   NN/Sch
Wilson, Christopher James.
Uganda in the Days of Bishop
Tucker. London: Macmillan,
1955.   NN/Sch
Wilson, Jesse R. "They Want
Us Everywhere." Missions:
An International Baptist Maga-
zine (147:1, Ja. , 1949), pp.
21-4.   Pam. File, DHU/R

k. Ethiopia (See also I-B)
Barsotti, Giulio. Etiopia Cris-
tiana; Prefazione di Piero
Bargelini. Milano: Editrice
Ancora, 1939.   NN/Sch
Bergama, Stuart. Rainbow Em-
pire; Ethiopia Stretches Out
Her Hands. Grand Rapids,
Mich. : W. B. Eerdmans Pub.
Co. , 1932.   NN/Sch
Christy, David. Ethiopia: her
Gloom and Glory, as Illustrated
in the History of the Slave
Trade and Slavery, the Rise
of the Republic of Liberia,
and the Progress of African

Missions. With an introd. by W. P. Strickland. New York: Negro Universities Press, 1969. NN/Sch; CtY-D "Originally published in 1857 by Rickey, Mallory & Webb."

Cooksey, Joseph James. A Serious Aspect of the Abyssinian Situation... London: New Mildmay Press, 1935. NN/Sch

Flickinger, Daniel Kumler. Ethiopia: or, Thirty Years of Missionary Life in Western Africa... Dayton: United Brethren Publishing House, 1885. DHU/MO

Gobat, Samuel. Journal of Three Years' Residence in Abyssinia. Proceeded by an Introduction, Geographical and Historical, on Abyssinia. Trans. from the French by Rev. Sereno D. Clark. Accompanied with a Biographical Sketch of Bishop Gobat, by Robert Baird... New York: M. W. Dodd, 1850. NN/Sch

Lamble, Thomas Alexander. Boot and Saddle in Africa. Philadelphia: The Blakiston Co., Distributed by Fleming H. Revell Co., New York and London, 1943. NN/Sch

Lucatello, Enrico. Ventidue Anni in Etiopia: la Missione di Monsignor Giustino de Jacobis. Roma: Annali della Missione, 1936. NN/Sch

Massaia, Guglielmo, (Cardinal). ...I Miei Trentacinque Anni di Missione Nell'alta Etiopia. Memorie Storiche... Roma: Coop. Tipografica Manuzio, 1921-30. NN/Sch

Rice, Esme Ritchie (ed.). Eclipse in Ethiopia and its Corona Glory. Toronto: Evangelical Publishers, 1938. NN/Sch

Salviac, Martial de. ...Un Peuple Antique: ou, Une Colonie Gauloise au Pays de Ménelik Les Galla, Grande Nation Africaine. Cahors F. Plantade, Imprimeur de L'eveche, 1900. NN/Sch

Sottochiesa, Gino. ...La Religione in Etiopia... Torino: Tip. G. Damonte, 1936. NN/Sch

Trimingham, John Spencer. The Christian Church and Missions in Ethiopia (Including Eritrea and the Somaliland.) London: World Dominion Press, 1950. NN/Sch

Waldmeier, Theophilus. The Autobiography of Theophilus Waldmeier, Missionary; Being an Account of Ten Years' Life in Abyssinia; and Sixteen Years in Syria. London: S. W. Partridge & Co., 1886. NN/Sch

l. Rhodesia--Northern and Southern, Zambia, Zimbabwe

Beyond the Waters and that Thunder; A book about Northern Rhodesia. Westminster: Universities Mission to Central Africa, 1930. NN/Sch Written by the Rev. A. S. B. Ranger, the Rev. G. H. Hewitt, the Rev. W. F. P. Ellis and others; edited by the U. M. C. A. Publications Committee.

Butt, G. E. My Travels in North West Rhodesia: or, A Missionary Journey of Sixteen Thousand Miles. London: E. Dalton, 19--. NN/Sch

Mackintosh, Catharine Winkworth. The New Zambesi Trail; A Record of Two Journeys to North-Western Rhodesia (1903 and 1920). London: Marshall, 1922. NN/Sch

Masters, Henry. In Wild Rhodesia. A Story of Missionary: Enterprise and Adventures Where Livingstone Lived,

(Masters, H. cont.)
Laboured and Died.   London:
F. Griffiths, 1920.   NN/Sch
Shaw, Mabel.   God's Candle-
lights; an Educational Venture
in Northern Rhodesia.   Lon-
don: The Livingstone Press,
1936.   DHU/MO; NN/Sch
Smith, Edwin William.   The Way
of the White Fields in Rho-
desia. A Survey of Christian
Enterprise in Northern and
Southern Rhodesia.   London:
World Dominion Press, 1928.
                              NN/Sch
"List of African tribes in
Southern Rhodesia."
Von Hoffman, Carl.   Jungle Gods.
New York: Holt, 1929.
                              NN/Sch
Wallis, John Peter Richard (ed.).
The Matabele Mission, a Se-
lection from the Correspond-
ence of John and Emily Mof-
fat, David Livingstone and
Others, 1858-1878.   London:
Chatto & Windus, 1945.
                              NN/Sch
(Government Archives of
Southern Rhodesia.   Oppen-
heimer Series. No. 2).

m. Cameroon
Beanland, Lillian L.   African
Logs.   Illustrated by Lois Mc-
Neil.   n. p., 1945.   NN/Sch
"Copyright...by the Board
of Foreign Missions of the
Presbyterian Church in the
U. S. A.
Christiansen, Ruth.   ...For the
Heart of Africa. Minneapolis:
Augsburg Pub. House, 1956.
                              NN/Sch
Christol, Frank.   ...Quatre ans
au Cameroun. Paris: Soci-
éte des Missions Evangéliques
de Paris; 1922.   NN/Sch
Dussercle, Roger.   ...Du Kilima-
ndjaro au Cameroun.   Mon-
seigneur F. X. Vogt (1870-
1943). Paris: La Colombe,
1954.

Halsey, Abram W.   "Romance of
Cameroun Mission."   Mis-
sionary Review (40: My., 1917),
pp. 330-8.   DHU/R
Horner, Norman Aste.   "Protestant and Roman Catholic Missions Among the Bantu of
Cameroun: A Comparative
Study." Doctoral dissertation,
Hartford, 1956.
Hitcher, B.   "Basel Mission in
the Southern Cameroons."
Missionary Review (35:My.,
1912), pp. 375-6.   DHU/R
Johnson, Thomas Lewis. Africa
for Christ. Twenty-Eight
Years a Slave. London: Alex-
ander and Shepheard, 1892.
                              NN/Sch
Mackenzie, Jean Kenyon.   Afri-
can Adventurers. West Med-
ford, Mass.: Central Commit-
tee on the United Study of For-
eign Missions, 1917. NN/Sch
--Black Sheep; Adventures in
West Africa.   New York:
Houghton Mifflin Co., 1916.
                              NN/Sch
Skolaster, Hermann.   Die Pallot-
tiner in Kamerun; 25 Jahre
Missions-Arbeit.   Limburg-
Lahn: Kongregation der Pal-
lotiner, 1924.   NN/Sch
Zoa, Jean.   "The African Church
Now." International Documen-
tation on the Contemporary
Church.   North American Edi-
tion. (No. 10: Sept. 26,
1970), pp. 45-9.   DHU/R
Archbishop of Yaounde,
Cameroon, opinions on the fu-
ture of the Catholic Church in
Africa.

n. Sierra Leone
Bacon, Ephraim.   Abstract of
a Journal of Ephraim Bacon,
Assistant Agent of the United
States, to Africa; with an
Appendix, containing extracts
from Proceedings of the
Church Missionary Society
in England, for the Years

1819-20. To which is pre-
fixed an Abstract of the Journal of the Rev. J. B. Cates...
on an Overland Journey, performed in Company with Several Natives, in the months of
February, March, and April,
1819. The Whole Showing the
Successful Exertions of the
British and American Governments in the Repressing the
Slave Trade. Philadelphia: S.
Potter & Co., 1821. NN/Sch

Charlesworth, Maria Louisa,
Africa's Mountain Valley;
or The Church in Regent's
Town, West Africa ...
London: Seeley, Jackson and
Halliday, 1874.   NN/Sch

Harris, J. H. "Dawn in Darkest
Africa." Missionary Review
(37: Sept., 1914), pp. 685-92.
                      DHU/R

Hughson, Shirley Carter. The
Green Wall of Mystery; Ven-
ture and Adventure in the
Hinterland of West Africa.
Holy Cross Press, 1928.
                      NN/Sch

Marais, Barend J. Colour, Un-
solved Problem of the West.
Cape Town: H. S. Timmins,
1962.   NN/Sch

Medbery, Rebecca B. Memoir
of William G. Crocker, Late
Missionary in West Africa
Among the Bassas, Including
a History of the Bassa Mission. Boston: Gould, Ken-
dall, & Lincoln, 1847.
                      NN/Sch

Mills, Job Smith. Mission Work
in Sierra Leone, West Africa.
Dayton, Ohio: United Brethren Pub. House, 1898.
                NN/Sch;DHU/MO

Olson, Gilbert W. Church
Growth in Sierra Leone.
Grand Rapids, Mich.: Wm.
Eerdmans Pub. Co., 1969.
                      DHU/R

Peacock, Amjogollo E. "Missionary Work in Sierra Le-

one." Masters thesis, Howard University, 1940.

Pierson, Arthur Tappan. Seven
Years in Sierra Leone. The
Story of the Work of William
A. B. Johnson, Missionary of
the Church Missionary Society
from 1816-1823 in Regent's
Town, Sierra Leone, Africa.
New York: Fleming H. Re-
vell, 1897.   NN/Sch

"Sierra Leone." Christian Spectator (8:1, Ja., 1826), pp.
48-9.   DHU/R
    Effect of missionary educa-
tion on "liberated Africans."

Thompson, George. Thompson
in Africa: or, An Account of
the Missionary Labors, Sufferings, Travels, and Observations of George Thompson
in Western Africa, at the
Mendi Mission. New York:
Printed for the author, 1852.
            DHU/MO; NN/Sch

Tyng, Stephen Higginson. A
Memoir of the Rev. W. A. B.
Johnson, Missionary of the
Church Missionary Society, in
Regent's Town, Sierra Leone,
Africa. New York: R. Carter
& Bros., 1853.   NN/Sch

o. Liberia

Anderson, Robert Earle. Liberia, America's African
Friend. Chapel Hill: University of North Carolina Press,
1952.   NN/Sch

Bane, Martin J. The Catholic
Story of Liberia. New York:
McMullen, 1950.
            DHU/MO; NN/Sch

Bellamy, V. Nelle. "The Li-
brary and Archives of the
Church Historical Society:
Domestic and Foreign Mis-
sionary Society Papers, Li-
beria Papers, 1822-ca. 1911."
Historical Magazine (37:1,
Mr., 1968), pp. 77-82.
                      DHU/R

Browne, George D. "History of
the Protestant Episcopal Mis-
sion in Liberia up to 1838."
Historical Magazine of the
Protestant Episcopal Church
(39:1, Mr., 1970), pp. 17-27.
                            DHU/R
Camphor, Alexander Priestley.
Missionary Story Sketches:
Folklore for Africa. With an
introduction by the Rev. M.
C. B. Mason. Cincinnati: Jen-
nings and Graham; New York:
Eaton and Mains, 1909.
                            NN/Sch
Negro author.
Cox, Melville Beverid. Remains
of Melville B. Cox, Late Mis-
sionary to Liberia. With a
Memoir. Boston: Light &
Horton, 1835.   NN/Sch
Edited by Gershom F. Cox.
Crummell, Alexander. The Fu-
ture of Africa: being Ad-
dresses, Sermons, etc., de-
livered in the Republic of Li-
beria. New York: Scribner,
1862.   NN/Sch
Negro author.
Emery, M. T. Bishop Auer of
Cape Palmas. Hartford, Conn.:
Junior Auxiliary Pub. Co.,
n. d.   NN/Sch
Flora, George R. New Turns on
the Liberia Road; a Mission
Study Book. Philadelphia:
Board of Foreign Missions and
Women's Missionary Society of
the United Lutheran Church in
America, 1945.   NN/Sch
Green, Ashbel. Presbyterian
Missions, by Ashbel Green;
With Supplemental notes by
John C. Lowrie. New York:
A. D. F. Randolph, 1895.
                            NN/Sch
Gurley, Ralph R. Life of Jehudi
Ashmun Late Colonial Agent
in Liberia... with a Brief
Sketch of the Life of the Rev.
Lott Carey... Washington,
D. C.: Printed by J. C. Dunn,
1835.   DHU/R

Harris, John Hobbis. Africa:
Slave or Free? With Preface
by Sir Sydney Olivier. London: Student Christian Movement, 1919. DHU/R; CtY-D
Haywood, Delores C. and Patricia L. Davis. "The Domestic and Foreign Missionary
Society Papers. The Liberia
Papers: 1822-1939." Historical Magazine of the Protestant
Episcopal Church (39:1, Mr.,
1970), pp. 91-94. DHU/R
Article describes papers.
Hening, E. History of the Afri-
can Mission of the Protestant
Episcopal Church in the United
States, with Memoirs of Deceased Missionaries and Notices of Native Customs. New
York: Stanford and Swords,
1850.   NN/Sch
Jordan, Lewis Garnett. Pebbles
from an African Beach. Phila-
delphia: Lisle-Carey Press,
1917.   NN/Sch
Negro author.
Methodist Church (United States)
Conference. Liberia. Journal
of Sessions... Monrovia: 19-
                            NN/Sch
Nunns, Theodora. The Land of
Storms and Hope. A short
history of the English Church
in South Africa. Wynberg:
Rustica Press, 1921. NN/Sch
Payne, John. A Full Descrip-
tion of the African Field of
the Protestant Episcopal
Church with Statistics from
All the Mission Stations. (Cor-
rected to 1st January, 1866)...
New York: Foreign Committee
of the Board of Missions,
1866?   NN/Sch
Peabody, George Barh-Fofoe.
Barh-Fofoe: a Bassa Boy.
Story of His Childhood and
Youth at His Home in the Doh
Country, and at the Mission
School in Quibie Country, near
Marshall, Liberia, West
Coast, Africa. Told by Him-

self. Lancaster, Pa.: New
Era Printing House, 1891.
　　　　　　NN/Sch
Negro author.
Ramsaur, William Hoke. The
Letters of William Hoke Ram-
saur; compiled by his Friends
Elwood Henry Haines, Jeannie
Ogden Miller Cornell and his
Sister, Mary Alexander Ram-
saur. Jacksonville, Fla.:
1928.　　　　　NN/Sch
Rice, Edwin Botts. Historical
Sketch of the African Mission.
New York: Church Missions
House, 1903.　　　NN/Sch
Seebach, Margaret Rebecca.
Man in the Bush. Philadel-
phia: The Board of Foreign
Missions and the Women of
the United Lutheran Church in
America, 1945.　　NN/Sch
Sibley, James. L. Liberia...
Old and New: a Study of its
Social and Economic Back-
ground with Possibilities of
Development. Garden City,
N.Y.: Doubleday, 1928.
　　　　　　NN/Sch
Smith, Lucius Edwin. Heroes
and Martyrs of Modern Mis-
sionary Enterprise, a Record
of Their Lives and Labors.
Including a Historical Review
of Earlier Missions. Provi-
dence, R.I.: O.W. Potters,
1857.　　　　　NN/Sch
Williams, Walter B. Adventures
with the Krus in West Africa.
New York: Vantage Press,
1955.　　　　　NN/Sch

p. Guinea
Barrow, A.H. Fifty Years in
Western Africa: Being a Rec-
ord of the Work of the West
Indian Church on the Banks of
the Rio Pongo. London: So-
ciety for Promoting Christian
Knowledge, 1900.　NN/Sch

q. Portuguese Africa
Alves Correia, Manuel. ...
Missões Franciscanas Portu-
guesas de Moçambique e da
Guiné. Braga, Tip. das Mis-
soes franciscanas.　NN/Sch
Barmento, Alexandre. ...Temas
Angolanos. Lisboa: Tipo-
grafia Ideal, 1957.　NN/Sch
pp. 51-64, Missions in
Angola.
Berthoud, Paul. Les Negrès
Gouamba; ou, Les Vingt Pre-
mières Années de la Mission
Romande. Lausanne: Le
Conseil de la Mission Romande,
1896.　　　　　NN/Sch
Brasio, Antonio Duarte. Monu-
menta Missionaria Africa.
Ocidental... Coligida e Ano-
tada pelo Padre Antônio Brasio
... Lisboa: Agencia Geral do
Utramar. Divisão de Publica-
cões e Biblioteca, 1952.
　　　　　　NN/Sch
Cancela, Luis Lourenco. Sur-
presas do Sertão; Cartas de
um Missionário a Seus So-
brinhos. Lisboa: Editorial
L.I.A.M., 1946.　NN/Sch
Cushman, Mary Floyd. Mis-
sionary Doctor, the Story of
Twenty Years in Africa, by
Mary Floyd Chushman, M.D.
New York: Harper & Bros.,
1944.　　　　　NN/Sch
Grenfell, W.D. The Dawn
Breaks; The Story of Mission-
ary Work at Sao Salvador,
Portuguese Congo. London:
Carey Press, 1948. NN/Sch
Maio, Augusto. No Coraco da
Africa Negra. Lisbon: Edi-
torial L.I.A.M., 1947.
　　　　　　NN/Sch
Missions, Angola.
Parsons, M.E. "Revival in An-
gola, West Africa." Mission-
ary Review (62; Ja., 1939),
p. 40.　　　　　DHU/R
Tucker, John T. Angola, the
Land of the Blacksmith Prince.
London: World Dominion

(Tuker, J. T. cont.)
Press, 1933.   NN/Sch

r. General
"Africa." Quarterly Register of
the American Education So-
ciety (3:1, Ag., 1830), pp.
30-37.   DHU/R
African Education Commission,
1923-1924. "Education in East
Africa; a Study of East, Cen-
tral and South Africa by the
Second African Education Commission Under the Auspices of
the Phelps-Stokes Fund, in
Cooperation with the Interna-
tional Education Board; Report
Prepared by Thomas Jesse
Jones, Chairman of the Com-
mission." New York: Phelps-
Stokes Fund.   NN/Sch
"African Missionary in Africa."
Missionary Review (28; Oct. -
Nov., 1905), pp. 739-43, 805-
16.   DHU/R
The African Squadron. Petition
of the Committee of the Church
Mission Society Deprecating
the Diminishing or Removal of
the Squadron. n.p., 1850.
                      DHU/MO
"Africa's Challenge to the Church."
National Council Outlook (5;
Feb., 1955), pp. 18+.
                      DHU/R
"After Lincoln." By a Mission-
ary. Christian Century (59:
17, Apr. 29, 1942), pp. 564-
65.   DHU/R
A letter by a missionary
concerning the mistreatment
of Negroes in the United
States.
Allen, Belle Jane. A Crusade
of Compassion for the Healing of the Nations. A Study
of Medical Missions for Wom-
en and Children; Compiled by
Belle J. Allen, edited by Caroline Atwater Mason. West
Medford, Mass.: The Central
Committee on the United

Study of Foreign Missions,
1919.   NN/Sch
Anderson, Llewellyn Kennedy.
Bridge to Africa. New York:
Board of Foreign Missions of
the Presbyterian Church in the
United States of America, For-
eign Missions and Overseas
Interchurch Services, 1952.
                      NN/Sch
--"When Twenty-Six Thousand
Africans were Converted; an
Experience of the Church in
West Africa." Missionary Re-
view (62; My., 1939), pp.
233-5.   DHU/R
Anderson, William T. "The
Church in African Universities."
Clergy Review (53:3, Mr.,
1968), pp. 191-8.   DCU/Th
"Anti-Christian Movements in
Africa." Missionary Review of
the World (33; 1910), pp. 723-
40.   DHU/R
Baird, James B. Children of Af-
rica. Chicago: F. H. Revell
Co., 1910.   NN/Sch
Barclay, Wade Crawford. The
Methodist Episcopal Church,
1845-1939: Widening Horizons,
1845-95. (Vol. III of the His-
tory of Methodist Missions).
New York: Board of Missions
of The Methodist Church,
1957.   DHU/R
Chapter IX, Expanding For-
eign Missions--Africa.
Bartlett, S. C. Historical Sketch
of the Missions of the American Board in Africa. Boston:
Pub. by the Board, 1880.
                      DHU/MO
Beach, Harlan Page. A Geogra-
phy and Atlas of Protestant
Mission; their Environment,
Forces, Distribution, Methods,
Problems, Results and Prospects at the Opening of the
Twentieth Century. New York:
Student Volunteer Movement
for Foreign Missions, 1901-
1903.   NN/Sch
Beaver, R. Pierce (ed.). Chris-

tianity and African Education.
Grand Rapids, Mich.: William B. Eerdman's Pub. Co.,
1966. DHU/R
Bell, William Clark. African
Bridge Builders. New York:
Friendship Press, 1936.
NN/Sch; DHU/MO
Bernardi, Bernardo. The Migwe: A Failing Prophet. Oxford: Oxford University
Press, 1959. DHU/R
Bliss, Edwin M. The Encyclopedia of Missions. Descriptive, Historical, Biographical Statistical. New York: Funk
& Wagnalls, 1891. DHU/R
Includes Africa and West
Indies.
Blyden, Edward Wilmot. Philip
and the Eunuch; or the Instruments and Methods of Africa's
Evangelization. A discourse
delivered in the Park Street
Church, Boston, U.S.A., Sunday, Oct. 22, 1882. Cambridge; John Wilson and Son,
1883. DHU/MO
Booth, Newell Snow. The Cross
Over Africa. New York:
Friendship Press, 1945.
NN/Sch
--This is Africa South of the
Sahara. New York: Friendship Press, 1959. NN/Sch
Bourne, Henry Richard Fox.
Slavery and Its Substitutes in
Africa. A Paper Submitted to
the Anti-Slavery Conference,
Held in Paris in August, 1900.
London: Aborigines Protection Society, 1900? CtY-D
Brain, B. "Africaner, a Twice-Born Black Man." Missionary
Review (35; Jl., 1912), pp.
487-94. DHU/R
Brown, Ina Corinne. Training
for World Friendship; a Manual in Missionary Education for
Leaders of Young People.
Nashville, Tenn.: Cokesbury
Press, 1929. NN/Sch; DHU/R
Brown, John Tom. Among the

Bantu Nomads. London:
Seeley, Service & Co., 1925.
DHU/MO
"Gives customs, religious
beliefs, and history of the
Bechuana."
--The Apostle of the Marshes:
The Story of Shomolekae.
London: The Religious Tract
Society, 1925. NN/Sch
Burton, E.D. and A.K. Parker.
"Expansion of Christianity in
the Twentieth Century." Biblical World (41; Je., 1913),
pp. 402-7. DHU/R
Butler, Annie Robins. By the
Rivers of Africa, from Cape
Town to Uganda; with a Map
and Sixty Illustrations. London: Religious Tract Society,
188?. NN/Sch
Capper, Joseph. The Negro's
Friend. Consisting of anecdotes, designed to exemplify
the moral, intellectual, and
religious attainments of the
African race, and the cruelties and oppressions to which
they have been subjected by
the Europeans. 2nd ed. London: S. Bagster, n.d.
DHU/MO
Carey, Lott. "Letters, Addresses, etc. Throwing Light on
the Career of." Journal of
Negro History (7:4, Oct.,
1922), pp. 427-48. DHU
Carpenter, George Wayland. ...
The Way in Africa. New
York: Friendship Press,
1959. NN/Sch
"A selected reading list,"
pp. 161-65.
Chadwick, W. and J.J. Willis.
"Kekuyu Missionary Conference." Missionary Review of
the World (37; Mr., 1914),
pp. 208-13. DHU/R
Church Conference on African
Affairs. New York: African
Committee of the Foreign Missions and Conference of North
America, 1942. DHU/MO

--Otterbein College, 1942.
Christian Action in Africa.
Report of the Church Confer-
ence on African Affairs held
at Otterbein College, Wester-
ville, Ohio, June 19-25, 1942.
New York: Africa Committee
of the Foreign Missions Con-
ference of North America,
1942.   DHU/MO
"Chart, Showing Societies at
Work in the Dark Continent."
Missionary Review (37; Je.,
1914), p. 422.   DHU/R
Chirgwin, A. M. The Forward
Tread. London: The Living-
ston Press, 1932.   DHU/MO
Christianity and Native Rites.
London: Central Africa Home
Press, 1956.   NN/Sch
Clendenen, Clarence C. and
Peter Duignan. Americans in
Black Africa Up to 1865.
Stanford University: The
Hoover Institution on War,
1964.   DHU/R
    Part II, Missionaries and
colonization, societies, revo-
lution and peace.
Coldham, Geraldine E.   A Bib-
liography of Scriptures in Af-
rican Languages. London:
British and Foreign Bible So-
ciety, 1966.   DLC
Commission on the Enlistment of
Educated Negroes for Work in
Africa. "The Task of the
Christian Church in Africa."
Arcadius S. Trawick (ed.).
The New Voice in Race Ad-
justment. (New York: Stu-
dent Volunteer Movement,
1914), pp. 201-9.   DHU/R
Conference of Mission Boards
Engaged in Work in the Conti-
nent of Africa, New York, 1917.
The Christian Occupation of
Africa: the Proceedings of a
Conference of Mission Boards
Engaged in Work in the Conti-
nent of Africa, Held in New
York City, November 20, 21
and 22, 1917, together with

the Findings of the Conference.
New York: Committee of Reference and Counsel of the
Foreign Missions Conference
of North America, 1917.
                   NN/Sch
...Congress of Africa, ...At-
lanta, 1895. Africa, and the
American Negro. Addresses
and Proceedings of the Congress on Africa, held under
the Auspices of the Stewart
Missionary Foundation for Af-
rica of Gammon Theological
Seminary, in Connection with
the Cotton States and Interna-
tional Exposition, December
13-15, 1895. Ed. Prof. J.W.
E. Bowen, Secretary of the
Congress. Atlanta: Gammon
Theological Seminary, 1896.
    DHU/MO; NN/Sch
Conover, Helen F. Africa South
of the Sahara. Washington:
Library of Congress, 1957.
                   DHU/MO
Cooley, John K. Baal, Christ,
and Mohammed; Religion and
Revolution in North Africa.
London: John Murray, 1967.
                   DHU/R
    Part III "Christian Mis-
sionaries and Moslem Rulers."
Coppinger, William. Winning
an Empire. Hampton, Va.:
Normal School Steam Press,
1884.   NN/Sch
Crawford, Daniel. Thinking
Black: 22 Years Without a
Break in the Long Grass of
Central Africa. New York:
Doran, 1912.   NN/Sch
Cripps, Arthur S. "Saint Francis
of Assisi: His Mission to Af-
rica and Elsewhere: 700
Years Ago and Now." The
East and the West (24; Oct.,
1926), pp. 289-96. DHU/R
Culwick, Arthur Theodore.
Good Out of Africa. Living-
stone, Northern Rhodesia:
The Rhodes-Livingstone Insti-
tute, 1942.   DHU/MO

"Dan Crawford of Africa." Literary Digest (47; Sept. 20, 1913), pp. 474-5.   DHU
Davis, John Merle. The Cinema and Missions in Africa.
                    NN/Sch
    "Reprinted from the International Review of Missions for July, 1936.
Dealtry, William. Duty and Policy of Propagating Christianity. A discourse delivered before the Church Missionary Society for Africa and the East, May 4, 1813. Pub. at the request of the General Meeting. London: Sold by L. B. Seeley, 1813.
                    NN/Sch
Dean, Christopher. The African Traveler; or, Prospective Missions in Central Africa. Boston, Mass.: Sabbath School Society, 1838.   DHU/MO
De la Cote des Esclaves aux rives du Nil, par une Religieuse Missionnaire. Lyon: Librairie E. Vitte Venissieux, Soeurs Missionnaires de N. D. des Aportres, 1931. NN/Sch
Delany, Martin Robinson and Robert Campbell. Search for a Place: Black Separatism and Africa, 1860. Introduction by Howard H. Bell. Ann Arbor: University of Michigan Press, 1969.   DHU/R
    Chapter 10, "Missionary Influence," pp. 102-6.
Dempsey, James. Mission on the Nile. New York: Philosophical Library, 1956.
                    NN/Sch
Devresse, L. Le Captaine Joubert. Leverville, Congo Belge: Bibliotheque de l'Etoile, 1951.   NN/Sch
Dougall, James W. C. Christians in the African Revolution. Edinburgh: The Saint Andrew Press, 1963.   DHU/R
"Dramatizing Missions: Work of Converting Africans Filmed

by Harmon Foundation." Newsweek (12; Oct. 17, 1938), p. 27.   DHU
Dubois, Henri Marie. ...Chez les Betsiléos; Impressions et Croquis. Paris: Casterman, 1907.   NN/Sch
--...Le Répertoire Africain. Rome: Sodalite de S. Pierre Claver, 1932.   NN/Sch
DuPlessis, Johannes. The Evangelisation of Pagan Africa; a History of Christian Missions to the Pagan Tribe of Central Africa. Published under the auspices of the University of Stellenbosch. Cape Town: Juta, 1930.   NN/Sch
Ellis, Alfred B. The Yoruba-Speaking Peoples of the Slave Coast of West Africa. Their Religion, Manners, and Customs, Laws, Languages, etc. London: Chapman & Hall, 1894.   DHU/MO
Evans, Stanley George. Christians and Africa... London: Society of Socialist Clergy and Ministers, 1950. NN/Sch
Faduma, Orishetukeh. "Success and Drawbacks to Missionary Work in Africa." J. W. E. Bowen (ed.). Africa and the American Negro: Addresses and Proceedings of the Congress on Africa. (Miami, Fla.: Mnemosyne Publishing, Inc., 1969), pp. 125-36.   DHU/R
Fahs, Charles Harvey. The Open Door; a Challenge to Missionary Advance. Cincinnati: Jennings & Pye, 1903.
                    NN/Sch
Fisher, A. B. "Mission Among the African Pygmies." Missionary Review of the World (27; Apr., 1904), pp. 297-8.
                    DHU/R
Fisher, Lena Leonard. Under the Crescent and Among the Kraals; a Study of Methodism in Africa. Boston, Mass.: The Women's Foreign Mis-

(Fisher, L. L. cont.)
sionary Soc. Methodist Epis-
copal Church, 1917. NN/Sch
Fisher, Miles Mark. "Lott
Carey, the Colonizing Mis-
sionary." Journal of Negro
History (7:4, Oct., 1922), pp.
380-418.   DHU
Negro author.
Floyd, Olive Beatrice. Partners
in Africa. New York: The
National Council, Protestant
Episcopal Church, 1946?
                        DHU/MO
Forde, H. A. Black and White
Mission Stories. New York:
E. & J. B. Young & Co., 1881.
                        NN/Sch
Forsberg, Malcolm. Land Be-
yond the Nile. New York:
Harper, 1958.   NN/Sch
Fox, William. A Brief History
of the Wesleyan Mission on
the Western Coast of Africa.
Including biographical sketches
of all the missionaries who
have died in that important
field of labour. With some
account of the European settle-
ments, and of the slave-trade.
London: Aylott & Jones, 1851.
                           CtY-D
Fraser, Donald. Africa Idylls;
Portraits & Impressions of
Life on a Central African Mis-
sion Station... London:
Seeley, Service, 1923. NN/Sch
--The Future of Africa. London:
Church Missionary Society,
1911.   NN/Sch
--The New Africa. New York:
Missionary Education Move-
ment of the United States and
Canada, 1928.   DHU/MO
--Winning a Primitive People:
Sixteen Year's Work Among
the Warlike Tribe of the
Ngoni and the Senga and Tum-
buka Peoples of Central Africa.
New York: E. P. Dutton &
Co., 1914.   NN/Sch
"Freedmen for Africa." The
Church at Home and Abroad

(2; Ag., 1887), pp. 166-67.
                          DHU/R
Discusses possibility of
Negroes as Missionaries in
Africa.
Freeman, Thomas Birch. Jour-
nal of Various Visits to the
Kingdoms of Ashanti, Aku,
and Dahomi, in Western Af-
rica... London: Sold by J.
Mason, 1844.   NN/Sch
Negro author.
Furlong, C. W. "White Fathers
of North Africa." Scribner's
Magazine (41; Feb., 1907),
pp. 140-51.   DHU
Gammon Theological Seminary.
Stewart Missionary Founda-
tion on Africa. Africa and
the American Negro. Ad-
dresses and Proceedings of
the Congress on Africa...
Dec. 13-15, 1896.   DHU/MO
Gavan Duffy, Thomas. Mission
Tours - Africa,... or, For
Short Let's Go. Boston:
Propagation of the Faith Of-
fice, 1928.   NN/Sch
"General Statistics of Missions
in Africa." Missionary Review
of the World (35; Je., 1912),
p. 460.   DHU/R
George, Poikail John. "Racist
Assumptions of the 19th Cen-
tury Missionary Movement."
International Review of Mis-
sion (59:235, Jl., 1970), pp.
271-84.   DHU/R
Gingyera-Pincwa, A. G. G. "The
Missionary Press and the De-
veloping of Political Aware-
ness in the Decade 1952-62."
Dini Na Mila (4:2, My., 1970),
pp. 35-61.   DHU/R
Goerner, H. C. "Race Factor in
World Missions." Review
and Expositor (59; Jl., 1959),
pp. 288-94.   DLC; CtY-D
Grahame, Nigel B. M. Arnot of
Africa, a Fearless Pioneer,
a Zealous Missionary and a
True Knight of the Cross.
New York: George H. Doran

Co., 1926.   DHU/MO
Grayston, E. Alison. ... Africa;
Comp. by E. Alison Grayston
and Clifton Ackroyd. London:
Edinburgh House, 1950.
                               NN/Sch
Groves, Charles Pelham. Jesus
Christ and Primitive Need:
A Missionary Study in the
Christian Message... London:
The Epworth Press, 1934.
                               CtY; NcD
--"Missionary and Humanitarian
Aspects of Imperialism from
1870-1914." L. H. Gann and P.
Duignan (eds.). Vol. 1 of
Colonialism in Africa: 1870-
1960. (New York: Cambridge
University Press, 1969), pp.
462-96.   DLC
--The Planting of Christianity in
Africa. London: Lutterworth
Press, 1948-1955. DHU/MO
Hallack, Cecily Rosemary. The
Legion of Mary. New York:
Crowell, 1950.   NN/Sch
Hammond, E. W. S. "Africa in
its Relation to Christian Civili-
zation." J. W. E. Bowen, (ed.).
Africa and the American Ne-
gro: Addresses and Proceed-
ings of the Congress on Af-
rica. (Miami, Fla.: Mne-
mosyne Publishing, Inc., 1969),
pp. 205-10.   DHU/R
Harnack, H. "Principles of Pro-
testant Missions." Missionary
Review of the World (24; Apr.,
1901), pp. 286-7.   DHU/R
Harr, Wilbur C. "The Negro as
an American Protestant Missionary in Africa." Doctoral
dissertation, University of
Chicago, 1945.
Harris, J. H. "Day of Opportunity in West Central Africa."
Missionary Review (35; Sept.,
1912), pp. 673-81.   DHU/R
Hartzell, Joseph C. (bp.).
"American Methodism in Africa." Missionary Review (32;
Ag., 1909), pp. 565-76.
Negro author.   DHU/R

--The Continent of Africa." Ar-
cadius S. Trawick (ed.). The
New Voice in Race Adjustments
(New York: Student Volunteer
Movement, 1914), pp. 115-20.
                               DHU/R
Haynes, George Edmund. Africa,
Continent of the Future. New
York: Association Press;
Geneva, Switzerland: World's
Committee of Young Men's
Christian Associations, 1950.
                               NN/Sch
Negro author.
Heard, William Henry. The
Bright Side of African Life.
Philadelphia: A. M. E. Publish-
ing House, 1898.
                    DHU/MO; OWibfU
Negro author.
--The Missionary Fields of West
Africa. Philadelphia: A. M. E.
Book Concern. n. d. DHU/MO
Helser, Albert David. Africa's
Bible; the Power of God Unto
Salvation. New York: Sudan
Interior Mission, 1951.
                               DHU/MO
--The Glory of the Impossible.
New York: Evangelical Pub-
lishers, 1940.   DHU/MO
Holden, Edith. Blyden of Li-
beria. An account of the life
and labors of... New York:
Vantage Press, 1966. DHU/R
Holmes, John Beck (bp.). His-
torical Sketches of the Mis-
sions of the United Brethren
for Propagating the Gospel
Among the Heathen from Their
Commencement to the Year
1817. London: Printed for
the author and sold by J. Nis-
bet, 1827.   NN/Sch
Hotchkiss, Willis Ray. Sketches
from the Dark Continent.
Cleveland, O.: The Friends
Bible Institute and Training
School, 1901.   NN/Sch
"How Missionaries Work in Africa; Extracts from Letters of
Pastors, Teachers, Doctors,
and Industrial Missionaries of

("How Missionaries ... cont.)
the American Presbyterian
Mission in West Africa."
Missionary Review (62; Ja.,
1939), pp. 2, 20-8.   DHU/R
Huckel, W. "Des Religions de
l'Afrique. Journal des Mes-
sions Evangéliques Paris
(Apr., 1922), pp. 315-33.
OO; CtY.
Hughes, W. Dark Africa and
Way Out, or A Scheme for
Civilizing and Evangelizing
the Dark Continent. New
York: Negro Universities
Press, 1969.   DHU/R
Jackson, Samuel Macauley. Bib-
liography of Foreign Missions.
New York: Funk & Wagnalls,
1891.   NN/Sch
James, Cyril L.R. A History
of Pan-African Revolt. Wash-
ington, D.C.: Drum & Spear
Press, 1969.   DHU/R
"Religious revolts in the
New Colonies," chapter iv.
James, J.A. The Path to the
Bush. Boston, Mass.: Sab-
bath School Society, 1843.
DHU/MO
Johnson, Samuel. The History
of the Yorubas from the Earli-
est Times to the Beginning of
the British Protectorate. Lon-
don: G. Routledge & Sons,
1921.   DHU/MO
Chapter III, Religion, pp.
26-39.
Johnston, Halcro. "The Mis-
sionary Attitude Towards Ne-
gro Labour in Africa." The
East and the West (1:3, Jl.,
1903), pp. 264-74.   DHU/R
Johnston, James. Missionary
Landscapes in the Dark Conti-
nent... New York: A.D.F.
Randolph & Co., 1892.
DHU/MO
Kingston, Vera. An Army With
Banners; the Romance of Missionary Adventure. London:
S. Low, Marston & Co., Ltd.,
1931.   NN/Sch

Kirkpatrick, Lois. Methodist at
Work in Africa, A Source for
those Studying about Africa.
Boston: The Methodist Pub-
lishing House, 1945. NN/Sch
Knak, Siegfried. Zwischen Nil
und Tafelbai; eine Studie Li er
Evangelium, Volkstum und
Zivilisation, am Beispiel der
Missionsprobleme unter den
Bantu, von d. Siegfried Knak
... 1.-3. Tausend. Berlin:
Heimatdienst-verlag, 1931.
NN/Sch
Krapf, Ludwig. Travels, Re-
searches, and Missionary La-
bors, During an Eighteen
Year's Residence in Eastern
Africa; Together with Journeys
to Jagga, Usambara, Ukam-
bani, Shoa, Abyssinia, and
Khartum; a Coasting Voyage
from Mombaz to Cape Delgado.
Boston: Ticknor & Fields.
DHU/MO; NN/Sch
Kumm, Herman Karl Wilhelm.
The Sudan; a Short Compendium
of Facts and Figures About the
Land of Darkness. London:
Marshall Bros., 1907.
NN/Sch
Latourette, Kenneth S. The
Great Century in the Ameri-
cas, Australasia, and Africa,
A.D. 1800-1914. New York:
Harper & Bros., 1943.
DHU/R
In History and Expansion
of Christianity, vol. 5.
Livingstone, David. Dr. Living-
stone's Cambridge Lectures,
Together with Prefatory Let-
ter by the Ref. Prof. Sedg-
wick... Cambridge: Deighton,
Bell & Co., 1858. NN/Sch
Livingstone, William Pringle.
Christina Forsyth of Fingo-
land; the Story of the Loneli-
est Woman in Africa. New
York: Hodder and Stoughton,
1918.   NN/Sch
Lloyd, Albert Bushnell. In
Dwarf Land and Cannibal

Country; a Record of Travel
and Discovery in Central
Africa. New York: C. Scrib-
ner's Sons, 1899.   NN/Sch
Lloyd, Thomas Ernest. African
Harvest. London: Lutter-
worth Press, 1953. NN/Sch
Luke, James. Pioneering in
Mary Slessor's Country. Lon-
don: Epworth Press, 1929.
                     NN/Sch
Macdonald, Allan John. Trade,
Politics and Christianity in
Africa and the East. London:
Longmans, Green, 1916.
                     NN/Sch
Macgregor, J. K. "Christian
Missions and Marriage Usage
in Africa." International Re-
view of Missions (24; 1935),
pp. 379-91.   DHU/R
MacGregor-Hastie, Roy. Africa,
Background for Today. New
York: Criterion, 1967.
                     DHU/R
    Chapter 5 and 8, informa-
tion on "Ethiopia, the first
Christian Empire & Mission-
ary Influence in West Africa."
Mackenzie, Jean Kenyon. An
African Trail. West Medford,
Mass.: The Central Commit-
tee on the United Study of
Foreign Missions, etc., 1917.
                     DHU/MO
Mason, Madison Charles B.
Solving the Problem: a Se-
ries of Lectures. Chicago:
n. p., 1917.   NN/Sch
    Negro author.
Mathews, Basil Joseph. Black
Treasure; the Youth of Africa
in a Changing World. New
York: Friendship Press, 1928.
                     NN/Sch
--Consider Africa. New York:
Friendship Press, 1936.
                     NN/Sch
Mbiti, John. "The Future of
Christianity in Africa (1970-
2000)." Communio Viatorum
(13:1-2, Spr., 1970), pp. 19-
38.   DHU/R

Methodist Overseas Missions;
Gazetteer and Statistics.
New York: n. p., 1946.
                     NN/Sch
Miller, Basil William. Twenty
Missionary Stories from Af-
rica. Grand Rapids: Zonder-
van Pub. House, 1951.
                     NN/Sch
Morrison, James H. The Mis-
sionary Heroes of Africa.
New York: George H. Doran
Co., 1922.   NN/Sch
Mott, John Raleigh. The Deci-
sive Hour of Christian Mis-
sions... New York: Student
Volunteer Movement for For-
eign Missions, Association
Press, 1911.   DHU/MO
Mouezy, Henri. ...Assinie et le
Royaume de Krinjabo, Histoire
et Coutumes. Paris: Larose,
1953.   NN/Sch
Mueller, John Theodore. Great
Missionaries to Africa. Grand
Rapids, Mich.: Zondervan
Pub. House, 1941. NN/Sch
Multi-Racial Conference on Chris-
tian Responsibility Toward
Areas of Rapid Social Change.
Johannesburg, 1959. Chris-
tian Responsibility Toward
Areas of Rapid Social Change;
Report of the Multi-Racial Con-
ference Held at the University
of Witwatersrand... from 7 to
10 Dec. 1959. Johannesburg:
Voortrekkerpers Beperk, 1960.
                     NN/Sch
Murray, Albert Victor. The
School in the Bush; A Criti-
cal Study of the Theory and
Practice of Native Education
in Africa. New York: Long-
mans, Green & Co., 1929.
                     NN/Sch
Nassau, Robert Hamill. Crowned
in Palm Land. A Story of
African Mission Life...
Philadelphia: J. B. Lippincott
& Co., 1874.   NN/Sch
--"Ibiya--a West African Pastor."
Missionary Review of the

(Nassau, R. H. cont.)
World (37; Je., 1914), pp.
442-4.   DHU/R
--My Ogowe: Being a Narrative
of Daily Incidents During Six-
teen Years in Equatorial West
Africa. New York: The Neal
Pub. Co., 1914.   NN/Sch
Naylor, Wilson Samuel. Day-
break in the Dark Continent.
Livingstone ed. New York:
Missionary Education Move-
ment of the United States and
Canada, 1915. DHU/R;NN/Sch
Nevinson, Henry W. A Modern
Slavery. New York: Schocken
Books, 1968.   DHU/R
  Chapter VII, Savages and
  Missions.
North, Eric McCoy. The King-
dom and the Nations. West
Medford, Mass.: The Central
Committee on the United Study
of Foreign Missions, 1921.
                          NN/Sch
Notice sur la Société des Mis-
sions Evangéliques, Chez les
Peuples non Chretiens. Paris:
Chez J. J. Risler, Librairie,
1839.   DHU/MO
Oldham, Joseph Houldsworth.
The Remaking of Man in Af-
rica. London: Oxford Uni-
versity Press, H. Milford,
1931.   NN/Sch
Orchard, Ronald Kenneth. Africa
Steps Out. London: Edinburgh
House, 1952.   NN/Sch
Overs, Walter Henry. Stories
of African Life. New York:
E. S. Gorham, 1924. NN/Sch
Parsons, Ellen C. Christus
Liberator; an Outline Study of
Africa. New York: Macmil-
lan, 1905. DHU/MO; NN/Sch
--A Life for Africa; Rev. Adol-
phus Clemens Good, Ph. D.
American Missionary in Equa-
torial West Africa. 2nd ed.
New York: Fleming H. Re-
vell, 1900. DHU/MO; NN/Sch
Patton, C. "Continental Pro-
gram for Africa." Mission-

ary Review (41; Ja., 1918),
pp. 29-36.   DHU/R
p'Bitek, Okot. "DeHellenising
the Church." East Africa
Journal (6:8, Ag., 1969), pp.
8-10.   DHU/MO
"Peril to Missionary Africa."
Literary Digest. (56; Feb. 9,
1918), p. 33.   DHU/R
Phillips, Ray Edmund. The Bantu
are Coming; Phases of South Africa's Problem. London: S. C.
M. Press, 1930.   NN/Sch
  The Christian Mission in
  relation to industrial problems in Asia and Africa--the
  official statement of the International Missionary Council,
  pp. 219-36.
Pierson, Arthur Tappan. "Khama,
the Good--Christian Chief of
Africa." Missionary Review of
the World (24; Feb., 1901),
pp. 93-9.   DHU/R
--The Miracle of Missions; or,
The Modern Marvels in the
History of Missionary Enterprise. New York: Funk &
Wagnalls Co., 1895. NN/Sch
--"One of the Miracles of Missions." Missionary Review of
the World (32; Je., 1908), pp.
418-22.   DHU/R
Quatrefoges de Breau, Armond,
i. e. Jeon Louis Armond de.
The Pygmies. By A. de Qua-
trefoges, late Prof. of An-
thropology at the Museum of
Natural History, Paris. Tr.
by Frederick Starr. New
York: Macmillan Co., 1895.
                         DHU
  "Religious beliefs of the
  Hottentots and the Bushmen."
Ransom, C. N. "South Africa, a
Burden, a Vision, and a
Duty." Missionary Review of
the World (26; Je., 1903), pp.
427-30.   DHU/R
Richards, Charles Granston.
Krapf, Missionary and Ex-
plorer. London: Nelson,
1950.   NN/Sch

Robinson, James Herman. Tomorrow, is Today. Philadelphia: Christian Education Press, 1954. DHU/R
Negro author.

Roome, William John Waterman. Can Africa be Won? London: A. & C. Black, 1927. NN/Sch

Roosevelt, T. "African Missions." Missionary Review (34; Ja., 1911), pp. 55-6. DHU/R

Roseberry, Robert Sherman. The Niger Vision. A Modern Miracle of Missions. The Record of the Opening of the Western Soudan to the Lighthouse along the Niger with its Tributaries, Program for Immediate Evangelization of Vast Pagan Areas. Harrisburg, Pa.: Christian Publications, 1934. NN/Sch

Ross, Emory. African Heritage. New York: Friendship Press, 1952. DHU/MO

Rutherford, J. "North Africa from a Missionary Point of View." Missionary Review of the World (34; Je., 1911), pp. 415-24. DHU/R

Sailer, Thomas Henry Powers. Christian Adult Education in Rural Asia and Africa. New York: Friendship Press, 1943. NN/Sch

Sharp, W. "Cardinal Lavigerie's Work in North Africa." Atlantic (74; Ag., 1894), pp. 214-27. DHU

Shepherd, William Henry. "Response of Africa to the Gospel." Arcadius S. Trawick, (ed.). The New Voice in Race Adjustments. New York: Student Volunteer Movement, 1914. pp. 120-28. DHU/R
Negro author.

Shillito, Edward. Craftsmen All; Fellow Workers in the Younger Churches... New York: Friendship Press, 1933. DLC; NN/Sch

Simon, Jean Marie, (bp.). Bish-

op for the Hottentots; African Memories, 1882-1909. Translated by Angeline Bouchard. New York: Benriger, 1959. NN/Sch

Smith, Edwin William. The Golden Stool: Some Aspects of the Conflict of Cultures in Africa. London: Holborn Pub. House, 1927. DHU/MO

--Knowing the African. London: United Society for Christian Literature, 1946. NN/Sch

Speer, Robert Elliott. Missions and Modern History; a Study of the Missionary Aspects of Some Great Movements of the Nineteenth Century. New York: Fleming H. Revell Co., 1904. NN/Sch

Stanley, M. W. "Friends Industrial Mission in Africa." Missionary Review (40; Nov., 1917), pp. 815-22. DHU/R

Stauffer, Milton Theobald, ed. ...Thinking with Africa. Chapters assembled and edited. New York: Published for the Student Volunteer Movement for Foreign Missions by the Missionary Education Movement of the United States and Canada, 1927. DHU/MO

Stewart, James. Dawn in the Dark Continent. New York: Felming H. Revell Co., 1903. DHU/MO

Talbot, Percy. "Aspects of West African Religions," Edinburgh Review (220; Jl., 1914), pp. 96-114. DHU

The Task of the Christian Church; a World Survey. London: World Dominion Press, 1926. NN/Sch

Taylor, John Vernon. ...Christianity and Politics in Africa. London: Penguin Books, 1957. DHU/MO;OWibfU; NN/Sch

Taylor, Stephen Earl. The Price of Africa. New York: Young People's Missionary Movement, 1902. NN/Sch

(Taylor, S. E. cont.)
    The forward mission study
    courses; ed. by A. R. Wells
    and S. E. Taylor.
Taylor, William (bp.). The
    Flaming Torch in Darkest
    Africa. New York: Eaton &
    Maine, 1898.   NN/Sch
Thompson, R. Ward. "The
    Ethiopian Movement and the
    Order of Ethiopia." The East
    and West. Review for the
    Study of Missions (2; 1904),
    pp. 375-97.   DHU/R
Thornton, Douglas Montagu.
    Africa Waiting; or, The Prob-
    lem of Africa's Evangelization.
    London: Student Volunteer
    Missionary Union, 1898.
                          NN/Sch
Tyler, Josiah. "Missionary Ex-
    periences Among the Zulus."
    J. W. E. Bowen, (ed.). Afri-
    can and the American Negro:
    Addresses and Proceedings of
    the Congress on Africa. (Mi-
    ami, Fla.: Mnemosyne Pub-
    lishing Inc., 1969), pp. 117-
    18.   DHU/R
Walker, Frank Deaville. The
    Call of the Dark Continent;
    A Study in Missionary Prog-
    ress, Opportunity and Urgency.
    London: Wesleyan Methodist
    Missionary Society, 1911.
                          NN/Sch
Walker, Samuel Abraham. Mis-
    sions in Western Africa,
    Among the Soosoos, Bulloms,
    &c. Being the First Under-
    taken by the Church Mission-
    ary Society for Africa and the
    East. With an introduction
    containing: I. A Sketch of
    Western Africa; with a descrip-
    tion of the principal tribes in-
    habiting that coast. II. A
    Brief History of the Slave
    Trade to the Present Day.
    III. Some Account of the Early
    African Churches. IV. A Con-
    densed Survey of all the Mis-
    sionary Exertions of Modern

Times, in Favor of Africa.
    Dublin: W. Curry, 1845.
                      CtY-D; NN/Sch
Wall, Martha. Splinters from
    an African Log. Chicago:
    Moody Press, 1960. NN/Sch
Wallace, Archer. Blazing New
    Trails. With an introduction
    by Rev. George A. Little.
    New York: Doubleday, Doran,
    1928.   NN/Sch
Wallbridge, Edwin Angel. The
    Demerara Martyr. Memoirs
    of the Rev. John Smith, Mis-
    sionary to Demerara. Lon-
    don: C. Gilpin, 1848. CtY-D
Wambutda, Daniel N. "An Afri-
    can Looks at Christian Mis-
    sions in Africa." Practical
    Anthropology (17:4, Jl-Ag.,
    1970), pp. 169-76. DHU/R
Ward, A. "Missionaries in
    Egypt." Nineteenth Century
    (48; Ag., 1900), pp. 207-18.
                          DHU
Ward, Gertrude. Letters from
    East Africa. London: Uni-
    versities' Mission to Central
    Africa, 1901.   NN/Sch
--The Life of Charles Alan
    Smythies, Bishop of the Uni-
    versities' Mission to Central
    Africa. London: Office of the
    Universities' Mission to Cen-
    tral Africa, 1899.   NN/Sch
Watt, Rachel S. In the Heart of
    Savagedom. Reminiscences of
    life and adventure during a
    quarter of a century of pioneer-
    ing missionary labours in the
    wilds of East Equatorial Africa.
    London: Marshall, 192-?
                          NN/Sch
Webster, Allan Neill. ...Mada-
    gascar. London: Society for
    the Propagation of the Gospel
    in Foreign Parts, 1932.
                          NN/Sch
Weitfrecht, H. U. "A Study of Af-
    rican Missions." Church Mis-
    sionary Review (74; Dec., 1923),
    pp. 227-34.   DHU/R
Wenzel, Kristen. "The Relation-

ship Between Religious Be-
liefs and Missionary Attitudes
Held Towards Black Africa:
A Study of Protestant and
Catholic Clergymen Serving
Churches Within the Five
Boroughs of New York City."
Doctoral dissertation, The
Catholic University of Amer-
ica, 1970.

West, E. Courtenay. "The Call
From Africa." East and the
West (24; Apr., 1926), pp.
156-65.   DHU/R
    Discusses evangelization
potential in Africa.

Westermann, Diedrich. The
Missionary and Anthropological Research. London: Ox-
ford University Press, International African Institute,
1948.   DHU/MO

Wilcox, W. D. "Need of Industrial Missions in Africa." Biblical World (41; Feb., 1913),
pp. 103-8.   DHU/R

Wilson, Frank T. "Future of
Missionary Enterprise in Africa South of the Sahara."
Journal of Negro Education
(30; Sum., 1961), pp. 324-
33.   DHU
    Negro author.

Woman's Congress of Missions,
Chicago, 1893. Women in Mis-
sions; Papers and Addresses
Presented at the Woman's
Congress of Missions, October
2-4, 1893, in the Hall of Co-
lumbus, Chicago. Compiled by
Rev. E. M. Wherry. New
York: American Tract Society,
1894.   NN/Sch

Woodworth, C. Historic Corre-
spondences in Africa and
America. A discourse delivered before the faculty and
students of Atlanta University,
May 27, 1888, by C. L. Woodworth. Boston: Beacon Press,
1889.   NN/Sch

Wrong, Margaret. Africa and
the Making of Books; Being

a Survey of Africa's Need of
Literature. New York: Inter-
national Committee on Chris-
tian Literature for Africa,
1934.   NN/Sch
--West African Journey, in the
Interests of Literacy and
Christian Literature, 1944-45.
London: Livingstone Press,
1946.   DHU/MO; NN/Sch

The Young African Prince; or,
Memoirs of Naimbana. Bos-
ton: Printed and sold by Lincoln & Edmands, Cornhill,
1822.   NN/Sch
    Religious conversion of an
African prince.

Vaughan, Edward Thomas. A
Sermon Preached at St. Andrew by the Wardrobe and St.
Anne Black Friars, on Tuesday, May 2, 1815, before the
Church Missionary Society for
Africa and the East, being
their Fifteenth Anniversary;
also the Report of the Committee to the Annual Meeting,
held on the Same Day and a
List of Subscribers and bene-
factors. London: Whittingham & Rowland, 1815.
                         NN/Sch

Vernier, Charles. Islamisme et
Christianisme et Afrique.
Montauban: Imprimeri Cooperative (Ancien Maison Granie,
1908.)   NN/Sch

Zwemer, Samuel Marinus. The
Unoccupied Mission Fields of
Africa and Asia. New York:
Student Volunteer Movement
for Foreign Missions, 1911.
                         NN/Sch

s. Other areas

American Sunday School Union.
History of Madagascar; Embracing the Progress of the
Christian Mission and an Account of the Persecution of the
Native Christians. Philadelphia: American Sunday School

(Amer. S. S. Union cont.)
Union, 1839.   NN/Sch
Bane, Martin J.   Catholic Pio-
neers in West Africa. Dublin:
Clonmore & Reynolds, 1956.
                      NN/Sch
Beacham, C.   New Frontiers in
the Central Sudan. Toronto:
Evangelical Publishers, 1928.
                      NN/Sch
Beiderbecke, Heinrich.   Life
Among the Hereros in Africa;
the Experiences of H. Beider-
becke, Lutheran Pastor. Ren-
dered into English by J. A.
Weyl... New York: E. Kauf-
mann, 1923.   NN/Sch
Bickersteth, E.   Memoirs of
Simeon Wilhelm, a Native of
the Susoo Country, West Af-
rica; Who Dies at the House
of the Church Missionary So-
ciety, London, Aug. 29, 1817;
Aged 17 Yrs. Together with
Some Accounts of the Super-
stitions of the inhabitants of
West Africa. New Haven: S.
Converse, 1819.   DHU/MO
Billy, Ed. de . En Côte d'Ivoire;
Mission Protestante d'A. O. F.,
par E. de Billy. Paris: La
Société des Missions Evan-
geliques, 1931.   NN/Sch
Broadbent, Samuel. A Narrative
of the First Introduction of
Christianity Amongst the Baro-
long Tribe of Bechuanas,
South Africa; With a Brief
Summary of the Subsequent
History of the Wesleyan Mis-
sion to the Same People. Lon-
don: Wesleyan Mission House,
1865.   NN/Sch
Clark, Samuel. Missionary
Memories. Cape Town: Meth-
odist Book Depot & Publishing
House, 1927.   NN/Sch
Crouzet. ...Dix ans d'Apostolat
Dans le Vicariat Apostolique
de Madagascar Meriodional,
1896-1905. Lille: Desclee,
de Brouwer et cie, 1912.
Daigre, Father. ...Oubangui-

Chari; Témoignage sur son
Evolution (1900-1940). Issou-
dun, Indre: Dillen & Cie,
1947.   NN/Sch
Dubois, Henri Marie. La Mission de Madagascar Betsiléo.
PP. Jésuites Français (Province de Champagne) Son Histoire, son Organisation, ses
Oeuvres. Lille, France: Procure des Missions, 1925.
                      NN/Sch
Ellis, William. History of Madagascar. Comprising also the
Progress of the Christian Mission Established in 1818; and
an Authentic Account of the
Persecution and Recent Martyrdom of the Native Christians.
Comp. chiefly from original
documents, by the Rev. Wm.
Ellis, London: Fisher, Son &
Co., 1838.   NN/Sch
-- Madagascar Revisited. Describing the events of a new
reign and the revolution which
followed; setting forth also the
persecutions endured by the
Christians, and their heroic
sufferings, with notices of the
present state and prospects of
the people... London: J. Murray, 1867.   NN/Sch
--The Martyr Church. A narrative of the introduction, progress, and triumph of Christianity in Madagascar. With notices of personal intercourse
and travel in that island. London: J. Snow, 1870. NN/Sch
Faure, Jean. ... Togo Champ de
Mission. Paris: Société des
Missions Evangéliques, 1943.
                      NN/Sch
Fenton, Thomas. Black Harvester... London: Cargate Press,
n. d.   NN/Sch
Fintan, Father. Light and Laughter in Darkest Africa. Dublin:
M. H. Gill & Son, 1943.
                      NN/Sch
Fisher, Ruth B. On the Borders
of Pigmy Land. Chicago:

F. H. Revell Co. , 1905.
NN/Sch
Fisher, William Singleton. Af-
rica Looks Ahead. The life
stories of Walter and Anna
Fisher of Central Africa. Lon-
don: Pickering & Inglis, 1948.
NN/Sch
Flickinger, Daniel Kumler and
William McGee. Missions of
the United Brethren in Christ.
History of the origin, devel-
opment, and condition of mis-
sions among the Sherbro and
Mendi tribes, in Western Af-
rica. Dayton, O.: United
Brethren Publishing House,
1885.   DHU/MO
Fouroadier, Etienne. ...La Vie
Héroique de Victoire Rasoa-
manrivo. Paris: Dillen, 1937.
NN/Sch
Gale, William Kendell. Church
Planting in Madagascar. With
a foreword by Dr. T. Coch-
rane... London: The World
Dominion Press, 1937.
NN/Sch
Giffen, John Kelly. "Fifteen
Years of Progress in Egypt."
Missionary Review of the
World (27; Nov. , 1904), pp.
835-41.   DHU/R
Gorja, Joseph. La Côté d'Ivoire
Chretienne. Lyon: E. Vitte,
1915.   NN/Sch
Goyau, Georges. ...Un Grand
"Homme," Mere Javouhey,
Apôtre des Moirs; Avec Qua-
tre Gravures Hors Texte.
Paris: Plon, 1929. NN/Sch
Groffier, Valérien. ...Héros
Trop Qubliés de Notre Epopée
Coloniale. Afrique Occident-
ale, Centrale et Orientale.
Lyon: E. Vitte, 1928.
NN/Sch
Groselaude, Étienne. ...Un
Parisien à Madagascar; Aven-
tures et Impressions de Voy-
age. Ouvrage Illustré de 138
Gravures. Paris: Hachette,
1898.   NN/Sch

Guilcher, Rene François. ...
La Société des Missions Afri-
caines; ses Origines, sa Na-
ture, sa Vie, ses Oeuvres.
Lyon: Procure des Missions
Africaines, 1956.   NN/Sch
Guinness, Fanny Emma. The
New World of Central Africa;
With a History of the First
Christian Mission on the Con-
go. Chicago: F. H. Revell,
1890.   NN/Sch
Hardyman, J. Madagascar on
the Move. London: Living-
stone Press, 1950. DHU/MO
Hayford, Mark Christian. West
Africa and Christianity. A
lecture delivered at the Ro-
chester Theological Seminary,
N. Y. , U. S. A. , September
28th, 1900, by Rev. Mark C.
Hayford... London: Pub. for
the author by the Baptist Tract
and Book Society, 1903.
NN/Sch
Hepburn, James Davidson.
Twenty Years in Khama's
Country and Pioneering Among
the Batauana of Lake Ngami;
told in the letters of the Rev.
J. D. Hepburn. London: Hod-
der, 1895.   NN/Sch
Hurst, Leonard. There Blos-
soms Red. London: Living-
stone Press, 1949. NN/Sch
Joseph, Gaston,   ...
Côte d'Ivoire. Paris: A.
Fayard, 1944.   NN/Sch
Kilham, Hannah. The Claims of
West Africa to Christian In-
struction. London: Harvey
and Darton, 1830. DHU/MO
Kinch, Emily Christmas. West
Africa, An Open Door. Phila-
delphia: Pr. by the A. M. E.
Book Concern, 1917.
NN/Sch; CtY-D
Knight-Bruce, George Wyndham
Hamilton, (bp.). Memories of
Mashonaland. London: E.
Arnold, 1895.   NN/Sch
Lacy, Creighton, (ed.). Chris-
tianity Amid Rising Men and

(Lacy, C. cont.)
Nations, by Barbara Ward...
New York: Association Press,
1965.   NN/Sch; NcD
"These nine papers emerge
from an interdisciplinary symposium sponsored by the Di-
vinity School of Duke Univer-
sity with the aid of the Ford
Foundation (April 9-12, 1954)."
La Vaissiere, Camille de. His-
toire de Madagascar, ses
Habitants et ses Missionnaires,
par le p. de La Vaissiere...
Paris: V. Lecoffre, 1884.
                    NN/Sch
Lhande, Pierre. Madagascar,
1832-1932. Paris: Plon,
1932.   NN/Sch
Light and Darkness in East Af-
rica. A missionary survey of
Uganda, Anglo-Egyptian Sudan,
Abyssinia, Eritrea, and the
three Somalilands. London:
World Domion Press, 1927.
                    NN/Sch
Livingstone, David. ...Family
Letters, 1841-1856... Edited
with an introduction by I.
Schapera. London: Chatto
& Windus, 1959.   NN/Sch
Livingstone, William Pringle.
Mary Slessor of Calabar; Pio-
neer Missionary. New York:
Doran, 1916?   NN/Sch
Mackenzie, John. Day-Dawn in
Dark Places. A story of wan-
dering and work in Bechuana-
land. London: Cassell, 1883.
                    NN/Sch
Madagascar for Christ; Impres-
sions of Nine Missionary Visi-
tors to Madagascar, July to
October, 1913. Paris: P.M.S.,
1914.   NN/Sch
McFarlan, Donald Maitland. Cal-
abar, the Church of Scotland
Mission, 1846-1946. London:
T. Nelson, 1946.   NN/Sch
McLanahan, Samuel. Isabella A.
Nassau of Africa. New York:
Women's Board of Foreign
Missions of the Presbyterian

Church, 190-.   NN/Sch
Nystrom, (Mrs.) Gertrude Evelyn.
Seeking Kenya's Treasures.
The life of Charles F. Johns-
ton, pioneer missionary of the
Africa Inland Mission. Grand
Rapids, Mich.: Zondervan
Pub. House, 1949.   NN/Sch
Oliver, Roland. The Missionary
Factor in East Africa. Lon-
don: Longmans, Green, 1952.
                    NN/Sch
Padwick, C. E. Temple Gairdner
of Cairo. London: Society
for Promoting Christian Knowl-
edge, 1930.   MH; CtY
Story of an Anglican mis-
sionary in Egypt during the
first quarter of the twentieth
century. Missions in Egypt.
Reading, Joseph Hankinson. The
Ogowe Band. A narrative of
African travel. Philadelphia:
Reading & Co., 1890. NN/Sch
Richardson, James. Lights and
Shadows; or Chequered Experiences Among Some of the
Heathen Tribes of Madagascar.
The London Missionary Socie-
ty, 1877.   NN/Sch
Schön, James Frederick. Journals of the Rev. James Fred-
erick Schon and Mr. Samuel
Crowther, who, with the Sanc-
tion of Her Majesty's Govern-
ment, Accompanied the Expedi-
tion up the Niger, in 1841, in
Behalf of the Church Mission-
ary Society. ... London: Hat-
chard & Son, 1842. NN/Sch
Sibree, James. Fifty Years in
Madagascar: Personal Experiences of Mission Life and Work
... Boston: Houghton Mifflin,
1924.   NN/Sch
Springer, John McKendree. The
Heart of Central Africa; Miner-
al Wealth and Missionary Opportunity. New York: The
Methodist Book Concern,
1909.   NN/Sch
Tildsley, Alfred. The Remarkable Work Achieved by Rev.

Dr. Mark C. Hayford, in
Promotion of the Spiritual and
Material Welfare of the Natives of West Africa, and Proposed Developments. London:
Morgan & Scott, 1926.
DHU/MO; NN/Sch
Victor, Osmund. The Salient of
of South Africa. London: Society for the Propagation of
the Gospel in Foreign Parts,
1931. NN/Sch

t. Malawi (Nyasaland)
Ambali, Augustine. Thirty
Years in Nyasaland. West-
minster, London: Universities' Mission to Central Africa, 1923.
Negro author.
Barnes, Bertram H. Johnson
of Nyasaland. A study of the
life and work of William Percival Johnson... Archdeacon
of Nyasa, missionary, pioneer, 1876-1928. London:
Universities Mission to Central Africa, 1933.
Booth, Joseph. Africa for the
African. Dedicated first to
Victoria, Queen of Great Britain, second, to the British
and American Christian people,
third, and specially to the
Afro-American people of the
United States of America.
Nyasaland, East Central Africa: n. p. 1897. NN/Sch
Douglas, Arthur Jeffreys. Arthur Douglas, Missionary on
Lake Nyasa. The story of his
life. London: Universities'
Mission to Central Africa,

1912. NN/Sch
Johnson, William Percival. My
African Reminiscences, 1875-
1895. Westminster, London:
Universities' Mission to Cen-
tral Africa, 1924. NN/Sch
Livingstone, William Pringle.
Laws of Livingstonia. A nar-
rative of Missionary adventure
and achievement. London:
Hodder and Stoughton, 1921.
NN/Sch
Macdonald, Duff. Africans; or,
The Heart of Heathen Africa.
London: Simpkin, Marshall
& Co., 1882. NN/Sch
Maclean, Norman. Africa in
Transformation. London: J.
Nisbet & Co., Ltd., 1914.
NN/Sch
Mackintosh, Catharine Winkworth.
...Some pioneer Missions of
Northern Rhodesia and Nyasa-
land. Livingstone, Northern
Rhodesia: Rhodes-Livingstone
Museiu, 1950. NN/Sch
Pineau, Henry. Evêque, Roi
des Brigands. Monseigneur
Dupont, Premier Vicaire Apos-
tolique du Nyassa (1850-1930).
Paris: La Province de France
de Pères Blancs, 1937.
NN/Sch
Shepperson, George. Independent
African; John Chilembwe and
the Origins, Settings and Sig-
nificance of the Nyasaland Na-
tive Rising of 1915. Edin-
burgh: University Press,
1958. NN/Sch
Wishlade, R. L. Sectarianism in
Southern Nyasaland. London:
Oxford University Press,
1965. DHU/MO

2. Independent Churches and Movements

Barrett, David B. "The African
Independent Churches." World
Christian Handbook (New

York: Abingdon Press, 1967),
pp. 24-28. DHU/R
Becken, H. J. "On the Holy

(Becken, H. J. cont.)
Mountain: A Visit to the New
Year's Festival of the Naza-
retha Church on Mount Nhlan-
gakazi, 14 January, 1967."
Journal of Religion in Africa
(1:2, 1967), pp. 138-49.
                          DHU/R
Bertsche, James E. "Kimbangu-
ism: A Challenge to Mission-
ary Statesmanship." Practi-
cal Anthropology (13:1, Ja. -
Feb., 1966), pp. 13-33.
                          DHU/R
Brown, Kenneth I. "Worshiping
with the African Church of the
Lord (Aladura)," Practical
Anthropology (13:2, Mr. -Apr.,
1966), pp. 59-84.   DHU/R
Cameron, W. M. "The Ethiopian
Movement and the Order of
Ethiopia." The East and the
West (2; Jl., 1904), pp. 375-
97.   DHU/R
A discussion of "Ethiopian-
ism" in South Africa.
Crane, William H. "The Kim-
ganguist Church and the Search
for Authentic Catholicity."
Christian Century (87:22, Je.
3, 1970), pp. 691-95. DHU/R
Deals with first independent African Church admitted
to the World Council of
Churches.
Dennett, Richard E. The Re-
ligious and Political System
of the Yoruba. Nigerian
studies. London: Macmillan
& Co., 1910.   DLC
Fehderau, Harold W. "Enthusi-
astic Christianity in an African Church." Practical Anthropology (8:6, Nov. -Dec.,
1961), pp. 279-80; 282.
                          DHU/R
-- "Kimbanguism: Prophetic
Christianity in Congo." Practical Anthropology (9:4, Jl. -
Ag., 1962), pp. 157-78.
                          DHU/R
Haliburton, G. M. "The Prophet
Harris and His Work in Ivory

Coast and Western Ghana."
Doctoral dissertation, Univer-
sity of London, 1966.
Hayward, Victor E. W. (ed.).
African Independent Church
Movements. London: Edin-
burgh House, 1963. DHU/MO
"The Kimbanguist Church in the
Congo." Ecumenical Review
(19:1, Ja., 1967), pp. 29-36.
                          DHU/R
Mitchell, Robert C. "Towards
the Sociology of Religious In-
dependency." Journal of Religion in Africa (III:1, 1970),
pp. 2-21.   DHU/R
Mitchell, Robert Cameron. "Re-
ligions Protest and Social
Change: The Origins of the
Aladura Movement in Western
Nigeria." Robert I. Rotberg
and Ali A. Mazrui (eds.).
Protest and Power in Black
Africa (New York: Oxford Uni-
versity Press, 1970), pp.
458-96.   DHU/R
Peel, John D. Y. "Syncretism
and Religious Change." Comparative Studies in Society and
and History (10:2, Ja., 1968),
pp. 121-41.   DHU/R
A study of the independent
churches in Western Nigeria.
Puller, F. W. "The Ethiopian
Order." East and West (1:1,
Ja., 1903), pp. 75-91.
                          DHU/R
Articles explore the connec-
tion between the "Ethiopian
Movement" in South Africa
and the A. M. E. Church.
Richardson, Lincoln. "Congo's
Kimbanguist Church." Presby-
terian Life (23:14, Ag. 1,
1970), pp. 18-21, 32-34.
                          DHU/R
Roberts, Andrew D. "The Lumpa
Church of Alice Lenshina."
Robert I. Rotberg and Ali A.
Mazrui (eds.). Protest and
Power in Black Africa (New
York: Oxford Univ. Press,
1970), pp. 513-68.   DHU/R

Sales, Jane. "Worship in African Separatist Churches."
Missionary Research Library:
Occasional Bulletin (22:4, Apr.
1971), pp. 1-11.   DHU/R
Thomas, George B. "Kimbangu-
ism, African Christianity."
International Documentation
on the Contemporary Church
(Mar. 13, 1971), pp. 2-29.
                        DHU/R
Turner, Harold W., ed. "Bib-
liography of Modern African
Religious Movements: Supple-
ment 1." Journal of Religion
in Africa (1:3, 1968), pp. 173-
210.   DHU/R
-- History of an African Inde-
pendent Church. Oxford:
Clarendon Press, 1967.
            DHU/MO; OWibfU
-- "The Litany of an Independent
West African Church." Prac-
tical Anthropology (7:6, Nov. -
Dec., 1960), pp. 256-62.
                        DHU/R
-- "Pagan Features in West Af-
rican Independent Churches."
Practical Anthropology (12:4,
Jl. -Ag., 1965), pp. 145-51.
                        DHU/R
-- "The Place of Independent Re-
ligious Movements in the Mod-

ernization of Africa." Journal
of Religion in Africa (2:1,
1969), pp. 43-63.   DHU/R
-- "A Typology for African Religious Movements." Journal
of Religion in Africa (1:1,
1967), pp. 1-34.   DHU/R
Van der Post, Laurens. The
Dark Eye in Africa. New
York: William Morrow & Co.,
1955.   DHU/MO
    David Stirling and the Cap-
ricorn Society, formulated in
British Africa, dedicated to
forming a new society free of
hate, color and religious dis-
crimination.
Walls, A. F., ed. "Bibliography of
the Society for African Church
History." Journal of Religion in
Africa (1:1, 1967), pp. 46-94.
                        DHU/R
Welbourn, Frederick Burkewood.
A Place to Feel at Home; a
Study of Two Independent
Churches in Western Kenya.
London: Oxford Univ. Press,
1966.   NN/Sch
Welton, Michael R. "The Holy
Aruosa: Religious Conserva-
tism in a Changing Society."
Practical Anthropology (16:1,
Ja. -Feb., 1969), pp. 18-27.
                        DHU/R

3. Recent Status

a. West Africa
Agbebi, Mojola. The Christian
Handbook, New Calabar, West
Africa. n. p., n. d.   NN/Sch
Baeta, C. G. Prophetism in Gha-
na. London: SCM Press,
1962.   DHU/MO
Belshaw, Harry. Facing the Fu-
ture in West Africa. London:
Cargate Press, 1951. NN/Sch
Faduma, Orishetukeh. "Religious
Beliefs of the Yoruba People,
West Africa." J. W. E. Bowen,
(ed.). Africa and the Amer-
ican Negro: Addresses and
Proceedings of the Congress

on Africa. (Miami, Fla. :
Mnemesyne Publishing Co.,
1969), pp. 31-6.   DHU/R
Forbes, Edgar Allen. "The
American Church on the West
Coast of Africa." Spirit of
Missions (74:8, Ag., 1909),
pp. 673-81.   DHU/R
    Illus. account of missionary
activity in Liberia.
Lasbrey, Bertram. "The Church
in Nigeria: Its Position and
Its Opportunity." The East and
the West (23; Apr., 1925), pp.
113-18.   DHU/R

Leone, John Sierra. "First Impressions of Sierra Leone." The Church Missionary Review (63; My., 1912), pp. 272-78. DHU/R

Morton, William P. "An Outline of the Cosmology and the Cult Organization of the Oyo Yoruba." Africa (34; 1964), p. 243. DHU/MO

Parratt, J. K. "Religious Change in Yoruba Society-A Test Case." Journal of Religion in Africa (2:2, 1969), pp. 113-28. DHU/R

Pilkington, F. "The Church in Nigeria." African Affairs (56), pp. 158-60. DHU

Sackey, Isaac. "A Brief History of the A. M. E. Zion Church, West Gold Coast District 1903-1953." Pam File; DHU/R

Truly, Mary Elizabeth. "Baptist Educational Program for Girls in Nigeria." D. R. E. thesis, Southwestern Baptist Theological Seminary, 1960.

Varney, Peter D. "Religion in a West African University." Journal of Religion in Africa, (2:1, 1969), pp. 1-42. DHU/R

"Western Africa." The American Quarterly Register (6:2, Nov., 1833), pp. 93-4. DHU/R

b. East Africa

"African Islands." The American Quarterly Register (6:2, Nov., 1833), pp. 96-8. DHU/R

Bordeaux, Henry. L'Épopée Noir: La France en Afrique Occidentale. Paris: Denoël et Steele, 1936. NN/Sch

"Eastern Africa." The American Quarterly Register (6:2, Nov., 1833), p. 96. DHU/R

Kamfer, Pieter P. Die Volksorganiese Sendingmetode. By Bruno Gutmann. Amsterdam: Swets & Zeitlinger, 1955. NN/Sch

Summary in English.

Hastings, Adrian. Church and Mission in Modern Africa. Bronx, N. Y.: Fordham University Press, 1968. DHU/R

Kingsnorth, John S. Come Back Africa; the Review of the Work of 1962. London: Universities' Mission to Central Africa, 196-. NN/Sch

Miller, Paul M. Equipping for Ministry in East Africa. Dodoma, Tanzania Cential: Tanganyika Press, 1969. DHU/R

Tanner, R. E. S. "Married Clergy in East and Central Africa: The Clash of Roles." Heythrop Journal (11:3, Jl., 1970), pp. 278-93. DHU/R

Walker, R. H. "Christian Unity in East Africa." The Church Missionary Review (50; Oct., 1909), pp. 621-23. DHU/R

Westink, D.E. "The Orthodox Church in East Africa." Ecumenical Review (20:1, Ja., 1968), pp. 33-43. DHU/R
A discussion of the African Greek Orthodox Church.

c. South Africa

Bobo, John. "Congregation Explores on-the-job Christianity." National Council Outlook (8; Sept., 1958), pp. 11-12. DHU/R

Brayshaw, E. Russell. "The Racial Problems of South Africa." Friends Intelligencer (109:33, Ag. 16, 1952), pp. 467-69. DHU/R

Carsten, Kenneth N., an interview with. "South Africa, the Churches and the Future." Concern (8:22, Dec. 15, 1966), pp. 4-7. DHU/R

Cawood, Lesley. The Churches and Race Relations in South Africa. Johannesburg: South African Institute of Race Relations, 1964. NcD; DLC

DeBeer, Z. J. Multi-Racial South

African: The Reconciliation of Forces. Issued under the auspices of the Institute of Race Relations. London: Oxford Univ. Press, 1961.
A&M; DHU/MO
Du Preez, Andries Bernardus. Eiesoortige Ontwikkeling Tot Volksdiens, die Hoop van Suid-Afrika. Kaapstad: H. A. U. M. , 1959.
--Inside the South African Crucible. Kaapstad, So. Africa: H. A. U. M. , 1959.
DLC; NN/Sch
Dutch Reformed Conference of Church Leaders, Pretoria, 1953. Christian Principles in Multi-Racial South Africa; A Report. Pretoria: n. p. , 1954. Conference held Nov. 17-19, 1953.
Du Toit, Stefanus. Holy Scripture and Race Relations, with Special Application to South African Conditions. Potchefstroom: Pro Rege-Pers, 1960.
DLC; NcD
Hurley, Denis E. Apartheid: A Crisis of the Christian Conscience. Delivered under the auspices of the South African Institute of Race Relations. Pietermaritzburg: Printed by the National Witness, 1964.
NN/Sch
Inter-Racial Conference of Church Leaders, Johannesburg, 1954. God's Kingdom in Multi-Racial South Africa; A Report on the Inter-Racial Conference of Church Leaders, Johannesburg, 7-10 December, 1954. Johannesburg: Printed by Voortrekkerpers Beperk, 1955?
NN/Sch
Jackman, Stuart Brooke. The Numbered Days. London: SCM Press, 1954.
DHU/R; NN/Sch; DLC
Keet, B. Wither--South Africa? Translated by N. J. Marquard. Stellenbosch, University Pub-

lishers and Booksellers, 1958.
NN/Sch
Kotzé, Jacobus Cornelius Gideon. Principle and Practice in Race Relations, According to Scripture. Stellenbosch, S. C. A. Publishers, 1962. DLC; NcD
Landman, W. A. A Plea for Understanding; A Reply to the Reformed Church in America. Cape Town: N. G. Kerkuitgewers for the Information Bureau of the Dutch Reformed Church in South Africa, 1968.
DLC
"Liberal Wins South Africa Church Election." Christian Century (79; Nov. 7, 1962), p. 1346.
DHU/R
Milingo, Emmanuel. "Patronado and Apartheid. Text of a radio speech delivered as a Easter Sermon. March 29, 1970." International Documentation on the Contemporary Church, North American Edition. (No. 10; Sept. 26, 1970), pp. 51-57. DHU/R
Archbishop of Lusaka, Zambia discusses the moral duty of the Catholic Church to censure the government.
Mitchell, Constance. "History and Development of the Seventh-Day Adventist Church in the Union of South Africa." Master's thesis, Howard University, 1959.
Nash, J. O. "The Church of the Province of South Africa." The Church Overseas (3; 1930), pp. 268-78. DHU/R
Noble, Walter James. The Black Trek; From Village to Mine in Africa. London: Livingstone Press, 1931. NN/Sch
Paton, Alan. The Long View. Edward Callan, (ed.). New York: Frederick A. Praeger, 1968. DHU/R
Chapt. II is entitled "Christian Conscience in a Racial Society."

(Paton, A. cont.)
--"The Price of Segregation:
The Effects of Apartheid on
Culture." Social Action (34:
8, Apr., 1968), pp. 19-25.
                              DHU/R
Pistorius, Philippus Villiers.
No Further Trek. Johannes-
burg: Central News Agency,
1957.   DLC
Pitts, S. G. "Churches Protest
South Africa Law." Christian
Century (74; Je. 5, 1957), pp.
714-16.   DHU
Reaves, A. "South Africa: the
Sin of Racism." Christian
Century (78; Dec. 13, 1961),
pp. 1490-3.   DHU
Reeves, Richard Ambrose, (bp.).
South Africa, Yesterday and
Tomorrow: A Challenge to
Christians. London: Gol-
lancz, 1962. DHU/R; NcD
--"South African Church vs.
Racism." Christian Century
(74; Ag. 7, 1957), pp. 936-9.
                              DHU
"The Responsibility of United
States Catholics and Racism
in Southern Africa." IDOC
International North American
Edition. (May 29, 1971), pp.
6-15.   DHU/R
Ross, Emory. ...Colour and
Christian Community. De-
livered under the auspices and
in the 25th anniversary year
of the South African Institute
of Race Relations, by Emory
Ross, at Johannesburg on 4
August 1954, and at Cape
Town on 6 August 1954. Jo-
hannesburg, S. A., Institute of
Race Relations, 1954. NN/Sch
Sachs, Bernard. The Road from
Sharpeville. London: D. Dob-
son, 1961.
              DHU/R; NN/Sch; DLC
Schneider, T. "The Divine Names
in the Tsonga Bible." The
Bible Translator (21:2, Apr.,
1970), pp. 89-99.   DHU/R
Setiloane, Gabriel M. "Youth

Work in African Churches in
South Africa." Ecumenical Re-
view (15:2, Ja., 1962), pp.
144-48.   DHU/R
Sheerin, John B. "South African
Bishops Defy the Government."
Catholic World (185; Sept.,
1957), pp. 401-2.   DHU/R
Shepherd, Robert Henry Wishat.
"Apartheid in South Africa's
Churches." Christian Century
(76:4 Ja. 28, 1959), pp. 103-
5.   DHU
"A Sick Church." Target (74;
June, 1970), p. 1.   DHU/R
An examination of the Angli-
can Church of Uganda, Rwan-
da and Burundi.
"South Africa." The American
Quarterly Register (6:2, Nov.,
1833), pp. 94-6.   DHU/R
"South African Churches Race
Against Time." Christian
Century (74:27, Jl. 31, 1957),
pp. 910-11.   DHU
"South African Racists Fear the
Light." Christian Century (79;
My. 30, 1962), p. 682. DHU
Southern Africa: A Time for
Change. George M. Daniells,
ed. New York: Friendship
Press, 1969.   DHU/R
"Effort on part of the church
to emphasize the deepening
plight of Southern Africa, the
backgrounds of its current
crisis and its future."
Sundkler, Bengt G. M. "Bantu
Messiah and White Christ."
Practical Anthropology (7:4;
Jl.-Ag., 1960), pp. 170-6.
                              DHU/R
Wadlow, Rene. "An African
Church and Social Change."
Practical Anthropology (16:6,
Nov.-Dec., 1969), pp. 257+.
                              DHU/R
"White Man's God: Apartheid
and the Churches." Time
(70; Jl. 29, 1957), p. 21.
                              DHU
"Witness Against Odds in South
Africa." Christian Century

(79:27 Jl. 4, 1962), p. 832.
DHU/R
Zulu, A. H. "Message from Africa." Christian Century (79: 3 Jan. 10, 1962), pp. 60-1.
DHU/R
Zululand, Wilmot. "A Native Episcopate for South Africa." East and the West (19; Ja., 1921), pp. 50-53.   DHU/R

d. Central Africa

Andersson, Efraim. Messianic Popular Movements in the Lower Congo. London: William Heinemann, Ltd., 1958.
CtY-D; DHU/MO

Broomfield, Gerald Webb. Towards Freedom. With a foreword by the Archbishop of New York. London: The Universities' Mission to Central Africa, 1957.   NN/Sch

Cline, Catherine Ann. The Church and the Movement for Congo Reform." Church History (32:1, Mr., 1963), pp. 45-56.

Coxill, H. Wakelin. "The Growth of the Church in the Congo." The East and West Review (5:1, Ja., 1939), pp. 62-9.   DHU/R

Fehderau, Harold W. "Planting the Church in the Congo, and the Merging Situation Today." Practical Anthropology (8:1, Ja.-Feb., 1961), pp. 25-30.
DHU/R

Hetherwick, Alexander. The Gospel and the African; The Croall Lectures for 1930-1931 on the Impact of the Gospel on a Central African People. Edinburgh: T. & T. Clark, 1932.   NN/Sch

Jadot, Jean. "The Church in the Congo." Catholic World (201:1, 204, Jl., 1965), pp. 247-53.   DHU/R

Jones, Arthur Gordon. Bridge of Friendship. London: Car-

gate Press, 1955.   NN/Sch

Keable, Robert. Darkness or Light; Studies in the History of the Universities' Mission to Central Africa. Illustrations to the theory and practice of missions; with a preface by the Rt. Rev. Frank Weston. London: Universities' Mission to Central Africa, 1914.
NN/Sch

Keller, Jean. "The Churches of Equatorial Africa." Practical Anthropology (10:1, Ja.-Feb., 1963), pp. 27-31.   DHU/R

Lasbrey, Bertram. Problems of a Church in Tropical Africa: The Niger Diocese." East and West Review (4:4, Oct., 1938), pp. 312-19.   DHU/R

Morris, Colin M. Anything but This; the Challenge of Race in Central Africa. London: United Society for Christian Literature, 1958.   NN/Sch

Parr, Martin W. "Church and State in Equatoria." East and West Review (5:3, Jl., 1939), pp. 214-19.   DHU/R

"South Africa: Geography and Natural Divisions." The American Quarterly Register (5:1, Ag., 1832), pp. 46-55.
DHU/R

e. General

Akeley, Delia J. (Denning). Jungle Portraits: with Original Photographs. New York: Macmillan Co., 1930.
DHU/MO

All-Africa Church Conference, Ibadan, Nigeria, 1958. "The Church in Changing Africa; Report of the All-Africa Church Conference, Held at Ibadan, Nigeria, January 10-19, 1958." New York: International Missionary Council, 1958.   NN/Sch

Asamoa, F.A. "The Christian Church and African Heritage."

(Asamoa, F. A. cont.)
International Review of Missions (44; 1955), pp. 292-301.
                              DHU/R
Baeta, C. G. "The Younger
Churches: An African View-
point." Religion in Life (34:
1, Wint., 1964-65), pp. 15-
24.   DHU/R
Bailey, J. Martin. "World Spot-
light Hits Africa." United
Church Herald (13:11, Dec.,
1970), pp. 44-7.   DHU/R
   "Churches collide with
white regimes in South Af-
rica, Rhodesia and Angola."
Banks, Arthur Leslie, (ed.).
The Development of Tropical
and Subtropical Countries with
Particular Reference to Africa.
London: Arnold, 1954.
                              DHU/MO
Barrett, David B. Schism and
Renewal in Africa: An Analy-
sis of Six Thousand Contempo-
rary Religious Movements.
New York: Oxford University
Press, 1968.   DLC
Beetham, Thomas. Christianity
and New Africa. London:
Pall Mall Press, 1967. DLC
Blomjous, Joseph. "The Church
in a Developing World."
Cross Currents (20:3, Sum.,
1970), pp. 287-314. DHU/R
   Church in Africa today.
Bowen, John Wesley Edward,
(ed.). Africa and the Ameri-
can Negro. Atlanta: Frank-
lin Press, 1896.   DHU/MO
Cash, W. Wilson. "Church Build-
ing in East Africa." East and
West Review (4:1, Ja., 1938),
pp. 21-28.   DHU/R
Coan, Josephus R. "The Mis-
sionary Presence in Africa."
A. M. E. Church Review (104:
246, Apr.-Je., 1971), pp. 65-
72.   DHU/R
   Negro author.
Comhaire, J. L. "Religious
Trends in African and Afro-
American Urban Societies."

Anthropology Quarterly (1; Ja.,
1928), pp. 95-108.   DHU
Conference on Christian Citizen-
ship in a Multi-Racial Society,
Rosettenville, South Africa, 1949.
The Christian Citizen in a
Multi-Racial Society: A Re-
port of the Rosettenville Con-
ference, July, 1949. With
Aids to Study and Discussion.
Strand, C. P.: Christian Coun-
cil of South Africa, 1949.
                          NN/Sch
Considine, John J. "Africa-
Birth of a Great Black Church."
Catholic World (190:1, 136,
Nov., 1959), pp. 93-100.
                          DHU/R
Damboriena, Prudencio. Tongues
As of Fire: Pentacostalism
in Contemporary Christianity.
Washington: Corpus Books,
1969.   DHU/R
   Chapter 9, Mission and
Ecumenism.
Desai, Ram, (ed.). Christianity
in Africa as Seen by Africans.
Denver: Swallow, 1962.
                 NN/Sch; DHU/MO
Dovlo, C. K. Africa Awakes.
Accra: Scottish Mission Book
Depot, 1952.   DHU/MO
   Some of the problems fac-
ing Africa today as seen from
the Christian point of view.
Fanon, Frantz. The Wretched of
the Earth. New York: Grove
Press, 1963.
   Author discusses the part
that religious rivalries play in
developing nations. DHU/R
Fueter, Paul D. "The African
Contribution to Christian Edu-
cation." Practical Anthropol-
ogy (11:1, Ja.-Feb., 1964),
pp. 1-13.   DHU/R
Herskovits, Melville J. "Afri-
can Gods and Catholic Saints
in New World Negro Belief."
American Anthropologist (38;
Oct.-Dec., 1937), pp. 635-
45.   DCU/AN
Hess, Mahlon M. "African Po-

litical Systems and African Church Polity." Practical Anthropology (4:5, Sept. -Oct., 1957), pp. 170-84. DHU/R

International Missionary Council. Assembly, Accra, 1957-1958. Minutes of the Assembly of the International Missionary Council, Ghana, December 28th, 1957 to January 8th, 1958. London: International Missionary Council, 1958?
NN/Sch

-- Dept. of Social and Industrial Research. Modern Industry and the African. An inquiry into the effect of the copper mines of Central Africa upon native society and the work of Christian missions made under the auspices of the Dept. of Social and Industrial Research of the Inter-Missionary Council... London: Macmillan & Co., 1933. DHU/MO

Johnson, Thomas Sylvester. The Story of a Mission. London: S. P. C. K., 1953. DHU/MO

Karefa-Smart, John. The Halting Kingdom; Christianity and the African Revolution. New York: Friendship Press, 1959.
NN/Sch
Negro author.

Kitagawa, D. "Church and Race in Today's Africa." Christian Century (78; No. 20, May 17, 1961), pp. 620-2. DHU

Kiwanicka, Joseph. "Silver Jubilee of Colored Bishop." St. Augustine's Messenger (31:9, Nov., 1954), pp. 313-17.
DHU/R
"Biographies of African Bishops."

Lagos, Frank Melville. "The Future of the Church in Africa." The East and the West (22; Apr., 1924), pp. 125-36. DHU/R

Lavanoux, Maurice. "African Religious Art Looks Forward." Catholic World (190:1, 136,

Nov., 1959), pp. 107-11.
DHU/R
Loth, Heinrich. Kolonialismus Unter der Kutte. Berlin: Dietz, 1960. NN/Sch

Makunike, Ezekiel C. "Voices for the New Africa." Ecumenical Press Service (Je., 1971), pp. 3-4. DHU/R

Martin, Denis. "Christianity and Development in Africa." Cross Currents (15; Wint., 1965), pp. 19-31. DHU/R

Mitchell, Robert E. and Harold W. Turner (comp.). A Comprehensive Bibliography of Modern African Religious Movements. Evanston, Ill.: Northwestern Univ. Press, 1966.
DHU/MO

Montgomery, H. H. "Education in Tropical Africa." East and West (23; Ja., 1925), pp. 1-7. DHU/R
An evaluation of Missionary education in Africa.

Moore, Clark D. and Ann Dunbar. Africa Yesterday and Today. New York: Frederick A. Praeger, 1969. DHU/R
pp. 350-7 missionaries and the Peace Corps.

Morris, Colin M. "The Cross Over Africa." Christian Century (87:22, Je. 3, 1970), pp. 688-91. DHU/R

-- Out of Africa Crucible; Sermons from Central Africa. London: Lutterworth Press, 1960. NN/Sch

Neill, Stephen C. "Crisis in Tropical Africa." The Ecumenical Review (3:1, Oct., 1950), pp. 14-25. DHU/R

Nelson, Robert G. "God's Church in Africa." World Call (53:7, Jl. -Ag., 1971), pp. 22-23.
DHU/R

Nketa, J. H. "The Contribution of African Culture to Christian Worship." International Journal of Missions (47:4, 1958), pp. 265-78. DHU/R

Noble, Frederic Perry. "Outlook for African Missions in the Twentieth Century." J. W. E. Bowen (ed.). Africa and the American Negro: Addresses and Proceedings of the Congress on Africa. (Miami, Fla.: Mnemosyne Publishing Inc., 1969), pp. 61-67.   DHU/R

--The Redemption of Africa; A Story of Civilization. With maps, statistical tables and select bibliography of the literature of African Missions... Chicago: F. H. Revell, 1899.
NN/Sch

Oosthuizer, Gerhardus C. Post-Christianity in Africa: A Theological and Anthropological Study. Grand Rapids, Mich.: Eerdmans, 1968.
DHU/MO
"A study of Christian and nativistic movements."

Pawelzik, Fritz, (ed.). I Lie on My Mat and Pray: Prayers by Young Africans. New York: Friendship Press, 1964.
DHU/R

Pratt, S. A. J. "Spiritual Conflicts in a Changing African Society." Ecumenical Review (8:2, Ja., 1956), pp. 154-62.
DHU/R

Rawson, David P. "Africa's Social and Political Demands on the Church." Practical Anthropology (16:1, Mr.-Apr., 1969), pp. 75-83.   DHU/R

Reyburn, William D. "Africanization and African Studies." Practical Anthropology (9:3, My.-Je., 1962), pp. 97-110.
DHU/R
Discusses the subtle reorientation of Christianity as it is exposed to African influences.

-- "Conflicts and Contradictions in African Christianity." Practical Anthropology (4:5, Sept.-Oct., 1957), pp. 161-69.
DHU/R

--"The Message of the Old Testament and the African Church-- I." Practical Anthropology (7:4, Jl.-Ag., 1960), pp. 152-56.   DHU/R

--"Sickness, Sin and the Curse: The Old Testament and the African Church--II." Practical Anthropology (7:5, Sept.-Oct., 1960), pp. 217-22.   DHU/R

Rotberg, Robert I. A Political History of Tropical Africa. New York: Harcourt, Brace, 1965.   DHU/MO
Conflict between Christian and Islamic traditions in Africa.

Samarin, William J. "Gbeya Prescientific Attitudes and Christianity." Practical Anthropology (6:4, Jl.-Ag., 1959), pp. 179-82.   DHU/R

Stevens, D. A. "African Christianity and the Sacraments." East and West (22; Oct., 1924, pp. 339-45.   DHU/R

Stock, Eugene. "A Notable African Bishop," Church Missionary Review (68; Ag., 1917), pp. 323-32.   DHU/R

Tanner, R. E. S. "Priestly Classes in East and Central Africa." The Heythrop Journal (12:2, Apr., 1971), pp. 175-91.
DHU/R

Thompson, Vincent B. Africa and Unity; The Evolution of Pan-Africanism. New York: Humanities Press, 1969.
DHU/MO
Information on religious overtones and undertones in the African resistance.

Trobisch, Walter A. "Church Discipline in Africa." Practical Anthropology (8:5, Sept.-Oct., 1961), pp. 200-06.   DHU/R

Zanzibar, Frank. "Mr. Keable's Indictment of African Priests." East and West (17; Ja., 1919), pp. 165-75.   DHU/R

II.   Christianity and Slavery in the New World

A.   SLAVERY IN THE WEST INDIES AND SOUTH AMERICA

Beattie, John and John Middleton,
(eds.). Spirit Mediumship and
Society in Africa. New York:
Africana Pub. Co., 1969.
                        DHU/R
Bennett, J. Harry. Bondsmen
and Bishops; Slavery and Ap-
prenticeship on the Codrington
Plantations of Barbados, 1710-
1838. Berkeley: University of
California Press, 1958.
                        CtY-D
Bird, Mark Baker. The Black
Man; or, Haytian [sic] Inde-
pendence. Deduced from his-
torical notes, and Dedicated to
the government and people of
Hayti. New York: Published
by the author, 1869. NN/Sch
Bleby, Henry. Romance Without
Fiction: or, Sketches from the
Portfolio of an Old Missionary.
London: Published for the au-
thor at The Wesleyan Confer-
ence Office, 1872.   NN/Sch
Breathett, George. "Religious
Protectionism and the Slave in
Haiti." Catholic Historical Re-
view (55:1, Apr., 1969), pp.
26-39.   DHU/R
Buchner, J. H. The Moravians
in Jamaica. History of the
Mission of the United Breth-
ren's Church to the Negroes in
the Island of Jamaica, from
the Year 1754-1854... London:
Longman, Brown & Co., 1854.
                        DHU/MO
Bury, Herbert. A Bishop
Amongst Bananas. Milwaukee:
Young Churchman Co., 1911.
                        NN/Sch

Caswell, Henry. The Martyr of
the Pongas being a Memoir of
the Rev. Hamble James Lea-
cock, Leader of the West Indian Mission to Western Africa.
London: Rivingtons, 1857.
                        NN/Sch
Chaplin, David. "Caribbean Ecumenism." International Review
of Missions (60:238, Apr.,
1971), pp. 186-91.   DHU/R
Coke, Thomas, (bp.). A History of the West Indies; Containing the natural, civil, and
ecclesiastical history of each
island; with an account of the
missions instituted in those islands, from the commence-
ment of their civilization; but
more especially of the Missions which have been established in that Archipelago by
the Society late in connexion
with the Rev. John Wesley...
Liverpool: Printed by Nuttall,
Fisher & Dixon, 1808.
              DHU/MO; NN/Sch
The Conference: or, Sketches of
Wesleyan Methodism. In two
parts. By the author of
"Amusements of a Mission,"
...Bridgeton, West N. J.: J.
Clarke, 1824.   DHU/MO
   Part II contains short sec-
tions on bringing God to the
blacks of South and West Africa and the slaves of the West
Indies.   DHU/MO
Copley, Esther. A History of
Slavery and its Abolition. Lon-
don: Houlston & Stoneman,
1839.   NN/Sch

Drew, Samuel. The Life of the
Rev. Thomas Coke. Including
in detail his various travels
an extraordinary missionary
exertions, in England, Ireland,
America, and the West Indies.
New York: Published by T.
Manson and G. Lane, for the
Methodist Episcopal Church,
at the Conference Office, 200
Mulberry Street; J. Collord,
printer, 1837.   NN/Sch
Hill, Clifford. "From Church to
Sect: West Indian Religious
Sect Development in Britain."
Journal for the Scientific Study
of Religion (10:2, Sum. , 1971),
pp. 114-23.   DHU/R
"Written by a Fellow of the
Martin Luther King Founda-
tion," London, England.
Hovey, Sylvester. Letters from
the West Indies; Relating Es-
pecially to the Danish Island
St. Croix, and the British Islands Antigua, Barbadoes and
Jamaica. New York: Gould
and Newman, 1838.   NN/Sch
Knibb, William. Facts and Doc-
uments Connected in the Late
Insurrection in Jamaica, and
the Violations of Civil and
Religious Liberty Originating
Out of It. London: Holds-
worth & Ball, 1832.   DLC
-- and Peter Borthwick. Colonial
Slavery. Defense of the Baptist missionaries from the
charge of inciting the late rebellion in Jamaica. A discussion Dec. 15, 1832, at Bath.
London: Published at the
Tourist Office, 1832.   DLC
Latimer, James. "The Foundations of Religious Education in
the Spanish West Indies."
Journal of Negro Education
(39:1, Win. , 1970), pp. 70-75.
                        DHU/R
-- "The Foundations of Religious
Education in the French West
Indies." Journal of Negro Education (40:1, Wint. , 1971),

pp. 91-8,   DHU/R
Moore, Joseph Grassle. Re-
ligion of Jamaican Negroes;
A study of Afro-Jamaican Ac-
culturation. Ann Arbor,
Mich.: University Microfilms,
1940.   DLC
Murray, William. "Christianity
in the West Indies." Schaff,
Philip and S. I. Prime. Evan-
gelical Alliance Sixth General
Conference. Held in New York
Oct. 2-12, 1873. (New York:
Harper & Bros. , 1874), pp.
133-36.   DHU/R
Oldendorp, Christian Georg
Andreas. C. G. A. Oldendorps
Geschichte der Mission der
Evangelischen Bruder auf den
Caraibischen Inseln S. Thomas.
S. Croix und S. Jan Heraus-
gegben durch Johann Jakob
Bossart... Barby: Bey C. F.
Laux, und in Leipzig in Com-
mission bey Weidmanns Erben
und Reich, 1777.   NN/Sch
Orjala, Paul. Haiti Diary: The
Intimate Story of a Modern
Missionary Couple's First Two
Years in a Foreign County.
Compiled from the letters of
Paul Orjala and edited by
Kathleen Spell. Kansas City,
Mo.: Beacon Hill Press, 1953.
                     NN/Sch
Pitman, Frank Wesley. "Slavery
on British West India Planta-
tions in the Eighteenth Century."
Journal of Negro History (11:
4, Oct. , 1926), pp. 584-660.
                        DHU
Religious instruction of the
slaves.
Ramos, Arthur. ...Las Culturas
Negras en el Nuevo Mundo; Ver-
sion Española de Ernestina de
Champourcin, Glosario de Voces.
Mexico: Fondo de Cultura
Económica, 1943.   NcD
Ramsay, James. An Essay on
the Treatment and Conversion
of African Slaves on the Bri-
tish Sugar Colonies. London:

J. Phillips, 1784. DLC; FSU
Riot in Barbadoes, and Destruc-
tion of the Wesleyan Chapel
and Mission House. London:
J. & T. Clarke, Printers, St.
John-Square, 1823.   NN/Sch
Rose, George Henry, (Sir)...
A Letter on the Means and
Importance of Converting the
Slaves in the West Indies to
Christianity. By the Rt. Hon.
Sir G. H. Rose. London: J.
Murray, 1823.   NN/Sch
Smith, Robert W. "Slavery and
Christianity in the British
West Indies." Church History
(19:3, Sept., 1950), pp. 171-
86.   DHU/R
Society for the Conversion and
Religious Instruction and Edu-
cation of Negro Slaves in the
British West Indian Islands.
n. p., n. d.   DHU/MO
Truman, George. Narrative of
a Visit to the West Indies, in
1840 and 1841. By George
Truman, John Jackson and
Thos. B. Longstreth. Phila-
delphia: Merrihew and Thomp-
son, Printers, 1844. NN/Sch
A missionary journey by
members of the Society of
Friends to various islands of
the Lesser Antilles. Slavery
in the West Indies.
Walker, Frank Deaville. The
Call of the West Indies; the
Romance of Methodist Work
and Opportunity in the West
Indies and Adjacent Regions.
London: Cargate Press,
193-.   NN/Sch

Watson, Richard. Sermons and
Sketches of Sermons... New
York: Pub. by T. Mason and
G. Lane, for Methodist Epis-
copal Church, 1838. NN/Sch
"The religious instruction
of slaves in the West India
colonies advocated and defend-
ed; preached before the Wes-
leyan Methodist Missionary Society, in the new chapel,
City-road, London, April 28,
1824."   NN/Sch
Weiss, H. "One Suriname;"
Handbook Voor Zendingsstudie.
Den Hang: Boekhandel van den
Zendings-Studie-Raad, 1911.
                     NN/Sch
West Indian Societies for the Instruction and Christian Education of the Negro Slaves.
Bristol: Wright and Bagnall,
n. d.   DHU/MO
West Indian Mission. Prepared
for the American Sunday School
Union and Revised by the Com-
mittee of Publication. Phila-
delphia: American Sunday-
School Union, 1834. NN/Sch
White, Newman Iney. "Racial
Traits in the Negro Song."
Sewanee Review (28; Jl., 1920),
pp. 396-404.   DHU
Wilberforce, William. An Appeal to the Religion, Justice,
and Humanity of the Inhabitants of the British Empire, in
Behalf of the Negro Slaves in
the West Indies. London:
Printed for J. Hatchard & Son,
1823.   DHU/MO

B.   RELIGIOUS INSTRUCTION OF THE SLAVES

An Address to the Presbyterians
of Kentucky, Proposing a
Plan for the Instruction and
Emancipation of Their Slaves,
By a Committee of the Synod

of Kentucky. Newburyport:
Whipple, 1836.   NcD
Adger, John Bailey. The Re-
ligious Instruction of the
Colored Population. A ser-

(Adger, J. B. cont.)
mon, preached by the Rev.
John Adger, in the Second
Presbyterian Church, Charleston, S. C., May 9th, 1847.
Published by request. Charleston: T. W. Haynes, 1847.
                           CtY-D; NcD
Association for the Religious Instruction of the Negroes in
Liberty County, Georgia. ...
4th Annual report. DHU/MO
           (4th); NN/Sch (5th)
Bacon, Thomas. Four Sermons
Preached at the Parish Church
of St. Peter in Talbot County,
in the Province of Maryland,
Two Sermons on Black Slaves,
and two for the Benefit of a
Charity Working-School, in the
Above Parish, For the Maintenance and Education of Orphans and Poor Children, and
Negroes. London: Printed by
J. Oliver, 1753. Reprinted at
Bath, by R. Cruttwell, 1783.
                                  DLC
--Four Sermons. Upon the Great
and Indispensible Duty of all
Christian Masters and Mistresses to Bring up their Negro
Slaves in the Knowledge and
Fear of God. London: J.
Oliver, 1750.   DLC
Bible. Parts of the Holy Bible,
Selected for the Use of Negro
Slaves in the British-West India
Islands. London: Printed by
Law and Gilbert, 1808.   TNF
Bolton, S. C. "South Carolina and
the Reverend Doctor, Francis
Le Jau: Southern Society and
the Conscience of an Anglican
Missionary" Historical Magazine of the Protestant Episcopal
Church (40:1, Mar., 1971), pp.
63-79.   DHU/R
"Religious instruction to Negro Slaves and Indians."
Bruner, Clarence Vernon. "The
Religious Instruction of the
Slaves in the Antebellum
South." Doctoral dissertation,

George Peabody College,
1933.   NcD; DLC
Campbell, Robert Fishburne.
Some Aspects of the Race
Problem in the South. A
paper by Rev. Robert F.
Campbell... 2d ed. N. C.:
The Citizen Company, 1899.
                           NN/Sch
A Catechism for the Religious
Instruction of Persons of
Color. Charleston: Printed
for the author., 1844.
                  NN/Sch; NcD
"The subjects have been
treated in accordance with the
views of the Protestant Episcopal Church."
Charleston, S. C. Meeting on
Religious Instruction of Negroes. Proceedings of the
Meeting in Charleston, S. C.,
May 13-15, 1845, on the Religious Instruction of the Negroes, Together with the Report of the Committee, and
the Address to the Public.
Pub. by Order of the Meeting. Charleston, S. C.: Pr.
by B. Jenkins, 1845.
                  DLC; NN/Sch
Daniel E. Huger, chairman of the meeting and of the
standing committee.
Child, Lydia Maria (Francis).
Anti-Slavery Catechism. Newburyport: C. Whipple, 1839.
                           CtY-D
Clark, Elmer Talmage. ... The
Negro and His Religion...
Nashville: Cokesbury Press,
1924.   DLC; NN/Sch
Reprinted from "Healing
Ourselves; the First Task of
the Church in America."
Dickson, Andrew Flinn. Plantation Sermons, or, Plain and
Familiar Discourses for the
Unlearned. Philadelphia:
Presbyterian Board of Publication, 1856.
              DHU/MO; DLC; NcD

"The Established Virginia
Church and the Conversion of
Negroes and Indians, 1620-
1760." Journal of Negro His-
tory (46:1, Jan., 1961), pp.
12-23.   DHU/MO
Fickling, Susan Maria Markey.
Slave-Conversion in South
Carolina, 1830-1860. Colum-
bia, S. C.: University of South
Carolina, 1924.
                    DHU/MO; DLC
Fisk University.   Social Science
Institute.   God Struck Me
Dead: Religious Conversion
Experiences and Autobiogra-
phies of Negro Ex-Slaves.
Nashville: Social Science In-
stitute, 1945.
          DCU; DLC; CtY-D; NN/Sch
Gibson, Edmund.   A Letter of
the Lord Bishop of London to
the Masters and Mistresses
of Families in the English
Plantations Abroad.   Exhort-
ing Them to Encourage and
Promote the Instruction of
Their Negroes in the Chris-
tian Faith.   London: n. p.,
1727.   DLC; NN/Sch
Glennie, Alexander.   Sermons
Preached on Plantations to
Congregations of Negroes.
Charleston: A. B. Hiller,
1844.   NN/Sch; NcD
Goodwin, Morgan.   Some Proposals Toward Propagating of
the Gospel in Our American
Plantations. ... To which is
Prefixed Mr. Morgan Good-
win's Brief Account of Reli-
gion in the Plantations.   With
the Causes of Neglect and De-
cay thereof in Those Parts.
London: G. Sawbridge, 1708.
                              DLC
-- Trade Preferr'd Before Re-
ligion and Christ Made to
Give Place to Mammon: Rep-
resented in a Sermon Relating
to the Plantations.   London:
B. Took, 1685.   CtY; DLC
(Rare Book Room).

"On the Duty of Giving Re-
ligious Instruction to Slaves."
... The Happy Negro; Being a
True Account of a Very Extra-
ordinary Negro in North Amer-
ica, and of an Interesting Con-
versation He Had With a Very
Respectable Gentleman From
England.   To Which is Added,
The Grateful Negro. London:
Printed by W. Clowes for the
Religious Tract Society, 1830.
          NN/Sch; DHU/MO; TNF
Hoff, John F. Manual of Religious
Instruction; Specially Intended
for the Oral Teaching of Col-
ored Persons but Adapted to
the General Use in Families and
Schools.   Richmond, Va.: P.
B. Price, 1857.
          DHU/MO;   NcD
"Instruction of Slaves."   Christian
Spectator (8:2, Feb., 1826),
p. 102.   DHU/R
Effects of Missionary ef-
forts on "liberated Africans."
Jackson, James Conroy.   "The
Religious Education of the
Negro in South Carolina Pri-
or to 1850." Historical Maga-
zine (36:1, Mr., 1967), pp.
35-61.   DHU/R
Jackson, Luther P.   "Religious
Development of the Negro in
Virginia from 1760-1860."
Journal of Negro History (16:
2, Apr., 1931), pp. 168-239.
                              DHU
--"Religious Instruction of Ne-
groes, 1830-1860 with Special
Reference to South Carolina."
Journal of Negro History (15:
1, Ja., 1930), pp. 72-114.
                              DHU
Jernegan, Marcus W.   "Slavery
and Conversion in the Ameri-
can Colonies." American His-
torical Review (21:3, Apr.,
1916), pp. 504-27.   DHU
Jones, Charles Colcock.   A Cate-
chism for Colored Persons.
Charleston: Observer Office
Press, 1834.   NcD

(Jones, C. C. cont.)
--A Catechism of Scripture Doc-
trine and Practice for Fami-
lies and Sabbath schools De-
signed also for the Oral In-
struction of Coloured Persons.
Philadelphia: Presbyterian
Board of Publication, 1852.
                              NcD
--The Religious Instruction of the
Negroes. A Sermon, Deliv-
ered Before Associations of
Planters in Liberty and M'-
Intosh Counties, Georgia, by
the Rev. Charles Colcock
Jones,... Princeton, N. J.:
D'hart & Connolly, 1832.
                              NcD
--The Religious Instruction of the
Negroes in the United States.
Savannah: T. Purse, 1842.
       DHU/R; NN/Sch; NcD
Reprinted 1969, Kraus Re-
print Co.
--Suggestions on the Religious In-
struction of the Negroes in
the Southern States: Together
With an Appendix Containing
Forms of Church Registers,
Form of a Constitution, and
Plans of Different Denomina-
tion of Christians. Philadel-
phia: Presbyterian Board Pub-
lication, 1847. NcD; NN/Sch
Knight, Edgar Wallace. A Docu-
mentary History of Education
in the South Before 1860...
Chapel Hill: University of
North Carolina Press, 1949-
53.   NN/Sch
Knox, William. Three Tracts
Respecting the Conversion and
Instruction of the Free Indians
and Negro Slaves in the Colo-
nies. London: n. p., 1768.
                         DHU/MO
Letters Respecting a Book,
"Dropped From the Catalogue"
of the American Sunday School
Union... New York: American
and Foreign Anti-Slavery So-
ciety. William Harned, Pub.
Agent... 1848.   DHU/MO

McNeilly, James Hugh. Religion and Slavery; a Vindication of the Southern Churches.
Nashville, Tenn.: Publishing
House of the M. E. Church,
South, 1911.
       NN/Sch; NcD; FSU
McTyeire, H. N. Duties of Masters to Servants. A History
of Methodism. Nashville,
Tenn.: n. p., 1884. NN/Sch
Meade, William. Pastoral Let-
ter... on the Duty of Affording
Religious Instruction to those
in Bondage. Delivered in the
year 1834-. Reprinted by the
Convocation of Central Virgin-
ia in 1853. Richmond: Elly-
son, 1853. In his sermons,
v. 2, no. 4.   NcD
--Sermons, Dialogues and Narra-
tives for Servants, to be Read
to them in Families; Abridged
Altered, and Adapted to their
Condition, Chiefly by the
Right Rev. William Meade,
D. D. Richmond: Southern
Churchman, 1836.   NcD
Nisbet, Richard. The Capacity
of Negroes for Religious and
Moral Improvement, consid-
ered; With Cursory Hints, to
Proprietors and to Govern-
ment, for the Immediate Meli-
oration of the Condition of
Slaves in the Sugar Colonies.
London: James Philips, 1789.
                              DLC
Palmer, Benjamin M. A Plain
and Easy Catechism Designed
Chiefly for the Benefit of Col-
oured Persons, to Which Are
Annexed Suitable Prayers and
Hymns. Charleston, S. C.:
Observer Office Press, 1828.
                               GU
Pennington, Edgar Legare. The
Reverend Francis Le Jau's
Work Among Indians and Ne-
gro Slaves. Baton Rouge:
Franklin Press, 1935?
                   NN/Sch; DHU
"Reprinted from the Journal

of Southern History, vol. I,
no. 4, November 1935."
-- ...Thomas Bray's Associates,
and Their Work among the
Negroes... Worcester, Mass.:
The Society, 1939.
          DHU/MO; NN/Sch
Perkins, Haven P. "Religion for
Slaves: Difficulties and
Methods." Church History
(10:3, Sept., 1941), pp. 228-
45.   DHU/R
Pitman, Frank Wesley. "Fetish-
ism, Witchcraft, and Chris-
tianity Among the Slaves."
Journal of Negro History (2:4,
Oct., 1926), pp. 650-68.
                   DHU/MO
Plumer, William Swan. Thoughts
on the Religious Instruction
of the Negroes of this Country.
First Published in the Prince-
ton Review. Princeton, N.J.:
Printed by J.T. Robinson,
1848. DLC; NcD; NN/Sch
Raymond, Charles A. "The Re-
ligious Life of the Negro
Slave." Harper's Monthly (27;
1863), pp. 479-88; 676-82;
816-25.   DAU
The Religious Instruction of the
Black Population. Extracted
from the Southern Presbyter-
ian Review, n.p., n.d. NcD
Religious Instruction of the
Slaves. London: Ellerton and
Henderson, n.d.   DHU/MO
Richmond, Legh.   The African
Servant; an Authentic Narra-
tive. New York: American
Tract Society. (Publications)
no. 53.   NN/Sch
Ryland, Robert.   The Scriptural
Catechism for Colored People,
the Church Members Guide.
Richmond: Harrold & Murry,
1948.   DLC
Shirmer, Charles Frederic.
Account for the Mission Es-
tablished by the Protestant
Church of the United Brethren
Among the Negroes in Toba-
go.   Extracted from the Re-

ports and Diaries of the Missionary, Received by the Secretary of the Brethren's Society for the Furtherance of
the Gospel Among the Heathen
in the Year 1799. London:
Printed by J. Marshall, 1799.
                   NN/Sch

Singleton, George A. "Religious
Instruction of the Negro in
the United States Before the
Rebellion." Master's thesis,
University of Chicago, 1929.
Negro author.
Smedes, Susan Dabney (ed.).
Memorials of a Southern
Planter. New York: James
Pott and Co., 1900. DHU/MO
   Pro-Slavery argument, pic-
tures of a good master giving
moral and religious training
to his slaves.
Thomas, Thomas E. Review of
the Rev. Dr. Junkn's Synodi-
cal Speech in Defense of Amer-
ican Slavery: Delivered Sep-
tember 19th and 20th, and
Published December, 1843;
With an Outline of the Bible
Argument Against Slavery.
Cincinnati: Daily Atlas Office,
1844.   OWoC
Thornwell, James Henley. A
Review of Rev. J.B. Adger's
Sermon on the Religious In-
struction of the Coloured Pop-
ulation. Charleston, S.C.:
Burges, James and Paxton,
Printers, 1847.   NcD
--The Rights and the Duties of
Masters. A Sermon Preached
at the Dedication of a Church
Erected in Charleston, S.C.,
for the Benefit and Instruction
of the Coloured Population.
Charleston, S.C.: Press of
Walker & James, 1850.
                NcD; NN/Sch
Trew, J.M. An Appeal to Chris-
tian Philanthropy of the People
of Great Britain and Ireland,
in Behalf of the Religious In-

(Trew, J.M. cont.)
structions and Conversion of
Three Hundred Thousand Negro Slaves. London: M.
Richardson, Cornhill, 1826.
            DHU/MO
Vibert, Faith. "The Society for
the Propagation of the Gospel
in Foreign Parts: Its Work
for the Negroes in North

America Before 1783." Journal of Negro History (18:2,
Apr., 1933), pp. 171-212.
            DHU/MO
Wilson, G.R. "The Religion of
the American Negro Slave:
His Attitude Toward Life and
Death." Journal of Negro History (7: 1, Ja., 1923), pp.
27+.   DHU/MO

C.   SLAVERY AND BIBLICAL INTERPRETATION

Allen, Isaac. Is Slavery Sanc-
tioned by the Bible? A
Premium Tract of the Amer-
ican Tract Society. Boston:
American Tract Society, 1860.
DLC; CtY-D; NcD
"American and Foreign Anti-
Slavery Society." Shall We
Give Bibles to Three Millions
of American Slaves? New
York: American and Foreign
Anti-Slavery Society, 1847.
            NN/Sch
American Reform Tract and
Book Society. The Bible Gives
No Sanction to Slavery, by a
Tennessean. Cincinnati, O.:
American Reform Tract and
Book Society, n.d. DHU/MO
--Hebrew Servitude and Ameri-
can Slavery. Cincinnati, O.:
American Reform Tract and
Book Society, n.d. DHU/MO
Tract no. 2. Pamphlets
on Slavery and Christianity,
vol. 2.
--Slavery and the Bible. Cin-
cinnati, O.: American Re-
form Tract and Book Society,
n.d.   DHU/MO
--A Tract for Sabbath Schools.
Cincinnati, O.: American Re-
form Tract and Book Society,
n.d.   DHU/MO
Tract No. 7. On Evils of
Slavery and Christianity,
Pamphlets on Slavery and
Christianity, vol. 11.

An Ancient Landmark, or The
Essential Element of Civil and
Religious Liberty: Dedicated
to the Young Men of New Eng-
land. By a Pastor. Middle-
town: C.H. Pelton, 1838.
            DHU/MO
Pamphlets on Slavery and
the Church.
Armstrong, George Dodd. The
Christian Doctrine of Slavery.
New York: Negro Universities
Press, 1969.
DLC;DHU/R; DHU/MO; CtY-D
Reprint of the 1857 ed.
Bacon, Thomas. Sermons Ad-
dressed to Masters and Serv-
ants, and Published in the
Year 1743 [sic]... Now Re-
published with other Tracts
and Dialogues on the Same
Subject, and Recommended to
all Masters and Mistresses
to be Used in their Families.
By the Rev. William Meade.
Winchester, Va.: John Heis-
kell, Printer, 1813. DHU/MO
Barnes, Albert. An Inquiry into
the Scriptural Views of Slav-
ery. Philadelphia: Perkins
and Purves, 1846. DHU/MO
Bartlett, T.R. The Black Apostle;
Ancient Biblical History of the
Black or Negro Race, Proven
by the Holy Bible... by J.
Justice (Pseud.) Shreveport:
Shreveport Journal, 1946.
            DHU/MO

Beecher, Charles. The God of
the Bible Against Slavery.
New York: American Anti-
Slavery Society. 1855.
                              CtY-D
Berdiaev, Nikolai Aleksandrovich.
Slavery and Freedom. London:
G. Bles, the Centenary Press,
1943.   DLC
    Philosophical account of
    effect of slavery on human na-
    ture.
Bible. English. Selections.
Scripture Evidence of the Sin-
fulness of Injustice and Op-
pression. Respectfully sub-
mitted to Professing Chris-
tians, in Order to Call Forth
their Sympathy and Exertions,
on Behalf of the Much-Injured
Africans. London: Harvey
and Darton, 1828.   NN/Sch
The Bible Gives no Sanction to
Slavery. By a Tennessean.
Cincinnati, O.: American Reform Tract and Book Society,
n. d.   NcD; DLC
The Bible on the Present Crisis.
The Republic of the United
States, and its Counterfeit
Presentment; the Slave Power
and the Southern Confederacy;
the Copperhead Organization
and the Knight of the Golden
Circle; the Civil War in Which
They are Involved, its Duration
and Final Results, Described
in Daniel and the Revelations,
and Other Prophecies of the
Old and New Testaments.
New York: S. Tousey, 1863.
              CtY-D; DHU/MO
The Bible View of Slavery Reconsidered. Letter to the
Right Rev. Bishop Hopkins.
Philadelphia: Henry B. Ashmead, 1863.   NcD
Birney, James Gillespie. Letter
to Ministers and Elders, on
the Sin of Holding Slaves and
the Duty of Immediate Emancipation. Mercer County, Ky.;
Sept. 2, 1834. New York:

S. W. Benedict & Co., 1834.
                         DHU/MO
--The Sinfulness of Slaveholding
in all Circumstances; Tested
by Reason and Scripture.
Detroit: C. Wilcox, 1846.
                         DHU/MO
Bolles, John R. A Reply to
Bishop Hopkins' View of Slav-
ery, and a Review of the
Times. Philadelphia: J. W.
Daughaday, 1865.   NN/Sch
Boole, William H.   Antidote to
Rev. H. J. Van Dyke's Pro-
Slavery Discourse. Delivered
in the M. E. Church, Mount
Vernon, New York, on Sunday,
January 13, 1861. New York:
E. Jones & Co., Printers,
1861.   NN/Sch
Booth, Abraham.   Commerce in
the Human Species, and the
Enslaving of Innocent Persons,
Inimical to the Laws of Moses,
and the Gospel of Christ.   A
Sermon Preached in the Little
Prescot Street, Goodman's
Fields, London, Ja. 29, 1792.
Philadelphia: Reprinted and
sold by Daniel Lawrence,
1792. NmU; PPU; PPULC
Bourne, George. The Book and
Slavery Irreconcilable. With
Animadversions Upon Dr.
Smith's Philosophy. Philadel-
phia: J. M. Sanderson & Co.,
1816.   DHU/MO; NN/Sch
-- A Condensed Anti-Slavery
Bible Argument, by a Citizen
of Virginia. New York: S. W.
Benedict, 1845.
      DHU/MO; NN/Sch; CtY-D
Brisbane, William Henry.   Slave-
holding Examined in the Light
of the Holy Bible. New York:
The American and Foreign
Anti-Slavery Society, 1849.
           NN/Sch; DHU/MO
-- Speech of the Rev. Wm. H.
Brisbane, Lately a Slaveholder
in South Carolina; Containing
an Account of the Change in
his Views on the Subject of

(Brisbane, W. H. cont.)
Slavery. Delivered before the
Ladies' Anti-Slavery Society
of Cincinnati, February 12,
1840. Hartford: S. S. Cowles,
1840.   DHU/MO; NN/Sch
Brooke, Samuel. Slavery and
the Slave-Holder's Religion;
as Opposed to Christianity.
Cincinnati: the Author, 1845.
            DHU/MO; DLC
--Slavery and the Slave-Holder's
Religion. Cincinnati: Spar-
hawk and Lytle, 1845.
            DLC; DHU/MO
Broomfield, Gerald Webb. The
Chosen People or the Bible,
Christianity and Race. London: Longmans, Green & Co.,
1954.   DHU/MO
    A study to re-examine
what the Bible and Christianity
says about racial distinction.
Buckingham, G. The Bible Vindicated from the Charge of Sus-
taining Slavery. Columbus:
Temperance Advocated Office,
1837.   CtY
Cannon, N. Calwell. The Rock
of Wisdom; an Explanation of
the Sacred Scripture. To
which are added several in-
teresting hymns. n. p., 1833.
                NN/Sch
Chautard, Leon. Escape from
Cayenne... Salem, Mass.:
Printed the Observer Office,
1857.   DHU/MO
    Contains a brief discussion
of slavery as a destruction of
God's work.
Cheever, George Barrell. The
Commission from God, of the
Missionary Enterprise, Against
the Sin of Slavery; and the Re-
sponsibility on the Church and
Ministry for its Fulfilment.
An Address, Delivered in
Tremont Temple, Boston,
Thursday, May 27th, 1858.
Before the American Mission-
ary Association. Boston, J.
P. Jewett, 1858. CtY-D; DLC

    Tracts for thinking men
and women, no. 3.
The Child's Book on Slavery or
Slavery Made Plain. ... Cincinnati: American Reform
Tract and Book Society, 1857.
                DHU/MO
    "Slavery goes against the
Bible and many Biblical passages are given as examples."
Christy, David. Cotton Is King:
or, The Culture of Cotton,
and Its Relation to Agriculture,
Manufactures and Commerce;
to the Free Colored People;
and to Those Who Hold that
Slavery Is in Itself Sinful;
by an American. Cincinnati:
Moore, Wilstach, Keys & Co.,
1855.   DHU/MO
Cobb, Howell. A Scriptural Ex-
amination of the Institution of
Slavery in the United States.
Georgia: Printed for the Au-
thor, 1856.   DLC
Colver, Nathaniel. The Fugi-
tive Slave Bill; or God's
Laws Paramount to the Laws
of Men. A Sermon, Preached
on Sunday, October 20, 1850
... Pub. by Request of the
Church. Boston: J. W. Howes
& Co., 1850.
            NN/Sch; DHU/MO
Cronan, Edward P. The Dig-
nity of the Human Person.
New York: Philosophical Li-
brary, 1955.   DLC
Day, Norris. A Lecture Upon
Bible Politics... Montpelier,
Poland and Briggs, 1846.
                DHU/MO
De Bow, James Dunwoody Brown-
son. ... The Interest in Slavery
of the Southern Non-Slave-
holder. The Right of Peace-
ful Secession. Slavery in the
Bible. Charleston: Evans &
Cogswell, 1860. (1860 Associ-
ation. Tracts no. 5). NN/Sch
Dickey, James H. A Review of
a Summary of Biblical Antiqui-
ties Compiled for the Use of

Sunday School Teachers, and
for the Benefit of Families, by
John W. Nevin... Ripley:
Pub. by the Abolition Society
of Paint Valley. Printed by
Campbell and Palmer, 1834.
DHU/MO
Does The Bible Sanction Slavery?
Pamphlets on Slavery and
Christianity, vol. 1.
DHU/MO; NN/Sch
Doulophilus. Slaveholding
Proved to be Just and Right
to a Demonstration From the
Word of God. South Caro-
lina: n.p., 1846. DHU/MO
Pamphlets on Slavery and
Christianity, vol. 1.
Drisler, H. A Reply on the
"Bible View of Slavery, by
J.H. Hopkins, D.D., Bishop
of the Diocese of Vermont."
Broadway, Loyal Publicatons
Society, 1863.
NN/Sch; CtY-D; DHU/MO
[Dudley, Miss Mary]. Scripture
Evidence of the Sinfulness of
Injustice and Oppression; Re-
spectfully Submitted to Pro-
fessing Christians, in Order
to Call Forth Their Sympathy
and Exertions on Behalf of
the Much Injured Africans.
London: Harvey and Darton,
1828. DHU/MO
Duncan, James. A Treatise on
Slavery. In Which is Shown
Forth the Evil of Slaveholding
Both from the Light of Nature
and Divine Revelation. Vevay:
Indiana Register Office, 1824.
DHU/MO
Easton, Hosea. An Address De-
livered Before the Coloured
Population, of Providence,
Rhode Island on Thanksgiving
Day, Nov. 27, 1828. Boston:
David Hooton, 1828. DLC
Elliott, Charles. The Bible
and Slavery: In which the
Abrahamic and Mosaic Disci-
pline is Considered in Connec-
tion with the Most Ancient

Forms of Slavery as Related
to Roman Slavery and the Dis-
cipline of the Apostolic
Churches... Cincinnati: L.
Swarmstedt & A. Poe, 1857.
DHU/MO; CtY-D; NN/Sch
--Sinfulness of American Slavery:
Proved from the Wrongs; its
Contrariety to Many Scriptur-
al Commands, Prohibitions,
and Principles and to the
Christian Spirit; and From its
Evil Effects; Together with
Observations on Emancipation,
and the Duties of American
Citizens in Regard to Slavery
...ed. by Rev. B.F. Tefft...
Cincinnati: Pub. by L. Swarm-
stedt & J.H. Power, 1851.
DHU/MO; CtY-D; A&M
Epps, Archie C. "The Christian
Doctrine of Slavery: A Theo-
logical Analysis." Journal of
Negro History (46:4, Oct.,
1961), pp. 243-49. DHU
Esquisses de Doctrines Chre-
tiennes et Notes Introductives
a quelques Livre du Nouveau
Testament. Port-au-Prince:
Imp. 'Etat, 1950. DHU/MO
An Essay on Slavery: Its In-
justifiableness Proved from
the Old and New Testament:
the State of the Negro Slaves
Investigated and an Equitable
Plan for their Gradual Eman-
cipation Proposed... By an
Eye-witness. London: Pr.
for John and Henry L. Hunt,
1824. NN/Sch; DHU/MO
Ethics of American Slavery, Being a Vindication of the Word
of God and Pure Christianity
in all Ages, from Complicity
with Involuntary Servitude and
Demonstration that American
Slavery is a Crime in Substance and Concomitants, by
an American Citizen. New
York: Ross and Tousey, 1861
DHU/MO
Evangelicus. Onesimus or the
Directions to Christian Mas-

(Evangelicus cont.)
ters, in Reference to their
Slaves, Considered. Boston:
Gould, Kendall & Lincoln,
1942.   NcD; PU
Ewart, David. A Scriptural
View of the Moral Relations
of African Slavery. Charles-
ton, S. C.: Walker Evans &
Co., 1859.   DLC
Fee, John Gregg. Anti-Slavery
Manual: or, The Wrongs of
American Slavery Exposed by
the Light of the Bible and of
Facts; With a Remedy for the
Evil... New York: William
Harned, 1851.   DHU/MO
--Non-Fellowship With Slave-
Holders the Duty of Christians.
New York: John A. Gray,
1851.   DHU/MO
--The Sinfulness of Slave-Holding,
Shown by Appeals to Reason
and Scripture. New York: John
A. Gray, 1851.   DHU/MO
Fitzgerald, W. P. N. A Scrip-
tural View of Slavery and
Abolition. New Haven: n. p.,
1839.   DHU/MO
Fletcher, Thomas. The Ques-
tion, "How Far is Slavery
Prohibited by the Christian
Religion and the Holy Scrip-
tures?" Impartially Examined.
London: Robson, Blades & Co.,
Printers, 1828.   DLC
Ford, Theodore P. God Wills
the Negro; an Anthropological
and Geographical Restoration
of the Lost History of the
American Negro People, Be-
ing in Part a Theological In-
terpretation of Egyptian and
Ethiopian Backgrounds; comp.
from Ancient and Modern
Sources with a Special Chap-
ter of Eight Negro Spirituals.
Chicago: Geographical Inst.
Press, 1939.   DHU/MO
A Friend to Mankind. Argument
from Scripture, for and
Against the African Slave
Trade, as Stated in a Series

of Letters Lately Published
in the Glasgow Courier.
Glasgow: n. p., 1792.   DLC
Frost, Maria Goodell. Gospel
Fruits: or, Bible Christianity
Illustrated; a Premium Essay
... Cinn. American Reform
Tract and Book Society, 1856.
                        DHU/MO
Gallaudet, Thomas H. Jacob
and His Songs; or The Second
Part of a Conversation Be-
tween Mary and Her Mother.
Prepared for the American
Sunday School Union. Phila-
delphia: American Sunday
School Union, 1832. DHU/MO
Ganse, Hervey Doddridge.
Bible Slaveholding not Sinful;
A Reply to "Slaveholding Not
Sinful, by Samuel B. Howe,
D. D." New York: R. & R.
Brinkerhoff, 1856.
                    NN/Sch; CtY-D
Garrison, William Lloyd. Lec-
tures of George Thompson,
With a Full Report of the
Discussion Between Mr.
Thompson and Mr. Borthwick,
the Pro-Slavery Agent, held
at the Royal Amphitheatre,
Liverpool, (Eng.) and which
Continued for Six Evenings
wih Unabated Interest: Com-
piled From Various English
Editions also, a Brief History
of his Connection with the
Anti-Slavery Cause in England.
Boston: Knapp, 1836. DHU/R
Giddings, Joshua R. The Con-
flict Between Religious Truths
and American Fidelity. Speech
of Mr. Giddings, of Ohio, Up-
on the Issues Pending Before
the American People in Re-
gard to Freedom and Slavery
Delivered in Committee of the
Whole House on the State of
the Union, Feb. 26, 1858.
Washington, D. C.: Buell &
Blanchard, n. d.   DHU/MO
Granger, Arthur. The Apostle
Paul's Opinion of Slavery and

Emancipation. A Sermon
Preached to the Congregational Church and Society in Mer-
iden, at the Request of Several Respectable Anti-abolition-
ists. Middletown: Pr. by C.
H. Pelton, 1837.   NN/Sch
Green, Beriah. The Chattel
Principle and Abhorrence of
Jesus Christ and the Apostles:
or, No Refuge for American
Slavery in the New Testament.
New York: American Anti-
Slavery Society, 1839.
          DHU/MO; NN/Sch
Hague, William. Christianity
and Slavery. A review of the
correspondence between Rich-
ard Fuller and Francis Way-
land on domestic slavery,
considered as a Scriptural
Institution. Boston: Gould,
Kendall & Lincoln, 1847.
          NN/Sch; DHU/MO
Hall, Barnes M. The Fugitive
Slave Law. A sermon, by B.
M. Hall. Schenectady: Riggs,
printer, 1850.   NN/Sch
Hamilton, W. T. The Duties of
Masters and Slaves Respec-
tively: or, Domestic Servitude
as Sanctioned by the Bible:
A Discourse Delivered in the
Government Street Church,
Mobile, Ala. ...Dec. 15,
1844. Mobile: Brooks, 1845.
          NN/Sch; NcD
Harris, Raymund. Scriptural
Researches on the Licitness of
the Slave Trade, Shewing its
Conformity with the Principles
of Natural and Revealed Re-
ligion, Delineated in the Sa-
cred Writings of the Word of
God. Liverpool: Pr. by H.
Hodgson, 1788.
          NN/Sch; DHU/MO
Harrison, William Pope. The
Gospel Among the Slaves. A
Short Account of Missionary
Operations Among the African
Slaves of the Southern States.
Compiled from original

sources and edited by W. P.
Harrison... Nashville, Tenn.:
Publishing House of the M. E.
Church, South, 1893.
          NcD; DHU/MO; DLC
Hatch, Reuben. Bible Servitude
Pre-Examined: With Special
Reference to Pro-Slavery In-
terpretations and Infidel Ob-
jections... Cincinnati: Apple-
gate & Co., 1862. DHU/MO
Hayne, J. E. Has the Ministry
of This Great Church of God
"sold itself" to Work Evil in
Sight of the Lord!" Acts 20:
20-30. Charleston, S. C., Aug.
23, 1902. n. p.: John G.
Thurlong, printer, n. d.
          DHU/MO
Higginson, Thomas Wentworth.
...Does Slavery Christianize
the Negro? ...New York:
American Anti-Slavery Society,
1855. DHU/MO; CtY-D; DLC
Hodgman, Stephen Alexander.
The Great Republic Judged,
but not Destroyed; or, The
Beginning and End of Slavery
and the Justice of God Dis-
played in the Doom of Slave-
holders... New York: R.
Craighead, Printer, 1865.
          DHU/MO
--The Nation's Sin and Punish-
ment; or, The Hand of God
Visible in the Overthrow of
Slavery. By a Chaplain of the
U. S. Army, who has been,
Thirty Years, a Resident of
the Slave State. New York:
American News Co., 1864.
          DHU/MO
Holmes, Daniel. Dialogue on
Slavery, and Miscellaneous
Subjects, Based on the Word
of God. Dayton, O.: Gazette
Book and Job Rooms, 1854.
          DLC
Hopkins, John Henry. Bible
View of Slavery. New York:
n. p., 1863.   NN/Sch
--Letter from the Right Rev.
John H. Hopkins, on the Bible

(Hopkins, J. H. cont.)
View of Slavery. New York:
Pr. by W. F. Kost, 1861.
                          NN/Sch
--A Scriptural Ecclesiastical,
and Historical View of Slavery,
From the Days of the Patri-
arch Abraham, to the Nine-
teenth Century. Addressed to
the Right Rev. Alonzo Potter
... New York: W. S. Pooley
& Co., 1864.
              FSU; DHU/MO; CtY-D
Hopkins, Josiah. An Inquiry
Whether We "Ought to Obey
God Rather Than Men," in a
Review of a Sermon Preached
by the Rev. J. C. Lard at
Buffalo, N. Y. entitled "The
Higher Law," its Application
to the "Fugitive Slave Bill."
Cleveland: Smead and Cowles,
1851.   DHU/MO
Hosmer, William. The Higher
Law, in its Relations to Civil
Government: With Particular
Reference to Slavery, and the
Fugitive Slave Law... Auburn,
N. Y.: Derby and Miller, 1852.
                            CtY-D
Houghton, James. Slavery Im-
moral; Being a Reply to a
Letter in Which an Attempt is
Made to Prove That Slavery is
not Immoral. Dublin: James
McGlashan, 1847. DHU/MO
Hughes, W. An Answer to the
Rev. Mr. Harris's "Scriptur-
al Researches on the Licit-
ness of the Slave Trade."
London: Pr. for T. Cadell,
in the Strand, 1788. DHU/MO
...Is Negro Slavery Sanctioned
by Scriptures? London: Eller-
ton & Henderson, n. d.,
                          DHU/MO
Jocelyn. Conflict Between
Christianity and Slavery. Re-
printed from the American
Missionary for May 1860.
n. p., n. d.   DHU/MO
Johnson, Clifton Herman (ed.).
God Struck Me Dead: Reli-

gious Conversion Experiences
and Autobiographies of Ex-
Slaves. Philadelphia: Pilgrim
Press, 1969.
                   DHU/R; CtY-D
Keefer, Justus. Slavery: Its
Sin, Moral Effects and Cer-
tain Death. Also, the Lan-
guage of Nature, Compared
With Divine Revelation, in
Prose and Verse...With Ex-
tracts from Eminent Authors.
Baltimore: J. Keefer, 1864.
                          DHU/MO
Law, William. An Extract from
a Treatise on the Spirit of
Prayer, or the Soul Rising
out of the Vanity of Time into
the Riches of Eternity, with
Some Thoughts on War...And
Considerations on Slavery.
Philadelphia: Jos. Cruikshank,
1780.   DLC
Lawrence, John. The Slavery
Question. Dayton, O.: Pub.
by Order of the Trustees of
the Conference Printing Es-
tablishment of the United
Brethren in Christ. Vonnieda
& Kumler, Agents, 1854.
                          NN/Sch
Lee, Luther. Slavery; a Sin
Against God. Syracuse: Wes-
leyan Methodist Book Room,
1853.   NN/Sch
Leighton, Nathan. The Bible and
Pulpit for Freedom; Ameri-
can Slavery in Conflict with
the Bible. Why Should not
the Ministry Show it? New
York: John A. Gray's Fire-
Proof Printing Office, 1858.
              DHU/MO; DHU/R
Pamphlets on Slavery and
Christianity, vol. 11.
Le Roy, Alexandre, (bp.). The
Religion of the Primitives.
New York: Negro Universities'
Press, 1969. NN; NcD; PCC
Reprint of the 1922 ed.
Lounsbury, Thomas. The
Touchstone of Truth, Applied
to Modern Abolition; or Seven

Lectures in Answer to the
Question, "What Do the Scrip-
tures Teach on the Subject of
Slavery?"   Geneva, N. Y.:
Scotten & Van Brunt, 1844.
                          NcD
Lovejoy, Joseph Cammet. The
Robbers of Adullam; or, A
Glance at "Organic Sin." A
Sermon Preached at Cam-
bridgeport, Nov. 27, 1845.
... Boston: D. H. Ela, Printer,
1845.   DHU/MO
Lovejoy, Owen. The Supremacy
of the Divine Law. A Sermon
Preached at Princeton, Bureau County, Illinois. n. p.
1842.   DHU/MO
Lundy, John Patterson. Review
of Bishop Hopkins' Bible View
of Slavery, by a Presbyter of
the Church in Philadelphia.
Philadelphia: n. p. , 1863.
            NN/Sch; CtY-D
Lyons, Adelaide Avery.   Religeious Defense of Slavery in
the North. (Ser. XIII, p. 5-
34 in Historical papers of the
Trinity College Historical Society.)   Durham, N. C.: 1919.
            NcD; DLC; CtY
Macbeth, James. The Church
and the Slaveholder; or, Light
and Darkness: an Attempt to
Prove, from the Word of God
and from Reason, that to Hold
Property in Man is Wholly
Destitute of Divine Warrant,
is a Flagrant Crime, and De-
mand Excommunication.
Earnestly and Respectfully Ad-
dressed to the Members of the
Approaching Assembly of the
Free Church of Scotland, and
to the Churches Generally.
Edinburgh: J. Johnston, etc. ,
etc. , 1850.   DLC
Marsh, Leonard. Review of a
"Letter from the Right Rev.
John H. Hopkins, Bishop of
Vermont, on the Bible View
of Slavery," by a Vermonter.
Burlington: Free Press,

1861.   CtY-D
M'Caine, Alexander. Slavery
Defended From Scripture,
Against the Attacks of the
Abolitionists, in a Speech De-
livered Before the General
Conference of the Methodist
Protestant Church, in Balti-
more, 1842. Baltimore: Pr.
by W. Wooddy, 1842.
            NcD; NN/Sch
McKeen, Silas. A Scriptural
Argument in Favor of With-
drawing Fellowship from
Churches and Ecclesiastical
Bodies Tolerating Slavehold-
ing among Them... New
York: American and Foreign
Anti-Slavery Society, 1848.
            DHU/MO; DLC
McWright, A. The Sin of Slave-
holding: in Two Sermons,
Preached in the Methodist Epis-
copal Church, Madison, Wisc. ,
April 15th and 22d, 1860.
Madison, Wis.: Atwood, Rub-
lee & Reed, Printers, 1860.
                       NN/Sch
Meredith, Thomas. Conserva-
tive Pro-Salvery Typical Argu-
ments." The Biblical Recorder
(9; Oct. 5, 12, 19, 26, Nov.
2, 1844).   NcD
Morris, Robert. Slavery; its
Nature, Evils, and Remedy.
A Sermon Preached to the
Congregation of the Presby-
terian Church, Newton, Pa.
on the Sabbath Morning, July
27, 1845. Philadelphia: Wm.
S. Martien, 1845. DHU/MO
Morse, Samuel Finley Breese.
... An Argument on the Ethi-
cal Position Relation to the
Politics of the Day. New
York: 1863. (Papers from the
Society for the Diffusion of
Political Knowledge. no. 12)
                       NN/Sch
Morse, Sidney Edwards. The
Bible and Slavery. From the
N. Y. Observer of Oct. 4,
1855. New York: n. d.   DLC

84 Afro-American Religious Studies

Nelson, William Stuart. "The
Christian Church and Slavery
in America." Howard Univer-
sity Review (2:1, 1925), pp.
41-71. DHU/MO; NN/Sch
Negro author.
Nevin, John W. A Review of a
Summary of Biblical Antiqui-
ties, Compiled for the Use of
Sunday School Teachers, and
for the Benefit of Families.
Ripley: Pr. by Campbell and
Palmer, 1834. DHU/MO
Pamphlets on Slavery and
Christianity, vol. 1.
Nevin, Robert. The Bible Versus
Slavery: a Tract for the
Times. Londonderry: James
and John Hampton, 1863.
NcD
Newman, Louis C. "The Bible
View of Slavery" Reconsidered;
Letter to the Rt. Rev. Bishop
Hopkins. NN/Sch
(In: Loyal Publication So-
ciety. Tracts, no. 39, pt. 2.
1864.)
The North and South Misrepre-
sented and Misjudged; or, A
Candid View of our Present
Difficulties and Danger, and
their Causes and Remedy.
Philadelphia: Pr. for the Au-
thor, 1861. NN/Sch
... The Nutshell. The System
of American Slavery "Tested
by Scriptures," being "a
Short Method" with Pro-
slavery D. D.'s whether Doc-
tors of Divinity, or of Democ-
racy... 2nd ed. New York:
Published for the Author,
1862. DHU/MO
Owen, Robert Dale. The Wrong
of Slavery, the Right of Eman-
cipation, the Future of the Af-
rican Race in the United
States... Philadelphia: J. B.
Lippincott & Co., 1864.
DHU/MO; CtY-D
Parker, Theodore. The Law of
God and the Statutes of Men.
A Sermon, Preached at the

Music Hall, in Boston, June
18, 1854. Boston: B. B. Mussey & Co., 1854. DLC
--A Sermon on Slavery, Deliv-
ered Ja. 31, 1841, Repeated
Jun. 4, 1843, and now Published by Request. Boston:
Thurston & Torrey, 1843.
DLC
Patton, William Weston. An At-
tempt to Prove that Pro-
Slavery Interpretations of the
Bible Are Productive of Infi-
delity. Hartford: W. H. Bur-
leigh, 1846. OO
-- Slavery--The Bible--Infidelity.
Pro-Slavery Interpretations of
the Bible, Productive of Infi-
delity. Hartford: W. H. Bur-
leigh, 1847. DHU/MO
--Slavery and Infidelity: or,
Slavery in the Church Ensures
Infidelity in the World. Cin-
cinnati: Amer. Reform Book
and Tract Society, 1856.
NcD; DHU/MO
Paulding, James K. Slavery in
the United States. New York:
Negro University Press, 1968.
DHU/R
Originally pub. in 1936.
"Opposition of Slavery to the
Law of God."
Perry, Lewis. "Adin Ballou's
Hopedale Community and the
Theology of Anti-Slavery."
Church History (29:3, Sept.,
1970), pp. 372-89. DHU/R
Perry, Nathaniel. Dialogues on
Freetrade, Freesoil, Slavery
and Abolition. Boston: The
Author, 1851. NN/Sch
Perry, Rufus Lewis. The Cu-
shite; or, The Descendants of
Ham as Found in the Sacred
Scriptures, and in the Writings
of Ancient Historians and Po-
ets from Noah to the Christian
Era. Springfield, Mass.:
Wiley & Co., 1893. DHU/MO
Negro author.
Phelps, Amos Augustus. Letters
to Professor Stowe and Dr.

Bacon, on God's Real Method
with Great Social Wrongs, In
which the Bible is Vindicated
from Grossly Erroneous In-
terpretations. New York:
Wm. Harned, 1848. DHU/MO
Priest, Josiah. Bible Defense
of Slavery, or, The Origin,
History, and Fortunes of the
Negro Race. Louisville, Ky.:
W. A. Bush, 1851.
              NN/Sch; DHU/MO
--Slavery, as it Relates to the
Negro or African Race, Ex-
amined in the Light of Circum-
stances, History and the Holy
Scriptures; with an Account
of the Origin of the Black
Man's Color, Causes of His
State of Servitude and Traces
of His Character as well in
Ancient as in Modern Times:
With Strictures on Abolition-
ism. Albany: Pr. by C. van
Benthuysen & Co., 1845.
                        NN/Sch
Prindle, Cyrus. Slavery Illegal.
A Sermon, on the Occasion of
the Annual Fast, April 12,
1850. Delivered in the Wesleyan Methodist Church, Shel-
burne, Vt. Burlington: Tuttle
& Stacy, 1850.   NN/Sch
The Pro-Slavery Argument; as
Maintained by the Most Distinguished Writers of the
Southern States. Charleston:
Walker, Richards & Co.,
1852.   DHU/R
pp. 181-285, The Morality
of Slavery.
Ramsey, James. Examination of
the Rev. Mr. Harris' Scriptural Researches on the Licitness of the Slave-Trade. London: James Phillips, 1788.
                        DLC
Raphall, Morris J. Bible View
of Slavery. A Discourse Delivered at the Jewish Synagogue "Bnai Jeshurum" New
York, on the Day of National
Fast, January 4, 1861. New

York: Rudd & Carleton, 1861.
                     DHU/MO
Pamphlets on Slavery and
Christianity, vol. 11.
Remarks on Bishop Hopkins'
Letter on the Bible View of
Slavery. n. p., n. d.   NcD
Remarks on the Immediate Abol-
ition Lecture of Rev. Mr.
Phelps, Delivered in the 2d
Baptist Church in Taunton,
Sunday Evening, May 24,
1834. By a Hearer. Taunton,
Mass.: E. Anthony, Printer,
1834.   NN/Sch
A Resemblance and a Contrast
Between the American Negro
and the Children of Israel in
Egypt; or, the Duty of the
Negro to Contend Earnestly
for His Rights Guaranteed Un-
der Constitution, 1902.
                     DHU/MO
Review of a "Letter from the
Right Rev. John Hopkins,
Bishop of Vermont, on the
Bible View of Slavery," by a
Vermonter. Burlington: Free
Press Print, 1861.
           DHU/MO; DHU/Sch
Robinson, Robert. Slavery In-
consistent with the Spirit of
Christianity. A Sermon,
Preached at Cambridge, Feb.
10, 1788. Cambridge: J.
Archdeacon, Printer to the
University, 1788. DLC; OO
Sawyer, Leicester Ambrose.
A Dissertation on Servitude:
Embracing an Examination of
the Scripture Doctrines on the
Subject... New Haven: Durrie
& Peck, 1837.   NN/Sch
Schaff, Philip. Slavery and the
Bible. A Tract for the Times.
Chambersburg, Pa.: M. Kief-
fer & Co.'s Caloric Printing
Press, 1861.   NN/Sch
Also in, Mercersburg Re-
view (10:4, Oct., 1858), pp.
614-20.   DHU/R
Shanks, Caroline L. "The Bib-
lical Anti-Slavery Argument

(Shanks, C. L. cont.)
of the Decade 1830-1840."
Journal of Negro History (16:
2, Apr. , 1931), pp. 132-57.
DHU/MO

Sharp, Granville. The Just
Limitation of Slavery on the
Laws of God, Compared with
the Unbound Claims of the Af-
rican Traders and British
American Slave Holders...
London: Pr. for B. White &
Co. Dilly, 1776.   NN/Sch

--The Law of Passive Obedience,
or, Christian Submission to
Personal Injuries. Wherein
is Shown that the Several
Texts of Scripture, which
Command the Entire Submission of Servants or Slaves to
Their Masters, Cannot Au-
thorize the Latter to Exact
an Involuntary Servitude, Nor
in the Least Degree, Justify
the Claims of Modern Slave
Holders... London: Pr. for
B. White and C. Dilly, 1776.
DHU/MO

--The Law of Retribution: or,
A Serious Warning to Great
Britain and Her Colonies,
founded on Unquestionable Ex-
amples of God's Temporal
Vengeance Against Tyrants,
Slave Holders and Oppressors
... London: B. White, 1776.
NN/Sch

--Serious Reflections on the
Slave Trade and Slavery.
Wrote in March, 1797. London: Pr. by W. Calvert,
1805.   NN/Sch

--Slavery. Proving from Scriptures Its Inconsistency with
Humanity and Religion in Answer to a Late Publication
Entitled "The African Slave
Trade for Negro Slaves Shown
to be Consistent with Principles of Humanity and with
the Laws of Revealed Religion."
Burlington: Pr. and sold by
Isaac Collins, 1773. NN/Sch

Sihler, Wilhelm. Die Sklaverei
im Lichte der Heiligen
Schrift Betrachtet. Baltimore,
n. p. , 1863.   NN/Sch

Slavery and the Bible. Cincin-
nati, O. : American Reform
Tract and Book Society, n. d.
NcD; DHU/MO

Slavery vs. the Bible; A Correspondence between the General Conference of Maine and
the Presbytery of Tombechee,
Miss. by Cyrus P. Grosve-
nor. Worcester: Spooner and
Howland, 1840.   DHU/MO

Smith, E. An Inquiry into Scriptural and Ancient Servitude,
in which it is Shown that Neither was Chattel Slavery;
with the Remedy for American Slavery... Mansfield, O. :
Pub. by the Author at the
Western Branch Book Concern
of the Wesleyan Methodist
Connection of America, 1852.
DHU/MO

Smith, Goldwin. Does the Bible
Sanction American Slavery?
... Cambridge: Sever & Fran-
cis, 1863.
DHU/MO; NN/Sch; CtY-D

Smith, Jeremiah. Is Slavery
Sinful? Being Partial Discus-
sions of the Proposition,
Slavery is Sinful, between
Ovid Butler, Esq., a Bishop
of the Christian Church at
Indianapolis, Ind... Indianap-
olis: H. H. Dodd & Co. ,
Printers, and Book Binders,
1863.   DHU/MO

Stowe, Harriet Elizabeth (Beech-
er). The Christian Slave. A
Drama Founded on a Portion
of Uncle Tom's Cabin. Dra-
matized by Harriet Beecher
Stowe, Expressly for the
Readings of Mrs. Mary E.
Webb. Boston: Phillips,
Sampson, 1855.   NN/Sch

Streeter, S.W. American Slavery, Essentially Sinful. A
Sermon. Oberlin, O. : J. M.

Fitch, 1845.   DHU/MO
Stringfellow, Thornton. A Brief
Examination of Scripture
Testimony on the Institution
of Slavery, in An Essay, First
Published in the Religious
Herald and Republished by Re-
quest... Richmond: Relig. Her.
1841.   CtY-D
-- Slavery; its Origin, Nature
and History. Its Relation to
Society, to Government, and
to True Religion,...to Human
Happiness and Divine Glory.
Considered in the Light of
Bible Teachings, Moral Jus-
tice and Political Wisdom.
Alexandria, Va.: Pr. at the
Virginia Sentinel Office, 1860.
DHU/MO; CtY-D; NN/Sch
Stuart, Charles. A Memoir of
Granville Sharp, to which is
Added Sharp's "law of Pas-
sive Obedience," and an Ex-
tract from his "Law of Retri-
bution." New York: The Amer-
ican Anti-Slavery Society, 1836.
                          NN/Sch
Stuart, Moses. Conscience and
the Constitution with Remarks
on the Recent Speech of the
Hon. Daniel Webster in the
Senate of the United States
on the Subject of Slavery.
Boston: Cricker & Brewster,
1850.   CtY-D; NN/Sch
Sunderland, LaRoy. The Testi-
mony of God Against Slavery; a
Collection of Passages from the
Bible, which Show the Sin of
Holding and Treating the Human
Species as Property... Boston:
Pub. by D.K. Hitchcock, 1838.
NN/Sch; DHU/MO; CtY-D
Thompson, Joseph Parrish. Chris-
tianity and Emancipation; or,
The Teachings and the Influence
of the Bible Against Slavery.
New York: A.D.F. Randolph,
1863.   NN/Sch; DHU/MO
--Teachings of the New Testa-
ment on Slavery. New York:
J.H. Ladd, 1856.   NN/Sch

Thompson, L. The Ethics of
American Slavery, being a
Vindication of the Word of
God and a Pure Christianity
in all Ages, from Complicity
with Involuntary Servitude;
and a Demonstration that
American Slavery is a Crime
in Substance and Concomitants,
by an American Citizen. New
York: Ross & Tousey, 1861.
                          NN/Sch
Thompson, Thomas. The Afri-
can Trade for Negro Slaves
Shewn to be Consistent with
Principles of Humanity, and
with the Laws of Revealed
Religion. Canterburg: Pr.
and sold by Simmons and
Kirby, sold also by Robert
Baldwin, Bookseller in Pater-
Noster Row, London, 1893.
                          DHU/MO
Tyler, Edward R. Slaveholding
"A Malum in se," or, Invari-
ably Sinful... Hartford: S.S.
Cowles, 1839.   DHU/MO
Vail, Stephen Montford. The
Bible Against Slavery, with
Replies to the "Bible View of
Slavery, by John H. Hopkins,
Bishop of Diocese of Vermont;
and to "A Northern Presby-
ter's Second Letter and Minis-
ters of the Gospel," by Na-
than Lord, late President of
Dartmouth College; and to
"X" of the New Hampshire
Patriot. Concord: Fogg, Hadley & Co., printer, 1864.
                   NcD; NN/Sch
Vernon, B.J. History of Jamaica. London: J. Hodges,
1790.   DLC
pp. 306-38. Religion of the
first Africans brought to this
country.
View of the Subject of Slavery
Contained in the Biblical Rep-
ertory for April, 1836, in
which the Scriptural Argument
it is Believed, is very Clearly
and Justly Exhibited. Pitts-

(View of the Subject... cont.)
burgh: A. Jaynes, Printer,
1836.   NN/Sch
Ward, James Wilson. Slavery
a Sin That Concerns Non-
Slaveholding States. A Ser-
mon Delivered on the Day of
the Annual Fast in Mass.,
Mr. 28, 1839. Boston: I.
Knapp, 1839.   NHi; MB
Ward, Jonathan. Father Ward's
Letter to Professor Stuart.
n. p., 1837.   DHU/MO
    Pamphlets on Slavery and
    Christianity, vol. 1. Priest
    writes letter for publication
    refuting Professor Stuart's
    argument justifying slavery
    by the Bible.
Warren, Ebenezer W. Nellie
Norton: or, Southern-Slavery
and the Bible. A Scriptural
Refutation of the Principal
Arguments Upon Which the
Abolitionists Rely. A Vindi-
cation of Southern Slavery
from the Old and New Testa-
ments. Macon, Ga.: Burke,
Boykin, 1864.   CtY-D
Webb, James Morris. The
Black Man, the Father of
Civilization. Proven by Bib-
lical History... Chicago, Ill.:
Wm. H. Poole, Printer, 1914.
                        DHU/MO
Weld, Theodore Dwight. The
Bible Against Slavery; or, An
Inquiry into the Genius of the
Mosaic System, and the Teach-
ings of the Old Testament on
the Subject of Human Rights.
Pittsburgh: United Presby-
terian Board of Publication,
1864.
    DHU/MO; CtY-D; NN/Sch
Wheaton, N. S. A Discourse on
St. Paul's Epistle to Philemon;
Exhibiting the Duty of Citizens
of the Northern States in Re-
gard to the Institution of Slav-
ery Delivered in Christ Church,
Hartford, Dec. 22, 1850.
Hartford: Case, Tiffany and

Co., 1851.   DLC
White, B. Modern Apostasy,
Slavery, the Two-Horned
Beast, and his Image. Re-
spectfully Dedicated to the
American People. Cincinnati:
n. p., 1856.   NN/Sch
White, William S. The Gospel
Ministry in a Series of Let-
ters From a Father to His
Sons. Philadelphia: Presby-
terian Board of Publications,
1860.   ICRL
Wiley, Calvin Henderson.
Scriptural Views of National
Trials; or, The True Road
to Independence and Peace of
the Confederate States of
America. Greensboro, N. C.:
Sterling, 1863.   NcD
Williston, Seth. Slavery not a
Scriptural Ground of Division
in Efforts for the Salvation
of the Heathen. New York:
M. W. Dodd, 1844.
    DLC; NcD; DHU/MO
Wisner, William C. The Bibli-
cal Argument of Slavery.
New York: 1844.   NN/Sch
Wolcott, Samuel T. The Bible
Against Oppression. Cincin-
nati, O.: American Tract So-
ciety, n. d.   DHU/MO
Woolman, John. Considerations
on Slavery, Addressed to the
Professors of Christianity of
Every Denomination, and Af-
fectionately Recommended to
their Sober Unprejudiced Attention. Baltimore: Pr. by T.
Maud, 1821.   NN/Sch
    Part 2 has title: Consid-
    erations on the keeping of Ne-
    groes.
Words for Working Men. First
Series. Slavery and the Bible.
n. p., n. d.   DHU/MO
Wright, Henry Clarke. Anthropology; or, The Science of
Man: In Its Bearing on War
and Slavery, and on Argu-
ments from the Bible, Marriage, God, Death, Retribu-

tion, Atonement and Government in Support of These and
Other Social Wrongs. In a

Series of Letters to a Friend
in England. Cincinnati: E.
Shepard, 1850.   DLC

D. SLAVERY, NEGROES, AND THE CHURCH

1. General

The Abrogation of the Seventh
Commandment by the Ameri-
can Churches. New York:
D. Ruggles, 1835.   DHU/MO
Action of the Church in Frank-
lin, Mass., in Regard to the
American Tract Society and
the American Board. New
York: J. A. Gray, 1854.
DHU/MO
Adams, John Greenleaf (ed.).
Our Day: A Gift for the
Times. Boston: B. B. Mussey,
1848.   NN/Sch
    Prose and poetry, "The
Alleged Inferiority of the Af-
rican Race, by Rev. C. Stet-
son:" pp. 66-7. "The Fugi-
tive Slave, by Rev. Henry
Bacon:" pp. 77-8. "Anniver-
sary Week in Boston, by J.
G. Adams:" pp. 83-105. "To
Frederick Douglass, by J. G.
Adams:" pp. 106-7. "A De-
mon to be Exercised, by Rev.
G. G. Strickland:" pp. 157-9.
"Thomas Clarkson, by J. G.
Adams:" pp. 171-7.
Adams, William. Christianity
and Civil Government: A Dis-
course Delivered on Sabbath
Evening, November 10, 1850.
New York: Charles Scribner,
1851.   DHU/MO
"An Address to Ministers and
Christian Masters." n. p.
1829.   DHU/MO
"An Address to the Churches, on
the Subject of Slavery."
Georgetown, O.: D. Ammen
and Co., 1831.   DHU/MO
The African Observer. A
Monthly Journal Containing

Essays and Documents Illus-
trative of the General Charac-
ter, and Moral and Legal Ef-
fects of Negro Slavery. Phila-
delphia: Apr. 1827-Mr. 1828.
(Edited by Enoch Lewis, a
Consistent Contributor to the
Genius of Universal Emancipa-
tion.)   DLC; NcD
Allard, Paul. Les Esclaves
Chrétiens Depuis les Premiers
Temps de l'Église Jusqu'à la
Pin de la Dominatic Romaine
en Occident. 5. ed. Paris:
J. Gabalda, 1914.   CtY
Allen, Benjamin Russell. The
Responsibilities and Duties of
American Citizens. A ser-
mon, preached in the Congre-
gational Church, South Ber-
wick, Me., Thanksgiving Day,
Dec. 19, 1850. Boston:
Crocker and Brewster, 1851.
NN/Sch
Allen, George. "Report of a
Declaration of Sentiments on
Slavery, Dec. 5, 1837 (to a
Committee of the Convention
of Ministers of Worcester
County)." Worcester: Henry
J. Howland, 1838. DHU/MO
--Resistance to Slavery Every
Man's Duty. A Report on
American Slavery; Read to the
Worcester Central Association,
Mr. 2, 1847. Boston: Wm.
Crosby & H. P. Nichols, 1847.
DHU/MO
--Speech on Ministers Leaving a
Moral Kingdom to Bear Testi-
mony Against Sin; Liberty in
Danger, from the Publication
of its Principles; the Consti-

(Allen, G. cont.)
tution a Shield for Slavery;
and the Union Better than
Freedom and Righteousness.
Boston: I. Knapp, 1838.
                    DHU/MO
Allen, Joseph Henry. A Reign
of Terror. A Sermon
Preached in Union Street
Church, Bangor, Je. 1, 1856.
Bangor: S.S. Smith, 1856.
                    DLC
Allen, William G. The Ameri-
can Prejudice Against Color.
An Authentic Narrative Show-
ing How Easily the Nation Got
into an uproar. London: W.
& F. G. Cash, 1853. DHU/MO
American and Foreign Anti-
Slavery Society. An Address to
the Anti-Slavery Christians of
the United States. New York:
Printed by J.A. Gray, 1852.
DHU/MO; NN/Sch; CtY-D;
                    DLC
American Anti-Slavery Reporter.
Monthly. New York: Vol. 1,
No. 2, Feb. 1834; Vol. 1,
No. 5, My. 1834; and Vol. 1,
No. 8, Ag 1834.   DLC
American Anti-Slavery Society.
Slavery and the American
Board of Commissioners for
Foreign Missions. New York:
1859.   CtY-D
American Board of Commission-
ers for Foreign Missions. ...
Report of the Committee on
Anti-Slavery Memorials, Sep-
tember, 1845. With a His-
torical Statement of Previous
Proceedings. Boston: Press
of T.R. Marvin, 1845.
                    CtY-D
American Missionary Association.
Missionary Boards in Relation
to Slavery, Caste, and Polyg-
amy. From the American
Missionary, "Extra, May,
1854." New York: American
Missionary Association, 1854.
                    DHU/MO
American Reform Tract and

Book Society. Agitation--the
Doom of Slavery. Cincinnati,
O.: American Reform Tract
and Book Society, n.d.
                    DHU/MO
Tract no. 4. Pamphlets on
Slavery and Christianity, vol.
2.
--On Slavery. Cincinnati, O.:
American Reform Tract and
Book Society, n.d. DHU/MO
Tract no. 3. Pamphlets on
Slavery and Christianity, vol.
2.
--Opinion of Mrs. Stowe on Ex-
cluding Slaveholders from the
Church. American Reform
and Tract and Book Society,
n.d.   DHU/MO
Pamphlets on Slavery and
Christianity, vol. 2.
American Tract Society. Action
of the Church in Franklin,
Mass., in Regard to the Amer-
ican Board. New York: J.A.
Gray, 1854.   DHU/MO
--The Enormity of the Slave
Trade; and the Duty of Seek-
ing the Moral and Spiritual
Elevation of the Colored Race.
Speeches of Wilberforce, and
Other Documents and Records.
New York: American Tract So-
ciety, 1846.   DHU/MO
Anti-Slavery Convention of Amer-
ican Women. "An Appeal to the
Women of the Nominally Free
States, Issued by an Anti-
Slavery Convention of Ameri-
can Women." New York: W.S.
Dorr, 1837. Boston: I. Knapp,
1838.   DHU/MO
Anti-Slavery Tracts. New York:
1855-1856.   DHU/MO
Nos. 4, 12, 16, 17, and
19. Church and Slavery.
Armistead, Wilson. Five Hun-
dred Thousand Strokes for
Freedom. A Series of Anti-
Slavery tracts, of which Half
a Million are now First Is-
sued by the Friends of the
Negro. London: W. & F.

Cash, 1853. Nos. 19; 22; 29;
31; 33; 45; 52; 55; 67; and
82.   DHU/MO
--A Tribute for the Negro being
a Vindication of the Moral,
Intellectual and Religious
Capabilities of the Colored
Portion of Mankind; with Particular Reference to the African Race. Illustrated by numerous biographical sketches,
facts, anecdotes, etc. n. p.
1848.   DHU/MO; INRE
Atkins, Thomas. African Slavery.
A Reply to the Letter of Bishop Hopkins, of Vermont on
This Important Subject. New
York: W. C. Green, n. d.
                       DHU/MO
--American Slavery Just Published: A Reply to the Letter
of Bishop Hopkins, of Vermont, on this Important Subject. New York: Scobell,
n. d.   DHU/MO
Attempt to Enlist Religion on the
Side of Colonial Slavery Exposed. London: Ellerton and
Henderson, 1830.   NcD
Austin, James Trecothick. Remarks on Dr. Channing's
Slavery. Boston: Russell,
Shattuck, and J. H. Eastburn,
1835.   CtY-D
Bacon, Leonard. A Discourse
Preached in the Center Church
in New Haven, Aug. 27, 1828,
at the Funeral of Jehudi Ashmun; Colonial Agent of the
American Colony of Liberia.
With the Address at the Grave
by R. R. Gurley. New Haven:
Hezekiah Howe, 1828. MH-AH
    Bacon was a colonization-
ist and bitter opponent of im-
mediate emancipation. He was
also opposed to slavery and
to the organized anti-slavery
effort.
--The Higher Law. A Sermon
Preached on Thanksgiving Day,
Nov. 27, 1851. New Haven:
B. L. Hamlen, 1851. DHU/MO

Baird, Robert. The Progress
and Prospects of Christianity
in the United States of America; With Remarks on the Subject of Slavery in America,
and on the Intercourse Between British and American
Churches. London: Partridge
and Oakey, 1851.
    DLC; DHU/R; NN/Sch
Balme, Joshua Rhodes. American States, Church, and Slavery. New York: Negro Uni-
versities Press, 1969. DLC;
    DHU/R; NcD; CtY-D
    Reprint of the 1862 ed.
Barnes, Albert. The Church
and Slavery. Philadelphia:
Parry & McMillan, 1857.
                       DHU/MO
Barnes, William. American
Slavery. A Sermon, Preached
at Hampton, Conn., Apr. 14,
1843, the Day of the Annual
Public Fast. Hartford: Elihu
Geer, 1843.   DLC
Bassett, John Spencer. ...Slav-
ery in the State of North Caro-
lina. Baltimore: John Hop-
kins Press, 1899. NN/Sch
Baxter, Richard. A Christian
Directory: Or, a Summary of
Practical Theologie, and
Cases of Conscience. London:
n. p., 1673.   DLC
Beaver, Robert Pierce (ed.).
Christianity and African Edu-
cation: The Papers of a Con-
ference at the University of
Chicago. Grand Rapids,
Mich.: Wm. Eerdmans Pub.
Co., 1966.   NN/Sch
Beecher, Charles. The Duty of
Disobedience to Wicked Laws.
A Sermon on the Fugitive
Slave Law... New York: J. A.
Gray, Printer, 1851.DHU/MO
--A Sermon on the Nebraska
Bill. New York: Oliver and
Bros., 1854.   DHU/MO
Beecher, Henry Ward. Speeches
of Rev. Henry Ward Beecher
on the American Rebellion,

Delivered in Great Britain in
1863. New York: F. F. Lov-
ell & Company, 1887.
                      DHU/MO
Beecher, Lyman. The Ballot
Box a Remedy for National
Crimes. A Sermon Entitled,
"The Remedy for Dueling by
Rev. Lyman Beecher, D.D.,
Applied to the Crime of Slave-
holding." Boston: I. Knapp,
1841.   DLC
Berry, Philip. A Review of the
Bishop of Oxford's Counsel to
the American Clergy, With
Reference to the Institution of
Slavery. Also Supplemental
Remarks on the Relation of
the Wilmot Proviso to the In-
terests of the Colored Class.
Washington, D.C.: Wm. M.
Morrison; New York: Stanford
& Swords, 1848.
                   NcD; DHU/MO
Bidlake, John. Slave Trade. A
Sermon Preached at Stonehouse
Chapel, on Dec. 28, 1788.
Second ed. Plymouth: M. Hay-
don & Son, 1789.   CtY
Birney, James Gillespie. The
American Churches, the Bul-
warks of American Slavery.
By an American. Newbury-
port: Charles Whipple, 1835.
DHU/R; DLC; NN/Sch; CtY-
                  D; DHU/MO
--Mr. Birney's Second Letter.
To the Ministers and Elders
of the Presbyterian Church in
Kentucky. n.p., 1834.
                      DHU/MO
Bodo, John R. The Protestant
Clergy and Public Issues.
Princeton University Press,
1954.   NN/Sch
   Slavery and the Church.
Bowditch, William Ingersoll.
God or Our Country. Review
of the Rev. Dr. Putnam's
Discourse Delivered on Fast
Day, Entitled "God and Our
Country." Boston: I.R. Butts,
1847.   DLC

Boyd, William K. (ed.). "Bene-
fit of Clergy as Applied to
Slaves." Journal of Negro
History (8:4, Oct., 1923),
pp. 443-7.   DHU
British and Foreign Anti-Slavery
Society, London. American Slavery and British Christians of
all Denominations...in May,
1845 Showing the Connection
of American Religious Bodies
With Slavery and the Article
Entitled "The Silent Men"
From the "Anti-Slavery Re-
porter" of July, 1853. Lon-
don: British and Foreign Anti-
Slavery Society, 1854.
                  DLC; DHU/MO
Brookes, Iveson L. Defence of
the South Against the Re-
proaches and Incroachments
of the North. n.p., 1850.
                         CtY-D
   Reply to an article in the
Christian Review for January,
1849, on the extension of
slavery.
--A Defence of Southern Slavery.
Against the Attacks of Henry
Clay and Alex'r. Campbell...
By a Southern Clergyman.
Hamburg, S.C.: Pr. by Robinson & Carlisle, 1851.
                         CtY-D
   This pamphlet contains a
review of Mr. Clay's Letter
on Emancipation and strictures on Mr. Campbell's
'Tract for the people of Kentucky.' - Pref.
Brown, James. American Slav-
ery, in its Moral and Political Aspects Comprehensively
Examined; to Which is Sub-
joined an Epitome of Ecclesi-
astical History, Shewing the
Mutilated State of Modern
Christianity. Oswego: Printed
by G. Henry, 1840. DHU/R
Brown, Solyman. Union of Ex-
tremes: a Discourse on Liberty and Slavery, as They
Stand Related to the Justice,

Prosperity, and Perpetuity of
the United Republic of North
America... New York: Pr.
by D. Fanshaw, 185? NN/Sch
Brown, William B. Religious
Organizations, and Slavery.
Oberlin: J. M. Fitch, 1850.
DHU/MO; NcD; DLC
Brunner, John H. The Union of
the Churches. New York:
Phillips & Hunt, n. d.
NB; NcD
Section on Slavery and
Church. Church Union versus
Church Schisms.
Burleigh, Charles. Reception of
George Thompson in Great
Britain. Compiled from Vari-
ous British Publications. Bos-
ton: I. Knapp, 1836. CtY-D
Burt, Jairus. The Law of Chris-
tian Rebuke, a Plea for Slave-
Holders. A Sermon Delivered
at Middle-town, Conn., Be-
fore the Anti-Slavery Conven-
tion of Ministers and Other
Christians, Oct. 18, 1843.
Hartford: N. W. Goodrich &
Co., 1843.   DLC
Buswell, James Oliver. Slavery
Segregation, and Scripture.
Grand Rapids: Eerdmans,
1964. DHU/R; NN/Sch; CtY-D
Cade, John B. "Out of the
Mouths of Ex-Slaves: V. Re-
ligion and Recreation of Ac-
tivities." Journal of Negro
History (20:3, Jl., 1934), pp.
327-34.   DHU
Cairns, Earle Edwin. Saints
and Society; the Social Impact
of Eighteenth Century English
Revivals and its Contemporary
Relevance. Chicago: Moody
Press, 1960.   CtY-D
Capen, Nahum. Letter to Rev.
Nathanial Hall, of Dorchester,
Mass., by Nahum Capen Con-
cerning Politics and the Pul-
pit. Boston and Cambridge:
J. Munroe & Co., 1855.
DLC; NN/Sch
"A protest directed against

the activity of ministers of the
Gospel in the anti-slavery
movement."
Caste and Slavery in the Ameri-
can Church. By a Churchman.
New York and London: Wiley
and Putnam, 1843. DHU/MO
Channing Edward. History of
the United States. New York:
Macmillan Co., 1932, v. 5,
pp. 204-41.   DHU
Chapter VII contains a
brief discussion of feelings of
the church relative to the
question of slavery.
Cheever, George Barrell.
God's Way of Crushing the
Rebellion. A Sermon at the
Church of the Puritans. New
York, Sept. 29, 1861. New
York: n. p., 1861.
DLC; DHU/MO
--The Sin of Slavery, The Guilt
of the Church, and the Duty of
the Ministry. An Address De-
livered Before the Abolition
Society at New York, on Anni-
versary Week 1858. Boston:
J. P. Jewett and Co.; Cleve-
land: H. P. B. Jewett, 1858.
DLC
Christian, John. A Christian
Experience of Grace, by John
Christian, (colored man) a
Baptist. Columbus, Ga.:
n. p., 1859.   DHU/MO
A broadside.
The Christian Citizen. Negro
Emancipation from the Law of
Love and Service Involved in
White Supremacy. Gaffney,
S. C.: n. p., n. d.   DHU/MO
Christianity Versus Treason and
Slavery. Religion Rebuking
Sedition... Philadelphia: H. B.
Ashmead, 1864.
DHU/MO; DLC
Christy, David. Pulpit Politics;
or, Ecclesiastical Legislation
on Slavery, in its Disturbing
Influences on the American
Union. New York: Negro Uni-
versities Press, 1969. DLC;

(Christy, D. cont.)
DHU/R; DHU/MO; CtY-D;
NcD
Church Anti-Slavery Society.
Proceedings of the Convention
Which Met at Worcester,
Mass. March 1, 1859. New
York: John F. Trow, 1859.
DLC
Church Anti-Slavery Society of
the United States. Circular--
Declaration of Principles and
Constitution. Worcester:
n. p. , 1859.   DLC
Clark, Rufus Wheelwright. Con-
science and Law. A Dis-
course Preached in the North
Church, Portsmouth, New
Hampshire, on Fast Day, Apr.
3, 1851. Boston: Tappan &
Whittemore; Portsmouth: S.
A. Badger, 1851. DHU/MO
--A Review of the Rev. Moses
Stuart's Pamphlet on Slavery,
Entitled Conscience and the
Constitution. Boston: C. C. P.
Moody, 1850.DHU/MO; CtY
Clarke, Walter. The American
Anti-Slavery Society at War
with the Church. A discourse,
delivered before the First
Congregational Church and So-
ciety, in Canterbury, Conn. ,
June 30th, 1844. Hartford:
Press of E. Geer, 1844.
NN/Sch; DLC
Clay, Cassius M. Cassius M.
Clay's Appeal to All Follow-
ers of Christ in the American
Union. n. p. , n. d. DHU/MO
Cohen, Chapman. Christianity,
Slavery and Labour. London:
Issued for the Secular Society,
Limited, by the Pioneer
Press, 1936.   NN/Sch
Cole, Arthur C. The Irrepres-
sible Conflict, 1850-1856. A
History of American Life.
New York: Macmillan Co. ,
1934.   DHU/R
Chapter X, "The Challenge
to the Church."
Colver, Nathaniel. "Slavery or

Freedom Must Die." The
Harper's Ferry Tragedy: A
Symptom of a Disease in the
Heart of the Nation; or the
Nation, from Which There is
no Escape but in the Destruc-
tion of Slavery Itself. A Ser-
mon Preached.. .Dec. 11,
1859. Published by Request
of the Congregation. Cincin-
nati: Office of the Christian
Luminary, 1860.   DLC
Conflict Between Christianity and
Slavery. From the American
Missionary for May, 1860.
DHU/MO
Pamphlets on Slavery and
Christianity, vol. 1.
Congregational Union of Scotland.
Address of the Congregation-
al Union in Scotland to Their
Fellow Christians in the
United States, on the Subject
of American Slavery. New
York: American and Foreign
Anti-Slavery Society, 1840.
DHU/MO
Conway, Moncure Daniel. The
Golden Hour. Boston: Tick-
nor & Fields, 1862. DHU/MO
Conway was the son of a
Virginia slaveholder; a Meth-
odist, then Unitarian minis-
ter; and a strong anti-slavery
writer.
Couch, Paul. ...Just Rulers, a
Sermon... Boston: Leavitt
and Alden, n. d.   DHU/MO
Crothers, Samuel. The Gospel
of the Jubilee. An Explana-
tion of the Typical Privileges
Secured to the Congregation
and Pious Strangers by the
Atonement on the Morning of
the Jubilee. Lev. , XXV, 9046.
Reprint from the Author's Edi-
tion of 1893. With an Intro-
duction by Rev. John Rankin.
Cincinnati: American Reform
Tract and Book Society, 1856.
DLC
--The Gospel of the Typical
Servitude; the Substance of a

Sermon Preached in Greenfield, Ja. 1, 1834. Published by the Abolition Society of Paint Valley (Ohio), Hamilton: Gardener & Gibbon, 1835. DHU/MO

--Strictures on African Slavery. Published by the Abolition Society of Paint Valley (Ohio). Rossville: Butler Co., Ohio, Taylor Webster, 1833. DHU/MO

Cuffel, Victoria. "The Classical Greek Concept of Slavery." Journal of the History of Ideas (17:3, Jl.-Sept., 1966), pp. 323-42. DHU/R

Curry, Daniel. The Judgements of God, Confessed and Deprecated. A Sermon Preached on the Occasion of the National Fast, Aug. 3, 1849... n.p., 1849. DHU/MO

[Curtis, Gegorge Ticknor]. Observations on the Rev. Dr. Gannett's Sermon, Entitled "Relation of the North to Slavery." Republished from the Editorial Columns of the Boston Courier, of June 28th, and 30th, and July 6th, 1854. Boston: Redding and Co., 1854. DHU/MO

Dana, James. The African Slave Trade. A Discourse Delivered in the City of New-Haven, September 9, 1790, before the Connecticut Society for the Promotion of Freedom. New Haven: Pr. by T. and S. Green, 1791. NN/Sch; CtY-D

Davies, Samuel. The Duty of Christians to Propagate their Religion among Heathens, Earnestly Recommended to the Masters of Negroe Slaves in Virginia. A Sermon Preached in Hanover, January 8, 1757. London: Pr. by J. Oliver, 1758. DLC

--Letters from the Rev. Samuel Davies, Shewing the State of Religion (particularly among the Negroes) in Virginia. Likewise an Extract of a Letter for a Gentleman in London to his friend in the country, being some observations on the foregoing. London: n.p., 1757. DLC

Davis, David Brion. The Problem of Slavery in Western Culture. Ithaca, N.Y.: Cornell University Press, 1966. CtY-D; DHU/R; NN/Sch;

Davis, Owen. Sketches of Sermons, Delivered by Rev. Owen Davis, in the First Free Bethel Church, in West Centre Street, Boston. Boston: Pr. for the Author, 1837. DLC

De Charms, Richard. A Discourse on the True Nature of Freedom and Slavery. Delivered before the Washington Society of the New Jerusalem, in View of the One Hundred Eighteenth Anniversary of Washington's Birth. Philadelphia: J. H. Jones, Printer, 1850. NN/Sch

Deeming, D. D. Anti-Spoonerism; or, The Reactionary Forces of the Negro. With a Scriptural View of the "Equality of Man." Also, Considerations on the Dogma of "Man Has No Property in Man." New York: Ross & Tousey, 1860. CtY-D

Dexter, Henry Martyn. Our National Condition, and its Remedy. A Sermon, Preached in the Pine Street Church, Boston, on Sunday, June 22, 1856. Boston: J. P. Jewett & Co., 1856. NN/Sch

Dollar, George W. "Churches and the Civil War." Bibliotheca Sacra (118:472, Oct.-Dec., 1916), pp. 327-33. DHU/R

Dorough, Charles D. "Religion in the Old South; a Pattern of Behavior and Thought."

(Dorough, C.D. cont.)
Doctoral dissertation, University of Texas, 1947.
Douglass, Frederick. "The Free Church and Slavery." Philip S. Foner, (ed.). The Life and Writing of Frederick Douglass. Vol. I. (New York: International Publishers, 1950), pp. 173-9.   DHU/R
Speech given in Glasgow, Scotland, May 29, 1846. Negro author.
Drummond, Andrew Landale. Story of American Protestantism. Boston: Beacon Press, 1931.   NN/Sch
Slavery and the Church, pp. 286-92.
Duffield, George. A Sermon on American Slavery: its Nature, and the Duties of Christians in Relation to It. Detroit: J.S. and S.A. Bagg, Printers, 1840. DHU/MO; DLC; NcD
Dumond, Dwight Lowell. Antislavery: The Crusade for Freedom in America. Ann Arbor: University of Michigan Press, 1949.
                          DHU/MO; DHU/R
--Anti-Slavery Origins of the Civil War in the United States. Ann Arbor, Mich.: University of Michigan Press, 1939.
                          DHU/MO
"Earlier phases of the evangelical attack on slavery."
--A Bibliography of Anti-slavery in America. Ann Arbor: University of Michigan Press, 1961.   DHU/R
Edge, Frederick Miles. Slavery Doomed; or, The Contest Between Free and Slave Labour in the United States. London: Smith, Elder & Co., 1860.
                          NN/Sch
Slavery and the church, pp. 166-74.
Edwards, Jonathan. The Injustice and Impolicy of the Slave Trade, and of the Africans:

Illustrated in a Sermon Preached before the Conn. Society for the Promotion of Freedom, and for the Relief of Persons Unlawfully Holden in Bondage at their Annual Meeting in New Haven, September 15, 1791...4th ed. Newburyport: Charles Whipple, 1834. DHU/MO; CtY; NN/Sch
Ellison, John Malcus. The Story of the Hamitic Peoples in the Holy Bible. Philadelphia: A. J. Holman Co., 194-.
                          NN/Sch
Negro author.
Emery, E.B. Letters from the South, on the Social, Intellectual, and Moral Condition of the Colored People... Boston: T. Todd, Printer, 1880.
                          DHU/MO
Evangelical Consociation, Rhode Island. Fellowship with Slavery. Report Republished from the Minutes of the Evangelical Consociation, Rhode Island. Cin.: American Reform and Book Society, 1853. DHU/MO
Evangelical Union Anti-slavery Society of the City of New York. Address to the Churches of Jesus Christ, by the Evangelical Union Anti-slavery society, of the City of New York, Auxiliary to the Am. A.S. Society. With the Constitution, Names of Officers, Board of Managers, and Executive Committee. April, 1839. New York: Pr. by S.W. Benedict, 1839.   DHU/MO
Evans, Joshua. A Journal of the Life, Travels, Religious Experiences and Labors in the Work of the Ministry. Phila.: J. & I. Comly, 1837.
                          NNC
Fast Day Sermons; or, The Pulpit on the State of the Country. New York: Rudd & Carleton, 1861.   NN/Sch
Father Ward's Letter to Profes-

sor Stuart. Brentwood, N. H. :
August, 1837.   DHU/MO
Pamphlets on slavery and
Christianity, vol. 1.
Faulkner, William J. "The Influence of Folklore Upon the
Religious Experience of the
Ante-Bellum Negro." Journal
of Religious Thought (24:2,
Aut.-Wint. , 1967-68), pp. 26-
8.   DHU/R
Fawcett, Benjamin. A Compas-
sionate Address to the Chris-
tian Negroes in Virginia, and
other British Colonies in
North America. With an Ap-
pendix, Containing Some Ac-
count of the Rise and Prog-
ress of Christianity among
that Poor People. 2d ed.
Salop: Pr. by F. Eddowes
and F. Cotton, 1756.   DLC
The Fellowship of Slaveholders
Incompatible with a Christian
Profession. New York: American Anti-Slavery Society,
1859.   DLC
Fish, Carl Russell. The Rise
of the Common Man. New
York: Macmillan Co. , 1927.
                         DLC
Vol. 6, split of Baptists
and Methodists over slavery.
Fish, Henry Clay. Freedom or
Despotism. The Voice of our
Brother's Blood: Its Source
and Its Summons. A Dis-
course Occasioned by the Sum-
ner and Kansas Outrages.
Preached in Newark, June 8,
1856. Newark, N. J. : Doug-
lass & Starbuck, 1856. DLC
Fisher, George Elisha. The
Church, the Ministry, and
Slavery. A Discourse, Deliv-
ered at Rutland, Mass. , July
14, 1850. Worcester: Pr. by
H. J. Howland, 1850.
        DLC; NN/Sch
Fitzgerald, John. Christian
Slaveholders Disobedient to
Christ; or, Ten Thousand Eng-
lish Christians Invited to Pro-

test Actively Against the Sin
of the Church in the United
States; And to Cease from
Purchasing the Produce of
Slave Labour. London: W. H.
Dalton, 1854.   ICN
Fitzhugh, George. Sociology for
the South or the Failure of a
Free Society. Richmond:
Morris, 1854. CtY; NN
Fletcher, John. Studies on
Slavery, in Easy Lessons.
Compiled into Eight Studies,
and Subdivided into Short Les-
sons for the Convenience of
Readers. Natchez: J. Warner,
1852.   NN/Sch; CtY-D
Forman, Jacob Gilbert. The
Fugitive Slave Law; a Dis-
course Delivered in the Con-
gregational Church in West
Bridgewater, Mass. , Nov. 17,
1850. Boston: Wm. Crosby
and H. P. Nichols, 1850.
                     DHU/MO
Foster, Daniel. An Address on
Slavery. Delivered in Danvers,
Mass. , by Daniel Foster,
Pastor of the Free Evangeli-
cal Church of North Danvers,
in Compliance with the Re-
quest of the Voters of Danvers.
Boston: B. Marsh, 1849.
                       CtY-D
Foster, Stephen Symonds. The
Brotherhood of Thieves; or,
A True Picture of the Ameri-
can Church and Clergy: a
Letter to Nathaniel Barney, of
Nantucket. Boston: Anti-
Slavery Office, 1844. DHU/MO;
DLC; NcD; NN/Sch
Fox, George. Gospel Family
Order, Being a Short Dis-
course Concerning the Order-
ing of Families, Both of
Whites, Blacks and Indians.
Philadelphia: n. p. , 1701.
                         DLC
Christian conscience sec-
tion discusses Negro slaves
on the new plantations.

Free Church Anti-Slavery Society. An Address to the Office-Bearers and Members of the Free Church of Scotland, on her Present Connexion with the Slaveholding Churches of America. From the Committee of the Free Church Anti-Slavery Society. Edinburgh: Charles Ziegler, 1847.
DHU/MO
--The Sinfulness of Maintaining Christian Fellowship with Slave-Holders. Strictures on the Proceedings of the Last General Assembly of the Free Church of Scotland, Regarding Communion with the Slave-Holding Churches of America, Respectfully Addressed to the Office-Bearers and Members of that Church. From the Committee of the Free Church Anti-Slavery Society. Edinburgh: C. Ziegler, 1846.
DHU/R
Friends of the Missions. ...For the Missions. The Apostolate in Africa... Quebec: The Model Print Shop, 1911.
NN/Sch
Frothingham, Frederick. Significance of the Struggle Between Liberty and Slavery in America. New York: American Anti-Slavery Society, 1857.   NN/Sch
Fuller, Edward J. A Fast Sermon, Delivered April 7, 1836, Before the Calvinistic Church and Society in Harwick, Mass. ...Brookfield, Mass.: E. & L. Merriam, Printers, 1836.   NN/Sch
Furfey, Paul H. The Respectable Murderers; Social Evil and Christian Conscience. New York: Herder and Herder, 1966.   DHU/R
Slavery and the church, pp. 29-49.
Furness, William Henry. Christian Duty. Three Discourses

Delivered in the First Congregational Unitarian Church of Philadelphia May 28, June 4, and June 11, 1854. Philadelphia: Merrihew & Thompson, 1854.   DLC
--Put Up They Sword. A Discourse Delivered Before Theodore Parker's Society, at the Music Hall, Boston, Sunday, March 11, 1860... Boston: R. F. Wallcut, 1860.
DHU/MO
--The Right of Property in Man. A Discourse Delivered in the First Congregational Unitarian Church, July 3, 1859. Philadelphia: C. Sherman & Sons, 1859.   DLC
Galpin, William. The Churchmen and His Churchmanship. Things Which the Christian Ought to Know and Believe to His Soul's Health. Muskegon, Mich.: The Parish Printer, n. d.   DHU/MO
-- Some Why Nots of the Church. Muskegon, Mich.: The Parish Printery, n. d.   DHU/MO
Gannett, Ezra Stiles. Peace--Not War. A Sermon Preached in the Federal Street Meetinghouse, Dec. 14, 1845... Boston: J. Dowe, 1845.
DHU/MO
--Relations of the North to Slavery. A Discourse Preached in the Federal Street Meeting House, in Boston June 11, 1854. Boston: Crosby, Nichols and Co., 1854.
DHU/MO; CtY-D
Garlick, Phyllis Louisa. Towards Freedom; Evangelicals and Slave Emancipation... London: Church Missionary Society, 1933.   CtY-D
Gaustad, Edwin Scott. A Religious History of America. New York: Harper & Row, 1966.   NN/Sch
Slavery and the church, pp. 179-201.

Christianity and Slavery   99

Glasgow Anti-Slavery Meeting.
Free Church Alliance with
Manstealers. Send Back the
Money. Great Anti-Slavery
Meeting in the City Hall, Glas-
gow, Containing Speeches De-
livered by Messrs. Wright,
Douglass and Buffum from
America, and by George
Thompson of London; with a
Summary Account of a Series
of Meetings held in Edin-
burgh, by the above Named
Gentlemen. Glasgow: G. Gal-
lie, 1846.   NN/Sch
   Speech of Frederick Doug-
lass, pp. 19-24.
Glasgow Emancipation Society.
Address by the Committee of
the Glasgow Emancipation So-
ciety of the Ministers of Re-
ligion in Particular and the
Friends of Negro Emancipation in General on American
Slavery. Glasgow: Aird &
Russell, 1836.   DHU/MO
-- The American Board of Commissioners for Foreign Missions, and the Rev. Dr.
Chalmers, on Christian Fellowship with Slaveholders: An
Address by the Glasgow Emancipation Society to Christians
of all Denominations, but Especially to Members of the
Free Church of Scotland.
Glasgow: Pr. by D. Russell,
sold by G. Gallie, 1845. DLC
Godwyn, Morgan. The Negro
and Indians Advocate: Suing
for Their Admission into the
Church. London: Pr. for
the author by J.D., 1680.
               CtY; ViU; NcD
Goodell, William. Come Outer-
ism. The Duty of Secession
from a Corrupt Church. New
York: American Anti-Slavery
Society, 1845. CtY; MH; OO
--One More Appeal to Professors of Religion, Ministers,
and Churches Who Are Not
Enlisted in the Struggle

Against Slavery. Boston: J.
W. Alden, n.d.   DHU/MO
"New England Anti-Slavery
Tract Association, No. 7."
--A Voice From America,
Touching the Evangelical Al-
liance and the Wrongs of the
Slave... Newcastle: W.B.
Leighton, n.d.   DHU/MO
Goodwin, Daniel Raynes. South-
ern Slavery in its Present
Aspects: Containing a Reply
to a Late Work of the Bishop
of Vermont on Slavery...
Philadelphia: J.B. Lippincott,
& Co., 1864.
               DHU/MO; CtY-D
Goodwin, Morgan. The Revival:
or Directions for a Sculpture,
Describing the Extraordinary
Case and Diligence of Our
Nation, in Publishing the
Faith Among Infidels in Amer-
ica and Elsewhere. Broad-
side. Rare Book Room.
                        RPJCB
Gouge, William. Of Domestical
Duties: Eight Treatises.
London: George Millery,
1622.   DFO
   Includes duties of masters
and slaves.
Green, Beriah. Belief Without
Confession. A Sermon,
Preached at Whitesboro, New
York. Utica: R.W. Roberts,
1844.   CtY; PHi; OClWHi
"I am opposed to slavery;
but am not an abolitionist."
--The Church Carried Along; or,
The Opinions of a Doctor of
Divinity on American Slavery.
New York: W.R. Dorr, 1836.
   CtY; PPrHi; OO
--Four Sermons, Preached in the
Chapel of the Western Reserve
College, on Lord's Days, Nov.
18, and 25, and Dec. 2, and
9, 1832. Cleveland: Office of
the Herald, 1833. DHU/MO
Green, Fletcher M. "Northern
Missionary Activities in the
South 1846-1861." Journal of

(Green, F. M. cont.)
the Southern History (21:2,
My., 1955), pp. 147-72. DHU
Greene, Lorenzo J. "Slavehold-
ing New England and Its
Awakening Conversion of the
Slaves." Journal of Negro His-
tory (13:4, Oct., 1928), pp.
492-533.   DHU
Greenslade, Stanley Lawrence.
The Church and the Social Order; A Historical Sketch.
London: SCM Press, 1948.
                      NN/Sch
    pp. 109-14 Slavery and
the Church.
Greville, Robert Kaye. Slavery
and the Slave Trade in the
United States of America;
and the Extent to Which the
American Churches are In-
volved in Their Support.
Edinburgh: W. Oliphan & Sons,
1845.   DLC
Griggs, Leverett Stearns. Fugi-
tives From Slavery. A Dis-
course Delivered in Bristol,
Conn., on Fast Day, Apr. 10,
1857. Hartford: D. B. Moseley,
1857.   NN/Sch
Grimes, Leonard A. "Impris-
oned in Richmond, Va., For
Assisting Fugitive Slaves to
Escape From Slavery, a
Lovely Disciple." Wm. J.
Simmons, (ed.). Men of
Mark... (Cleveland, O.: Geo.
M. Rewell & Co., 1887), p.
662.   DHU/R
Grimké, Angelina Emily. Ap-
peal to the Christian Women
of the South. New York: Amer.
Anti-Slavery Society, 1836.
                      DHU/MO
Grimké, Sarah Moore. An
Epistle to the Clergy of the
Southern States. New York:
American Anti-Slavery Society.
1936.   DHU/MO; NN/Sch
    "On slavery."
Grosvenor, Cyrus Pitt. A Re-
view of the "Correspondence"
of Messrs Fuller and Wayland

on the Subject of American
Slavery. To Which is Added
a Discourse by Roger Willi-
ams, Printed in London, 1692
on "the Hierling Ministry."
Utica: Pub. at the Christian
Contributor Office, 1847.
                      NN/Sch
Hall, Nathaniel. The Limits of
Civil Obedience. A Sermon
Preached in the First Church,
Dorchester, Ja. 12, 1851.
Boston: W. Crosby and H. P.
Nichols, 1851.   DLC
Hall, P. W. Thoughts and In-
quiry on the Principles and
Tenure of the Revealed and
Supreme Law, Shewing the
Utter Inconsistency and Injus-
tice of Our Penal Statutes, and
the Illicit Traffic and Practice
of Modern Slavery. With
Some Grounds of a Plan for
Abolishing the Same. To
Which is Added a Letter to a
Clergyman on the Same Sub-
ject. London: J. Ridgway,
1792.   DHU/MO
Hammon, Jupiter. An Address
to the Negroes in the State
of New-York. By Jupiter Ham-
mon, Servant of John Lloyd,
Jun. Esq. of the Manor of
Queen's Village, Long Island
... New York: Pr., Philadelphia, reprinted by Daniel
Humphreys, in Spruce Street,
near the Drawbridge, 1787.
Tarrytown, N. Y.: Reprinted
W. Abbatt, 1925.   DLC
Harlow, Ralph Volney. Gerrit
Smith; Philanthropist and Re-
former. New York: H. Holt
& Co., 1939.   DHU/MO
    Based on primary sources
makes a strong plea for abolition of slavery for religious
reasons.
Harris, Eugene. Two Sermons
on the Race Problems, Ad-
dressed to Young Colored Men,
by One of Them. Nashville,
Tenn.: n.p., 1895.   DHU/MO

Negro author.

Harris, John "The Church and
Slavery: A Great Opportunity."
The Church Overseas (6;
1933), pp. 205-9.   DHU/R

Hart, Albert B. Slavery and
Abolition, 1831-1841. London:
Harper & Bros., 1906.
                          DHU/R
Schism in churches over
slavery issue.

Haven, Gilbert, (bp.). National
Sermons. Sermons, speeches
and Letters on Slavery and
its War, from the Passage of
the Fugitive Slave Bill to the
Election of President Grant.
Boston: Lee & Shepard, 1869.
                          NN/Sch

Haynes, Lemuel. Universal
Salvation, a Very Ancient
Doctrine; With Some Account
of the Life and Character of
the Author. A Sermon De-
livered at Rutland, West Parish in the Year 1805. Boston:
Pr. by David Carlisle, 1807.
                          DHU/MO
Negro author.

Helper, Hinton Rowan. The Im-
pending Crisis of the South:
How to Meet It. New York:
A. B. Burdick, 1859.
                  CtY-D; DHU/MO

Henson, Herbert Hensley, (bp.).
Christianity and Slavery. London: Rivingtons, 1887.
                          CtY-D
Bishop of Durham, 1863-
1947.

Hersey, John. An Appeal to
Christians, on the Subject of
Slavery... Baltimore: Arm-
strong & Plaskitt, 1833.
                          DHU/MO

Higginson, Thomas Wentworth.
"Man Shall Not Live by Bread
Alone." A Thanksgiving Sermon, Preached in Newbury-
port, Nov. 30, 1848. New-
buryport: Charles Whipple,
1848.   DLC
--Massachusetts in Mourning.

A Sermon Preached in Wor-
chester, on Sunday June 4,
1854... Boston: James Munroe and Co., 1854. DHU/MO

Hillhouse, William. The Crisis,
No. 1-2; or Thoughts on Slavery Occasioned by the Missouri Question. New Haven:
A. H. Maltby & Co., 1820.
                          DLC

Hodges, Charles Edward. Dis-
union Our Wisdom and Our
Duty. New York: American
Anti-Slavery Society, 1855.
                          CtY-D

Holcombe, William Henry. Suggestions as to the Spiritual
Philosophy of African Slavery,
Addressed to the Members
and Friends of the Church of
the New Jerusalem. New
York: Mason Bros., 1861.
                          NN/Sch

Hosmer, William. Slavery and
the Church... Auburn, N.Y.:
W. J. Moses, 1853. DHU/MO;
DLC; NN/Sch; CtY-D

Hough, J. Our Country's Mission; or, The Present Suffering of the Nation Justified by
its Future Glory. A Dis-
course Preached at Williston,
Vermont, on the Day of the
National Fast, August 4th,
1864. By Rev. J. W. Hough.
Burlington: Free Press Print,
1864.   CtY-D

Humphrey, Heman. Dr. Hum-
phrey's Charges Against Slavery. Extracts from a Dis-
course Delivered at Pittsfield,
on the National Fast Day.
Jan. 4, 1861. Boston: American Tract Society, 1861.
                          NN/Sch

The Independent. Politics and
the Pulpit: A Series of Articles which Appeared in the
Independent, during the year
1850. To Which is Added an
Article from the Independent
of Feb. 21, 1850, Entitled
"Shall We Compromise?"

(The Independent cont.)
New York: W. Harned, 1851.
DHU/MO; DLC
Jay, William. An Address to
the Anti-Slavery Christians of
the United States. New York:
J.A. Gray, n.d.   DHU/MO
--An Examination of the Mosaic
Laws of Servitude... New
York: M.W. Dodd, 1854.
NN/Sch; DHU/MO; CtY-D
-- A Letter to the Committee
Chosen by the American Tract
Society, to Inquire into the
Proceedings of its Executive
Committee, in Relation to
Slavery. New York: n.p.,
1857.   DLC; NN/Sch
Jeffrey, George. The Pro-Slav-
ery Character of the Ameri-
can Churches, and the Sin of
Holding Christian Communion
with Them. A Lecture De-
livered at the Request of the
Free Church Anti-Slavery So-
ciety, Edinburgh: Charles
Ziegler, 1847.   DHU/MO
Jenkins, William S. Pro Slavery
Thought in the Old South.
Chapel Hill, N.C.: Univ. of
North Carolina Press, 1935.
DHU/MO
Jessup, Lewis. God's Honour;
or, The Christian's Statesman.
A Sermon Preached in Mills-
bury, June 15, 1856. Worces-
ter: Chas. Hamilton, 1858.
TNF
Johnson, Evan M. "The Com-
munion of Saints." A Dis-
course delivered in St. Mi-
chael's Church, Brooklyn,
N.Y., on Sunday, the 26th of
March, A.D., 1848. Brooklyn:
I. Van Anden, 1848. DHU/MO
Jones, Absalom, & Allen, Richard.
A Narrative of the Proceedings
of the Black People, During
the Late Awful Calamity in
Philadelphia, in 1793; and a
Refutation of Some Censures,
Thrown Up on Them in Some
Late Publications. n.p., 1794.

DLC; DHU/R
(In reply to a vicious at-
tack upon Negroes by Matthew
Carey colonizationist.)
Also in, Negro Protest
Pamphlets, A Compendium.
New York: Arno Press, 1969.
Jones, John Richter, Slavery
Sanctioned by the Bible. The
First Part of a General Trea-
tise on the Slavery Question.
Philadelphia: J.B. Lippincott,
1861.   NN/Sch
Jullan, George Washington.
Speeches on Political Ques-
tions, 1850-1871. With an
introd. by L. Maria Child.
New York: Hurd and Hough-
ton, 1872.   NN/Sch
Slavery and the church, pp.
67-82.
Junkin, George. The Integrity
of our National Union, vs.
Abolitionism: An Argument
from the Bible in Proof of the
Position that Believing Mas-
ters Ought to be Honored and
Obeyed by their Own Servants,
and Tolerated in, not Excom-
municated from, the Church
of God: Being Part of a Speech
Delivered Before the Synod of
Cincinnati, on the Subject of
Slavery, September 19th and
20th, 1843. Cincinnati, O.:
Pr. by R.P. Donogh, 1843
DLC; NcD; NN/Sch
Kemble, Frances Anne. The
View of Judge Woodward and
Bishop Hopkins on Negro
Slavery at the South. Illus-
trated from the Journal of a
Residence on Georgian Planta-
tion. Philadelphia: n.p.,
1863.   CtY-D
Kennedy, John Herron. Sympa-
thy, Its Foundation and Legiti-
mate Exercise Considered, in
Special Relation to Africa. A
Discourse Delivered on the
4th of July, 1828. in the Sixth
Presbyterian Church. Philadel-
phia: W.F. Geddes, 1828. DLC

Ker, Leander. Slavery, Consistent with Christianity. Jefferson City, Mo.: Pr. by W. Lusk & Son, 1842. DHU/MO

Kettell, George F. A Sermon on the Duty of Citizens, with Respect to the Fugitive Slave Law. White Plains, N. Y.: Eastern States Journal, 1851. DLC

Kiefl, Franz Xaver. Die Theorien des Modernen Sozialismus über Den Ursprung des Christentums. Zugleich ein Kammentar zu 1 Kor. 7, 21, von F. X. Kiefl. Kempten und Muchen: Kosel, 1915. NN/Sch; DLC

Kingsford, Edward. The Claims of Abolitionism Upon the Church of Christ, Candidly Examined. A Sermon Delivered at the Baptist Church, Harrisburg, on the Morning of Sabbath, February 18th, 1838. Pub. by Request of Several Members of the Senate and House of Representatives of the Legislature of Pennsylvania. Harrisburg: Pr. by E. Guyer, 1838. DLC

Klein, Herbert S. Slavery in the Americas: a Comparative Study of Virginia and Cuba. Chicago: University of Chicago Press, 1967. DHU/R
    Pt. III is entitled "Anglicanism, Catholicism, and the Negro Slave."

Krebs, John Michael. The American Citizen. A Discourse on the Nature and Extent of our Religious Subjection to the Government under which we Live... New York: Charles Scribner, 1851. DHU/MO; CtY-D

Lacy, Charles L. A Sermon Preached in Falling Spring Valley, West Va. October 19, 1876. Lacy on His Return Home, Twelve Years After His Escape from Slavery. Together with an Account of His Flight from Bondage, and a Brief Account of His Miraculous Escape from Death. Also, Good News Received by Letters from Friends. Cleveland: T. C. Schenck, 1880. CtY-D

Lafon, Thomas. The Great Obstruction to the Conversion of Souls at Home and Abroad. An Address... New York: Union Missionary Society, 1843. DHU/MO

Lane Seminary. Fifth Annual Report of the Trustees; Together with the Laws of the Institution, and a Catalogue of the Officers and Students. Cincinnati: Corey & Fairbank, 1834. DLC
    Contains statement by faculty concerning the late controversy with students over slavery.

--Fourth Annual Report of the Trustees of the Cincinnati Lane Seminary; Together with a Catalogue of the Officers and Students. Lane Seminar: Students Typographical Association, n. p., 1834. DLC
    Seminary was actively involved in the slavery issue.

Larroque, Patrice. De L'Esclavage Chez les Nations Chrétiennes. Paris: Librairie Etrangère de Bohne et Schultz, 1860. NN/Sch; CtY-D

Lay, Benjamin. All Slave-Keepers That Keep the Innocent in Bondage, Apostates Pretending to Lay Claim to the Pure and Holy Christian Religion; of What Congregation So Ever; but Especially in Their Ministers, by Whose Example the Filthy Leprosy and Apostacy Is Spread Far and Near. Philadelphia: Pr. for the Author, 1737. DLC

Lechler, Gotthard Victor. Sklaverei und Christentum. Leip-

(Lechler, G. V. cont.)
zig: Druck von A. Edelmann,
1877-78.   CtY-D
Le Jau, Francis. The Carolina
Chronicle, 1706-1717. Berke-
key: University of California,
Press, 1956.   CtY-D
A Letter to an American Plant-
er, From His Friend in Lon-
don. Printed by H. Reynell,
1781.   DLC
The letter is dated Oct. 1,
1770.
Letters Addressed to Dorothy
Ripley, From Several Afri-
cans and Indians, on Subjects
of Christian Experience...
Chester: J. Heminway, 1807.
                          DHU/MO
Lewis, Evan. An Address to
Christians of All Denomina-
tions, on the Inconsistency of
Admitting Slave-Holders to
Communion and Church Mem-
bership... Philadelphia: S. C.
Atkinson, Printer, 1831.
                     DHU/MO; DLC
Published by order of the
Pennsylvania Society for Pro-
moting the Abolition of Slav-
ery.
-- Address to the Coloured
People of Philadelphia. De-
livered at Bethel Church,
Mr. 12, 1833. Philadelphia:
J. Richards, 1833. DHU/MO
Liberty or Slavery; the Great
National Question. Three
Prize Essays on American
Slavery... Boston: Congrega-
tional Board of Publication,
1857.   NN/Sch; NcD
Locke, Mary S. Anti-Slavery in
America From the Introduc-
tion of African Slaves to the
Prohibition of the Slave Trade.
Gloucester, Mass.: Peter
Smith, 1965. (Radcliffe Col-
lege Monographs, no. 11)
                          DHU/R
"Aims to trace the early
development of anti-slavery
sentiment under the influence

of religious and ethical principles and of political theo-
ries."
Loguen, Jermain Wesley. Cor-
respondence Between the Rev.
H. Mattison and Rev. J. W.
Loguen, on the Duty of Minis-
ters to Allow Contributions in
the Churches in Aid of Fugi-
tives Slaves and the Obligation of Civil Government and
the Higher Law. Syracuse,
N. Y.: J. E. Masters, 1857.
                          DHU/MO
London Emancipation Committee's
Tract. The Rev. John Wadding-
ton and American Slavery.
London: W. M. Watts, 1860.
                          DHU/MO
London Missionary Society. The
London Missionary Society's
Report of the Proceedings
Against the Late Rev. J.
Smith, of Demerara... Who
was Tried Under Martial Law,
and Condemned to Death, on
a Charge of Aiding and Assist-
ing in a Rebellion of the Ne-
gro Slaves. London: F. West-
ley, 1824.   CtY-D
Long, John Dixon. Pictures of
Slavery in Church and State;
Including Personal Reminis-
cences, Biographical Sketches,
Anecdotes, etc., etc. With
and Appendix, Containing the
Views of John Wesley and
Richard Watson on Slavery.
New York: Negro Universities
Press, 1969.
              DHU/MO; DHU/R; DLC
Reprint of the 1857 ed.
Longstreet, Augustus Baldwin.
Letters on the Epistle of
Paul to Philemon, or the
Connection of Apostolical
Christianity with Slavery.
Charleston: Jenkins, 1845.
                            NcD
Lotz, Adolf. Sklaverei, Staats-
kirche und Freikirche; die
Englischen Bekenntnisse im
Kampf um die Aufhebung von

Sklavenhandel und Sklaverei.
Leipzig: B. Tauchnitz, 1929.
                              NN/Sch
Love, Horace Thomas. Slavery
in Its Relation to God. A
Review of Rev. Dr. Lord's
Thanksgiving Sermin, in Fav-
or of Domestic Slavery, En-
titled the Higher Law, in Its
Application to the Fugitive
Slave Bill. Buffalo: A. M.
Clapp & Co., 1851.   DLC
Love, William Deloss. The Re-
opening of the African Slave
Trade. Milwaukee: n. p.,
1860?   CtY-D
From the advanced sheets
of 'The New Englander,' for
Feb., 1860, v. 18.
Lovewell, Lyman. A Sermon
on American Slavery Preached
in New Hudson, Michigan,
June 18, 1854. Detroit: Baker
and Conover, 1854.   OO
Macdonald, Eugene Montague.
A Short History of the Inquisi-
tion, what it was and what it
Did; to which is Appended an
Account of Persecutions by
Protestants, Persecutions of
Witches, the War Between Re-
ligion and Science, and the
Attitude of the American
Churches Toward African
Slavery... New York: The
Truth Seeker Company, 1907.
                              NN/Sch
March, Daniel. The Crisis of
Freedom. Remarks on the
Duty which all Christian Men
and Good Citizens Owe to
their Country in the Present
State of Public Affairs. Nash-
ua, N. H.: Pr. by Dodge and
Noyes, 1854.   NN/Sch
Marvin, Abijah Perkins. Fugi-
tive Slaves: A Sermon
Preached in North Congrega-
tional Church, Winchendon,
Apr. 11, 1850. Boston: J. P.
Hewett & Co., 1850.   DLC
Massie, James William. Slavery
the Crime and Curse of Amer-

ica: An Expostulation with the
Christians of That Land. Lon-
don: John Snow, 1852.
                    CtY; MB; ICN
Mather, Cotton. Rules for the
Society of Negroes, 1693.
New York: n. p., 1888.
                              CtY-D
May, George. A Sermon on the
Connection of the Church with
Slavery. Lowell, Mass.: W.
H. Stevens, 1845.   NN
May, Samuel Joseph. Address
of Rev. Mr. May, on Emanci-
pation in the British West In-
dies; Delivered in the First
Presbyterian Church in Syra-
cuse, August 1, 1845. Syra-
cuse: J. Barber, 1845.
                              DHU/MO
McCabe, Joseph. ... Christianity
and Slavery. Girard, Kan.:
Haldeman-Julius Co., 1927.
                              NN/Sch
Meacham, Standish. Henry
Thorton of Clapham, 1760-
1815. Cambridge: Harvard
University Press, 1964.
                              CtY-D
Minutes of the Fifth Annual Con-
vention for the Improvement
of the Free People of Colour
in the United States, held by
adjournments in the Wesley
Church, Philadelphia from the
First to the Fifth of June,
inclusive, 1835. Philadelphia:
Pr. by Wm. P. Gibbons,
Sixth and Cherry Streets, 1934.
                              DHU/MO
Moore, H. E. "The Attitude of
the Church Toward Slavery and
Serfdom from 325 to 1200
A. D." Quarterly Journal (11:
1, Ja., 1942), pp. 13-45.
                              DHU/MO
Morrill, Anson Peaslee. Mes-
sage of Governor Morrill, to
the Legislature of the State of
Maine, January 6, 1855. Au-
gusta: Stevens & Blaine, 1855.
                              NcD
Morse, Jedidiah. A Discourse

(Morse, J. cont.)
Delivered at the African
Meeting-House in Boston.
July 14, 1808, in Grateful
Celebration of the Abolition
of the African Slave-Trade,
by the Governments of the
United States, Great Britain
and Denmark. Boston: Pr.
by Lincoln & Edmands, 1808.
                           NN/Sch
Morse, Sidney Edwards. Premium Questions on Slavery,
Each Admitting of a Yes or
No Answer; Addressed to the
Editors of the New York Independent and New York Evan-
gelist, by Sidney E. Morse,
lately editor of the New York
Observer. New York: Harper
& Bros., 1860.   NN/Sch
Moulton, Phillips. "John Woolman's Approach to Social Ac-
tion--As Exemplified in Relation to Slavery." Church History (35:4, Dec., 1966), pp.
399-410.   DHU/R
Mudge, Zachariah Atwell. The
Christian Statesman; A Por-
traiture of Sir Thomas Fe-
well Buxton; with sketches of
British Anti-Slavery Reform.
New York: Carlton & Porter,
1865.   NN/Sch
Negro Slavery. No. XVIII.
Attempt to Enlist Religion on
the Side of Colonial Slavery
Exposed. London: Ellerton
and Henderson, Printers,
183-. Pam. File; NcD
-- A Review of Five Books:
Each Dealing with the Subject
of Slavery. Reprinted from
the American Quarterly Review.   NN/Sch
Phila., n.p., 1832?
Nelson, Isaac. Slavery Supported by the American Church
and Countenanced by Recent
Proceedings in the Free
Church of Scotland. A Lecture Delivered at the Request
of the Free Church Anti-

Slavery Society. Edinburgh:
C. Ziegler, 1847. DHU/MO
Newcomb, Harvey. The "Negro
Pew" Being an Inquiry Con-
cerning the Propriety of Dis-
tinctions in the House of God
on Account of Color. Boston:
Isaac Knapp, 1837.
                     DHU/MO; DLC
Offley, Greenburg W. God's
Immutable Declaration of His
Own Moral and Assumed Nat-
ural Image and Likeness in
Man, Declared. (Genesis 1:
26-27...) New Bedford: Mer-
cury Stern Printing House,
1875.   DHU/MO
Ohio State Christian Anti-Slavery
Convention, Columbus, 1859.
Proceedings of the Ohio State
Christian Anti-Slavery Con-
vention, held at Columbus,
August 10, and 11, 1859.
Columbus: n.p., 1859. DLC
Parker, Joel and A. Rood. The
Discussion Between Rev. Joel
Parker, and Rev. A. Rood,
on the Question "What are the
Evils Inseparable from Slav-
ery," which was Referred to
by Mrs. Stowe, in "Uncle
Tom's Cabin." Reprinted from
the Phil. Christian Observer
of 1846. New York: S.W.
Benedict; Phila.: H. Hooker,
1852.   DHU/MO
Parsons, Theophilus. Slavery.
Its Origin, Influence, and
Destiny. Boston: W. Carter,
1863.   CtY-D
Patterson, Caleb Perry. ... The
Negro in Tennessee, 1790-
1865... Austin, Tex., The
University, 1922. (University
of Texas Bulletin no. 2205:
Feb. 1, 1922).   NN/Sch
Patterson, James. A Sermon
on the Effects of the Hebrew
Slavery as Connected with
Slavery in This Country.
Preached in the 7th Presby-
terian Church in the City of
Phila....July 4, 1825. Phila.:

Christianity and Slavery

107

S. Probasco, 1825. DHU/MO
Patton, William Weston. Conscience and Law; or, A Discussion of Our Comparative Responsibility to Human and Divine Government: With an Application to the Fugitive Slave Law. New York: M. H. Newman, 1850.
DHU/MO; NN/Sch
--Reminiscences of the Late Rev. Samuel Hopkins, D.D., of Newport, R.I. Illustrative of His Character and Doctrines, with Incidental Subjects... Providence, R.I.: Isaac H. Cady, 1843.
DHU/MO
--Thoughts for Christians Suggested by the Case of Passmore Williamson: A Discourse Preached in the Fourth Congregational Church, Hartford, Conn., Oct. 7, 1855. Hartford, Conn.: Montague & Co., 1855. DHU/MO
Paxton, John D. Letters on Slavery; Addressed to the Cumberland Congregation, Virginia... Their Former Pastor. Lexington, Ky.: Abraham T. Skillman, 1833.
DHU/MO
Peabody, William Bourne Oliver. An Address, Delivered at Springfield, Before the Hampden Colonization Society, July 4th, 1828. Springfield: Pr. by S. Bowles, 1828. CtY-D
Perkins, Justin. American Slavery; In Connection with American Christianity. Our Country's Sin. A Sermon Preached to the Members and Families of the Nestorian Mission, at Oroomiah, Persia, July 3, 1853. Boston: John P. Jewett and Co., 1854.
DHU/MO; NN/Sch
Pierpont, John. National Humiliation. A Sermon, Preached in Hollis Street Church, Apr. 2, 1840. Boston: Samuel N.

Dickinson, 1840. MB; MH
Pierre, C. E. "The Work of the Society for the Propagation of the Gospel in Foreign Parts Among the Negroes in the Colonies." Journal of Negro History (1:4, Oct., 1916), pp. 349-60. DHU/MO
Pillsbury, Parker. The Church as It Is; or, The Forlorn Hope of Slavery. Concord, N.H.: Pr. by the Republican Press Association, 1885.
DLC; CtY-D; DHU/MO
Porter, Dorothy (ed.). Negro Protest Pamphlets. New York: Arno Press, 1969. DHU/MO
Anti-Slavery pamphlets written by Absolom Jones, Daniel Coker, Nathaniel Paul and Hosea Easton.
Negro author.
Porter, Noah. Civil Liberty. A Sermon, Preached in Farmington, Conn., July 13, 1856. New York: Pudney & Russell, 1851. DLC
--Two Sermons on Church Communion and Excommunication, with a Particular View to the Case of Slaveholders, in the Church. Hartford: Case, Tiffany & Co., 1853.
CtY; NNC
Posey, Walter Brownlow. Frontier Mission; a History of Religion West of the Southern Appalachians to 1861. Lexington: University of Kentucky Press, 1966. NN/Sch
Potter, Alonzo. Christian Philanthropy. A Discourse, Preached in St. George's Church, Schenectady, Sunday Evening Ja. 13, 1833, Before the African School Society. Schenectady, N.Y.: S.S. Riggs, 1833. DLC
The Praying Negro. An Authentic Narrative. [Andover, Flagg and Gould, 1818]. NcD
"Present State of the Slavery Question." Quarterly Chris-

("Present State ... cont.)
tian Spectator (8:1, Mr. ,
1836), pp. 112-27.   DHU/R
A discussion of the book
Slavery, by Wm. E. Channing.
Boston, 1835.
Purvis, Robert.   A Tribute to
the Memory of Thomas Ship-
ley, the Philanthropist. De-
livered at St. Thomas' Church,
Nov. 23, 1836. Published by
Request.   Philadelphia; Mer-
rihew and Gunn, 1838.
                              DHU/MO
Putnam, George.   Our Political
Idolatry.   A Discourse Deliv-
ered in the First Church in
Roxbury, on Fast Day, Apr.
6, 1843. Boston: Wm. Crosby
& Co., 1843.   DLC
--The Sign of the Times.   A
Sermon, Preached Mar. 6,
1836. Boston: Charles J.
Hindee, 1836.   OO
Rankin, John.   An Address to the
Churches; in Relation to Slav-
ery. Delivered at the First
Anniversary of the Ohio State
Anti-Slavery Society. By Rev.
John Rankin. With a Few In-
troductory Remarks, by a
Gentleman of the Bar... Me-
dina: Pr. at the Anti-Slavery
Office, 1836.   DLC
--Letters on American Slavery,
Addressed to Mr. Thomas
Rankin, Merchant at Middle-
brook, Augusta Co., Va.
Boston: I. Knapp, 1838.
               CtY-D; NN/Sch
"Religion Among Slaves." (From
the London Methodist Magazine,
being extracts" Mr. Hyde's
Journal, dated Parham, Antigua,
May 7, 1821). Christian Spec-
tator (12:3, Dec., 1821), pp.
656-57.   DHU/R
Religious and Slavery Convention,
Boston, 1846. The Declara-
tion and Pledge Against Slavery,
Adopted by the Religious and
Anti-Slavery, Convention, held
at Marlboro Chapel, Boston,

February 26, 1846. Devereux
& Seaman, Printers, 1846.
                       NN/Sch
Reynolds, Grant. Religious Education of the Negro During
the Colonial Period. New York:
n. p. , n. d.   NN/Sch
Negro author.
Reynolds, Elhanan W.   The Re-
lations of Slavery to the War:
and the Position of the Clergy
at the Present Time. Three
Discourses, Preached at
Watertown, N. Y. Watertown,
N. Y.: Sold at the Bookstores
and at Rand's, 1861.   DLC
Richmond, Legh. Annals of the
Poor: Consisting of the Dairy-
man's Daughter, the African
Servant, and the Young Cot-
tager. With a Brief Memoir
of the Author, and an Intro-
ductory Letter, by the Rev.
Joel Hawes. Springfield, Mass.:
G. & C. Meriman, 1852.
                       NN/Sch
Richmond, Thomas.   God Dealing
with Slavery. God's Instru-
mentalities in Emancipating the
African Slave in America.
Spirit Message from Franklin,
Lincoln, Adams, Jackson,
Webster, Penn, and others, to
the Author. Chicago: Religio-
philosophical Publishing House,
1870.   DHU/MO
Right of Petition. New England
Clergymen. Remarks of
Messrs. Everett, Mason, Pet-
itt and others on the Memorial
from Some 3,050 Clergymen of
all Denominations and Sects in
the Different States in New
England, Remonstrating Against
the Passage of the Nebraska
Bill. Senate of the U. S. , Mar.
14, 1854. Washington, D. C.:
Buell & Blanchard, Printers,
1854.   CtY-D
Ring, Rodney Everett. "The
Early Christian Church and
the Problem of Slavery."
Master's thesis, University of

Chicago, 1950.

Root, David. A Tract for the
Times and for the Churches;
Being the Substance of a Dis-
course Delivered at South
Boston, June, 1845. Boston:
A. J. Wright, 1845.   OO

Ross, Frederick Augustus. Position of the Southern Church
in Relation to Slavery, as Illustrated in a Letter of Dr.
F. A. Ross to Rev. Albert
Barnes. With an Introduction
by a Constitutional Presbyterian. New York: John A.
Gray, 1857.   NcD

Ross, William Stewart. Chris-
tianity and the Slave Trade.
By Saladin (pseud.) London:
W. Stewart, 1894.
      CtY-D; NN/Sch

Russo, Pasquale. Negro Slavery;
or Crime of the Clergy; a
Treatise on Chattel and Wage
Slavery, Presenting a Brief
Historical Discussion of the
Negro Problem in America.
Chicago, Ill.: Modern School
of Pedagogy, 1923.
      DHU/MO; DLC

Schaff, Philip. "The Influence
of the Early Church on the
Institution of Slavery." Mercersburg Review (10:4, Oct.,
1858), pp. 614-20. DHU/R

Schaub, Friedrich. Studien Zur
Geschichte der Sklaverei im
Frühmittel-Alter. Von dr.
Friedrich Schaub. Berlin und
Leipzig: W. Rothschild, 1913.
      NN/Sch; CtY-D; DLC

Schouler, James. History of
the United States. New York:
Dodd, Mead & Co., 1894-99.
      DHU/R
    Schism in the churches
over slavery.

Scott, Michael. Experiment in
Time. London: The Africa
Bureau, 1954.   DHU/MO
    A Sermon on Africa
preached by Rev. Michael
Scott at New York Cathedral,

New York City.

Sears, Edmund Hamilton. Revolution or Reform. A Dis-
course Occasioned by the
Present Crisis. Preached at
Wayland, Mass., Sunday,
June 15, 1856. Boston: Crosby, Nichols, 1856.   CtY-D

Separation From Sin and Sinners.
Should Christians Withdraw
Themselves from Sinners?
American Reform Tract and
Book Society.   DHU/MO
    Pamphlets on Slavery and
Christianity, vol. 1.

A Sermon Intended to Enforce
the Reasonable and Duty, on
Christian, as well as Political, Principles of the Abolition of the African Slave-
Trade. By Rev. J.M., Lon-
don: Sold by J. Johnson. St.
Paul's Church-yard, 1788.
      DHU/MO

A Sermon on the Relations and
Prospects of the United States
in Regard to Slavery. In the
Liberty Preacher, June, 1851.
Milwaukee, Wis.: June, 1851.
      DHU/MO

Sewall, Samuel. "The Selling
of Joseph." Merle Curti, Willard Thorp, (eds.), et al.
American Issues. (Chicago: J.
B. Lippincott Co., 1960), pp.
65-7.   DHU
    Slavery and the church and
Puritanism and the Negro.

Should the Free Church hold
Fellowship with Slave-Holders?
and, Should the Money Lately
Received from Slaveholding
Churches be Sent Back? Re-
spectfully Addressed to the
Members of the Free Church
of Scotland by a Member of
the Free Church. Linlithgow:
A. Waldie, 1846. DHU/MO

Sipkins, Henry. An Oration on
the Abolition of Slave Trade.
Delivered in the African
Church in the City of New
York, January 2, 1869, By

(Sipkins, H. cont.)
Henry Sipkins, a Descendent
of Africa. New York: Pr. by
J. C. Totten, 1809.
                DHU/MO; NN/Sch
Negro author.
A Sketch of the African Slave
Trade and the Slavery of the
Negroes Under Their Chris-
tian Masters in the European
Colonies. n. p., n. d. DHU/MO
...Slaveholding Piety. London:
Sold by W. and F. G. Cash,
1853.   DLC
"Slavery and the Church: Let-
ters." Journal of Negro His-
tory (10:4, Oct., 1925), pp.
754-58.   DHU
Slavery in America; With Notices
of the Present State of Slav-
ery and the Slave Trade
Throughout the World. Con-
ducted by the Rev. Thomas
Price, D. D. No. 1-14. July
1836-Aug. 1837. London: G.
Wightman, 1837.   DLC
Smectymnuus, (pseud.). Slavery
and the Church. Two letters
Addressed to Rev. N. L. Rice
D. D., in Reply to his Let-
ters to the Congregational
Deputation, on the Subject of
Slavery. Also a Letter to Rev.
Nehemiah Adams, D. D., in
Answer to the "South Side
View of Slavery." By Smecty-
mnuus. Boston: Crocker &
Brewster, 1856.   DLC
Smith, Henry B. Report on the
State of Religion in the United
States of America Made to the
General Conference of the
Evangelical Alliance, at Am-
sterdam, 1867. New York:
U. C. Roger, 1867. DHU/MO
Smith, Timothy L. Revivalism
and Social Reform in Mid-
Nineteenth Century America.
New York: Abingdon Press,
1957.   DHU/R
    Chapters XII and XIII
Churches and Slavery.
Smith, William Andrew. Lectures

on the Philosophy and Prac-
tice of Slavery, as Exhibited
in the Institution of Domestic
Slavery in the United States:
With the Duties of Masters to
Slaves. Ed. by Thos. O.
Summers. Nashville, Tenn.:
Stevenson & Evans, 1856.
                                CtY-D
    "The substance of lectures
...delivered to the classes in
moral science in Randolph
Macon College."
South Middlesex Conference of
Churches. The Political Duties
of Christians. A Report
Adopted at the Spring Meeting
of the South Middlesex Confer-
ence of Churches, April 18,
1848. Boston: Andrews &
Prentiss, 1848.   DLC
Spear, Samuel Thayer. The
Law-Abiding Conscience and
the Higher Law Conscience;
with Remarks on the Fugitive
Slave Question; a Sermon,
Preached in the South Presby-
terian Church, Brooklyn, Dec.
12, 1850. New York: Lambert
& Lane, Stationers and Print-
ers, 1850.   NN/Sch
Spike, Robert W. "Our Churches
Sin Against the Negro."
Look (My., 1965).   DHU
Stampp, Kenneth M. The Pe-
culiar Institution. Slavery in
the Ante-Bellum South. New
York: Vintage Books, 1956.
                                DHU/R
    Religion and slavery, pp.
156-62.
Stanton, Robert Livingston. The
Church and the Rebellion a
Consideration Against the
Government of the United
States; and the Agency of the
Church, North and South, in
Relation Thereto. New York:
Derby & Miller, 1864.
            NN/Sch; DLC; GAU; NcD
Stanton, William Ragan. The
Leopard's Spots: Scientific
Attitudes Toward Race in

America, 1815-1859. Chicago: University of Chicago Press, 1960.   DHU/MO; CtY-D

Steele, J.   The Substance of an Address Delivered by Rev. J. Steele in the Associate Reformed Synod of the West at Their Meeting in Steubenville, on the Evening of October 16th, 1829, on the Question of Making the Holding of Slaves a Term of Communion in the Church.   Washington: Guernsey Co., Ohio: Hamilton Robb, 1830.   OO; OOXM

Stephenson, George Malcolm. The Puritan Heritage. New York: Macmillan, 1952.
                    NN/Sch
   Slavery and the church, pp. 271-73.

Stone, Thomas Treadwell.   An Address Before the Salem Female Anti-Slavery Society, at its Annual Meeting, December 7, 1851.   Salem: W. Ives & Co., Printers, 1852.
                    CtY-D

Stowe, Mrs. Harriet Elizabeth (Beecher).   Mrs. H. B. Stowe on Dr. Monod and the American Tract Society; Considered in Relation to American Slavery ... Edinburgh: Repr. for the Edinburgh Ladies' Emancipation Society, 1858.   DLC

Strom, Herbert Edward.   Conscience and Law: the Debate in the Churches over the Fugitive Slave Law of 1850. New Haven: n.p., 1969.
                    CtY-D

Strong, Josiah. Our Country: Its Possible Future & Its Present Crisis.   New York: The American Home Missionary Society, 1885.   DLC

Sumner, Charles.   Final Protest for Himself and the Clergy of New England Against Slavery in Kansas and Nebraska.   Speech of Hon. Charles Sumner, on the Night of the Passage of the Kansas and Nebraska Bill.   In Senate of the United States, May 25, 1854. Washington, D. C.: Buell & Blanchard, Printers, 1854.
                    CtY-D

Sunderland, La Roy.   Antislavery Manual, Containing a Collection of Facts and Arguments on American Slavery.   New York: Pr. by S. W. Benedict, 1837.   CtY-D

Sweet, William Warren.   The Story of Religion in America. New York: Harper & Bros., 1930.   DHU/R
   Discusses the part of religion in the events leading to the Civil War, including the controversy over slavery.

Tannenbaum, Frank.   Slave and Citizen: The Negro in the Americas.   New York: Alfred A. Knopf, 1947.   DHU/MO

Tappan, Lewis.   Letters Respecting a Book "Dropped from the Catalogue" of the American Sunday School Union in Compliance with the Dictation of the Slave Power. New York: American and Foreign Anti-Slavery Society, 1848.
                    DHU/MO; DLC

Taylor, Joe G.   "Negro Slavery in Louisiana."   Doctoral dissertation, Louisiana State University, 1951.

Thayer, William Makepeace.   A Sermon on Moses' Fugitive Slave Bill, Preached at Ashland, Mass., November 3, 1850.   Boston: Pr. by C. P. Moody, 1850.   NN/Sch

Thompson, Andrew.   Slavery Condemned by Christianity. Edinburgh: Wm. Whyte and Co., 1847.   DHU/MO
   Pamphlets on Slavery and Christianity, vol. 1.

Thompson, George, and Wright, Henry Clarke.   The Free Church

(Thompson, G. and Wright, H. C.
cont.)
of Scotland and American
Slavery. With an Appendix
Containing the Deliverances
of the Free Church on the
Subject of Slavery, 1844, 1845,
and 1846, and Other Valuable
Documents. Edinburgh: Scot-
tish Anti-Slavery Society,
1846.   DLC
Thompson, Joseph Parrish. The
Duties of the Christian Citi-
zen. A Discourse, by Joseph
P. Thompson, Pastor of the
Broadway Tabernacle Church.
New York: S. W. Benedict,
1848.   DLC
Thomson, Andrew Mitchell.
Slavery Condemned by Chris-
tianity. Edinburgh: W. Whyte
and Co. , 1847. DHU/MO;DLC
"Thoughts on the Discussion of
Slavery." Christian Spectator
(7:3, Ag. , 1865), pp. 405-08.
                                    DHU/R
Article is initialed S. H.
Three Letters from the Reverend Mr. George Whitfield...
Letter III: To the Inhabitants
of Maryland, Virginia, North
and South Carolina Concerning Their Negroes. Philadelphia: Pr. & Sold by B. Frank-
lin, 1740.   DLC
Tyler, Alice. Freedom's Fer-
ment. New York: Harper,
1962.   DHU/R
Slavery, controversy and
religion, pp. 463-503.
Tyson, Bryan. The Institution
of Slavery in the Southern
States, Religiously and Moral-
ly Considered in Connection
with our Sectional Troubles.
Washington, D. C. : H. Polkinhorn, Printer, 1863.
                                    CtY-D
United States. 33d Cong. , 1st
Session, 1853-1854. Senate.
Right of Petition New England
Clergymen. Remarks of
Messrs. Everett... Mason,

Pettit, Douglas, Butler, Sew-
ard, Houston, Adams and
Badger. On the Memorial
From Some 3, 050 Clergymen
of all Denominations and Sects
in New England... Washington:
Buell & Blanchard, Printers,
1854.   DHU/MO
Union Anti-Slavery Society. How
the Action of the Churches
Towards the Anti-Slavery
Cause Promotes Infidelity.
Issued by the Union Anti-
Slavery Society. n. p. , n. d.
                                    DHU/MO
Vail, Stephen Montford. The
Church and the Slave Power.
A Sermon Preached before the
Students of the Methodist Bib-
lical Institute, Concord, New
Hampshire, February 23,
1860. Pub. by the Students.
Concord: Fogg, Hadley & Co. ,
1860.   DLC
Van der Linde, Jan M. Heren,
Slaven, Broeders; Momenten
Uit de Geschiedenis der Slav-
ernij. Nijkerk; G. F. Callen-
bach, 1963.   NN/Sch
Van Dyke, Henry Jackson. Giv-
ing Thanks for all Things.
A Sermon Preached in the
First Presbyterian Church of
Brooklyn on Thanksgiving-day,
Nov. 29, 1860. New York:
G. F. Nesbitt and Co. , Print-
ers, 1860.   NN/Sch
Veal, Frank Richard. "The Atti-
tude of the Ante-Nicean Fath-
ers toward Slavery Prior to
325 A. D. " B. D. Paper,
School of Religion, Howard
University, 1937.
Wallace, Cyrus Washington. A
Sermon on the Duty of Minis-
ters to Oppose the Extension
of American Slavery, Preached
in Manchester, N. H. , Fast
Day, April 3, 1857. Manches-
ter, N. H. : Steam Printing
Works of Fisk & Gage, 1857.
Washington, L. Barnwell. "The
Use of Religion for Social Con-

trol in American Slavery."
Master's thesis, Howard University, 1939.
    Negro author.
Warren, Edwin R. The Free
Missionary Principle, or,
Bible Missions. A Plea for
Separate Missionary Action
from Slaveholders... Boston:
J. Howe, 1847.   DHU/MO
Whipple, Charles King. The
Family Relation, as Affected
by Slavery. Cincinnati: American Reform Tract and Book
Society, 1858. (American Reform Tract and Book Society.
Tracts no. 40.)   CtY-D
--Relations of Anti-Slavery to
Religion. New York: American Anti-Slavery Society,
1855.
        DHU/MO; NN/Sch; CtY-D
    (Anti-Slavery Tracts, no.
19)
--Slavery and the American
Board of Commissioners for
Foreign Missions. New York:
American Anti-Slavery Society, 1859.   DLC
Wilkinson, James Garth. The
African and the True Christian, his Magna Charta. A
Study in the Writings of
Emanuel Swedenborg. London: J. Speirs, 1892.
                NN/Sch; DLC
Willey, Austin. The History of
the Anti-Slavery Cause in
State and Nation. Portland:
n. p., 1886.
    Section on slavery and the
church.
Williams, Thomas Scott. The
Tract Society and Slavery.
Speeches of Chief Justice Williams, Judge Parsons, and
Ex-Governor Ellsworth: Delivered in the Center Church,
Hartford, Conn. at the Anniversary of the Hartford Branch
of the American Tract Society.
January 9th, 1859. Hartford:
Steam Press of E. Geer,

1859.   NN/Sch
Wolcott, Samuel T. Separation
from Slavery. Being a Consideration of the Inquiry,
"How Shall Christians and
Christian Churches Best Absolve Themselves from all
Responsible Connection with
Slavery?" Boston: American
Tract Society, n. d.
        DHU/MO; CtY-D
    Prize essay by Church
Anti-Slavery Society.
Woolman, John. Considerations
on Keeping Negroes; Recommended to the Professors of
Christianity of Every Denomination. Part Second. Philadelphia: B. Franklin and D.
Hall, 1762.   DLC
Woolridge, Nancy Bullock. "The
Slave Preacher--Portrait of
a Leader." Journal of Negro
Education (14; Wint., 1945),
pp. 28-37.   DHU/MO
Worcester, Mass., Convention of
Ministers of Worcester County,
on the Subject of Slavery,
1837-1838. Proceedings of
the Convention of Ministers
of Worcester County, on the
Subject of Slavery; Held at
Worcester, 1838. Worcester:
Mass. Spy Office, 1838.
                DHU/MO
A Word to Members of the Free
Church, in Reference to the
Proceedings of the General
Assembly of 1847, on the
Question of Communion with
Slave-Holding Churches. By
a Free Churchman. Edinburgh: Charles Ziegler...
1847.   DHU/MO
Wright, Henry Clarke. Duty of
Abolitionists to Pro-Slavery
Ministers and Churches. Concord, N. H.: Pr. by J. R.
French, 1841.
        NN/Sch; CtY-D; DLC
--Christian Church; Anti-Slavery
and Non-Resistance Applied
to Church Organizations.

(Wright, H. C. cont.)
Boston: Anti-Slavery Office,
1841. DLC; NNC; OClWHi
--Christian Communion with
Slaveholders: Will the Alliance
Sanction It? Letters to Rev.
John Angell James, D.D. and
Rev. Ralph Wardlaw, D.D.,
Shewing their Position in the
Alliance. Rochdale: J. Hall,
1846.   DLC
--American Slavery: Two Let-

ters from H. C. Wright to the
Liverpool Mercury, Respecting
the Rev. Drs. Cox and Olin,
and American Man-Stealers.
Dublin: Webb and Chapman,
1846.   MH
The first of the two letters
appeared in the Manchester
Examiner, Sept. 26, 1846 and
second in the Liverpool, Mercury, Oct. 9, 1846

2. Roman Catholic Church

Allen, Cuthbert Edward. "The
Slavery Question in Catholic
Newspapers, 1850-1865."
United States Catholic Histori-
cal Society Records and Stud-
ies, (26; 1936), pp. 99-179.
                          DGU
Andrews, Rena M. "Slavery
Views of a Northern Prelate."
Church History (3:1, Mr.,
1934), pp. 60-78. DHU/R
Blied, Benjamin J. Catholics
and the Civil War. Milwaukee,
Wisc.: n.p., 1945.
          NcD; CtY-D; NN/Sch
Brokhave, Joseph D. Francis
Patrick Kenrick's Opinion on
Slavery. Washington, D.C.:
Catholic University of Ameri-
can Press, 1955. DCU; DLC
The Catholic Church and the
Question of Slavery. Balti-
more: n.p., 1855. NN/Sch
In issue of the Metropoli-
tan, v.3, no. 5, June, 1955.
Clarke, Richard Frederick.
Cardinal Lavigerie and the
African Slave Trade. New
York: Longmans, Green,
1889.   CtY-D
Decker, Vincent de. Sous le
Signe de la Croix; des Hor-
reurs de la Traite aux Pre-
mières Caravanes. n.p.,n.d.
                        NN/Sch
Decleene, Arnold. Het Rassen-

vraagstuk Door een Katholiek
Gezien. Antwerpen: Uitgeverij
"De Schelde," 1937.   DLC
Ellis, John Tracy. American
Catholicism. Chicago: Univer-
sity of Chicago Press, 1956.
                        NN/Sch
Slavery and the church.
--Documents of American Catho-
lic History. Milwaukee:
Bruce Pub. Co., 1956.
Slavery and the church.
England, John. Letters of the
Late Bishop England to the
Hon. John Forsyth on the
Subject of Domestic Slavery.
Baltimore: J. Murphy, 1844.
                        NN/Sch
Fave, Armand Joseph. Confér-
ence sur l'Esclavage. Pa-
négyri que de Saint Pierre
Claver... Grenobe: Baratier,
1888.   NN/Sch
Fitton, James. The Influence
of Catholic Christian Doc-
trines on the Emancipation of
Slaves. Boston: n.p., 1863.
                          DLC
Fransioli, Joseph. ...Patriotism,
a Christian Virtue. A Ser-
mon Preached...at St. Peter's
(Catholic) Church, Brooklyn,
July 26, 1863. New York:
n.p., n.d. 1863. DHU/MO
Gannon, Michael Valentine.
Rebel Bishop: the Life and

Era of Augustin Verot. Milwaukee: Bruce Pub. Co., 1964.   CtY-D
Gibbons, James. Our Christian Heritage. Baltimore: J. Murphy and Co., 1889.   NN/Sch
  Slavery and the church, pp. 416-37.
Gochet, Jean Baptiste. La Traite des Nègres et la Croisade Africaine, Comprenant la Lettre Encyelique de Léon XIII sur l'Esclavage, le Discours du Cardinal Lavigeri à Paris, les Temoignages des Grands Explorateurs: Livingstone, Cameron, Stanley, des Missionnaires. Français, etc. Ainsi que l'Organisation des Sociétés Anties Clavagistes en France et en Europe. Paris: Ch. Poussielgue, 1891.
                            NN/Sch; NcD
Holland, Timothy J. "Catholic Church and the Negro in the United States Prior to the Civil War." Doctoral dissertation, Fordham University, 1950.
Imbart de la Tour, Joseph Jean Baptiste. L'Esclavage en Africae et la Croisade Notre. Paris: Maison de la Bonne Press, 1891.   NN/Sch
La Faye, Jean Baptiste de. A Voyage to Barbary, for the Redemption of Captives; Performed in 1720 by the Mathuren-Trinitarian Fathers... Barbary, n.p., 1735. CtY-D
Lavigerie, Charles Martial Allemand. Documents sur la Foundation de l'Oeuvre Antiesclavagiste. Saint-Cloud: Imprimerie Vve E. Belin et Fils, 1889.   NN/Sch
--L'Esclavage Africain. Conference Faite dans L'Eglise de Saint-Sulpice à Paris. Paris: A la Procure des Missions d'Afrique, 1888.   CtY-D
--Slavery in Africa; a Speech by Cardinal Lavigerie made

at the Meeting Held in London July 31, 1888. Presided over by Lord Granville, Former Minister of English Foreign Affairs. Boston: Cashman, Keating, 1888.   CtY-D
Letter of an Adopted Catholic, Addressed to the President of the Kentucky Democratic Association of Washington City on Temporal Allegiance to the Pope, and the Relations of the Catholic Church and Catholics, both Native and Adopted, to the System of Domestic Slavery and Its Agitation in the U.S. n.p., 1856.   NcD
Manaricua, Andres E. de. El Matrimonio de los Esclavos; Estudio Histórico Juridico Hasta la Fijacion De la Disciplina en el Derecho Canonico. Romae: A Pud Aedes Universitates Gregorianae, 1940.
                                        NcD
  Slavery and the Catholic Church.
Miller, Richard Roscoe. Slavery and Catholicism. Durham, N.C.: North State Publishers, 1957.
  DHU/MO; DLC; NcD;
                            NN/Sch
Pilkington, George, (ed.). Folhetos de Pilkington. Rio de Janeiro: Typographia de Laemmert, 1841.   NN/Sch
Rice, Madeleine Hooke. American Catholic Opinion in the Slavery Controversy. New York: Columbia University Press, 1944.
  DHU/MO; NN/Sch; NcD
Rigord. Observations sur Quelques Opinions Relatives l'Esclavage, Emites & la Chambre des Pairs l'Occasion de la Discussion de la Loi Sur le Régime. Martinique: Typographie de E. Ruelle, 1845.
                            NN/Sch
Wight, Willard E. "Bishop Verot and the Civil War." The

(Wight, W. E. cont.)   (47:2, Jl., 1961), pp. 153-66.
Catholic Historical Review   DHU/R

3. Congregational Church (United Church of Christ)

An Affectionate Expostulation
with Christians in the United
States of America, Because
of the Continuance of Negro
Slavery Throughout Many Dis-
tricts of Their Country, Ad-
dressed by the Minister,
Deacons, and Members of the
Congregational Church, Joined
by the Congregation, Assem-
bling in Mill Street Chapel,
Perth. Glasgow: Geo.
Geo. Gallie, n. d.   DHU/MO
Allen, George. "Mr. Allen's
Report of a Declaration of
Sentiments on Slavery, Dec.
5, 1837." Worcester: H. J.
Howland, 1838.   CtY-D
--"Mr. Allen's Speech on Minis-
ters Leaving a Moral Kingdom
to Bear Testimony Against
Sin; Liberty in Danger, from
the Publication of its Prin-
ciples the Constitution a
Shield for Slavery; and the
Union Better than Freedom and
Righteousness." Boston: I.
Knapp, 1838. DHU/MO; CtY-D
Bacon, Leonard. Review of
Pamphlets on Slavery and
Colonization. First published
in Quarterly Christian Specta-
tor, for Mar. 1833. New
Haven: A. H. Maltby, 1833.
                             CtY
--Slavery Discussed in Occasion-
al Essays, from 1833 to 1846.
New York: Baker and Scrib-
ner, 1846.   CtY-D
--Two Sermons Preached to the
First Church in New Haven,
on the Day of Fasting. Viz.;
Good Friday, the 10th of Ap-
ril, 1857. New Haven: Thos.
H. Pease, 1857. DHU/MO
Bassett, George W. Slavery

Examined by the Light of Nature. Sermon Preached at
the Congregational Church,
Washington, D. C., Feb. 28,
1858. Washington, D. C.: n. p.,
1858.   DHU/MO; NN/Sch
Beeson, Lewis (ed.). Congre-
gationalism, Slavery and the
Civil War. Lansing: Michi-
gan Civil War Centennial Ob-
servance Commission, 1965.
                              DLC
Blodgett, C. How to Win a
Brother. A Discourse Deliv-
ered in the Congregational
Meeting House, Pawtuckett;
July 10, 1842. Pawtuckett:
Chronicle Press, 1842.
                          DHU/MO
Boynton, Charles Brandon.
Separation From Sin and Sin-
ners. Cincinnati: American
Reform Tract Society, n. d.
                          DHU/MO
--Thanksgiving Sermon by Rev.
C. B. Boynton D. D. Chaplain
of the House of Representa-
tives, and Pastor of the
First Congregational Church,
Washington, D. C., delivered
November 29, 1866. Alex-
andria, Va.: Pr. at the "Vir-
ginia State Journal" Job Of-
fice, 1866.   DHU/MO
Bulkley, Charles Henry Augustus.
Removal of Ancient Landmarks
or the Causes and Conse-
quences of Slavery Extension.
A Discourse Preached to Sec-
ond Congregational Church of
West Winsted Conn., Mr. 5,
1854.   DLC; CtY
Bushnell, Horace. The Census
and Slavery; a Thanksgiving
Discourse, Delivered in the
Chapel at Clifton Springs,

N.Y., November 29, 1860.
Hartford: L.E. Hunt, 1860.
CtY-D; DHU/MO
--A Discourse on the Slavery
Question. Delivered in the
North Church, Hartford,
Thursday Evening, Jan. 10,
1839. Hartford: Case, Tif-
fany & Co., 1839.
DHU/MO; CtY-D
--The Northern Iron. A Dis-
course Delivered in the North
Church, Hartford, on the An-
nual State Fast, April 14,
1854... Hartford: E. Hunt &
Son, 1854.   CtY-D
Cheever, George Barrell. The
Fire and Hammer of God's
Word Against the Sin of Slav-
ery. Speech of George B.
Cheever, D.D. at the Anni-
versary of the American Abo-
lition Society, May, 1858.
New York: American Abolition
Society, 1858. CtY-D; DHU/R
--God Against Slavery: and the
Freedom and Duty of the Pul-
pit to Rebuke It, as a Sin
Against God. Cincinnati: Amer-
ican Reform Tract and Book
Society, 1859.   A&M;
DHU/MO; DHU/R; CtY-D
--The Guilt of Slavery and the
Crime of Slave-Holding Demon-
strated from the Hebrew and
Greek Scriptures... Boston:
J.P. Jewett & Co., 1860.
NN/Sch; CtY-D; DHU/MO
--The Salvation of the Country
Secured by Immediate Emanci-
pation. A Discourse by Geo.
B. Cheever Delivered in the
Church of the Puritans, Sab-
bath Evening, Nov. 10, 1861.
New York: J.A. Gray, 1861.
CtY-D
Cheever, Henry Theodore. A
Tract for the Times, on the
Question, Is It Right to With-
hold Fellowship from Churches
or from Individuals that Tol-
erate or Practise Slavery!
Read by Appointment, before

the Congregational Ministers'
Meeting, of New London Coun-
ty, Ct. ...New York: J.A.
Gray, Printer, 1859. NN/Sch
Clark, Calvin Montague. Amer-
ican Slavery and Maine Con-
gregationalists; a Chapter in
the History of the Development
of Anti-Slavery Sentiment in
the Protestant Churches of the
North. Bangor, Me.: The
Author, 1940.
NcD; NN/Sch; CtY-D
Cleaveland, Elisha Lord. The
Patriot's Song of Victory. A
Thanksgiving Discourse, for
Recent Military Successes,
Delivered in the Third Congre-
gational Church, New Haven,
September 11, and Repeated
by Request, in the Same
Place, September 18, 1864.
By Elisha Lord Cleaveland
...New Haven: T.H. Pease,
1864.   CtY-D
Congregational Churches in Mas-
sachusetts. General Association.
Report of the Committee of
Correspondence with Southern
Ecclesiastical Bodies on Slav-
ery; to the General Associa-
tion of Massachusetts. Pub. by
the Vote of the Association.
Salem: J.P. Jewett and Co.,
1844.   DLC; NN/Sch
Congregational Home Missionary
Society. Home Missions and
Slavery: A Reprint of Sever-
al Articles, Recently Pub. in
the Religious Journals; with an
Appendix. New York: J.A.
Gray, 1857.   DLC
Convention of Congregational Min-
isters of Massachusetts. Report
of the Committee on Slavery,
to the Convention of Congregational Ministers of Massachusetts. Presented May 30,
1849. Boston: Press of J.R.
Marvin, 1849.
NN/Sch; CtY-D; NcD; DHU/MO
Dickinson, James Taylor. A
Sermon, Delivered in the Sec-

(Dickinson, J. T. cont.)
ond Congregational Church,
Norwich, on the Fourth of
July, 1834, at the Request of
the Anti-Slavery Society of
Norwich and Vicinity. Norwich: Anti-Slavery Society,
1834. Also, Rochester: Hoyt
& Porter, 1835.   DHU/MO
Dickinson, Noadiah Smith. Slavery: the Nation's Crime and
Danger. A Sermon Preached
in the Congregational Church,
Foxborough, Mass., Sept. 30,
1860. Boston: Press of G.
Noyes, 1860.   NN/Sch
Dunlop, John. American Slavery.
Organic Sins: or, The Iniquity
of Licensed Injustice. Edin-
burgh: W. Oliphant and Sons,
1846.   NN/Sch
Finney, Charles G. An Autobiog-
raphy. Westwood, N. J.: Flem-
ing H. Revell Co., 1876.
                    DHU/R
    Chapter 25, views on slav-
    ery and church.
Forman, Jacob Gilbert. The
Christian Martyrs; or, The
Conditions of Obedience to the
Civil Government; A Discourse
by... Minister of the Second
Congregational Church in Nan-
tucket;... To Which is Added, a
Friendly Letter to Said Church
and Congregation on the Pro-
Slavery Influences that Occa-
sioned His Removal. Boston:
W. Crosby and H. P. Nichols,
1851.   DHU/MO
Forster, Daniel. Our Nation's
Sins and the Christian's Duty.
A Fast Day Discourse, by Dan-
iel Forster, Minister in Charge
of the Congregational Church of
Concord, Mass., Delivered Ap-
ril 10, 1851. Boston: White &
Potter, Printers, 1851.   DLC
Foster, Eden Burroughs. A North-
Side View of Slavery... A Ser-
mon on the Crime Against
Freedom, in Kansas and Wash-
ington. Preached at Henniker,

N. H., August 31, 1856. Concord: Jone & Cogswell, Printers, 1856.   CtY-D; NN/Sch
--The Rights of the Pulpits, and
Perils of Freedom. Two Dis-
courses Preached in Lowell,
Sunday, June 25, 1854. Low-
ell: J. J. Judkins, 1854.
                    DHU/MO
Gillett, Francis. A Review of the
Rev. Horace Bushnell's Dis-
course on the Slavery Ques-
tion, Delivered in the North
Church, Hartford, January 10,
1839. Hartford: S. S. Cowles,
1839.   DHU/MO; CtY-D
Green, Beriah. Iniquity and a
Meeting. A Discourse Deliv-
ered in the Congregational
Church, Whitesboro, (N. Y.),
Jan. 31, 1841. n. p., n. d.
                    DHU/MO
Gulliver, J.P. The Lioness and
Her Whelps. A Sermon on
Slavery Preached in the Broad-
way Congregational Church,
Norwich, Connecticut. Decem-
ber 18, 1859. Norwich: Man-
ning Perry & Co., 1860.
                DHU/MO; CtY-D
Hall, Nathaniel. The Iniquity:
A Sermon in The First Church,
Dorchester, on Sunday Dec. 11,
1859. Nathaniel Hall. Boston:
Pr. by J. Wilson & Son, 1859.
                    CtY-D
--The Moral Significance of the
Contrasts Between Slavery and
Freedom. A Discourse
Preached in the First Church,
Dorchester, May 10, 1864...
Boston: Walker, Wise & Co.,
etc., 1864. DHU/MO; CtY-D
--Righteousness and the Pulpit:
A discourse Preached in the
First Church, Dorchester, on
Sunday, Sept. 30, 1855. Bos-
ton: Crosby, Nichols, 1855.
                NN/Sch; CtY-D
--Truth Not to Be Overthrown
Nor Silenced: A Sermon
Preached at Dorchester, Sun-

day, Jan. 27, 1861. Boston:
Pr. by J. Wilson, 1861.
                    CtY-D
--Two Sermons on Slavery and
its Hero-Victim. Boston: Pr.
by J. Wilson & Son, 1859.
                    NN/Sch
Hartford, Conn. Fourth Con-
gregational Church. The Unani-
mous Remonstrance of the
Fourth Congregational Church.
Hartford, Conn. Against the
Policy of the American Tract
Society on the Subject of Slav-
ery. New York: American
Anti-Slavery Society, 1855.
DHU/MO; NN/Sch; NcD; DLC;
                    GAU
Haynes, Lemuel. The Influence
of Civil Government on Reli-
gion. A Sermon Delivered at
Rutland, West Parish, Sept.
4, 1798...At the Annual Free-
men's Meeting...Pastor of a
Church in Rutland. Rutland,
Vermont, Pr. by John Walker,
1798.   DHU/MO
    Negro author.
Home Missions and Slavery. A
Reprint of Several Articles,
Recently Published in the Re-
ligious Journals; with an Ap-
pendix. New York: J.A. Gray,
Printer, 1857.   CtY-D
Humphrey, Heman. Parallel Be-
tween Intemperance and the
Slave Trade. An Address De-
livered at Amherst College,
July 4, 1828. Amherst: J.S.
and C. Adams, 1828. CtY-D
James, Horace. Our Duties to
the Slave. A Sermon Preached
Before the Original Congrega-
tional Church and Society, in
Wrentham, Mass. on Nov. 28,
1846. Boston: Richardson &
Filmer, 1847.
            DLC; DHU/MO
McEwen, Able. A Sermon,
Preached in the First Congre-
gational Church, New London,
Conn., on the Day of Thanks-
giving, November 28, 1850.

New London: Daniels & Bacon,
1851.   CtY-D
The National Entail. A Sermon
Preached to the First Congregational Church in Brookline,
on The 3rd July, 1864. Boston: Wright & Potter, 1864.
                    CtY-D
New York City (New York),
Church of the Puritans (Congregational). Reply of the Church
of the Puritans to the Protest
of their Late Deacons, also
to a "Letter" Addressed to
the Church by Sundry Individuals, July 15, 1857. New
York: W.C. Bryant, Printers,
1857.   CtY-D
Nott, Samuel. The Necessities
and Wisdom of 1861. A supple-
ment to the 6th ed. of Slavery
and the Remedy. Boston:
Crocker & Brewster, 1861.
                    CtY-D
--The Present Crisis: With a
Reply and Appeal to European
Advisers, from the 6th ed. of
"Slavery and the Remedy."
Boston: Crocker & Brewster,
1860.   CtY-D
--Slavery and the Remedy; or,
Principles and Suggestions for
a Remedial Code, With a Re-
view of the Decision of the
Supreme Court in the Case of
Dred Scott. New York: Apple-
ton, 1857.   CtY-D
Patten, William. On the Inhu-
manity of the Slave-Trade, and
the Importance of Correcting
It. A Sermon, Delivered in
the Second Congregational
Church, Newport, Rhode Is-
land, Aug. 12, 1792. Provi-
dence: J. Carter, 1793. DLC
Patton, William Weston. The
American Board and Slave-
holding. Hartford: W.H. Burleigh, Printer, 1846.
CtY-D; DHU/MO; DLC
--Freedom's Martyr. A Discourse on the Death of the
Rev. Charles T. Torrey.

(Patton, W. W. cont.)
  Hartford: Wm. H. Burleigh,
  1846.   DHU/MO
--The Unanimous Remonstrance
  of the Fourth Congregational
  Church, Hartford, Conn. ,
  Against the Policy of the Am-
  erican Tract Society on the
  Subject of Slavery. Hartford:
  Silas Andrus & Son, 1855.
                           DHU/MO
Pennington, James W. C. (bp.).
  Covenants Involving Moral
  Wrong are not Obligatory up-
  on Man: A Sermon, Delivered
  in the Fifth Congregational
  Church, Hartford, Nov. 17,
  1842. Hartford: J. C. Wells,
  1842.   DLC
--A Two Years' Absence; or, A
  Farewell Sermon, Preached in
  the Fifth Congregational
  Church. Nov. 2d, 1845. Hart-
  ford: H. T. Wells, 1845.
     Negro author.
Putnam, George. God and Our
  Country. A Discourse Deliv-
  ered in the First Congrega-
  tional Church in Roxbury, on
  Fast Day, April 8, 1847.
  Boston: W. Crosby and H. P.
  Nichols, 1847.   CtY-D
Quint, Alonzo Hall. The Chris-
  tian Patriot's Present Duty. A
  Sermon Addressed to the
  Mather Church and Society, Ja-
  maica Plain, Mass. , April 28,
  1861, by the Pastor. Boston:
  Hollis & Gunn, 1861.   CtY-D
Root, David. A Fast Sermon on
  Slavery. Delivered April 2,
  1835, to the Congregational
  Church and Society in Dover,
  N. H. Dover: Pr. at the En-
  quirer Office, 1835. DHU/MO
--Liberty of Speech and the
  Press. A Thanksgiving Ser-
  mon Delivered November 26,
  1835, to the Congregational
  Church and Society in Dover,
  N. H. Dover: Pr. at the En-
  quirer Office, 1835. DHU/MO
--A Memorial of the Martyred

Lovejoy...Delivered in Dover,
  N. H. Published by Request.
  Dover: n. p. , 1837. DHU/MO
Salter, William. Slavery and the
  Lessons of Recent Events. A
  Sermon Preached in the Con-
  gregational Church. Burling-
  ton: Dec. 4, 185-? DHU/MO
Sanders, William Davis. Two
  Anti-Slavery Sermons Deliv-
  ered in 1853 and 1854. Edited
  by David Sanders Clark. Wash-
  ington, 1964.   NcD
Senior, Robert C. "New England
  and Congregationalist and the
  Anti-Slavery Movement, 1830-
  1860." Doctoral dissertation,
  Yale University, 1954. NcD
Sexton, Jessie Ethelyn. Congre-
  gationalism, Slavery and the
  Civil War. Lewis Beeson,
  editor. Lansing: Michigan Civil War Centennial Observance
  Commission, 1966.   NcD
Starkey, Marion Lens. The Congregational Way; the Role of
  the Pilgrims and their Heirs
  in Shaping America. Garden
  City: Doubleday, 1966.
                           NN/Sch
  "The abolitionists:" pp.
  215-25.
Stetson, Caleb. A Discourse on
  the State of the Country, De-
  livered in the First Church in
  Medford, on the Annual Fast
  April 7th, 1842. Boston: J.
  Munroe, 1842.   CtY-D
Storrs, Richard Salter. Ameri-
  can Slavery, and the Means of
  its Removal. A Sermon,
  Preached in the First Congre-
  gational Church, Braintree,
  April 4, 1844. Boston: T. R.
  Marvin, 1844.   CtY-D
The Tables Turned. A Letter to
  the Congregational Association
  of New York, Reviewing the
  Report of Their Committee on
  "The Relation of the American
  Tract Society to the Subject of
  Slavery." By a Congregational-
  ist Director. Boston: Crocker

& Brewster, 1855.
   CtY-D; NN/Sch
Thompson, L. The Nation's Danger. A Discourse Delivered in the Congregational Church, West Amesbury, on the Day of the Annual State Fast, April 10, 1856. Boston: J. M. Hewes, Printer, 1856. CtY-D
Tilton, Theodore. The American Board and American Slavery. Speech of Theodore Tilton, in Plymouth Church, Brooklyn, January 28, 1860. Reported by Wm. Henry Burr. n. p., 1860.   CtY-D
Weiss, John. Discourse Occasioned by the Death of Convers Francis, D.D. Delivered Before the First Congregational Society, Watertown, April 19, 1863. Cambridge: Priv. Print., 1863. CtY-D
--Northern Strength and Weakness. An Address on Occasion of the National Fast, April 30, 1863. Delivered in Watertown. Boston: Walker, Wise, 1863. CtY-D
West Brookfield. Anti-Slavery Society. An Exposition of Difficulties in West Brookfield, Connected with Anti-Slavery Operations, Together with a

Reply to Some Statements in a Pamphlet Put Forth by "Moses Chase, Pastor of the Church," Purporting to be a "Statement of Facts in the Case of Deacon Henshaw." By the Board of Managers of the W. B. Anti-Slavery Society. West Brookfield, Mass.: The Anti-Slavery Society, 1844. NN/Sch
Whipple, Charles King. Relation of the American Board of Commissioners for Foreign Missions to Slavery. Boston: R. F. Wallcut, 1861.
    NcD; CtY-D
Whitcomb, William Charles. A Discourse on the Recapture of Fugitive Slaves, Delivered at Stoneham, Mass., Nov. 3, 1850. Boston: Pr. by C. C. P. Moody, 1850. CtY-D; NN/Sch
Withington, Leonard. A Bundle of Myrrh. Thanksgiving Sermon Preached Nov. 28, 1850, at Newbury, First Parish. Newburyport, C. Whipple, 1851.
   CtY-D; DHU/MO
Wyatt-Brown, Bertram. Lewis Tappan and the Evangelical War Against Slavery. Cleveland: Press of Case Western Reserve University, 1969.
    CtY-D

4. Disciples of Christ (Christian Churches)

Crain, James Andrew. The Development of Social Ideas Among the Disciples of Christ. St. Louis, Mo.: Bethany Press, 1969. DHU/R; DLC
Fife, Robert Oldham. Alexander Campbell and the Christian Church in the Slavery Controversy. Bloomington, Ind.: 1960.   INU
 Typewritten ms.

Haynes, Nathaniel Smith. The Disciples of Christ in Illinois and Their Attitude Toward Slavery. NN/Sch
 (In Illinois State Historical Society. Papers in Illinois History and Transactions for the Year 1913. Springfield, 1914. pp. 52-59)

5. Friends - Quakers

Alexander, Ann. An Address
to the Inhabitants of Charles-
ton, South Carolina. Philadel-
phia: Kimber, Conrad, 1805.
                          INRE
Alexander, Stella. Quaker Testimony Against Slavery and
Racial Discrimination. An
Anthology Compiled by Stella
Alexander. London: Friends
Home Service Committee,
1958.   INRE; DHU/R
American Tract Society. New
York Branch. Testimony of Five
of the Society's Founders.
Historical facts limiting its issues to publications in which
Evangelical Christians agree.
n. p. , n. d.   DLC
Applegarth, Albert C. ...
Quakers in Pennsylvania. Bal-
timore: Johns Hopkins Press,
1892. (Johns Hopkins Univer-
sity Studies in Historical and
Political Science, 10th ser. ,
viii-ix).
Aptheker, Herbert. "The Quakers and Negro Slavery." Journal of Negro History (25:3,
Jl. , 1940), pp. 331-62.
                       DHU/MO
"Corrects the impression
that Quakers were always
'Anti-slavery' it shows the
gradual evolution."
Association for the Care of Colored Orphans of Philadelphia.
Annual Report. 1st- 1836.
            INRE (1892)
Association of Friends for Promoting the Abolition of Slavery
and Improving the Condition of
the Free People of Color.
Annual Report. Philadelphia:
n. p. , 1846. DLC; NcD
Association of Friends for the
Aid and Elevation of the Freedmen. Philadelphia. Annual Report. Philadelphia: n. p. ,

1865.   DLC; NcD
Bassett, William. Letters to a
Member of the Society of
Friends, in Reply to Objec-
tions Against Joining Anti-
Slavery Societies. Boston:
Isaac Knapp, 1836. DHU/MO
-- Society of Friends in the
United States: Their View of
the Anti-Slavery Question, and
Treatment of the People of
Color. Compiled from Origi-
nal Correspondence. Darling-
ton: J. Wilson, 1840.   PHC
Benezet, Anthony. A Caution to
Great Britain and her Colo-
nies, in a Short Representa-
tion of the Calamitous State
of the Enslaved Negroes in
the British Dominions. Phila-
delphia: Printed; London: Re-
printed and Sold by J. Phil-
lips, 1784.   CtY-D
Restricted circulation.
--Notes on the Slave Trade.
Cruikshank, n.d. INRE.
--Observations on the Enslaving,
Importing and Purchasing of
Negroes; with Some Advice
Thereon, Extracted from the
Epistle of the Yearly Meeting
of the People Called Quakers,
Held in London in 1748. Germantown: Christopher Sower,
1760.   DHU/MO; FSU
--A Serious Address to the Rulers
of America, on the Inconsistency of Their Conduct Respecting
Slavery: Forming a Contrast Be-
tween the Encroachments of Eng-
land on American Liberty, and
American Injustice in Tolerating
Slavery. London: J. Phillips,
1783.   DHU/MO
--A Short Account of the Religious Society of Friends, Commonly Called Quakers. Philadelphia: Kimber and Conrad,
1814.   DHU/MO

Quakers views on slavery.
--Some Historical Account of
Guinea, its Situation, Produce
and the General Disposition of
its Inhabitants. With an Inquiry
into the Rise and Progress of
Slave-Trade, its Nature and
Lamentable Effects. Also a
Republication of the Sentiments
of Several Authors of Note, on
this Interesting Subject; par-
ticularly an Extract of a Trea-
tise, by Granville Sharp. By
Anthony Benezet... Philadel-
phia: Pr. by J. Cruikshank,
1771.   INRE
--Views of American Slavery,
Taken a Century Ago. An-
thony Benezet, John Wesley...
Philadelphia: Pub. by the As-
sociation of Friends for the
Diffusion of Religious and Use-
ful Knowledge, 1858.   INRE
Birkett, Mary. A Poem on the
African Slave Trade. 2d ed.
Dublin: J. Jones, 1792.
                        INRE
Birney, James Gillespie. Cor-
respondence Between James
G. Birney, of Kentucky, and
Several Individuals of the So-
ciety of Friends. Haverhill:
Essex Gazette, 1835.
                     DHU/MO
Bousell, John. The Standard of
the Lord of Hosts Exalted;
the Banner of the Prince of
Peace Displayed. Being a
Message unto the King... to
take Away the Heavy Burthen
of Tithes and to Set at Liberty
the African Slaves. n. p.: Pr.
for the Author, 1790. INRE
A Brief Sketch of the Schools for
Black People, and their Des-
cendants, Established by the
Religious Society of Friends
in 1770. Philadelphia: Pub.
by Direction of the Committee
Having Charge of the Schools,
Friends Bookstore, 1867.
                        INRE
Candler, John. Narrative of a

Recent Visit to Brazil, by
John Candler and Wilson Bur-
gess; to Present an Address
on the Slave-Trade and Slav-
ery, issued by the Religious
Society of Friends. London:
E. Marsh, 1853.   INRE
Carland, Fernando Gale. South-
ern Heroes; or, The Friends
in War Time. Cambridge:
Riverside Press, 1895.
Chace, Elizabeth (Buffum). Two
Quaker Sisters. From the
Original Diaries of Elizabeth
B. Lovell, with an Introduc-
tion by Malcolm R. Lovell,
foreword by Rufus M. Jones.
New York: Liveright Publish-
ing Corp., 1937.
      INRE; DHU/MO; CtY-D
Chandler, Elizabeth Margaret.
Essays, Philanthropic and
Moral, by Elizabeth Margaret
Chandler: Principally Relating
to the Abolition of Slavery in
America... Phila.: Chapman,
1845.   INRE
Child, Lydia Maria (Francis).
Isaac T. Hopper: a True Life.
Boston: J. P. Jewett, 1853.
                        CtY-D
--The Progress of Religious
Ideas, Through Successive
Ages. New York: C. S. Fran-
cis & Co., 1855.   NN/Sch
Clarkson, Thomas. Cries of Af-
rica, to the Inhabitants of
Europe; or, A Survey of that
Bloody Commerce Called the
Slave-trade. London: Harvey
and Darton, 1821?   CtY-D
--The History of the Rise, Prog-
ress, & Accomplishment of
the Abolition of the African
Slave-Trade, by the British
Parliament... Philadelphia:
Pub. by J. P. Parke, 1808.
Brown & Merritt, Printers.
                        CtY-D
Coleman, Elihu. A Testimony
Against that Anti-Christian
Practice of Making Slaves of
Men... New Bedford: 1733;

(Coleman, E. cont.)
   Reprinted A. Shearman, 1825.
        NN/Sch; INRE
Curtis, Anna L. Stories of the
   Underground Railroad, by Anna
   L. Curtis; Foreword by Rufus
   M. Jones, Illustrated by Wm.
   Brooks. New York: The Island
   Workshop Press Co-op., Inc.,
   1941.   INRE
Danforth, Mildred E. A Quaker
   Pioneer: Laura Haviland, Su-
   perintendent of the Under-
   ground. New York: Exposi-
   tion Press, 1961.   CtY-D
Dillon, Merton Lynn. Benjamin
   Lundy and the Struggle for
   Negro Freedom. Urbana:
   University of Illinois Press,
   1966.   CtY-D
Drake, Thomas E. "Joseph
   Drinker's Pleas for the Ad-
   mission of Colored People to
   the Society of Friends, 1795."
   Journal of Negro History (37:
   1 Ja., 1947), pp. 110-12.
                              DHU/M
--Quakers and Slavery in Amer-
   ica. New Haven: Yale Uni-
   versity Press, 1950.
                         DHU/R; CtY-D
Edgerton, Walter. A History of
   the Separation in Indiana Year-
   ly Meeting of Friends Which
   Took Place in the Winter of
   1842 and 1843 on the Anti-
   Slavery Question... By Walter
   Edgerton. Cincinnati: Pugh,
   Printer, 1856. INRE; NcD
Evans, William. Journal of the
   Life and Religious Service of
   William Evans, a Minister of
   the Gospel in the Society of
   Friends. Philadelphia: n. p.,
   1870.   DHU/MO
Forbush, Bliss. Elias Hicks, a
   Quaker Liberal. New York:
   Columbia University Press,
   1956.   NN/Sch
Forster, John. Slavery Incon-
   sistant with Justice and Good
   Policy, by Philanthropos.
   Lebanon, O.: McLean and

   Hale, 1812.   INRE
Forster, William. Memoirs.
   Edited by Benjamin Seebohm.
   London: A.W. Bennett, 1865.
                              CtY-D
Free Produce Association of
   Friends of Philadelphia. An
   Address to Our Fellow Mem-
   bers of the Religious Society
   of Friends on the Subject of
   Slavery and the Slave-Trade
   in the Western World, by
   Philadelphia Free Produce
   Association of Friends. Phila-
   delphia: n. p., 1894.   DLC
Friends, Society of. American
   Friends Service Committee.
   Some Quaker Approaches to
   the Race Problem. Philadel-
   phia: American Friends Serv-
   ice Committee, 194-. INRE
--Baltimore Yearly Meeting.
   A Review of a Pamphlet En-
   titled, "A Defence of the Re-
   ligious Society of Friends who
   Constitute the Yearly Meeting
   of Baltimore Against Certain
   Charges Circulated by Joseph
   John Gurney." Baltimore:
   Pr. by John D. Toy, 1840.
                            DHU/MO
--Friends Board of Control.
   (Representing the Yearly Meet-
   ings of the West) Committee
   on Freedmen. Report, Third
   Month, 1865. Cincinnati, O.:
   R.W. Carroll, 1865. INRE
--Indiana Yearly Meeting. Mis-
   sionary Board. Annual Report
   of the Missionary Board, for
   Southland, to Indiana Yearly
   of Friends. v. 1. 1864. Rich-
   mond, Ind.: 1864-   INRE
-- -- The Discipline of the So-
   ciety of Friends, of Indiana
   Yearly Meeting, Revised by
   the Meeting Held at White
   Water in the Year 1854, and
   Printed by Direction of the
   Same. Cincinnati: A. Pugh,
   Printer, 1854.   NN/Sch
      pp. 89-91, Slavery and the
   Church.

---- Report of Indiana Yearly
Meeting's Executive Committee for the Relief of Colored
Freedman. Richmond: Hollo-
way & Davis, 1864.   INRE
--Institute for Colored Youth.
... Annual Report of the Board
of Managers of the Institute for
Colored Youth. Philadelphia:
1852.   INRE
-- London. The Case of Our
Fellow Creatures, the Op-
pressed Africans, Respectful-
ly Recommended to the Seri-
ous Consideration of the Leg-
islature of Great Britain by
the People Called Quakers.
London: Pr. by James Phil-
lips, George Yard, Lombard
Street, 1783.   DHU/MO
--London Yearly Meeting. An
Address to the Inhabitants of
Europe on the Iniquity of
Slave Trade; Issued by the
Religious Society of Friends,
Commonly Called Quakers, in
Great Britain and Ireland.
London: W. Phillips, 1822.
                     DHU/MO
---- An Appeal on the Iniquity
of Slavery and the Slave-Trade
... London: E. Marsh, 1844.
                     INRE
---- An Appeal to the Inhabit-
ants of Europe, on Slavery
and the Slave-Trade. Issued
on Behalf of the Religious So-
ciety of Friends in Gt. Brit.
London: Harvey and Darton,
1839.   INRE
-- Appel sur l'Iniquité de
L'Esclavage et de la Traite
des Noirs, Adopté de la Part
de L'Assemblée Annuelle de
la Sociéte Religieuse Dite des
Amis, Réunie en Son Assemblée Annuelle de 1844. Paris:
Firmin Didot Friès, 1845.
                     NN/Sch
---- Beroep op de Goddeloosheid
der Slavernij en van den Slav-
enhandel, Nitgegeven door de
Jaarlijksche Vergadering van

het Godsdiestig Genootschap,
der Vrienden. Gehouden in
London, 1844. Amsterdam:
Gedrukt Bij C.A. Spin & Zoon,
1845.   NN/Sch
---- Committee on the Negro
and Aborigines Fund. Reports
of the Committee... Presented
to the Yearly Meetings of
1854 and 1855... London:
Book and Tract Depository of
the Society of Friends, 1855.
                     INRE
---- Observations on the Inslaving, Importing and Purchasing
of Negroes; with Some Advice
thereon, Extracted from the
Epistle of the Yearly Meeting
of the People called Quakers.
Held at London in the year
1748... 2nd ed. Germantown:
Pr. by Christopher Sower,
1760.   INRE
---- Proceedings in Relation to
the Presentation Address of
the Yearly Meeting... on the
Slave-Trade and Slavery to
Sovereigns and those in Authority in the Nations of Europe... London: Newman,
1854.   INRE
---- Proceedings in Relation to
the Presentation of the Address of the Yearly Meeting of
the Religious Society of Friends,
on the Slave-Trade and Slavery,
to Sovereigns and Those in Authority in the Nations of Europe, and in Other Parts of
the World, Where the Christian Religion is Professed.
Cincinnati: Pr. by E. Morgan
and Sons, 1855. NN/Sch; NcD
---- Proceedings in Relation to
the Presentation of the Address of the Yearly Meeting
of the Religious Society of
Friends, on the Slave-Trade
and Slavery, to Sovereigns
and those in Authority in the
Nations of Europe, and in
Other Parts of the World
Where the Christian Religion

(Friends, Soc. of. London Yearly
Meeting, cont.)
  is Professed. New York: J.
  Egbert, 1856.   NN/Sch
-- New England Yearly Meeting.
  An Appeal to the Professors
  of Christianity, in the South-
  ern States and Elsewhere, on
  the Subject of Slavery: by the
  Representatives of the Yearly
  Meeting of Friends for New
  England. Providence: Pr. by
  Knowles and Vose, 1842.
                         CtY-D
--New York Yearly Meeting.
  Address to the Citizens of
  the United States of America
  on the Subject of Slavery,
  from the Yearly Meeting of
  the Religious Society of Friends
  (called Quakers) Held in New
  York. New York: New York
  Yearly Meeting of Friends,
  1837.   CtY-D
-- -- An Address of Friends of
  the Yearly Meeting of New-
  York, to the Citizens of the
  United States, Especially to
  Those of the Southern States,
  Upon the Subject of Slavery.
  New York: M. Day, 1844.
                    NN/Sch; CtY-D
-- -- Address of the Yearly
  Meeting of the Religious So-
  ciety of Friends, Held in the
  City of New York in the Sixth
  Month 1852, to the Professors
  of Christianity in the United
  States, on the Subject of Slav-
  ery. New York: J. Egbert,
  Printer, 1852.   DHU/MO
-- -- Third Report of a Commit-
  tee of the Representatives of
  New York Yearly Meeting of
  Friends Upon the Condition
  and Wants of the Colored
  Refugees. New York: n.p.,
  1864.   CtY-D
-- Philadelphia Yearly Meeting.
  An Address to the Quarterly,
  Monthly and Preparative Meet-
  ings, and the Members there-
  of, Composing the Yearly

Meeting to Have Charge of the
Subject of Slavery. Philadelphia: Pr. by J. Richards,
1839.   CtY-D
-- -- A Brief Statement of the
Rise and Progress of the Testimony of the Religious Society of Friends, against Slavery and the Slave-Trade. Pub.
by Direction of the Yearly
Meeting, Held in Philadelphia,
in the Fourth Month, 1843.
Philadelphia: Pr. by J. and
W. Kite, 1843.
        INRE; DHU/R; CtY-D
-- -- An Exposition of the Afri-
can Slave Trade, from the
Year 1840-1850, Inclusive,
Prepared from Official Docu-
ments, and Published by Di-
rection of the Representatives
of the Religions Society of
Friends, in Pennsylvania, New
Jersey, and Delaware. Phila-
delphia: J. A. Rakestraw,
Printer, 1851.   DHU/MO
-- -- Memorial...on the African
Slave Trade. Philadelphia: J.
& W. Kite, 1840.   INRE
-- -- Slavery and the Domestic
Slave Trade, in the United
States. By the Committee ap-
pointed by the late Yearly
Meeting of Friends held in
Philadelphia, in 1839. Phila.:
Pr. by Merrihew and Thomp-
son, 1841.   INRE
-- -- A View of the Present
State of the African Slave
Trade. Published by Direction
of a Meeting Representing the
Religious Society of Friends
in Pennsylvania, New Jersey,
&c. Philadelphia: W. Brown,
Printer, 1824.   CtY-D
-- The Appeal of the Religious
Society of Friends in Pennsyl-
vania, New Jersey, Delaware,
etc., to their Fellow-Citizens
of the United States on Behalf
of the Colored Races. Philadelphia: Friends' Book Store,
1858.   NcD

Friends' Association of Philadelphia and its Vicinity for the Relief of Colored Freedmen. Report of the Executive Board. First, 1864. Philadelphia: 1864. DHU/MO; INRE
--Statistics of the Operations of the Executive Board of Friends' Association of Philadelphia, and its Vicinity, for the Relief of Colored Freedmen, as Presented to a Public Meeting of Friends, held at Arch St. Meeting House, Philadelphia, 1st Month, 1864. Together with the Report of Samuel R. Shipley, President of the Board, of his Visit to the Campus of the Freedmen on the Mississippi River. Inquirer Print. Office, 1864. INRE; NN/Sch; DHU/MO

Green, Beriah. The Martyr. A Discourse, in Commemoration of the Martyrdom of the Rev. Elijah P. Lovejoy, Delivered in Broadway Tabernacle, New York; and in the Bleeker Street Church, Utica. (New York): American Anti-Slavery Society, 1838. DHU/MO

Hicks, Elias. Journal of the Life and Religious Labours of Elias Hicks. Written by Himself. New York: Isaac T. Hopper, 1832. DHU/MO

Hilty, Hiram H. "North Carolina Quakers and Slavery." Doctoral dissertation, Duke University, 1969. INRE

Irish, David. Observations on a Living and Effectual Testimony Against Slavery. Introduced with Some Remarks upon Excess and Superfluity. Recommended to the Consideration of the Members of the Society of Friends. New York: Pr. for the Author, 1836. DHU/MO

Ivimey, Joseph. The Utter Extinction of Slavery an Object of Scripture Prophecy: A Lecture the Substance of Which was Delivered at the Annual Meeting of the Chelmsford Ladies' Anti-Slavery Association, in the Friend's Meeting-House, on Tuesday the 17th of April, 1832. With Elucidatory Notes. London: Sold by G. Wightman, 1832. DHU/MO; NN/Sch; CtY-D

James, Sydney Vincent. A People Among People; Quaker Benevolence in Eighteenth-Century America. Cambridge: Harvard University Press, 1963. NN/Sch

Janney, Samuel M. The Life of George Fox; with Dissertations, or, his Views Concerning the Doctrines, Testimonies and Discipline of the Christian Church... Phila.: Lippincott, Grambo and Co., 1853 DHU/MO

Jones, Rufus Matthew. The Quakers in the American Colonies. New York: Russell & Russell, 1962. NN/Sch

Jordan, Richard. A Journal of the Life and Religious Labors of Richard Jordan a Minister of the Gospel in the Society of Friends, Late of Newton, in Gloucester County, New Jersey. Phila.: For Sale at Friends Book Store, 1877. NN/Sch

Jorns, Auguste. The Quakers as Pioneers in Social Work (Studien Uber die Sozialpolitik der Quaker). New York: Macmillan, 1931. DHU/R; NN/Sch Bibliographical note: p. 7.

Keene, Calvin. "Friends and Negro Slavery." Friends Intelligencer (109:3, Ja., 19, 1952), pp. 33-4. DHU/R

Keith, George. An Exhortation & Caution to Friends Concerning Buying or Keeping Negroes. New York: Wm. Bradford, 1893. Philadelphia, 1889. NN/Sch

(Keith, G. cont.)
--The First Printed Protest
Against Slavery in America.
Philadelphia: n. p., 1889.
      CtY-D
  "Reprinted from 'The
Pennsylvania Magazine of His-
tory and Biography.'"
Lerner, Gerda. The Grimké
Sisters from South Carolina;
Rebels Against Slavery. Bos-
ton: Houghton Mifflin, 1967.
      CtY-D
McKiever, Charles. Slavery and
the Emigration of North Caro-
lina Friends. Murfreesboro,
N. C.: Johnson Pub. Co.,
1970.   INRE
Marriott, Charles. An Address
to the Religious Society of
Friends, on the Duty of De-
clining the Use of the Products
of Slave Labor... New York:
I. T. Hopper, 1835.
    CtY-D; DHU/MO
Miles, Edward. Reform in
Earnest or Truth Over All...
London: Bennett, 1859.
      INRE
Mordell, Albert. Quaker Mili-
tant, John Greenleaf Whittier...
Boston and New York: Hough-
ton Mifflin Co., 1933.
      DHU/MO
Niles, John Milton. Speech of
Mr. Niles, of Connecticut, on
the Petition of a Society of
Friends in Pennsylvania: Pray-
ing for the Abolition of Slavery
in the District of Columbia.
In Senate, Feb. 15, 1836.
Washington: Blair & Rives,
1836.   DHU/MO
The Non-Slaveholder. v. 1-5,
1846-50; n. s. v. 1-2, 1853-54.
Philadelphia: Merrihew and
Thompson, 1846-54.   INRE
Nuermberger, Ruth Anna (Ketring).
The Free Produce Movement;
a Quaker Protest Against Slav-
ery. Durham, N. C.: Duke
University Press, 1942.
    CtY-D; NN/Sch

Also in, Trinity College Historical Society, Historical Papers (ser. 25), 1942.
    DLC; NcD; CtY
Observations on the Inslaving Im-
porting and Purchasing of Ne-
groes, with Some Advice
Thereon Extracted From the
Epistle of the Yearly Meeting
of the People Called Quakers.
Held at London in the Year
1748. n. p., 1760. DHU/MO
Osborn, Charles. Journal of the
Faithful Servant of Christ,
Charles Osborn, Containing an
Account of Many of His Trav-
els and Exercises in the Serv-
ice of the Lord, and in De-
fense of the Truth, as It is in
Jesus. Cincinnati: A. Pugh,
1854.   DLC; INRE
--A Testimony Concerning the
Separation Which Occurred in
Indiana Yearly Meeting of
Friends, in the Winter of
1842-43; Together with Sundry
Remarks and Observations Particularly on the Subjects of
War, Slavery and Colonization.
Centreville, [Ind. ?]: R. Vaile,
1849.   DLC
Philadelphia Free Produce Association of Friends. An Address
to Our Fellow Members of the
Religious Society of Friends
on the Subject of Slavery and
the Slave-Trade in the Western World. Philadelphia: n. p.,
1849.   INRE
Pickett, Clarence Evan. ...For
More Than Bread; an Autobiographical Account of Twenty-
two Years' Work with the American Friends Service Committee. Boston: Little, Brown,
1953.
  Slavery and the Church-
Friends, Society of, pp. 369-
72.
Rhoads, Samuel. Considerations
on the Use of the Productions
of Slavery... 2d ed. Philadelphia: Merrihew and Thompson,

1845.   DLC; INRE
Rose, Ralph. American Friends
and Race Relations. London:
Friends Home Service Com-
mittee, 1954.   INRE
Siebert, Wilbur Henry. A Quaker Section of the Underground
Railroad in Northern Ohio.
Columbus: Heer, 1930. INRE
Smucker, Orden C. "The Influence of the Quakers in the
Abolition of Negro Slavery in
the United States." Master's
thesis, University of Chicago,
1933.
Thomas, Allen Clapp. The Attitude of the Society of Friends
Towards Slavery in the Seven-
teenth and Eighteenth Centuries, Particularly in Relation
to its Own Members. n. p.,
n. d.   DHU/R; CtY-D
(In American Society of
Church History. Papers. New
York & London, 1879. 24.5
cm. vol. viii, p. 263-99.)
                    CtY-D; DHU/R
Watson, Frank D. A Quest in
Interracial Understanding by
Frank D. Watson. Foreword
by Henry J. Cadbury. Oc-
tober, 1935. Prepared under
Direction of Sub-commission
for Race Relations and Attitudes of the Five Years Meeting and the Committee on Race
Relations of Philadelphia Year-
ly Meetings.   INRE
Weeks, Stephen Beauregard.
Southern Quakers and Slavery:

a Study in Institutional History.
Baltimore: The Johns Hopkins
Press, 1896. DHU/R; CtY-D
Wigham, Eliza. The Anti-Slavery
Cause in America and its
Martyrs. London: Bennett,
1863.   INRE
Woodson, Carter G. "Anthony
Benezet." Journal of Negro
History (2:1, Ja., 1917), pp.
37-50.   DHU/MO
"Author regards him as the
greatest Quaker anti-slavery
leader."
Negro author.
Woolman, John. A Journal of the
Life, Gospel Labours, and
Christian Experiences of that
Faithful Minister of Jesus
Christ. n. p., Pr. by Thos.
Hurst, 1840.   DHU/MO
Woolman, John. Extracts on the
Subject of Slavery, from the
Journal and Writings of John
Woolman, of Mount Holly, New
Jersey, a Minister of the So-
ciety of Friends, in the City
of New York. New York: M.
Day and Co., 1840.   DLC
--Selections from the Writings of
John Woolman...Dublin: Pr. by
C. Benthaus, 1823. DHU/MO
Zilversmit, Arthur. The First
Emancipation; the Abolition of
Slavery in the North. Chicago:
Univ. of Chicago Press, 1967.
                        DHU/R
Chapter 3, Quakers and
slavery.

6. Methodist Episcopal (United Methodist)

Abbey, Richard. Peter, Not an
Apostle, But a Chattel With a
Strange History. Nashville:
Southern Methodist Pub.
House, 1885.   NcD
Adams, C. An Address to the
Abolitionists of the Methodist
Episcopal Church. Boston:

Reid & Rand, 1843.   NcD
Alexander, Gross. "The History
of the Methodist Church,
South." Vol. 2. American
Church History Series. New
York: Christian Literature
Co., 1894.

An Appeal on the Subject of Slavery; Addresses to the Members of the New England and New Hampshire Conferences of the Methodist Episcopal Church. Together with a Defense of Said Appeal in Which is Shown the Sin of Holding Property in Man. Boston: Davis H. Ela, 1835. DHU/MO

Asbury, Francis. The Heart of Asbury's Journal. New York: Eaton & Mains, 1904. NN/Sch

Baker, George C. An Introduction to the History of Early New England Methodism, 1789-1839. Durham, N.C.: Duke University Press, 1941. DLC "Methodism and Slavery Problem."

Bascom, Henry Bidleman. Methodism and Slavery; with other Matters in Controversy between the North and the South; Being a Review of the Manifesto of the Majority in Reply to the Protests of the Minority... in the Case of Bishop Andrew. Frankfort: Hodges, 1845. NcD; DLC

Bassett, John Spencer. North Carolina Methodism and Slavery. In Historical Paper of the Trinity College Historical Society. Durham, N.C.: 1900. NcD

Beeson, Lewis. The Methodist Episcopal Church in Michigan During the Civil War. Lansing: Civil War Centennial Observance Commission, 1965. DLC

Betker, John P. The M.E. Church and Slavery, as Described by Revs. H. Mattison, W. Hosmer, E. Bowen, D.D., D. DeVinne, and J.D. Long, With a Bible View of the Whole Subject. Syracuse: S. Lee, 1859. DLC

Bond, T.E. "The Methodist Episcopal Church, South." Methodist Quarterly Review (31:2, Apr.

1849; 33:3, Jl., 1851), pp. 282-302; 396-428. DHU/R Discusses the problem of slavery and its effects on Methodism in the South.

Bowen, Elias. Slavery in the Methodist Episcopal Church. Auburn: Wm. J. Moses, Printer, 1850. DHU/MO

Bradburn, Samuel. An Address to the People Called Methodists. Concerning the Criminality of Encouraging Slavery. 5th ed. London: M. Gurney, n.d. CtY; PHC

Brownlow, William Gannaway. Ought American Slavery to be Perpetuated? A Debate Between Rev. W.G. Brownlow and Rev. A Pryne. Held at Phila., Sept. 1858. Philadelphia: J.B. Lippincott & Co., 1858. DHU/MO; CtY-D

--A Sermon on Slavery: A Vindication of the Methodist Church, South: Her Position Stated. Delivered in Temperance Hall, in Knoxville, on Sabbath August 9th 1857, to the Delegates and Others in Attendance at the Southern Commercial Convention. Knoxville: Kinsloe & Rice, 1857. DHU/MO

Bruce, J.G. A Sermon on the Deity of Instructing Slaves. Delivered Sabbath Evening, August 23, 1846. Georgetown: Wise, 1846. NcD; DLC

Bucke, Emory S. History of American Methodism. New York: Abingdon Press, 1964. DHU/R V.1, "Methodists Churches for Negroes" pp. 601-17. Position on Slavery, pp. 251-56.

Buckley, James M. History of Methodism. New York: Harper & Bros., 1898. DHU/R Vol. 2, Slavery issue and the Methodist Church.

Caldwell, John H., (bp.). Slav-

ery and Southern Methodism:
Two Sermons Preached in the
Methodist Church in Newman,
Georgia. Newman, Ga.: Pr.
for the Author, 1865.
                    DHU/MO
Carman, Adam. An Oration De-
livered at the Fourth Anniver-
sary of the Abolition of the
Slave Trade, in the Methodist
Episcopal Church, in Second
Street, N.Y., Jan. 1, 1811.
New York: Totten, 1811. MBU
Carter, Cullen T. History of
the Tennessee Conference.
Nashville: The Author, 1948.
                            IEG
Information on Negro work
1828-1832 and 1862-1866.
Cartwright, Peter. Autobiography
of ... The Backwoods Preacher.
New York: Carleton & Porter,
1856.   DHU/MO; NN/Sch
Clark, Davis Wasgatt, (bp.).
Life and Times of Rev. Eli-
jah Hedding... By Rev. D.W.
Clark, D.D. With an introduc-
tion by Rev. Bishop E.S.
Janes. New York: Carlton &
Phillips, 1856.   NN/Sch
Clark, Robert Donald. The Life
of Matthew Simpson. New
York: Macmillan, 1958.
                    NN/Sch
Coggeshall, Samuel Wilde. An
Anti-Slavery Address, Deliv-
ered in the Methodist Episco-
pal Church, Danielsonville,
Conn., Jul. 4, 1849. West
Killingly: E. B. Carter, 1849.
                    MBU; OO
Coke, Thomas, (bp.). Journal
& Addresses, etc. London:
1789-1790.   NN/Sch
Information about Harry
Hoosier, known as "Black
Harry" a preacher.
Coles, George. Heroines of
Methodism; or, Pen and Ink
Sketches of the Mothers and
Daughters of the Church. New
York: Carlton & Porter, 1857.
                    NN/Sch

Collyer, Isaac J. P. Review of
Rev. W.W. Eell's Thanksgiving
Sermon, Delivered in the Meth-
odist Episcopal Church, New-
buryport, Dec. 29, 1850...
Newburyport: C. Whipple, 1851.
                    NN/Sch
Crane, Jonathan Townley. Chris-
tian Duty in Regard to Ameri-
can Slavery. A Sermon
Preached in the Trinity Meth-
odist Episcopal Church, Jersey
City, on Sabbath Morning, De-
cember 11, 1859. Jersey City:
R. B. Kashov, 1860. NN/Sch
Debate on "Modern Abolitionism,"
in the General Conference of
the Methodist Episcopal Church,
Held in Cincinnati, May, 1836.
With Notes. Cincinnati, O.:
Anti-Slavery Society, 1836.
                    DHU/MO
DeVinne, Daniel. The Methodist
Episcopal Church and Slavery.
A Historical Survey of the Relation of the Early Methodists
to Slavery. New York: F. Hart,
1857.   NN/Sch; DHU/MO
Elliott, Charles. History of the
Great Secession from the Meth-
odist Episcopal Church in the
Year 1845. Cincinnati: Sworm-
stedt & A. Poe, 1855.   DLC
Fuller, Erasmus Q. An Appeal
to the Records: a Vindication
of the Methodist Episcopal
Church, in its Policy and Pro-
ceedings Toward the South.
Cincinnati: Hitchcock and Wal-
den, 1876.   CtY-D
Garber, Paul Neff. The Methodists Are One People. Nashville: Cokesbury, 1939.
                    DHU/R
Slavery and racial issues
divide Methodists.
Gravely, William B. "Methodist
Preachers, Slavery and Caste:
Types of Social Concern in
Antebellum America." The
Duke Divinity School Review
(34:3, Aut., 1969), pp. 209-29.
                Pam. File; DHU/R

Gross, Alexander. "History of
the Methodist Episcopal Church,
South." American Church History Series, Vol. 11 (New York:
Christian Literature Co.,
1894), pp. 1-142.   DHU/R
Guice, John Asa. "American
Methodism and Slavery to
1844." Bachelor paper, School
of Religion, Duke University,
1930.
Harris, William Logan. The
Constitutional Powers of the
General Conference, with a
Special Application to the Sub-
ject of Slaveholding. Cincin-
nati: Methodist Book Concern,
1860.   NcD
Harrison, William Pope. Meth-
odist Union, Threatened in
1844, Was Formally Dissolved
in 1848 by the Legislation of
Dr. (afterward Bishop) Simp-
son in the Northern General
Conference of 1848; Whereby
the Reunion of Episcopal
Methodism was Rendered For-
ever Impossible... Nashville:
Pub. House, Meth. Episcopal
Church, South, 1892. DLC; NcD
    "Appeared in the Quarterly
Review under the caption:
'Bishop Simpson as a Politi-
cian.'"
Henkle, Moses Montgomery. The
Life of Henry Biddleman Bas-
com... Louisville: Morton &
Griswold, 1854.   NN/Sch
Horton, Joseph P. "Religious
and Educational Contributions
of the Methodists to the
Slaves." Bachelor of Divinity
thesis, Southern Methodist Uni-
versity.
How the Action of the Churches
Towards the Anti-Slavery
Cause Promotes Infidelity. Is-
sued by the "Union Anti-Slavery
Society," Composed of Mem-
bers of the M. E. Church.
                        DHU/MO
    Pamphlets on Slavery and
Christianity, vol. 1.

Johnston, Robert. Four letters
to Rev. J. Caughey, Method-
ist Episcopal Minister, on the
Participation of the American
Methodist Episcopal Church in
the Sin of American Slavery.
Dublin: Samuel J. Machen,
1841. TNF; MH; ICN; OClWHi
Lee, Luther. Slavery Examined
in the Light of the Bible.
Syracuse, N.Y.: Wesleyan
Methodist Book Room, 1855;
Detroit: Republished by Negro
History Press, 1969. CtY-D
Lee, Umphrey and William W.
Sweet. A Short History of Meth-
odism. New York: Abingdon
Press, 1956.   DHU/R
    pp. 151-53, attitude of
church on slavery.
Macmillan, Margaret (Burnham).
The Methodist Episcopal
Church in Michigan During the
Civil War. Lewis Beeson,
editor. Lansing, Mich.: Civil
War Centennial Observance
Commission, 1965.   NcD
Mason, C. B. "The Methodist
Episcopal Church and the
Evangelization of Africa." J.
W. E. Bowen, (ed.). Addresses
and Proceedings of the Con-
gress of Africa. (Miami, Fla.:
Mnemosyne Pub., Inc., 1969),
pp. 143-48.   DHU/R
Mathews, Donald G. "Anti-Slav-
ery Piety, and Institutionalism:
the Slavery Controversies in
the Methodist Episcopal Church,
1780-1814..." Doctoral disser-
tation, Duke University, 1962.
--Slavery and Methodism. A
Chapter in American Morality,
1780-1845. Princeton, N.J.:
Princeton University Press,
1965.   DHU/MO; DHU/R
Matlack, Lucius C. The Anti-
slavery Struggle and Triumph
in the Methodist Episcopal
Church. New York: Phillips
& Hunt, 1881.
          DHU/MO; NN/Sch; NcD
--The History of American Slav-

ery and Methodism, from
1780 to 1849; and History of
the Wesleyan Methodist Connection of America. New York:
n. p. , 1849.
    NcD; DHU/MO; NN/Sch
--Narrative of the Anti-Slavery
Experience of a Minister in
the Methodist Episcopal
Church, Who Was Twice Re-
jected by the Philadelphia
Annual Conference, and Final-
ly Deprived of License to
Preach for Being an Abolition-
ist. Philadelphia: Merrihew
& Thompson, 1845. OO; DLC
Mattison, Hiram. The Impend-
ing Crisis of 1860; or, the
Present Connection of the
Methodist Episcopal Church
with Slavery and our Duty in
Regard to it... New York:
Mason Bros. , 1859.
    DHU/MO; CtY-D
M'Carter, J. Mayland. Border
Methodism and Border Slavery.
Being a Statement and Review
of the Action of the Philadel-
phia Annual Conference Con-
cerning Slavery, at its Late
Session at Easton, Pa. , In-
cluding the Case of Rev. J. D.
Long; the Slaveholding Among
Members of the Body; the Ex-
tent and Character of Slave-
holding in our Territory: and
"the Crushing Out" of Rev. J.
S. Lame since the Late Ses-
sion of the Conference. Phila-
delphia: Collins, Printer, for
Sale by Higgins & Perkinpine,
1858.   NcD
Macmillan, Margaret B. "Michigan Methodism in the Civil
War." Methodist History (3;
Jan. , 1965), pp. 26-38.
    DHU/R
Merrill, Stephen E. The Organ-
ic Union of American Methodism. Cincinnati: Cranston &
Stowe, 1892.
    ICU; GEO
Methodist Episcopal Church.

General Conference, 1836.
"Modern Abolitionism" in the
General Conference of the...
Held in Cincinnati, May, 1836.
Cincinnati: Anti-Slavery So-
ciety, 1836.   DLC
Mitchell, Joseph. "Traveling of
Preacher and Settled Farmer."
Methodist History (5; Je. ,
1967), pp. 3-14.   DHU/R
"Slaveholding interest in
Southern Methodism."
Norwood, John Nelson. The
Schism in the Methodist Epis-
copal Church, 1844: a Study of
Slavery and Ecclesiastical Poli-
tics... Alfred, N. Y. : Alfred
University, 1923.
    DHU/R; CtY-D; NcD
Parks, William Justice. A Di-
ary-Letter Written from the
Methodist General Conference
of 1844 by the Rev. W. J.
Parks, edited by the Franklin
Nutting Parker... Atlanta, Ga. :
The Library, Emory Univer-
sity, 1944.   NcD; CtY-D
Peck, George. Slavery and the
Episcopacy: Being an Exami-
nation of Dr. Bascom's Re-
view of the Reply of the Ma-
jority to the Protest of the Mi-
nority of the Late General Con-
ference of the M. E. Church,
in the Case of Bishop Andrew.
... New York: G. Lane & C.
B. Tippett, 1845.   NcD
Phelan, Macum. A History of
Early Methodism in Tennessee.
Nashville: Cokesbury Press,
1924.   IEG
Slavery and Methodism.
Posey, Walter Brownlow. "Influ-
ence of Slavery Upon the Meth-
odist Church in the Early
South and Southwest." Mississippi Valley Historical Review
(17:4, Mr. , 1931), pp. 530-
42.   DHU
Pullen, Wm. H. The Blast of a
Trumpet in Zion, Calling upon
Every Son and Daughter of
Wesley, in Great Britain and

(Pullen, W. H. cont.)
Ireland, to Aid Their Breth-
ren in America in Purifying
Their American Zion from
Slavery. London: Webb, Mill-
ington & Co., 1860.   DLC
Redford, A. H.   History of the
Organization of the M. E.
Church in Kentucky. Nash-
ville: Southern Methodist Pub-
lishing House, 1868-70. DLC
Schreyer, George Maurice.
"Methodist Work Among the
Plantation Negroes in the
South Carolina Conference from
1829 to 1865." B. D. thesis,
Duke University, 1939.   NcD
Scott, Orange. Address to the
General Conference of the
Methodist Episcopal Church.
A Member of that Body; Pre-
sented During its Session in
Cincinnati, Ohio, May 19,
1836. New York: H. R. Piercy,
1836.   DHU/MO
--Appeal to the Methodist Epis-
copal Church. Boston: David
H. Ela, 1838. DHU/MO; NcD
--The Grounds of Secession from
the M. E. Church: or, Book
for the Times; Being an Ex-
amination of Her Connection
with Slavery, and Also of Her
Form of Government; Revised
and Corrected. To Which is
Added Wesley upon Slavery.
New York: L. C. Mallock,
1851. OO; NcD; TNF; MH;
            GAU; CtY-D
--The Life of Rev. Orange Scott:
Compiled from his Personal
Narrative, Correspondence,
and Other Authentic Sources
of Information. In two Parts.
By Lucius C. Matlack. New
York: Prindle and D. C. Matlack, 1851.   NN/Sch
--The Methodist E. Church and
Slavery. Containing Also the
Views of the English Wesley-
an Methodist Church with Re-
gard to Slavery, and a Trea-
tise on the Duty of Seceding

from All Pro-Slavery Churches.
Boston: Orange Scott, 1844.
                          MBU
--The Wesleyan Anti-Slavery Re-
view, Containing an Appeal to
the Methodist Episcopal
Church. No. 1, 1838. Boston:
David H. Ela, 1838.   PHi
Simpson, Matthew. Cyclopedia
of Methodism... Philadelphia:
Louis H. Everts, 1881.
                        DHU/R
Relation of Methodism to
the slave trade. p. 803f.
Slicer, Henry. Speech of Rev.
Henry Slicer. Delivered in the
General Conference at Indianap-
olis 28th May, 1856, on the
subject of the Proposed Change
in the Methodist Discipline,
making Non-slaveholding a
Test or Condition of Member-
ship in Said Church. Washing-
ton: Polkinhorn, n. d.   NcD
Stevens, Abel. An Appeal to the
Methodist Episcopal Church,
Concerning What Its General
Conference Should Do on the
Question of Slavery. New York:
Trow, 1859.   OClWHi
--A Compendious History of Am-
erican Methodism. New York:
Eaton & Mains, n. d. DHU/R
Slavery question in general
conferences of the Methodist
Church, pp. 524-28.
Stokes, James Carlisle. "The
Methodist Episcopal Church,
South and the American Negro
from 1844 to the Setting up of
the Colored Methodist Episco-
pal Church." Doctoral disser-
tation, Boston University,
1938.
Swaney, Charles Baumer. Epis-
copal Methodism and Slavery,
with Sidelights on Ecclesiastical Politics. Boston: R. G.
Badger, 1926. NcD; CtY-D
Sweet, William Warren. Methodism in American History.
Nashville: Abingdon Press,
1954.   DHU/R

Contains information on
Missionary Activities and Slav-
ery in the Methodist Church.
--The Methodist Episcopal
Church and the Civil War.
Cincinnati: Methodist Book
Concern, 1933.   ODW
Taylor, Thomas J.   Essay on
Slavery, as Connected with the
Moral and Providential Gov-
ernment of God, as an Ele-
ment of Church Organization.
With Miscellaneous Reflec-
tions on the Subject of Slavery.
New York: J. Longking, Print-
er, 1851.
     DHU/MO; NN/Sch; NcD
Thompson, George.   The Sub-
stance of Mr. Thompson's
Lecture on Slavery, Delivered
in the Wesleyan Chapel, Ir-
well Street, Salford, Manchester, (Eng.).   Manchester, Pr.
by S. Wheeler; Boston: Repr.
by I. Knapp, 1836.   CtY-D

At head of title: Can any
circumstances justify men in
holding their fellow-men in
slavery, without incurring guilt
by so doing?   The question an-
swered.
Wesley, John. ... Thoughts Upon
Slavery, Published in the Year
1774. New York: n. p. , 1835.
          DHU/R; NN/Sch
     Issue of the Wesleyan Extra,
v. 1, no. 1, April, 1835.
Whipple, Charles King.   The
Methodist Church and Slavery.
New York: American Anti-
Slavery Society, 1859.   DLC
Williams, Thomas L. "The Meth-
odist Mission to the Slaves."
Doctoral dissertation.   Yale
University, 1943.
"Words for Working Men." Fourth
Series.   Westley's Thoughts
on Slavery. n. p., n. d.
                    DHU/MO

7.   Presbyterian

Aikman, William.   The Future of
the Colored Race in America:
Being an Article in the Pres-
byterian Quarterly Review of
July, 1862.   New York: An-
son D. F. Randolph, 1862.
                    DHU/MO
Armstrong, George Dodd. A
Discussion on Slaveholding.
Philadelphia: J. M. Wilson,
1858.   NN/Sch; DLC
Barber, Verle L. "The Slavery
Controversy and the Presby-
terian Church." Doctoral dis-
sertation, University of Chi-
cago, 1928.   NcD
Barnes, Albert.   Life at Three-
Score: A Sermon Delivered
in the First Presbyterian
Church, Philadelphia.   Phila-
delphia: Perry & McMillan,
1859.   DHU/MO
-- Our Position.   A Sermon,

Preached before the General
Assembly of the Presbyterian
Church in the United States, in
the Fourth Presbyterian Church
in the City of Washington, May
20, 1852. New York: New-
man & Ivison, 1852. DHU/MO
Basker, Roosevelt A. "Pro-
Slavery Arguments of Southern
Religious Leaders as Illus-
trated by the Old School Pres-
byterians." Master's thesis,
University of Chicago, 1935.
Beman, Nathan Sidney Smith.
Antagonisms in the Moral and
Political World.   A Discourse
Delivered in the First Presby-
terian Church, Troy, New York,
on Nov. 18, 185.   New York:
A. W. Scribner & Co. , 1858.
                    DHU/MO
Bittinger, Joseph Baugher. A
Plea for Humanity.   A Ser-

(Bittinger, J. B. cont.)
mon Preached in the Euclid
Street Presbyterian Church,
Cleveland, Ohio. Cleveland:
Medall Cowles & Co., 1854.
                              CtY
Blanchard, Jonathan. A Debate
on Slavery. Held in the City
of Cincinnati, on the First,
Second, Third, and Sixth days
of Oct., 1845, upon the Ques-
tion: Is Slavery in itself Sin-
ful, and the Relation between
Master and Slave, a Sinful
Relation? Affirmative: Rev. J.
Blanchard. Negative: N. L.
Rice. Cincinnati: W. H. Moore
& Co.; New York: M. H. New-
man, 1846. CHU/MO; CtY-D
-- and N. L. Rice. Is Slave-Hold-
ing in Itself Sinful, and the
Relation Between Master and
Slave, A Sinful Relation? De-
bate on Slavery: Held in the
City of Cincinnati, on the
first, second, third, and sixth
days of October, 1845. New
York: Arno Press, 1969.
                              DHU/R
"Reprint of 1946 edition."
Bourne, George. An Address
to the Presbyterian Church
Enforcing the Duty of Exclud-
ing all Slaveholders from the
"Communion of Saints." New
York: n. p., 1833.
          DLC; CtY; NN/Sch
          Signed: Presbyter.
--Man Stealing and Slavery De-
nounced by the Presbyterian
and Methodist Churches, To-
gether with an Address to All
the Churches. Boston: Garri-
son & Knapp, 1834.
DHU/MO; DLC; NN/Sch; NcD
--Picture of Slavery in the United
States of America. Middletown,
Conn.: E. Hunt, 1834.
          DHU/MO; NN/Sch
Caruthers, Eli Washington. "To
the Colored People." (Eli
Washington Caruthers Collec-
tion, Duke University.)

An Anti-slavery sermon by
a Presbyterian minister. NcD
Cleveland, Charles Dexter. Slavery and Infidelity. Letter to a
Certain Elder of a Certain
Presbyterian Church. n. p.,
n. d.   DHU/MO
Collier, Casa. Meet Ngombi...
New York: Board of Foreign
Missions of the Presbyterian
Church, U. S. A., 1934.
                           NN/Sch
Cross, Jasper W. "John Mil-
ler's Missionary Journal, 1816-
1817: Religious Conditions in
the South and Midwest." Jour-
nal of Presbyterian History
(47:3, Sept., 1969), pp. 226-
61.   DHU/R
Mentions efforts to preach
to "Blacks."
Davidson, Robert. History of the
Presbyterian Church in the
State of Kentucky with a Pre-
liminary Sketch of the Churches
in the State of Kentucky. New
York: Carter, 1847. DHU/R
Chapter 13 Slavery and the
Church.
Davis, J. Treadwell. "The Pres-
byterians and the Sectional
Conflict." Southern Quarterly
(8:2, Ja., 1970), pp. 117-33.
          Pam. File; DHU/R
Drury, Clifford Merrill. ...
Presbyterian Panorama. Phila-
delphia: Board of Christian
Education, Presbyterian
Church in the United States of
America, 1952.   NN/Sch
The Enormity of the Slave Trade,
and the Duty of Seeking the
Moral and Spiritual Elevation
of the Colored Race... New
York: American Tract Socie-
ty, 1846.   NN/Sch
Foster, Robert V. "A Sketch of
the History of the Cumberland
Presbyterian Church." Ameri-
can Church History Series,
Vol. 11. (New York: Christian
Literature Co., 1894), pp.
258-309.   DHU/R

"The General Assembly of 1856;
Constitutional Power Over
Slaveholding." Presbyterian
Quarterly Review (5:18, Sept.,
1856), pp. 312-27.   DHU/R
"The General Assembly of 1857:
Slavery." The Presbyterian
Quarterly Review (6:22, Sept.,
1857), pp. 233-46.   DHU/R
Gibbs, Jonathan C. The Great
Commission, a Sermon
Preached Oct. 22, 1856, Be-
for a Convention of Presby-
terian and Congregational Min-
isters in the Shiloh Presby-
terian Church, Corner Prince
and Marion Streets, New York.
New York: Daily...1857.
                       DHU/MO
Gilliland, James, and Crothers,
Samuel. Two Letters on the
Subject of Slavery from the
Presbytery of Chillicothe, to
the Churches under Their
Care. Hillsborough: Whetstone
and Buxton, 1830.   NN
"Title varies."
Green, Beriah. Sermons and
Other Discourses. With Brief
Biographical Hints. New York:
S. W. Green, 1860.
               DHU/MO; NN/Sch
--Things for Northern Men to
do: A Discourse Delivered on
the Lord's Day Evening, July
17, 1836, in the Presbyterian
Church, Whitesboro, N. Y.
New York: Pub. by Request,
1836.   CtY-D
Griffin, Edward Dorr. A Plea
for Africa. A Sermon
Preached Oct. 26, 1817, in the
First Presbyterian Church in
the City of New York before
the Synod of New York and
New Jersey, at the Request of
the Board of Directors of the
African School Established by
the Synod. New York: Gould,
Printer, 1817.
               CtY-D; NN/Sch
Howard, Victor B. "The Slavery
Controversy and a Seminary

for the Northwest." Journal
of Presbyterian History (43:4,
Dec. 1965), pp. 227-53.
                       DHU/R
Jack, Thomas C. "History of
the Southern Presbyterian
Church." American Church
History Series, vol. 11 (New
York: Christian Literature
Co., 1894), pp. 313-479.
                       DHU/R
Slavery and the church.
Johnson, Herrick. The Nation's
Duty: Thanksgiving Sermon,
Preached in the Third Presby-
terian Church, Pittsburgh,
Thursday, November 27, 1862,
by the Pastor, Rev. Herrick
Johnson. Pittsburgh: Pr. by
W. S. Haven, 1862.   CtY-D
Kay, John. The Slave Trade in
the New Hebrides; being Pa-
pers Read at the Annual Meet-
ing of the New Hebrides Mis-
sion, held at Aniwa, July 1871,
and Published by the Authority
of the Meeting. Edited by the
Rev. John Kay, Coatbridge,
Secretary Presbyterian Church
of Scotland. Edinburgh: Ed-
monston & Douglas, 1872.
                       CtY-D
Kull, Irving Stoddard. "Presbyterian Attitudes Toward Slavery." Church History (7:2,
Je., 1938), pp. 101-114.
                       DHU/R
Lord, John Chase. "The Higher
Law," in Its Application to the
Fugitive Slave Bill. A Sermon on the Duties Men Owe to
God and to Governments. De-
livered at the Central Presby-
terian Church, Buffalo, on
Thanksgiving day. New York:
Published by Order of the "Un-
ion Safety Committee," 1851.
                       CtY-D
Lord, Nathan. A Letter of In-
quiry to the Ministers of the
Gospel of All Denominations,
on Slavery. By a Northern
Presbyterian. Boston: Little,

(Lord, N. cont.)
  Brown and Co., 1854.
    DHU/MO; CtY-D
--A Northern Presbyter's Second
  Letter to Ministers of the Gos-
  pel of All Denominations on
  Slavery... New York: D. Ap-
  pleton and Co., 1855.
    CtY-D; DHU/MO
Lyon, James A. "Slavery and the
  Duties Growing Out of the Re-
  lation." Southern Presbyterian
  Review (16; Jl., 1863), pp. 1-
  37.   DLC; KyLxCB
McGill, Alexander Taggart. The
  Hand of God with the Black
  Race. A Discourse Delivered
  before the Pennsylvania Colo-
  nization Society. Philadelphia:
  W. F. Geddes, 1862. CtY-D
McLeod, Alexander. Negro Slav-
  ery Unjustifiable. A Dis-
  course, by Alexander McLeod,
  A. M., Pastor of the Reformed
  Presbyterian Congregation in
  the City of New York. New
  York: T. & F. Swords, 1802.
    DLC; NN/Sch
Memminger, C. G. Lecture Be-
  fore the Young Men's Library
  Association of Augusta, Geor-
  gia Shewing African Slavery to
  be Consistent With the Moral
  and Physical Progress of a
  Nation. Augusta: W. S. Jones,
  1851.   NNUT
Miller, Samuel. The Life of
  Samuel Miller, D. D., LL. D.,
  Second Professor in the Theo-
  logical Seminary of the Pres-
  byterian Church, at Princeton,
  New Jersey. Philadelphia:
  Claxton, Remsen and Haffel-
  finger, 1869.   NN/Sch
Moore, Edmund Arthur. Robert
  J. Breckinridge and the Slav-
  ery Aspect of the Presbyterian
  Schism of 1837. Chicago:
  n. p., 1935. NcD; DLC
    Also, Church History (4:4,
  Dec., 1935), pp. 282-94.
    DHU/R
Murray, Andrew Evans. Presby-

terians and the Negro; a History. Philadelphia: Presbyterian Historical Society, 1966.
    CtY-D; INU; DHU/MO
Nevin, Edwin Henry. The Religion of Christ at War with
  American Slavery, or, Reasons
  for Separating from the Presbyterian Church. Mt. Vernon:
  Wm. H. Cochran, Printer,
  1849.   DHU/MO
"Note: The General Assembly's
  Answer to the Protest on Slavery." The Presbyterian Quarterly Review (6:24, Mr., 1858,
  pp. 686-90.   DHU/R
    Letters received in refer-
  ence to the General Assembly
  of 1857 on Slavery. For original Statement see Presbyterian
  Review (6:22, Sept. 1857), pp.
  233-43.
--The Presbyterian Quarterly Review (6:23, Dec., 1857), pp.
  521-27.   DHU/R
    Letters received in refer-
  ence to statement of the General Assembly of 1857 on
  Slavery. For original statement
  see Presbyterian Quarterly
  Review (6:22, Sept., 1857), pp.
  233-43.
Palmer, Benjamin M. The Duty
  of the South to Preserve and
  Perpetuate the Institution as
  It Now Exists. New York, n. p.,
  1861.   ICU
--The Rights of the South De-
  ferred in Pulpits... Mobile;
  J. Y. Thompson, 1860. NcD
Pickens, Andrew Lee. Anti-
  Slavery and Other Memories of
  Old Richmond Kirkworth. A
  Heterogeny of Abstracts and
  Outlines... Paducah, Ky.:
  Meridian States Research, 1943.
    CtY-D
Posey, Walter Brownlow. The
  Presbyterian Church in the Old
  Southwest, 1788-1838. Rich-
  mond, Va.: John Knox Press,
  1952.   NN/Sch
-- "The Slavery Question in the

Presbyterian Church in the Old
Southwest." Journal of Southern History (15:3, Ag., 1949),
pp. 311-24.   DHU
Presbyterian Church in the U. S. A.
Annual Reports of the Presbyterian Committee of Missions
for 1871-82. Committee Incorporated under the Name of
the Presbyterian Board of Missions for Freedom. Pitts-
burgh: n. p., 1883.   DLC
--The Distinctive Principles of
the Presbyterian Church in the
United States, Commonly
Called the Southern Presbyterian Church, as Set Forth in
the Formal Declarations, and
Illustrated by Extracts From
Proceedings of the General Assembly, from 1861-67; and of
the N. S. Assembly, from
1861-66. 2d ed. Richmond:
Presbyterian Committee of
Publication, n. d.   NcD
--Presbyteries. Chillicothe.
Two Letters on the Subject of
Slavery From the Presbytery
of Chillicothe to the Churches
Under Their Care. Hillsborough: Pr. by Whetstone & Bux-
ton, 1830.   NcD
    Microfilm copy (negative)
of the original in New York
Public Library.
-- Synod of Cincinnati. An Ad-
dress to the Churches, on the
Subject of Slavery; George-
town, Ohio, Aug. 5, 1831.
(Georgetown?) D. Ammen &
Co. (1831)   DLC
-- Synod of Kentucky. An Ad-
dress to the Presbyterians of
Kentucky, Proposing a Plan for
the Instruction and Emancipation of Their Slaves by a Com-
mittee of the Synod of Kentucky. Cincinnati: Taylor &
Tracy, 1835.   DLC
"Report on Slavery." The South-
ern Presbyterian Review (5:3,
Ja. 1852), pp. 380-94. DHU/R
"The Revival of the Slave Trade."

Southern Presbyterian Review
(11:1, 1 Apr. 1858), pp. 100-
136.   DHU/R
    Review of Reports of the
Committee to Whom was Re-
ferred the Message of Gov.
James H. Adams, Relating to
Slavery and the Slave Trade.
Columbia, S. C.: Steam Power
Press Carolina Times, 1857.
Rice, David. Slavery Inconsistent
with Justice and Good Policy,
by Philanthropos (pseud.) Together with a Twentieth Century Afterword. Lexington:
University of Kentucky Library
Associates, 1956. CtY-D; KYU
    (University of Kentucky Li-
brary Associates Keepsake no.
3)
Robinson, John. The Testimony
and Practice of the Presby-
terian Church in Reference to
American Slavery. With an
Appendix: Containing the Position of the General Assembly
(New School), Free Presbyterian Church, Reformed Presbyterian, Associate, Associate
Reformed, Baptist, Protestant,
Episcopal, and Methodist Episcopal Churches. Cincinnati: J.
D. Thorpe, 1852.
    DLC; DHU/MO; CtY-D
Rogers, Tommy W. "Dr. Frederick A. Ross and the Presbyterian Defense of Slavery."
Journal of Presbyterian History
(45:2, Je., 1967), pp. 112-24.
                         DHU/R
Ross, Frederick Augustus. Slavery Ordained of God... Philadelphia: J. B. Lippincott & Co.,
1857. CtY-D; DHU/R; NcD
Shedd, William Greenough Thayer.
The Union and the War. A
Sermon Preached November 27,
1862. New York: Scribner,
1863.   CtY-D
Slave Holding. A Disqualification
for Church Fellowships. A
Letter to Dr. Joshua L. Wilson and the First Presbyterian

(Slave Holding cont.)
Church, Cincinnati.   By "A
Brother. " n. p. , n. d. CtY-D
"Slavery. " Christian Spectator
(5:4, Dec. , 1833), pp. 631-
55.   DHU/R
Discussion of the work:
Letters on Slavery: Addressed
to the Cumberland Congrega-
tion, Virginia. By J. D. Pax-
ton, their former pastor. Lex-
ington, Kentucky, 1833.
--Southern Presbyterian Review
(9:3, Ja. 1856), pp. 345-64.
                        DHU/R
Sloane, James Renwick Wilson.
Life and Work of J. R. W.
Sloane D. D. Professor of The-
ology in the Reformed Presby-
terian Seminary at Allegheny,
Penn. , 1868-1886. .. New
York: A. C. Armstrong &
Son, 1888.   OWoC
--Review of Rev. Henry J. Van
Dyke's Discourse on "The
Character and Influence of
Abolitionism, " a Sermon
Preached in the Third Re-
formed Presbyterian Church,
Twenty-third Street, New York,
on Sabbath Evening, December
23, 1860. Also, by Special
Request, in the Church of the
Puritans (Rev. Dr. Cheever's
on Sabbath Evening, January
6, 1861. New York: W. Ew-
ing, 1861.   NN/Sch; CtY-D
Slosser, Gaius Jackson.   They
Seek a Country; the American
Presbyterians, Some Aspects.
Contributors: Frank H. Cald-
well. .. and Others. New York:
Macmillan, 1955.   NN/Sch
Smith, Asa Dodge.   Obedience
to Human Law. A Discourse
Delivered on the Day of Pub-
lic Thanksgiving, December
12, 1850, in the Brainerd
Presbyterian Church, New
York. New York: Leavitt,
1851.   CtY-D
Smith, Edward.   The Bible
Against Slavery.   An Address

Delivered in the Sixth Presby-
terian Church, Cincinnati,
March 19, 1843. n. p. , 1843.
                      DHU/MO
Smith, Gerrit. Letter of Gerrit
Smith to Rev. James Smylie,
of the State of Mississippi.
New York: Pub. by R. G. Wil-
liams, for the American Anti-
Slavery Society, 1837.
                        CtY-D
(The Anti-Slavery Examin-
er, No. 3)
--Letters of Rev. Dr. Schumaker
and Gerrit Smith. n. p. , 1838.
                      DHU/MO
Smith, H. Shelton. "The Church
and the Social Order in the
Old South As Interpreted by
James H. Thornwell, " Church
History (7:2, Je. , 1938), pp.
115-24.   DHU/R
Slavery and the church by
a Presbyterian minister.
--"Moral Crisis in a Troubled
South. " Journal of Religious
Thought (14; Aut. -Wint. ,
1956-57), pp. 37-42. DHU/R
Smylie, James. A Review of a
Letter, from the Presbytery
of Chillicothe, to the Presby-
tery of Mississippi, on the
Subject of Slavery. Woodville,
Mi. : Pr. by W. A. Norris and
Co., 1836.   NN/Sch
Spencer, Ichabod S. Fugitive
Slave Law. The Religious Du-
ty of Obedience to Law; A
Sermon Preached in the Sec-
ond Presbyterian Church in
Brooklyn, Nov. 24, 1850.
New York: M. W. Dodd, 1850.
                 DHU/MO; CtY-D
Stiles, Joseph Clay. Speech on
the Slavery Resolutions, De-
livered in the General Assem-
bly which Met in Detroit in
May Last. New York: M. H.
Newman & Co., 1850.
                    NcD; NN/Sch
Tappan, Lewis. Proceedings of
the Session of Broadway Taber-
nacle (New York City), Against

Lewis Tappen, with the Action
of the Presbytery and General
Assembly. New York: n.p.,
1839.   DHU/MO
Taylor, Hubert Vance. "Slavery
and the Deliberating of the
Presbyterian General Assembly, 1833-1838." Doctoral dissertation, Northwestern University, 1964.
Thomas, Alfred A. (ed.). Correspondence of Thomas Ebenezer Thomas, Mainly Relating to the Anti-Slavery Conflict in Ohio Especially in the
Presbyterian Church. n.p.,
1909. CtY-D; NcD; OWoC;
                        DHU/MO
Thompson, Ernest Trice. Presbyterians in the South... Richmond: John Knox Press, 1963.
Thompson, George. Discussion
on American Slavery, between
George Thompson and Robert
J. Breckinridge, Holden in the
Rev. Dr. Wardlaw's Chapel,
Glasgow, Scotland; on the Evenings of the 13th, 14th, 15th,
16th, 17th of June, 1836. Boston: I. Knapp, 1836.   CtY-D
Thompson, Robert E. A History
of the Presbyterian Churches
in the United States. New
York: The Christian Literature
Co., 1895.   DHU/R
    "American Church History
Series, Volume 6," Slavery
Issue.

Tinker, Reuben. The Gospel,
the Hope of Our Nation. A
Discourse on Occasion of the
Public Thanksgiving Delivered
in the Presbyterian Church.
Westfield, N.Y., Buffalo: T.
& M. Butler, Publishers,
1851.   DHU/MO
Two Letters on the Subject of
Slavery From the Presbytery
of Chillicothe to the Churches
under Their Care. Hillsborough: Whetstone and Buston,
1830.   DHU/MO
Union Anti-Slavery Society Auxiliary No. II. To the Congregation of the Western Presbyterian Church. Read and
adopted December 24, 1838.
Philadelphia: Pub. by Order of
the Society, 1838. DHU/MO
Vander Velde, Lewis George.
The Presbyterian Churches
and the Federal Union, 1861-
1869. Cambridge: Harvard University Press, 1932.
            CtY-D; DHU/R; NcD
White, William S. 4th of July
Reminiscences and Reflections:
A Sermon Preached in the
Presbyterian Church. Charlottesville: Pr. by R.C. Noel, 1840.
                            Vi
"Who is Responsible for the Present Slavery Agitation?" The
Presbyterian Quarterly Review
(8:32, Apr., 1860), pp. 529-
44.   DHU/R

8. Protestant Episcopal and Anglican

Addison, James Thayer. The
Episcopal Church in the United
States, 1789-1931. New York:
Scribner, 1951.   NN/Sch
    For Slavery and the Civil
War, see pp. 189-99.
Bangs, Nathan. A History of the
Methodist Episcopal Church.
New York: T. Mason & G.
Lane, 1839.   DLC

Birney, William. James G. Birney and his Times; the Genesis of the Republican Party.
New York: Bergman Publishers, 1969.   CtY-D
    "Anti-Slavery books before
1831:" pp. 382-3. Bibliographical footnotes.
Brooks, Phillips. Our Mercies
of Re-Occupation. A Thanks-

(Brooks, P. cont.)
giving Sermon, Preached at
the Church of the Holy Trinity, Philadelphia, November
26, 1863. Philadelphia: W. S.
& A. Martien, 1863. CtY-D
Clifton, Denzil T. "Anglicanism
and Negro Slavery in Colonial
America." Historical Magazine
of the Protestant Episcopal
Church (39:1, Mr., 1970), pp.
29-70.   DHU/R
Crummell, Alexander. "The Absolute Need of an Indigenous
Missionary Agency in Africa."
Africa and the American Negro: Addresses and Proceed-
ings of the Congress on Afri-
ca. Edited by J. W. E. Bowen
(Miami, Fla.: Mnemosyne Pub.
Inc., 1969), pp. 137-42.
                              DHU/R
Negro author.
--"Civilization a Collateral Agen-
cy in Planting the Church in
Africa." Africa and the Amer-
ican Negro: Addresses and
Proceedings of the Congress
on Africa. Edited by J. W. E.
Bowen (Miami, Fla.: Mnemo-
syne Pub. Inc., 1969), pp.
119-24.   DHU/R
Ellerbee, A. W. "The Episcopal
Church Among the Slaves."
American Church Review (7;
1855), pp. 429-37.   DLC
Holly, James Theodore (bp.). A
Vindication of the Capacity of
the Negro Race for Self-Gov-
ernment. New Haven: W. H.
Stanley, 1857.   NN/Sch
Negro author.
Jay, John. Caste and Slavery in
the American Church. By a
Churchman. New York: Wiley
and Putnam, 1843.
                    NN/Sch; CtY-D
--Slavery and the War: Speeches,
Letters... New York: n. p.,
1859-68.   DLC
--Thoughts on the Duty of the
Episcopal Church, in Relation
to Slavery: Being a Speech

Delivered in N. Y. A. S. Conven-
tion, Feb. 12, 1839. New
York: Piercy & Reed, 1839.
                              DLC
"New York Anti-Slavery So-
ciety."
Jay, William. A Letter to the
Right Rev. L. Silliman Ives,
Bishop of the Protestant Epis-
copal Church in the State of
North Carolina; Occasioned by
His Late Address to the Con-
vention of His Diocese... New
York: W. Harned, 1848.
                          DHU/MO
Klingberg, Frank J. "The African
Immigrant in Colonial Pennsyl-
vania and Delaware." Histori-
cal Magazine of the Protestant
Episcopal Church (11:1, Mr.,
1942), pp. 126-53. DCU/TH
--Anglican Humanitarianism in Colonial New York. Phila.: The
Church Historical Assoc., 1940.
                    NN/Sch; CtY-D
The S. P. G. program for Negroes in colonial New York.
--(ed.). The Carolina Chronicle
of Dr. Francis Le Jau, 1706-
17. Berkeley & Los Angeles:
University of California Press,
1956.   DLC
"Negro's condition in South
Carolina written by a Missionary."
--(ed.). Codrington Chronicle:
An Experiment in Anglican Al-
truism on a Barbados Plantation, 1710-1834." Berkeley
and Los Angeles: University
of California Press, 1949.
              NN/Sch; DLC; DHU/MO
-- "The S. P. G. Program for Negroes in Colonial New York."
Historical Magazine of the
Protestant Episcopal Church
(8:4, Dec., 1939), pp. 306-71.
                              DLC
Lines, Stiles Bailey. "Slaves and
Churchmen: The Work of the
Episcopal Church Among Southern Negroes, 1830-1860." Doctoral dissertation, Columbia

University, 1960.
McAll, Samuel. Slavery a
Cruse and a Sin. A Speech
Delivered at Bradford, York-
shire on Wednesday, Oct. 20,
1852, at the Autumnal Meeting
of the Congregational Union of
England and Wales... London:
Charles A. Bartlett, ca1852.
DHU/MO
Melish, William Howard.
Strength for Struggle; Social
Witness in the Crucible of our
Times. New York: Bromwell
Press, 1953. NN/Sch
Posey, Walter Brownlow. "The
Protestant Episcopal Church:
An American Adaptation."
Journal of Southern History
(25; Feb., 1959), pp. 3-30.
DHU
Seabury, Samuel. American
Slavery Distinguished from the
Slavery of English Theorists
and Justified by the Law of
Nature. New York: Mason
Bros., 1861. CtY-D
Shelling, Richard I. "William
Sturgeon, Catechist to the Ne-
groes of Philadelphia and As-
sistant Rector of Christ Church,

1747-1766." Historical Maga-
zine of the Protestant Episco-
pal Church (8:4, Dec., 1939),
pp. 388-401. DLC
Ward, Henry Dana. Diary: As
Rector of St. Jude's P.E.
Church, N.Y. City Services
for Others Including Wm. A.
Muhlenberg and Thos. Galla-
det, Marriages, Births,
Deaths; Church Government;
Elections of Bishops; "Wine
Bibbing" Bishops; his Family
and his School for Young La-
dies; Discipline, Teachers and
Servants; Current Events;
Slavery; Weather; Letter from
Fillmore, 1856, etc. n.p.,
1850-57. NN/Sch
View on slavery by a Prot-
estant Episcopal Minister.
Wilberforce, Samuel, (bp.). A
Reproof of the American
Church on the Subject of Slav-
ery. By the Bishop of Oxford.
To Which is Added, the Opin-
ions of Eminent Persons in
All Ages Regarding Slavery
and Oppression. London:
W. Tweedie, 1853. NN/Sch

9. Lutheran

Fortenbaugh, Robert. "American Luthern Synods and Slavery, 1830-1860." Journal of

Religion (13:1, Ja., 1933),
pp. 72-92. DHU/R

10. Unitarian Universalist Association

American Slavery. A Protest
Against American Slavery, by
One Hundred and Seventy
Three Unitarian Ministers.
Boston: B. H. Greene, 1845.
DLC
--Report of a Meeting of Mem-

bers of the Unitarian Body,
Held at the Freemasons' Tav-
ern, June 13th 1851. London:
E. T. Whitfield, 1851. DLC
Boston Courier. Observations
on the Rev. Dr. Gannett's
Sermon, entitled "Relation of

(Boston Courier cont.)
the North to Slavery." Republished from the editorial columns of the Boston Courier,
of June 28th and 30th, and
July 6th, 1854. Boston: Reading, 1854.   CtY-D
Channing, William Ellery. An
Address Delivered at Lenox,
on the first of August, 1842,
the Anniversary of Emancipation, in the British West Indies. Lenox, Mass.: J. G.
Stanly, 1842.   CtY-D
--The Duty of the Free States;
or, Remarks Suggested by the
Case of the Creole. Philadelphia: n. p., 1842.   CtY-D
--Emancipation. Boston: E. P.
Peabody, 1840.   CtY-D
--Letter of William E. Channing
to James G. Birney. Boston:
J. Munroe, 1837.   CtY-D
"Prepared for 'The Philan-
thropist,' an anti-slavery pa-
per, published at Cincinnati,
and edited by James G. Bir-
ney."
--Remarks on the Slavery Ques-
tion, in a Letter to Jonathan
Phillips, esq. Boston: J.
Munroe, 1839.   CtY-D
--Slavery Boston: J. Munroe,
1835.   DHU/MO; CtY-D
--The Works of William E. Chan-
ning. Boston: American Uni-
tarian Association, 1875.
                         DHU/R; CtY-D
Contains sermons on slav-
ery and the church.
Clarke, James Freeman. The
Rendition of Anthony Burns.
Its Causes and Consequences.
A Discourse on Christian Poli-
tics, Delivered in Williams
Hall, Boston, on Whitsunday,
June 4, 1854. Boston: Crosby
Nichols, 1854.
                         DHU/MO; CtY-D
"Published by request."
--Slavery in the United States.
A Sermon Delivered in Amory
Hall, on Thanksgiving Day,

November 24, 1842. Boston:
B. H. Greene, 1843.
                           NN/Sch; CtY-D
"Printed by friends for gra-
tuitous distribution."
Conway, Moncure Daniel. The
One Path; or, the Duties of
the North and South; A Dis-
course in the Unitarian
Church, Washington, Ja. 26,
1856. (Washington: 1856) DLC
--Virtue vs. Defeat. A Dis-
course Preached on November
9, 1856... in the Unitarian
Church. Cincinnati: Cincinnati
Gazette, 1856.   DHU/MO
Dean, Paul. A Discourse Deliv-
ered Before the African Soci-
ety, at Their Meetinghouse, in
Boston, Mass. on the Aboli-
tion of the Slave Trade by the
United States of America, July
14, 1819, at First Universal
Church in Boston. Boston:
Nathaniel Coverly, 1819. DLC
Dewey, Orville. A Discourse on
Slavery and the Annexation of
Texas. New York: C. S. Fran-
cis, 1844.   CtY-D
Frothingham, Octavius Brooks.
Colonization. New York: Amer-
ican Anti-Slavery, 1855.
                              CtY-D
--The Last Signs. A Sermon
Preached at the Unitarian
Church in Jersey City, on Sun-
day Morning, June 1, 1856.
New York: John A. Gray, 1856.
                           TNF; DLC
--The New Commandment: A
Discourse Delivered in the
North Church, Salem on June
4, 1854. Salem: Pr. at the
Observer Office, 1854.   DLC
Furness, William Henry. A Dis-
course Delivered, January 5,
1851 in the First Congregation-
al Unitarian Church. Philadel-
phia: n. p., 1851.   DHU/MO
-- A Discourse Occasioned by the
Boston Fugitive Slave Case,
Delivered in the First Congre-
gational Unitarian Church,

Phil., April 13, 1851. Phila.:
Merrihew and Thompson,
Printers, 1851.   DHU/MO
-- A Thanksgiving Discourse De-
livered in the First Congre-
gational Unitarian Church in
Phil., April 13, 1862. Phila.:
T. B. Pugh, 1862.   DHU/MO

Gannett, Ezra Stiles. The State
of the Country: A Discourse
Preached in the Federal Street
Meetinghouse in Boston, on
June 8, 1856. Boston: Cros-
by, Nichols and Co., 1856.
                      CtY-D
--Thanksgiving for the Union: A
Discourse Delivered in the
Federal Street Meetinghouse
in Boston, on Thanksgiving
Day, Nov. 28, 1850. Boston:
W. Crosby & H. P. Nichols,
1850.   CtY-D
Gannett, William C. Ezra Stiles
Gannett, Unitarian Minister in
Boston, 1824-1871. A Memoir
by His Son... Boston: Roberts
Bros., 1875.   DHU/MO
Hall, Edward Brooks. A Dis-
course Occasioned by the Death
of William Ellery Channing;
Delivered in the First Congre-
gational Church, Providence,
R. I., October 12, 1842.
Providence: B. Cranston, 1842.
                      CtY-D
Martin, John H. "The Unitarian
and Slavery." Bachelor of Di-
vinity thesis, University of
Chicago, 1954.
May, Samuel Joseph. Liberty or
Slavery, the Only Question.
Oration: Delivered on the
Fourth of July, 1856, at
Jamestown, Chautauque, Co.,
New York. Syracuse, N. Y.:
J. G. K. Truair, 1856. CtY-D
--Speech of Rev. Samuel J. May,
to the Convention of Citizens,
of Onondaga County, in Syra-
cuse, on the 14th of October,
1851, Called "to Consider the
Principles of the American

Government, and the Extent to
Which they are Trampled under
Foot by the Fugitive Slave Law,"
Occasioned by an Attempt to
Enslave an Inhabitant of Syra-
cuse. Syracuse: Agan & Sum-
mers, Printers, 1851. CtY-D
Palfrey, John Gorham. The
Inter-State Slave Trade. New
York: American Anti-Slavery
Society, 1855.   CtY-D
Parker, Theodore. Collected
Works, Containing Theological,
Polemical, and Critical Writ-
ings, Sermons, Speeches, and
Addresses, and Literary Mis-
cellanies. Edited by Frances
Power Cobbe. London: Trüb-
ner, 1863-71.   CtY-D
--The Effect of Slavery on the
American People. A Sermon
Preached at the Music Hall,
Boston, on Sunday, July 4,
1858. Boston: W. L. Kent,
1858.   CtY-D
--A False and True Revival of
Religion. A Sermon Delivered
at Music Hall, Boston, on Sun-
day, April 4, 1858. ...Bos-
ton: Wm. L. Kent & Co.,
1858.   DHU/MO
--A Letter to the People of the
United States Touching the
Matter of Slavery. Boston:
J. Munroe, 1848.   CtY-D
--The Nebraska Question. Some
Thoughts on the New Assault
upon Freedom in America, and
the General State of the Coun-
try in Relation thereunto, Set
Forth in a Discourse Preached
at the Music Hall, in Boston,
on Monday, Feb. 12, 1854.
Boston: B. B. Mussey, 1854.
                      CtY-D
--The New Crime Against Human-
ity. A Sermon, Preached at
the Music Hall, in Boston, on
Sunday, June 4, 1854. Boston:
B. B. Mussey, 1854. CtY-D
--A New Lesson for the Day: a
Sermon Preached at the Music
Hall, in Boston, on Sunday,

(Parker, T. cont.)
May 25, 1856. Boston: B. H.
Greene, 1856.   CtY-D
--The Present Aspect of Slavery
in America and the Immedi-
ate Duty of the North: A
Speech Delivered in the Hall
of the State House, before the
Massachusetts Anti-Slavery
Convention, on Friday Night,
January 29, 1858. Boston:
B. Marsh, 1858.   CtY-D
--The Relation of Slavery to a
Republican Form of Govern-
ment. A Speech Delivered at
the New England Anti-Slavery
Convention, Wednesday Morn-
ing, May 26, 1858. Rev. by
the author. Boston: W. L.
Kent, 1858.   CtY-D
--The Rival of Religion Which We
Need. A Sermon Delivered at
Music Hall, Boston, on Sun-
day, April 11, 1858. Boston:
W. L. Kent & Co., 1858.
                          DHU/MO
--A Sermon on the Dangers
which Threaten the Rights of
Man in America; Preached at
the Music Hall, on Sunday,
July 2, 1854. Boston: B. B.
Mussey, 1854.
              CtY-D; NN/Sch
--The Three Chief Safeguards of
Society, Considered in a Ser-

mon at the Melodeon, on Sunday, July 6, 1851. Boston:
Wm. Crosby and H. P. Nichols, 1851.   DHU/MO
--The Trial of Theodore Parker
for the "Misdemeanor" of a
Speech in Faneuil Hall Against
Kidnapping, before the Circuit
Court of the United States, at
Boston, Apr. 3, 1855. Bos-
ton: Pub. for the author, 1855.
                          DHU/MO
Peabody, Andrew Preston. Posi-
tion and Duties of the North
with Regard to Slavery. New-
buryport, Mass.: C. Whipple,
1847.   CtY-D
"Reprinted from the Chris-
tian Examiner of July, 1843."
Steinthal, S. Alfred. American
Slavery. A Sermon Preached
at Christ Church Chapel,
Bridgwater, on Sunday, May
the First, 1853. Bridgwater:
Pr. by J. Whitby, 1853.
                          CtY-D
Willson, Edmund Burke. The
Bad Friday: A Sermon
Preached in the First Church,
West Roxbury, June 4, 1854;
it Being the Sunday After the
Return of Anthony Burns to
Slavery. Boston: Pr. by J.
J. Wilson, 1854.   CtY-D

11.   Seventh Day Adventist

Nichol, Francis D. Reasons
For Our Faith. A Discus-
sion of Questions Vital... of
Certain Seventh-Day Adventist
Teachings. Takoma Park,

Washington: Review and Herald Pub. Assn., 1947.
                          DHU/R
Adventist and World Betterment, pp. 124-28.

12.   Baptist

American Baptist Free Mission
Society. Anti-Slavery Missions.
A Brief View of the Origin,
Principles and Operations of

the American Baptist Free
Mission Society. Bristol:
1851.   MB

-- -- Review of the Operations of the American Baptist Free Mission Society for the Past Year. Bristol: Mathews Bros., 1851.   MB

Biddell, William R. "The Baptism of Slaves in Prince Edward Island." Journal of Negro History (4:4, Oct., 1932), pp. 307-9.   DHU/MO

Boyd, Jesse Lansy. A History of Baptists in America, Prior to 1845. New York: American Press, 1957.   NN/Sch

Cutting, Sewall Sylvester. Influence of Christianity on Government and Slavery: a Discourse Delivered in the Baptist Church, in West Boylston, Mass., January 15, 1837. Worcester: Pr. by H. J. Howland, 1837.   DHU/MO; DLC

Daniel, W. Harrison. "Virginia Baptists and the Negro in the Antebellum Era." Journal of Negro History (56:1, Ja., 1971), pp. 1-16.   DHU/R

Free-Will Baptist Antislavery Society. Annual Report...Read at Sutton, Vt., Oct. 13, 1847. Dover: Wm. Burr, Printer, 1848.   DHU/MO

--Fifth Annual Report of the... Read at Lebanon, Maine, October 9, 1851. Dover: Wm. Bun, Printer, 1851. DHU/MO

Fuller, Richard. Domestic Slavery Considered as a Scriptural Institution: in a Correspondence Between Richard Fuller and Francis Wayland. New York: L. Colby, 1847.
NN/Sch; CtY-D

Furman, Richard. Rev. Dr. Richard Furman's Exposition of the Views of the Baptists, Relative to the Coloured Population of the United States, in a Communication to the Governor of South Carolina. Charleston: A. E. Miller, 1823.   DLC

Harvey, H. Memoir of Alfred Bennett, First Pastor of the

Baptist Church, Homer, N. Y. ...New York: Edward H. Fletcher, 1852.   DHU/MO

Hopkins, Samuel. A Dialogue Concerning the Slavery of the Africans! Shewing It to be the Duty and Interest of the American States to Emancipate all their Slaves. With an Address to the Owners of Such Slaves. Norwich (Conn.): Judah P. Spooner, 1776. New York: Repr. for Robert Hodge, 1785.
DLC

--A Discourse upon the Slave Trade and the Slavery of the Africans. Delivered in the Baptist Meeting House at Providence, before the Providence Society for Abolishing the Slave-Trade. At Their Annual Meeting, on May 17, 1793. Providence: J. Carter, 1793
DLC

Leavell, Zachery T. A Complete History of Mississippi Baptists. Jackson, Mississippi: Mississippi Baptists Pub. Co., 1904.   DLC
pp. 53-84, Negro Baptists.

Mathews, Edward. The Shame and Glory of the American Baptists; or, Slaveholders Versus Abolitionists. Bristol: T. Mathews, 1852.   CtY

Murdock, John Nelson. Our Civil War: its Causes and its Issues. A Discourse Delivered in the Baptist Church, Brookline, on the Occasion of the National Thanksgiving, August 6, 1863. Boston: Wright & Potter, Printers, 1863.
CtY-D

Posey, Walter Brownlow. "The Baptist and Slavery in the Lower Mississippi Valley." Journal of Negro History (41:2, Apr., 1956), pp. 117-30.
DHU

Putnam, Mary B. "The Baptists and Slavery, 1840-1845." Doctoral dissertation, Univer-

sity of Chicago, 1910.
Also pub. by G. Wahr,
1913.   NcD
Sweet, William Warren. Religion on the American Frontier:
The Baptists, 1783-1830, A
Collection of Source Material.
New York: Cooper Square Publishers, Inc., 1964.   DHU/R
Chapter V, Anti-Slavery Movements Among Baptists." Chapter XIV, "Documents Relating
to the Friends to Humanity or

the Anti-Slavery Baptists in
Kentucky and Illinois."
To Catholic Citizens! The Pope's
Bull, and the Words of Daniel
O'Connell. New York: J. H.
Ladd, 1856.   NN/Sch
Watkins, Richard H. "The Bap-
tists of the North and Slavery,
1856-1860." Foundations: A
Baptist Journal of History and
Theology (13:4, Oct. -Dec.
1970), pp. 317-32.   DHU/R

13. Reformed Church

Eekhof, Albert. De Negerpredi-
kant Jacobus Elisa Joannes
Capitein, 1717-1749, 's Graven-
hage: M. Nijhoff, 1917. CtY-D
Biography of a black mis-
sionary in Ghana.
How, Samuel Blanchard. Slaveholding not Sinful. Slavery,

the Punishment of Man's Sin,
its Remedy, the Gospel of
Christ. An Argument before
the General Synod of Reformed
Protestant Dutch Church, Oc-
tober 1855... New Brunswick,
N. J.: J. Terhune, 1856.
CtY-D; DHU/MO; NN/Sch

14. Moravian

Laing, Samuel. Slave-Holding
Missionaries. Correspondence
of Mr. S. Laing, with the
Secretary of the Edinburgh
Association in Aid of the
United Brethren's (Moravian)

Missions, on Their Holding
Slaves at Their Missionary
Stations in the Danish West
Indies Islands. Edinburgh:
Printed by W. Forrester,
1844.   NN/Sch

E. SLAVE REVOLTS

Cromwell, John W. "Aftermath
of Nat Turner's Insurrection."
Journal of Negro History (5:2,
Apr., 1920), pp. 208-34.
DHU/MO
Gruber, Jacob. Defendant. The
Trial of the Rev. Jacob Gru-
ber, Minister of the Method-
ist Episcopal Church, at the
March Term, 1819, in the
Fredrick County Court, for

a Misdemeanor. (The Charge
was Preaching in such man-
ner as to incite slave insur-
rection.) Fredricktown, Md.:
David Martin, 1819.   DLC
Wish, Harvey. "American Slave
Insurrections Before 1861."
Journal of Negro History (22:3,
Jl., 1937), pp. 299-320.
DHU/MO

F. ABOLITION, ABOLITIONISTS, AND COLONIZATION.

"The Abolition of Slavery."
Quarterly Christian Spectator
(6:2, Je., 1833), pp. 332-44.
                              DHU/R
A discussion of the book:
Lectures on Slavery and Its
Remedy, by Amos A. Phelps,
pastor of Pine Street Church,
Boston. Published by the New
England Anti-Slavery Society,
1834.
"Abstract from the Seventh Re-
port of the American Coloni-
zation Society." Christian
Spectator (6:4, Apr., 1824),
pp. 324-28.   DHU/R
"Address to the Clergy of All
Denominations on Colonization."
n. p., n. d.   DHU/MO
An Affectionate Expostulation with
Christians in the United States
of America, Because of the
Continuance of Negro Slavery
Throughout Many Districts of
Their Country. Glasgow: Alex.
Gardner, n. d.   DHU/MO
Agutter, William. The Abolition
of the Slave Trade Considered
in a Religious Point of View.
A sermon preached before the
corporation of the City of Ox-
ford, at St. Martin's Church,
on Sunday, February 3, 1788.
London: F. F. and C. Riving-
ton, 1788.   DHU/MO
American Colonization Society.
... Annual Report. Washington:
n. p., n. d.
      DHU/MO; CtY-D; NN/Sch
Armistead, Wilson. A Cloud
of Witnesses Against Slavery
and Oppression. Containing the
Acts, Opinions, and Sentiments of Individual and Societies in All Ages. Selected
from Various Sources and for
the Most Part Chronologically
Arranged... London: W.
Tweedie, etc., 1853. DHU/MO

-- A Tribute for the Negro Being
a Vindication of the Moral, Intellectual and Religious Capabilities of the Coloured Portion of Mankind; with Particular Reference to the African
Race. Illustrated by Numerous Biographical Sketches,
Fact, Anecdotes, etc. n. p.,
1848.   DHU/MO
Barnes, Gilbert H.   The Anti-
Slavery Impulse, 1840-1844.
New York: D. Appleton-Cen-
tury, 1933. DHU/MO; DHU/R
  Points out that "the religious conviction was translated in to the anti-slavery
  cause."
--and Dwight L. Dumond. Letters
of Theodore Dwight, Weld,
Angelina Grimke Weld, and
Sarah Grimke, 1822-1844.
Mass., P. Smith 1965. 2 vols.
                      DHU/MO
  "Discusses the connection
  between the anti-slavery move-
  ment and religious revivalism."
Barrow, David. Involuntary, Un-
merited, Perpetual, Absolute,
Hereditary Slavery Examined,
on Principles of Nature, Rea-
son, Justice, Policy and Scripture. Lexington: D. & C.
Bradford, 1808. NcD; NIC
Belfast Anti-Slavery Society. To
The Christian Churches of the
United States. The Address of
the Belfast Anti-Slavery So-
ciety. Belfast: H. M'Kendrick,
1841.   MBU
Bibb, Henry. Narrative of the
Life and Adventures of Henry
Bibb, An American Slave Writ-
ten by Himself. New York:
The Author, 1849.
            DHU/MO; NN/Sch
  Negro author.
-- "Speech." American and For-
eign Anti-Slavery Society.

(Bibb, H. cont.)
Annual Report New York, May
8, 1849, With Resolutions and
Addresses. (New York: A & F
Anti-Slavery Society, 1849.
                    NcD
Birney, Catherine H. The Grimke
Sisters. Sarah and Angelina
Grimke. New York: Haskell
House Publishers, 1970.
                    DHU/R
(Reprint of 1885 edition)
"The First American Women
Advocates of Abolition and
Woman's Rights."
Bowen, John Wesley Edward. An
Appeal to the King; the Ad-
dress Delivered on Negro Day
in the Atlanta Exposition, Oc-
tober 21, 1895. Atlanta; Ga.:
n.p., 1895.   DHU/MO
Bowley, Samuel. General Anti-
Slavery Convention. Address
of the Convention Held in Lon-
don From the 15th to the 22nd
June Inclusive, to Christian
Professors. London: Johnston
& Barret, Printers, 1843.
                    DHU/MO
Pamphlets on Slavery and
Christianity, vol. 1.
Brainerd, M. Life of Rev.
Thomas Brainerd for Thirty
Years Pastor of the Old Pine
Street Church, Phila. Phila.:
J. B. Lippincott, 1870.
                    DHU/MO
Brawley, Benjamin Griffin.
"Lorenzo Dow." Journal of
Negro History (1:3, Jl., 1916),
pp. 265-75.   DHU/MO
Dow, a white Protestant,
traveled north and south
preaching against slavery.
Brayton, Patience. A Short Ac-
count of the Life and Religious
Labours of Patience Brayton,
Late of Swansey, in the State
of Mass., Mostly Selected
From Her Own Minutes. New
York: Printed; London: Repr.
and sold by Wm. Phillips,
George-Yard, 1802. DHU/MO

Brooks, George S. Friend Anthony Benezet... Phila., University of Pennsylvania Press;
London: H. Milford, Oxford
University Press, 1937.
                    DHU/MO
Brown, Isaac Van Arsdale.
Memoirs of the Rev. Robert
Finley, D.D., late Pastor of
the Presbyterian Congregation
at Basking Ridge, New Jersey
and President of Franklin College, Located at Athens, in
the State of Georgia. With
brief Sketches of Some of His
Contemporaries, and Numerous Notes. New Brunswick:
Terhune & Letson, 1819.
                    DHU/R; CtY-D
Buchanan, George. An oration
upon the Moral and Political
Evil of Slavery. Delivered at
a Public Meeting of the Maryland Society, for Promoting the
Abolition of Slavery, and the
Relief of Free Negroes, and
Others Unlawfully Held in
Bondage, Baltimore, July 4,
1791. Baltimore: Philip Edwards, 1793.   DLC
Burgess, Thomas. Considera-
tions on the Abolition of Slav-
ery and the Slave Trade, Up-
on Grounds of Natural, Reli-
gious, and Political Duty.
Oxford: D. Prince and J.
Cooke, 1789.   NNC
Burleigh, Charles C. ...Slavery
and the North. New York:
American Anti-Slavery Society,
1855.   DHU/MO; NN/Sch
Anti-slavery tracts, no. 10.
Carrol, Daniel Lynn. Sermons
and Addresses on Various
Subjects. Philadelphia: Lind-
say & Blakiston, 1846.
                    NN; IU
Including: "A Paramount
Remedy for the African Slave
Trade."
Carroll, Kenneth L. "Religious
Influences on the Manumission
of Slaves." Maryland Histori-

ical Magazine (56; Je., 1961),
pp. 176-97. DAU
Caruthers, Eli Washington.
"American Slavery and the
Immediate Duty of Southern
Slaveholders." (Eli Washing-
ton Caruthers Collection,
Duke University.) NcD
Chandler, Elizabeth Margaret.
Essays, Philanthropic and
Moral, Principally Relating
to the Abolition of Slavery in
America. Philadelphia: n.p.,
1836. DLC
Cheever, George Barrell.
Rights of the Coloured Race to
Citizenship and Representa-
tion; and the Guilt and Conse-
quences of Legislation Against
Them. A Discourse Deliv-
ered in the Hall of Represent-
atives of the United States, in
Washington, D.C., May 29,
1864. New York: Francis &
Loutrel, 1864. DHU/MO
Child, Lydia Maria (Francis).
An Appeal in Favor of that
Class of Americans Called
Africans. Boston: Allen and
Ticknor, 1833.
DHU/MO; FSU
A review: Quarterly Chris-
tian Spectator (6:3, Sept.,
1834), pp. 445-56. DHU/R
Christian Anti-Slavery Convention.
The Minutes of the Christian
Anti-Slavery Convention As-
sembled April 17-20th, 1850.
Cincinnati: Ben Franklin Book
& Job Rooms, 1850. DLC
Clarke, James Freeman. Causes
and Consequences of the Af-
fair at Harper's Ferry. A
Sermon Preached in the Indi-
ana Place Chapel, on Nov. 6,
1859. Boston: Walker, Wise
& Co., 1859. DHU/R
Clarke was a Congregation-
al Clergyman of Cincinnati;
Editor or the "Western Mes-
senger," 1836-1839.
Clarkson, Thomas. An Essay on
the Impolicy of the African

Slave Trade. In Two Parts.
By the Rev. T. Clarkson. To
Which is Added, an Oration,
Upon the Necessity of Estab-
lishing at Paris, Society to
Promote the Abolition of the
Trade and Slavery of the Ne-
groes. By J.P. Brissot de
Warville. Philadelphia: Fran-
cis Bailey, 1788.
NN; DLC; DHU/MO
--A Letter to the Clergy of Vari-
ous Denominations, and to the
Slave-Holding Planters, in the
Southern Parts of the United
States of America. London:
Johnston and Barrett, 1841.
DHU/MO
Clough, Simon. A Candid Ap-
peal to the Citizens of the
United States, Proving that the
Doctrines Advanced and the
Measures Pursued by the Abo-
litionists, Relative to the Sub-
ject of Emancipation... New
York: A.K. Bertron, 1834.
DHU/MO; DLC
Cole, Charles Chester. The So-
cial Ideas of the Northern
Evangelists, 1826-1860. New
York: Columbia University
Press, 1954. (Columbia stud-
ies in the social sciences;
edited by the faculty of politi-
cal science of Columbia Uni-
versity, no. 580).
DHU/R; NN/Sch
"Colonization and Anti-Coloniza-
tion." Quarterly Christian Spectator (7:3, 4, Sept. and Dec.
1835), pp. 503-20; 521-40.
DHU/R
Remarks on the following
works: An Inquiry into the
Character and Tendency of the
American Colonization and
American Anti-Slavery Societies, by William Jay and Letters to the Hon. William Jay:
Being a Reply to his "Inquiry
into the American Colonization
and American Anti-Slavery Societies," by David M. Reese.

152   Afro-American Religious Studies

Converse, John Kendrick. A
Discourse, on the Moral, Legal and Domestic Condition of
our Colored Population... Burlington, Vt.: E. Smith, 1832.
                DHU/MO; CtY-D
Cornish, Samuel E. The Colonization Scheme Considered in
its Rejection by the Colored
People in its Tendency to Up-
hold Caste-in its Unfitness for
Christianizing and Civilizing
the Aborigines of Africa, and
for Putting a Stop to the African Slave-trade: In a Letter
to the Hon. Theodore Freling-
huysen and the Hon. Benjamin
F. Butler. Newark, N. J.:
A Guest, 1840.
                DHU/R; DLC
Correspondence Between Rev. H.
Mattison and Rev. J. S. Logu-
en, on the Duty of Ministers
to Allow Contributions in the
Churches in Aid of Fugitive
Slaves and the Obligation of
Civil Government and the High-
er Law. Syracuse: J. E. Mas-
ters, 1857.   DHU/MO
Cummings, George D. Life of
Mrs. Virginia Hale Hoffman
Late of the Protestant Episco-
pal Mission to Western Africa.
2d ed. ... Philadelphia: Lind-
say and Blakiston, 1859.
                DHU/MO
Dunham, Chester Forrester.
"The Attitude of the Northern
Clergy toward the South,
1860-65." Doctoral disserta-
tion, Chicago, 1939.
Foster, Stephen Symonds. "An
Abolitionist View of the Amer-
ican Church and Slavery."
Louis Ruchames (ed.). The
Abolitionists (New York: Cap-
ricorn Books, 1966,) pp. 179-
92.   DHU/R
Frothingham, Octavius Brooks.
Gerrit Smith; a Biography.
New York: G. P. Putnam &
Son, 1909.   DHU/MO
Furness, William Henry. The

Blessing of Abolition. A Dis-
course Delivered in the First
Congregation Unitarian Church.
Sunday, July 1, 1860. Phila-
delphia: C. Sherman & Son,
Printers, 1860.   NN/Sch
Garrettson, Freeborn. A' Dia-
logue between Do-Justice and
Professing-Christian. Dedi-
cated to the Respective and
Collective Abolition Societies,
and to all other Benevolent,
Humane Philanthropists, in
America. Wilmington: P. Bryn-
berg, (1820?),   DLC
Gibson, Bertha Askew. The Big
Three Then, the Big Job.
New York: Vantage Press,
1960.   DHU/MO
Negro author.
Story of the Israelites.
Giltner, John H. "Moses Stuart
and the Slavery Controversy:
A Study in the Failure of Mod-
eration." Journal of Religious
Thought (18:1, Wint. -Spr.,
1961), pp. 27-39.   DHU/R
Gray, Thomas. A Sermon, in
Boston, Before the African So-
ciety, 14th of July, 1818; the
Anniversary of the Abolition
of the Slave Trade. Boston:
Parmenter & Norton, 1818.
                NNC; CtY; DLC
Grimké, Angelina Emily. Slav-
ery in America. A Reprint of
an Appeal to the Christian
Women of the Slave States of
America. By Angelina E.
Grimké, of Charleston, South
Carolina. With Introduction,
Notes, and Appendix, by George
Thompson. Recommended to
the Special Attention of the
Anti-Slavery Females of Great
Britain. Edinburgh: Oliphant
and Sons, 1837.   DLC
Guthrie, John. Garrisonian Infi-
delity Exposed; in Two Letters
from the Rev. John Guthrie,
Greenock in Reply to George
Thompson... Glasgow: Pr. by
H. Nisbet, 1851.   DHU/MO

Hamilton, William. Address to the Fourth Annual Convention of the Free People of Color of the United States. Delivered at the Opening of Their Session in the City of New York, June 2, 1834. New York: S.W. Benedict & Co., 1834. CtY; NN/Sch
Negro author.

--An Address to the New York African Society, for Mutual Relief, Delivered in the Universalist Church, January 2, 1809. New York: 1809. NN/Sch
Typescript copy.

--An Oration Delivered in the African Zion Church, on the 4th Day of July 1827, in Commemoration of the Abolition of Domestic Slavery in this State. New York: Gray & Bunce, 1827. DLC; DHU/MO

Hart, Levi. Liberty Described and Recommended; in a Sermon, Preached to the Corporation of Freemen in Farmington, Sept. 20, 1774. Hartford: Watson, 1775. DLC (Microfilm)

Helm, T.G. "Wendell Phillips and the Abolition Movement." Reformed Church Review (20: 2, April, 1916), pp. 196-226. DHU/R

Holley, Myron. Address Delivered Before the Rochester Anti-Slavery Society, on the 19th January and Again, by Request of Several Citizens, at the Court House, in Rochester on the 5th Feb., 1837. Rochester: Hoyt & Porter, 1837. MH

Hough, John A. A Sermon Delivered before the Vermont Colonization Society, at Montpelier, October 18, 1826. Montpelier: Pr. by Walter, E.P., 1826. CtY-D

Houston, David. "John Woolman's in Behalf of Freedom." Journal of Negro History (2:2, Apr., 1917), pp. 126-38. DHU/MO
"Points out that Woolman's influence in 1758 was the first important movement toward abolition among the Quakers."

Howard, Victor B. "The Anti-Slavery Movement in the Presbyterian Church, 1835-1861." Master's thesis, Ohio State University, 1961. NcD

Howitt, William. Colonization and Christianity. A Popular History of the Treatment of the Natives by the Europeans in All Their Colonies. London: Longman, Orme, Brown, Green & Lingmans, 1838. DHU/MO

Hyde, A.B. "Wilberforce--A Study of Freedom." Methodist Review (Bimonthly) (83; Ja., 1901), pp. 46-52. DHU/R

Jay, John. Correspondence Between John Jay, Esq., and the Vestry of St. Matthew's Church, Bedford, N.Y. Bedford, N.Y.: n.p., 1862. DLC; NcD; MB; MBU

Jay, William. An Inquiry into the Character and Tendency of the American Colonization and American Anti-Slavery Societies. New York: Leavitt, Lord Co., 1856. DHU/MO

--Miscellaneous Writings on Slavery. Boston: J.P. Jewett, 1853. CtY-D; NN/Sch

--Reply to Remarks of Rev. Moses Stuart, Late Professor in the Theological Seminary at Andover on Hon. John Jay, and an Examination of His Scriptural Exegesis, Contained in His Recent Pamphlet Entitled "Conscience and the Constitution." New York: Pr. by J.A. Gray, 1850. CtY-D

Jocelyn, Simeon S. College for Colored Youth. An Account of the New Haven City Meeting and Resolutions, with Recommendations of the College,

(Jocelyn, S. S. cont.)
and Strictures upon the Doings
of New Haven. New York:
Published by the Committee,
1831.   RPB
Jones, Benjamin S. Abolitionrie-
ties: or Remarks on Some of
the Members of the Pennsylvania State Anti-Slavery Society for the Eastern District,
and the American Anti-Slavery,
Most of Whom Were Present
at the Annual Meetings, Held
in Philadelphia and New York
in May, 1840. n. p., n. d.
                    PHC; DHU; ICU
Lane Seminary Students (Theodore D. Weld). A Statement of
the Reasons Which Induced the
Students to Dissolve Their Con-
nection with That Institution.
Cincinnati: n. p., 1834.
                        DHU/MO
Leeds Anti-Slavery Association.
The Negro Mother or Christian
Steadfastness. New York: Ne-
gro Universities Press, 1969.
                            DLC
Lloyd, Arthur Young. The Slav-
ery Controversy, 1831-1860.
Chapel Hill: The University of
North Carolina Press, 1939.
                        NN/Sch
Lunn, Arnold Henry Moore. A
Saint in the Slave Trade Peter
Claver (1581-1654)... New
York: Sheed & Ward, 1935.
DHU/MO; DLC; GAU; NcD;
                        NN/Sch
MacMaster, Richard K. "Henry
Highland Garnet and the Afri-
can Civilization Society."
Journal of Presbyterian History
(48:2, Sum., 1970), pp. 95-
112.   DHU/R; NcD
Marsh, William H. God's Law
Supreme. A Sermon, Aiming
to Point Out the Duty of a
Christian People in Relation to
the Fugitive Slave Law; Deliv-
ered at Village Corners, Wood-
stock, Conn., Nov. 28, 1850;
and Subsequently Repeated by

Request, in Southbridge, Mass.
Worcester: Henry J. Howland,
1850.   DLC; MH
May, Samuel Joseph. A Dis-
course on the Life and Charac-
ter of the Rev. Charles Follen,
who Perished, Jan. 13, 1840,
in the Conflagration of the Lex-
ington. Delivered before the
Massachusetts Anti-Slavery So-
ciety, in the Marlborough
Chapel, Boston, April 17, 1840.
Boston: Henry L. Devereux,
1849.   DHU/MO
McGiffert, Arthur Cushman.
"Charles Grandison Finney."
Christendom (5:4, Aut., 1942),
pp. 496-506.   DHU/R
Influence of Finney upon
Anti-Slavery sentiment in the
Church.
"A Memorial to the White People
of that City, (Baltimore), Re-
specting African Emigration."
The Christian Spectator (9:1,
Ja., 1828), p. 55.   DHU/R
A Memorial on African Col-
onization by "The people of
colour in Baltimore at a meet-
ing in the African church."
Meridith, Robert. "A Conserva-
tive Abolitionist at Alton: Ed-
ward Beecher's Narrative."
Journal of Presbyterian His-
tory (42:1, Mr., 1964; 42:2,
Je., 1964), pp. 39-53; 92-103.
                        DHU/R
Miller, Samuel. A Sermon
Preached at Newark, October
22, 1823, before the Synod of
New Jersey, for the Benefit
of the African School under the
Care of the Synod. Trenton:
Pr. by G. Sherman, 1823.
                        NN/Sch
Moore, Wilbert E. "Slavery,
Abolition and the Ethical Valu-
ation of the Individual." Doc-
toral dissertation, Harvard Uni-
versity, 1940.
Mott, Lucretia (Coffin). A Ser-
mon to the Medical Students,
Delivered at Cherry Street

Meetinghouse, Philadelphia,
Feb. 11, 1849. Philadelphia:
W. B. Zeiber, 1849.   DLC
Newhall, Fales Henry. The Con-
flict in America. A Funeral
Discourse Occasioned by the
Death of John Brown of Ossa-
wattomie, who Entered into
Rest, from the Gallows, at
Charlestown, Virginia, Dec.
2, 1859. Preached at the Warren St. M. E. Church, Rox-
bury, Dec. 4. Boston: J. M.
Hewes, 1859.   CtY-D
Parker, Theodore. An Address
Delivered before the New York
City Anti-Slavery Society, at
its First Anniversary, Held at
the Broadway Tabernacle, May
12, 1854. New York: Amer-
ican Anti-Slavery Society,
1854.   DLC
  Parker was a renowned
  scholar and one of the most
  active and daring participants
  in the latter phases of the abolition movement.
Parrish, John. Remarks on the
Slavery of the Black Peoples:
Addressed to the Citizens of
the United States, Particularly
to Those Who are in Legislative or Executive Stations in
the General or State Government and Also to Such Individuals as Hold Them in Bondage. Philadelphia: Kimber,
Conrad & Co., 1806. DHU/MO
Paul, Nathaniel. Reply to Mr.
Joseph Phillips' Enquiry Respecting "The Light" In Which
the Operations of the American Colonization Society are
Viewed by the Free People of
Color on the United States.
London: n. p., 1832.   NjMD
Peabody, William Bourne Oliver.
The Duties and Dangers of
Those Who Are Born Free. A
Sermon, Preached at the An-
nual Election of Ja. 2, 1833,
before His Excellency Levi
Lincoln, Governor, and His

Honor Thomas L. Winthrop,
Lieutenant-Governor, the Hon-
orable Council and Legislature
of Massachusetts. Boston:
Dutton and Wentworth, 1833.
                           DLC
Peck, Nathaniel, and Thomas S.
Price. Report of Messrs. Peck
and Price, Who Were Ap-
pointed at the Meeting of the
Free Colored People of, Held
on the 25th of Nov., 1839.
Delegates to Visit British Gui-
ana, and the Island of Trini-
dad; for the Purpose of Ascer-
taining the Advantages to be
Derived by Colored People Mi-
grating to Those Places. Bal-
timore: n. p., n. d. DHU/MO
  Negro author.
Peckard, Peter. Justice and
Mercy Recommended Particu-
larly with Reference to the
Slave Trade. A Sermon
Preached before the University
of Cambridge... Cambridge:
Pr. by J. Archdeacon, Printer
to the University... 1788.
                        DHU/MO
Pillsbury, Parker. Acts of the
Anti-Slavery Apostles. Con-
cord, N. H.: Clague, Weg-
man, Schlict, & Co., Printer,
1883.   CtY-D; NN/Sch
Presbyterian and Congregational
Convention. The Minutes and Ser-
mon of the Second Convention;
Held in the Central Presbyteri-
an Church, Lombard Street,
Philadelphia, on the 28th Day
of October, 1858. New York:
Daly, Printer, 1858. NN/Sch
Priestly, Joseph. A Sermon on
the Subject of the Slave Trade;
Delivered to a Society of Prot-
estant Dissenters, at the New
Meeting in Birmingham; and
Published at Their Request...
Birmingham: Printed for the
Author by Pearson and Rolla-
son, 1788.   DHU/MO
Quarles, Benjamin. Black Aboli-
tionists. New York: Oxford

(Quarles, B. cont.)
  University Press, 1969.
                DHU/R
  Negro author.
  Chapter IV, Pulpit and
  Press.
Quincy, Ill. Anti-Slavery Concert
  for Prayer 1842. Narrative
  of Facts Respecting Alanson
  Work, Jas. E. Burr & George
  Thompson, Prisoners in the
  Missouri Penitentiary for the
  Alleged Crime of Negro Steal-
  ing, Prepared by a Commit-
  tee. Quincy, Ill.: Quincy
  Whig Office, 1842. DHU/MO
Rankin, John. The Soldier, the
  Battle, and the Victory; Being
  a Brief Account of the Work of
  Rev. J. Rankin in the Anti-
  Slavery Cause; by the Author
  of Life and Writings of Samuel
  Crothers Etc. Cincinnati:
  Western Tract & Book Society
  (1852).   PPPrHi
"Review of African Colonization:
  Thirteenth Annual Report of
  the American Society for Colonizing the free people of col-
  or in the United States; Washington, 1830. Third Annual Report of the Colonization Society of the State of Connecticut; New Haven, 1830. An
  Address delivered to the Colonization Society of Kentucky,
  at Frankfort, Dec. 12, 1829
  by Hon. Henry Clay; Lexington, Kentucky, 1829." Christian Spectator (10:3, Sept.,
  1830), pp. 459-82.   DHU/R
Review of Pamphlets on Slavery
  and Colonization. First Published in the Quarterly Christian Spectator, for March,
  1833. New Haven: Published
  and Sold by A. H. Maltby,
  1833.   CtY-D
"A Review of the 'Address to
  the Public,' by the Managers
  of the Colonization Society of
  Connecticut: With an Appendix. New Haven." Christian

Spectator (2:9, Sept., 1828),
  pp. 493-96.   DHU/R
"Reviews: Tenth and Eleventh
  Annual Report of the American
  Society for Colonizing the Free
  People of Color in the United
  States; Washington, 1827,
  1828." Christian Spectator (10:
  7, Jl., 1828), pp. 358-70.
                DHU/R
Rockwood, George J. George
  Barrell Cheever, Protagonist
  of Abolition. In Proceedings
  of the American Antiquarian
  Society, v. 4, 46, pt. 1,
  April 15, 1936.   DHU/MO
Root, David. The Abolition
  Cause Eventually Triumphant.
  A Sermon Delivered Before
  the Anti-Slavery Society of
  Haverhill, Mass. August, 1836.
  Andover: Gould and Newman,
  1836.   DHU/MO
Ruchames, Louis. The Abolition-
  ist: A Collection of Their
  Writings. New York: Capricorn
  Books, 1963.   DHU/R
Ruggles, David. The Abrogation
  of the Seventh Commandment
  By the American Churches.
  New York: n. p., 1835.
                DHU/MO
  Pamphlets on Slavery and
  Christianity, vol. 1.
  Negro author.
--An Antidote for a Poisonous
  Combination Recently Prepared
  by a "Citizen of New York,"
  Alias Dr. Reese, Entitled "An
  Appeal to the Reason and Reli-
  gion of American Christians,"
  Also David Meredith Reese
  "Humburgs"... New York: W.
  Stuart, 1838. DHU/MO; CtY-D
Sherwin, Oscar. "The Armory of
  God." New England Quarterly
  (18:1, Mr., 1945), pp. 70-82.
                DGU
  "Summarizes the religious
  arguments of the Abolitionists
  and illustrates the use of Bib-
  lical sanctions on both sides
  of the Civil War."

Simmons, George Frederick.
Two Sermons on the Kind
Treatment and on the Emanci-
pation of Slaves. Preached at
Mobile on Sunday the 10th,
and Sunday the 17th of May,
1840. Boston: W. Crosby &
Company, 1840.   DHU/MO
"Slavery and Colonization." Chris-
tian Spectator (5:1, Mr., 1833),
pp. 145-68.   DHU/R
A rebuttal of William Lloyd
Garrison's attack on the Amer-
ican Colonization Society.
Smith, Gerrit. Sermons and
Speeches of Gerrit Smith. New
York: Ross and Tousey, 1861.
DLC
Spring, Gardiner. Memoirs of
the Rev. Samuel J. Mills,
Late Missionary to the South
Western Section of the United
States and Agent of the Ameri-
can Colonization Society. New
York: Evangelical Missionary
Society, J. Seymour Printer,
1820.   NN/Sch
Staiger, C. Bruce. "Abolition-
ism and the Presbyterian
Schism of 1837-1838." Mis-
sissippi Valley Historical Re-
view (36:3, Dec. 1949), pp.
391-414.   DHU
Stanton, Henry B(rewster). De-
bate at the Lane Seminary,
Cincinnati. Speech of James
A. Thome, of Kentucky, De-
livered At the Annual Meeting
of the American Anti-Slavery
Society, May 6, 1834. Boston:
Garrison & Knapp, 1834.
DHU/MO
Stearns, Oliver. The Gospel Ap-
plied to the Fugitive Slave
Law: A Sermon Preached to
the Third Congregational So-
ciety of Hingham on Sunday,
March 2, 1851. Boston: Wm.
Crosby and H. P. Nichols, 1851.
DHU/MO
Stowe, Lyman Beecher. Saints,
Sinners and Beechers...Indi-
anapolis: The Bobbs-Merrill

Co., 1934.   DHU/MO
Chapter III, Activities of
Lyman Beecher, President of
Lane Theological Seminary,
Cincinnati, Ohio, in the Abo-
lition Movement.
Stuart, Charles. Oneida and Ober-
lin, or a Call, Addressed to
British Christians and Philan-
thropists Affectionately Inviting
their Prayers and their Assis-
tance in Favor of the Chris-
tians... Bristol: Pub. by
Wright and Albright, 1841.
DHU/MO
Tappan, Lewis. Letter to the
Convention of Ministers and
Representatives of the Evan-
gelical Branches in the Church
in Brooklyn, New York. n. p.:
John A. Gray and Green,
1866.   DHU/MO
Thompson, George (ed.). Slavery in America. A Reprint of
an Appeal to the Christian
Women of America by Ange-
lina E. Grimke of Charleston,
South Carolina. Edinburgh:
William Oliphant and Son,
1837.   DLC
Tracy, Joseph. Colonization and
Missions. A Historical Exami-
nation of the State of Society
in Western Africa, as Formed
by Paganism and Muhammedan-
ism, Slavery, the Slave Trade
and Piracy, and of the Reme-
dial Influence of Colonization
and Missions. By Joseph Tracy,
Secretary of the Massachusetts Colonization Society.
Published by the Board of
Managers. 4th ed. Boston:
Press of T.R. Marvin, 1845.
DHU/MO; CtY-D
Troxler, George. "Eli Caruthers:
A Silent Dissenter in the Old
South." Journal of Presbyterian History (45:2, Je., 1967),
pp. 95-111.   DHU/R
Underground Railroad. Letter
From an Unidentified Quaker
of Short Creek, Harrison

(Underground Railrod cont.)
County, Ohio, Signed "X. Y.
Z.," to "A. B. C." ("to the
Care of Thomas Perkins");
Lynchburg, Virginia, Feb. 21,
1844, Relating to Slavery and
the "Underground Railroad,"
4 p. Accompanied by a Type-
written Transcript. NN/Sch
Van Dyke, Henry Jackson. The
Character and Influence of
Abolitionism. A Sermon
Preached in the First Presby-
terian Church, Brooklyn, on
the Sabbath Evening, Dec. 9,
1860. New York: D. Apple-
ton & Co., 1860.   NN/Sch
Ward, Samuel. "Speech" Amer-
ican and Foreign Anti-Slavery
Society. Annual Report, New
York, May 8, 1849. With
Resolutions and Addresses.
New York: A & F, Anti-Slav-
ery Society, 1849. pp. 13-15.
                            NcD
Negro author.
Whipple, Charles King. The
Non Resistance Principle:
with Particular Application to
the Help of Slaves by Aboli-
tionists. Boston: R. F. Wall-
cut, 1860.   CtY-D
Williams, Peter. An Oration
on the Abolition of the Slave
Trade; Delivered in the Afri-
can Church, in the City of
New York, January, 1808...
New York: Printed by Samuel
Wood, 1808.   DHU/MO
Negro author.

G.   THE FREEDMAN--RECONSTRUCTION.

Alvord, John Watson. "Letters
from the South Relating to the
Condition of Freedmen, Ad-
dressed to Major General O.
O. Howard Commissioner
Bureau R., F., and A. L."
Washington, D. C.: Howard
University Press, 1870.
                        DHU/MO
American Missionary Association.
What Remains of Slavery and
the Slave Trade, the Freed-
men and Africa. Papers and
Addresses at the Twenty-Ninth
Anniversary of the American
Missionary Association, with
Facts and Statistics. New
York: American Missionary
Association, 1875.
            NN/Sch; DHU/MO
--Woman's Work for the Lowly,
as Illustrated in the Work of
the American Missionary As-
sociation Among the Freedmen.
Boston: South Boston Inquirer
Press, 1873.   DHU/MO
Anscombe, Francis Charles.
"The Contribution of the Quak-
ers to the Reconstruction of
the South." Master's thesis,
University of North Carolina,
1926.
Arnold, S. G. "Education Among
the Freedmen." Methodist
Quarterly Review (60:1, Ja.,
1878), pp. 43-67.   DHU/R
"Black Lilly." The Church at
Home and Abroad (3; Ja.,
1888), pp. 62-64.   DHU/R
Tribute to the faith of a
daughter of a slave.
The Board of Freedmen's Mis-
sions of the United Presbyterian
Church. Our Work Among the
Freedmen. n. p.: Published
by the Board of Freedmen's
Missions of the United Presbyterian Church, 1911.
                        DHU/MO
Boyle, Sarah Patton. The De-
segregated Heart: A Virginian's Stand in Time of Transition. New York: William Morrow & Co., 1962. DHU/MO
Brewe, H. Peers. "The Protestant Episcopal Freeman's Com-

mission, 1865-1878." His-
torical Magazine of Protestant
Episcopal Church (26:4, Dec.,
1967), pp. 361-81. DCU/TH
Bruce, Philip A. ... The Planta-
tion Negro as a Freeman; Ob-
servations on His Character,
Condition and Prospects in
Virginia. New York: Putnam,
1889.   DHU/MO; NN/Sch
Carroll, J. M.   History of Texas
Baptists. Dallas: Baptist
Standard Pub. Co., 1923.
                    NN/Sch
        Chapter 43, Religious work
among the Negroes during Re-
construction 1867-75.
Donald, Henderson Hamilton.
   ...The Negro Freedman; Life
Conditions of the American Ne-
gro in the Early Years After
Emancipation. New York: H.
Schuman, 1952.
        DHU/MO; NN/Sch
Douglass, Harlan Paul.   Chris-
tian Reconstruction in the
South. New York: The Pil-
grim Press, 1909.
        NN/Sch; CtY-D; DHU/MO
Fleming, Walter Lynwood. Docu-
mentary History of Reconstruc-
tion. Cleveland: A. H. Clark,
1906.   DHU/R
"Freedmen or Free Men?" The
Church at Home and Abroad.
(3; Apr., 1888), p. 373.
                      DHU/R
Geppert, Dora Higbee. In "God's
Country," a Southern Romance
...With Introduction by Henry
Watterson. New York: Ameri-
can Publishers Corporation,
1897.   DHU/MO
Girardeau, J. L. "Our Ecclesi-
astical Relation to the Freed-
man." Southern Presbyterian
Review (18; 1867), pp. 2-6.
        DLC; KyLxCB
Grimké, Francis James. The
Religious Aspect of Recon-
struction. A Discourse Deliv-
ered at the Second Annual
Convocation for Pastors and

Christian Workers, Under the
Direction of the School of The-
ology, Howard University, Feb-
ruary 19th, 1919. Washington,
D. C.: n. p., 1919.   DHU/R
Negro author.
Haven, Gilbert (bp.). An Appeal
to Our People for Our People.
New York: n. p., 1875. DLC
Holland, Frederic May. Fred-
erick Douglass: the Colored
Orator. New York: Funk &
Wagnalls Co., 1895. DHU/R
        Chapter X, "Is God Dead?"
Jervey, Edward D. "Motives
and Methods of the Methodist
Episcopal Church in the Per-
iod of Reconstruction." Meth-
odist History (4; Jl., 1965),
pp. 17-25.   DHU/R
Litwack, Leon F. North of Slav-
ery: the Negro in the Free
States, 1790-1860. Chicago:
Univ. of Chicago Press, 1961.
                      NN/Sch
        Negro church, pp. 187-
213.
McKelvey, Blake. "Penal Slavery
and Southern Reconstruction."
The Journal of Negro History
(30:2, Apr., 1935), pp. 153-
79.   DHU/MO
Morrow, Ralph E. "The Methodist Episcopal Church, the
South, and Reconstruction,
1865-1880." Doctoral dissertation, Indiana University,
1954.
--Northern Methodism and Reconstruction. East Lansing,
Mich.: Michigan State University Press, 1956.
        DHU/MO; NN/Sch
Osborne, William. "Slavery Sequel: A Freeman's Odyssey."
Jubilee (3; Sept., 1955), pp.
10-23.   DCU/HU
Pearne, Thomas H. "The Freedmen." Methodist Quarterly Review (37; Ja., 1877), pp. 462-
80.   DHU/R; DLC
Pierce, Paul Skeels. The Freedmen's Bureau. A Chapter in

(Pierce, P. S. cont.)
the History of Reconstruction.
New York: Haskell House
Publishers, Ltd. 1971. DHU/R
"Reprint of 1904 edition.
Chapter I, Work of religious
and benevolent societies and
Freedmen's Aid Societies.
Presbyterian Church in the U. S. A.
Board of Missions for Freedmen.
Annual Report of the Board of
Missions for Freedmen of the
Presbyterian Church in the
United States of America.
Pittsburgh: n. p. , 186-. NN/Sch
1874-75-83-84-87-88. DHU/MO
1871-1885.
Rankin, Charles Hays. "The
Rise of Negro Baptist
Churches in the South Through
the Reconstruction Period."
Master's thesis, New Orleans
Baptist Theological Seminary,
1955.
Richardson, Joe M. The Negro
in the Reconstruction of Flor-
ida, 1865-1877. Tallahassee;
The Florida State University,
1965.   DHU/MO
Chapter 8, Negro religion.
Sweet William Warren. "Negro
Churches in the South: A
Phase of Reconstruction."
Methodist Review (Quarterly)
(104; My. , 1921), pp. 405-18.
                          DHU/R
Taylor, Alrutheus A. The Negro in South Carolina During
the Reconstruction. Washington, D. C. : The Association
for the Study of Negro Life
and History, 1924. DHU/MO

Negro author.
Also, Journal of Negro
History (9:3, Jl. , 1924), pp.
241-364.   DHU
--The Negro in the Reconstruction of Virginia. Washington,
D. C. : Assn. for Study of Negro Life and History, 1926.
                     DHU; NN/Sch
Also, Journal of Negro His-
tory (11:3, Jl. , 1926), pp.
243+.   DHU
Wallace, Jesse Thomas. "His-
tory of the Negroes of Mis-
sissippi from 1865-1890."
Doctoral dissertation, Colum-
bia University, 1928.
Warfield, B. B. "A Calm View
of the Freedmen's Case." The
Church at Home and Abroad
(1; Ja. , 1887), pp. 62-65.
                          DHU/R
Waterbury, Maria. Seven Years
Among the Freedmen. Chi-
cago: T. B. Arnold, 1890.
                         NN/Sch
Williamson, Jolt. After Slavery.
The Negro in South Carolina
During Reconstruction, 1861-
1877. Chapel Hill: University
of North Carolina Press, 1965.
                          DHU/R
Chapter on Religion, With-
drawal and Reformation.
Wright, Elizur. "The Sin of Slav-
ery and its Remedy; Contain-
ing Some Reflections on the
Moral Influence of American
Colonization." Louis Ruchames
(ed.). The Abolitionists (New
York: Capricorn Books, 1966),
pp. 58-60.   DHU/R

H. SPIRITUALS, GOSPEL SONGS, MUSIC, POETRY.

Adams, Charles G. "Some As-
pects of Black Worship."
Andover Newton Quarterly (11:
3, Ja. , 1971), pp. 124-38.
Pam. File; DHU/R
Negro author.

Allen, William F. & Charles
Pickard Ware, (et al.). Slave
Songs of the United States.
New York: A Simpson & Co. ,
1867.   DHU/MO

Armstrong, Mary F. and Helen
W. Ludlow (et al.). Hampton and
Its Students... New York: G.
Putnam's Sons, 1874.   DHU/R
    Includes fifty cabin and
    plantation songs arranged by
    Thomas P. Fenner.
Barton, William E. "Hymns of
the Negro." New England Mag-
azine (n. s.) (19; Ja., 1899),
pp. 609-24.   CtY
--Old Plantation Hymns: A Col-
lection of Hitherto Unpublished
Melodies of the Slave and the
Freedman, with Historical and
Descriptive Notes. New York:
Samson, Wolffe and Co., 1899.
                        DHU/MO
    (In New England Magazine,
    v. 19, p. 443-56.)
Bell, W. B. "Everybody's Parish."
Crisis (62:3, Mr., 1955), pp.
133-38.   DHU/MO
    The Church of the Trans-
    figuration at 5th Ave. & 29th
    St., N.Y.C., where Negroes
    were once harbored during a
    post-Civil War riot.
Bontemps, Arna W. "Rock
Church Rock." Sylvester C.
Watkins. Anthology of Amer-
ican Negro Literature. (New
York: Random House, 1944)
                        DHU/MO
    Gospel Singers and their
    religious orientation.
Botkin, Benjamin Albert, (ed.).
...Negro Religious Songs and
Services... Phonodisc. Li-
brary of Congress, Division
of Music, Recording Labora-
tory Album 10 (AAFS 46-AAFS
50), 1943. DHU/R; NN/Sch
Bradford, R. "Swing Low, Sweet
Chariot; Religious Rites of the
Southern Negro." Colliers (96;
Sept. 21, 1935), pp. 16-17+.
                        DHU
Brewer, John Mason. American
Negro Folklore... Chicago:
Quadrangle Book, 1968.
                        DHU/MO
    Negro author.

Oral Negro sermons.
--The Word on the Brazos; Ne-
gro Preacher Tales from the
Brazos Bottoms of Texas.
Austin: University of Texas
Press, 1953.
                DHU/R; NcD; FSU
--"Songs of the Slave." Lippin-
cott's Magazine (2; 1868), pp.
617.   DHU
Burlin, Natalie. Negro Folk-
Song-Hampton Series, Books
I, II, III and IV. New York:
G. Schirmer, 1918-19.
                        DHU/MO
    Vols. I and II are spiritu-
    als, v. III and IV are work
    songs and play songs.
Chapman, Maria Weston. Songs
of the Free and Hymns of
Christian Freedom. Boston:
I. Knapp, 1836.   DLC
Chambers, Herbert A. The
Treasury of Negro Spirituals.
New York: Emerson Books,
1959.   DHU/R; A&M
    Score and lyrics.
Chirgwin, A.M. "Vogue of the
Negro Spiritual." Edinburgh
Review (247; Ja., 1928), pp.
57-74.   DHU
Christensen, A.M.H. Afro-Amer-
ican Folk Lore. New York:
Negro Universities Press,
1892.   DHU/R
Cohen, Lily Young. Lost Spiritu-
als, by Lily Young Cohen,
with Thirty-Six Illustrations by
Kenneth K. Pointer, and Forty-
One Plates of Musical Compo-
sitions as Composed by Ne-
groes and Set Down in Music
by the Author. New York: W.
Neale, 1928. NcD; DLC;
                        DHU/R
Connelly, Marcus Cook. The
Green Pastures, a Fable, Sug-
gested by Roark Bradford's
Southern Sketches, "Ol' man
Adam an' his chillun," New
York: Farrar and Rinehart,
1930.
NcD; DHU/R; DLC; NN/Sch

(Connelly, M. C. cont.)
Attempts "to present certain aspects of a living religion in the terms of its believers... thousands of negroes in the deep South."
Courlander, Harold. Negro Folk Music, U.S.A. New York: Columbia University Press, 1963.
DHU/R; FSU; A&M
pp. 52-56, Spirituals that may have originally been sermons.
Cox, John Harrington. Folk Songs of the South. Collected Under the Auspices of the West Virginia Folklore Society. Cambridge, Mass.: Harvard University Press, 1925.
DHU/MO
Most of these songs are songs of the Whites of the mountains, but they throw light on the origin of many Negro songs.
Davis, Henderson S. "The Religeious Experience Underlying the Negro Spiritual." Doctoral dissertation, Boston, 1950.
Dett, Robert Nathaniel, (ed.). Religious Folk-Songs of the Negro as Sung at Hampton Institute. Hampton, Va.: Hampton Institute Press, 1927. DHU/MO; NN/Sch; DHU/R
Negro author.
Dundes, Alan. The Study of Folklore. New Jersey: n.p., 1965.   DHU
Federal Writers Project. Lay My Burden Down. A Folk History of Slavery. Chicago: University of Chicago Press, 1945.   DHU/MO
Fenner, Thomas Putnam. Religious Folk-Songs of the Negro as Sung at Hampton Institute. Hampton, Va.: Hampton Institute Press, 1924.   DHU
142 songs arranged for mixed voices.
-- Religious Folk Songs of the

Negro as Sung on the Plantation. Arranged by the Musical Directors of the Hampton Normal and Agricultural Institute ... Hampton, Va.: The Institute Press, 1909.
DHU/MO; NN/Sch
Fichter, Joseph H. "Negro Spirituals and Catholicism." Interracial Review (35; Sept., 1962), pp. 200-203. DCU/SW
Fisher, Miles Mark. Negro Slave Songs in the United States. Ithaca, N.Y.: Cornell University Press, 1953.
DHU/R
Negro author.
Funk, Joseph, (comp.). A Compilation of Genuine Church Music. Winchester: The Pub. at the Office of the Republican, 1832.   DLC
Garnett, Thomas Clifton. "A Comparative Study of Ancient Hebrew and American Negro Folk-song." B.D. Paper, School of Religion, Howard University, 1937.
Gaul, Harvey B. "Negro Spirituals." New Music Review (17; 1918), pp. 47-51. DCU/MU
George, Zelma Watson. A Guide to Negro Music: An Annotated Bibliography of Negro Folk Music, and Art Music by Negro Composers or Based on Negro Thematic Material. Ann Arbor: University Microfilms, 1954.   FSU; DHU/MO
Negro author.
Gloucester, Henry. The Songs of Freedom. Collection of Songs for Anti-Slavery Meetings. Portland: B. Thurston, 1855.
DLC
Hall, Frederick. Negro Spirituals, Arranged for Mixed Voices. Winona Lake, Ind.: The Rodeheaver Co., n.d.
DHU/R
Negro author.
Hare, Maud Cunney. Negro Musicians and Their Music.

Christianity and Slavery 163

Washington, D. C.: The Asso-
ciated Publishers, 1936.
A&M; DHU/MO
Negro author.
Hatfield, Edwin Francis (Comp.).
Freedom's Lyre: or, Psalms,
Hymns and Sacred Songs, for
the Slave and His Friends.
New York: S.W. Benedict,
1840.   DLC
Henry, George W. The Golden
Harp or Camp-Meeting Hymns,
Old and New. Set to Music.
Auburn: Wm. G. Moses, 1865.
                      DHU/MO
Hepburn, D. "Big Bonanza in
Gospel Music." Sepia (12; Mr.,
1963), pp. 13-18.   DHU/MO
Herskovits, Melville J. "Social
History of the Negro." C.
Murchison (ed.). Handbook of
Social Psychology (Worcester,
Mass.: Clark University
Press, 1935.   DHU/R
Place of Music in Negro
Religious Service.
"Higher Music of Negroes."
Literary Digest. (45; Oct. 5,
1912), p. 565.   DHU
Higginson, Thomas Wentworth.
"Negro Spirituals." Atlantic
Monthly (19; 1867), pp. 685-
94.   DHU
Howe, R. "The Negro and his
Songs." Southern Workman.
(51; Je., 29, 1912), pp. 381-
87.   DHU/MO
Jackson, Bruce Harold (ed.).
The Negro and His Folklore in
19th Century Periodicals.
Austin: University of Texas
Press, 1967.
DLC; INU; A&M
Church music, pp. 20-133.
Jackson, George Pullen. Spiritu-
al Folk-Songs of Early Amer-
ica 250 Tunes and Texts with
Introduction and Notes by
George P. Jackson. New York:
J. J. Augustin, Publisher,
1953.   DHU/MO
Jackson, John H. "The Ethical
Implications of the Negro

Spiritual." Bachelor of Divin-
ity thesis, Union Theological
Seminary, 1945.
Jackson, Mahalia. "Mahalia:
Songbird for God." Negro Di-
gest (10; Jl., 1961), pp. 8-
12.   DHU/MO
"James Cleveland: Top U.S.
Gospel Singer." Sepia (14;
My., 1965), pp. 54-9.
                      DHU/MO
James, Willis Laurence. "The
Romance of the Negro Folk
Cry in America." Phylon (16;
Spr., 1965), pp. 15-30.
                      DHU/MO
Material on the rise and
amazing spread of Gospel
singing.
Jessye, Eva A. My Spirituals.
New York: Robbins Engel,
Inc., 1927.   CLU
Johnson, Hall. The Green Pas-
tures Spirituals, Arranged for
Voice and Piano. New York:
C. Fisher, 1930.
                FSU; DHU/MO
Johnson, James Weldon and J.R.
Johnson. Book of American Ne-
gro Spirituals. New York:
Viking, 1940.   DHU/R
Negro author.
Words and music of 120
spirituals.
Jones, Le Roi. Blues People.
New York: William Morrow &
Co., 1963.   DHU/R
Music and religion produced
by being Black in America.
Keesee, Robert E. "The Origin
and Development of Negro
Spirituals." The Journal of
Religious Education of the A.
M.E. Church (30:3, Mr.-My.,
1970), pp. 11-13.   DHU/R
Kelly, Raymond. "Gospel Music
and Its Use in Three Urban
Churches." B.D. Paper,
School of Religion, Howard Uni-
versity, 1968.
Kennedy, Robert Emmet. Black
Cameos. New York: Aond
Co., Boni, 1924.   DHU

(Kennedy, R. E. cont.)
    A series of stories of Ne-
gro life, through which are
interwoven the words and music of numerous Negro songs.
--More Mellows. New York:
Dodd, Mead & Co., 1931.
        NcD; DLC; NN/Sch
Kerlin, Robert Thomas. "Can-
ticles of Love and Woe, Ne-
gro Spirituals." Southern
Workman (50; Feb., 1921), pp.
62-4.   DHU/MO
King, Dearine E. "A Compara-
tive Study of Standard Hymns
and Gospel Songs." Master's
thesis, Howard University,
1940.
    Negro author.
King, Willis J. "The Negro
Spirituals and the Hebrew
Psalms." Methodist Review
(Bimonthly) 114, My., 1931),
pp. 318-26.   DHU/R
    Negro author.
Krehbiel, Henry Edward. Afro-
American Folksongs, a Study
in Racial and National Music.
New York: Schirmer, 1914.
DHU/MO; A&M; FSU
    "Religious character of the
folksongs."
Kruger, E. T. "Negro Religious
Expression." American Jour-
nal of Sociology (38:1, Jl.,
1932), pp. 22-31.   DHU
Locke, Alain. The New Negro.
New York: Atheneum, 1969.
                        DHU/R
    Negro spirituals, pp. 199-
213.
Lomax, Alan. The Rainbow Sign.
A Southern Documentary. New
York: Duell, Sloan & Pearce,
1959.   DHU/MO
    An introduction to Ameri-
can Negro folk religion, pp.
3-20, cf.
Lomax, J.A. "Self-Pity in Ne-
gro Folk Songs." Nation
(New York) (105; Ag. 9,
1917), pp. 141-5.   DHU
Marsh, J. B. T. The Story of

the Jubilee Singers. With
Their Songs. Boston: Hough-
ton, Mifflin, 1881.
        DHU/MO; FSU
McIlhenny, Edward Avery. Befo'
de War Spirituals; Words and
Melodies. Boston: The Chris-
topher Publishing House, 1933.
                        CtY-D
    "The numbers... represent
the real singing of real Lou-
isiana spirituals by Louisiana
Negroes."
McLaughlin, Wayman B. "Sym-
bolism and Mysticism in the
Spiritual." Phylon (24; Sept.,
1963), pp. 69-77. DHU/MO
Murphy, Jeannette Robinson.
"Survival of African Music in
America." Popular Science
(55; 1899), pp. 6-60.
            DGU/S; DCU/ST
--"The True Negro Music and
its Decline." Independent (55;
1903), pp, 1723-30. DCU/ST
Niles, A. "Rediscovering the
Spirituals." Nation (New York)
(123; Dec. 8, 1926), pp. 598-
600.   DHU
Odum, Howard Washington. The
Negro and his Songs in the
South. Hatboro, Pa.: Folk-
lore Assoc., 1964. DHU/R
    Religious songs of the Ne-
gro.
Owen, Anna Kranz. "Negro
Spirituals: Their Origin, De-
velopment and Place in Amer-
ican Folk-Song." Musical Ob-
server (19; 1921), pp. 12+.
                      DLC; OO
Peabody, Charles. "Negro Mu-
sic." Southern Workman (33;
My., 1904), pp. 305+.
                        DHU/MO
Perkins, A.E. "Negro Spirituals
From the Far South." Journal
of American Folk-lore. (35;
Jl., 1922), pp. 223-49. DLC
Pike, G.D. The Jubilee Singers
and their Campaigns for
Twenty-Thousand Dollars.
Boston: Lee and Shepard,

1884.   VIU; FSU
Pound, Louise. "The Ancestry of
a Negro Spiritual." Modern
Language Notes (33; 1918); pp.
442-4.   CtY; DCU; MH
Pratt, Waldo S. & Boyd, Charles
N. "Negro Music." George
Groves. Dictionary of Music
and Musicians (New York:
Macmillan Co., 1920), vols.
5 & 6.   DHU
Proctor, Henry Hugh. "The
Theology of the Songs of the
Southern Slaves," Southern
Workman. (36; Nov. -Dec.,
1907), pp. 584-652. DHU/MO
Puckett, Newell Niles. "Reli-
gious Folk-Beliefs of Whites
and Negroes." Journal of Ne-
gro History (16:1, Ja., 1931),
pp. 9-35.   DHU
Ricks, George Robinson. "Some
Aspects of the Religious Music of the United States Negro: an Ethnomusicological
Study with Special Emphasis on
the Gospel Tradition." Doctoral dissertation, Northwestern University, 1960.
Robinson, Archibald Thomas.
Rays of Heavenly Light, Church
of God Holiness Hymnal. Asheville, N. C., n. p., 1941.
Negro author.
Rodeheaver's Negro Spirituals.
Winona Lake, Ind.: Rode-
heaver, Hall-Mack Co., n. d.
                       DHU/R
Fifty-one spirituals, original melodies, many of which
are printed here for the first
time.
Songs of the Free, and Hymns
of Christian Freedom... Boston: I. Knapp, 1836. DHU/MO
Stacy, George W. Anti-Slavery
Hymns, Designed to Aid the
Cause of Human Rights. Containing Original Hymns written
by Abby H. Price, and Others
of Hopedale Community, with
a Choice Selection from Other
Authors. Hopedale, Mass.:

Community Press, 1844. DLC
Sweet, William Warren. Revival-
ism in America. New York:
C. Scribner's Sons, 1944.
                       DHU/R
Negroes and the revival,
p. 154.
Talbot, Edith Armstrong. "True
Religion in Negro Hymns."
Southern Workman (51; My. -
Jl., 1922), pp. 213+.
                       DHU/MO
Taylor, Marshall W. Planta-
tion Melodies. Cincinnati:
Marshall W. Taylor, 1883.
                       DHU/MO
Negro author.
Thurman, Howard. Deep River:
Reflections on the Religious
Insight of Certain of the Ne-
gro Spirituals. New York:
Harper & Row, 1955. DHU/R
Negro author.
--Disciplines of the Spirit. New
York: Harper and Row, 1963.
                       DHU/R
--The Negro Spiritual Speaks of
Life and Death. New York:
Harper, 1947.
          OWibfU; DHU/R
Waugh, E. "All God's Children,
a Sunday on the Sea Islands."
Travel (77; My. 1941), pp.
26-9.   DLC
Weman, Henry. African Music
and the Church in Africa.
Uppsala: Lundequistska Bok-
handeln, 1960.   DHU/MO
Deals with both African in-
digenous religious music and
Christian congregational adap-
tation of western church mu-
sic.
Wesley, Charles Harris. "The
Folk-Song from the Historical
Point of View." Howard Uni-
versity Record (My., 1919),
                       DHU/MO
Negro author.
White, Newman Inly. American
Negro Folk-Songs. Cambridge:
Harvard University Press,
1928.   DHU/MO

(White, N.I. cont.)
    Contains music.
Williams, John G. "De Ole Plan-
    tation." Charleston, S.C.:
    Walker, Evans, & Cogswell
    Co., Printers, 1895.   DLC
    Contents--Preface.--An
    old-time Saturday night meet-
    ing.--Brudder Coteny's Ser-
    mons.--Glimpses of a vanished
    past: Two pictures of old
    plantation life.
Williams, M.L.   "What I learned
    From God About Jazz." Sepia
    (6; Apr., 1958), pp. 57-60.
                               NN/Sch
Work, John Wesley.   "Negro

Folk-Song." Opportunity (1;
    Oct., 1923), pp. 292-4.
                               DHU/MO
Work, Frederick J. (ed.). Folk
    Songs of the American Negro.
    Introduced by John W. Work.
    Nashville, Tenn.: n.p., 1907.
                               DHU/MO
    91 Negro spirituals ar-
    ranged mostly for mixed
    voices.
Wright, Jeremiah. "The Treat-
    ment of Biblical Passages in
    Negro Spirituals." Master's
    thesis, Howard University,
    1969.

III.	The Negro and the American Religious Life
[for contemporary status, see section V]

A.	RELIGIOUS DEVELOPMENT OF THE NEGRO

1.	The Negro Church

(Note:	All items marked with an asterisk (*) check libraries
listed for holdings.)

a.	Denominations
1.	African Methodist Episcopal

Adams, Revels A.	Cyclopedia of
African Methodism in Missis-
sippi.	Natchez, Mississippi:
n. p. , 1902.	DLC; ISAR
*African Methodist Episcopal
Church.	Annual State Conferences.
DLC; DHU/MO; DHU/R; GAU;
TNF; NcD-D; CtY-D; NcSalL
--Articles of Association of the
African Methodist Episcopal
Church of the City of Phila-
delphia in the Commonwealth
of Pennsylvania.	Philadelphia:
Historic Publications, 1969.
DLC
Reprint of the 1799 ed. ,
with "The founding of Mother
Bethel and the African Method-
ist Episcopal Church 1799; a
bibliographical note, by Max-
well Whiteman" added.
--Bishop's Address to the Mem-
bers and Friends of the Afri-
can Methodist Episcopal
Church in America.	n. p. ,
1872.	GAU
--Bishops' Council.	Committee on
Deaconesses.	Deaconess Manual
of the African Methodist Epis-
copal Church.	n. p. , 1902.
NN/Sch
Negro author.

Written by Bishop Abraham
Grant, Chairman at the Com-
mittee, appointed by the Bish-
ops' Council, July 19, 1901.
--Board of Education.	Report.
n. p. , The Board, 1884.	TNF
*--Catechisms...	DLC; GAU;
NN/Sch; OWibfU; NcSalL;
DHU/MO; NcD; CtY-D
--Conferences.	South Carolina.
Some Mountain Peak Charac-
ters in the Early Days of Af-
rican Methodism and the Dan-
iel A. Payne Memorial Chau-
tauquas...	Columbia, S. C.:
Allen University Press, n. d.
NcD
--Constitution of the Preacher's
Meeting of the African Method-
ist Episcopal Church of Balti-
more and Vicinity.	Baltimore,
Md.: n. p. , n. d.	DHU/MO
*--Dept. of Christian Education.
Quadrennial Report to the Ses-
sion of the African Methodist
Episcopal Church.	19- .	GAU;
NN/Sch; DLC; DHU/MO;
NcSalL
*--Doctrine and Discipline...	DLC;
OWibfU; NcSalL;	DHU/MO
--14th Episcopal District.	Two
in One, Bright and Dark Side
of West Africa, by John H.
Clayborn Presiding Bishop,
14th Episcopal District.

167

(A. M. E. Church cont.)
Little Rock, Ark. : D. M. Wells
& Sons, 1945.
"Report to the bishops of
the A. M. E. Church of the
first visit to the 14th Episcopal District to Africa. "
--General Conference, 1936.
The Episcopal Address Presented by Bishop William Alfred Fountain to the Thirtieth
General Conference of the Af-
rican Methodist Episcopal
Church, New York City, N. Y.
May 6, 1936. Pub. by Order
of the General Conference of
the African Methodist Episco-
pal Church. Philadelphia: A.
M. E. Book Concern, 1936.
DHU/MO; NN/Sch; GAU;
                OWibfU; NcSalL
*--General Conference. Journal
of the... Quadrennial Session
of the General Conference of
the African Methodist Episco-
pal Church. 1820- GAU;
NcSalL; DHU/MO; DLC; TNF;
                OWibfU
*-- -- Official Directory... GAU;
DHU/MO; DLC; NcSalL;
OWibfU; CtY-D; NcD
*-- -- Dept. of Finance. Quad-
rennial Report... TNF; OWibfU;
DLC; GAU; NcSalL; DHU/MO
*-- -- Reports of the Quadrennial
Sessions... NN/Sch; DHU/MO;
NcSalL; OWibfU; CtY-D; TNF
-- Hand Book, A. M. E. Church,
1909. Nashville, Tenn. : Afri-
can Methodist Episcopal Church
Sunday School Union Pub.
House, 1910. NN/Sch; GAU;
                TNF
--Home and Foreign Missionary
Dept. Annual Reports... 18--.
NN/Sch; OWibfU; GAU; DLC;
                NcSalL; DHU/MO
*-- Hymnal, Adapted to the Doc-
trines and Usages of the Afri-
can Methodist Episcopal
Church. Philadelphia: A. M. E.
Book Concern, 1915. DLC;
DHU/MO; OWibfU; NcSalL; GAU

-- Illinois Conference, 39th Ses.
An Appeal to the President
and Congress of the United
States. Resolution on the Proposed Exposition Commemora-
tive of the Semi-Centennial of
the Negroes' Freedom in America. Passed by the Illinois Conference of the A. M. E. Church,
at Springfield, Illinois, September, 1910. Springfield: n. p. ,
1910.
--Journal of Negro Education (29;
Sum. , 1960), pp. 319-22.
                DHU
--Liturgy and Ritual. A. M. E.
Church Liturgy. Philadelphia:
A. M. E. Book Concern, 1911.
NN/Sch; DLC; OWibfU; GAU;
                DHU/MO
-- Missions and Mission Conferences. Indian Mission... Pro-
ceedings of the 28th Session
of the Indian Mission Annual
Conference. Nashville, Tenn. :
1907.   DLC
-- Philadelphia. Centennial His-
torical Souvenir of "Mother"
Bethel A. M. E. Church. Phila-
delphia Historical Society,
1916.   GAU
--Reprint of the Discipline of the
African Methodist Episcopal
Church, with Historical Pref-
ace and Notes, by C. M. Tan-
ner... Atlanta, Ga. : Counts
Printing Office, 1916. DLC;
GAU; CtY-D; TNF; NN/Sch
-- Survey of the Colleges and
Schools of the Colored Method-
ist Episcopal Church. Comp.
by J. A. Bray. n. p. , J. W.
Perry, n. d.   NcD
-- Woman's Home and Foreign
Missionary Society. Constitution
and By-Laws of the Woman's
Home and Foreign Missionary
Society. Adopted at Chicago,
Ill. May, 1928. n. p. , 1929.
NN/Sch; OWibfU; FSU; CtY-D;
                NcSalL
*-- -- Report... Charleston, S. C. :
n. d. CtY-D; DLC; DHU/MO;

NcSalL; GAU; OWilbfU
*--Yearbook. NN/Sch; NcSalL;
OWibfU; GAU; DLC
*--Young People's Congress, At-
lanta, 1914. Official Programme;
Connectional, Young People's
Congress of the African M. E.
Church, Atlanta, Georgia, July
8 to 12, 1914... Nashville,
Tenn.: A. M. E. S. S. Union
Print, 1914. NN/Sch; DLC;
DHU/R; OWibfU; GAU;
                          DHU/MO
--"Report." John Henry Barrows
(ed.). The World's Parliament
of Religions. Vol. II (Chicago:
Parliament Publishing Co.,
1893), pp. 1394-96. DHU/R
Anderson, Robert. The Life of
Rev. Robert Anderson, Born
the 22d day of February in the
Year of Our Lord 1819, and
Joined the Methodist Episcopal
Church in 1839. This Book
Shall be Called The Young
Men's Guide; or, The Brother
in White... Atlanta, Ga.:
Foote & Davies Co., 1900.
          NN/Sch; DHU/MO; GAU
Arnett, Benjamin W. (ed.). The
Budget, Containing Annual Re-
ports of the General Officers
of the African M. E. Church
of the United States of Amer-
ica. Xenia, O.: Torchlight
Printing Co., 1881. DHU/MO
Negro author.
--(ed.). The Budget of 1904.
African Methodist Episcopal
Church History. Philadelphia:
Lampton & Collett, 1924.
          DHU/MO; OWibfU
--(ed.). Centennial Budget Containing an Account of the Celebration (Nov. 1887) in the
Different Parts of the Church,
and the Principal Address Delivered in Bethel Church,
Phil., Pa., Together with the
Portrait of Each Bishop and
his Wife, Also the Portrait
and Sketch of Many of the
Prominent Men of Church...

Dayton, O.: Christian Pub. Co.,
ca. 1888.
DHU/MO; OWibfU; DLC
Negro author.
--(ed.). Proceedings of Semi-Cen-
tenary Celebration... 1874. Cin-
cinnati: H. Watkins, 1874. GAU
Barrows, John Henry (ed.). The
World's Parliament of Reli-
gions. Chicago: The Parlia-
ment Pub. Co., 1893.
                    ISAR; DHU/R
A. M. E. Congress, pp.
1394-6.
Batten, J. Minton. "Henry M.
Turner: Negro Bishop Extra-
ordinary." Church History (7:
3, Sept., 1938), pp. 231-46.
                          DHU/R
Baxter, Daniel Minort. Back to
Methodism. Philadelphia:
A. M. E. Book Concern, 1926.
          DHU/MO; NN/Sch
-- Bishop Richard Allen and His
Spirit. Philadelphia: A. M. E.
Book Concern, 1923.
          OWibfU; DLC; NN/Sch
Bentley, D. S. Brief Religious Re-
flections. Practical Studies for
Christians. In Three Chapters.
Philadelphia: A. M. E. Publish-
ing House, n. d.   DHU/MO
Negro author.
Berry, Lewellyn Longfellow. A
Century of the African Meth-
odist Episcopal Church, 1840-
1940. New York: Gutenberg
Printing Co., Inc., 1942.
DHU/MO; GAU; WilbfU; CtY-
                    D; NN/Sch
Negro author.
Blake, Charles C. Handbook for
Members of the A. M. E.
Church. n. p., n. d. OWibfU
Brooks, William Sampson, (bp.).
Footprints of a Blackman;
the Holy Land. St. Louis:
Eden Publishing House Print,
1915.   DHU/MO
Negro author.
--Three Addresses by Bishop
W. Sampson Brooks, A. M. E.
Bishop of Texas. n. p., n. d. GAU

The Budget, Containing Annual
Reports of the General Offi-
cers of the African Methodist
Episcopal Church of the United
States of America; With Facts
and Figures, Historical Data
of the Colored Methodist
Church in Particular, and
Universal Methodism in Gen-
eral... 1881- Xenia, O.: 1881-
TNF; NN/Sch; DLC (1881-1904)
Butler, William H. H. A. M. E.
Church Ecclesiastical Judicial
Practice. Philadelphia: A. M. E.
Book Concern, 1914. DHU/MO
　　　OWibfU; GAU
Butt, Israel LaFayette. History
of African Methodism in Vir-
ginia; or, Four Decades in
the Old Dominion. Introduc-
tion by Rev. Benjamin F. Lee
... Hampton, Va.: Hampton
Institute Press, 1908.
DLC; NN/Sch; OWibfU
Caldwell, J. C. Constitution of
the Allen League of the A. M.
E. Church by General Secre-
tary. Nashville, Tenn.: A. M.
E. Publication Department,
1914.　　　　　　　OWibfU
Coan, Josephus Roosevelt. Dan-
iel Alexander Payne: Chris-
tian Education. Philadelphia:
A. M. E. Book Concern, 1935.
Negro author.　　　DHU/MO
Cox, John Morris. "A Study of
the Religious Education Pro-
gram of the African Methodist
Episcopal Churches in the Dis-
trict of Columbia." Master's
thesis, Howard University,
1938.
Negro author.
Davis, James A. The History
of Episcopacy, Prelastic and
Moderate; with an Introduction
by the Rev. B. T. Tanner.
Nashville: A. M. E. Church Sun-
day School Union, 1902. NN/Sch
Negro author.
Davis, Monroe H. The Dogmas
and Precepts of the Fathers.
Nashville: A. M. E. Sunday

School Union, 1948.
　　　　　ISAR; OWibfU
Early, Sarah J. W. "Early Pro-
cedures of A. M. E. History in
Series: Life and Labors of
Rev. Jordan W. Early." A. M.
E. Church Review (104:246,
Apr. -Je., 1971), pp. 15-18.
Negro author.
-- The Life and Labors of Rev.
Jordan Early. Edited by
George A. Singleton. Nash-
ville Publishing House, A.
M. E. Church Sunday School
Union, 1894.　　　　DHU/R
INF; OWibfU; NN/Sch
Embry, James Crawford, (bp.).
Digest of Christian Theology...
Philadelphia: A. M. E. Book
Concern, 1890. DLC; NN/Sch
Negro author.
--"Our Father's House" and Fam-
ily Past, Present, and Future.
Philadelphia: A. M. E. Book
Concern, 1893.　　　　　CN
Encyclopedia of the African Meth-
odist Episcopal Church, com-
piled by Bishop R. R. Wright,
Jr. Philadelphia: The Book
Concern of the AME Church,
1947.　　　TNF; DHU/R
Fountain, William A. (bp.). The
Episcopal Address Presented
by... to the Thirtieth General
Conference of the African Meth-
odist Episcopal Church. New
York City, N. Y. May 6, of the
General Conference. Philadel-
phia: A. M. E. Book Concern,
May 6, 1936.　　　DHU/MO
Gaines, Wesley John (bp.). Afri-
can Methodism in the South;
or, Twenty-Five Years of
Freedom. Atlanta, Ga.: Frank-
lin Publishing Co., c1890.
DHU/MO; GAU; TNF; NN/Sch
Negro author. African Meth-
odist Episcopal Church.
--The Negro and the White Man.
... Phila.: A. M. E. Pub. House,
1897.　　　　　　DHU/MO
Gibson, A. B. B. The African
Methodist Shield (improved)

For the Benefit of the Members Sunday Schools, Allen Christian Endeavor League and Missionary Societies of the African Methodist Episcopal Church. A Companion of the Gibson Handbook, The Gibson Catechism. Macon, Ga.: n.p., 1919.   NN/Sch

Gist, Grace. "Educational Work of the African Methodist Episcopal Church." Master's thesis, Howard University, 1949.

Green, A.R. The Life of the Rev. Dandridge F. Davis of the African Methodist Episcopal Church, and His Ministerial Labor. Pittsburgh, Pa.: Pr. at Herald Office, 1850.
         DHU/MO; NN/Sch

Greene, Sherman L., Jr. "Rationale Underlying the Support of Colleges Maintained by the African Methodist Episcopal Church." Journal of Negro Education (29; Sum., 1960), pp. 319-22.   DHU
Negro author.

Gregg, Howard D. Richard Allen and Present Day.. Social Problems. Nashville: A.M.E. Sunday School Union, 19--. GAU
Negro author.

Griffin, Eunice. The Rise of American Missions, The African Methodist Episcopal Church. New York: Coker Press Books, 1960.   DLC; CtY-D; NN/Sch

Grimes, William W. Thirty-three Years' Experience of an Itinerant Minister of the A.M. E. Church. Lancaster, Pa.: S. Speaker, Printer, 1887.
         TNF

Gullins, William Richard. The Heroes of the Virginia Annual Conference of the A.M.E. Church. Norfolk, Va.: 1899.
         DLC; NN/Sch
Negro author.

Handy, James Anderson. Scraps of African Methodist Episco-

pal History. Philadelphia; A. M.E. Book Concern, 1901. NN/Sch; TNF; DHU/MO; OWibfU
Negro author.

Hanson, V.W. (ed.). The World Congress of Religions of the World Columbian Exposition. Chicago: Monarch Book Co., 1894, pp. 1002+.   IEG

Heard, William Henry. From Slavery to the Bishopric in the A.M.E. Church. New York: Arno Press, 1969.
DLC; TNF; DHU/MO; CtY-D; OWibfU

Historical Records Survey. Inventory of the Church, Michigan Conference. Prepared by the Historical Records Survey Program, Division of Professional and Service Projects, Work Projects Administration, Michigan State Administrative Board, Sponsor. Michigan Historical Collections, Co-Sponsor. Detroit, Mich.: The Michigan Historical Records Survey Project, 1940.
         DLC; CtY-D

Hodges, Ruth H. "Materials for a Program of Creative Art Activities in the Christian Education of Children." Doctoral dissertation, New York University, 1965.
A handbook for teachers' use in the African Methodist Episcopal Church.

Hopes, W.K. (ed.). African Methodist Episcopal Church Liturgy. Philadelphia: A.M.E. Book Concern, 1947. OWibfU

"How AME's Elect Bishops." Ebony (11; Ag., 1956), pp. 17-20.   DHU/MO

Isaacs, Esther B. The Leader of Young Women's Auxiliary. Young People's Department. Woman's Parent Mite Missionary Society of the African Methodist Episcopal Church. n.p.: Brady-Wolfe Co., 1934.

(Isaacs, E. B. cont.)
                              NN/Sch
Negro author.
Jackson, Edward Junius. The
A. M. E. Layman. Tampa, Fla. :
Tampa Bulletin Print, n. d.
                              NN/Sch
Negro author.
Jenifer, John Thomas. Centen-
nial Retrospect History of the
African Methodist Episcopal
Church. Nashville: Sunday
School Union Print, 1915.
                   DHU/MO; NN/Sch
--Who Was Richard Allen and
What Did He Do? Baltimore:
n. p., 1905.   NN/Sch
Johnson, James H. A. The Epis-
copacy of the AME Church,
or the Necessity for an Ample
Force of Bishops. Baltimore:
Hoffman & Co, 1888. DHU/MO
--The Pine Tree Mission. Balti-
more: J. Lanahan, Bookseller,
1893.   NN/Sch
Negro author.
Johnson, John Albert. Private
Journal. Bermuda: n. p.,
1889.   NN/Sch
Johnson, Henry Theodore. Di-
vine Logos. Boston: A. M. E.
Pub. Co., 1890.   DLC
Negro author.
Jordan, Artishia. The African
Methodist Episcopal Church in
Africa. New York: Board of
Missions, African Methodist
Episcopal Church, 1960.
                   OWibfU; CtY-D
Negro author.
Jordan, Casper Leroy, (comp.).
The Benjamin William Arnett
Papers at Carnegie Library.
Wilberforce, O. : Wilberforce
Univ., 1958. DHU/MO; NcD
Negro author.
Lane, Isaac. Autobiography.
With a Short History of the A.
M. E. Church in America and
of Methodism. Nashville:
Publishing House of M. E.
Church, South, 1916.
                            DHU/MO

Leach, William H. "Sees Great
Race in the Making. Cleve-
land Conference." Christian
Century (49:23, Je., 1932),
p. 750.   DHU/R
Report on the 29th Gener-
al Conference of the AME
Church at Cleveland, Ohio.
Lee, Benjamin Franklin. Some
Statistics of the African
Methodist Episcopal Church,
1916. Xenia, O. : Aldine Pub.
House, 1916?   NN/Sch
Negro author.
Lee, Jarena. Religious Experi-
ence and Journal... Giving an
account of Her Call to Preach
the Gospel. Rev. and Cor.
From the Original Manuscript,
Written by Herself. Phila. :
Pub. for the Author, 1849.
                   DHU/MO; NN/Sch
Long, Charles Sumner. History
of the A.M. E. Church in Flor-
ida. Philadelphia: A. M. E.
Book Concern, 1939.
                   DHU/MO; OWibfU
Mathews, Marcia M. Richard
Allen. Baltimore: Helicon,
1963. NN/Sch; A&M; NcD;
                              DLC
Michigan Historical Records Sur-
vey. Inventory of the Church
Archives of Michigan African
Methodist Episcopal Church,
Michigan Conference. Detroit:
The Michigan Historical Rec-
ords Survey Project, 1940. IEG
Mixon, W. H. History of the Af-
rican Methodist Episcopal
Church in Alabama, with bio-
graphical sketches with Intro-
duction by Rt. Rev. Henry
McNeil Turner. n. p., n. d.
                          NcD; TNF
Negro author.
Morgan, Joseph H. Morgan's
History of the New Jersey Con-
ference of the A. M. E. Church
from 1872-1887, with Bio-
graphical Sketches of Members
of the Conference. Camden,
N. J. : S. Chew, 1887.   TNF

Morris, Samuel Solomon. An
African Methodist Primer. A
Digest of the History, Beliefs
Organization and Operation of
the African Methodist Episco-
pal Church. Gary, Ind.: Har-
ris Printing Co., n.d. DHU/R
    Negro author.
Newsome, Effie Lee. "Quinn
Rides." The Negro Journal of
Religion (5:7, Sept., 1939), p.
9.   DHU/R
    Work of William Paul Quinn
as an itinerant AME minister.
Newton, Alexander Herritage.
Out of the Briars; an Auto-
biography and Sketch of the
Twenty-ninth Regiment, Con-
necticut Volunteers. With
intro. by J. P. Sampson. Mi-
ami, Fla.: Mnemosyne Pub.
Co., 1969, 1910.
        TNF; DLC; NN/Sch
Norris, John William. The A.
M. E. Episcopacy; a Paper
Read before the Baltimore
A. M. E. Preachers' Meeting.
Baltimore: Afro-American
Co., 1916.   NN/Sch
"Oldest A.M. E. Church." Ebony
(9; Mr., 1954), pp. 17-20.
                    DHU/MO
Palmer, John Moore. Was Rich-
ard Allen Great? Sermon
Delivered by Rev. John M.
Palmer, Allen Chapel A. M. E.
Church, Lombard Street,
above Nineteenth, Philadelphia,
Sunday Evening, February 20,
'98. Philadelphia: Weekly
Astonisher Print., 1898.
                    NN/Sch
Parks, H. B. Africa. The
Problem of the New Century
The Party of the AME Church
is to have in its Solution...
New York: Board of... Home
and Foreign Missionary Dept.
of the AME Church, 1899.
                    DHU/MO
Payne, Daniel Alexander, (bp.).
The African Methodist Episco-
pal Church in Its Relations to

the Freedmen. Address Be-
for the College Aid Society,
Marietta, Ohio, November 7,
1868. Xenia: Torchlight Co.,
1868.   NcD
    Negro author.
--Bishop Payne's First Address
to the Philadelphia Annual
Conference of the First A. M.
E. Church, May 16, 1853.
Philadelphia: C. Sherman,
1853.   NN/Sch
-- History of the African Method-
ist Episcopal Church. New
York: Arno Press, 1969.
DHU/MO; DLC; DHU/R;
            OWibfU
-- The Moral Significance of the
XVth Amendment.   OWibfU
    Transcript.
--Recollection of Seventy Years.
Nashville: A. M. E. Sunday
School Union, 1888. NN/Sch;
DHU/R; DHU/MO; DLC
-- The Semi-Centenary and Ret-
rospection of the African Meth-
odist Episcopal Church in the
United States. Baltimore:
Sherwood and Co., 1866.
        INF; NN/Sch
-- Sermons Delivered Before the
General Conference of the A.
M. E. Church, Indianapolis,
Ind., May 1888. Stenographi-
cally Reported. Edited by Rev.
C. S. Smith. Nashville, Tenn.:
Publishing House, AME Sun-
day School Union, 1888.
                    NN/Sch
--A Treatise on Domestic Edu-
cation... Cincinnati: Pr. by
Cranston & Stowe, 1889.
            DHU/MO; NN/Sch
Perry, Naomi. "The Education
Work of the African Methodist
Episcopal Church Prior to
1900." Master's thesis, How-
ard University, 1900.
Pottinger, John Leo. A Manual
for Church Members. Phila.:
Reading Press, 1942. DHU/R;
OWibfU; NN/Sch; DLC
    Negro author.

Ransom, Reverdy Cassius (bp.).
African Methodist Social
Creed. n. d.   OWibfU
Negro author.
Transcript.
--Christianity, The Church and
the Episcopacy: An Address
at the Bishops' Council of the
A. M. E. Church, Baltimore,
Maryland, February 19, 1942.
                              OWibfU
Transcript.
--The Pilgrimage of Harriet
Ransom's Son.   Nashville:
A. M. E. Sunday School Union,
1950.   DHU/MO
--Preface to History of A. M. E.
Church. Nashville, Tenn. : A.
M. E. Sunday School Union,
1950.   OWibfU
--Year Book of Negro Churches.
Wilberforce: Authority of
Bishops of the A. M. E.
Church, 1936.   DHU/R
With statistics of records
of achievements of Negroes in
the United States.
The Reformed Zion Union Apos-
tolic Church.   Discipline...
                              ISAR
A group that left the A. M.
E. and formed this church
shortly after the Civil War.
Reid, Gaines S. (bp.).   The
Church and the Layman.
Man's Duty to God; a Place
for Positive and Dynamic Sup-
port of the Christian Church.
Foreword by Bishop George
W. Barber. New York: Expo-
sition Press, 1959.
                DHU/R; DHU/MO
Roman, Charles Victor.   Fraternal Message from the African Methodist Episcopal
Church to the Methodist Church
of Canada. Nashville: Hemp-
hill Press, 1920.
                DHU/MO; NN/Sch
Negro author.
Rush, Christopher.   Short Account of the Rise and Progress
of the African Methodist Epis-

copal Church in America.
Written by the Aid of George
Collins. Also a View of the
Church Order of Government
from Authors Relative to Epis-
copacy. New York: The Au-
thor, 1843.   TNF; DHU/MO
Negro author.
Sampson, John Patterson. Ad-
dress of Rev. J. P. Sampson,
D. D. , Presiding Elder of the
New England Conference of the
A. M. E. Church, at the 46th
Annual Convention of the Mon-
mouth County Sunday School
Association. Ocean Grove,
N. J. : n.p. , n.d.   NN/Sch
Negro author.
Shorter, Susie I.   The Heroines
of African Methodism... at the
Octogenial Celebration of Bish-
op Daniel A. Payne, Feb. 24,
1891. Jacksonville, Fla. : ca.
1891.   DHU/MO
Singleton, George Arnett.   The
Autobiography of George Ar-
nett Singleton.   Boston: Forum
Publishing Co. , 1964.
                              DHU/MO
Negro author.
--The Romance of African Meth-
odism: a Study of the Afri-
can Methodist Episcopal
Church. New York: Exposi-
tion Press, 1952.
         DHU/R; INF; NN/Sch
Speech on the eligibility of
colored members to seats in
the Georgia Legislature, pp.
203-18.
Smith, Charles Spencer, (bp.).
Dedicatory Services at the
Publishing House of the A. M. E.
Church Sunday School Union,
Nashville, Tenn. , Sunday and
Monday, January 20-21, 1889.
Nashville, Tenn. : Publishing
House A. M. E. Church Sunday
School Union, 1894.
                        NN/Sch; DLC
Negro author.
--Episcopal Address, Delivered
by Bishop Chas. S. Smith.

D. D., May, Nineteen Hundred
Twelve to the Twenty-Fourth
General Conference of the Af-
rican Methodist Episcopal
Church, Kansas City, Missouri.
Nashville, Tenn.: Sunday
School Union Print, 1912.
DHU/MO
--Glimpses of Africa, West and
Southwest Coast, Containing
the Author's Impressions and
Observations During a Voyage
of Six Thousand Miles from
Sierra Leone to St. Paul de
Loanda and Return, Including
the Rio del Ray and Came-
roons Rivers, and the Congo
River from its mouth to Ma-
tadi, by C. S. Smith. Intro-
duction by Bishop H. M. Turn-
er... Nashville, Tenn.: Pub-
lishing House A. M. E. Church
Sunday School Union, 1895.
NN/Sch
--A History of the African Meth-
odist Episcopal Church. New
York: Johnson Reprint Co.,
1968. (c1922) DHU/MO; TNF;
GAU; OWibfU
--The Relations of the British
Government to the Natives of
South Africa. Address of
Bishop C. S. Smith, Resident
Bishop of the African Method-
ist Episcopal Church in South
Africa, 1904-1906, Delivered
at the Negro Young People's
Christian and Education Con-
gress, in Convention Hall,
Washington, D. C., Wednesday,
August 1, 1906.
Smith, David. Biography of Rev.
David Smith, of the A. M. E.
Church; Being a Complete His-
tory, Embracing Over Sixty
Years Labor in the Advance-
ment of the Redeemer's King-
dom on Earth. Including "The
History of the Origin and De-
velopment of Wilberforce University." Xenia, O.: Pr. at
the Xenia Gazette Office,
1881.   NN/Sch

Negro author.
Smith, James H. Vital Facts
Concerning the African Meth-
odist Episcopal Church. Nash-
ville: A. M. E. Book Concern,
1914. DHU/MO; OWibfU;
NN/Sch
Sterrett, N. B. Annual Sermon
Delivered at the Commence-
ment of Allen University,
1906. The Development of the
Will Power. Charleston, S. C.:
John J. Furlong, Printer, n. d.
DHU/MO
Negro author.
Steward, Theophilus Gould.
From 1864 to 1914, 50 Years
in the Gospel Ministry. Phila-
delphia: A. M. E. Book Con-
cern, 1914.
Negro author.
--Genesis Pre-read or, The
Latest Conclusion of Physical
Science Views in their Rela-
tion to Mosaic Record, to
which is Added an Important
Chapter on the Direct Evi-
dences of Christianity, by
Bishop J. P. Campbell. Phila-
delphia: A. M. E. Book Rooms,
1885.   DHU/MO
Tanner, Benjamin Tucker (bp.).
An Apology for African Meth-
odism. Baltimore: n. p., 1867.
TNF; GAU; NN/Sch; CtY-D
Negro author.
--The Dispensations in the His-
tory of the Church and the In-
terregnums. Kansas City:
The Author, 1899. DHU/MO
--Hints to Ministers, Especially
Those of the African Method-
ist Episcopal Church. Wilber-
force, O.: Industrial Student
Printers, 1900.   NN/Sch
--An Outline of Our History and
Government for African Meth-
odist Churchmen, Ministerial
and Lay in Catechetical Form.
Two Parts with appendix. ...
Introduction by B. F. Lee.
Philadelphia: Grant, Faires &
Rodgers, Printers, 1884.

(Tanner, B. T. cont.)
DHU/R; DHU/MO; TNF
Tanner, Carlton Miller. A Man-
ual of the African Methodist
Episcopal Church, Being a
Course of Twelve Lectures for
Probationers and Members.
Philadelphia: A. M. E. Publish-
ing House, 1900.
NN/Sch; DLC
Negro author.
Tolbert, Horace. The Sons of
Allen. Xenia, O.: n. p.,
1906.   IE G; OWibfU
Townsend, Vince M. Fifty-
Four Years of African Meth-
odism; Reflections of a Pre-
siding Elder on the Law and
Doctrine of the African Meth-
odist Episcopal Church. New
York: Exposition Press, 1953.
DHU/R; TNF; OWibfU; DLC;
NN/Sch
Turner, Henry McNeil, (bp.).
"The Church of the Lord."
Journal of African History
(3:1,   1962), pp. 91-100.
DHU/MO
Negro author.
--The Genius and Theory of
Methodist Polity; or, The Ma-
chinery of Methodism. Prac-
tically Illustrated Through a
Series of Questions and An-
swers. Approved by the Gen-
eral Conference of the A. M. E.
Church. Philadelphia: Publi-
cation Dept., A. M. E. Church,
1885.   NN/Sch; DHU/MO
--Turner's Catechism; Being a
Series of Questions and An-
swers, Upon Some of the Car-
dinal Topics of Christianity.
Designed for the General Use
of Adults, by... Edited by B.
T. Tanner.. Part 1st. Phila-
delphia: A. M. E. Church Book
Rooms, 1917.
TNF; GAU; OWibfU
Washington, R. Francis. The
Philosopher Looks at Life.
Detroit: Missionary Press,
1953.   OWibfU

Wayman, Alexander Walker, (bp.)
Cyclopaedia of African Meth-
odism. Baltimore: Methodist
Episcopal Book Depository,
1882. DHU/MO; TNF; NN/Sch
Negro author.
--The Life of Rev. James Alex-
ander Shorter, One of the
Bishops of the African Meth-
odist Episcopal Church. Bal-
timore: J. Lanahan, 1890.
DHU/MO
--Manual, or Guide Book for
the Administration of the Dis-
cipline of the African M. E.
Church. Philadelphia: Afri-
can Methodist Episcopal Book
Rooms, 1886. GAU; DHU/MO
--My Recollections of African
M. E. Ministers. Philadelphia:
African Methodist Episcopal
Book Rooms, 1881.
NN/Sch; DHU/MO; GAU
Wesley, Charles Harris. Richard
Allen, Apostle of Freedom.
Washington, D. C.: The As-
sociated Publishers, Inc.,
1935.
DHU/R; GAU; TNF; NN/Sch
Negro author.
Wilberforce University, Wilber-
force, O. Carnegie Library.
The Levi Jenkins Coppin Col-
lection at Carnegie Library,
Wilberforce University, Wil-
berforce, Ohio. Compiled by
Casper LeRoy Jordan, Chief
Librarian. Wilberforce, O.:
Wilberforce University, 1957.
NN/Sch; OWibfU
-- Committee on Law and Publi-
cation. Laws and Historical
Sketch of Wilberforce Univer-
sity Near Xenia, Greene
County, Ohio, Belonging to
The African M. E. Church of
America... Committee on Law
and Publication. Rev. Benja-
min W. Arnett. Rev. J. P.
Underwood. D. A. Payne...
Cincinnati: R. Clarke & Co.,
Printers, 1876.
NN/Sch; OWibfU

Wright, Richard Robert, (bp.).
"African Bishop in Africa:
The Story of Missionary's
Journey." Missionary Review
of the World (60:12, Dec.,
1937), pp. 589-91.   DHU/R
Negro author.
--The Bishops of the African
Methodist Episcopal Church.
Nashville: Pr. by the A.M. E.
Sunday School Union, 1963.
DHU/R; TNF; INU; DLC
--(ed.). ...Centennial Encyclo-
pedia of the African Methodist
Episcopal Church, Containing
Principally the Biographies of
the Men and Women, Both
Ministers and Laymen, Whose
Labors During a Hundred Years,
Helped Make the A.M. E.
Church What it is; Also Short
Historical Sketches of Annual
Conferences Educational Insti-
tutions, General Departments,
Missionary Societies of the
A.M. E. Church, and General
Information About African
Methodism and the Christian
Church in General; Being a
Literary Contribution to the
Celebration of the One Hun-
dredth Anniversary of the For-
mation of the African M. E.
Church... Philadelphia: n.p.,
1916.   DHU/R
--87 Years Behind the Black Cur-
tain. An autobiography. Phila-
delphia: Rare Book Co., 1965.
TNF; DLC; OWibfU
--The Encyclopedia of the Afri-
can Methodist Episcopal Church
...2d ed. Containing Princi-
pally the Biographies of the
Men and Women, Both Minis-
ter and Laymen, Whose Labors
During a Hundred and Sixty
Years, Helped Make the AME
Church What it is; also Short
Historical Sketches of Annual
Conferences, Educational Insti-
tutions, General Departments,
Missionary Societies of the
AME Church. Philadelphia:

n.p., 1947.   DHU/R
--What the Negro Gives his
Church: Two Cents. Phila-
delphia: African Methodist
Episcopal Sunday School Union,
1940.   DLC
--Who's Who in the General Con-
ference, 1924, Containing
Sketches and Pictures of Bish-
ops, General Officers, College
Presidents, Delegates and Al-
ternates, Lay and Ministerial,
and their Wives, Who are
Members of the General Con-
ference of the A.M. E. Church,
Convening at Louisville, Ken-
tucky, May 1924. Philadelphia:
A.M. E. Book Concern, 1924.
NN/Sch
Yancy, J. History of the Con-
nectional Departments of the
African Methodist Episcopal
Church. Waco, Tex.: n.p.,
n.d. Negro author. DHU/R
Yearbook and Historical Guide to
African Methodist Episcopal
Church. E.D. Adams, ed. Co-
lumbia, S.C.: Bureau of Re-
search and History, 1955.
GAU
Yearbook of Negro Churches
With Statistics and Records of
Achievements of Negroes in
the United States. Wilberforce,
O.: Pr. at Wilberforce Univer-
sity, 1935. OWibfU; DHU/MR;
CtY-D; DHU/MO (1939-40);
DLC; NN/Sch
"Published by authority of
the bishops of the A.M. E.
Church."

ii. African Methodist Episcopal Zion.

Adams, Donald Conrad. "A Comparative Study of the Social
Functions of the Highway
Church of Jesus of the Apostolic Faith of T.B., Maryland
and the Grace Methodist Church
of Chapel Hill, Maryland."
B.D. Paper, School of Reli-

(Adams, D. C. cont.)
gion, Howard University,
1966.
*African Methodist Episcopal
Zion Church. Annual State Con-
ference. DLC; NcSalL;
DHU/MO; DHU/R; NcD-D;
CtY-D; GAU
*--Catechisms... DHU/R; GAU;
DHU/MO; NcSalL; NN/Sch;
DLC
*--Code on the Discipline of the
African Methodist Episcopal
Zion Church. DLC; DHU/MO;
OWibfU; GAU; NcSalL; NN/Sch
*--Christian Education Dept. Re-
port. Chicago: n. p. , n. d.
DLC; NcSalL; DHU/MO;
NN/Sch
*--Department of Foreign Missions.
...Quadrennial Report...
Washington, D. C.: n. p. , n. d.
DHU/MO; DLC; GAU; NcSalL;
NN/Sch; CtY-D
*--The Doctrines and Disciplines
of the African Methodist Epis-
copal Zion Church in America
... New York: n. p. , 18-.
TNF; DLC; NcSalL; GAU;
DHU/MO
--General Conference. Protest
of the A. M. E. Zion Church,
New York City, Against the
Ordination of Bishops, by the
Extraordinary General Confer-
ence, to be Held in Harris-
burg, Pa. , September 20th,
1866, with the Articles of
Consolidation. New York:
Zion's Standard, n. d.   NcD
--Hand Book, 1856-1960. Edit-
ed and Compiled by Willie G.
Alstork. Washington, D. C.:
n. p. , n. d.   DNH/R
*-- Hymnals... DLC; DHU/R;
NN/Sch; NcSalL
*--Message of the Bishops... to
the General Conference. Chi-
cago: n. p. , n. d.   DLC; GAU;
NcSalL
*-- ... Year Book, 1906- New
Bern, N. C.: n. p. , 1906-.
DLC; DHU/MO; NcSalL; GAU

--Zion's Sesquicentennial, A. M.
E. Zion Church, 1796-1946.
Official Souvenir Journal...
Sept. 8-22, 1946. New York
City, N. Y. New York: n. p. ,
1946.   NN/Sch; NcSalL
Anderson, James H. Biographi-
cal Souvenir Volume of the
Twenty-third Quadrennial Ses-
sion of the General Conference
of the African Methodist Epis-
copal Zion Church. Big Wes-
ley AMEZ Church, Philadel-
phia, Pa. , May 8-30, 1908.
Philadelphia: n. p., 1908.
                          NN/Sch
Bradley, David Henry. A His-
tory of the A. M. E. Zion
Church. 2 vols. Nashville:
Parthenon Press, 1956-70.
DHU/R; NN/Sch; DLC; CtY-D
Negro author.
Clement, George Clinton, (bp.).
Boards for Life's Building.
...Introduction by Rev. Thos.
W. Wallace... Cincinnati, O. :
Pr. for the Author by The
Caxton Press, 1924.
             NN/Sch; DHU/MO
Coleman, Clinton R. "A Study of
A Black Ghetto Church, The
Pennsylvania Avenue A. M. E.
Zion Church, Baltimore,
Maryland." M. Div. Paper,
School of Religion, Howard
University, 1971.
Negro author.
Davenport, William Henry. The
Anthology of Zion Methodism.
Charlotte, N. C. : A. M. E.
Zion Publishing House, 1925.
                          NN/Sch
Negro author.
--Membership in Zion Methodism;
the Meaning of Membership in
the A. M. E. Zion Church. Char-
lotte, N. C. : A. M. E. Zion Pub-
lishing House, 1936.   DLC
Davis, Arnor S. "A Proposed
Program of Christian Education
for Juniors in Galbraith Afri-
can Methodist Episcopal Zion
Church, Washington, D. C."

Master's thesis, Howard University, 1958.

Eichelberger, James William. "African Methodist Episcopal Zion Church: The Rationale and Policies upon which Maintenance of its Colleges is Based." Journal of Negro Education (29; Sum., 1960), pp. 323-29.   DHU
Negro author.

--The Religious Education of the Negro; an Address Delivered at the International Convention of Religious Education, Toronto, Canada, June 26, 1930. Chicago: The Herald Press, 1931.   DHU/MO; DLC

Harris, Cicero R. Historical Catechism of the A. M. E. Zion Church. For use of Families and Sunday Schools. Charlotte, N. C.: A. M. E. Zion Publication House, 1922.
NN/Sch; DHU/R
Negro author.

Hood, James Walker (bp.). The Negro in the Christian Pulpit or, The Two Characters and Two Destinies, as Delineated in Twenty-One Practical Sermons... Raleigh: Edwards Broughton Co., 1884.
DHU/MO; NN/Sch
Negro author.

--One Hundred Years of the African Methodist Episcopal Zion Church; or, The Centennial of African Methodism. New York: A. M. E. Zion Book Concern, 1895.
DHU/MO; TNF; NN/Sch; NcD

--Sermons by J. W. Hood... Vol. II. York, Pa.: P. Anstadt & Sons, n. d.
NN/Sch; DHU/R

--Sketch of the Early History of the African Methodist Episcopal Zion Church With Jubilee Souvenir And an Appendix. n. p., 1914.   NN/Sch

Hood, Solomon Porter. Sanctified Dollars; How We Get

Them, and Use Them. Philadelphia, Pa.: A. M. E. Book Concern, 1908.
Negro author.

Jones, Singleton T. (bp.). Sermons and Addresses of the Late Rev. Bp. Singleton T. Jones, D. D., of the African Methodist Episcopal Zion Church, with a Memoir of his Life and Character. York, Pa.: P. Anstadt & Sons, 1892.
DHU/MO; NN/Sch
Negro author.

Livingstone College, Salisbury, N. C. Carnegie Library. An Index to Biographical Sketches and Publications of the Bishops of the A. M. E. Zion Church. Compiled by Louise M. Rountree. Salisbury, N. C.: n. p., 1963.
DHU/MO; NcD; DLC

Medford, Hampton Thomas, (bp.). Zion Methodism Abroad. Giving the Rise and Progress of the A.M. E. Zion Church on its Foreign Fields. n. p., 1937.
NN/Sch; DHU/R
Negro author.

Miller, John J. History of the A. M. E. Zion Church in America... York, Pa.: Teacher's Journal Office, 1884.   GAU

Milles, John H. The Right Hand of Fellowship. n. p., 1963.
DHU/R
"A manual on church membership and responsibility written by a A. M. E. Z. minister."

Moore, John J., (bp.). History of the A. M. E. Zion Church in America. Founded 1796, in the City of New York, Compiled and Published by John Jamison Moore. York, Pa.: Teachers Journal Office, 1884.
DHU/MO; TNF; NN/Sch
Negro author.

Powell, Jacob Wesley. Bird's Eye View of the General Conference of the African Methodist Episcopal Zion Church with

(Powell, J.W. cont.)
Observations on the Progress
of the Colored People of
Louisville, Kentucky... Boston, Mass.: The Lavalle
Press, 1918.   NcD
Negro author.
--Echoes of Christian Education.
Miss M. Leonessa Powell,
Secretary. Malden, Mass.:
1934.   DLC
Van Catledge, John. "A Criti-
cal Evaluation of the Inter-
mediate Senior Curriculum of
the African Methodist Episco-
pal Zion Church." Doctoral
dissertation, Hartford, 1943.
Walls, William Jacob, (bp.).
Joseph Charles Price: Edu-
cator and Race Leader. Bos-
ton: The Christopher Pub-
lishing House, 1943. DHU/MO
Negro author.
-- Living Essentials of Our
Methodism. n.p., n.d. DHU/R
Negro author.
--The Romance of a College.
New York: Vantage Press,
1963.   DHU/R
Founding and history of
Livingstone College, Salisbury,
N. C.
Walton, O.M. "A.M.E. Zion
Has Lively Session." Chris-
tian Century (73:24, Je. 13,
1956), pp. 732-33. DHU/R
Wheeler, Benjamin F. Cullings
from Zion's Poets. Mobile,
Ala.: n.p., 1907.   DHU/R
Negro author.
"Short biographies and pic-
tures of some A.M.E. Zion
bishops along with their re-
ligious poetry."
--The Varick Family. Mobile,
Ala.: n.p., 1907.
DHU/R; DHU/MO
Descendants of James Var-
ick, founder of the African
Methodist Episcopal Zion
Church.

iii. Christian Methodist Episcopal.

Bailey, Augustus Ceasar. The
Passion Week. Jackson, Tenn.:
Publishing House of the A.M.
E. Church, 1935.   ISAR
Negro author.
Brown, Lorenzo Quincy. "A
Study of the Sunday School Lit-
erature Provided for the Inter-
mediate Department of the
Colored Methodist Episcopal
Church." Master's thesis,
Howard University, 1940.
Byers, Theodore F. "A Compara-
tive Study of Dropouts and
Nondropouts Among the Con-
gregational Methodist Episco-
pal Church and the Montello
Ingram Baptist Church."
M. Div. Paper, School of
Religion, Howard University,
1971.
Negro author.
Cade, John B. Holsey, The In-
comparable. New York: Pa-
geant Press, 1964.
DLC; DHU/MO; A&M
Negro author.
About Bishop Lucius Henry
Holsey, 1842-1920, of the
Christian Methodist Episcopal
Church.
Carter, Randall Albert, (bp.).
A Century of Progress in
Christian Journalism; The
Christian Index. Jackson,
Tenn.: C.M.E. Publishing
House, 1967.   ISAR
Negro author.
*Christian Methodist Episcopal
Church. Annual Conference
Yearbooks... GAU; NN/Sch
NcSalL
*--The Doctrines and Disciplines
...GAU; DLC; NN/Sch;
DHU/MO
*--Episcopal Addresses to Quad-
rennial Session...
DLC; GAU; DHU/MO; NcSalL
*--Quadrennial Reports... GAU;
NN/Sch; DLC; DHU/MO;

NcSalL
--Songs of Love and Mercy.
Adapted to the Use of Sunday
Schools, Epworth Leagues Re-
vivals, Prayer Meetings and
Special Occasions. By Rev.
F. M. Hamilton and Bishop L.
H. Holsey. Memphis, Tenn.:
Publishing House of the C. M.
E. Church, 1968. Originally
pub. in 1904. Scores and
words. Pam. File; DHU/R
--State and District Programs...
GAU; DHU/R; NcSalL; NN/Sch
*--State Annual Conference. Sou-
venir Programs... DHU/R;
GAU; NcSalL; NN/Sch; DLC
*--Youth Conferences... GAU;
NN/Sch; DHU/MO; NcSalL
*--General Board of Religious
Education. Annual Reports.
GAU; DHU/R; DLC; DHU/MO
--General Board of Christian
Education. Christian Education
in the C. M. E. Church... A
Handbook for Workers in
Christian Education. Jackson,
Tenn.: Christian Methodist
Episcopal Church, 1961.
DHU/R
Colclough, J. G. The Spirit of
John Wesley Gibbert. Nash-
ville: Cokesbury Press, 1925.
IEG
Coleman, C. D. "Christian Meth-
odist Episcopal Church: The
Rationale and Policies upon
Which Support of its College
is Predicated." Journal of
Negro Education (29; Sum.,
1960), pp. 315-18.   DHU
Hamilton, Fayette M. Plain Ac-
count of the Colored Method-
ist Episcopal Church in Amer-
ica... Nashville: n. p., 1887.
DHU/MO
Negro author.
Holsey, Lucius Henry, (bp.).
Autobiography, Sermons, Ad-
dresses, and Essays of Bish-
op L. H. Holsey. Atlanta, Ga.:
Franklin Printing and Publish-
ing Co., 1898.

DHU/MO; NN/Sch
Negro author.
--The Race Problem. Atlanta,
Ga.: By the author, 1899.
DHU/MO
McAfee, Sara Jane. History of
the Woman's Missionary So-
ciety in the Colored Methodist
Episcopal Church, Comprising
its Founders, Organizations,
Pathfinders, Subsequent Devel-
opments and Present Status.
Phenix City, Ala.: Phenix City
Herald, 1945.
DHU/MO; NN/Sch
Newborn, Captolia D. "Proposals
for Developing a Program of
Education at William Institu-
tional C. M. E. Church." Doc-
toral dissertation, Columbia
University, Teachers College,
1955.
Pettigrew, M. C. From Miles to
Johnson. Memphis, Tenn.:
C. M. E. Publishing House,
1970.   DHU/R
Negro author.
"One Hundred Years of
Progress 1870-1970 of the
Christian Methodist Episcopal
Church."
Phillips, Charles Henry, (bp.).
From the Farm to the Bish-
opric: An Autobiography.
Nashville: Parthenon Press,
1937.   DHU/MO
Negro author.
--The History of the Colored
Methodist Episcopal Church in
America; Comprising its Or-
ganization, Subsequent Devel-
opment, and Present Status.
Jackson, Tenn.: Publishing
House, C. M. E. Church, 1898.
DHU/MO; NN/Sch
"Biography of the author,
by J. W. Smith;" p. 7-18.
Sideboard, Henry Yergan. "The
Historical Background of the
Colored Methodist Episcopal
Church." B. D. Paper, School
of Religion, Howard Univ.,
1938. Negro author.

Thrall, Homer S. History of
Methodism in Texas. Houston:
Cushing, 1872.   IEG
Formation of the C. M. E.
Church.

iv. National Baptist

Johnson, Robert Ross. The
Mountain of Olivet. A His-
torical Sketch of Negro Bap-
tists in Rochester, N. Y.
Rochester, N. Y. : n. p. , 1946.
                        SCBHC
Xerox copy.
McGuire, U. M. "A Baptist
Golden Jubilee." Baptist (21),
pp. 1068-9.   SCBHC
Morris, Charles S. "Fiftieth
Anniversary of Negro Bap-
tists." Baptist (11), pp.
1095+.   SCBHC
Newman, Albert H. (ed.). A
Century of Baptist Achieve-
ment... Philadelphia: Ameri-
can Baptist Publication So-
ciety, 1901.   SCBHC
Palmer, F. B. "Negro Baptist
Work in Colorado." Baptist
(10; 1929), pp. 694+.
                        SCBHC

v. Progressive National Baptist Convention.

Tinney, James S. "Progressive
Baptists." Christianity Today
(15:1, Oct. 9, 1970), pp. 42-
3.   DHU/R

vi. National Baptist Convention, U. S. A. Inc. --Negro
Baptist in general.

Adams, C. C. and Marshall A.
Talley. Negro Baptists and For-
eign Missions. Philadelphia:
The Foreign Mission Board of
the National Baptist Convention,
U. S. A. , Inc. , 1944.
                 DHU/MO; DLC
*American National Baptist Con-
vention. Journal... Louisville:

Courier-Journal Job Printing
Co., 18-.
   NN/Sch; DHU/MO; GAU;
                          DLC
Asher, Jeremiah. Autobiography
with Details of a Visit to Eng-
land, and Some Account of the
History of the Meeting Street
Baptist Church, Providence,
Rhode Island and of Shiloh
Baptist Church, Philadelphia,
Pa. ... Philadelphia: Pub. by
Author, 1862.   DHU/MO
Negro author.
Baptist Advance. The Achieve-
ments of the Baptist of North
America for a Century and a
Half. Nashville: Broadman
Press, 1964.   DHU/R
pp. 186-226 Negro Baptists.
The Baptist Standard Hymnal
with Responsive Readings. A
New Book for All Services.
Edited by Mrs. A. M. Town-
send. Nashville: S. S. Pub.
Bd. , National Baptist Conven-
tion, 1924.   SCBHC
Baugh, J. Gordon. Historical
Account of the First African
Baptist Church. Philadelphia:
The Author, 1904.   DLC
Benedict, David. A General His-
tory of the Baptist Denomina-
tion, in America and in Other
Parts of the World. Boston:
n. p. , 1813. DLC; CtY-D
Bennett, Ambrose Allen. The
Preacher's Weapon... Nash-
ville, Tenn.: Sunday School
Publishing Bd. , National Bap-
tist Convention, U. S. A. ,
1922.   NN/Sch
Negro author.
"Blunting and Cutting Edge; Res-
olution Adopted by National
Baptist Convention, U. S. A. ,
Inc. , Tulsa." Christian Cen-
tury (82:28, Jl. 14, 1965),
pp. 883-4.   DHU/R
Boone, Theodore S. Beginnings
in Negro Baptist History.
Narration by Dr. T.S. Boone
with Musical Background by

Theodore Harris, Organist,
the Baronaires Quartette, the
Mass Choir, of King Solomon
Baptist Church. Phonodisc,
Shann Custom Recording, 1964.
                                TNF
--Negro Baptist Chief Executives
in National Places. Detroit:
n. p., 1948.   DLC
   Negro author.
--Negro Baptist in Pictures and
History; A Negro Baptist
Historical Handbook. Detroit:
Voice of Destiny, 1964. DLC
--A Social History of Negro Bap-
tists. Detroit: Historical
Commission, National Baptist
Convention, U. S. A., 1952.
                                DLC
Booth, L. Venchael. Who's
Who in Baptist America...
Cincinnati, O.: n. p., 1960.
                              DHU/R
   Negro author.
   Includes leaders and workers
   in the National Sunday School
   and Baptist Training Union
   Congress.
Boothe, Charles Octavius. The
Cyclopedia of the Colored Bap-
tists of Alabama, Their Lead-
ers and Their Work. Birming-
ham: Alabama Pub. Co.,
1895.   DLC; NcD
Borders, William Holmes. Men
Must Live as Brothers. Twen-
ty Sermons Which Were First
Preached in the Wheat Street
Baptist Church, Atlanta. At-
lanta: n. p., 1947.   DLC
   Negro author.
-- Sermons. Philadelphia: Dor-
rance and Company, 1939.
                         DHU/MO; DLC
-- Seven Minutes At the "Mike"
in the Deep South. Atlanta:
B. F. Logan Press, 1943.
                         DHU/MO; DLC
-- Thunderbolts. Atlanta, Ga.:
B. F. Logan Press, 1943.
                                SCBHC
-- Twenty-Fifth Pastoral Anniver-
sary of Rev. & Mrs. William

Holmes Borders, 1937-1962.
n. p., n. d. DLC; DHU/MO;
                         NN/Sch
   "What Street Baptist Church,
Atlanta, Ga."
Boyd, Richard Henry. A Story
of the National Baptist Publish-
ing Board. The Why, How,
When, Where, and By Whom
it Was Established... With an
appendix by Rev. C. H. Clark.
Nashville: n. p., n. d.
                         DHU/MO; TNF
Brawley, Edward Macknight, (ed.).
The Negro Baptist Pulpit; a
Collection of Sermons and Papers on Baptist Doctrine and
Missionary and Educational
Work, by Colored Baptist Ministers. Philadelphia: American Baptist Publication Society,
1890.   DHU/MO; DLC; TNF
   Negro author.
-- The Special Duty of Baptists
to Circulate the Bible. Peters-
burg, Va.: Mitchell Manufac-
ture Co., 1893.   DHU/MO
Brooks, Charles H. Official His-
tory of the First African Bap-
tist Church. Philadelphia: The
Author, 1922.   DLC
Brooks, Walter H. "The Prior-
ity of the Silver Bluff Church
and Its Promoters." Journal
of Negro History (7:2, Apr.,
1922), pp. 172-96. DHU/MO
   Traces the growth of the
   Negro Baptist Church at Silver
   Bluff, S. C. and its influence
   on the establishment of other
   Baptist Churches.
   Negro author.
-- "Unification and Division
Among Colored Baptists. With
diagram." Crisis (30; My.,
1925), pp. 20-2.
Casey's Fork (Ky.). Baptist
Meeting House Church Book,
May 3, 1818 to Aug. 3, 1856.
                                SCBHA
   Contains a list of members,
   and a list of "coullered breth-
   ren."

Chandler, Russell. "Negro Baptists Praise God and Country." Christianity Today (15:1, Oct. 9, 1970), pp. 42-4.   DHU/R

Clinton, George Wylie, (bp.). Christianity Under the Searchlight. Nashville, Tenn.: National Baptist Pub. Board, 1909.   NN/Sch
Negro author.

Cole, S. W. R. Sermons Outlined. 9th ed. Nashville: National Baptist Publishing Board, 1940.   SCBHC
Bound with it: J. P. Robinson's Sermons and Sermonettes.

Davis, Felix L. The Young Men as an Important Force, or the Young Men as an Important Active Spiritual Power on the Field; Address Delivered by Elder Felix L. Davis... to the Twenty-Eighth Annual Session of the Ministerial and Deacons' Convention of Eastern Association of Indiana Baptist, Held With the Howard's Chapel Baptist Church, New Albany, Ind. ... August the 9th, 1911. n. p., 1911.   DLC

Davis, John W. "George Liele and Andrew Bryan, Pioneer Negro Baptist Preachers." Journal of Negro History (3: 2, Apr. 1918), pp. 119-27.
                                DHU/MO

Dehoney, Wayne. Baptists See Black. Waco, Texas: Word Books, 1969.   DHU/R
Negro Baptists ministers in the south and their struggle for racial justice.

Dillard, James A. "Developing Music Activities in the Negro Church with Emphasis Expecially on the Concord Baptist Church of Christ, Brooklyn, New York." Doctoral dissertation, Columbia University, Teachers College, 1951.

Durden, Lewis Minyon. ..."The Small Negro Baptist Church

in Washington, D. C., It's Existing Program of Religious Education and Methods for Improving it..." Master's thesis, Howard University, 1942.

Ellison, John M. "Policies and Rationale Underlying the Support of Colleges Maintained by the Baptist Denomination." Journal of Negro Education (29; Sum., 1960), pp. 330-38.
                                DHU
Negro author.

"First Negro Baptist Church." Sepia (6:53, Ja., 1958). DLC

Fisher, Miles Mark. "History of Olivet Baptist Church of Chicago." Master's thesis, University of Chicago, 1922.
Negro author.

Fowler, Andrew. "A Study of Social Welfare Work of the Shiloh Baptist Church, 1939." B. D. Paper, School of Religion, Howard University, 1940.

Fuller, Thomas Oscar. History of the Negro Baptists of Tennessee. Memphis, Tenn.: Haskins Print, 1936.
DHU/MO; DLC; GAU; TNF

General Association of the Colored Baptists in Kentucky. Diamond Jubilee... The Story of Seventy Five Years of the Association and Four Years of Convention Activities... Louisville, Ky.: American Baptist, 1943.   GAU; TNF

-- Golden Jubilee of the General Association of Colored Baptists in Kentucky. Louisville: Mayers Printing Co., 1915.   GAU

Hacher, Leroy C. "The History and Program of the Zion Baptist Church." B. D. Paper, School of Religion, Howard University, 1937.

Harris, Solomon Parker. The External Relations of a Baptist Church. n.p. 1936.   TNF

Hester, William H. One Hundred and Five Years by Faith. Twelfth Baptist Church, n. p.,

1946.   GAU
Hicks, William. History of
Louisiana Negro Baptists,
1804-1914. Nashville: Nation-
al Baptist Pub. Board, 1915.
                        DHU/MO
    Negro author.
--Nails to Drive, Drawn from
    the Word of God and the His-
    tory of the Earliest Beginnings
    of Negro Missionary Baptists
    in America. Los Angeles:
    n. p. , 1947.   DLC
Hill, Andrew William. Some
    Signs of an Orthodox Baptist
    Church. Aiken, S. C. : Ideal
    Printing Press, 1920? TNF
Hill, Richard Hurst. History of
    the First Baptist Church of
    Charleston, West Va. n. p. ,
    n. d.   DHU/MO
    Negro author.
Historical Records Survey. Di-
    rectory of Negro Baptist
    Churches in the United States.
    Prepared by Illinois Histori-
    cal Records Survey, Division
    of Community Service Pro-
    grams, Work Projects Admin-
    istration. Sponsored by the
    Governor of Illinois. Chicago:
    Illinois Historical Records Sur-
    vey, Illinois Public Records
    Project, 1942.   NcD;
    DHU/MO; DLC; TNF; DHU/R
        Reproduced from typewrit-
    ten copy.
--Virginia. Inventory of the
    Church Archives of Virginia.
    Prepared by the Historical
    Records Survey of Virginia,
    Division of Professional and
    Service Projects, Work Pro-
    jects Administration. Spon-
    sored by the Virginia Conser-
    vation Commission. Negro
    Baptist Churches in Richmond.
    Richmond, Va. : The Histori-
    cal Records Survey of Vir-
    ginia, 1940. DHU/MO; DLC
        Reproduced from typewrit-
    ten copy.
Holmes, Edward A. "George

Liele: Negro Slavery's Proph-
    et of Deliverance. " Founda-
    tions (9:4, Oct. -Dec. , 1966),
    pp. 333-45.   DAU/W
        One of the founders of and
    pastors of the First African
    Baptist Church, Savannah, Ga. ,
    between the years 1780-88.
Jackson, Benjamin Franklin.
    "An Adequate Program of Re-
    ligious Education for the Small
    Negro Baptist Church in
    Northwest Baltimore Which
    Has Inadequate Facilities. "
    Master's thesis, School of Re-
    ligion, Howard University,
    1942.
Jackson, Joseph Harrison. Many
    but One; the Ecumenics of
    Charity. New York: Sheed &
    Ward, 1964. NN/Sch; DHU/R
    Negro author.
--A Voyage to West Africa and
    Some Reflections on Modern
    Missions. Philadelphia: n.p. ,
    1936.   DLC
Jackson, Joseph Julius. A Com-
    pendium of Historical Facts of
    the Early African Baptist
    Churches. Bellefontaine, O. :
    n. p. , 1922.   DLC
    Negro author.
Johnson, R.J. History of Walk-
    er Baptist Association of
    Georgia... Augusta, Ga. :
    Chronicle Job Print, 1909.
                          NcD
Johnson, William A. "A Study of
    Leadership Training of Negro
    Baptist Ministers Attending the
    Chicago Baptist Institute. "
    Master's thesis, University of
    Chicago, 1944.
Koger, Azzie Briscoe. Negro
    Baptist of Maryland. Balti-
    more: Clarke Press, 1946.
    DHU/MO; DLC; TNF
Lewis, Thomas P. Condensed
    Historical Sketch of Taber-
    nacle Baptist Church, Augusta,
    Georgia, from its Organiza-
    tion in 1885 to February, 1904.
    Augusta, Ga. : The Georgia

(Lewis, T. P. cont.)
Baptist Book Print, 1904.
DHU/MO
Negro author.
Negro church in Georgia.
Love, Emanuel King. History of
the First African Church,
From Its Organization, Janu-
ary 20th, 1788, to July 1st,
1888. Including the Centenni-
al Celebration, Addresses,
Sermons, etc. Savannah, Ga. :
The Morning News Print.,
1888. DHU/MO; TNF; NcD
*Maryland State & District of Co-
lumbia Missionary Baptist Con-
vention. Minutes of the Annual
Session. Baltimore: Press of
H. S. Patterson, n.d.
DHU/MO; GAU; DLC
Meachum, John B. An Address
to all the Colored Citizens of
the United States. Philadelphia:
Pr. for the Author, by King
and Baird, 1846. NN/Sch
Negro author.
Morris, Charles S. Pastor
Henry N. Jeter's Twenty-five
Years Experience with the
Shiloh Baptist Church, and her
History, Corner School and
Mary Streets, Newport, R. I.
... Providence: Remington
Print. Co., 1901. TNF
*National Baptist Convention.
Benefit Association. Report...
Nashville: National Baptist
Publishing Board, 1905-.
DHU/MO; GAU
*-- Young People's Union Board.
Reports... Nashville: National
Baptist Publishing Board, n. d.
DHU/MO; GAU
-- "The Deplorable Conditions of
the Visible Church of Our
Day." Proceedings of the
Sixty-Third Annual Session of
the National Baptist Conven-
tion, U. S. A., Inc. Chicago,
Sept., 1943. DHU/MO
*-- Journal ... Nashville, Tenn. :
National Baptist Publishing
Board, n. d.

DHU/MO; NN/Sch; GAU
National Baptist Convention of
America. National Baptist Pub-
lishing Board. Golden Gems; a
Song Book for Spiritual and
Religious Worship for the
Church, the Choir, the Pew,
the Sunday School and the
Various Auxiliaries This Book
is Presented After Careful
Compilation and Offered to a
Discriminating Public. Nash-
ville, Tenn. : National Bap-
tist Pub. Board, 19--.
NN/Sch; GAU
National Baptist Publishing Board.
Annual Report. v. 1, 1897 -
Nashville, Tenn. : n. p., 1897.
TNF
1916, 1920.
Negro Baptist Year Book. The
Negro Baptist Year Book.
Fiscal Year Ending August
31, 1906. Compiled by Sam-
uel W. Bacote... Kansas City,
Mo., n. p., n. d. DHU/MO
Negro Baptists of Georgia. Sta-
tistical Report of Negro Bap-
tists of Georgia for the Year
1915; Rev. D. D. Crawford,
Statistician. Macon, Ga. :
William Pullins, Printer, 1915.
GAU
New England Baptist Convention.
The 1923 and 1924, State of
Country, New England and
Baptist Convention... At Mt.
Zion Baptist Church, Newark,
N. J., June 13-18, 1923. Writ-
ten by Rev. L. B. Brooks,
Pastor, Mt. Ararat Baptist
Church, Rutherford, N. J.
Forty-ninth Annual Session
June 13-18, 1923. DHU/MO
New York City (New York).
Abyssinian Baptist Church.
Annual Reports 31st.
TNF; NN/Sch
Mim.
-- The Articles of Faith, Church
Discipline and By-Laws...New
York: J. Post, 1933. NN/Sch
Ohsberg, Harry O. "The Race

Problem and Religious Education Among Baptists in the U. S. A." Doctoral dissertation, University of Pittsburgh, 1964.

Olivet Baptist Church. Greetings of Olivet Baptist Church Celebrating the Seventy-Second Anniversary of the Church and Six Years Pastorate of Dr. L. K. Williams, 1922. Compiled by Madeline Hawkins. DHU/MO

Parrish, Charles H. Golden Jubilee of the General Association of Colored Baptists in Kentucky. The Story of Fifty Years' Work from 1865-1915, Including Many Photos and Sketches... Louisville, Ky.: Mayes Printing Co., 1915.
　　　　　　　　　　TNF

Pastor Henry N. Jeter's Twenty-Five Years Experience with the Shiloh Baptist Church and Her History. Corner School and Mary Streets, Newport, R. I. (Pref. by Charles S. Morris). Providence: Remington Print. Co., 1901. NN/Sch

Pegues, Albert Witherspoon. Our Baptist Ministers and Schools. Springfield, Mass.: Wiley and Co., 1892.
　　　　　　　　　　DHU/MO

Pelt, Owen D. and R. L. Smith. The Story of the National Baptist. New York: Vantage Press, 1960. DHU/R
Negro author.

Person, I. S. An Open Door. Augusta, Ga.: Georgia Baptist Book Print, 1901. NN/Sch
Negro author.

Piepkorn, Arthur C. "The Primitive Baptists of North America." Concordia Theological Monthly (42:5, May, 1971), pp. 297-314. DHU/R
Some information on "Black Primitive Baptists."

Pius, N. H. An Outline of Baptist History. Nashville, Tenn.: National Baptist Publishing

Board, 1911.
　　　DHU/MO; TNF; GAU
"The Beginning of Negro Baptist History." Contains information about early Negro Baptist Organizers.

Quarles, Benjamin. "Ante-Bellum Relationships Between the First African Baptist Church of New Orleans and White Agencies." The Chronicle (18; Ja., 1955), pp. 26-36. NcD
Negro author.

Ransome, William Lee. Christian Stewardship and Negro Baptists. Richmond, Va.: National Ministers' Institute, Virginia Union University. Richmond, Va.: Brown Print Shop, Inc., 1934.
　　　　　　　　DHU/MO; DLC
Negro author.

--History of the First Baptist Church and Some of her Pastors, South Richmond, Va. By W.L. Ransome, Assisted by the Following Committee: C. H. Munford, Mary V. Binga, Mary V. Nelson and others... Richmond: n. p., 1935.

-- An Old Story for this New Day, and Other Sermons and Addresses. Richmond: Central Pub. Co., 1954. DHU/R

Reid, Barney Ford. A Brief History of Teachers' Training Work as Connected with the Baptist State Sunday School Convention of Kentucky. Louisville: The Convention, 1928. DLC

Reid, Ira De A. The Negro Baptist Ministry: An Analysis of its Profession, Preparation, and Practices. Philadelphia: H & L Advertising Co., 1951. Negro author. DLC

Reid, Stevenson N. History of Colored Baptists in Alabama; Including Facts About Many Men, Women and Events of the Denomination... Gadsden, Ala.: n. p., 1949. DLC

Reynolds, Mary C.   Baptist Mis-
sionary Pioneers Among Ne-
groes.   Sketches Written by
Mary C. Reynolds and others.
n. p. , 1915?   GAU; NN/Sch
Semple, Robert Baylor.   A His-
tory of the Rise and Progress
of the Baptist in Virginia.
Richmond, Va. :   Pitt & Dickinson, 1894.   NcD
Snyder, John.   "The Baptists."
Crisis (20; My. , 1920), pp.
12-14.   DHU/MO
Spencer, David.   Early Baptist of
Philadelphia.   Philadelphia:
W. Syckelmoore, 1877.
          CtY-D; NN
Stackhouse, Perry J.   Chicago
and the Baptists.   Chicago:
University of Chicago Press,
1933.   DLC
Stewart, Maria W.   Productions
of Mrs. Maria W. Stewart
Presented to the First Afri-
can Baptist Church & Society,
of the City of Boston.   Boston:
Friends of Freedom and Vir-
tue, 1835.   NN/Sch
     Negro author.
Stokes, Olivia P.   "An Evalua-
tion of the Leadership Train-
ing Program Offered by the
Baptist Educational Center,
Harlem, N. Y. , with Recom-
mendations for its Improve-
ment."   Doctoral dissertation,
Teachers College, Columbia
University, 1952.
Thomas, Edgar G.   The First
African Baptist Church of
North America. . . Savannah,
Ga. : n. p. , 1925.
     DHU/MO; NcD; DHU/R; TNF
     Negro author.
"Thomas Paul, Pioneer Baptist
Organizer."   David P. Adams,
(ed.).   Great Negroes Past
and Present (Chicago: Afro-
Am. Publishing Co. , 1963),
p. 80.   DHU/R
     In 1805 Thomas Paul (1773-
1831) organized a congrega-
tion of free Negroes in a Bap-

tist church on Jay Street in
Boston.
Thompson, Patrick H.   The His-
tory of Negro Baptists in Mis-
sissippi.   Jackson, Miss. :
Bailey Print. Co. , 1898.
                          CtY-D
Tupper, H. A. (ed.).   The First
Century of the First Baptist
Church of Richmond, 1780-
1880.   Richmond: C. McCar-
thy, 1880.   DLC; Vi
Tyms, James Daniel.   The Rise
of Religious Education Among
Negro Baptists; a Historical
Case Study.   New York: Ex-
position Press, 1906.
          TNF; DHU/R; NcD
     Negro author.
Washington, D. C. Nineteenth
Street Baptist Church.   One Hun-
dred Anniversary of the Nine-
teenth Street Baptist Church.
Washington, D. C. : 1839-1939.
Fifty-Seventh Anniversary,
Rev. Walter H. Brooks, D. D. ,
1882-1939.   Washington: Pr.
by Murray Bros. , Inc. , 1939.
                     DHU/R; TNF
Williams, Lacey Kirk.   First
Annual Address of Dr. L. K.
Williams, President, National
Baptist Convention, September
5-10, 1923.   DHU/MO
     Negro author.
--"Lord ! Lord !" Special Occasion Sermons and Addresses
of Dr. L. K. Williams, edited
by Theodore S. Boone. . . Ft.
Worth, Tex. : Historical Commission, National Baptist Convention, U. S. A. , Inc. , 1942.
                          DLC
vii. National Convention of
America.

Baptists. Kentucky.   General
Association of Colored Baptists.   Diamond Jubilee of the
General Association of Colored Baptists in Kentucky; the
Story of Seventy-Five Years
of the Association and Four

Years of Convention Activities.
Published per Order of the
General Association, by the
Diamond Jubilee Commission
... Louisville, Ky.: Ameri-
can Baptist, 1943. SCBHC
Boyd, Archard H. The Separate
or "Jim Crow" Car Laws or
Legislative Exactments of
Fourteen Southern States. Re-
ply in Compliance With a Res-
olution of the National Baptist
Convention, September 19,
1908. Lexington, Ky.: Nash-
ville, Tenn. National Baptist
Publishing Board, 1909.
            DLC; NN/Sch
Bradley, Fulton C. "An Evalua-
tion of the Junior Sunday
School Curriculum Material of
the National Baptist Conven-
tion, United States of Ameri-
ca, Inc." M.A. thesis, How-
ard University, 1957.
Brooks, Walter H. "The Evolu-
tion of the Negro Baptist
Church." Journal of Negro
History (7:1, Ja., 1922), pp.
11-22.   DHU/MO
Negro author.
Clanton, Solomon T. A Special
Meeting in Behalf of the Amer-
ican Baptist Publication So-
ciety Held at Indianapolis, Ind.,
Sept. 18-19, 1889... SCBHC
Negro author.
Jordan, Lewis Garnett. The
Baptist Standard Church Di-
rectory and Busy Pastor's
Guide. n.p.: Sunday School
Publication Board of National
Baptist Convention, 1929.
            DHU/MO
Negro author.
--In Our Stead. Foreign Mis-
sions Board of the National
Baptist Convention. Phila-
delphia: n.p., n.d. OWibfU.
-- Negro Baptist History, U.S.A.
1750, 1930. Nashville, Tenn.:
The Sunday School Publishing
Board, N.B.C., 1930.
DHU/MO; DLC; TNF; NcD

--On Two Hemispheres Being the
Life Story of Lewis G. Jordan
as Told by Himself. n.p.,
n.d.
--Up the Ladder in Foreign
Missions. Nashville, Tenn.:
National Baptist Pub. Board,
1901.
            DLC; NN/Sch
Negro author.
Moses, William Henry. The
Colored Baptist Family Tree
... Nashville, Tenn.: Sunday
School Publishing Board of
Natl. Baptist Convention of
U.S., 1925. GAU; DHU/MO
Negro author.
--The White Peril... Philadel-
phia: Lisle-Carey Press,
1919. DHU/MO; NN/Sch
*National Baptist Convention, Inc.
Annual Report of the Auditor
of the National Baptist Con-
vention of the United States of
America. n.p., 1915.
TNF; DLC; NN/Sch; DHU/MO
-- Evangelical Board. Report of
the National Baptist Evangeli-
cal Board... Kansas City, Mo.:
Sept. 6-12, 1916. Nashville:
N.B.P.B., 1916.   TNF
*-- Home Mission Board. Report
... Nashville, National Bap-
tist Publishing Board, 189-.
    DHU/MO; GAU; NN/Sch
-- Journal of the National Baptist
Convention... v.1, 1881- n.p.,
The Convention, 1881. TNF
1892-3; 1897-1902; 1915.
The National Baptist Hymnal Ar-
ranged for Use in Churches,
Sunday Schools and Young
People's Societies, R.H.
Boyd, editor; William Ros-
burgh, Musical editor. 3rd ed.
Nashville, Tenn.: Natl. Bap-
tist Publishing Board, 1903.
            SCBHC
    pp. 440-3 "Articles of
faith which should be adopted
by Baptist churches at the
time of organization."

National Baptist Sunday School
Convention of the U.S. 1st Con-
vention, 1869. OClWHi; ViU
"Negro Baptists of the National
Baptist Convention Throng
Chicago." Baptist (2), pp.
1080+.   SCBHC

viii. General Negro Churches--
Negro Church-related Colleges
--Methodist Historical Society

Anderson, H. C. Annual Report
Delivered to Members and
Friends of New Prospect Bap-
tist Church, Williamston, S. C.
and Mountain Spring Baptist
Church, Route No. 2 Ander-
son, S. C. by the Pastor Rev.
H. C. Anderson.   SCBHC
Ashanin, C. B. "Afro-American
Christianity: Challenge and
Significance." Journal of Re-
ligious Thought (16:2, Sum. -
Aut., 1959), pp. 109-20.
                        DHU/R
-- "Negro Protestantism in Cris-
is." Journal of Religious
Thought (20:2, Aut. -Win.,
1963-64), pp. 123-30. DHU/R
Augusta, Ga. Tabernacle Baptist
Church. Condensed Historical
Sketch. By Thomas P. Lewis,
with an Introduction by Rev.
C. T. Walker.   SCBHC
Baptists. North Carolina. Neuse
River Baptis Association. Min-
utes of the...Annual Session
of the Neuse River Baptist
Association...1st, 1869- Wel-
don, N. C.: n. p., 1869. NcD
1869-1923 as Neuse River
Missionary Baptist Associa-
tion.
Bare, Paul W. "The Negro
Churches in Philadelphia."
Master's thesis, Drew University, 1931.
Blanton, Robert J. "The Future
of Higher Education Among Negroes." Journal of Negro Education (9:2, Apr., 1940), pp.
177-82.   DHU/MO

p. 179, Establishment of
faculty for Theology Depart-
ment at Howard University.
Boston. Twelfth Baptist Church.
...One Hundred and Five
Years by Faith, a History of
the Twelfth Baptist Church...
Boston, Massachusetts, Rev.
William H. Hester, D. D.,
Pastor. Boston: n. p., 1946.
                        SCBHC
Bowen, J. W. E. "The Call of the
Christian Pulpit--An Appeal of
a Negro Minister to Negro
Students." Arcadius S. Tra-
wick, (ed.). The New Voice
in Race Adjustments. (New
York: Student Volunteer
Movement, 1914), pp. 93-6.
                        DHU/R
Brooklyn, New York. Mount Leb-
anon Baptist Church. Souvenir
Journal... 1905-1955.
                        SCBHC
Brunner, Edmund De S. Church
Life in the Rural South; a
Study of the Opportunity of
Protestantism Based Upon Da-
ta from Seventy Counties.
New York: George H. Doran
Co., 1923.   DHU/R
Chapter 9, The Negro Rur-
al Church.
Burdette, Mary G. Twenty-Nine
Years' Work Among Negroes.
Chicago: W. B. H. M.S., 1906.
                        SCBHC
Bureau of Governmental Re-
search, Detroit. The Negro in
Detroit... Prepared for the
Mayor's Inter-Racial Commit-
tee by a Special Survey Staff
under the General Direction of
the Detroit Bureau of Govern-
mental Research, Inc. De-
troit: n. p., 1926. 12 v. in 3.
                        NN/Sch
Negro author.
V. 3, "The Negro and the
Church."
Burgess, Margaret E. Negro
Leadership in a Southern City.
Chapel Hill: Univ. of North

Carolina Press, 1962. DHU/R Negro religious institutions in a typical urban center in the middle south.

Carroll, H. K. "The Present Religious Condition of America." J. H. Barrows, (ed.). The World's Parliament of Religions. Vol. II. (Chicago: Parliament Publishing Co., 1893), pp. 1162-65. DHU/R

Carter, Edward Randolph. Biographical Sketches of our Pulpit. Atlanta: J. P. Harrison and Co., 1888. GAU; NN/Sch

Carter, Eugene J. Once a Methodist; Now a Baptist. Why? ...and "What Baptists Believe and Practice," by R. H. Boyd; "Boyd's National Baptist Pastor's Guide;" "The Negro's Place in Ancient History and in American Life at the Present Day." Nashville: National Baptist Publishing Board, 1905. SCBHC

"Churches, Early Negro, in Kingston, Jamaica and Savannah, Georgia." Journal of Negro History (1:1, Ja., 1916), pp. 69-92. DHU

Coleman, John W. "Criteria for Evaluating a Program of Education for Professional Workers in Oklahoma Metropolitan Negro Baptist Churches." Doctoral dissertation, Oklahoma A & M University, 1956.

Colored Baptist Home Missionary Society. The State of Illinois. Proceedings...1844. Alton, Ill. : Pr. at the Telegraph Office, 1844. SCBHC Lacks pp. 5-6.

Cook, Richard Briscoe. Story of the Baptists...33rd Thousand. Baltimore: R. H. Woodward & Co., 1891. SCBHC The supplementary chapter is entitled "The Colored Baptists."

Corey, Charles H. History of the Richmond Theological Seminary with Reminiscences of Thirty Years' Work Among the Colored People of the South. Richmond, Va. : J. W. Randolph Co., 1895. DHU; DHU/MO; FSU

Cromwell, John W. "First Negro Church in the District of Columbia." Journal of Negro History (7:1, Ja., 1922), pp. 64-106. DHU/MO

Daniel, Robert P. "Impact of the War Upon the Church Related College and University." Journal of Negro Education (11:3, Jl., 1942), pp. 359-64. DHU Negro author.

-- "Relationship of the Negro Public College and the Negro Private and Church Related College." Journal of Negro Education (29; Sum., 1960), pp. 388-93. DHU

Daniel, William Andrew. "Negro Theological Seminary Survey." Doctoral dissertation, University of Chicago, 1925.

Dean, Emmett S., (ed.). Victory for Christian Work and Worship... Nashville: National Baptist Publishing Board, 1918. SCBHC 165 hymns, & 1 p. of index.

Dorey, Frank David. "Negro College Graduates in Schools of Religion." Christian Education (29; Sept., 1946), pp. 350-58. DHU/R

Douglass, Harlan Paul. The Springfield Church Survey. (Massachusetts). New York: Geo. H. Doran Co., 1926. DHU/R

Dowling, John. Sketches of New York Baptists. Rev. Thos. Paul and the Colored Baptist Churches. (In the Baptist Memorial and Monthly Chronicles Vol. 8, No. 9, Sept. 1849, p. 295-301). SCBHC

Dyson, Walter. Howard Univer-
sity, The Capstone of Negro
Education. A History: 1867-
1940. Washington, D. C.:
Graduate School, Howard Uni-
versity, 1941.   DHU/R
  Chapter 16, Religion.
Elmira, New York. Monumental
Baptist Church. Historical
Sketch of the Elmira Monu-
mental Church. In Chemung
Association Minutes for 1934.
p. 11-13.   SCBHC
Fisher, Miles Mark. "The
Crozer Family and Negro Bap-
tists." Chronicle (8; Oct. 4,
1945), pp. 181-7.   SCBHC
  Negro author.
-- "Separated not Segregated."
Chronicle (14:2, Apr., 1951),
pp. 87-93.   SCBHC
-- A Short History of the Baptist
Denomination. Nashville: Sun-
day School Pub. Board, 1933.
                          DHU/R
Gray, Henderson. History of
Monumental Baptist Church,
West Philadelphia, Pa., June
30, 1891. n.p., n.d. SCBHC
  Rev. W. H. Davenport,
  Pastor.
Greenleaf, Jonathan. A History
of the Churches of All De-
nominations, in the City of
New York, From the First
Settlement to the Year 1848.
New York: E. French, 1846.
                          NN/Sch
Haley, James. Afro-American
Encyclopedia; or the Thoughts,
Doings and Sayings of the
Race... Sermons... History of
Denominations. Nashville:
Haley & Florida, 1895.
                          DHU/MO
Hampton Negro Conference. An-
nual Report, Hampton Negro
Conference. Hampton, Va.:
Hampton Institute Press,
1898-. 1908-1912, CtY-D;
1898-1912, DHU/MO
  "Report of first conference
July 1897 is contained in (Sept.

1897) Southern Workman.
Hargett, Andrew H. "Teaching
of Religion in State Colleges
for Negroes." Journal of Ne-
gro Education (22; Win., 1953),
pp. 88-90.   DHU
Harris, William Frederick.
"Methodism and Her Secession"
Methodist Review (Quarterly)
(77:1, Ja., 1928), pp. 72-81.
                          DHU/R
  Includes brief section on
  Negro Secessions.
Harvey, W. "National Baptists
in Foreign Missions." Mis-
sion (Dec., 1968), p. 32.
  "Historical Survey of Negro
  Natl. Baptists, Inc."
Hirsch, Leo H. "The Negro and
New York, 1783-1865." Jour-
nal of Negro History (16:4,
Oct., 1931), pp. 382-473.
                          DHU
  Includes a discussion of the
  church.
Hodges, George Washington.
Early Negro Church Life in
New York. n.p., 1945.
  DHU/MO; NN/Sch; NcD
  Negro author.
Jamaica, New York. Amity
Baptist Church. Twenty-Fifth
Anniversary, 1916-1941.
n.p., n.d.   SCBHC
Jeter, Henry Norval. Forty-
Two Years Experience as
Pastor... Brief Fifty Years
History of the New England
Baptist Missionary Convention,
by Rev. H. N. Jeter, D. D.
n.p., n.d.   SCBHC
--Pastor Henry N. Jeter's Twen-
ty-Five Years Experience with
the Shiloh Baptist Church and
Her History... Newport, R. I.:
Providence, Remington Print-
ing Co., 1901.   SCBHC
Kennard, Richard. A Short His-
tory of the Gilfield Baptist
Church of Petersburg, Virgin-
ia. Compiled by Wm. H.
Johnson. Petersburg: Owen,
1903.   SCBHC

Kennedy, P. Baptist Directory and Year Book 1892-1893. Henderson, Ky.: n.d. SCBHC
Negro author.

Kingsley, Harold M. "The Negro Goes to Church." Opportunity (7:3, Mr., 1929), pp. 90-91. DHU/MO

Lee, J. Oscar. "Racial Inclusion in Church Related Colleges in the South." Journal of Negro Education (22; Win., 1953), pp. 16-25. DHU

Lenski, Gerhard Emmanuel. The Religious Factor: A Sociological Study of Religion's Impact on Politics, Economics, and Family Life. Garden City, N.Y.: Doubleday, 1961. DHU/R; INU; NN/Sch
Based on a survey made in the Detroit area.

Look Magazine. Religions in America: a Completely revised and Up-to-Date Guide to Churches and Religious Groups in the U.S. New York: Simon and Schuster, 1963. DHU/R; INU
pp. 296-300, Negro religions.

Lucas, George W. "Negro Baptists, the Stormiest Protestants." Negro Digest (Jan., 1962), pp. 32-40. SCBHC

MacKerrow, P. A Brief History of the Coloured Baptists of Nova Scotia, and Their First Organization as Churches, A. D. 1832. ...Halifax, N.S.: Nova Scotia Printing Co., 1895. SCBHC

Magee, J.H. The Night of Affliction and Morning of Recovery. An Autobiography. By Rev. J.H. Magee, Pastor of the Union Baptist Church. 2nd ed. Cincinnati, O.: Pub. by the Author, 1873. SCBHC
Negro author.

Marrs, Elijah P. Life and History of Rev. Elijah P. Marrs, First Pastor of Beargrass

Baptist Church... Louisville: Bradley & Gilbert Co., 1885. SCBHC
Negro author.

Mays, Benjamin Elijah. "The Significance of the Negro Private and Church Related College." Journal of Negro Education (29:3, Sum., 1960), pp. 245-51. DHU/MO
Negro author.

-- "Present Status of and Future Outlook for Racial Integration in the Church Related White Colleges in the South." Journal of Negro Education (21; Sum., 1952), pp. 350-52. DHU

McKinney, Richard Ishmael. "Religion in Negro Colleges." Journal of Negro Education (13; Fall, 1944), pp. 509-19. DHU

Mead, Frank Spencer. Handbook of Denominations in the United States. New York: Abingdon Press, 1956. INU; DHU/R
Brief history and current statistics on Negro churches in America.

Murray, Florence. The Negro Handbook. New York: Macmillan, 1949. DHU/R
Negro author.
pp. 288-99, membership of Negro churches.

National Jubilee Melodies. Nashville, Tenn.: Natl. Baptist Publishing Board, n.d. SCBHC

Negro Baptists - Halifax, Nova Scotia. Cornwallis Street Baptist Church. Halifax, N.S.: Royal Print, n.d. SCBHC

Negro Year Book, An Annual Encyclopedia of the Negro. Tuskegee Institute, Ala.: Negro Year Book Publishing Co., 1912. DHU/MO; DHU/R
Short historical facts, denominational statistics.

New Brunswick, New Jersey.
Ebenezer Baptist Church. His-
tory of the Ebenezer Church.
In Central N. J. Association
Minutes for 1896, p. 33.
SCBHC
New Rochelle, New York. Beth-
esda Baptist Church. Yearbook,
1939. n. p, n. d.   SCBHC
New York City, (New York)
Abyssinian Baptist Church. The
Abyssinian School of Religious
Education and Community
House Activities. N. Y. :
n. p. , n. d.   SCBHC
-- 32nd Annual Report of the
Subscribing Members and
Friends... from May 1, 1929,
Including April 30, 1930.
n. p. : Hayley Press, n. d.
SCBHC
--The Opening and Dedication
Programme of the New Abys-
sinian Baptist Church and
Community House... 1923.
N. Y. : New York Age Press,
n. d.   SCBHC
New York City, (New York) Bap-
tist Education Center. (Negro
Auxiliary). Minutes and Corre-
spondence, 1925-1955.
SCBHC
-- Greater New York Federation
of Churches. The Negro
Churches of Manhattan (New
York City). A Study Made in
1930. New York: n. p. , n. d.
SCBHC
Niebuhr, Helmut Richard. The
Social Sources of Denomina-
tionalism. New York: Holt,
Rinehart and Winston, Inc. ,
1929.   DHU/R
Oliver, Pearleen. A Brief His-
tory of the Colored Baptists
of Nova Scotia, 1782-1953. In
Commemoration of Centennial
Celebrations of the African
United Baptist Association of
Nova Scotia, Inc. n. p. , 1953.
SCBHC
Pearson, Colbert Hubert. A
Non-Denominational Program

of Christian Education for a
Group of Negro Churches Serv-
ing the Negro Community of
Englewood, New Jersey. New
York, n. p. , 1948. DHU/MO
Microfilm.
Philadelphia, Pa. Shiloh Baptist
Church. Articles of Faith and
Covenant. Philadelphia: W. G.
F. Brinckloe, Printer, 1861.
SCBHC
Bound with J. Asher's
autobiography.
-- -- A Century of Faith and
Service; Shiloh Baptist Church,
Philadelphia, Pennsylvania,
1842-1942; Centennial Jubilee
and Anniversary Celebration,
September 4, October 29,
1942. Rev. W. H. R. Powell,
Pastor. Philadelphia: n. p. ,
1942.   SCBHC
Powell, Adam Clayton, (Jr.).
The One Hundred Thirtieth
Anniversary of the Abyssinian
Baptist Church and the First
Anniversary as Pastor of A.
Clayton Powell, Jr.   New
York: n. p. , 1938.   SCBHC
Powell, Ruth Marie. Lights and
Shadows. The Story of the
American Baptist Theological
Seminary, 1924-1964. n. p. ,
1964.   SCBHC
Rand, Earl W. "An Analysis of
the Boards of Control of a
Group of Selected Negro Prot-
estant Church Related Col-
leges." Doctoral dissertation,
Indiana University, 1952.
-- "Negro Private and Church
College at Mid-century." Jour-
nal of Negro Education (22;
Wint. , 1953), pp. 77-9. DHU
-- "Selection of Board Members
in Negro Church-related Col-
leges." Journal of Negro Edu-
cation (25; Wint., 1956), pp.
79-82.   DHU
Religious Services in the Second
African Church, Philadelphia,
at the Ordination and Installa-
tion of the Rev. Andrew Har-

ris as Pastor of Said Church, on the 13th of April, 1841. Philadelphia: Isaac Ashmead, 1841.   DHU/MO
Richmond, Va. First Baptist Church. "Reminiscences of the First African Church, Richmond, Va." By Basil Manly, Jr. The Baptist Memorial and Monthly Chronicle (14; 1855), pp. 262-65; 289-92; 321-27; 353-56.   SCBHC
Robert, Mattie A. Our Immediate Need of an Educated Colored Ministry. n. p. , 1878.
                SCBHC
Rochester, New York. Mount Olivet Baptist Church. Operation Expansion. Oct. , 1954. n. p. , n. d.   SCBHC
Rohrer, John H. , (ed.). The Eighth Generation Grows Up: Cultures and Personalities of the New Orleans Negroes. New York: Harper & Row, 1960.   DHU/R
  pp. 30-34, Negroes, and the church in New Orleans.
Rosten, Leo, (ed.). A Guide to the Religions of America; The Famous Look Magazine Series on Religion, Facts, Figures, Tables, Charts, Articles and Comprehensive Reference Material on Churches and Religious Groups in the United States. New York: Simon & Schuster, 1963.   DHU/R
Rusling, G. W. "A Note on Early Negro Baptist History." Foundation (XI, Oct. -Dec. , 1968), pp. 362-68.   NcD
Russell, Daniel Hames. History of the African Union Methodist Protestant Church. Philadelphia: Union Star Book & Job Print. & Pub. House, 1920.   DLC
St. Paul, Minn. Pilgrim Baptist Church. 1863 Centennial 1963. St. Paul, F.D. Fredell, n.d.
                SCBHC
  Rev. Floyd Massey, Jr. ,

Pastor.
Sargent, Charles J. Negro Churches and the American Baptist Convention. New York: n. p. , 1966. SCBHC
  Delivered by the pastor of the Union Baptist Church, Stamford, Conn. , at the Ministers and Missionaries Benefit Board Annual Luncheon, Kansas City, May 11, 1966.
Savannah, Georgia. First African Baptist Church. Constitution and Rules of Order of the F. A. B. Church, Savannah, Ga. Savannah: Morning News Steam Printing House, 1887.
                SCBHC
  Short History of the African Union Meeling and School-House. Erected in Providence (R. I.) in the Years 1819, '20, '21; with Rules for its Future Government. Published by Particular Request. Providence: Brown and Danforth, 1821.
                NcD
Simms, James M. The First Colored Baptist Church in North America, Constituted at Savannah, Georgia, January 20, A. D. 1788. Philadelphia: Lippincott, 1888. SCBHC
Sims, David. "Religious Education in Negro Colleges and Universities." Journal of Negro History (5:2, Apr. , 1920), pp. 166-208.   DHU/MO
Spence, Hartzell. The Story of America's Religions. Published in Cooperation with the Editors of Look Magazine. New York: Rinehart & Winston, 1960.   NN/Sch
  History and statistics on Negro churches.
Spencer, Dwight. Home Missions and the Negroes. New York: American Baptist Home Missions Society, n. d. SCBHC
Stakely, Charles Averett. History of the First Baptist Church of Montgomery, Ala-

bama, with Sketches of the
Other Baptist Churches of the
City and County, in Papers
Presented at the Hundredth
Anniversary of the First Bap-
tist Church Celebrated in
Montgomery, November 29-
December 1, 1929. Together
with a Reprint of the Church's
Declaration of Faith, Constitu-
tion, Covenant, and By-Laws
... The History Written and the
Papers Collected and Compiled
in Chapters. Montgomery,
Ala.: The Paragon Press,
1930.
    p. 67-72: the colored Bap-
tist churches of Montgomery.
Steele, Henry M. Common Life
Among Negro Baptists in
Georgia, Between the Years
1874-1904. n. p., 1967.
                        SCBHC
    Paper in Baptist history
for Dr. W. S. Hudson, Dec. 1,
1967.
Stevenson, J. D. "Tuskegee's
Religious Work." Southern
Workman (39; Jl., 1910), pp.
401+.   DHU/MO
Sweet, William Warren. The
American Churches. New York:
Abingdon, 1948.   DHU/MO
    Religious affiliations of
American Negroes.
Talbert, Horace. The Sons of
Allen. Together with a Sketch
of the Rise and Progress of
Wilberforce University, Wil-
berforce, Ohio. Xenia, O.:
The Aldine Press, 1906.
            DHU/MO; DLC
    Negro author.
Tankerson, Richard Earl. "Some
Sociological Factors Effecting
the Organic Merger of the
A. M. E. Zion, and C. M. E.
Churches," B. D. Paper,
School of Religion, Howard
University, 1967.
    Negro author.
Thirkield, Wilbur Patterson.

The Training of Physicians
and Ministers for the Negro
Race. Washington, D. C.:
Howard University, 1909.
                        DHU/R
Trent, William J. "Relative
Adequacy of Sources of In-
come of Negro Church-re-
lated Private Colleges." Jour-
nal of Negro Education (29;
Sum., 1960), pp. 356-67.
                        DHU
Tupper, H. A. The Foreign Mis-
sion of the Lutheran Baptist
Convention. Philadelphia:
American Baptist Publication
Society, n. d.   DHU/MO
United States. Census Bureau.
Negroes in the United States.
Washington, D. C.: Govt. Prtg.
Office, 1915.   DHU/R
    Negro churches, pp. 45-53.
-- -- Religious Bodies, 1906,
1916, 1926, 1936... Washing-
ton, D. C.: Govt. Prtg. Office,
1910-1941.   DHU/R
    Statistics on Negro church-
es.
-- Work Project Administration,
New Jersey. The Negro Church
in New Jersey. Emergency
Education Project. Hacken-
sack, N. J.: n. p., 1938.
                DLC; NN/Sch
    Mim.
Unofficial Inter-Racial Confer-
ence on Christian Education for
Negroes under Baptist Auspices.
    Christian Education for Ne-
groes under Baptist Auspices;
Proceedings of an Unofficial
Interracial Conference of the
Hundred Texas Baptist Leaders,
Nov. 4, 1941, Baptist Building,
Dallas, Texas. Sponsored and
Published by the Board of
Trustees... Bishop College,
Marshall, Texas. Marshall,
Tex.: n. p., 1941. NN/Sch
Vass, Samuel Nathaniel. How
to Study and Teach the Bible.
Teacher Training Book, Na-
tional Baptist Convention,

U. S. A. Nashville, Tenn.:
Sunday School Pub. Board,
1922. Negro author. NN/Sch
-- Our Needs as Colored People.
Philadelphia: A. B. P. S., n. d.
                          SCBHC
-- Principles and Methods of Re-
ligious Education. Nashville,
Tenn.: Sunday School Publish-
ing Board, 1932.
              DHU/MO; NN/Sch
Vincent, A. B. Address Deliv-
ered Before the Baptist State
Sunday School Convention,
Warrenton, N. C., Sept. 19,
1895. Raleigh: n. p., 1896.
                          SCHBC
Walker, T. C. "How We May
Improve. Our Colored
Churches in the Country."
Arcadius S. Trawick, (ed.).
The New Voice in Race Ad-
justments (New York: Student
Volunteer Movement, 1914),
pp. 139-45.   DHU/R
Wallace, S. B. "Behold we are
Servants this Day." The In-
dustrial Status of the Colored
People of the District of Co-
lumbia. A Sermon Delivered
at the Israel C. M. E. Church,
Washington, D. C., December
30, 1894. Union League Pub-
lication, no. 5, n. d. DHU/MO
Negro author.
Washington, D. C. Shiloh Baptist
Church. Fiftieth Anniversary
(1863-1913). n. p., n. d.
                          SCBHC
Weatherford, Willis Duke. Amer-
ican Churches and the Negro;
an Historical Study from Early
Slave Days to the Present.
Boston: Christopher Pub.
House, 1957.
            DHU/R; INU; GAU
Weaver, Robert C. "Negro Private and Church Related Col-
lege: A Critical Summary."
Journal of Negro Education
(29; Sum., 1960), pp. 394-
400.   DHU
Negro author.

Webster, Sherman N. "A Study
of the Patterns of Adult Edu-
cation in Selected Negro
Churches." Doctoral disserta-
tion, Indiana University, 1959.
West, C. S. "A Colored Church
Self-Sustaining." The Church
at Home and Abroad (4; Jl.,
1888), p. 43.   DHU/R
A letter.
White, Eugene Walter. That
They Might Know. A Book of
Gospel Sermons. Baltimore:
Clarke Press, 1952. SCBHC
Whitted, J. A History of the Ne-
gro Baptists of North Carolina.
Raleigh: Edwards and Brough-
ton, Printing Co., 1908.
            DHU/MO; GAU; SCBHC
Woman's American Baptist Home
Mission Society. From Ocean to
Ocean; the Annual Report of
the Missionaries Medical Edu-
cational and Evangelistic...
New York: 19- .
              NN/Sch; DHU/MO
-- Suggestions for Meetings. Bos-
ton: W. A. B. H.M. S., 1902.
                          SCBHC
A mission study manual designed for the study of the
Negro.
Contains music.
Wood River (Illinois) Baptist
Association. A Historical Sketch
of the Wood River Baptist Association of the State of Illinois for the State of Illinois
for the Past Fifty Years,
(1838-1888). In Wood River
Baptist Association Minutes
for 1888. pp. 44-58.
                          SCBHC
Work, Monroe N., (ed.). Negro
Year Book. An Annual En-
cyclopedia of the Negro. Tuskegee, Ala.: Tuskegee Institute, Negro Year Book Co.,
1912-47.   DHU/MO
Statistics on the Negro
church.
Negro author.

Wright, Stephen J. "Some Criti-
cal Problems Faced by the
Negro Church Related College."
Journal of Negro Education
(29; Sum., 1960), pp. 339-44.
                              DHU
Yearbook of American Churches.
New York Council Press,
National Council of Churches
in America, 1916.   DHU/R
Published yearly. Included
are short histories of Negro
churches in addition to sta-
tistics.
Yonker, Thomas Walter. "The
Negro Church in North Caro-
lina, 1700-1900." Master of
Arts thesis, Duke University,
1955.
Yonkers, N.Y. Messiah Church
and Sunday School. "Historical
Sketch." Agnes Kirkwood.
Church and Sunday School Work
in Yonkers, pp. 473-83.
                              SCBHC

b. Storefront Churches and Sects
i. Churches of God

"Church Celebrates 50th Anniversary; Church of God in
Christ Lauds Founder."
Ebony (13; Mr., 1958), pp.
54-6+.   DHU/MO
Massey, James Earl. An Introduction to the Negro Churches
in the Church of God Reformation Movement. New York:
Shining Light Survey Press,
1957.   DHU/MO
Negro author.

ii. Holiness Church

Battle, Allen O. "Status Per-
sonality in a Negro Holiness
Sect. Doctoral dissertation,
Catholic University, 1961.
Johnson, Benton. "Do Holiness
Sects Socialize in Dominant
Values?" Social Forces (39;
My., 1961), pp. 309-16. DHU

Parsons, A. "Pentecostal Im-
migrants: Study of an Ethnic
Central Church." Practical
Anthropology (14; Nov., 1967),
pp. 249-66.   DHU/R

iii. Daddy Grace--House of
Prayer.

Alland, Alexander. "Possession
in a Revivalistic Negro
Church." Journal for the Sci-
entific Study of Religion (1:2,
Spr., 1962), pp. 204-13.
                      DHU/R
Deals with United House of
Prayer (Daddy Grace).
"Daddy Grace; Millionaire With
a Bible." Our World (8; Oct.,
1953), pp. 50-3.
                 DLC; DHU/MO
"Daddy Grace to Use Fire Hose
on 300." Amsterdam News
(Jl. 28, 1956).   DHU/MO
Whiting, Albert N. "The United
House of Prayer for All
People." A case study of a
Charismatic Sect." Doctoral
dissertation, American Univer-
sity, 1952.

iv. Cults and Sects, General

Bach, Marcus. They Have
Found a Faith. Indianapolis:
Bobbs-Merrill Co., 1946.
                      DHU/R
Chapter 6, The Kingdoms
of Father Divine.
Boaz, R. "My Thirty Years
With Father Divine." Ebony
(20; My., 1965), pp. 88+.
                      DHU/MO
Braden, Charles Samuel. These
Also Believe. New York:
Macmillan Co., 1950. DHU/R
See Chapter I, "The Peace
Mission Movement of Father
Divine."
Brean, H. "Prophet Jones in
Church and At Home." Life
(17; Nov. 27, 1944), pp. 22+.
                      DLC

Cantril, Hadley. The Psychology of Social Movements. New York: Wiley, 1941.
DHU/R; INU
Includes section on Father Divine and his Kingdom.
-- and Muzafu Sherif. "The Kingdom of Father Divine." Journal of Abnormal and Social Psychology (33; Apr., 1938), pp. 147-67.   DHU

Clark, Elmer T. The Small Sects in America. Nashville, Tenn.: Abingdon, 1937, 1949.
DHU/R; INU
Chapter 4, Negro sects, distinguishing five types of "charismatic" sects, most of them offshoots of regular churches, and all of them characterized by revivalism, emotionalism, and evangelism.

Daniel, Vattel Elbert. "Ritual in Chicago's South Side Churches for Negroes." Master's thesis, University of Chicago, 1940. DLC; CtY-D

Denlinger, S. "Heaven is in Harlem." Forum Century (95; Apr., 1936), pp. 211-18.
DCU/St

"The Dini Ya Israel." Sepia (14; Je., 1965), pp. 42-5.
DHU/MO

"Father Divine is Dead." Sepia (14; Nov., 1965), pp. 76-81.
DHU/MO

Fauset, Arthur H. Black Gods of the Metropolis. Philadelphia: University of Pennsylvania Press, 1944. DHU/MO
"Negro cults in the city."

Fisher, Miles Mark. "Organized Religion and the Cults." Crisis (44; Ja. 1937), pp. 8-10+.   DHU/MO
Negro author.

Garvey, Marcus. "The Back to Africa Movement: 1922." Bradford Chambers, (ed.). Chronicles of Black Protest (New York: The New America Library, 1968). DHU/MO

Garvey founded the African Orthodox Church, a black Christ and black Madonna.
Negro author.

Harris, Sara and Harriet Crittendon. Father Divine: Holy Husband. Garden City, N.Y.: Doubleday, 1953.
DHU/MO; INU

Harris, Sara. The Incredible Father Divine. London: Allen, 1954.   DHU/MO; INU

Hoshor, John. God is in a Rolls Royce; The Rise of Father Divine, Madman, Menace or Messiah. New York: Hillman-Curl, 1936. DHU/MO

Howell, C.V. "Father Divine: Another View; Reply to F.S. Mead." Christian Century (53:41, Oct., 7, 1936), p. 1332.   DHU/R

Jones, Raymond Julius. A Comparative Study of Religious Cult Behavior Among Negroes, With Special Reference to Emotional Group Conditioning Factors. Washington, D.C.: Pub. by the Graduate School for the Division of the Social Sciences, Howard University, 1939. DHU/R; CtY-D
Negro author.

Kelley, H. "Heaven Incorporated." American Magazine (121; Ja., 1936), pp. 40-1.
DHU

Lips, Julius. "God's Chillun Negerseklen in Washington." Mass und Werte, Zurich: (3:1, 1939), pp. 89-116.
NN/Sch
"Negro Cults, Solomon Lightfoot Michaux and Father Divine."

Lockley, Edith. "The Negro Spiritualist Churches of Nashville." Master's thesis, Fisk University, 1935.

Onwauchi, Patrick C. "Religious Concepts and Socio-Cultural Dynamics of Afro-American Religious Cults of St. Louis

(Onwauchi, P. C. cont.)
Missouri." Doctoral disser-
tation, St. Louis University,
1963.
Ottley, Roe. New World A-
Coming. Boston: Houghton
Miflin Co., 1943.   DHU/R
  Chapter 7, "I Talked with
God," an early account of the
Father Divine movement.
Parker, Robert A. The Incred-
ible Messiah: the Deification
of Father Divine. Boston:
Little, Brown & Co., 1937.
                       DHU/R; DLC
Rasky, Frank. "Harlem's Re-
ligious Zealots." Tomorrow
(9; Nov., 1949), pp. 11-17.
                       DHU/R
  Elder Lightfoot Solomon
Michaux, "Happy Am I Proph-
et," and Mother Rosa Artinus
Horne, "Pray for Me Priest-
ess."
"Second Front in Harlem: Elder
Michaux and His Choir."
Time (40; Dec. 21, 1942), pp.
74+.   DHU
"Spiritual Churches, Sects
Mark 35- Years of Growth."
Ebony (15; Oct., 1960), pp.
69+.   DHU/MO
Tallant, Robert. Voodoo in New
Orleans. New York: The
Macmillan Co., 1946.
                       DHU/MO
Tinker, E. L. "Mother Cather-
ine's Castor Oil; Visiting the
High Priestess of a Negro
Cult in New Orleans." North
American Review (230; Ag.,
1930), pp. 148-54.   DHU
Tyms, James Daniel. "A Study
of Four Religious Cults Op-
erating Among Negroes."
Master's thesis, Howard Uni-
versity, 1938.
  Negro author.
Williams, Chancellor. Have
You Been to the River? New
York: Exposition Press,
1952.   DHU/R
  Negro and cults, fiction.

Negro author.

v. Storefront Churches
Eddy, Norman G. "Store-front
Religion." Religion in Life
(28:1, Win., 1958-59), pp.
68-85.
Harrison, Ira E. "The Store-
front Church as a Revitaliza-
tion Movement." Hart M.
Nelsen & Raytha L. Yokley,
et al. The Black Church in
America (New York: Basic
Books, 1971), pp. 240-45.
                       DHU/R
  Also in Review of Religious
Research (7; Spr., 1966), pp.
160-63.
Hill, Hilley. "The Negro Store-
front Churches in Washington,
D. C." Master's thesis, How-
ard University, 1947.
  Negro author.
"Old Lafayette Gets Religion;
Harlem Theater Made Famous
by Lafayette Players Becomes
Live Wire Church." Our
World (8; Apr., 1953), pp.
48-51.   DHU/MO; DLC
Reapsome, J. W. "Storefront
Chapel that Grew and Grew."
Moody Monthly (68; Dec.,
1967), pp. 28-32.   DHU/R
Reid, Ira De A. "Storefront
Churches and Cults." Sher-
man, Richard B. The Negro
and the City (Englewood Cliffs.
N. J.: Prentice-Hall, 1970),
pp. 104-09.   DHU/R
  Negro author.
Schermerhoun, Richard A. These
Our People; Minorities in
American Culture. Boston:
D. C. Heath, 1949. DHU/MO
  Storefront church.
Sherman, Richard B., (ed.).
The Negro and the City. Engle-
wood, N.J.: Prentice Hall,
1970.   DHU/R
  Chapter V, storefront
churches and cults.
"Store-front Church." Our
World (7; My., 1952), pp.

62-5. DHU/MO; DLC
Williams, Chancellor. "The
Socio-Economic Significance
of the Store-Front Church
Movement in the United States
Since 1920." Doctoral disser-
tation, American University,

1949.   DHU/R
Negro author.
Willoughby, W. "Storefront
Churches: Social Stabilizers."
Christianity Today (13:16,
My. 9, 1969), pp. 44-5.
                          DHU/R

2. Negroes--Religion

a. Black Jews

"Black Jew-Hatred in Historical
Perspective." Jewish Specta-
tor (Ja. 1969), pp. 2+.   NN
"Black Migrants to a Promised
Land." Life (68:19; My., 22,
1970), pp. 65-8.   DHU
Resettlement of thirty-four
members of (Black) Hebrew-
Israelites in Israel.
Brotz, Howard. The Black Jews
of Harlem: Negro National-
ism and the Dilemmas of Ne-
gro Leadership. New York:
Free Press of Glencoe, 1964.
DHU/R; INU; DLC
Ehrman, Albert. "Exploration
and Responses." Journal of
Ecumenical Studies (8:1, Win.,
1971), pp. 103-14.   DHU/R
"Black Judaism in New
York."
"New York's Negro Jews." Lit-
erary Digest (100; Mr. 2,
1929), p. 27.   DHU
Wartgker, H. "Black Judaism.
in New York." Harvard Journal of Negro Affairs (1; 1967);
pp. 12-44.   DLC

b. Black Muslims

Ashmore, Harry S. The Other
Side of Jordan. New York:
W. W. Norton & Co.
DHU/MO; INU
Baldwin, James. The Fire Next
Time. New York: Dial Press,
1963. DHU/R; CtY-D
Negro author.

Berger, Morroe. "The Black
Muslims." Horizon (6; Ja.
1964), pp. 48-65. DAU; DGU
Bontemps, Arna Wendell and
Jack Conroy. "Registered with
Allah." David M. Reimers,
(ed.). The Black Man in
America Since Reconstruction
(New York: Thomas Y. Cro-
well, 1970), pp. 263-90.
INU; DHU/MO
Taken from Arna Bontemps
and Jack Conroy Anyplace But
Here (New York: Hill & Wang,
Inc., 1966), pp. 216-41.
Copyright 1945, 1966.
Originally published as They
Seek a City. Discusses the
origin and growth of the Black
Muslims.
Breitman, George. The Last
Year of Malcolm X: the Evo-
lution of a Revolutionary. New
York: Merit Publishing, 1967.
DLC; INU; DHU/R
--(ed.). Malcolm X Speaks.
New York: Merit Publishers,
1965.   DHU/R
Brown, L. P. "Black Muslims
and the Police." Journal of
Criminal Law, Criminology
and Police Science (56; Mr.,
1965), pp. 119-26.
DAU; DLC
Burns, W. Haywood. "Black
Muslims in America: A Re-
interpretation." Race 5; Jl.,
1963), pp. 26-37.   DLC
California. Investigation; Para-
military Organizations in California. Sacramento: 1965.

(California cont.)
(In Misc. doc. , Vol. 1429).
NcD/L
Investigation of actions of
Black Muslims.
Calverley, Edwin Elliott. Negro
Muslims in Hartford. Hart-
ford: Hartford Seminary
Foundation, 1965. INU
Clark, Kenneth Bancroft. The
Negro Protest: James Bald-
win, Malcolm X, Martin Lu-
ther King, talk with Kenneth
B. Clark. Boston: Beacon
Press, 1963. NcD; DHU/R
Clark, Michael. "Rise in Racial
Extremism." New York Times
Jan. 25, 1960. DHU
"Constitution Law-Black Muslim-
ism is a Religion Within the
Meaning of the First Amend-
ment." Georgia Bar Journal
(24; My. , 1962), pp. 519+.
DHU/L
Crabitès, P. "American Negro
Mohammedans." Catholic
World (136; Feb. , 1933), pp.
559-66. DHU
"Discretion of Director of Cor-
rections not Abused in Refus-
ing to Grant Black Muslims
Prisoners Rights Afforded
Other Religious Groups."
UCLA Law Review (9; Mr. ,
1962), pp. 501+. DLC
Drimmer, Melvin, (ed.). Black
History, a Reappraisal. New
York: Doubleday, 1969.
DHU/R
pp. 440+ On the role of
Martin Luther King. pp. 454+
The Black Muslims as a pro-
test movement.
Eddy, George Norman. Black
Racist Religion. Boston: n. p. ,
1962. Pam. File, NcD
Edwards, H. "Black Muslim
and Negro Christian Family
Relationships," Journal of
Marriage and Family (Nov. ,
1968), p. 604. DHU/R
"8, 500 Crowd Armory to Hear
Muhammed." Amsterdam

News (Ag. 6, 1960). DHU/MO
Elkholy, Abdo A. "Religion and
Assimilation in two Muslim
Communities in America."
Doctoral dissertation, Prince-
ton University, 1960.
"The End of Malcolm X." Sepia
(14; My. , 1965), pp. 14-19.
DHU/MO
Essien-Udom, Essien Udosen.
Black Nationalism; a Search
for an Identity in America.
Chicago: University of Chicago
Press, 1963.
DHU/R; INU; CtY-D
Haley, Alex. "Mr. Muhammed
Speaks." Readers Digest (76;
Mr. 1960), pp. 110-14. DHU
Hatchett, John F. "The Moslem
Influence Among American
Negroes." Journal of Human
Relations (10; Sum., 1962),
pp. 375-82. DHU
Hentoff, Nat. "Elijah in the
Wilderness." Reporter (23;
Ag. 4, 1960), pp. 37-40.
DLC
Hernton, Calvin C. "White Lib-
erals and Black Muslims."
Negro Digest (12; Oct. , 1963),
pp. 3-9. DLC
Howard, John R. "Becoming a
Black Muslim: A Study of
Commitment Processes in a
Deviant Political Organization,"
Doctoral dissertation, Stanford
University, 1965.
Howell, Hazel W. "Black Mus-
lim Affiliation as Reflected in
Attitudes and Behavior of Ne-
gro Adolescents With its Ef-
fect on Policies and Adminis-
trative Procedures in Schools
of two Eastern Cities, 1961-
64." Doctoral dissertation,
Columbia University, 1966.
Illo, John. "The Rhetoric of
Malcolm X." The Columbia
University Forum (9:2, Sept. ,
1966), pp. 5-12.
Pam. File, DHU/R
Karpas, Melvin Ronald. The
Black Muslims as the Negro

Segregationalists. Chicago:
Chicago Teachers College,
1964.   INU
Kirman, J. M. "Challenge of the
Black Muslims." Social Education (27; Nov., 1963), pp.
365-68.   DHU; DAU
Krosney, Herbert. "America's
Black Supremacists." Nation
(192; My., 6, 1961), pp. 390-
92.   DHU
Lacey, Leslie A. "African Re-
sponses to Malcolm X." Le-
Roi Jones and Neal Larry,
(eds.). Black Fire (New York:
William Morrow and Co.,
1968).   DHU/MO
Laue, James E. "A Contempo-
rary Revitalization Movement
in American Race Relations;
The Black Muslims." Social
Forces (42; Mr., 1964), pp.
315-23.   DGU; DAU
Leiman, Melvin. "Malcolm X."
Liberation (10:2, Apr., 1965),
pp. 25-27.   DHU/R
Lincoln, Charles Eric. "The
Black Muslims." Progressive
(26:12, Dec., 1962), p. 43.
                          DGU
Negro author.
-- "Extremist Attitudes in the
Black Muslim Movement."
New South (18:1, Ja., 1963),
pp. 3-10.   DHU/R
-- The Black Muslims in Amer-
ica. Boston: Beacon Press,
1961.
"This book originated as a
dissertation... in the Graduate
School of Boston University."
-- My Face is Black. Boston:
Beacon Press, 1961.
                   DHU/R; INU
-- Sounds of the Struggle: Per-
sons and Perspectives of the
Civil Rights. New York: Mor-
row, 1967.   DHU/R; INU
pp. 32-75+, Black Muslims.
Little, Malcolm. The Autobiog-
raphy of Malcolm X. New
York: Grove Press, 1965.
                   DHU/R; INU

Negro author.
-- (Malcolm X). "Malcolm X and
the Black Muslims, 1964."
Bradford Chambers, (ed.).
Chronicles of Black Protest.
(New York: The New Ameri-
can Library, 1968.)
                       DHU/MO
pp. 200-11.
-- Malcolm X Speaks: Selected
Speeches and Statements. New
York: Grove Press, 1966.
                   DHU/R; INU
-- The Speeches of Malcolm X at
Harvard. Edited, with an in-
troductory essay by Archie
Epps. New York: W. Morrow,
1968.   NcD
Lomax, Louis E. The Negro Re-
volt. New York: Harper,
1962.   DHU/R; INU
pp. 164-177, Black Muslims.
Negro author.
-- When the Word is Given: A
Report on Elijah Muhammad,
Malcolm X and the Black Mus-
lim World. Cleveland: World
Pub. Co., 1963.
                CtY-D; DHU/R
Maesen, William A. "Watchtower
Influences on Black Muslim
Eschatology: An Exploratory
Story." Journal for the Scien-
tific Study of Religion (9:4,
Win., 1970), pp. 321-25.
                       DHU/R
Martin, Walter Ralston. The
Kingdom of the Cults: An An-
alysis of the Major Cults Sys-
tems in the Present Christian
Era. Grand Rapids: Zonder-
van Pub. Co., 1965.   INU
"The Meaning of Malcolm X."
The Christian Century (82:14,
Apr. 7, 1965), pp. 431-33.
                       DHU/R
Moon, Henry L. "Enigma of
Malcolm X." Crisis (72; Apr.,
1965), pp. 226-7. DHU/MO
Morsell, John A. "Black Na-
tionalism." Journal of Inter-
group Relations. (3; Win.,
1961-62), pp. 5-11.   DLC

"Muslims Ask Leaders to Rally."
Amsterdam News (My. 28,
1960).   DHU/MO
N'Daye, Jean Pierre. Les Noirs
aux Etats-Unis Pour les Af-
ricains. Paris: n.p., 1964.
                               INU
Parenti, Michael. "The Black
Muslims: From Revolution to
Institution." Social Research
(31; 1964), pp. 175-94. DGU
Poole, Elijah (Elijah Muhammed).
How to Eat to Live. Chicago:
Muhammed Mosque of Islam
No. 2, 1967.   NcD
-- Message to the Blackman.
Chicago: Muhammad Mosque
of Islam No. 2, 1965.
                        INU; NcD
-- "What the Muslims Believe."
Harvey Wish, (ed.). The Ne-
gro Since Emancipation.
(Englewood Cliffs, N.J.:
Prentice-Hall, Inc., 1964),
pp. 181-2.   DHU/R
Poulard, Grady E. "The Black
Muslims: Racism on the Re-
bound." United Church Herald
(5:8, Apr. 19, 1962), pp. 14-
15.   DHU/R
Negro author.
Raab, Earl, ed. American Race
Relations Today. Garden City,
N.Y.: Doubleday, 1962.
                          DHU/MO
pp. 179-90, Black Mus-
lims.
Record, Wilson. "Extremist
Movements Among American
Negroes." Phylon (17; Spr.,
1956), pp. 17-23. DHU/MO
Black Muslims.
-- "The Negro Intellectual and
Negro Nationalism." Social
Forces (32; Oct., 1954), pp.
10-18.   DHU
"The Right to Practice Black
Muslim Tenents in State Pris-
ons." Harvard Law Review
(75; Feb., 1962), pp. 837+.
                          DHU/L
Rose, Arnold M. Assuring Free-
dom to the Free. Detroit:

Wayne State University, 1964.
                          DHU/MO
"The Black Muslims as a
Protest Movement," by C.
Eric Lincoln.
Samuels, Gertrude. "Feud Within
the Black Muslims." New
York Times Magazine, Mr.
22, 1964.   DLC
-- "Two Ways: Black Muslims
and NAACP." New York
Times Magazine, May 12,
1963.   DLC
Schaller, Lyle E. "Black Mus-
lims and White Protestants."
Christian Advocate (7; Feb.
14, 1963), pp. 9+.
                    DHU/R; DAU/W
Shack, William S. "Black Mus-
lims: A Nativistic Religious
Movement Among Negro Amer-
icans." Race (3; Nov., 1961),
pp. 57-67.   DLC
Sharrieff, Osman. Islam in
North America. Chicago:
n.p., 1961.   DLC
Sherwin, Mark. The Extremists.
New York: St. Martin's
Press, 1964.   INU
pp. 190-212, Black Mus-
lims.
Spellman, A.B. "Interview with
Malcolm X." Monthly Review
(May, 1964).   DHU
Thorne, Richard. "Integration
or Black Nationalism; Which
Route Will Negroes Choose?"
Negro Digest (12; Ag., 1963),
pp. 36-47.   DHU
Vernon, Robert. The Black
Ghetto. Preface by Rev. Al-
bert B. Cleage, Jr., Introduc-
tion by James Shabazz. New
York: Merit Publishers, 1965.
                          DHU/R
"Articles originally ap-
peared in the socialist news-
paper, The Militant.
Williams, Daniel Thomas. The
Black Muslims in the United
States: a Selected Bibliogra-
phy. Tuskegee, Ala.: Hollis

Burke Frissell Library, Tuskegee Institute, 1964. CtY-D

c. Migrations--Effect on Religion

Barton, John W. "Negro Migration." Methodist Quarterly

Review (74:1, Ja., 1925), pp. 84-101.   DHU/R
Beynon, Erdmann D. "Voodoo Cult Among Negro Migrants in Detroit." American Journal of Sociology, (43; My., 1938), pp. 894-907.   DHU

3.   Evaluation and Aspects of Negro Religion and Church

Abbott, Ernest H. Religious Life in America: A Record of Personal Observation. New York: Outlook Co., 1902.
            DHU/R; NN/Sch
    For Negro Church, see pp. 81-104.
-- "Religious Tendencies of Negroes." Outlook (69; 1901), p. 1070.   DCU/SW
Ackiss, Thelma D. "Changing Pattersn of Religious Thought Among Negroes." Social Forces (23; Dec. 1944), pp. 212-15.   DHU
Aldrich, G. B. "Church and the Negro." Commonweal (9; Feb. 13, 1929), pp. 432-3.
Allensworth, A. M. "The Great Children's Preacher of the Gospel, Chaplain of the 24th Infantry of the U. S., Presidential Elector, Agent of the American Baptist Publication Society." Simmons, Wm. J., (ed.), Men of Mark... (Cleveland, O.: Geo. M. Rewell & Co., 1887), p. 843. DHU/R
American Baptist Home Mission Society. The Christian Education of the Negro. n. p., 1910.
            NN/Sch
"American Negro Churches, Membership and Contributions; Table." Missionary Review of the World (59; Je., 1936), p. 36.   DHU/R
"Are Negroes Losing Religion?" Ebony (5; Ag., 1950), pp. 44-45.   DHU/MO
Arnett, Benjamin W. Colored

Sunday Schools. Nashville: A. M. E. Sunday School Union, 1896.   OWibfU
    Negro author.
Arnold, Benjamin. "A Negro Looks at His Church." Zion's Herald (116; Je. 22, 1939), p. 800.   DLC; CtY-D
"Baha'i a Way of Life for Millions." Ebony (20; Apr., 1965), pp. 48-50+.   DHU/MO
Baker, Ray Stannard. Following the Color Line: An Account of Negro Citizenship in the American Democracy. New York: Doubleday, Page & Co., 1908.   DHU/MO
Bardolph, Richard. "Negro Religious and Educational Leaders in 'Who's Who in America,' 1936-1955." Journal of Negro Education (26:2, Spr., 1957), pp. 182-92.   DHU/R
Beatty-Brown, Florence Rebekah. "The Negro as Portrayed by the St. Louis Post-Dispatch from 1920-1950." Doctoral dissertation, University of Illinois, 1951.
Berrigan, P. F. "Christianity in Harlem." Commonweal (81; Nov. 27, 1964), pp. 323-5.
            DHU
Billings, R.A. "The Negro and His Church: A Psychogenetic Study." Psychoanalytic Review (21; Oct., 1934), pp. 425-41.
            DHU/MED
Blacknall, O. W. "New Departure in Religion Among Negroes." Atlantic Monthly (52;

(Blacknall, O. W. cont.)
Nov., 1883), pp. 680-85.
                DHU; NN/Sch
"Blames Negro Ministry for Lag-
ging Churches." Christian
Century (67:33, Ag. 16, 1950),
p. 964.   DHU/R
Boatright, Mody Coggin. From
Hell to Breakfast, edited by
Mody C. Boatright and Donald
Day, Dallas: Southern Meth-
odist University Press, 1967.
                DLC; NN/Sch
   Publications of the Folklore
Society, no. 19.
Bowen, Trevor. Divine White
Right; A Study of Race Segre-
gation and Inter-Racial Coop-
eration in Religious Organiza-
tions and Institutions in the
United States, with a section
on "The Church and Education
for Negroes," by Ira De A.
Reid. New York and London:
Pub. for the Institute of Social
and Religious Research,
Harper & Bros., 1934.
        NN/Sch; DHU/R; DHU/MO
   Ch. 3-5, the Negro's
Church, Churches & Slavery
and Christian Associations.
Boyer, Laura F. Wanted--
Leaders! A Study in Negro
Development: Suggestions for
Groups Discussion and Indi-
vidual Study. New York: Pre-
siding Bishop and Council,
Dept. of Missions and Church
Extension, 1922.   NN/Sch
Bracey, John M. and August
Meier. Black Nationalism in
America. New York: The
Bobbs-Merrill Co., 1970.
                        DHU/R
   Pt. 1, Foundation of the
Black Community: the Church,
pp. 3-17+.
Bradley, L. Richard. "The
Curse of Canaan and the
American Negro." Concordia
Theological Monthly (42:2,
Feb., 1971), pp. 100-10.
                        DHU/R

Bragg, George Freeman. Afro-
American Church and Workers.
Baltimore, Md.: Church Advo-
cate Printers, 1904.
                DHU/MO; NN/Sch
   Negro author.
-- "Beginning of Negro Church
Work in the South." Living
Church (65; Ag. 20, 1921),
p. 505.   CtY; DLC
-- The First Negro Organization.
The Free African Society, Es-
tablished on April 12th, 1787.
Baltimore: Pub. by the author,
1927.   DHU/MO
--The First Negro Priest on
Southern Soil. Baltimore:
Church Advocate Print., 1909.
        DHU/MO; A&M; NN/Sch
-- How the Black Man Found the
Church. Baltimore, Md.:
n. p., n. d.   DHU/MO
Brawley, Benjamin Griffin. A
Prayer. Words by B. G.
Brawley, music by A. H. Ry-
der in (Atlanta, Ga.). At-
lanta: Baptist College Press,
1899.   DHU/MO
   Negro author.
-- A Short History of the Ameri-
can Negro. New York: The
Macmillan Co., 1917.
        DHU/R; DHU/MO; CtY-D
Brawley, Edward MacKnight. Sin
and Salvation. A Text Book on
Evangelism. Revised by Benja-
min Brawley. Philadelphia:
Judson Press, 1925.
                        DHU/MO
   Negro author.
Brisbane, Robert H. The Black
Vanguard. Valley Forge:
Judson Press, 1970. DHU/M
   Contains information on the
black church.
Brooks, Walter H. "Religion."
Washington Conference on the
Race Problem in the United
States. National Sociological
Society. How to Solve the Race
Problem (Washington, D. C.:
Beresford, Printer, 1904), pp.
212-27.   DHU/R

Minister of the Nineteenth
Street Baptist Church, Wash.,
D. C.
Negro author.
Brotz, Howard. Negro Social
and Political Thought, 1850-
1920; Representative Texts.
New York: Basic Books, 1966.
            CtY-D; DHU/R
Part two, Black Christians.
Brown, Archer W. Did Jesus
Christ Have Negro Blood in
Him? Wonder of the Century.
Newark, N. J.: Archer W.
Brown, 1908.   DHU/MO
Brown, Ina Corinne. The Story
of the American Negro. New
York: Friendship Press, 1936.
            DHU/R; OWibfU
Brown, M. R. "The Negro in
His Religious Aspect." South-
ern Workman (17; 1875), p.
498.   NIC
Brown, Williams Wells. The
Black Man: His Antecedents,
His Genius, and His Achieve-
ments... Miami, Fla.: Mne-
mosyne Pub. Co., 1969.
            DHU/R
Negro author.
"Originally published in
1865."
Buehrer, E. T. "Harlem's God."
Christian Century (52; Dec. 11,
1935), pp. 1590-3.   DHU/R
A Call Upon the Church for Pro-
gressive Action, to Elevate
the Colored American People.
Fall River: n.p., 1848. DLC
"Beginning with a protest
against the use of the term
"African" by churches of the
colored people, the writer de-
scribes the various Negro
churches of Philadelphia and
New York."
Canzoneri, Robert. I Do So Po-
litely, a Voice from the
South. Boston: Houghton Miff-
lin Co., 1965.   DHU/R
Chapters 7 and 9 on the
Negro church.
Carrington, William E. "Negro

Youth and the Religious Education Program of the Church."
Journal of Negro Education
(9; Jl., 1940), pp. 388-96.
            DHU
Carroll, Charles. The Tempter
of Eve; or the Criminality of
Man's Social, Political and Religious Equality with the Negro, and the Amalgamation to
which these Crimes Inevitably
Lead. Discussed in the Light
of the Scriptures. St. Louis:
The Adamic Pub. Co., 1902.
            DHU/MO
Carroll, H. K. "The Negro in
His Relations to the Church."
J. W. E. Bowen, (ed.). Africa
and the American Negro: Addresses and Proceedings of
the Congress on Africa. (Mi-
ami, Fla.: Mnemosyne Pub.
Co., 1969), pp. 215-18.
            DHU/R
-- "Religious Progress of Negroes." Forum (14; 1893), pp.
75+.   DHU
Carter, Edward Randolph. The
Black Side; a Partial History
of the Business, Religious and
Educational Side of the Negro
in Atlanta, Ga. Atlanta, Ga.:
n. p., 1894.   DHU/MO
Carter, Randall Albert, (bp.).
"What the Negro Church has
Done." Journal of Negro History (11:1, Ja., 1926), pp. 1-
7.   DHU
Negro author.
Catchings, L. Maynard. "The
Social Relevance of the School
of Religion of Howard University: A Study of the Bachelor
of Divinity Curriculum Content
and its Bearing upon the Social Purpose of the School and
the Social Obligation Felt by
its Graduates. B.D. Paper,
School of Religion, Howard
University, 1941.
Cayton, Horace. "E. Franklin
Frazier: A Tribute and a Review." Review of Religious

(Cayton, H. cont.)
Research (5; Spr., 1964), pp.
137-42.
Review of Frazier's post-
humously published the Negro
Church.
Cheshire, Joseph B. The Church
in the Confederate States.
n.p., 1912.   GAU
pp. 106-34, The Church
and the Negro.
Chivers, W.R. "Religion in Negro Colleges." Journal of Negro Education (9; Ja., 1940),
pp. 5-12.   DHU/MO
Clark, William A. "Sanctifica-
tion in Negro Religion." Social
Forces. (15; My., 1937), pp.
544-51.   DHU
Cleaver, Eldridge. Soul on Ice.
New York: McGraw-Hill,
1968.   DHU/R
Negro author.
pp. 30-39 his religious con-
victions.
Clement, Rufus E. "The Church
School as a Factor in Negro
Life." Journal of Negro History (12:1, Ja., 1927), pp. 5-
12.   DHU/MO
Clemes, W.W. "Heaven Comes
to Harlem." Negro Digest
(8:5, My., 1950), pp. 66-71.
            DHU/MO
"East Harlem church brings
useful Christianity to people in
urban ghetto."
Clinton, George W. "Evangelism." Arcadius S. Trawick,
(ed.). The New Voice in Race
Adjustments. (New York: Student Volunteer Movement,
1914), pp. 107-12.   DHU/R
Negro author.
Clyde, Nathana Lore. ...The Application of the Teachings and
Example of Christ to the Relationship of the Native Citizen to the Immigrant, by Nathana L. Clyde. First prize,
1913. A Practical Application
of Christianity to the American Race Problem, by William

Burkholder. Second prize,
1913. Lawrence: University
of Kansas, 1913. (Hattie Eliza-
beth Lewis memorial essays in
applied Christianity).
            NN/Sch
Cockin, Frederic Arthur, (bp.).
The Problem of Race; Being
Outline Studies Based on
"Christianity and the Race
Problem," by J.H. Oldham...
By F. A. Cockin... London:
Student Christian Movement,
1924.   NN/Sch
Coles, R. "When I Draw the
Lord He'll Be a Real Big
Man." The Atlantic (My, 1966),
p. 69.   DHU
Conference on Education for Ne-
groes in Texas. Proceedings
of the Tenth Educational Con-
ference. The Negro Church in
Texas as an Educational Agen-
cy. Ed. and Comp. by John
B. Cade and Walter R. Harri-
son. Bul. v. 31, no. 1.
Hempstead, Tex.: Prairie
View State Normal & Industri-
al College, Prairie View Col-
lege Branch, 1939.   NN/Sch
Conference on Science, Philosophy
and Religion in their Relation to
the Democratic Way of Life.
Perspectives on a Troubled
Decade: Science, Philosophy,
and Religion, 1939-1949.
Tenth Symposium, ed. by Lyman Bryson, Louis Finkelstein
(and) R.M. MacIver, New
York: Conference on Science,
Philosophy and Religion in
their Relation to the Democratic Way of Life, Inc. New
York: Harper, 1950. DHU/R
Conference on the Relation of the
Church of the Colored People of
the South. Conference on the Re-
lation of the Church to the Colored People of the South.
Protestant Episcopal Church,
n.p., 1883.   DHU/MO
Coppin, Levi J., (bp.). "The
American Negro's Religion for

the African Negro's Soul."
Independent (54; Mr. 27, 1902),
pp. 748-50.   DHU
    Negro author.
-- Episcopal Addresses Deliv-
    ered by Bishop Levi J. Cop-
    pin. Philadelphia: A. M. E.
    Book Concern, May, 1916.
                            DHU/MO
-- Fifty-two Suggestive Sermon
    Syllabi. Philadelphia: A. M. E.
    Book Concern, 1910. DHU/MO
-- Fifty Years of Religious Prog-
    ress: an Emancipation Ser-
    mon. Delivered on the occa-
    sion of the Emancipation
    Semi-Centennial, Philadelphia,
    Pa., Sunday, September 14th,
    1913. Philadelphia: A. M. E.
    Book Concern Printers, 1913.
                            NN/Sch
-- Key to Scripture Interpreta-
    tion. Philadelphia: A. M. E.
    Publishing House, 1895.
                            DHU/MO
-- Unwritten History. Philadel-
    phia: A. M. E. Book Concern,
    1919.   NN/Sch; A&M
Cromwell, John Wesley. "First
    Negro Churches in the District
    of Columbia." Journal of Ne-
    gro History (8; Ja., 1922),
    pp. 64-106.   DHU/MO
    Negro author.
-- The Negro in American His-
    tory... Washington, D. C.:
    The American Negro Acad-
    emy, 1914. DHU/R; NN/Sch
    Chapters 16, 17, Negro
    Church, Slavery.
Crook, Roger H. No South or
    North. St. Louis, Mo.:
    Bethany Press, 1959.
                    CtY-D; NN/Sch
Curran, Francis X. Major
    Trends in American Church
    History... New York: The
    American Press, 1946.
                            NN/Sch
    Negro Church, pp. 107-20.
Daniel, Vattel Elbert. "Negro
    Classes and Life in the
    Church." Journal of Negro

Education (13; Wint., 1944),
    pp. 19-29.   DHU
-- "Ritual and Stratification in
    Chicago Negro Churches."
    American Sociological Review
    (7; Je., 1942), pp. 353-58.
                            DHU/R
    Described types of behavior
    in ecstatic cults.
Daniel, William Andrew. The
    Education of Negro Ministers,
    based upon a Survey of Theo-
    logical Schools for Negroes in
    the United States made by
    Robert L. Kelly and W. A.
    Daniel. New York: Geo. H.
    Doran Co., 1925.   DHU/R
Darrow, Clarence and R. E.
Jones. "The Religion of the
    American Negro." Crisis (38;
    My., 1931), pp. 190-92.
                            DHU/MO
Davenport, F. M. "The Religion
    of the American Negro." Ec-
    lectic Magazine of Foreign
    Literature (145; Dec., 1905),
    pp. 609-14.   DLC
Davie, Maurice Rea. Negroes in
    American Society. New York:
    McGraw-Hill Book Co., 1949.
            DHU/R; CHU/MO; CtY-D
Diggs, James R. "Negro Church
    Life." Voice of the Negro (1:
    2, Feb., 1904), pp. 46-50.
        DHU/MO; DLC; NN/Sch
Dodson, Dan. "The Role of In-
    stitutional Religion in Ethnic
    Groups of Dallas." Master's
    thesis, Southern Methodist
    University, 1936.
Dollard, John. Caste and Class
    in a Southern Town. New
    Haven: Pub. for the Institute
    of Human Relations by Yale
    University Press, 1937.
                    CtY-D; DHU/MO
    Chapter 11, caste patterns
    in religion.
Douglass, William. Annals of
    the First African Church, in
    the United States of America,
    Now Styled the African Epis-
    copal Church of St. Thomas,

(Douglass, W. cont.)
Philadelphia. Established by
Absalom Jones, Richard Allen
and others, in 1787, and
Partly from the Minister of
the Aforesaid Church. Phila-
delphia: King & Baird, 1862.
DHU/MO; NN/Sch
Negro author.
--Sermons Preached in the Afri-
can Protestant Episcopal
Church of St. Thomas, Phila-
delphia. Philadelphia: King &
Baird, 1854.
DHU/MO; NcD; NN/Sch
Dowd, Jerome. The Negro
Races, a Sociological Study.
New York: The Macmillan
Co., 1907. DHU/MO; CtY-D
Chapters 23-29, Negro
church.
Du Bois, William Edward Burg-
hardt. Darkwater; Voices from
Within the Veil. New York:
Harcourt, Brace & Howe,
1920. DHU/MO; DHU/R; CtY-D
Negro author.
-- The Gift of Black Folk; the
Negroes in the Making of
America. Boston: The Strat-
ford Co., 1924.   DHU/MO
Chapter 10, The Gift of
the spirit.
-- "The Negro Church in Phila-
delphia." Richard B. Sher-
man, (ed.). The Negro and
the City. (Englewood Cliffs,
N.J.: Prentice Hall, 1970),
pp. 100-04.   DHU/R
--The Negro Church; Report of
a Social Study Made under the
Direction of Atlanta University; Together with the Proceedings of the Eighth Conference for the Study of the Negro Problems, Held at At-
lanta University, May 26th,
1903. Atlanta, Ga.: The Atlanta University Press, 1903.
DHU/MO; DLC
-- "Negro Church." Political
Science Quarterly (19; Dec.,
1904), pp. 703-04.   DHU

-- "The Negro in the Black Belt:
Some Social Studies." Wash-
ington, D.C.: U.S. Dept. of
Labor Bulletin, (4:22, My.,
1899), pp. 401-17. DHU/MO
-- The Philadelphia Negro: A
Social Study. Philadelphia:
University of Pennsylvania
Press, 1899.   DHU/MO
-- "Religion of Negroes." New
World (9; 1900), p. 614.
DCU/RE
-- The Souls of Black Folk. Chi-
cago: A.C. McClurg and Co.,
1903. DHU/R; DHU/MO;
CtY-D
Negro Church, pp. 190-91.
Earnest, Joseph B. The Reli-
gious Development of the Ne-
gro in Virginia. Charlottes-
ville, Va.: Michie Co., 1914.
CtY-D; DLC; NN/Sch
Issued earlier as doctoral
dissertation, University of
Virginia.
Eason, James Henry. Pulpit
and Platform Efforts. Sancti-
fications vs. Fanaticism...
Nashville, Tenn.: National
Baptist Publishing Board,
1899.   DHU/MO; NN/Sch
Ebony. The White Problem in
America, by the Editors of
Ebony Magazine. Chicago:
Johnson Publishing Co., 1966.
DHU/R
Eddy, Ansel Doane. "Black
Jacob," a Monument of Grace.
The Life of Jacob Hodges, an
African who Died in Canandai-
gua, N.Y., Feb. 1842...
Philadelphia: American Sunday
School Union, 1842. DHU/MO
Edwards, V.A. "Religion and
Rural Life... A Description of
a Program for Rural Life Im-
provement Through the Church
in Rural Georgia Communities."
"A paper prepared at Fort
Valley College, Fort Valley,
Ga., 1943.
Eleazer, Robert Burns. Reason,
Religion, and Race. New

(Eleazer, R. B. cont.)
York: Abingdon-Cokesbury,
1950.   NN/Sch
Ellison, John Malcus. Negro
Organizations and Leadership
in Relation to Rural Life in
Virginia. Virginia Agricultural
Station, 1933.   DHU/MO
Negro author.
Also Doctoral dissertation,
Drew University.
-- and C. H. Hamilton. The Ne-
gro Church in Rural Virginia.
Blacksburg, Va.: Virginia
Polytechnic Institute, Virginia
Agricultural Bulletin 27340.
                          DHU/MO
Negro authors.
-- Tensions and Destiny. Rich-
mond: Knox Press, 1953.
                 DHU/MO; NN/Sch
Ely, Effie Smith. "American
Negro Poetry." Christian Cen-
tury (40; Mr. 22, 1923), pp.
366-67.   DHU/R
A discussion of religious
protest poetry.
Embree, Edwin Rogers. Amer-
ican Negroes, a Handbook.
New York: the John Day Co.,
1942.   DHU/MO; CtY-D
-- Brown America; the Story of
a New Race. New York: The
Friendship Press, 1936.
         DHU/R; DHU/MO; CtY-D
Encyclopedia of the Negro,
Preparatory Volume with Ref-
erence Lists and Reports, by
W. E. DuBois and Guy B.
Johnson...Prepared with the
Cooperation of E. Irene Diggs,
Agnes C. L. Donohugh, Guion
Johnson and Others. New
York: The Phelps-Stokes
Fund, Inc., 1946.
                 DHU/MO; CtY-D
Eubanks, John B. "Modern
Trends in the Religion of the
American Negro." Doctoral
dissertation, University of
Chicago, 1947.
Faduma, Orishatukeh. ...The
Defects of the Negro Church.

Washington, D. C.: The Acad-
emy, 1904.
       DHU/MO; DLC; NN/Sch
Felton, Ralph Almon. Go Down
Moses; a Study of 21 Success-
ful Negro Rural Pastors.
Madison, N. J.: Dept. of the
Rural Church, Drew Theologi-
cal Seminary, 1952.
                   DLC; DHU/R
-- These My Brethren; a Study
of 570 Negro Churches and
1542 Negro Homes in the Rur-
al South. Madison, N. J.:
Dept. of the Rural Church,
Drew Theological Seminary,
1950. DHU/R; CtY-D; NN/Sch
Ferm, Vergilius Ture Anselm.
The American Church of the
Protestant Heritage. New
York: Philosophical Library,
1953.   DHU/R; INU
Fickland, R. William. The Ideal
Christian Ministry. Philadel-
phia: A. M. E. Book Concern,
1910.   NN/Sch
Negro author.
Fisher, Miles Mark. "Negro
Church and the World War."
Journal of Religion (5:5, Sept.,
1925), pp. 483-99. DHU/R
Negro author.
Discusses effect of World
War I on the Negro Church.
-- "Negroes as Christian Minis-
ters." Journal of Negro Edu-
cation (4; Jan., 1935), pp.
53-9.   DHU
-- "Negroes Get Religion." Op-
portunity (14:5, My., 1936),
pp. 147-50.   DHU/MO
Flynn, R. O. "Cooperation Be-
tween Pastors of White and
Colored Churches." Arcadius
S. Trawick, (ed.) The New
Voice in Race Adjustments
(New York: Student Volunteer
Movement), pp. 183-8.
                          DHU/R
Ford, C. E. and G. Schinert.
"The Relation of Ethnocentric
Attitudes to Intensity of Reli-
gious Practice." Journal of

Educational Sociology (32; 1958), pp. 157-62.
DAU; DCU/ED; DGU

Forrest, Edna Mae. "The Religious Development of the Negro in South Carolina Since 1865." Master's thesis, Howard University, 1928.

Fowler, Andrew. "Negro Churches as Revealed by the U.S. Census of Religious Bodies for 1936." Master's thesis, Howard University, 1943.

Fox, William K. "Experiments in Southern Rural Religious Developments Among Negroes." Bachelor of Divinity thesis, University of Chicago, 1943.

Frazier, Edward Franklin. Black Bourgeoisie. Glencoe, Ill.: The Free Press, 1957.
DHU/R
Negro author.
"Rise of the Negro middle class in the United States with corresponding modifications in religious values and behavior." pp. 209-12.

-- The Negro Church in America. New York: Schocken Books, 1964.   DHU/R; DLC

-- ... The Negro in the United States. New York: Macmillan, 1949. DHU/R; NN/Sch; CtY-D
Negro church, pp. 334-66.

Frucht, Richard, (ed.). Black Society in the New World. New York: Random House, 1971.   DHU/R
Part V, Religion.

Fry, C. Luther. The United States Looks at its Churches. New York: Institute of Social and Religious Research, 1930.
DHU/R
Chart showing the white and Negro adult population in churches by sex, 1926.

Fuller, Thomas Oscar. Pictorial History of the American Negro; a Story of Progress

and Development Along Social, Political, Economic, Educational and Spiritual Lines. Memphis, Tenn.: Pictorial History, Inc., 1933.
DHU/MO; NN/Sch

"Future of the Negro Churches." Christian Century (47; Sept. 17, 1930), pp. 1110-11.
DHU/R

"Discussion." (47; Oct. 15, 1930), pp. 1252-3. DHU/R

Gandy, Samuel L. "Negro Church and the Adult Education Phases of its Program." Journal of Negro Education (14; Sum., 1945), pp. 381-4.
DHU
Negro author.

-- Prayers of a Chaplain. Petersburg: Virginia State College, 1955.
Mim. Pam. File; DHU/R

Garnet, Henry Highland. "If You Must Bleed, Let it Come All At Once." Thomas Wagstaff, (ed.). Black Power. The Radical Response to White America. Beverly Hills: Glencol Press, 1909, pp. 32-40.   DHU/R
Negro author.

-- The Past and the Present Condition, and the Destiny of the Colored Race: A Discourse Delivered at the Fifteenth Anniversary of the Female Benevolent Society of Troy, N.Y., Feb. 14, 1848... Troy: J.C. Kneeland & Co., 1848.
DHU/MO

Gelman, Martin. "Adat Boyt Moshe--the Colored House of Moses: A Study of a Contemporary Negro Religious Community and Its Leaders." Doctoral dissertation, University of Pennsylvania, 1965.

Gibson, John William. Progress of a Race; or, The Remarkable Advancement of the American Negro from the Bondage of Slavery, Ignorance and Pov-

erty to the Freedom of Citizenship, Intelligence, Affluence, Honor and Trust. Rev. and enl. by J. L. Nichols and Wm. H. Crogman. Naperville, Ill. : I. L. Nichols & Co. , (c1929).
DHU/MO; NN/Sch
Religion and the Negro, pp. 307-28.

Gibson, Joseph Kermit. "The Methodist Evangelistic Movement Among Negroes in America." Salisbury, N. C. : Bachelor of Divinity thesis, Livingstone College, 1948.
DLC

Gillard, John Thomas. "Negro's God." Catholic World (151; Je. , 1940), pp. 305-13.
DHU/R

Glenn, Norval D. "Negro Religion and Negro Status in the United States." Lous Schneider, (ed.). Religion Culture and Society. New York: Wiley, 1964.   DHU/R

Gordon, Asa Hines. The Georgia Negro, a History. Ann Arbor, Mich. : Edwards Bros. Inc. , 1937.   NN/Sch
Negro author.

Gordon, Buford F. , (bp.). Teaching for Abundant Living; Teaching Through Sharing and Guiding Experience. Boston: The Christopher Pub. House, 1936.   DHU/MO; NN/Sch
Negro author.

Green, Constance McLaughlin. The Secret City. A History of Race Relations in the Nation's Capital. Princeton, N. J. : Princeton University Press, 1967.   DHU/MO
Information on Negro churches in Washington, D. C.

Green, David B. "Folk Singing in Worship." Theology Today (26:3, Oct, 1969), pp. 323+.
DHU/R

Griffin, Clifford S. Their Brothers' Keepers. New

Brunswick, N. J. : Rutgers University Press, 1960. DLC
Chapter 1, Negro Church.

Griffin, John Howard. The Black Church and the Black Man. Dayton, O. : Pflaum, 1969.
DHU/R
Includes a recorded commentary of Rev. James Groppi and Rev. Albert Cleage.

Grimke, Francis James. A Call for a Revival Within the Church. Washington, D. C. : n. p. , n. d.   DHU/MO
Negro author.

-- "Christianity Is Not Dependent Upon the Endorsement of Men Great in Worldly Wisdom." Washington, D. C.: The Author, 1934.   DHU/MO

-- "Christianity Needs No New Center of Gravity." Washington, D. C. : The Author, 1934.
NjPT

-- "Christ's Program" for the Saving of the World. n.p. , n. d.
DHU/MO

-- The Church Faces the College Generation. n. p. : The Author, 1930.   NjPT; DHU/MO

-- Divine Fellowship. Washington, D. C. : The Author, n. d.
NjPT

-- Effective Christianity in the Present World Crisis. Wash. , D. C. : The Author, 1918.
DHU/MO

-- Italy and Abyssinia. Washington, D. C. , n. p. , n.d.
DHU/MO

-- Loyalty to One's Church. n. p. , The Author, n. d.   DHU/MO

-- Religious Attitudes of Negro Youth. Washington, D. C. : The Author, n. d.

-- Spiritual Life. Washington, D. C. : The Author, n. d.
NjPT

-- What Is the Trouble With the Christianity of Today? There is Something Wrong About it... Delivered at the Seventh Annual Convention of the School

(Grimke, F. J. cont.)
of Religion of Howard University, Washington, D. C., Nov.
20, 1923. Washington, D. C.:
n. p., 1923.   DHU/MO
Grissom, Mary Allen. The Negro
Sings a New Heaven... Chapel
Hill: The University of North
Carolina Press, 1930.
                        DHU/MO
Grout, L. "Religious Instruction
of Negroes." New England
Magazine (42; 1883), p. 723.
                        DLC
Gwaltney, Grace. "The Negro
Church and the Social Gospel,
1877-1944. Master's thesis,
Howard University, 1949.
Hamilton, Charles Horace. The
Negro Church in Rural Virginia. The Virginia Agricultural Experiment Station and
the Virginia State College for
Negroes Cooperating. Blacksburg, Va.: n. p., 1930.
                        CtY-D
Hammond, J. D. "The Relation
of the Southern White Man to
the Education of the Negro in
Church Colleges." Arcadius
S. Trawick, (ed.). The New
Voice in Race Adjustments.
(New York: Student Volunteer
Movement, 1914), pp. 57-61.
                        DHU/R
Hammond, Lilly Hardy. Southern Women and Racial Adjustment. Lynchburg, Va.: J. P.
Bell Co., 1917.
            DHU/MO; NN/Sch
"Hampton Ministers' Conference."
Southern Workman (54; Ag.,
1925), pp. 349+.   DLC
Handy, Robert T. "Negro Christianity and American Church
Historiography." Jerald C.
Brauch, (ed.). Reinterpretation in American Church History (Chicago: The University of Chicago, 1968), pp.
91-112.   DHU/R
Hanson, Geddes. "Black Seminarians and the Crisis in

Theological Education." Dimension, Theology in Church and
World (6:1, Fall, 1968), pp.
41-6. Pam. File; DHU/R
Harding, Vincent, "Religion and
Resistance Among Antebellum
Negroes, 1800-1860." August
Meier and Elliott Rudwick,
(eds.). The Making of Black
America: The Black Community in Modern America. New
York: Atheneum, 1969, vol. 1,
pp. 179+.   DHU/MO
    Negro author.
Hargett, Andrew H. "Religious
Attitudes as Expressed by Students of Savannah State College." Journal of Negro Education (20; Spr., 1951), pp.
237-40.   DHU
Harrison, Walter R. "The Attitudes of the Negro Towards
the Church." Doctoral dissertation, Cornell University,
1945.
Hartshorn, William N. An Era
of Progress and Promise,
1863-1910; the Religious, Moral and Educational Development of the American Negro
Since his Emancipation. Boston: The Priscilla Publishing
Co., 1910. DHU/MO; NN/Sch
Harvey, M. L. "Negro Youth and
the Church." Missionary Review of the World (59; Je.,
1936), pp. 306-7.   DHU/R
Haynes, George Edmund. "The
Church and the Negro Spirit."
Survey Graphic (6:6, Mr. 1,
1925), pp. 695-97; 708-9.
            Pam File; DHU/R
    Negro author.
Haynes, Leonard L. The Negro
Community Within American
Protestantism, 1619-1844.
Boston: Christopher Pub.
House, 1953.
    DHU/R; DHU/MO; NN/Sch
    Negro author.
Haygood, Atticus G. "The Negro
in the South." Quarterly Review of the M.E. Church,

South (10; Jl., 1891), pp. 300-
15.   DLC; CtY
Hedgley, David R. "The Attitude of Negro Pastors in Chicago Toward Christian Education." Master's thesis, University of Chicago, 1935.
Henning, C. Garnett. "The Edu-
cational Task of the Negro
Church." Journal of Religious
Education (30:1, Sept., 1969),
p. 13.   DHU/R
Hewitt, Doris W. The Relation-
ship of Security and Religiosity
of the Low-Income Southern
Negro Youth. Tallahassee:
n. p., 1965.   FSU
Hickok, C. T. The Negro in
Ohio, 1802-1870. Cleveland:
n. p., 1896.   DHU/MO
Hill, Daniel Grafton. "The Ne-
gro in Oregon: A Survey."
Master's thesis, University of
Oregon, 1932.   NN/Sch
Negro author.
Hoffman, Mamie G. "A Survey
of Sunday Schools in the Ne-
gro Churches of the Chicago
Church Federation." Doctors
dissertation, University of
Chicago, 1933.
Holland, Jerome Heartwell. "Role
of Negro Church as an Organ
of Protest." Journal of Negro
Education (11; Ja., 1942), pp.
165-69.   DHU/MO
Holly, Alonzo P. God and the
Negro... Nashville: National
Baptist Publishing Board, 1937.
                       DHU/R
Biography and photographs
of Negro ministers.
Negro author.
Howard University, Washington,
D. C., Department of Sociology
and Anthropology. Religion and
Magic Among Negroes in
Washington, D. C. Washing-
ton, D. C.: Howard Univer-
sity, 1946.   DHU/MO
-- Graduate School. Division of
the Social Sciences. ...The In-
tegration of the Negro into

American Society. Papers Con-
tributed to the Fourteenth Annual Conference of the Division of the Social Sciences,
May 3, and 4, 1951. Edited
by E. Franklin Frazier.
Washington, D. C.: Pub. by the
Howard University Press for
the Graduate School, Howard
University, 1951.   DHU/R
Negro church by Frank D.
Dorey.
Hughley, Judge Neal. Rethink-
ing Our Christianity. Philadel-
phia: Dorrance & Co., 1842.
                      DHU/R
Negro author.
Imes, G. Lake. "A Service of
the Country Church in Helping
the Negro." Arcadius S. Tra-
wick, (ed.). The New Voice
in Race Adjustments. (New
York: Student Volunteer Move-
ment, 1914), pp. 145-53.
                      DHU/R
Negro author.
"Is There Too Much Rock'n Roll
in Religion?" Color (11; Ja.,
1957), pp. 12-13.   TNF
Jackson, Algernon Brachear.
The Man Next Door. Phila-
delphia: Neaula Publishing
Co., 1919.
Negro author.
Negro church, pp. 53-76.
Jenkins, John J. "The Structure
and Function of the American
Negro Church in Race Integra-
tion." Doctoral dissertation,
Boston, 1952.
Jernagin, W. H. "President's Ad-
dress to the Fraternal Council
of Negro Churches in Ameri-
ca, Washington, D. C. 1938."
Negro Journal of Religion (4:
6, Jl., 1938), pp. 8+.
                      DHU/R
Johnson, Charles S. Growing
Up in the Black Belt. Wash-
ington, D. C.: American Coun-
cil on Education, 1941.
                   INU; DHU/MO
Negro author.

(Johnson, C. S. cont.)
Rurgal Negro church.
-- Shadow of the Plantation.
Chicago: University of Chicago
Press, 1934.
-- "Youth and the Church." Hart
M. Nelsen & Raytha L. Yok-
ley et al. The Black Church
in America. (New York:
Basic Books, 1971), pp. 91-9.
                                   DHU/R
Increasing numbers of young
blacks in plantation areas
early become dissatisfied with
their church.
Johnson, Edward A. A School
History of the Negro Race in
America from 1619 to 1890...
Philadelphia: Sherman & Co.,
1892.   DHU/MO
Chapter 30, "Religious
Progress."
Johnson, Frederick E. The So-
cial Work of the Churches:
A Handbook of Information.
New York: Department of Re-
search and Education, Feder-
al Council of the Churches of
Christ in America, 1930.
                                   DHU/R
Johnson, Guion. The Church and
the Race Problem in the
United States; a Research
Memorandum Prepared by
Guion Griffis Johnson and Guy
B. Johnson with the assistance
of Edward Nelson Palmer...
New York: n.p., 1940.
                                   NN/Sch
Johnson, Henry Theodore. Pulpit,
Pew and Pastorate... n.p.,
1902. DHU/MO; NN/Sch
Negro author.
Johnson, James Weldon. God's
Trombones. New York: Viking,
1927.   DHU/R
Descriptions of Negro ser-
mons.
Johnson, Mordecai W. "Editorial
Comment. Tribute to the
President Emeritus, Daniel
G. Hill." Journal of Religious
Thought (18; Win. -Spr., 1961),

p. 3.   DHU/R
Johnston, Henry Halcro. "Negro
and Religion." Current Literature (49; Ag., 1910), pp.
187-8.   DLC
Johnston, Ruby. The Develop-
ment of Negro Religion. New
York: Philosophical Library,
1954.   DHU/R; INU; DLC
Negro author.
-- The Religion of Negro Protestants; Changing Religious Attitudes and Practices. New
York: Philosophical Library,
1956.
DHU/R; CtY-D; INU; DLC
Johnstone, Ronald L. "Militant
and Conservative Community
Leadership Among Negro
Clergymen." Doctoral dissertation, University of Michigan,
1963.
Jones, Summerfield Frances.
"The Church as a Factor in
the Economic Progress of the
Negro in America." Master's
thesis, Howard University,
1928.
Jordan, Winthrop D. "The Re-
sulting Pattern of Separation
in Negro Churches." Hart M.
Nelsen & Raytha L. Yokley,
et al. The Black Church in
America (New York: Basic
Books, 1971), pp. 49-53.
                                   DHU/R
Triumph of racial prejudice
over Christian ideals.
-- White Over Black: American
Attitudes toward the Negro,
1550-1812. Chapel Hill: Pub-
lished for the Institute of Early
American History and Culture
at Williamsburg, Va., by the
University of North Carolina
Press, 1968. CtY-D; DHU/R
Chapter 5, the Negro
church.
Jowers, Joseph Bebee. "Negro
Baptists and Methodists in
American Protestantism; As-
pects and Trends, 1957."
Doctoral dissertation, New

School of Social Research, 1958.
Karon, Bertram P. The Negro Personality. New York: Springer Publishing Co., 1958. DHU/MO
Investigation of the effects of culture.
Kealing, H. T. "Race Rich in Spiritual Content." Southern Workman (33; Ja., 1904), pp. 41+. DHU/MO
Kletzing, Henry F. Progress of a Race; or, The Remarkable Advancement of the Afro-American Negro from the Bondage of Slavery, Ignorance and Poverty, to the Freedom of Citizenship, Intelligence, Affluence, Honor and Trust. With an Introduction by Booker T. Washington... Atlanta, Ga. & Naperville, Ill.: J. L. Nichols & Co., 1898. DHU/MO; NN/Sch
Kyles, Lynwood W., (bp.). "The Contribution of the Negro to the Religious Life of America." Journal of Negro History (11:1, Ja., 1926), pp. 8-16. DHU/MO
Negro author.
Lamar, J. S. "Religious Future of the Negroes of the South." Christian Quarterly (6; 1874), p. 211. CtY
Lambert, R. E. "Negroes and the Church." Commonweal (75; Oct. 20, 1961), pp. 90-2. DHU
Lander, Ernest M. A History of South Carolina. Chapel Hill: University of North Carolina Press, 1960. NN/Sch
Negro church, pp. 163-8.
Lawrence, Charles Radford. "Negro Organizations in Crisis: Depression, New Deal, World War II." Doctoral dissertation, Columbia University, 1952.
Lawton, Samuel Miller. ...The Religious Life of South Caro-

lina Coastal and Sea Island Negroes. Nashville, Tenn.: George Peabody College for Teachers, 1939. DLC
Also Doctoral dissertation.
Leading Afro-Americans of Vicksburg, Mississippi; Their Enterprises, Churches, Schools. Vicksburg: Biographa, 1908. DLC
Lee, J. Oscar. "Religion Among Ethnic and Racial Minorities." Annals of the American Academy of Political and Social Science (332; Nov., 1960), pp. 112-24. DHU; DLC
-- "Religious Life and Needs of Negro Youth." Journal of Negro Education (19; Sum., 1950), pp. 298-309. DHU
Lee, R. L. Racial Episcopacy--Reasons. Greenville, Miss.: M. Kanaga, 1915. DLC
Lehman, H.C. and Witty, P.A. "Church and Sunday School Attendance of Negro Children." Religious Education (22; Ja., 1927), pp. 50-6. DHU/R
Leiffer, Murray H. The Layman Looks at the Minister. Nashville: Abingdon-Cokesbury Press, 1946. DHU/R
Chapter 7, The minister and social ideas.
LeMone, Archie. "The Afro-American Churches." Ecumenical Review (20:1, Ja., 1968), pp. 44-52. DHU/R
"Letters Showing the Rise and Progress of the Early Negro Churches of Georgia and the West Indies." Journal of Negro History (1; Ja., 1916), pp. 69-92. DHU/MO
Levine, M. H. "The Negro in the Bible." Negro Digest (14; Ja. 1965), pp. 82-3. DHU/MO
Lewis, Hylan G. Blackways of Kent. Chapel Hill: University of North Carolina Press, 1955. DHU/MO

(Lewis H. G. cont.)
Negro author.
Chapter 6, Religion and
Salvation.
-- "The Social Life of the Negro
in a Southern Piedmont Town."
Doctoral dissertation, Univer-
sity of Chicago, 1952.
Lewis, John Henry. Social Serv-
ices in Negro Churches."
Master's thesis, University of
Chicago, 1914.
Licorish, David Nathaniel. To-
morrow's Church in Today's
World; a Study of the Twenti-
eth-Century Challenge to Re-
ligion. New York: Exposi-
tion Press, 1956. DHU/MO
Negro author.
Loguen, Jermain Wesley. The
Rev. J.W. Loguen, As a
Slave and As a Freeman. New
York: Negro Universities
Press, 1968. DHU/R; FSU
Negro author.
Originally published in 1859
by Rev. J.W. Loguen.
Love, Edgar. "Role of the
Church in Maintaining the
Morale of the Negro in World
Wars I and II." Journal of
Negro Education (12; Sum.,
1943), pp. 502-10.   DHU
Mannoni, O. "The Lament of the
Negro." Cross Currents (1;
Sum., 1951), pp. 1-11.
                               DHU/R
Margolies, Edward. Native
Sons: A Critical Study of
Twentieth Century Negro-Amer-
ican Authors. Philadelphia:
Lippincott, 1969.   DLC
A chapter entitled, "The
Negro Church: James Bald-
win and the Christian Vision."
Markoe, William M. "Negro
Morality and a Colored Clergy."
America (26; Nov. 12, 1921),
pp. 79-81.   DLC
Marty, Martin E. Righteous Em-
pire: The Protestant Experi-
ence in America. New York:
The Dial Press, 1970. DHU/R

Chapter 3, The Overlooked
Protestant, The Black Ameri-
can.
Marx, Gary T. Protest and
Prejudice; A Study of Belief
in the Black Community. New
York: Harper & Row, 1969.
                               DHU/R
-- "Religion: Opiate on Inspira-
tion of Civil Rights Militancy
Among Negroes." Benjamin
Quarles. The Negro in the
Making of America. New York:
Macmillan, 1964. DHU/MO
Pp. 362-75.
Mays, Benjamin Elijah. "The
American Negro and the Chris-
tian Religion." Journal of Ne-
gro Education (8:3, Jl., 1939),
pp. 530-8.   DHU/R
Negro author.
-- The Christian in Race Rela-
tions. West Haven, Conn. :
Promoting Enduring Peace,
Inc., 1952.   CtY-D
Negro author.
Lecture given at the Yale
Divinity School.
-- "Christian Youth and the Race."
Crisis (46:11, Dec., 1939),
pp. 364+.   DHU/MO
-- "Christianity in a Changing
World." National Educational
Outlook Among Negroes (1:4,
Dec., 1937), pp. 18+.
                               DHU/MO
-- "Christianizing and Democra-
tizing America in This Genera-
tion." Journal of Negro Edu-
cation (14:4, Fall, 1945), pp.
527-34.   DHU/MO
Commencement address,
Howard University, June 8,
1945.
-- "The Church Surveys World
Problems." Crisis (44; Oct. ,
1937), pp. 299+.   DHU/MO
-- Contributing Editor. Vergilius
Ferm, (ed.). Encyclopedia of
Religion (New York: Philo-
sophical Library, 1945)
                               DHU/R
-- "The Development of the Idea

of God in Contemporary Negro
Literature." Doctoral dissertation, University of Chicago,
1935.
-- "Fifty Years of Progress in
the Negro Church." Pitts-
burgh Courier Apr. 8, 1950.
                DHU/MO; NN/Sch
-- "The Inescapable Christ." G.
Paul Butler, (ed.). Best Ser-
mons Vol. 2 (New York:
Harper & Bros., Publishers,
1946), pp. 26-32.   DHU/R
-- "The Negro Church in Amer-
ican Life." Christendom (5:
3, Sum., 1940), pp. 387-98.
                DHU/R
-- "The Negro in the Christian
Ministry." A. M. E. Church
Review (75:200, Ap. -Je.,
1959), pp. 21-9.   DHU/R
-- "Negroes and the Will to Jus-
tice." Christian Century (59:
43, Oct., 1942), pp. 1316-7.
                DHU
-- The Negro's Church. New
York: Institute of Social and
Religious Research, 1933.
                DHU/R; OWibfU
-- The Negro's God, as Re-
flected in His Literature.
New York: Negro Universi-
ties Press, 1969.
        DHU/R; DLC; CtY-D
Reprint of the 1938 ed.
-- "The Religious Life and Needs
of Negro College Students."
Journal of Negro Education
(9; Jl., 1940), pp. 332-43.
                DHU/R
-- "Religious Roots of Western
Culture." Child Study (30;
Fall, 1953).   HQ
-- Seeking to Be Christian in
Race Relations. New York:
Friendship Press, 1946.
    DLC; DHU/R; DHU/MO
-- "The Training of Negro Min-
isters." National Outlook
Among Negroes (3:2, Nov. -
Dec., 1939), pp. 16+.
                DHU/MO
-- "Who Will Preach to Negroes

in the Year 2000?" Chicago
Defender, Ag. 1955.
                DHU/MO
-- "World Churchmen Score
Prejudice." Crisis (44; Nov.,
1937), pp. 340+.   DHU/MO
Mead, Frank Spencer. "God in
Harlem." Christian Century
(53; Ag. 26, 1936), pp. 1133-
5.   DHU/R
Meier, August and Elliot M.
Rudwick. From Plantation to
Ghetto: An Interpretive His-
tory of American Negroes.
New York: Hill and Wang,
1966.   DHU/R
For a discussion of the de-
velopment and the impact of
the Negro churches on ghetto
dwellers in the ante-bellum
cities, see pp. 74-80.
Meier, August. "Negro Racial
Thought in the Age of Booker
T. Washington, circa 1880-
1915..." Doctoral disserta-
tion, Columbia University,
1957.   NN/Sch
Church and race relations,
pt. 5.
Mencken, H. L. "The Burden of
Credulity." Opportunity (9:2,
Feb., 1931), pp. 40-1.
                DHU/MO
Miller, Kelly. Out of the House
of Bondage. New York: The
Neal Publishing Co., 1914.
                DHU/MO; CtY-D
Negro author.
-- "Religion and Education."
Voice of the Negro (1:4, Apr.,
1940), pp. 163-5. DHU/MO
Miller, William Robert. "The
Negro Church in the U. S. A."
Risk (10:1, 1968.)   DLC
Montgomery, Leroy Jeremiah.
Two Distinct Religions, Chris-
tianity and the Religion of
Jesus Christ. Houston: In-
former Publishing Co., n. d.
                DHU/MO
Negro author.
Muelder, Walter. "Recruitment
of Negroes for Theological

(Muelder, W. cont.)
Studies." Review of Religious
Research (5:3, Spr., 1964),
pp. 152-6.   DHU/R
Myrdal, Gunnar. An American
Dilemma. New York: Harper
& Bros., 1944.
      INU; DHU/R; CtY-D
      Chapter 40, vol. II, The
      Negro church.
The National Encyclopedia of the
Colored Race: Editor in
Chief, Clement Richardson...
Montgomery, Ala.: National
Publishing Company, Inc.,
1919.   NN/Sch
      Negro author.
      Negro church, pp. 573-8.
National Urban League, Dept. of
Research and Community Projects. A Survey of the Economic and Cultural Conditions of
the Negro Population of Louisville, Kentucky and a Review
of the Program and Activities
of the Louisville Urban League
in Cooperation with the Louisville Health and Welfare Council and the Louisville Community Chest, by J. Harvey
Kerns, Assistant Director,
Dept. of Research and Community Projects, National Urban League... Jan.-Feb.,
1948.   NN/Sch
Negro Christian Student Conference, Atlanta, 1914. The New
Voice in Race Adjustment;
Addresses and Reports Presented at the Negro Christian
Student Conference. Atlanta,
Ga., May 14-18, 1914. A.M.
Trawick, editor... New York:
Student Volunteer Movement,
1914.   A&M;
DHU/MO; NN/Sch; DHU/R
"The Negro Church." Political
Science Quarterly (19; Dec.,
1904), pp. 702-3. DHU; DLC
"Negro Emotionalism Passing."
Literary Digest (115; Mr. 4,
1933), p. 22.
      DHU/R; DHU

"Negro God Has Realms on
Earth." Newsweek (2; Dec. 23,
1933), p. 26.   DHU/R
"Negroes in Missouri." The
Church at Home and Abroad
(3; My., 1888), pp. 479-80.
      Religious orientation of Ne-
      groes in Missouri.
Nelson, William Stuart. The
Christian Way in Race Rela-
tions. New York: Harper,
1948. DHU/R; DHU/MO;
                   NN/Sch
      Negro author.
Newby, Idus. Jim Crow's De-
fense. Baton Rouge, La.:
University of Louisiana Press,
1965.   DHU/R
      Bible justification for seg-
      regation.
Newton, John B. The Colored
Commission. Alexandria,
Va.: Hill Print, 1888, p. 60-
5. (In: The Negro and the
Church: v. 1).   NN/Sch
Newton, Percy John. The Road
to Happiness and Other Es-
says. Boston: Chapman
Grimes, 1955.   DHU/MO
      Negro author.
North Carolina. State Board of
Public Welfare. The Negro Pop-
ulation of North Carolina,
1945-1955, by John R. Lar-
kins, Consultant on Negro
Work. Raleigh: n.p., 1957.
                   NN/Sch
Odum, Howard Washington. So-
cial and Mental Traits of the
Negro: Research into the
Conditions of the Negro Race
in Southern Towns, a Study in
Race Traits, Tendencies and
Prospects. New York: Co-
lumbia University, 1910.
                   NN/Sch
Payne, Daniel Alexander, (bp.).
"Speech." Anti-Slavery Con-
ference, Held in Paris, in the
Salle Herz, on the Twenty-
Sixth and Twenty-Seventh, Au-
gust 1867... London: Pub. by
the Committee on the British

and Foreign Anti-Slavery So-
ciety, n. d. pp. 24-6.
Penn, Irvine Garland. "Negro
Religious and Social Life."
Missionary Review (45:6, Je.,
1922), pp. 447-53.   DHU/R
Negro author.
Secretary of the Board of
Education for Negroes of the
Methodist Episcopal Church.
The Philadelphia Colored Di-
rectory; A Handbook of the
Religious, Social, Political,
Professional, Business and
Other Activities of the Ne-
groes of Philadelphia. Com-
piled by R. R. Wright, Jr.,
assisted by Ernest Smith.
Colored Directory Co., 1907.
                      DHU/MO
Pipes, William Harrison. "Old
Time Negro Preaching: An
Interpretative Study." Doc-
toral dissertation, University
of Michigan, 1945.
-- Say Amen, Brother! Old-
time Negro Preaching: a
Study in American Frustration.
New York: William-Frederick
Press, 1951.
     DHU/R; DHU/MO; DLC
Pipkin, James Jefferson. The
Negro in Revelation, in History,
and in Citizenship; What the
Race has Done and is Doing.
New York: Thompson Publish-
ing Co., 1902. DLC; TNF
-- The Story of a Rising Race.
St. Louis: N. D. Thompson,
1902.   DHU/MO
Pleasants, D. M. "The Negro
Methodist Since 1784." Cen-
tral Christian Advocate (135:
23, Dec. 1, 1960), pp. 4-6.
                       DHU/R
Ploski, Harry A.   The Negro
Almanac. New York: Bell-
wether Publishing Co., 1967.
          DHU/R; INU
Negro church, pp. 793-815.
Poinsett, Alex.   Common Folk
in an Uncommon Cause. Chi-
cago: Liberty Baptist Church,

1962.   DHU/MO
Negro author.
-- "Negroes and the Christian
Church." Ebony. The Negro
Handbook. Chicago: Johnson
Publishing Co., 1966, pp. 307-
8. Includes membership sta-
tistics.   DHU/R
-- "The Religion, Negroes and
the Christian Church." Ebony
Editors. The Negro Handbook
Chicago: Johnson Publishing
Co., 1966, pp. 307-8. DHU/R
Pollard, Myrtle E. "Harlem as
It Is." BAA and M. B. A. thes-
is, City College of New York,
1936-37.   NN/Sch
Negro author.
"Typescript." Section on
Negro Church.
Pope, Liston. "The Negro and
Religion in America." Review
of Religious Research (5:3,
Spr., 1964), pp. 142-52. DHU/R
Poteat, Ervin M. "The Contribu-
tion of the Negro Race to the
Interpretation of Christianity."
Arcadius S. Trawick, (ed.).
The New Voice in Race Adjust-
ments. (New York: Student
Volunteer Movement, 1914)
                       DHU/R
Powdermaker, Hortense. After
Freedom, A Cultural Study of
the Deep South. New York:
Viking Press, 1939.
                DHU/R; NN/Sch
Chapter IV, Religion and
superstition.
Powell, Adam Clayton, Sr. "Give
Me That Old Time Religion."
Negro Digest (8; My., 1950),
pp. 19-21.   DHU/MO
Negro author.
Powell, Adam Clayton, Jr. "Rock-
ing the Gospel Train." Negro
Digest (9:6 Apr., 1951), pp.
10-13. Negro author. DHU/MO
"Powell Wins Council Seat."
The New York Age (Nov. 15,
1941).   DHU/MO
Preston, J. T. L. "Religious Ed-
ucation of Negroes." New

(Preston, J. T. L. cont.)
England Magazine (37; 1878),
p. 680.   DLC
Price, Thomas. Christianity
and Race Relations. London:
SCM Press, 1954.
                NN/Sch; CtY-D
"Progress for Negro Sunday
Schools." Religious Education
(8; Ag., 1913), pp. 283-4.
                          DHU/R
Protestant Church Directory...
of Metropolitan New York,
Including Nassau and West-
chester Counties. New York:
Protestant Council of the City
of New York, 1933.
                    NN/Sch; DLC
Puckett, Newbell Niles. "Folk
Beliefs of the Southern Ne-
gro." Thesis, Yale Univer-
sity, 1925.
-- "The Negro Church in the
United States." Social Forces
(4; Mr., 1926), pp. 581-87.
                            DHU
Quayle, W. A. The Black Man
and Christ. n. p.: Freed-
men's Aid Society of the
Methodist Episcopal Church,
n. d.   IEG
Ransom, Reverdy Cassius, (bp.).
The Industrial and Social Con-
dition of the Negro: A
Thanksgiving Sermon, Nov. 26,
1896 at Bethel A. M. E. Church
Chicago.   OWibfU
    Negro author.
    Transcript.
-- The Mission of the Religious
Press... an Address Before
the General Conference of the
A. M. E. Church in Kansas
City, Mo., May 16, 1912.
New York: American Negro
Press, 1912.
                 NN/Sch; OWibfU
-- The Negro: the Hope or the
Despair of Christianity. Bos-
ton: Ruth Hill Publisher,
1935.   NN/Sch
Reid, Ira De A. "Let Us Pray!"
Opportunity (4:45, Sept.,

1926), pp. 274-78. DHU/MO
    Discusses Negro churches
    in the city.
Reimers, David Morgan. "Prot-
estant Churches and the Ne-
gro: A Study of Several Ma-
jor Protestant Denominations
and the Negro from World
War One to 1954." Doctoral
dissertation, University of
Wisconsin, 1961.
"The Religion of the American
Negro." New World (19; Dec.,
1900).   DCU/RE
"Religious Life of the Negro."
North American Review (181;
Jl., 1905), pp. 20-23. DHU
Renard, Alice. "A Negro Looks
at the Church." Commonweal
(46:9, Je. 13, 1947), pp.
209-12.   DHU
Reuter, Edward Byron. The
American Race Problem. A
Study of the Negro. New
York: Thomas Y. Crowell Co.,
1927.   DHU/R; DHU/MO
    The church and religious
    life of the Negro, p. 13.
Richardson, Harry Van Buren.
Dark Glory, a Picture of the
Church Among Negroes in the
Rural South. New York: Pub.
for Home Missions Council of
North America and Phelps-
Stokes Fund by Friendship
Press, 1947.
        DHU/R; DHU/MO; DLC
    Negro author.
-- "The Negro in American Re-
ligious Life." John P. Davis,
(ed.). The American Negro
Reference Book (Englewood
Cliffs, N. J.: Prentice-Hall,
1966, pp. 396-413. DHU/R
-- "The New Negro and Religion."
Opportunity (11; Feb. 1933),
pp. 41-4.   DHU/MO
-- "The Rural Negro Church; a
Study of the Rural Negro
Church in Four Representative
Southern Counties to Determine
Ministerial Adequacy. Doctor-
al dissertation, Drew Theologi-

cal Seminary, 1945.
Richardson, Lee and Goodman.
In and About Vicksburg.
Vicksburg, Miss.: Gibraltar,
1890.   DLC
Richie, Willis Temple. "The
Contribution of the Negro
Churches of Washington, D. C.,
to the Problem of the Soldier,
Defense Worker and the
Parishioner During World War
II." Master's thesis, Howard
University. 1943.
Richings, G. F. Evidences of
Progress Among Colored
People. Philadelphia: G. S.
Ferguson, 1904.
                  DHU/R; NN/Sch
Riddick, John Hudson. "Preacher,
Councilman, Deputy Marshal."
Willim J. Simmons, (ed.).
Men of Mark... (Cleveland, O.:
M. Rewell & Co., 1887), p.
752.   DHU/R
Roberts, James Deotis. "The
Negro's Contribution to Re-
ligious Thought in America."
Swarthmore College Bulletin
Alumni Issue. (68:2, Oct.,
1970), pp. 7-14.
             Pam. File; DHU/R
Robertson, Archibald Thomas.
That Old-Time Religion.
Boston: Houghton Mifflin,
1950.   NN/Sch
Rogers, Cornish R. "The Black
Minister and his Family."
The Christian Ministry (2:4,
Jl. 1971), pp. 19-20. DHU/R
Negro author.
Roman, Charles Victor. "The
Church in Relation to Growing
Race Pride." Arcadius S.
Trawick, (ed.). The New
Voice in Race Adjustments
(New York: Student Volunteer
Movement, 1914), pp. 40-50.
                          DHU/R
Negro author.
Rooks, Charles Shelby. "A
Cross to Bear." Journal of
Religious Thought (20:2, 1963-
64), pp. 131-5.   DHU/R

Negro author.
"Goal of excellence for Negro seminarians."
-- "The Shortage of Negro Theological Students." Christianity
and Crisis (25:2, Feb., 1965),
pp. 20-23.   DHU/R
-- (ed.). Toward a Better Ministry: A Report of the Consultation on the Negro in the
Christian Ministry. Held at
the Blue Ridge Assembly, Inc.,
Black Mountain, N. C., Oct.
5-7, 1965. Sponsored by the
Edward W. Hazen Foundation
and the Fund for Theological
Education, Inc., 1965.
             Pam. File, DHU/R
Rudwick, Elliot M. W. E. B. Du-
Bois: A Study in Minority
Group Leadership. Philadelphia: The University of Pennsylvania Press, 1961.
                        DHU/MO
Russell, James S. "Church Work
Among Negroes." Spirit of
Missions (86; Nov., 1921),
pp. 737-39.   DHU/R
-- "Past and Present Among the
Negroes of Southern Virginia."
Spirit of Missions (74:4, Apr.,
1909), pp. 307-10.   DHU/R
Rutledge, A. "God's Dark Children." Outlook (155; Jl. 23,
1930), pp. 446-8.   DHU
Salisbury, W. Seward. Religion
in American Culture. Home-
wood, Ill.: Dorsey Press,
1964.   DHU/R
pp. 472-5, Negro church.
Schab, Fred. "Attitudinal Differences of Southern White and
Negro Adolescent Males Regarding the Home, School, Religion and Morality." Journal
of Negro Education (40:2, Spr.
1971), pp. 108-10.   DHU/R
Scheiner, Seth M. The Negro
Church and the Northern City
1890-1930. William G. Shade
and Roy C. Herrenkohl (eds).
Seven on Black (Philadelphia:
L. B. Lippincott, 1969), pp.

(Scheiner, S. M. cont.)
91-117.   DHU/R
Shockley, Grant S. "Improvement of the Status and In-
Service Education of Negro
Methodist Accepted Supply
Pastors." Doctoral dissertation, Teachers College, Columbia University, 1952.
Schomburg, Arthur Alfonso.
"The Negro and Christianity."
Opportunity (2; Dec. , 1924),
pp. 362-64.   DHU/MO
Sinclair, Georges H. "The Re-
ligious Attitudes of Forty In-
stitutionalized Protestant
Girls With Implications for
Christian Education. A Com-
parative Study." Doctoral
dissertation, Hartford Semi-
nary Foundation, 1964. "Ra-
cial differences were included
in this comparative study."
Sisk, Glenn N. Churches in the
Alabama Black Belt, 1875-
1917." Church History (23:2,
Je. , 1954), pp. 153-74.
                     DHU/R
Smith, Allen Hart. The Negro
Church; a Critical Examina-
tion of the Christian Church
Among Negroes in the United
States. New Haven: Yale
University Divinity School,
1961.   CtY-D; DHU/R
Typescript.
"Study... presented in con-
junction with the Special Hon-
ors Program of Yale Univer-
sity Divinity School... 1960-
1961."
Speaks, R. L. "Will the Negro
Remain Protestant?" Chris-
tian Century (7:22, Je. 2, 1954),
pp. 668-9.   DHU/R
Sperry, Willard Learoyd. Reli-
gion in America. New York:
Macmillan Co. , 1946.
          NN/Sch; DHU/R
Negro churches, pp. 181-
98.
Stelzle, Charles. American Social and Religious Conditions.

New York: Revell, 1912.
                     NN/Sch
Stevens, George E. "The Ne-
gro Church in the City." The
Missionary Review of the
World (49; Je. , 1926), pp.
435-39.   DHU/R
Strange, Robert (bp.). ...
Church Work Among the Ne-
groes in the South... Chi-
cago: Western Theological
Seminary, 1907.
          NcD; CtY-D
Sutherland, Robert L. "An An-
alysis of Negro Churches in
Chicago." Doctoral disserta-
tion, University of Chicago,
1930.
Tarter, Charles L. "The De-
velopment of a Program of
Cooperation Among Some Ne-
gro Churches in the Fourth
Ward of Paterson, New Jer-
sey." Doctoral dissertation,
Teachers College, Columbia
University, 1952.
Thirkield, Wilbur Patterson, (bp.)
"Constructive Sunday School
Work Among Colored People."
Religious Education (7; Oct. ,
1912), pp. 445-50. DHU/R
-- "The Peril of the Negro
Church." Opportunity (11:7,
Jl. , 1933), pp. 213-15.
                     DHU/MO
Thomas, Isaac Lemuel. Sepa-
ration or Continuity, Which?
Or a Colored Man's Reply to
Bishop Foster's Book, "Union
of Episcopal Methodisms."
Baltimore: H. H. Smith,
1893.   NjMD
Negro author.
Thomas, James S. "A Study of
the Social Role of the Negro
Rural Pastor in Four Selected
Southern Areas." Doctoral dis-
sertation, Cornell University,
1952.
Tobias, Channing H. 'Negro
Thinking Today." Religion in
Life (13:2, Spr. , 1944), pp.
204-12.   DHU/R

Trawick, Arcadius, (ed.). The
Negro Voice in Race Adjust-
ments. Addresses and Re-
ports Presented at the Negro
Christian Student Conference,
Atlanta, Georgia, May 14-18,
1914. New York: Student Vol-
unteer Movement, 1914.
DHU/R
Trawick, Arch, (Mrs.). "The
Social Message of the Church."
Arcadius S. Trawick, (ed.).
The New Voice in Race Adjust-
ments. (New York: Student
Volunteer Movement, 1914),
pp. 62-5.   DHU/R
Trollope, Frances. Domestic
Manners of the Americans.
New York: A.A. Knopf, 1949.
DHU
pp. 237-41, camp meetings
and the Negro.
Turner, Henry McNeal, (bp.).
"There is No Manhood Future
in the United States for the
Negro." Thomas Wagstaff,
(ed.). Black Power. The
Radical Response to White
America. Beverly Hills:
Glencoe Press, 1969, pp. 50-
55.   DHU/R
Negro author.
Urges Negroes to emigrate
to Africa.
Tyms, James Daniel. "Church
and This New Generation."
Journal of Religious Thought
(18; Win.-Spr., 1961), pp. 57-
65.   DHU
Negro author.
United States Census Bureau.
"Religion Reported by the Ci-
vilian Population of the United
States: March, 1957." Current
Population Reports, (ser. p.
20; 79, 1958).
Walker, C.T. "The Negro Church
as a Medium for Race Expression." Arcadius S. Trawick,
(ed.). The New Voice in Race
Adjustments. (New York: Student Volunteer Movement, 1914)
pp. 50-54.

Negro author.
Walker, George Gilbert. "Col-
ored People and their Reli-
gious Organizations." Living
Church (65; My. 7, 1921), pp.
15-16.   CtY; DLC
Walker, Harry J. ...The Negro
in American Life. New York:
Oxford Book Co., 1954.
NN/Sch
Negro author.
Evaluation of the Negro
church in American life.
Walsh, Francis Augustine, (ed.).
The Religious Education of the
Negro; Papers Read at the
National Congress of the Con-
fraternity of Christian Doc-
trine, New York...October,
1936... Cincinnati: Benziger
Bros., 1937. DHU/MO; NcD
Waltz, Alan K. and Robert L.
Wilson. "Ministers' Attitudes
Toward Integration." Phylon
(19; Sum., 1958), pp. 195-98.
DHU/MO
Washington, Booker Taliferro
and W.E.B. Du Bois. "Religion
in the South," The Negro in
the South. Philadelphia: Geo.
W. Jacobs & Co., 1907.
DHU/R; NN/Sch
Negro authors.
Washington, Booker Taliaferro.
"The Religious Life of the
Negro." North American Re-
view (181; Jl., 1905), pp. 20-
23.   DHU
Negro author.
-- The Story of the Negro. New
York: Doubleday, Page & Co.,
1909. 2 vols.   DHU/MO
"The Negro preacher and
the Negro church."
Washington, Joseph R. "Are
American Negro Churches
Christian?" Theology Today
(20; Apr., 1963), pp. 76-86.
DHU/R
Negro author.
Watson, J.J. "Churches and Re-
ligious Conditions Among the
Negroes." Annals of the Am-

(Watson, J. J. cont.)
erican Academy (49; Sept.,
1913), pp. 120-28.   DHU
Watson, James Jefferson. "The
Religion of the Negro." Doc-
toral dissertation, University
of Pennsylvania, 1912.
Weatherford, Allen Ericson.
"Recreation in the Negro
Church in North Carolina."
Journal of Negro Education
(13; Fall, 1944), pp. 499-508.
                           DHU
Weatherford, Willis Duke. The
Negro from Africa to America.
New York: Doran, 1924.
                        NN/Sch
Negroes and the church, pp.
298-337.
-- Negro Life in the South, Pres-
ent Conditions and Needs,
With a Special Chapter on the
Economic Condition of the Ne-
gro, by G. W. Dyer... New
York: Young Men's Christian
Association Press, 1910.
        DHU/R; NN/Sch
Negro church, pp. 117-46.
Webber, W. "Witness and Serv-
ice in East Harlem." Interna-
tional Review of Missions (54;
Oct., 1965), pp. 441-46.
                          DHU/R
Weisenburger, Francis P. "Wil-
liam Sanders Scarborough:
Scholarship, The Negro Reli-
gion and Politics." Ohio His-
tory (72; Ja., 1963), pp. 25+.
                            NcD
Wengatz, John Christian. Mir-
acles in Black. New York:
Fleming H. Revell Co., 1938.
                        DHU/MO
Wesley, Charles Harris. "The
Religious Attitudes of Negro
Youth." Journal of Negro His-
tory (21:4, Oct., 1936), pp.
376-93.   DHU/MO
Negro author.
Wharton, Vernon Lane. The Ne-
gro in Mississippi, 1865-1890.
Chapel Hill: University of
North Carolina Press, 1947.

Negro church, pp. 256-65.
White, Horace A. "Who Owns the
Negro Churches?" Christian
Century (55; Feb. 9, 1938),
pp. 176-77.   DHU/R
Whither the Negro Church? Semi-
nar Held at Yale Divinity
School, New Haven, Conn.,
April 13-15, 1931. n. p., n. d.
                        DHU/MO
Wiley, Bell Irvin. Southern Ne-
groes, 1861-1865. New Haven,
Conn.: Yale University Press,
1965.   CtY; DHU/R
Chapter 6, Religious life.
Williams, George Washington.
History of the Negro Race in
America from 1619 to 1880.
New York: Putnam, 1883.
                          DHU/R
Negro author.
Williams, Kenny Jackson. They
Also Spoke. Nashville: Town-
send Press, 1970. DHU/R
Written by daughter of the
President of the National Bap-
tist Convention, U. S. A. Has
many references to Negro
church.
Negro author.
Wilson, Elizabeth L. "Minority
Groups in Bronx Churches: A
Study of the Extent of Partici-
pation of Negro Minority
Groups in Protestant Churches
in the Bronx, New York City."
Master's thesis, Columbia
University, 1945.
Wilson, Gold Refined. "The Re-
ligion of the American Negro
Slave: His Attitude Toward
Life and Death." Journal of
Negro History (8:1, Ja., 1923),
pp. 41-71.   DHU/MO
Wilson, Robert L. "The Associ-
ation of Urban Social Areas in
Four Cities and the Institution-
al Characteristics of Local
Churches in Five Denomina-
tions." Doctoral dissertation,
Northwestern University, 1958.
Includes social rank, urbani-
zation and segregation.

Wolfram, Walter A. and Ralph
W. Fosold. "A Black English
Translation of John 3:1-21
with Grammatical Annotations."
The Bible Translator (20:2,
Apr. , 1969), pp. 48-54.
            DHU/R
Woodson, Carter Godwin. The
African Background Outlined;
or, Handbook for the Study of
the Negro. Washington, D. C. :
Association for the Study of
Negro Life and History, 1936.
            DHU/R; NN/Sch
Negro church, pp. 363-92.
Negro author.
-- The History of the Negro
Church. Washington, D. C. :
The Associated Publishers,
1945.   DHU/R; DHU/MO; DLC;
                OWibfU
Woofter, Thomas J.   The Basis
of Adjustment.   Boston: Ginn
& Co. , 1925.
Negro church, pp. 212-34.
Work, Monroe N.   "Contribu-
tions of Black People to the
Kingdom of God. " Student
World (16; Apr. , 1923), pp.
43-45.   CtY; DLC
Negro author.
-- "Negro Church and the Com-
munity. " Southern Workman
(37; Ag. , 1908), pp. 428+.
                DHU/MO
-- and William E. B. Du Bois.
The Negro Ministry in the
Middle West.   Hart M. Nelson
& Raytha L. Yokley, et al.
The Black Church in America
(New York: Basic Books, 1971)
pp. 265-268.   DHU/R
Also in DuBois, W. E. B. ,
The Philadelphia Negro.
Wright, James Martin. ... The
Free Negro in Maryland,

1634-1860.   New York: Columbia University, 1921.
                NN/Sch
(Studies in History, Econ-
omics and Public Law; ed. by
the faculty of Political Science
of Columbia University, v. 97,
no. 3, whole no. 222).
Negro church.
Wright, Richard. 12 Million
Black Voices; a Folk History
of the Negro in the United
States. New York: The Viking Press, 1941.
            DHU/MO; CtY-D
Negro author.
Wright, Richard Robert. "Social
Work and Influence of the Negro Church. " Annals of the
American Academy (30; Nov.
1907), pp. 509-21.   DHU/R
Negro author.
Wynn, Daniel Webster. "Do Negroes Lack a Sense of Mission?" Religious Education
(59:2, Mr. -Apr. , 1964), pp.
168-70.   DHU/R
Negro author.
Yates, Walter L. "An Analysis
of the Influence of War-Service
upon the Religious Views of
Eight Hundred Negro Ex-serv-
ice Men in the District of Co-
lumbia, United States of Amer-
ica, World War II. "
Master's thesis, Howard
University, 1947.
Yinger, J. Milton. Religion, Society and the Individual. New
York: The Macmillan Co. ,
1957.   DHU/R
Young, Viola Mae. Little Helps
for Pastors and Members.
Rosebud, Ala. : n. p. , 1909.
                NN/Sch
Negro author.

4. Negro Ministers, Priests, and Laity--Writings

Adams, Henry. "A Faithful
Pastor, a Good Man." Wm.
J. Simmons, (ed.). Men of
Mark (Cleveland, O.: Geo. M.
Rewell & Co., 1887), p. 798.
                          DHU/R
Alexander, William T. History
of the Colored Race in Amer-
ica. New Orleans: Palmetto,
1888.   DHU/MO
Allen, Richard. "First Bishop of
the A.M.E. Church, an Eminent Preacher, a Devout Man."
Wm. J. Simmons, (ed.). Men
of Mark... (Cleveland, O.:
Geo. M. Rewell & Co., 1887),
p. 491.   DHU/R
-- The Life Experience and Gospel of the Rt. Rev. Richard
Allen. To which is annexed
the rise and progress of the
African Methodist Episcopal
Church in the United States of
America. Containing a narrative of the yellow fever in the
year of Our Lord 1793. With
an address to the people of
color in the United States.
Written by himself and pub-
lished by his request. With
an introd. by Geo. A Singleton. New York: Abingdon
Press, 1960. DHU/R; A&M;
              DHU/MO; OWibfU
Alleyne, Cameron Chesterfield,
(bp.). The Negro Faces Chris-
tianity. n.p., 1946. NcSalL
     Negro author.
-- Our Pilgrim Vanguard. n.p.,
1950.   NcSalL
-- Religion and its Requirements.
n.p., n.d.   NcSalL
Alstork, John Wesley, (bp.).
"Greatest Need of the Negro
Race." W.N. Hartshorn. An
Era of Progress (Boston:
Priscilla Pub. Co., 1910), p.
400.   NcSalL
     Negro author.

Arnett, Benjamin W. and J.M.
Ashley. "Addresses of Bishop
B.W. Arnett and the Hon. J.
M. Ashley." J.H. Barrows,
(ed.). The World's Parlia-
ment of Religions. Vol. II
(Chicago: Parliament Publish-
ing Co., 1893), pp. 1101-04.
                          DHU/R
Arnett, Benjamin W., D.D.
"Financial Secretary of the
A.M.E. Church, the Statisti-
cian of his Church; Author,
Editor of the Budget, Legisla-
tor, Author of the Bill Wiping
Out the 'Black Laws' of
Ohio." Wm. J. Simmons, (ed.).
Men of Mark, Cleveland, O.:
George M. Rewell & Co.,
1887), p. 883.   DHU/R
-- "The Northwest Territory."
Address at the Music Hall,
Chicago, October 11, 1899."
Ohio Archaeological and His-
torical Quarterly. (8, 1908),
pp. 433-64.   NcD; DLC
     Negro author.
Asher, Jeremiah. Incidents in
the Life of Rev. J. Asher:
Pastor of Shiloh (Colored)
Baptist Church, Philadelphia.
With an Introduction by Wilson
Armistead. London: C. Gil-
pin, 1850.   DLC; NcD
Atwood, Jesse H. "The Atti-
tudes of Negro Ministers of
the Major Denominations in
Chicago toward Racial Divi-
sion in American Protestant-
ism." Doctoral dissertation,
University of Chicago, 1930.
Bacote, Samuel William, ed.
Who's Who Among the Colored
Baptists of the United States
... Kansas City, Mo.: Frank-
lin Hudson Publishing Co.,
1913-. DHU/MO; DLC; GAU
Baldwin, James. Go Tell It on
the Mountain. New York:

Knopf, 1953. DHU/R; DHU/MO
Negro author.
Fiction on Negro preacher.
Banks, William L.   Jonah, Verse
by Verse. New York: Vantage
Press, 1963.   DHU/MO
Negro author.
Beckett, L. M.   True Worship-
pers. A Sermon. Anacostia,
D. C.: n. p., 1911.   DHU/MO
Negro author.
Billingsley, Andrew. "Edward
Blyden: Apostle of Blackness."
The Black Scholar (2:4, Dec.
1970), pp. 3-12.   DHU/R
Negro author.
Bishop, Shelton Hale. The Ro-
mance of the Negro, by the
Rev. S. H. Bishop. New York:
n. p., 1910.   NN/Sch
Detached from the Spirit of
Missions, v. 75, no. 3, Mar.
1910.
Negro author.
-- The Wonder of Prayer. Green-
wich, Conn.: Seabury Press,
1959.   DHU/MO; NN/Sch
Blackson, Lorenzo D.   The Rise
and Progress of the Kingdoms
of Light and Darkness, or the
Reign of Kings, Alpha and
Abadon.   Philadelphia: J.
Nichols, 1867.   DHU/R
Negro author.
Blackwell, George L., (bp.).
Cloaks of Sin. n. p., 1904.
                      NcSalL
Negro author.
-- Man Wanted. n. p., 1907.
                      NcSalL
-- Model Homestead.   Boston:
Marshall Printers, 1893.
                      NcSalL
Blyden, Edward Wilmot. "The
Call of Providence to the
Descendants of Africa in
America." Howard Brotz, (ed.)
Negro Social and Political
Thought. New York: Basic
Books, 1950, pp. 112+.
                      DHU/R
Negro author.
-- Philip and the Church. Cam-

bridge: John Wilson and Son,
1883.   DHU/MO
Boddie, Charles E.   Giant in the
Earth: A Biography. Berne,
Ind.: Berne Witness Co.,
1944.   DHU/MO
Negro author.
Borders, William Holmes. God
is Real. Atlanta, Ga.: Fuller
Press, 1951.   DHU/MO
-- What Is That in Thine Hand?
and Other Sermons. n. p.,
n. d.
Negro author.
Bouey, Harrison N. "Missionary
to Africa, Agent American
Baptist Publication Society,
District Secretary." Wm. J.
Simmons, (ed.). Men of Mark
... (Cleveland, O.: Geo. M.
Rewell & Co., 1887), p. 951.
                      DHU/R
Boulden, Jesse Freeman. "Mem-
ber of the Lower House of the
Legislature of Mississippi in
Reconstruction Times, Agent
of the American Baptist Publi-
cation Society." Wm. J. Sim-
mons, (ed.). Men of Mark...
(Cleveland, O.: George M.
Rewell & Co., 1887), p. 707.
                      DHU/R
Bowen, John Wesley Edward.
"Letter to the Editor," Zion
Herald, 124 (Apr. 10, 1946),
p. 338.   DLC; CtY-D
Negro author.
-- What Shall the Harvest Be?
A National Sermon, or a Se-
ries of Plain Talks to the Col-
ored People of America, on
Their Problems, by the Rev.
J. W. E. Bowen... in the As-
bury Methodist Episcopal
Church, Washington, D. C.
n. p., n. d. NN/Sch;DHU/MO
-- and Penn I. Garland.   The
United Negro: His Problems
and Progress. Atlanta: D. E.
Luther Pub. Co., 1902.
                      DHU/MO
Bowen, Thomas J. Central Af-
rica.   Adventures and Mis-

(Bowen, T. J. cont.)
sionary Labors in Several
Countries in the Interior of
Africa from 1849 to 1856.
... Charleston, Southern Bap-
tist Publication Society, 1857.
DHU/MO; NN/Sch
Bragg, George Freeman. A
Bond Slave of Christ. Enter-
ing the Ministry Under Great
Difficulties. n. p. , n. d.
DHU/MO
Negro author.
-- The Hero of Jerusalem. In
Honor of the One Hundredth
Anniversary of the Birth of
General William Mahone of
Virginia. Baltimore: The Au-
thor, n. d.   DHU/MO
-- Heroes of the Eastern Shore:
Absalom Jones, the First of
the Blacks... Baltimore, Md.:
The Author, 1939.   CtY-D
-- Richard Allen and Absalom
Jones. Baltimore, Md.: The
Church Advocate Press, 1915.
DHU/MO; NN/Sch
-- Seven Speeches and Sermons
and a Tribute to Mrs. Nellie
G. Bragg, by the Rev. George
F. Bragg, Jr.... Baltimore:
n. p. , 1917-37.   NN/Sch
Bragg, George Tillman. The
Story of the First of the
Blacks, the Pathfinder, Ab-
salom , 1746-1818. Balti-
more, Md.: n. p. , 1929.
DHU/MO
Brawley, Benjamin Griffin.
Early Negro American Writers.
Freeport, N. Y.: Books for
Libraries Press, 1968. Rpr.
DHU/R
Negro author.
-- History of the English Hymn.
New York: Abingdon Press,
1932.   DHU/R
Brawley, Edward McKnight, D. D.
"Editor Baptist Tribune,
President of Selma University,
Sunday School Agent of South
Carolina." Wm. J. Simmons,
(ed.). Men of Mark... (Cleve-

land, O.: George M. Rewell
1887), p. 908.   DHU/R
Braxton, P.H. A. "Pastor of the
Calvary Baptist Church, Balti-
more, Maryland, Writer,
Speaker." Wm. J. Simmons,
(ed.). Men of Mark... (Cleve-
land, O.: George M. Rewell
& Co. , 1887), p. 1046.
DHU/R
Brooks, Walter H. The Pastor's
Voice. Washington, D. C. :
The Associated Press, 1945.
DHU/R
Negro author.
Brown, Annie E. Religious Work
and Travels. Chester, Pa. :
O. T. Pancoast, 1909.
NN/Sch
Brown, Hallie Q. Pen Pictures
of the Pioneers of Wilberforce.
Wilberforce, O. : Aldine Pub.
Co. , 1937.   DHU/MO
Negro author.
Brown, John M. "An Active
Bishop in the A. M. E. Church."
Wm. J. Simmons, (ed.). Men
of Mark... (Cleveland, O. :
George M. Rewell & Co. ,
1887), p. 1113.   DHU/R
Negro author.
Bruce, John Edward, comp.
Short Biographical Sketches of
Eminent Negro Men and Wom-
en in Europe and the United
States. With Extracts from
their Writing and Public Utter-
ances. Yonkers, N. Y. : Ga-
zette Press, 1910. DHU/MO
Bullock, Ralph W. In Spite of
Handicaps; Brief Biographical
Sketches with Discussion Out-
lines of Outstanding Negroes
Now Living Who Are Achiev-
ing Distinction in Various Lines
of Endeavor... with a Foreword by Channing H. Tobias.
New York: Associated Press,
1927.   DHU/MO
Bunton, Henry C. , (bp.). The
Challenge to Become Involved
in the Drama of Restoration.
n. p. , 1966. Pam. File; DHU/R

Negro author.
Burgan, I. M. "President of Paul
Quinn College, Educator, Pi-
oneer." Wm. J. Simmons,
(ed.). Men of Mark... (Cleve-
land, O.: George M. Rewell
& Co., 1887), p. 1086.
            DHU/R
Burgess, Lois F. No Boot
Straps. n. p., 1965. DHU/MO
Negro author.
Burroughs, Nannie Helen. Mak-
ing Your Community Christian.
Washington, D. C.: Woman's
Convention, n. d.   DHU/MO
Negro author.
-- What Do You Think? Wash-
ington, D. C.: n. p., 1950.
            NN/Sch
Butcher, Charles Simpson. "A
Historical Study of Efforts to
Secure Church Union Among
Independent Negro Method-
ists." B. D. Paper, School of
Religion, Howard University,
1939.
Cadbury, N. H. The Life of
Amanda Smith. Birmingham,
Ala.: Cornish, 1916. NcNjHi
A Negro evangelist.
Cain, Richard Harvey. "Bishop
of the A. M. E. Church, Con-
gressman, Senator in the
South Carolina Legislature,
President of Paul Quinn Col-
lege." Wm. J. Simmons, (ed.).
Men of Mark... (Cleveland, O.:
George M. Rewell & Co.,
1887), p. 866.   DHU/R
Caldwell, Josiah S., (bp.). "Fi-
nancial Department of the A.
M. E. Zion Church." I. G.
Penn. The United Negro (At-
lanta: Luther, 1902), pp. 524+.
Negro author.
-- "Greatest Need of the Negro
Race." W. N. Hartshorn, An
Era of Progress and Promise
(Boston: Priscilla Pub. Co.,
1910), pp. 399+.
-- "Young People's Societies as
a Religious Force in the
Church." I. G. Penn. The

United Negro (Atlanta: Luther,
1902), pp. 524+.
            NcSalL; DHU/R
Campbell, Israel. An Autobiog-
raphy. Bond and Free: or
Yearings for Freedom, From
my Green Brier House...
Philadelphia: By the Author,
1861.   SCBHC
Campbell, J. P. "Bishop of the
A. M. E. Church, the Theo-
logian of the Denomination."
Wm. J. Simmons, (ed.).
Men of Mark... (Cleveland,
O.: George M. Rewell & Co.,
1887), p. 1031.   DHU/R
Campbell, Matthew. "One of
God's Servants--Full of Years
and Work for Christ, a Thirty
Years' Pastorate." Wm. J.
Simmons, (ed.). Men of
Mark... (Cleveland, O.: Geo.
M. Rewell & Co., 1887), p.
719.   DHU/R
Carey, Lott. "First American
Missionary to Africa." Wm.
J. Simmons, (ed.). Men of
Mark... (Cleveland, O.:
Geo. M. Rewell & Co., 1887),
p. 506.   DHU/R; DHU/MO
Carter, Luther C., Jr. "Negro
Churches in a Southern Com-
munity." Doctoral disserta-
tion, Yale University, 1955.
Carter, Randall Albert, (bp.).
Canned Laughter. Cincinnati:
Caxton Press, 1923. DHU/MO
Negro author.
-- Feeding Among the Lilies.
Cincinnati: Caxton Press,
1923.   NN/Sch; DHU/MO
-- Gathered Fragments. Nash-
ville: The Parthenon Press,
1939. DHU/MO; NN/Sch
-- Morning Meditations and Other
Selections. Atlanta: Foote &
Davis Co., 1917.
            NN/Sch; DHU/MO
Cattell, Elizabeth. "A Quaker
Portrait: Barrington Dunbar."
Friends Journal (16:9, My. 1,
1970), pp. 257-58. DHU/R

Ceremonies Attending the Unveiling of the Monument Erected in the memory of Bishop Daniel Alexander Payne, Monday, May 21, 1894. At Laurel Cemetery, Baltimore, Maryland, Appendix-Sermon by Bishop A. W. Wayman, at the Funeral of Bishop Payne, Preached in Bethel A. M. E. Church, Baltimore, Dec. 5, 1893. Published by the Committee.   DHU/MO
Charlton, Huey Edward. "Stability of the Negro Family in a Southern Community." Doctoral dissertation, Temple University, 1958.
Clanton, Solomon T., Jr. A. B., B. D. "Instructor of Mathematics, Secretary of the American National Baptist Convention, Agent of the American Baptist Publication Society." Wm. J. Simmons, (ed.), Men of Mark ... (Cleveland, O.: Geo. M. Rewell & Co., 1887), p. 419.
                              DHU/R
Clement, George C., (bp.). Boards for Life's Building. Cincinnati: Caxton Press, 1924.   DHU/MO; NN/Sch
Clinton, George Wylie, (bp.). Christianity Under the Searchlight. Nashville, Tenn.: National Baptist Pub. Board, 1909.   NN/Sch
Negro author.
-- "The Church and Modern Industry." Elias B. Sandford. Federal Council of the Churches in America (New York: Revell Press, 1919), pp. 65+.
                              DHU/R
-- "The Negro as a Freeman." W. N. Hartshorn. An Era of Progress and Promise. (Boston: Priscilla Pub., 1910), pp. 43+.
                    NcSalL; DHU/R
-- The Negro in the Ecumenical Conference of 1901. n. p., n. d.   NcSalL
-- The Three Alarm Cries.

n. p., 1906.   NcSalL
-- "To What Extent is the Negro Uplifting the Race." D. W. Culp. Twentieth Century Negro Literature. (Atlanta: Nicholson, 1902), pp. 115+.
                    NcSalL; DHU/R
-- Tuskegee Lectures. n. p., 1907.   NcSalL
-- A Voice From the South. n. p., n. d.   NcSalL
Coker, Daniel. A Dialogue Between a Virginian and an African Minister... Baltimore: Printed by Benjamin Edes, 1810.   DHU/MO; DHU/R
Negro author.
Also, in Negro Protest Pamphlets: A Compendium. New York: Arno Press, 1969.
-- Journal of Daniel Coker... Baltimore: Edward J. Cole Publisher, 1820.   DHU/MO
Coleman, Charles Cecil, (bp.), Patterns of Race Relations in the South. New York: Exposition Press, 1949.
                    NcSalL; DHU/MO
Negro author.
Coleman, Lucretia H. Newman. Poor Ben, A Story of Real Life. Nashville: Publishing House of the A. M. E. Sunday Union, 1890.   DHU/MO
Life of Bishop B. W. Arnette of the A.M. E. Church.
Coles, Samuel B. Preacher with a Plow. Boston: Houghton Mifflin, 1957.
Negro author.
Confessions of a Negro Preacher. Chicago: The Canterbury Press, 1928.   DHU/MO
Conner, James Mayer. Elements of Success. Philadelphia: A. M. E. Book Concern, 1911.
                              NN/Sch
Cooper, Anna Julia (Haywood). Life and Writings of the Grimke Family. n. p., '51.
                    NN/Sch;   DHU/MO
Negro author.
Corrothers, James David. In

Spite of the Handicap; an Auto-
biography... With an Introduc-
tion by Ray Stannard Baker.
New York: George H. Doran
Co., 1916.   DHU/MO
    Negro author.
Crawford, Evans Edgar. "The
Leadership Role of the Urban
Negro Minister." Doctoral
dissertation, Boston Univer-
sity, 1957.
Crite, Allan Rohan. All Glory;
Brush Drawing Meditations on
the Prayer of Consecration.
Cambridge, Mass.: Society of
St. John the Evangelist, 1947.
         DHU/MO; NN/Sch
    Negro illustrator.
Crogman, W. H. The Negro:
His Needs and Claims. At-
lanta: n.p., 1883.   IEG
Cronon, Edmund D. Black
Moses; the Story of Marcus
Garvey... Madison, Wisc.:
The University of Wisconsin
Press, 1969.   DHU/MO
    Garvey's ideas on religion,
    pp. 177-83; 215.
Crummell, Alexander. Africa
and America: Addresses and
Discourses. Springfield,
Mass.: Willey, 1891.
         NN/Sch; A&M
    Missions - Africa, West,
    pp. 405-53.
    Negro author.
-- Charitable Institutions in Col-
ored Churches. Washington,
D.C.: R.L. Pendleton, 189?
         NN/Sch
-- Civilization the Primal Need
of the Race. Washington, D.C.:
The Academy, 1898. DHU/MO
    (American Negro Academy
    Occasional Papers, No. 3.)
-- Commonsense in Common
Schooling. A Sermon... n.p.,
n.d.   DHU/MO
-- A Defence of the Negro Race
in America from the Assaults
and Charges of Rev. L.J.
Tucker, D.D., of Jackson,
Miss. in Paper before the

"Church Congress" of 1882 on
the Relation of the Church to
the Colored Race. Prepared
and published at the request
of the colored clergy of the
Protestant Episcopal Church
... Washington: Judd & Det-
weiler, 1883.   DHU/MO
-- The Duty of a Rising Chris-
tian State to Contribute to the
World's Well-Being and Civilization, and the Means by
Which it May Perform the
Same. The Annual Oration
Before the Common Council
and the citizens of Monrovia,
Liberia-July 26, 1855. Lon-
don: Wertheim & Macintosh,
1856.   DHU/MO
-- The Greatest of Christ and
Other Sermons. New York:
Thomas Whittaker, 1882.
         NN/Sch; DHU/R
-- "Rector of St. Luke's Church,
Washington, D.C., Professor
of Mental and Moral Sciences,
in the College of Liberia,
Author." Wm. J. Simmons,
(ed.). Men of Mark... (Cleve-
land, O.: George M. Rewell
& Co., 1887), p. 530.
         DHU/R
-- The Race-Problem in Amer-
ica. Washington, D.C.: W.
R. Morrison, 1889. DHU/MO
-- Sermons Preached in Trinity
Church, Monrovia, West Af-
rica. Boston: Press of J.R.
Marion & Son, 1865. DHU/MO
Culp, D.W. Twentieth Century
Negro Literature. Atlanta:
Nicholson & Co., 1902.
         DHU/MO
    Chapters 18, 20 & 24 deal
    directly with the Negro
    Church; many other chapters
    are by black churchmen.
Current, William Chester. God's
Promise to His People, by
Homeless and Blind Billy...
Nashville, Tenn.: National
Baptist Publishing Board,
1908.   NN/Sch

Dale, Marcus. Shrewd Financier and General Manager, Business Capacity Shown." Wm. J. Simmons, (ed.). Men of Mark... (Cleveland, O.: Geo. M. Rewell & Co., 1887), p. 685.   DHU/R

Dangerfield, Abner Walker. Extracts on Religious and Industrial Training... Washington, D.C.: Murray Bros., Printers, 1909.   NN/Sch
   Negro author.

Davis, J. Arthur. Reformation and Unity... Can the Leopard Change His Spots, or the Afro-American His Status? Washington, D.C.: Hamilton Printing Co., 1913. NN/Sch
   "An open letter to the Afro-American ministry."

Davis, Noah. A Narrative of the Life of Rev. Noah Davis, a Colored Man. Written by Himself, at the Age of Fifty-Four. Printed Solely for the Author's Benefit. Baltimore: John F. Weishampel, Jr., 1859.   SCBHC

Day, Helen Caldwell. Color, Ebony. New York: Sheed & Ward, 1951.   NN/Sch
   Negro author.

-- Not Without Tears. New York: Sheed and Ward, 1954.
                           NN/Sch

Day, Richard Ellsworth. Rhapsody in Black. Philadelphia: Judson Press, 1953.
                 DHU/MO; DHU/R
   Life and preaching career of John Jasper, illiterate Negro 19th century minister.

DeBaptiste, Richard, D.D. "Corresponding Secretary and Beloved Disciple." Wm. J. Simmons, (ed.). Men of Mark ... (Cleveland, O.: Geo. M. Rewell & Co., 1887), p. 352.
                           DHU/R

D'Elia, Donald J. "Dr. Benjamin Rush and the Negro." Journal of the History of

Ideas, (30:3, Jl.-Sept., 1969), pp. 413-23.   DHU/R

-- "The Republican Theology of Benjamin Rush." Pennsylvania History (37; Apr., 1966), pp. 187-203.   DCU/SW; DGW

Derrick, W.B. "Minister of the A.M.E. Church, Pulpit Orator." Wm. J. Simmons, (ed.). Men of Mark... (Cleveland, O.: George M. Rewell & Co., 1887), p. 88.   DHU/R
   Negro. author.

Detweiler, Frederick G. The Negro Press in the United States. Chicago: University of Chicago Press, 1922.
                           DHU/MO
   Negro ministers, writers, and periodicals.

Dixon, William T. "Veteran Pastor of Concord Baptist Church, Brooklyn, New York." Wm. J. Simmons, (ed.). Men of Mark... (Cleveland, O.: George M. Rewell & Co., 1887), p. 718.   DHU/R

Douglass, Frederick. Ceremonies Attending the Unveiling of the Monument Erected to the Memory of Bishop Daniel Alexander Payne, Monday, May 21, 1894. At Laurel Cemetery, Baltimore, Maryland. ...Appendix-Sermon by Bishop A.W. Wayman, at the Funeral of Bishop Payne, Preached in Bethel A.M.E. Church, Baltimore, Dec. 5, 1893. n.p., n.d.   DHU/MO
   Address by Frederick Douglass, pp. 19-30.
   Negro author.

-- Why is the Negro Lynched? ... Reprinted by Permission from "The A.M.E. Church Review" for Memorial Distribution, by a few of his English Friends. Bridgewater: Pr. by John Whitby, 1895.   DHU/MO

Douglass, Robert Lewis. "The Life and Thought of Bishop Henry Clay Bunton." B.D. Pa-

per, School of Religion, Howard University, 1968.
Douglass, William. "A Clergyman of the Protestant Episcopal Church." William Wells
Brown. The Black Man (Mi-
ami, Fla.: Mnemosyne Pub.
Co., 1969), pp. 271-72.
                              DHU/R
Negro author.
Dupee, George Washington.
"Eminent Minister, Modera-
tor of the General Associa-
tion, Editor." Wm. J. Sim-
mons, (ed.). Men of Mark...
(Cleveland, O.: Geo. M. Re-
well & Co., 1887), p. 847.
                              DHU/R
Easton, Hosea. A Treatise on
the Intellectual Character and
Civil and Political Condition
of the Colored People of the
United States and the Preju-
dice Exercised Toward Them:
With a Sermon on the Duty of
the Church to Them... Bos-
ton: Pr. and pub. by Isaac
Knapp, 1837.   DHU/MO
Also in, Negro Protest
Pamphlets: A Compendium.
New York: Arno Press, 1969.
Elaw, Zilpha. Memoirs of the
Life, Religious Experience,
Ministerial Travels and Lab-
ours, of Mrs. Zilpha Elaw,
An American Female of Col-
our in London. Published by
the Authoress and Sold by T.
Dudley, 1846.   DHU/MO
Elizabeth a Colored Minister of
the Gospel, Born in Slavery.
Philadelphia: Tract Associa-
tion of Friends, 1889.
                              NN/Sch
Negro author. Tract no.
170.
Ellison, John Malcus. They
Who Preach. Nashville:
Broadman Press, 1956.
                       DHU/R; NN/Sch
Negro author.
Ewell, John L. A History of
the Theological Department

of Howard University. Wash-
ington, D. C.: Howard Univer-
sity, 1906.   DHU/MO
Faulk, John Henry. "Quickened
by de Spirit: Ten Negro Ser-
mons." Master's thesis, Uni-
versity of Texas, 1940.
Fleton, Ralph Almon. "Un-
trained Negro Clergy." Chris-
tian Century (72:5, Feb. 2,
1955), pp. 141-2.   DHU/R
Ferrill, London. "Pastor of a
Church Incorporated by a
State Legislature, an Old
Time Preacher, Hired by
Town Trustees to Preach to
Colored People." Wm. J.
Simmons, (ed.). Men of
Mark... (Cleveland, O.: Geo.
M. Rewell & Co., 1887), p.
321.   DHU/R
Ferry, Henry J. "Francis
James Grimke: Portrait of a
Black Puritan." Doctoral dis-
sertation, Yale University,
Graduate School, 1970.
Fields, J. B. "An Eloquent Bap-
tist Minister, Popular Histor-
ian, Lecturer, the Annihilator
of Ingersollism." Wm. J. Sim-
mons, (ed.). Men of Mark...
(Cleveland, O.: Geo. M. Re-
well & Co., 1887), p. 1016.
                              DHU/R
Finley, James B. History of
the Wyandot Mission. Cincin-
nati: Wright & Swormstedt,
1840.   NjMD
Fishel, Leslie H. and Benjamin
Quarles. Black America: A
Documentary History. New
York: Morrow, 1970. DHU/R
Fisher, Miles Mark. "Jobs for
Negro Preachers." Opportunity
(10:5, My., 1932), pp. 142-
43.   DHU/MO
Negro author.
-- The Master's Slave, Elijah
John Fisher. Philadelphia:
The Judson Press, 1922.
                              DHU/MO
Biography of the pastor of
Olivet Baptist Church, Geor-

(Fisher, M. M. cont.)
gia, written by his son, pas-
tor of White Rock Baptist
Church, Durham, N. C.
Floyd, Silas Xavier. "The
Apostle of the Second Com-
ing." Voice of the Negro (3:
6, Je., 1906), p. 441.
                        DHU/MO
Negro author.
-- The Gospel of Service, and
Other Sermons. Philadelphia:
American Baptist Publication
Society, 1902.   GAU
-- Life of Charles T. Walker,
D. D. ("The Black Surgeon,")
Pastor, Mt. Olivet Baptist
Church. Nashville: National
Baptist Publishing Board,
1902.   DHU/MO
Foley, Albert S. "Bishop Healy
and the Colored Catholic Con-
gress." Interracial Review
(28; 1954), pp. 79-80. DGU
-- God's Men of Color: The
Colored Catholic Priests of
the U. S. 1854-1954. New
York: Farrar, Straus, 1955.
                        DHU/R; INU
-- "Status and Role of the Negro
Priest in the American Cath-
olic Church." American Cath-
olic Sociological Review (16;
Je., 1955), pp. 83-92. DGU
-- "U. S. Colored Priests: Hun-
dred Years Survey." America
(49; Je. 13, 1953), pp. 295-
97.   DGU
Foote, Julia A. J. A Brand
Plucked from the Fire. An
Autobiographical Sketch. New
York: G. Hughes & Co.,
1879.   DHU/MO; DLC
Negro author.
Foster, Gustavus L. Uncle
Johnson, the Pilgrim of Six
Score Years. Philadelphia:
Presbyterian Board of Publi-
cation, 1867.
        Pam. File; NcD
Frazier, Edward Franklin. God
and War. n. p., n. d. DHU/MO
Negro author.

Gaddie, Daniel Abraham, D. D.
"From the Blacksmith Shop
to the Pulpit, Temperance
Advocate, Moderator of Fifty
Thousand Baptists." Wm. J.
Simmons, (ed.). Men of
Mark... (Cleveland, O.: Geo.
M. Rewell & Co., 1887), p.
647.   DHU/R
Galbreath, George, (bp.). "Bi-
ography." Carter G. Wood-
son. The History of the Ne-
gro Church. (Washington,
D. C.: Associated Publishers,
192-), pp. 105-6.
                DHU/R; NcSalL
Negro author.
Garland, Phyl. "The Unorthodox
Ministry of Leon H. Sullivan."
Ebony (26:7, May, 1971), pp.
112-20.   DHU/R
Garnet, Henry Highland. A
Memorial Discourse; Deliv-
ered in the Hall of the House
of Representatives, Washing-
ton, D. C., on Sabbath, Feb-
ruary 12, 1865. With an In-
troduction by James McCune
Smith. Philadelphia: J. M.
Wilson, c. 1865.   NN/Sch
Negro author.
-- "Minister, Missionary to Ja-
maica and Orator." Wm.
Wells Brown. The Black Man
(Miami, Fla.: Mnemosyne
Pub. Co., 1969), pp. 149-51.
                        DHU/R
-- "Minister Resident of Liberia,
Distinguished Minister of the
Gospel, and a Brilliant Ora-
tor." Wm. J. Simmons, (ed.).
Men of Mark... (Cleveland,
O.: Geo. M. Rewell & Co.,
1887), p. 656.   DHU/R
Glass, Victor Thomas. "An An-
alysis of the Sociological and
Psychological Factors Re-
lated to the Call to Christian
Service of the Negro Baptist
Ministers." Doctoral disser-
tation, Southern Baptist Theo-
logical Seminary, 1952.
Goens, Anna. How God Became

Real in Four Years: A Spir-
itual Experience. New York:
Exposition Press, 1957.
            DHU/MO
   Negro author.
Gordon, Buford F. , (bp.). The
Negro in South Bend. n. p. ,
n. d.   NcSalL
   Negro author.
-- Pastor and People. n. p. ,
1930.   NcSalL
-- The Quest of the Restless
Souls. n. p. , n. d.   NcSalL
-- Reflections in Prose and Po-
etry. n. p. , n. d.   NcSalL
Granderson, Elizabeth. Church
Chatter. New York: Pageant
Press, 1950.   DHU/MO
   Negro author.
Grandy, Moses. "Narrative of
the Life of"... Wm. L.
Katz, (ed.). Five Slave Narra-
tives (New York: Arno Press,
1969), pp. 35-6.   DHU/MO
Grant, John Henry. Am I a
Christian or Just a Church
Member? Which? Nashville,
Tenn. : The Author, n. d.
            NN/Sch
   Negro author.
Griffith, T. L. "Negroes in the
Baptist Denomination," Baptist
(8; 1927), pp. 872-3, 906-7.
            SCBHC
Grimke, Francis James. "Earnest
Words from a Colored Mis-
sionary." The Church at Home
and Abroad (1; Ja. , 1887), pp.
65-6.   DHU/R
   Negro author.
-- "Learned and Eloquent Presby-
terian Divine, Touching Me-
morial on Leaving Washington,
D. C." Wm. J. Simmons, (ed.).
Men of Mark... (Cleveland,
O. : Geo. M. Rewell & Co. ,
1887), p. 608.   DHU/R
-- A Look Backward Over a Pas-
torate of More Than Forty-
Two Years Over the Fifteenth
Street Presbyterian Church,
Washington, D. C. ... Deliv-
ered Oct. 14, 1923. Wash-

ington, D. C. , n. p. , 1923.
            DHU/MO
Gustafson, James M. "The
Clergy in the United States."
Daedalus (92; Fall, 1963), pp.
724-44.   DHU
   Includes material on the un-
satisfactory state of the Negro
Protestant Ministry and their
inadequate education.
Hall, A. L. The Ancient Mediae-
val and Modern Greatness of
the Negro. By Dr. A. L. Hall,
Memphis, Tenn. : n. p. , n. d.
            SCBHC
   Containing biographical
sketches.
Hall, Ernest N. "A Negro In-
stitutional Church." Southern
Workman (50; Mr. , 1921), pp.
113+. Illus.   DHU/MO
Harding, Vincent. "W. E. B. Du-
Bois and the Black Messianic
Vision." Freedomways (9:1,
Wint. , 1969), pp. 44-58.
            DHU/R
   Negro author.
Harlan, Howard Harper. John
Jasper--a Case History in
Leadership. Charlottesville:
University of Virginia, 1936.
   NcD; DLC; DHU/MO
Harvey, Claire. "The Black Wom-
an: Keeper of the Faith."
The Church Woman (35:9,
Nov. , 1969), pp. 15-18.
Pam. File; DHU/R
Hatcher, William Eldridge.
John Jasper, the Unmatched
Negro Philosopher and
Preacher. Chicago: Fleming
H. Revell & Co. , 1908.
            DHU/MO
Haygood, Atticus G. Our Chil-
dren... Macon & Atlanta, Ga. :
John W. Burke & Co. , 1876.
            DHU/MO
   Negro author.
Haynes, Lemuel. "A Distin-
guished Theologian." Wm. J.
Simmons, (ed.). Men of Mark
... (Cleveland, O. : Geo. M.
Rewell & Co. , 1887), p.

(Haynes, L. cont.)
677.   DHU/R
Negro author.
Henderson, George W. "Colored
Ministers." Southern Work-
man (33; Mr., 1904), pp.
174+.   DHU/MO
Henry, Romiche. A Question of
Life. New York: Vantage
Press, 1963.   DHU/MO
Negro author.
Henson, Josiah. Father Henson's
Story of His Own Life. Bos-
ton: John P. Jewett & Co.,
1858.
Higgins, (Sir) Godfrey. Jesus--
a Colored Man? Race Preju-
dice by Jerome David, The
Life of Jesus, by Members of
National Association for the
Advancement of Colored
People. Dallas, Tex.: n.p.,
n.d.   DHU/MO
Hill, Charles Leander. The
Evangel in Ebony. Boston:
Meador Publishing Co, 1960.
                        DHU/R
Negro author.
A book of sermons.
-- (tr.). The Communes of
Philip Melanchthon ... With
a Critical Introduction by the
Translator ... Boston: Meador
Publishing Co., 1944. DHU/MO
Hill, Daniel Grafton. Well-
Springs of Life (and other Ad-
dresses to College Youth) De-
livered at All University Re-
ligious Services in Andrew
Ranking Memorial Chapel,
Howard University. Washing-
ton, D. C., n.p., n.d.
    DHU/R; DHU/MO; NN/Sch
Hill, John Louis. When Black
Meets White. Cleveland:
The Argyle Pub. Co., 1924.
                        DHU/MO
Religion, pp. 60-80.
Holloman, John Lawrence Sulli-
van. "Eulogy for ..." by John
M. Ellison. Journal of Reli-
gious Thought (27:2, Sum.
Suppl., 1970), pp. 19-22.

                        DHU/R
Negro minister, Washing-
ton, D. C.
Holly, James Theodore, (bp.).
"First Negro American Bishop." Holly Alonzo, God and
the Negro. Nashville: National Baptist Publishing Board,
1937.   DHU/R
Negro author.
-- "Negro Minister of the Prot-
estant Episcopal Church."
Wm. Wells Brown. The
Black Man (Miami, Fla., Mne-
mosyne Pub. Co., 1969), pp.
274-76.   DHU/R
-- The Word of God Against Ec-
clesiastical Imperialism.
1880.   OWibfU
In Arnette Papers, v. 76.
Holmes, James H. "Pastor of a
Flourishing Church in Rich-
mond, Virginia. Wm. J. Sim-
mons, (ed.). Men of Mark...
(Cleveland, O.: Geo. M. Re-
well & Co., 1887), p. 666.
                        DHU/R
Negro author.
Hood, James Walker, (bp.). The
Plan of the Apocalypse.
York, Pa.: Anstadt & Sons,
1900.   NcSalL
Negro author.
"How the Stars See God." Ebony
(14; Apr., 1959), pp. 101-2.
                        DHU/MO
Hughes, Langston. The Gospel
Glory. A Passion Play. New
York: n.p., 1962. NN/Sch
Negro author.
Hurst, John H. "A. M. E. Bish-
op." Alonzo Holly God and
the Negro. Nashville, Tenn.:
Natl. Baptist Publication Bd.,
1937.   DHU/R
Negro author.
Imes, G. Lake. "Negro Minis-
ters and Country Life." Re-
ligious Education (7:2, Je.,
1912), pp. 169-75. DHU/R
Negro author.
"J. W. C. Pennington." Free
Presbyterian (Oct. 22,

1851). OWoC
Jackson, Andrew Webster. A
Sure Foundation. Houston,
Tex.: n. p., 1940. NN/Sch
Biographies of Negro min-
isters.
Jasper, John T. "De Sun Do
Move: The Celebrated Ser-
mon of a Negro Minister.
Richmond: Dietz Press, n. d.
DHU/R
-- "The Sun Do Move." Wm. J.
Simmons, (ed.). Men of Mark
... (Cleveland, O.: Geo. M.
Rewell & Co., 1887), p. 1064.
DHU/R
Biography of John T. Jas-
per.
Jenness, Mary. A Course for
Intermediates on the Negro in
America, Based Primarily on
Twelve Negro Americans.
New York: Council of Women
for Home Missions and Mis-
sionary Education Movement,
1936. DHU/MO; CtY-D;
NN/Sch
Biographies of Wm. Lloyd
Imes and Howard Thurman.
Jeter, Henry Norval. Baptist
Preacher. Wm. J. Simmons,
(ed.). Men of Mark... (Cleve-
land, O.: Geo. M. Rewell &
Co., 1887), p. 588. DHU/R
Johnson, Harvey. Eminent Bal-
timore Pastor Prominent in
the Councils of his Church.
Wm. J. Simmons, (ed.). Men
of Mark... (Cleveland, O.:
Geo. M. Rewell & Co., 1887),
p. 729. DHU/R
Johnson, Henry Theodore. Tus-
kegee Talks. Ministerial
Training and Qualification.
Philadelphia: Press of Inter-
national Printing Co., 1902.
DHU/MO; NN/Sch
Negro author.
Johnson, John Howard. A Place
of Adventure. Essays and
Sermons. Greenwich, Conn.:
Seabury Press, 1955.
DHU/MO

Negro author.
Johnson, Joseph A., (bp.). The
Soul of the Black Preacher.
n. p., 1970. DHU/R
Negro author.
Sermons and meditations
by a bishop of the Christian
Methodist Episcopal Church.
"Johnson, Mordecai W. Edwin
R. Embree. 13 Against the
Odds, New York: The Viking
Press, 1944. DHU/R
Biography of Baptist min-
ister and former president of
Howard University.
-- "The Faith of the American
Negro." Carter G. Woodson,
Negro Orators and Their Ora-
tions. (New York: Russell &
Russell, 1969), pp. 568-663.
DHU/R
Negro author.
Address delivered as one
of three commencement parts
at Howard University, June
22, 1922.
Johnson, W. Bishop. The
Scourging of the Negro. A
Sermon delivered at Second
Baptist Church, Washington,
D. C. By the Pastor... Sunday,
April 10, 1904 at 11:00 a. m.
Washington, D. C.: Beresford
Printer, 1904. DHU/MO
Johnson, William Henry. A
Sketch of the Life of Rev.
Henry Williams, D. D., Late
Pastor of the Gilfield Baptist
Church, Petersburg, Virginia,
with Ceremonies Incident to
his Death, and to the Erection
of a Monument to his Memory.
Petersburg, Va.: Fenn &
Owen, Printers, 1901.
SCBHC
Johnstone, Ronald L. "Negro
Preachers Take Sides." Re-
view of Religious Research
(2:1, Fall, 1969), pp. 81-89.
DHU/R
Data on sociological change
of Negro clergymen.

Jones, Daniel. "Presiding Elder
of the M. E. Church, his
Hair-Breadth Escapes." Wm.
J. Simmons, (ed.). Men of
Mark... (Cleveland, O.: Geo.
M. Rewell & Co., 1887), p.
583.   DHU/R
Jones, Robert E. "Qualifications
of the Minister." Arcadius S.
Trawick, (ed.). The New
Voice in Race Adjustments.
(New York: Student Volunteer
Movement, 1914), pp. 96-9.
                        DHU/R
    Negro author.
Jordan, Casper Leroy. "First
Freedom Rider." Negro Di-
gest (10; Aug. 1961), pp. 38-
42.   DHU/MO
    "About Bishop Reverdy C.
Ransom of the A. M. E.
Church."
Kelly, Edmund. Christian Letter
Writer, Lecturer and Author.
Wm. J. Simmons, (ed.). Men
of Mark... (Cleveland, O.:
Geo. M. Rewell & Co., 1887),
p. 291.   DHU/R
King, Willis J., (bp.). The
Spiritual Pilgrimage of Two
Christian Leaders... Saul of
Tarsus and John Wesley.
Monrovia, Liberia, W. Af-
rica: n.p., n.d.   DHU/MO
    Negro author.
LaFarge, John. "Aunt Pigeon's
108 Years." America (56;
Mr. 6, 1937), pp. 551+.
                        DLC
Lawson, R. C. The Anthropology
of Jesus Christ Our Kinsman
... New York: Church of
Christ, n.d.   DHU/MO
    Negro author.
Lee, Benjamin Franklin, D. D.
"Editor of the Christian Re-
corder, President of Wilber-
force University for Many
Years." Wm. J. Simmons,
(ed.). Men of Mark... (Cleve-
land, O.: Geo. M. Rewell &
Co., 1887), p. 922.   DHU/R
    Negro author.

Lee, John Francis. Building the
Sermon. Atlanta, Ga.: A. B.
Caldwell Publishing Co., 1921.
                        NN/Sch
    Negro author.
"Letters of Richard Allen and Ab-
salom Jones." Journal of Ne-
gro History (1; Oct., 1916),
pp. 436-43.   DHU/MO
Levine, Richard M. "The End
of the Politics of Pleasure."
Harper's Magazine (242:1451,
Apr., 1971), pp. 45-60.
                        DHU/R
    "The decline and fall of
Adam Clayton Powell, Prince
of Harlem."
Lewis, Carlos A. Catholic Ne-
gro Bishops; a Brief Survey
of the Present and the Past.
Bay St. Louis, Miss.: Divine
Word Publications, 1958.
                        CtY-D
Lewis, John W. The Life, La-
bors and Travels of Elder
Charles Bowles, of the Free
Will Baptist Denomination.
... Together with an Essay on
the Character and Condition of
the African Race. Watertown:
Ingalls and Stowell's Steam
Press, 1852. CtY-D; DHU/MO
Licorish, David Nathaniel. Ad-
ventures for Today. New
York: Fortuny's, 1939.
                        DHU/MO
    Negro author.
Lipscombe, E.H. "President of
the Western Union Institute,
Professor of Rhetoric and
Moral Philosophy, Preacher,
Editor of the Mountain Glean-
er." Wm. J. Simmons, (ed.).
Men of Mark... (Cleveland,
O.: George M. Rewell & Co.,
1887), p. 959.   DHU/R
Long, Charles H. Alpha: Myths
of Creation. New York: G.
Braziller, 1963.   DHU/R
    Negro author.
-- "The Death of God: Creativity
or Decadence, a Modest Re-
flection." Criterion (7:3, Spr.,

1968), pp. 15-18.
           Pam. File; DHU/R
Love, Emanuel King. "From the
Ditch to the Pastorate of 5000
Christians, Editor of the Cen-
tennial Record of Georgia,
Associate Editor." Wm. J.
Simmons, (ed.). Men of
Mark... (Cleveland, O.: Geo.
M. Rewell & Co., 1887), p.
481.   DHU/R
Lynch, Hollis R. Edward Wilmot
Blyden. Pan-Negro Patriot
1832-1912. London: Oxford
University Press, 1970.
                     DHU/R
Marrs, Elijah P. "Preacher,
Soldier, Treasurer." Wm. J.
Simmons, (ed.). Men of
Mark... (Cleveland, O.:
Geo. M. Rewell & Co., 1887),
p. 579.   DHU/R
   Negro author.
Martin, John Sella. "Negro
Presbyterian Minister." Wm.
Wells Brown. The Black Man
(Miami, Fla.: Mnemosyne
Pub. Co., 1969), pp. 241-45.
   Negro author.
Massey, James Earl. "When
Thou Prayest; an Interpreta-
tion of Christian Prayer Ac-
cording to the Teachings of
Jesus." Anderson, Ind.:
Warner Press, 1960. NN/Sch
   Negro author.
Mayard, Aurora. The Inner
Guidance. New York: Vantage
Press, 1965.   NN/Sch
   Negro author.
   On Christian life.
Mays, Benjamin E. Born to Re-
bel. New York: Scribner Co.,
1971.   DHU/R
   Autobiography of Baptist
minister and former President
of Morehouse College, Atlanta,
Ga.
   Negro author.
-- "College President Responds."
Social Action (29; Sept., 1962),
pp. 28-30.   DHU/R
-- "Color line Around the

World." Journal of Negro Education (6; Jl., 1937), pp. 134-
43.   DHU
-- "Democratizing and Christianizing America in this Generation." Journal of Negro Education (14; Fall, 1945), pp.
527-34.   DHU
-- "Education of Negro Ministers."
Journal of Negro Education
(2; Jl., 1933), pp. 342-51.
                     DHU
-- "Improving the Morale of Negro Children and Youth."
Journal of Negro Education
(19; Sum., 1950), pp. 420-25.
                     DHU
-- "Role of the Negro Community in Delinquency Prevention
Among Negro Youth." Journal
of Negro Education (28; Sum.,
1959), pp. 366-70.   DHU
-- "Role of the Negro Liberal
Arts College in Post-war Re-
construction." Journal of Ne-
gro Education (11; Jl., 1942),
pp. 400-11.   DHU
-- Weekly Columnist for the
Pittsburgh Courier since 1946.
                     DHU/MO
-- "Why I Believe There is a
God." Ebony (17; Dec. 1961),
p. 139.   DHU/MO
McAlpine, William H. "Baptist
Divine, President of a college,
editor of a weekly journal."
Wm. J. Simmons, (ed.). Men
of Mark... (Cleveland, O.:
Geo. M. Rewell & Co., 1887),
p. 524.   DHU/R
McClellan, G. E. "One Ministry;
Seabury Consultation on the
Training of Negro Ministers."
National Council Outlook (9;
My., 1959), pp. 6-8.
                     DHU/R
McDaniels, Geraldine. God is
the Answer. New York: Van-
tage Press, 1965. DHU/MO
   Negro author.
McDowell, Henry Curtis. Fred-
erick L. Brownlee: Heritage
of Freedom. Philadelphia:

(McDowell, H. C. cont.)
United Church Press, 1963.
          DHU/R
Biography of Negro mis-
sionary to Angola.
McGlotten, Mildred Louise. "Rev.
George Freeman Bragg, a
Negro Pioneer in Social Wel-
fare." Master's thesis, How-
ard University, 1948.
A Negro Protestant Episco-
pal priest.
McKay, John. The Life of Bish-
op Crowther, First African
Bishop of the Niger. London:
Sheldon Press, 1932. NN/Sch
"Largely based upon 'The
Black Bishop,' by Jesse Page,
and 'The Romance of the
Black River,' by Deaville
Walker."
McNeil, Jesse Jai. As the Days
So Thy Strength. Grand Rap-
ids, Mich.: Wm. E. Eerd-
mans, Pub. Co., 1960.
Negro author.
"A Book of Meditations."
Medford, Hampton Thomas, (bp.).
"Biography." Biographical
Encyclopedia of the World
(New York: Institute of Re-
search, 1946), p. 818.
          NcSalL
Negro author.
-- "Biography." J. C. Schwarz.
Religious Leaders of America.
(New York: The Author,
1941-42), p. 779.
          NcSalL; DHU/R
-- "Biography." Who's Who in
Colored America. New York:
Who's Who in Colored Ameri-
ca, 1930-32. NcSalL; DHU/R
Miller, Ernest J. "The Role of
Henry Highland Garnet."
Master's of Sacred Theology,
Union Theology Seminary,
1969.
Miller, George Frazier. The
Sacredness of Humanity. An-
nual Sermon of the Conference
of Church Workers (Episcopal)
Among Colored People at

St. Philips Church, New
York. Brooklyn: Frank R.
Chisholm, Printer, 1914.
          DHU/MO
Miller, Harriet Parks. Pioneer
Colored Christians. Clarks-
ville, Tenn.: W. P. Titus,
1911.   DHU/MO
Miller, Theodore Doughty. "The
Eloquent Pastor of Cherry
Street Baptist Church. Phila-
delphia, Pa., a Veteran Di-
vine Distinguished for Long
Service." Wm. J. Simmons,
(ed.). Men of Mark... (Cleve-
land, O.: Geo. M. Rewell &
Co., 1887), p. 260. DHU/R
Negro author.
"Minister Malcolm, Orator Pro-
fundo." Negro History Bulle-
tin (30; Nov., 1967), pp. 4-5.
          DHU/MO
Minister's Institute. Proceed-
ings; 1936, held at School of
Religion, Bishop College, Mar-
shall, Texas. Dean H. M.
Smith, director.   DHU/MO
"Ministers (Southern Negro)
Meet with Edwin M. Stanton
and General William T. Sher-
man." Journal of Negro His-
tory (16:1, Ja., 1931), pp.
88-94.   DHU
Minor, Richard Clyde. James
Preston Poindexter, Elder
Statesman of Columbus, Ohio.
Reprinted from the Ohio
State Archaeological Historical
Quarterly, July 1947. SCBHC
Mitchell, Henry H. Black
Preaching. Philadelphia: J.
P. Lippincott Co., 1970.
          DHU/R; DLC
Negro author.
Mitchell, Joseph. A Missionary
Pioneer or a Brief Memoir of
the Life and Labors and Death
of John Stewart (Man of Color)
Founder Under God of the Mis-
sions Among the Wyandotts,
at Upper Sandusky, Ohio.
New York: J. C. Totten, 1827.
TAMph; DLC; DHU/R; DHU/MO

Montgomery, Leroy Jeremiah.
An Analysis of Two Distinct
Religions: Organized Chris-
tianity and the Religion of
Jesus Christ. New York: New
Voices Pub. Co., 1956.
                        DHU/MO
Negro author.
Moon, Bertha Louise Hardwick.
The Bird on the Limb. New
York: Comet Press, 1959.
                        DHU/MO
Negro author.
Moorland, Jesse Edward. The
Demand and Supply of In-
creased Efficiency in the Ne-
gro Ministry. Washington,
D.C., 1909.
(American Negro Academy,
Washington, D.C. Occasional
papers, no. 13).   DHU/MO
Negro author.
Morant, John J. Mississippi Min-
ister. 1st ed. New York:
Vantage Press, 1958.
DLC; DHU/MO; NN/Sch; NcD
Negro author.
Morris, Madison C. B.   The
Gospel Message: Sermons and
Pulpit Talks. Delivered Ex-
temporaneously on Special Oc-
casions. New York: Eaton &
Mains, 1905.   NN/Sch
Negro author.
Morse, W. H. "Lemuel Haynes."
Journal of Negro History (4;
Ja., 1919), pp. 22-32.
                        DHU/MO
Negro minister.
Morton, Lena Beatrice. Man Un-
der Stress. New York: Philo-
sophical Library, 1960.
                        DHU/MO
Negro author.
"Negro Churches Need Educated
Ministry." Christian Century
(50; Ag. 23, 1933), p. 1052.
                        DHU/R
"Negro Pastor Nominated for
Presbyterian Moderator."
Concern (7; Dec. 1, 1965), p.
23.   DAU/W
"Negro Preachers Serving

Whites," The Negro History
Bulletin (3; Oct., 1939), p. 8.
                        DHU/MO
"New Catholic Bishop." (Editori-
al). Crisis (72; Oct., 1965),
p. 485.   DHU/MO
Newsome, Effie Lee. "The Ne-
gro Minister as an Emancipa-
tor." Negro Journal of Reli-
gion (4:10, Nov., 1938), p. 11.
                        DHU/R
-- "Saddlebag Saga." The Negro
Journal of Religion (5:1, Ja.,
1940), pp. 7+.   DHU/R
Early Negro Methodist
circuit riders.
Nichols, Decatur Ward, (bp.).
The Episcopal Addresses Presented to the Thirty-Fourth
Quadrennial Session of the
General Conference of the African Methodist Episcopal
Church at Chicago, Illinois,
May 1952. General Confer-
ence, 1952.   NcD
Offley, Greenbury W.A. Narra-
tive of the Life and Labors of
the Rev. G.W. Offley, a Col-
ored Man, and Local Preacher.
Written by Himself. Hart-
ford, Conn.: n.p., 1860. TNF
Olcott, John W. "Recollections
of Katy Ferguson." Southern
Workman (52; Sept., 1923),
p. 463. DHU/MO; CtY-D;
                        DLC
About the Negro woman who
founded the first Sunday School
in New York City.
Olmstead, Clifton E. "Francis
James Grimke (1850-1937)."
Hugh T. Kerr, (ed.). Sons of
the Prophets. Princeton,
N.J.: Princeton University
Press, 1963.   DHU/R
O'Neil, Michael J. Some Outstanding Colored People: In-
teresting Facts in the Lives of
Representative Negroes. Bal-
timore: Franciscan Sisters,
1943.   NN/Sch
"Only Negro Bishop: First Colored Prelate to be Conse-

(Only Negro Bishop cont.)
crated by Vatican in Past
1300 Years Visits Catholic
Centers in U. S." Ebony (50;
Je. , 1950), pp. 40+.
                    DHU/MO
Patterson, Bernardin J. "Re-
flection of a Negro Priest."
Catholic World (200:1, 199,
Feb. , 1965), pp. 269-76.
                    DHU/R
Patterson, S. J. "Presiding
Elder of the A. M. E. Church."
Holly Alonzo, God and the Ne-
gro (Nashville, Tenn. : Natl.
Baptist Pub. Board, 1937).
                    DHU/R
Negro author.
Paul, Nathaniel. An Address,
Delivered on the Celebration
of the Abolition of Slavery in
the State of New York, July
5, 1827... Albany: Printed
by John B. Van Stienbergh,
1827.   DHU/MO; DHU/R
Also in Negro Protest
Pamphlets; A Compendium.
New York: Arno Press, 1969.
Payne, Christopher. "Preacher,
Editor and Soliciting Agent."
Wm. J. Simmons, (ed.). Men
of Mark... (Cleveland, O. :
Geo. M. Rewell & Co. , 1887),
p. 368.   DHU/R
Negro author.
Payne, Daniel Alexander, (bp.).
"Bishop Daniel A. Payne's
Estimate of Abraham Lincoln."
Negro History Bulletin (9;
Feb. 1946), p. 111. DHU/MO
Negro author.
-- "Bishop of A. M. E. Church and
Author." Wm. Wells Brown.
The Black Man. (Miami, Fla. :
Mnemosyne Pub. Co. , 1969),
pp. 207-11.   DHU/R
-- "Senior Bishop of the A. M. E.
Church, Educator and Author,
the Scholar of the Denomina-
tion." Wm. J. Simmons, (ed.).
Men of Mark... (Cleveland,
O. : Geo. M. Rewell & Co. ,
1887), p. 1078.   DHU/R

Peck, W. H. "Negro Chruches in
Detroit; Reply to H. A. White."
Christian Century (55; Apr.
13, 1938), p. 468. DHU/R
Penn, Irvine Garland. The
Afro-American Press and its
Editors. Springfield, Mass. :
Willey & Co. , 1891. DHU/R
Biographies of Negro min-
isters and information about
early religious periodicals.
Negro author.
Pennington, James W. C. , (bp.).
An Address Delivered at New-
ark, N. J. at the First Anni-
versary of West Indian Eman-
cipation, August, 1839. New-
ark: Aaron Guest, Printer,
1839.   DHU/MO
Negro author.
-- "Biography." Wm. L. Katz,
(ed.). Five Slave Narratives.
New York: Arno Press,
1969.   DHU/MO
A early Presbyterian min-
ister.
-- The Fugitive Blacksmith: or,
Events in the History of
James Pennington, Pastor of
a Presbyterian Church, For-
merly a Slave in the State of
Maryland, United States.
3rd ed. London: Charles Gil-
pin, 1850.   DLC; DHU/R
Also in Bontemps, Anna,
(ed.). Great Slave Narratives.
Boston: Beacon Press, 1969,
pp. 193-267.
-- A Lecture Delivered before
the Glasgow Young Men's
Christian Association; and Al-
so Before the St. George's
Biblical Literary and Scientific
Institute... London...New
York: n. p. , n.d. DHU/MO
-- A Narrative of Events of the
Life of J. H. Banks, An Es-
caped Slave from the Cotton
State, Alabama in America.
Liverpool: M. Rourke,
Printer, 1861.   DHU/MO
-- "Negro Presbyterian Minister."
Wm. Wells Brown. The Black

Man. (Miami, Fla.: Mne-
syne Pub. Co., 1969), pp.
276-78.   DHU/R
-- "Speeches." Proceedings of
the General Anti-Slavery Con-
vention...Held in London
From Tuesday June 15th, to
Tuesday, June 20th, 1843.
(London: John Snow, 1843), pp.
16 f.   NcD
Perkins, A. E. Sunday School
Plans and Outlines. New Or-
leans: The Author, 1923.
          DHU/MO
     "Guide and aid for superin-
tendents, teachers, officers,
and Sunday School workers."
Negro author.
Perry, Rufus Lewis. "Ph. D.,
Editor, Ethnologist, Essayist,
Logician, Profound Student of
Negro History, Scholar in the
Greek, Latin and Hebrew Lan-
guages." Wm. J. Simmons,
(ed.). Men of Mark... (Cleve-
land, O.: Geo. M. Rewell &
Co., 1887), p. 620. DHU/R
Negro author.
Peterson, Daniel H. The Look-
ing-Glass: Being a True Re-
port and Narrative of the Life
Travels of ... a Colored
Clergyman. New York:
Wright, Printer, 1854.
          DHU/MO
Negro author.
Pettiford, William Reuben. "A
Successful Pastor, Trustee of
Selma University." Wm. J.
Simmons, (ed.). Men of
Mark... (Cleveland, O.: Geo.
M. Rewell & Co., 1887), p.
460.   DHU/R
Poindexter, James. "Advocate
of Human Rights, Minister of
the Gospel and Agitator, Di-
rector of the Bureau of For-
estry, Member of the Board
of Education of the City of
Columbus, Ohio." Wm. J.
Simmons, (ed.). Men of
Mark... (Cleveland, O.: Geo.
M. Rewell & Co., 1887), p.

394.   DHU/R
Ponton, M. M. Life and Times
of Henry M. Turner. The
Antecedent & Preliminary His-
tory of the Life & Times of
Bishop H. M. Turner, His
Boyhood Education & Public
Career... Atlanta: A. B. Cald-
well Pub., 1917. DHU/MO
Powell, Adam Clayton, Jr. "The
Early Years of Adam Powell."
Freedomways (7; Sum., 1967),
pp. 199-213.   DHU/R
-- Keep the Faith, Baby! New
York: Trident Press, 1967.
DHU/MO; DLC; GAU; NN/Sch
Negro author.
Powell, Adam Clayton, Sr.
Against the Tide; an Autobiog-
raphy. New York: R. R.
Smith, 1938. TNF; DHU/MO
Negro author.
-- Palestine and Saints in Ceas-
ar's Household. New York:
R. R. Smith, 1939.
DHU/MO; DLC; NN/Sch
-- Riots and Ruins. New York:
Richard R. Smith, 1945.
          NN/Sch
-- Upon This Rock. New York:
Abyssinian Baptist Church,
1949.   SCBHC
Price, Joseph, A. B. "President
of Livingston College. Great
Temperance Orator." Wm. J.
Simmons, (ed.). Men of Mark
... (Cleveland, O.: Geo. M.
Rewell & Co., 1887), p. 754.
          DHU/R
Proctor, Henry Hugh. Between
Black and White; Autobio-
graphical Sketches. Boston:
Chicago: the Pilgrim Press,
1925. DHU/MO; CtY-D
Negro author.
Negro ministers, chapters
6 & 7.
Progress of a Race; or, the Re-
markable Advancement of the
American Negro, from the
Bondage of Slavery, Ignorance,
and Poverty to the Freedom of
Citizenship, Intelligence, Af-

(Progress... cont.)
fluence, Honor and Trust.
Rev. and enl. by J. L. Nichols
...and William H. Crogman
...With Special Articles by
Well Known Authorities, Mrs.
Booker T. Washington, Charles
M. Melden...M. W. Dogan...
Albon L. Holsey..Naperville,
Ill: J. L. Nichols & Co.,
1920.   DHU/R
First edition published un-
der the title "The Colored
American." Biographies of
Negroes including ministers,
pp. 329-460.
Purce, Charles L., A. B. "Pres-
ident of Selma University,
Selma, Alabama." Wm. J.
Simmons, (ed.). Men of Mark
... George M. Rewell & Co.,
1887), p. 454.   DHU/R
Randolph, Edwin Archer. The
Life of Rev. John Jasper,
Pastor of Sixth Mt. Zion Bap-
tist Church, Richmond, Va.
From His Birth to the Present
Time, with his Theory on the
Rotation of the Sun. Rich-
mond, Va.: R. T. Hill & Co.,
1884.   DHU/MO
Ransom, Reverdy Cassius, (bp.).
Crispus Attacks, a Negro the
First to Die for American In-
dependence. An Address at
the Metropolitan Opera House,
Philadelphia, Pa. March 6,
1930.   OWibfU
Negro author.
Transcript.
-- Daniel Alexander Payne, The
Prophet of an Era.   OWibfU
Transcript.
--The Disadvantages and Oppor-
tunities of the Colored Youth.
Cleveland: Thomas & Mattel,
1894.   OWibfU
-- Heredity and Environment. An
Address at Literary Congress.
Indianapolis, Ind.: n. p., 1898.
                      OWibfU
Transcript.
-- Out of the Midnight Sky: A

Thanksgiving Day Address,
Nov. 30, 1893 in Mt. Zion
Congregational Church, Cleve-
land, Ohio.   OWibfU
Transcript.
-- Wendell Phillips... Centennial
Oration Delivered...in Ply-
mouth Church, Nov. 29, 1911.
Brooklyn: n. p., 1910.
                      NN/Sch
Reed, John M.   The Devil in
Holy Robes.   The Bible
Against Witchcraft, Fortune
Telling, Good, and Bad Luck.
Little Rock, Ark.: n. p., n. d.
                      DHU/R
Negro author.
Reiss, Julian J. "The Future is
Yours--Plan and Prepare."
Opportunity (25:2, Spr., 1947),
pp. 60-2, 115.   DHU/MO
Discusses Negro ministry
as a career.
Reynolds, Louis B.   The Dawn
of a Brighter Day: Light
Through the Darkness Ahead.
Nashville, Tenn.: The South-
ern Pub. Assn., 1945.
                      DHU/MO
Negro author.
Robinson, J. P.   Sermons and
Sermonettes. Nashville, Tenn.:
National Baptist Publishing
Board, 1909.   SCBHC
Bound up and issued with
S. W. R. Cole's Sermons Out-
lined... 1940.
Robinson, James Herman.   Ad-
venturous Preaching. Great
Neck, N.Y.: Channel Press,
1956.   DHU/R; DHU/MO;
                      DLC
Negro author.
-- Africa at the Crossroads.
Philadelphia: Westminster
Press, 1962.   NN/Sch
-- Road Without Turning. The
Story of Reverend James H.
Robinson; an Autobiography.
New York: Farrar Straus,
1950.   DHU/R; DLC
Rogers, Walter Charles.   A Man
of God. ... Boston, The Chris-

topher Publishing House,
1931. NN/Sch
Rooks, Charles Shelley. "Image
of the Ministry as Reflected
in the Protestant Fellowship
Program." Journal of Religious Thought (18:2, 1961-62),
pp. 317-48.
Negro author.
Rosenberg, Bruce A. The Art
of the American Folk Preach-
er. New York: Oxford Uni-
versity Press, 1970.
DHU/R; DLC
Roston, David W. "The Sleeping
Preacher" Major Perry, 1831-
1925. "Saluda County's Sleep-
ing Preacher Carries Mystery
to the Grave." n.p., n.d.
Pam. File; DHU/R
Negro author.
"Rural Preachers at Bettis."
Southern Workman (52; Sept.,
1923), pp. 422-24. DHU/MO
Rush, Christopher, (bp.). "Bi-
ography." Carter G. Woodson.
History of the Negro Church.
Washington, D.C.: Associ-
ated Pub., 1921. pp. 73; 90.
NcSalL; DHU/R
Negro author.
-- Writers Program. New York
City. Negroes at New York.
Biographical Sketches. New
York: 1938-41. 4 vols.
NN/Sch
Russell, Charles L. Light From
the Talmud. New York:
Block Pub. Co., 1942.
DHU/R; DHU/MO
Hebrew and English on op-
posite pages.
Negro author.
Rutledge, D. "Two Dynamic
Leaders for Baptists and Meth-
odists." Sepia (10; My.,
1961), pp. 64-7. DHU/MO
Savage, Horace C. Life and
Times of Bishop Isaac Lane.
Nashville: National Publishing
Co., 1958. DHU/MO
Negro author.
Schoener, Allon, (ed.). Harlem

on My Mind. Cultural Capi-
tal of Black America, 1900-
1968. New York: Random
House, 1968. DHU/R
Text and pictures of an
exhibit in the New York Met-
ropolitan Museum. "Political
Involvement of Negro minis-
ters in Harlem."
Schomburg, Arthur Alfonso.
"Two Negro Missionaries to
the American Indians, John
Warrant, and John Stewart."
Journal of Negro History (21:
4, Oct., 1936), pp. 394-415.
DHU
Scott, Nathan. Nathanael West.
Grand Rapids, Mich.: Eerd-
man's Publishing Co., 1971.
DHU/R
Negro author.
Scott, Nathan Alexander. The
New Orpheus. Essays To-
ward a Christian Poetic. New
York: S. Sheed & Ward,
1964. DHU/R; NN/Sch
Religion and literature.
Negro author.
-- The Tragic Vision and the
Christian Faith. New York:
Association Press, 1957.
DHU/R
Religion and literature.
Scott, Osborne S. "Chaplain
Teacher; Negro Minister In-
structs Chaplains in Army
School." Ebony (8; Feb.,
1953), pp. 67-70. DHU/MO
Shaw, Alexander P. "What Must
the Negro Do to Be Saved?"
Religion in Life (17:4, Aut.,
1948), pp. 540-48. DHU/R
A Black churchman dis-
cusses the Negro's responsi-
bility for solving the race
problem.
Negro author.
Shaw, Benjamin Garland, (bp.).
"Biography." Who's Who in
Colored America." (New York:
Who's Who in Col. America
Corp., 1938-40; 1950), pp. 464,
643. NcSalL; DHU/R

(Shaw, B. G. cont.)
Negro author.
Shaw, George Bernard. The Adventures of the Black Girl in
her Search for God. New
York: Dodd, Mead & Co. ,
1932.   DHU/MO
Shaw, Herbert Bell, (bp.). "Bi-
ography." Biographical Encyc-
lopedia of the World (New
York: Institute of Research,
1946), p. 817.   NcSalL
Negro author.
Shaw, James Beverly Ford.
Life and Work of Bishop Al-
exander Preston Shaw. Nash-
ville: Partheon Press, 1954.
                      NcLjHi
Shillito, Edward. "The Poet
and the Race Problem."
Christian Century (46; Jl. , 17,
1929), pp. 915-16.
         Pam. File; DHU/R
Countee Cullen's religious
poetry.
Simmons, William J. Men of
Mark: Eminent, Progressive,
and Rising. Cleveland: Geo.
M. Rewell & Co. , 1887.
                      DHU/R
Simms, Joseph D. Soul-Saving;
or, Life and Labors of Henry
M. Willis, Evangelist and
Missionary. Philadelphia:
Robert E. Lynch, 1886.
                      DHU/MO
Negro author.
Skinner, Tom. Black and Free.
Grand Rapids, Mich. : Eerd-
man's, 1968.   DHU/R
Negro author.
-- "I Preach the White Man's
Religion." Christian Life (28;
Jl. , 1966), pp. 21-25.
         Pam. File; DHU/R
Small, John Bryan, (bp.). A
Cordial and Dispassionate Dis-
cussion on Predestination, its
Spiritual Support. York, Pa. :
Dispatch Pub. Co. , 1901.
                      DLC
Negro author.
-- The Human Heart Illustrated

by Nine Figures of the Heart,
Representing the Different
Stages of Life, and Two Death-
Bed Scenes; the Wicked and
the Righteous. York, Pa. :
York Dispatch Print, 1898.
         DHU/MO; NN/Sch
-- Practical and Exegetical Pul-
piteer. York, Pa. : Anstadt
& Son, 1895.   NcSalL
-- Predestination: Its Scriptural
Import. York, Pa. : Dis-
patch, 1901.   NcSalL
Smith, Amanda (Berry). An
Autobiography. Chicago:
Meyers & Bros. , 1893.
                      DHU/MO
A Negro evangelist.
Smith, George. A Short Trea-
tise Upon the Most Essential
and Leading Points of Wesley-
an or Primitive Methodism.
Poultney, Vt. : L. J. Reynolds,
Printer, 1830.   NN/Sch
Negro author.
Smith, H. H. "John Jasper:
The Unmatched Negro Philoso-
pher and Preacher." Method-
ist Quarterly Review (72:2,
Jl. , 1923), pp. 466+. DHU/R
Smith, Hubert W. "Three Negro
Preachers in Chicago: A
Study on Religious Leadership."
Master's thesis, University of
Chicago, 1935.
Smith, John Wesley, (bp.).
"Greatest Need of the Negro
Race." W. N. Hartshorn. An
Era of Progress and Promise.
(Boston: Priscilla, 1910), pp.
398+.   NcSalL; DHU/R
Negro author.
Smith, Paul Dewey. Man's Re-
lationship and Duty to God...
New York: Carlton Press,
1964.   NN/Sch
Smothers, Felton C. I Am the
Beginning and the Ending; A
Book of Excerpts from Gene-
sis and the Revelations of St.
John, the Divine. Ed. & illus-
trated by Felton Smothers.
New York: Carlton Pr. ,

1961.   DHU/MO; A&M
Negro author.
Spearman, Aurelia L. P. What
Christ Means to Us. A Book
of Religious Verse. New
York: Carlton Press, 1964.
                            DHU/R
Negro author.
Spearman, Henry Kuhns. Soul
Magnets; Twelve Sermons
from New Testament Texts,
compiled as a Memorial by
Mrs. Elizabeth F. Spearman.
Philadelphia: Pr. by the A.
M. E. Book Concern, 1929.
                            NN/Sch
Negro author.
Speers, Wallace Carter. Lay-
men Speaking. New York:
Association Press, 1947.
                            DHU/MO
Negro author.
Spivey, Charles S. A Tribute to
the Negro Preacher, and Oth-
er Sermons and Addresses by
Charles S. Spivey... Wilber-
force, O.: Xenia, O., Eck-
erle Printing Co., 1942.
                    NN/Sch; OWibfU
Negro author.
Spywood, G. A. "Biography."
Carter G. Woodson. History
of the Negro Church (Washing-
ton, D. C.: Associated Pub-
lishers, 1926), p. 104.
                    NcSalL; DHU/R
Negro author.
Stange, Douglas C. "Payne,
Bishop Daniel Alexander: Prot-
estation of American Slavery."
Journal of Negro History (52:
1, Ja., 1967), pp. 59-64.
                            DHU
Stephenson, Isaiah H. First
Oration on Stephen the First
Martyr of the Christian
Church. n. p., 1898. DHU/MO
Negro author.
Stephenson, John W., M. D.
"Church Builder, Financier,
Druggist, His Methods." Wm.
J. Simmons, (ed.). Men of
Mark... (Cleveland, O.: Geo.

M. Rewell and Co., 1887), p.
820.   DHU/R
Stevens, Abel. Sketches & Inci-
dents; or, A Budget from the
Saddle-Bags of a Superannu-
ated Itinerant... George Peck,
ed. Cincinnati: Pub. by
Hitchcok & Walden, 1869.
                        NN/Sch; IEG
Stevenson, J. W. How to Get
and Keep Churches Out of
Debt and Also a Lecturer on
the Secret of Success in the
Art of Making Money. Al-
bany: Weed, Parsons & Co.,
1886.   DHU/MO
Negro author.
Steward, Theophilus Gould.
Fifty Years in Gospel Minis-
try. Philadelphia: A. M. E.
Book Concern, 1920. DHU/MO
Negro author.
Stewart, Maria W. Religion and
the Pure Principles of Moral-
ity the Sure Foundation on
which we Must Build. Pro-
ductions from the Pen of Mrs.
Maria W. Stewart, Widow of
the late James W. Stewart of
Boston. n. p., 1831. DHU/MO
Negro author.
Stokes, A. Jackson. Select Ser-
mons. n. p., 1914. SCBHC
Stroyer, Jacob. "Biography."
Wm. L. Katz, (ed.). Five
Slave Narratives. New York:
Arno Press, 1969. DHU/MO
About a early A. M. E. Min-
ister.
Swift, Job. Discourse on Reli-
gious Subjects... to which are
Prefixed, Sketches of his Life
and Character, and a Sermon
Preached at West-Ruthland on
the Occasion of his Death, by
the Rev. Lemuel Haynes...
Middlebury, Vt.: Pr. by Hunt-
ington & Fitch, 1805.
                            DHU/MO
Tanner, Benjamin Tucker, (bp.).
A. M., D. D. "Editor A. M. E.
Review, Twenty Years an Edi-
tor, for Many Years Editor of

250 Afro-American Religious Studies

(Tanner, B. T. cont.)
the Christian Recorder, Author of Ecclesiastical Works."
Wm. J. Simmons, (ed.).
Men of Mark... (Cleveland,
O.: Geo. M. Rewell & Co.,
1887), p. 985.   DHU/R
Negro author.
-- Color of Solomon--What? "My
Beloved is White and Ruddy."
A Monograph... with an Introduction by W. S. Scarborough.
Philadelphia: A. M. E. Book
Concern, 1895.   DHU/MO
-- Douglass Monthly. (1; Apr.
1859,) p. 64.   NcD
-- Joel, the Son of Pethuel; His
Personage; the Time in Which
He Lived, His Work, the Impression He made. n. p., 1905.
DHU/MO; NN/Sch
-- The Negro in Holy Writ.
Philadelphia, Pa.: n.p., 1902.
DHU/MO
-- The Negro's Origin. Philadelphia: African Methodist
Episcopal Depository, 1869.
DHU/MO
-- (ed.). Scriptural Means of
Producing an Immediate Revival of Pure Christianity in
the Ministry and Laity of Our
Church; Prize Essays. Philadelphia: A. M. E. Pub. Dept.,
1881.   DHU/MO
-- Theological Lectures. Nashville: A. M. E. Sunday School
Union Press, 1894. DHU/MO
-- ... To the Memory of Professor O. V. Catto. Respectfully
Inscribed to His Fellows of
the Institute for Colored Youth
and to the Pupils of the Same
with Considerations. n. p.,
1871.   NN/Sch
Tatum, E. Ray. Conquest or
Failure? Biography of J.
Frank Norris. Dallas: Baptist Historical Foundation,
1966.   DLC
Taylor, Bartlett. "Financier and
Church Builder, Christian
Pioneer." Wm. J. Simmons,

(ed.). Men of Mark... (Cleveland, O.: Geo. M. Rewell &
Co., 1887), p. 626.   DHU/R
Taylor, James B. Lives of Virginia Baptist Ministers. Richmond: Yale & Wyatt, 1837.
NNUT
Taylor, Marshall W., D. D.
"Editor of the Southwestern
Advocate, Brilliant Writer."
Wm. J. Simmons, (ed.). Men
of Mark... (Cleveland, O.:
George M. Rewell & Co.,
1887), p. 933.   DHU/R
Negro author.
-- The Fastest Bicycle Rider in
the World (Autobiography).
Worcester, Mass.: Wormley
Publishing Co., 1928.
DHU/MO
Life of a Negro minister of
the Methodist Episcopal Church.
-- The Life, Travels, Labors,
and Helpers of Mrs. Amanda
Smith, the Famous Negro Missionary Evangelist. Cincinnati:
Pr. by Cranston and Stowe for
the Author, 1888.   DHU/MO
Taylor, Preston. "Pastor of
the Church of the Disciples,
Nashville, Tennessee, General Financial Agent of the College, Big Contractor." Wm.
J. Simmons, (ed.). Men of
Mark... (Cleveland, O.: Geo.
M. Rewell & Co., 1887), p.
296.   DHU/R
Negro author.
Thompson, Daniel C. The Negro Leadership Class. Englewood Cliffs, N. J.: Prentice-
Hall, Inc., 1963.   DHU/R
Pp. 34-37, Occupational
characteristics of the Protestant ministry.
Thurman, Howard. The Creative
Encounter. New York: Harper & Row, Publishers, 1954.
DHU/R
Negro author.
-- Deep is the Hunger. New
York: Harper & Row, Publishers, 1951.   DHU/R

-- Footprints of a Dream. New
York: Harper & Row, Pub-
lishers, 1959.
-- "Interracial Church in San
Francisco." Social Action (11:
2, Feb. 15, 1945), pp. 27-8.
                                DHU/R
-- Meditations of the Heart. New
York: Harper & Row, Pub-
lishers, 1953.   DHU/R
-- Mysticism and the Experience
of Love. Wallingford, Pendle
Hill, Pa.: n. d.   DHU/R
Tilmon, Levin. A Brief Miscel-
laneous Narrative of the More
Early Part of the Life of L.
Tilmon, Pastor of a Methodist
Congregation in the City of
New York. Jersey City: W. W.
& L. A. Pratt, 1853. DHU/MO
Negro author.
  "Pastor of a Colored Meth-
odist Congregational Church in
the city of New York."
Tindley, Charles A. Book of
Sermons. Philadelphia: Edw.
T. Duncan, 1932.
                    DHU/MO; NN/Sch
Negro author.
Tolton, Augustus. "The First
and Only Native American
Catholic Priest of the African
Descent, though Both Parents,
on the Continent." Wm. J.
Simmons, (ed.). Men of Mark
... (Cleveland, O.: Geo. M.
Rewell & Co., 1887), p. 439.
                                DHU/R
Toomer, Jean. ...The Flavor
of Man... Philadelphia: Young
Friends Movement of the Phila-
delphia Yearly Meetings, 1949.
                                NN/Sch
Negro author.
  "Delivered at Arch Street
Meeting House, Philadelphia."
Tross, Joseph Samuel Nathaniel.
This Thing Called Religion.
... Charlotte, N. C.: n. p.,
1934.   DHU/MO
Truss, Matthew B. A Sketch of
the Life, Death and Funeral of
the Rev. Simon Smith, a Man

of Colour, and a Member of
the Methodist Episcopal
Church. Delivered by Matthew
B. Truss, One of the Same.
                                NN/Sch
Negro author.
Turner, Henry McNeal, (bp.).
D. D., LL. D. Bishop of A. M. E.
Church, Philosopher, Politi-
cian and Orator, Eminent Lec-
turer, Author, Intense Race
Man, United States Chaplain."
Wm. J. Simmons, (ed.). Men
of Mark... (Cleveland, O.:
George M. Rewell & Co.,
1887), p. 805.   DHU/R
Negro author.
-- "Races Must Separate, Asserts
Bishop Turner." C. E. Dorman,
et al. A Solution of the Negro
Problem Psychologically Con-
sidered. The Negro Not 'A
Beast'. (Atlanta: Franklin
Printing & Publishing Co.,
n. d.), pp. 30-1.   NcD
Negro author.
-- "Twelfth Bishop of the A. M. E.
Church." Journal of Religious
Education (30:1, Sept. 1969),
p. 4.   DHU/R
United States. Senate. The Race
Problem Speech. February
23-24, 1903. Washington, D. C.:
1903.   NcD; DLC
  Includes letter of Henry Mc-
Neal Turner to Hon. Benjamin
R. Tillman, Senator, South
Carolina.
Vandervall, Randall Bartholomew,
D. D. "A Self Made Man, A
Graduate from the School of
Adversity." Wm. J. Simmons,
(ed.). Men of Mark... (Cleve-
land, O.: Geo. M. Rewell &
Co., 1887), p. 572. DHU/R
Varick, James, (bp.). "Biogra-
phy." Dictionary of American
Biography (New York: Scrib-
ners), vol. 19, pp. 225-26.
                    NcSalL; DHU
Negro author.
Vassall, William F. The Origin
of Christianity; a Brief Study

(Vassall, W. F. cont.)
of the World's Early Beliefs
and their Influence on the
Early Christian Church, In-
cluding an Examination of the
Lost Books of the Bible. New
York: Exposition Press, 1952.
DHU/MO; NN/Sch
Negro author.
Vaughn, C. C. "State Grand
Chief of I. O. Good Samaritans
and Daughters of Samaria,
Preacher and Teacher." Wm.
J. Simmons, (ed.). Men of
Mark... (Cleveland, O. : Geo.
M. Rewell & Co. , 1887), p.
732.   DHU/R
Walls, William Jacob, (bp.).
Baseball: The Parable of Life.
n. p. , n. d.   NcSalL; DHU/R
Negro author.
-- "Biography." Biographical
Encyclopedia of the World
(New York: Institute of Re-
search, 1946), p. 824. NcSalL
-- Connectionalism and the Negro
Church. n. p. , n. d.   NcSalL
-- The Dream of the Youth. n. p. ,
n. d.   NcSalL
-- Glimpses of Memory. n. p. ,
n. d.   NcSalL
-- Harriet Tubman. n. p. , n. d.
DHU/R
-- Messages of Five Years. n. p. ,
n. d.   NcSalL
-- The Negro in Business and
Religion. n. p. , n. d.   NcSalL
-- Pastorates and Reminiscences.
n. p. , n. d.   NcSalL
-- Visions for the Times. n. p. ,
n. d.   NcSalL
--What Youth Wants. n. p. ,
n. d.   NcSalL
Walters, Alexander, (bp.). "Bi-
ography." Dictionary of
American Biography (New
York: Scribners), vol. 19,
no. 9.   NcSalL
Negro author.
-- "Biography." Who Was Who
in America (New York: 1897-
1942), p. 1295.   NcSalL
-- "Biography." Who's Who in

America (Chicago: Marquis Co. ,
1908; 1912; 1914; 1916).
-- "Biography." Who's Who in
American Methodism (New
York: E. B. Treat Co. , 1916),
p. 232.   NcSalL
-- Carter G. Woodson. History
of the Negro Church (Washing-
ton, D. C. : Associated Pub-
lishers, 1925), pp. 311-12.
NcSalL; DHU/R
-- Carter G. Woodson. Negro
Orators and Their Orations
(Washington, D. C. : Associ-
ated Publishers, 1925), p.
554.   NcSalL; DHU/R
-- "Financier and Pulpit Orator."
Wm. J. Simmons, (ed.). Men
of Mark... (Cleveland, O. :
George M. Rewell & Co. ,
1887), p. 340.   DHU/R
-- Frederick Douglass and His
Work. Nashville: National
Baptist Publishing Board,
1904.   NcSalL
-- "Greatest Need of the Negro
Race." W. N. Hartshorn. An
Era of Progress and Promise
(Boston: Priscilla, 1910), pp.
396+.   NcSalL
-- "A Letter to J. W. Thompson."
J. W. Thompson. Authentic
History of the Douglass Monu-
ment (Rochester: Rochester
Herald Press, 1908), p. 196.
NcSalL
-- My Life and Work. n. p. ,
1917.   NcSalL
-- "Possibilities of the Negro in
the Realm of Politics." W. H.
Ferris. The African Abroad
(New Haven: Tuttle, More-
house, Taylor, 1913), vol. 1,
pp. 379-81. DHU/MO; NcSalL
-- "What Should the Next Con-
gress Do?" Irving G. Penn.
The United Negro (Atlanta:
Luther, 1902), pp. 592+.
NcSalL
Ward, Samuel R. "Negro Pres-
byterian Minister." Wm. Wells
Brown. The Black Man. (Mi-
ami, Fla. : Mnemosyne Publi-

cation Co., 1969), pp. 284-5.
DHU/R
Negro author.
Ward, Thomas Playfair. The
Truth that Makes Men Free;
a Novel. New York: Pageant
Press, 1955.
A novel by a Negro Meth-
odist minister.
Warner, Andrew Jackson, (bp.).
"Biography." W. N. Hartshorn.
An Era of Progress and
Promise (Boston: Priscilla,
1910), pp. 409+.
NcSalL; DHU/R
Negro author.
Washington, Joseph R. Mar-
riage in Black and White.
Boston: Beacon Press, 1971.
DHU/R
Written by a black theol-
ogian.
Watson, Edgar Benton, (bp.).
"Biography." Who's Who in
Colored America (New York:
Who's Who in Colored Amer-
ica Corp.), 1930-40.
NcSalL; DHU/R
White, J. T. "Divine, Editor,
State Senator, Commissioner
of Public Works." Wm. J.
Simmons, (ed.). Men of Mark
... (Cleveland, O.: Geo. M.
Rewell & Co., 1887), p. 590.
DHU/R
White, W. J. "Editor of the
Georgia Baptist." Wm. J.
Simmons, (ed.). Men of Mark
... (Cleveland, O.: Geo. M.
Rewell & Co., 1887), p. 1095.
DHU/R
White, William Spottswood. The
African Preacher. An Authen-
tic Narrative... Philadelphia:
Presbyterian Board of Publi-
cation, 1849.
Negro author.
Whitman, A. A. "Author of a
Book of Poems, entitled,
'Not a Man, and Yet a Man,'
with Miscellaneous Poems."
Wm. J. Simmons, (ed.). Men
of Mark... (Cleveland, O.:

George M. Rewell & Co.,
1887), p. 1122. DHU/R
Negro author.
Whittier, A. Gerald. Christ-
mas Meditations. New York:
Carlton Press, 1961.
DHU/MO
Negro author.
Who's Who of the Colored Race;
A General Biographic Dic-
tionary of Men and Women of
African Descent. Chicago:
n. p., 1915. DHU/MO
Includes biographical
sketches of Negro ministers.
Why I Believe There is a God;
Sixteen Essays by Negro
Clergymen, with an Introduc-
tion by Howard Thurman.
Chicago: Johnson Publication
Co., 1965. DHU/R; NN/Sch
Wilkerson, James. Wilkerson's
History of His Travels and
Labors, in the United States,
as a Missionary, in Particu-
lar that of the Union Seminary,
Located in Franklin Co., Ohio,
Since he Purchased His Lib-
erty in New Orleans, La.,
Etc. Columbus, O.: n. p.,
1861. DLC
Williams, H. M. Preacher's
Text and Topic Book with One
Hundred Ordination Questions.
Nashville, Tenn.: National
Baptist Publishing Bd., 1909.
NN/Sch
Negro author.
Williams, Ethel L., (ed.). Bio-
graphical Directory of Negro
Ministers. New York: Scare-
crow Press, 1965. 1970 -
2d ed. DHU/R
Negro author.
Williams, Florence D. Guiding
Light. Baltimore: National
Baptist Training Union Board,
1962. DHU/MO
Williams, Henry Roger. The
Blighted Life of Methuselah.
Nashville, Tenn.: National
Baptist Publishing Board,
1908. NN/Sch

(Williams H. R. cont.)
Negro author.
Williams, Peter. A Discourse
Delivered on the Death of
Capt. Paul Cuffe, Before the
New York African Institution,
in the African Methodist Epis-
copal Zion Church October 21,
1817. New York: B. Young &
Co., Printer, 1817.
                    NN/Sch; DLC
Negro author.
Wise, Namon. The Namon Wise
Story. New York: Carlton
Press, 1964.   DHU/MO
Negro author.
"Woman of God: Dynamic Min-
ister Sponsors a Broad Social
Action Program." Our World
(6; Feb. 1951), pp. 42-45.
                    DHU/MO; DLC
Wood, John Wesley, (bp.). "Bi-
ography." Who's Who in
American Methodism (New
York: Who's Who in America
Corp., 1927-37).
NcSalL; DHU/MO; DHU/R
Negro author.
-- Lyrics of Sunshine. n. p.,
1922.   NcSalL
Woodson, Carter Godwin. The
Mis-Education of the Negro.
Washington, D. C.: The As-
sociated Publishers, 1933.
            DHU/MO; CtY-D
Chapter 14, Negro minis-
ters.
Negro author.
-- The Rural Negro. Washing-
ton, D. C.: Association for the
Study of Negro Life and His-
tory, 1930. DHU/MO; NN/Sch
Rural Negro Church.
Wright, Nathan. Let's Work To-
gether. New York: Haw-
thorn Books, 1968. DHU/MO
Negro author.
-- One Bread, One Body. Green-
wich, Conn.: Seabury Press,
1962.   DHU/MO
Wright, Richard Robert, Jr.,
(bp.). "Negro Companions of
Spanish Explorers." Ameri-

can Anthropologist (4; Je.,
1902), pp. 217-28. DHU/MO
Negro author.
-- The Negro in Pennsylvania:
A Study in Economic History
... Philadelphia: A. M. E.
Book Concern, 1912. DHU/MO
-- The Negro Problem... Phila-
delphia: A. M. E. Book Con-
cern, 1911.   DHU/MO
-- Self-Help in Negro Education.
Cheyne, Pa.: Committee of
Twelve for the Advancement
of the Interest of the Negro
Race, 1909.   DHU/MO
Wynn, Daniel Webster. Moral
Behavior and the Christian
Ideal. New York: American
Press, 1961.   DHU/MO
Negro author.
Wynn, Daniel Webster. Time-
less Issues. New York: Phil-
osophical Library, 1967.
                         DHU/R
"Sermons delivered by the
chaplain at Tuskegee Institute,
Alabama."
Negro author.
Yates, Walter L., (ed.). He
Spoke Now and They Speak:
A Collection of Speeches and
Writings of and on the Life
and Works of J. C. Price.
Salisbury, N. C.: Rowan Print-
ing Co., 1952.   DHU/R
Negro author.
About Bishop Joseph C.
Price, founder of Livingstone
College and supporter of the
Hood Theological Seminary of
the African Methodist Episcopal
Zion Church.
Yates, William. Rights of Col-
ored Men to Suffrage, Citizen-
ship and Trial by Jury: Be-
ing a Book of the Facts, Argu-
ments and Authorities, Histori-
cal Notices and Sketches of De-
bates with Notes. Philadelphia:
Merrihew & Gunn, 1838. NcD
p. 61 has repro. of Rev. P.
Williams' passport, an early
A. M. E. Zion minister.

5. Negroes in White Denominations

Adams, Elizabeth Laura. Dark
Symphony. New York: Sheed
& Ward, 1942.
   DHU/MO; NN/Sch
 A Negro woman's account
of her conversion to Roman
Catholicism.
Allen, L. Scott. "Toward Pre-
serving the History of the
Central Jurisdiction." Meth-
odist History (7; Oct. , 1968),
pp. 24-30. ISAR; DHU/R
Arnold, W. E. A History of
Methodism in Kentucky. Louis-
ville: Herald Press, 1936.
     IEG
 Pp. 268, 312 statements on
Negro members.
Baltimore, Maryland. Saint
James' First African Protestant
Episcopal Church. Origination,
Constitution, and By-Laws of
St. James' First African
Episcopal Church in the City
of Baltimore. Adopted Apr.
22, 1829. Baltimore, Pr. by
William Woody, 1829. NcD
Barber, Jesse Belmont. Climb-
ing Jacob's Ladder; Story of
the Work of the Presbyterian
Church U.S.A. Among the
Negroes. New York: Board
of National Missions, Presby-
terian Church in the U.S.A.,
1952. DHU/MO; DLC; NN/Sch
 Negro author.
Betts, Albert Dreems. History
of South Carolina Methodism.
Columbia, S. C. : Advocate
Press, 1952. IEG
 Chapters on "The Negro's
Share in Methodism" and "Our
Brother in Black."
Bolivar, William C. A Brief
History of St. Thomas' P. E.
Church. Philadelphia: The
Author, 1908. NN/Sch
Bowen, John Wesley E. "A
Psychological Principle in

Revelation." Methodist Re-
view (73; 1891), pp. 227-39.
   DHU/R; DLC
 Negro author.
Bragg, George Freeman. The
Attitude of the Conference of
Church Workers Among Col-
ored People Toward the Adap-
tation of the Episcopate to the
Needs of the Race. n. p. ,
1904.   DHU/MO
 Contains a list of ordina-
tions of colored men to the
ministry of the church.
 Negro author.
-- The Colored Harvest in the
Old Virginia Diocese. n. p. ,
1901.   DHU/MO
-- History of the Afro-American
Group of the Episcopal Church.
Baltimore, Md. : Church Ad-
vocate Press, 1922.
   DHU/R; NN/Sch
-- Men of Maryland. Baltimore,
Md. : Church Advocate Press,
1914.   DHU/MO
-- The Story of Old Stephen's,
Petersburg, Va. & the Origin
of the Bishop Payne Divnity
School. Baltimore: n. p. ,
1917.   DHU/MO
-- "The Whittingham Canon" The
Birth and History of the Mis-
sionary District Plan. Balti-
more: n. p. , n. d. NN/Sch
-- Yearbook and Church Direc-
tory of St. James First Afri-
can Episcopal Church. Balti-
more: Pub. by the Rector,
1934.   DHU/MO
Brooklyn. St. Philip's Church
(Protestant Episcopal). Golden
Jubilee Album of St. Philip's
P. E. Church (McDonough
Street) Brooklyn, New York.
Published in Connection with
the 50th Anniversary of the
Founding of the Church. New
York: Dodd Bros. , Printers,

(Brooklyn. St. Philip's Church
cont.)
    1949.   NN/Sch
Brooks, Jerome. "The Negro
Priest in White Parishes."
Religious Education (59:1, Ja. -
Feb. , 1964), pp. 73-76.
                        DHU/R
Brooks, William E. From
Saddlebags to Satellites. Nash-
ville: Parthenon Press, 1969.
                        ISAR
-- History and Highlights of Flor-
ida Methodism. Ft. Lauder-
dale, Fla. : Tropical Press,
Inc. , 1965.   ISAR
    Chapter on "Work Among
    Slaves, Freedman's Aid and
    Development of the Central
    Jurisdiction."
Brown, Ethelred. Jesus of Naza-
reth the World's Greatest Re-
ligious Teacher was Unitarian
... A Sermon Delivered on
Sunday Evening, March 14,
1943 ... at the Harlem Unitar-
ian Church. New York: n. p. ,
n. d.   DHU/MO
    Negro author.
Brydon, G. McClaren. The
Episcopal Church Among the
Negroes of Virginia. Rich-
mond, Va. : Richmond Press,
Inc. , 1937.
        NN/Sch; NcD; DHU/MO
Butsch, Joseph. "Negro Catho-
lics in the United States."
Catholic Historical Review (3:
1, Apr. , 1917), pp. 33-51.
                        DHU/R
Cadbury, Henry J. "Negro
Membership in the Society of
Friends." Journal of Negro
History (21:2, Apr. , 1936),
pp. 151-213.   DHU/R
Carrington, William Orlando.
Carry a Little Honey, and
Other Addresses. New York:
Fleming H. Revell Co. , 1936.
                DHU/R; NN/Sch
    Negro author.
"The Catholic Church and the
Negro." Ebony (13; Dec. ,

1957), pp. 19-22.
    Pam. File; DHU/R
Catto, William Thomas. History
of the Presbyterian Movement.
Philadelphia: J. M. Wilson,
1857.   DHU/MO
    A semi-centenary discourse
and history of the first African Presbyterian Church, Philadelphia, May 1857, from its
organization, including a notice
of its first pastor, John Gloucester, also appendix containing sketches of all the colored churches in Philadelphia.
Caution, Tollie L. "Protestant
Episcopal Church: Policies
and Rationale upon which Support of its Negro Colleges is
Predicated." Journal of Negro
Education (29; Sum. , 1960),
pp. 274-83.   DHU
    Negro author.
Centennial Methodist Conference,
Baltimore, 1884. Proceedings,
Sermon, Essays, and Addresses of the Centennial Methodist Conference Held in Mt.
Vernon Place Methodist Episcopal Church, Baltimore, Md. ,
December 9-17, 1884. With
a Historical Statement. Ed.
by H. K. Carroll, W. P. Harrison... and J. H. Bayliss...
New York: Phillips & Hunt;
Cincinnati: Cranston & Stowe,
1885.   NN/Sch
Chatham, J. G. "Southern Pente-
cost; Address, with Editorial
Comment." America (109;
Jl. 6, 1963), pp. 11-12. DHU
Chitty, Arthur Ben. "St. Augustine's College, Raleigh, North
Carolina." Historical Magazine of the Protestant Episcopal Church (35:3, Sept. 1966),
pp. 207-19.   DHU/R
Chritzberg, A. M. Early Methodism in the Carolinas. Nash-
ville: Publishing House of the
M. E. Church, South, 1897. IEG
    Pp. 32+, Negro churches.
Church, Roberta. "In the Steps

of Her Father." Ebony (14;
My., 1959), pp. 61-2.
        DHU/R; DHU/MO
    Roberta Church, daughter
of Robert R. Church, Jr. a
Tenn. politician, was Minority
Group's Consultant for Department of Labor and a member
of Memphis' Emmanuel Episcopal Church, founded in her
great-aunt's parlor.
The Church Standard. The
    Church and the Negro; Five
    Editorials from the Church
    Standard. Reprinted by Re-
    quest. Philadelphia: n. p.,
    1906.   NN/Sch; DLC
    Contents. -I. Race Sepa-
    ration; II. Religions division
    of races; III. the Opportunity
    of the Episcopal Church; IV.
    Evangelization; V. Bishop
    Nelson on church work among
    the Negroes.
Clair, Mathew Walker, (bp.).
    "Methodism and the Negro."
    Wm. K. Anderson, (ed.).
    Methodism (Nashville: The
    Methodist Pub. House, 1947),
    pp. 245-50.   ISAR; DHU/R
    Negro author.
Connell, Francis J. "Rights of
    the Catholic Negro." Ameri-
    can Ecclesiastical Review (114;
    1946), pp. 459-62.   DHU/R
Convocation of the Colored Clergy.
    Proceedings of the First Con-
    vocation of the Colored Clergy
    of the Protestant Church in the
    United States of America, Held
    at the Church of The Holy
    Communion, 6th Avenue and
    20th Streets, N. Y. City, Sep-
    tember 12th, 13th, and 14th,
    1883. Newark, N. J.: Star-
    buck and Durham, 1883.
        DHU/MO
Cooley, Timothy Mather.
    Sketches of the Life and Char-
    acter of the Rev. Lemuel
    Haynes... New York: Harper
    & Bros., 1837.   DHU/MO
    Negro pastor in Rutland,

Vt., in the later half of the
eighteenth century.
Cranston, Earl, (bp.). The Dy-
    namic of a United Methodism.
    Evanston: n. p., 1915.   IEG
Crapsey, Algernon Sidney. ...
    The Last of the Heretics.
    New York, Knopf, 1924.
        NN/Sch
    About St. Philips P. E.
    Church, New York City.
Crum, Mason. The Negro in the
    Methodist Church... New
    York: Editorial Department,
    Division of Education and Ci-
    vilization, Board of Missions
    and Church Extension, Meth-
    odist Church, 1951.
        NcD; OWibfU; A&M
Daniel, Everard W. The Church
    on Trial: A Sermon Preached
    Before the Conference of
    Church Workers Among Col-
    ored People. Philadelphia:
    n. p., 1916.   NN/Sch
    Negro author.
De Costa, Benjamin Franklin.
    Three Score and Ten. The
    Story of St. Philip's Church,
    New York City. A Discourse
    Delivered in the New Church,
    West Twenty-Fifth St., at its
    Opening, Sunday Morning,
    February 17, 1889. New York:
    Pr. for the Parish, 1889.
        NN/Sch
"Dedication of a Colored Church."
    The Church at Home and
    Abroad (2; Sept., 1887), p.
    272.   DHU/R
    Dedication of Negro Presby-
    terian Church in Tennessee.
"Dedication of a Colored Church
    and Installation of a Colored
    Pastor." The Church at
    Home and Abroad. (3; Ja.,
    1888), p. 62.   DHU/R
    Announcement of dedication
    of a Negro Presbyterian
    Church in Baltimore.
"Dedication of Mary Allen Semi-
    nary." The Church at Home and
    Abroad (4; Sept., 1888), pp.

("Dedication cont.)
261-63.   DHU/R
Announcement of the dedi-
cation of a boarding school for
Negro girls by the Presbyter-
ian Church.
Diggs, M. A. Catholic Negro
Education in the United States.
Washington: Pub. by the Au-
thor, 1936.   DHU/MO
Negro author.
Downs, Karl E. Meet the Negro.
Los Angeles: The Methodist
Youth Fellowship, Southern
California-Arizona Annual Con-
ference, 1943.
            DHU/MO; NN/Sch
Negro author.
Drewes, Christopher F. Half
a Century of Lutheranism
Among Our Colored People;
a Jubilee Book. St. Louis,
Mo.: Concordia Publishing
House Print, 1927.
            NN/Sch; NcD; DLC
Edwards, S. J. Celestine. From
Slavery to a Bishopric, or the
Life of Bishop Walter Hawkins.
London: John Kensit, 1891.
            IEG; DHU/MO
Bishop of the British Meth-
odist Episcopal Church of
Canada.
Negro author.
Fahey, Frank Joseph. "The So-
ciological Analysis of a Ne-
gro Catholic Parish." Doctor-
al dissertation, University of
Notre Dame, 1959.
Foley, Albert S. Bishop Healy:
Beloved Outcast. New York:
Farrar, Strauss & Young,
1954.   DHU/R
First Negro priest and
bishop of the United States.
Franklin, John Hope. Negro
Episcopalians in Ante-Bellum
North Carolina. New Bruns-
wick, N. J.: n. p., 1944.
            DHU/MO; NN/Sch; DHU/R
Reprinted from the Histor-
ical Magazine of the Episco-
pal Church, v. 13, September

1944.
Negro author.
Gaynor, W. C. "The Catholic
Negro in Louisiana." Anthro-
pos (9; 1914), pp. 539-45.
            DCU/AN
Georges, Norbert. Meet Brother
Martin. The Life of Blessed
Martin de Porres, Saintly
American Negro. New York
City: The Torch, 1936.
            DHU/MO
Gillard, John Thomas. "First
Negro Parish in the United
States." America (50; 1934),
pp. 370-72.   DGU
"A Glance at the Negro Aposto-
late." (Editorial). St. Augus-
tine's Messenger (30:9, Nov.
1953), pp. 260+.   DHU/R
Gloucester, John. A Sermon De-
livered in the First African
Presbyterian Church in Phila-
delphia on the First of Janu-
ary, 1830, Before the Differ-
ent Coloured Societies of Phil-
adelphia. Philadelphia, n.p.,
1839.   DHU/MO
Goin, Edward F. "One Hundred
Years of Negro Congregation-
alism in New Haven, Conn."
Crisis (19; Feb., 1920), pp.
177-81.   DHU/MO
Gordon, David M. The Lexing-
ton Conference and the Negro
Migration. Evanston: n. p.,
1957.   IEG
Graham, John H. Gammon's
Recruiting Progress and the
Replacement Needs of Central
Jurisdiction. Atlanta: n. p.,
1956.
-- The Role of Gammon Theolog-
ical Seminary in Ministerial
Training and Services for the
Negro Churches, 1940-1954.
Atlanta: n. p., 1956. GAITH
Seminary founded by the
Methodist Church for Negroes.
-- Mississippi Circuit Riders,
1865-1965. Nashville: Par-
thenon Press, 1967. DLC; NcD
Early Negro ministers.

-- A Study of Revel's Methodist
Church of Greenville, Mississippi. Atlanta: Interdenominational Theological Center, 1960.   GAITH
-- A Study of Wesley Methodist
Church York, South Carolina
Atlanta: Department of Soci-
ology, Gammon Theological
Seminary, 1959.   GAITH
Grill, C. Frederick. Methodism
in the Upper Fear Valley.
Nashville: Parthenon Press,
1966.   IEG
Grimke, Francis James. Anniversary Address on the Occasion of the Seventy-Fifth Anni-
versary of the Fifteenth Street
Presbyterian Church, Washington, D. C. Washington, D. C. :
R. L. Pendelton, Printer, 1916.
                      DHU/MO
   Negro author.
   Also in Woodson Carter G.
Francis J. Grimke, Washington, D. C. : Association Press,
1942.
-- An Argument Against the Union
of the Cumberland Presbyter-
ian Church and the Presbyter-
ian Church in the United States
of America... Washington,
D. C. : Hayworth Publishing
House, 1904.   NN/Sch
-- "The Battle Must Go On."
Crisis (XLI; Ag. , 1934), pp.
240-41.   DHU/MO
-- "Colored Men as Professors
in Colored Institutions." South-
ern Workman (LXIII; Dec. ,
1934), pp. 370-72.   DHU/MO
-- "Doctor Toyohiko Kagawa."
Pub. by the author, n. d.
                 DHU/MO; NjPT
-- Equality of Rights for All
Citizens, Black and White
Alike. Washington, D. C. :
The Author, 1909.   DHU/MO
-- Eulogy...of the Late Major
James E. Walker. Washing-
ton, D. C. : Mu-So-Lit. Club,
1916.   DHU/MO
-- Fifty Years of Freedom.

Washington, D. C.: The Au-
thor, 1913.   DHU/MO
-- Highest Values. Washington,
D. C. : The Author, n. d.
                       NjPT
-- Human Accountability. Pub.
by the Author, n.d.   NjPT
-- Jews...A Suffering Perse-
cuted People. Washington,
D. C. : The Author, 1934.
              NjPT; DHU/MO
-- Last Quadrennial Message to
the Race. Washington, D. C.:
The Author, 1929. DHU/MO
-- Lincoln University Alone of
Negro Institutions Shuts Out of
Its Trustee Board and Out of
Its Professorships. Pub. by
the Author, 1916.   DHU/MO
-- Man of Nazareth. Washing-
ton, D. C. : The Author, n. d.
                       NjPT
-- "The Negro and His Citizen-
ship," The Negro and the
Elective Franchise. Washing-
ton, D. C. : The American Ne-
gro Academy, Occasional Pa-
pers, No. 11, 1905. DHU/MO
-- The Negro and Political Par-
ties. Washington, D. C. : The
Author, n. d.   DHU/MO
-- Obedience to God. Washing-
ton, D. C. : The Author, n. d.
                       NjPT
-- One Thing Needful. Washing-
ton, D. C. : The Author, n. d.
                      DHU/MO
-- Prize Fighting (Four Tracts).
Washington, D. C.: The Au-
thor, n. d.   DHU/MO
-- Scotsboro. Washington, D. C. :
The Author, n. d.   DHU/MO
-- "The Second Marriage of Fred-
erick Douglass. " Journal of
Negro History (19; Jl. , 1934),
pp. 324-29.   DHU/MO
-- "Segregation." Crisis (41;
Je. , 1934), pp. 173-4.
                      DHU/MO
-- Senator Borah and the Negro.
Washington, D. C.: The Au-
thor, n. d.   NjPT
-- The Shame of Lincoln Univer-

(Grimke, F. J. cont.)
sity. Washington, D. C. : The
Author, 1926.   DHU/MO
-- Some Reflections Growing Out
of the Recent Epidemic of In-
fluenza That Affected Our
City. Washington, D. C. : The
Author, 1918.   DHU/MO
-- Suicide a Self-Murder. Wash-
ington, D. C. : The Author,
n. d.   DHU/MO
-- "Valiant Men and Free." Op-
portunity (12; Sept. , 1934),
pp. 276+.   DHU/MO
-- What Is to Be the Real Future
of the Black Man in This
Country? Washington, D. C. :
The Author, 1934.   DHU/MO
-- Wilson College Presbytery of
Washington City... Colorpho-
bia. Washington, D. C. : The
Author, n. d.   DHU/MO
-- A Word of Greeting to Col-
ored Soldiers. Washington,
D. C. : The Author, 1918.
                     DHU/MO
-- The Young People of Today
and the Responsibility of the
Home in Regard to Them.
Washington, D. C. : The Pres-
byterian Council, 1909.
                     DHU/MO
Grissom, W. L. History of Meth-
odism in North Carolina From
1772 to the Present Time.
Nashville: Publishing House
of the Methodist Episcopal
Church, South, 1905.   IEG
    Chapter XIV, Negroes.
Gulfside, Waveland, Mississippi.
A Summer Assembly and
Camp Ground for Religious,
Educational and Recreational
Purposes. n. p. , 1927.
                     NN/Sch
    Conducted, for Negroes, by
the Dept. of Rural Work,
Board of Home Missions and
Church Extension, Methodist
Episcopal Church.
Hargett, James H. The Black
Ministries Resource Book.
New York: United Church of

Christ, 1970.
    Pam. File; DHU/R
Mim.
    "The Black Situation in the
United Church of Christ."
Harris, Marquis LaFayette, (bp.)
Life Can Be Meaningful. Bos-
ton: Christopher Pub. House,
1951.   NN/Sch; DHU/MO
    Negro author.
Hepburn, D. "Negro Catholics of
New Orleans." Our World
(5; Apr. , 1950), pp. 14-31.
             DLC; DHU/MO
Hickman, Thomas Lloyd. "A
Study of the Status of Negroes
as Members of White Baptist
Churches in the State of North
Carolina, 1776-1863." Mas-
ter's thesis, School of Reli-
gion, Howard University, 1947.
Hodges, George Washington.
Touchstones of Methodism.
New York: The Compact Re-
flector Press, 1947. NN/Sch
    Negro author.
Hoss, Elijah E. Methodist Fra-
ternity and Federation. Nash-
ville: Publishing House, Meth-
odist Episcopal Church, South,
1913.   DLC
Jason, William C. "The Delaware Annual Conference of the
Methodist Church 1864-1965."
Methodist History (4:4, Jl. ,
1966), pp. 26-40.
                DHU/R; ISAR
Jones, John G. A Complete History of Methodism as Con-
nected With the Mississippi
Conference. Baton Rouge:
Claitors Book Store, 1966.
                        IEG
    Brief statements about Ne-
gro work.
Jones, Robert E. Fifty Years in
the Lombard Street Central
Presbyterian Church. Philadelphia: Edward Stern, 1894.
                     DHU/MO
    History of Second African
Presbyterian Church with biographies of Negro Presbyter-

ians.

Jordan, David M. Gradual Racial Integration in the Methodist Church. n. p., 1956. IEG

Kearns, H. C. , (O. P.) The Life of Blessed Martin de Porres. New York: Kennedy & Sons, 1937.   DHU/R

King, Willis J. , (bp.). History of the Methodist Church Mission in Liberia. n. p. , 1945. IEG
Negro author.

-- The Negro in American Life: An Elective Course. New York: The Methodist Book Concern, 1926. PCC; JiU; NN; PP; PPE
For young people on Christian race relationships.

-- "The Negro Membership of the (Former) Methodist Church in the (New) United Methodist Church." Methodist History (7; Apr. 3, 1969), pp. 32-43. ISAR

Kirrane, John Philip. "The Establishment of Negro Parishes and the Coming of the Josephites, 1853-1871." Master's thesis, Catholic University, 1932.

LaFarge, John. "The Cardinal Gibbons Institute. Commonweal (15; Feb. 17, 1932), pp. 433-34.   DLC

-- "Negro Apostolate." Commonweal (22; Jl. 5, 1935), pp. 257-9.   DHU

Lazenby, Marion Elias. History of Methodism in Alabama and West Florida. n. p. , 1960. ISAR
See chapter 32.

Love, J. Robert. Is Bishop Holly Innocent? Charges Specific Arguments, Canon Laws Involved in an Ecclesiastical Trial Held in Holy Trinity Church, Port-au-Prince, Hayti, the 4th of Sept. , 1882. n. p. , n. d.   NN/Sch
First Negro Bishop in the

Protestant Episcopal Church.

Martin, Isaac P. History of Methodism in the Holston Conference. Nashville: Holston Conference Historical Society, 1945.   IEG
Negroes and the Methodist Episcopal Church, South.

McFerrin, John B. History of Methodism in Tennessee. Nashville: Southern Methodist Publishing House, 1879. IEG
See pp. 85-196.

Methodist Episcopal Church. Minutes of the Lexington Conference of the Methodist Episcopal Church; Held in Park Street Methodist Episcopal Church, Cinn. , Ohio, March 25-30, 1908. Adopted by the Conference as its Official Record. Cincinnati: John W. Robinson, Edited and Published, 1908.
DHU/MO; GAU; NN/Sch

*-- Official Journal of State Conferences... DHU/MO; NN/Sch; GAU

-- Board of Foreign Missions. The Centenary Survey of the Board of Foreign Missions. The Methodist Episcopal Church. New York: Joint Centenary Committee, Methodist Episcopal Church, 1918.
NN/Sch

*-- Board of Missions. Journal of the Annual Meeting.
NN/Sch; DLC; DHU/MO

*-- Division of National Missions. Reports 194-.
NN/Sch; GAU; NJMD

*-- Conferences. Liberia. Journal of Session.
NN/Sch; DHU/MO; DLC

Mills, M. Gertrude. Christian Creative Science. Rendered at the State Federation of Colored Women Clubs. June 16-18, 1915. At Palatka, Fla. : Fla. Printing Co., 1915.
NN/Sch

Nail, Olin W. History of Texas
Methodism. Austin: Capital
Printing Co. , 1961.   IEG
     Methodism and the Negroes
     by I. B. Loud.
Nanna, John C. The Centennial
Services of Asbury Methodist
Episcopal Church. Wilming-
ton, Del. : Delaware Pub. Co. ,
1889.   NcD-D
     Information about the Afri-
     can Union Methodist Protestant
     Church Organized in 1865.
     Disciplines of 1871 and
     1895 contain information on it
     also.
Nelson, Clarence T. R. "A
     Study of Current Religious
     Education in the Lexington Con-
     ference of the Methodist
     Church." Master's thesis,
     Garrett Theological Seminary,
     1951.
Owens, I. V. "And Forbid Them
     Not." Crisis (57:2, Feb. ,
     1950), pp. 78-82.   DHU/MO
     The merger of the Presby-
     terian and Protestant Episco-
     pal Church in Cincinnati in
     organizing an interracial
     church.
Patton, Robert Williams. An
Inspiring Record in Negro Ed-
ucation; Historical Summary
of the Work of the American
Church Institute for Negroes
Delivered to the National Coun-
cil of the Protestant Episco-
pal Church, at the Request of
the Presiding Bishop, the Rt.
Rev. Henry St. George Tucker, D.D. , February 14, 1940.
New York: The National Council, Protestant Episcopal
Church, 1940.   NN/Sch
Peirce, Alfred M. A History
of Methodism in Georgia.
North Georgia Conference Historical Society, 1956.   IEG
     Founding of Clark College
     and Gammon Theological Sem-
     inary.

Perry, Calbraith Bourn. Twelve
Years Among the Colored
People. A Record of the
Work of Mount Calvary Chapel
of St. Mary the Virgin, Balti-
more. New York: J. Pott &
Co. , 1884.   NN/Sch
Peterson, Frank L. "Why the
     Seventh-Day Adventist Church
     Established and Maintains a
     Negro College (and Schools
     for below College grade)."
     Journal of Negro Education
     (29; Sum. , 1960), pp. 284-88.
                          DHU
Phillips, Henry L. In Memoriam
of the Late Rev. Alex Crum-
mell, D. D. of Washington,
D. C. An Address Delivered
before the American Negro
Historical Society, of Phila. ,
Nov. 1898, with an Introduc-
tory Address by Rev. Matthew
Anderson. Philadelphia: Cole-
man Printery, 1899. DHU/MO
Pool, Frank Kenneth. "The
     Southern Negro in the Method-
     ist Episcopal Church." Doc-
     toral dissertation, Duke Uni-
     versity, 1939.
Posey, Walter Brownlow. The
Development of Methodism in
the Old Southwest, 1883-1924.
Tuscaloosa, Ala. : Weather-
ford Printing Co. , 1933. IEG
     Chapter, "Negro and the
     Methodist Church."
Protestant Episcopal Church in
the U. S. A. Proceedings of the
First Convocation of Colored
Clergy, 1883. OWibfU; NN/Sch
     In Arnett Papers, v. 76.
-- Conference on the Relation of
the Church to the Colored
People of the South. n.p. ,
1883.   DHU/MO
-- National Council. Woman's
Auxiliary. Toward Understand-
ing Negro American. Leader's
Manual... New York: The Na-
tional Council, Protestant
Episcopal Church, 1936.
                          CtY-D

"Prepared by Leila W. Anderson, Esther Brown, field secretaries, Woman's Auxiliary." DLC
Richards, James McDowell. Brothers in Black, by J. McDowell Richards; A Sermon Preached as Retiring Moderator before the Presbytery of Atlanta. Atlanta: Southern Regional Council, 1946. NN/Sch
Ridgel, Alfred L. Africa and African Methodism. Atlanta: Franklin Printing and Publishing Co., 1896. TNMph
Riley, Walter H. Forty Years in the Lap of Methodism; History of Lexington Conference of Methodist Episcopal Church. Louisville, Ky.: Mayes Printing Co., 1915. NN/Sch
Roche, Richard J. "Catholic Colleges and the Negro Student." Doctoral dissertation, Catholic University of America, 1948. INU; DCU; DHU/MO; NcD
Satterwhite, John H. "John Stewart and the Mission to the Wyandott Indians." Forever Beginning. Lake Junaluska, N.C.: Association of Methodist Historical Societies, 1967. DHU/R
Negro author.
Scott, Allen L. "Toward Preserving the History of the Central Jurisdiction." Methodist History (7; Oct., 1968), pp. 24-30. DHU/R
Shaw, James Beverly Ford. The Negro in the History of Methodism. Nashville: Parthenon Press, 1954. DHU/MO; DHU/R; NN/Sch; DLC; IEG
Shipp, Albert M. A History of Methodism in the Holston Conference. Nashville: Holston Historical Conference, 1945. IEG
Sketon, D.E. History of Lexington Conference. n.p., 1950. ISAR

Former all-Negro conference of the United Methodist Church.
Slattery, John Richard. "Roman Catholic College for Negro Catechists." Catholic World (70; 1900), pp. 1+. DHU; DCU/HU
-- "The Seminary for the Colored Missions." Catholic World (46; 1888), pp. 541-50. DHU/R
Southern Baptist Convention. Annual Report of the Southern Baptist Convention 1932. 77th Session 87th Year. St. Petersburg, Fla. May 13-16, 1932. n.p., 1932. DHU/MO
Spalding, David. "The Negro Catholic Congresses, 1889-1894." Catholic Historical Review (55:3, Oct., 1969), pp. 337+. DHU/R
Springfield, Massachusetts, St. John's Congregational Church. The History of St. John's Congregational Church, 1844-1962. Springfield, Mass.: St. John's Congregational Church, 1962. A&M; DHU/MO
Steward, Theophilus Gould. Active Service: or Religious Work among U.S. Soldiers. A Series of Papers by our Post and Regiment Chaplains. New York: United States Army Aid Association, n.d. DHU/MO
Negro author.
Sweet, William Warren. Virginia Methodism. A History. Richmond: Whittel & Shepperson, 1955. IEG
Sylvester, H. "Negro Seminary; Techny Fathers Persevere at Their Task of Preparing Colored Priests." Commonweal (33; Apr. 11, 1941), pp. 615-16. DHU
Teba, Wea. The Book of Hymns; Selected Verses from the Protestant Episcopal Church, with New Hymn Tunes by Wea Teba (Taylor). New York: LeMers

(Teba, W. cont.)
Music Publishers, 1959.
                        NN/Sch
Negro composer.
"Permission to use several
of the enclosed hymn words
was graciously granted by the
church hymnal corporation."
Thirkield, Mary Haven. Eliza-
beth Lounes Rust. Cincinnati:
Jennings & Pye, 1903. GAITH
Thirkield, Wilbur Patterson.
Rev. Eleza H. Gammon. At-
lanta: n.p., 1892.   IEG
-- Separation or Continuity,
Which? or A Colored Man's
Reply to Bishop Foster's Book,
"The Union of the Episcopal
Methodisms." Baltimore: H.
H. Smith, 1893.   NJMD
Thomas, James S. "Rationale
Underlying Support of Negro
Private Colleges by the Meth-
odist Church." Journal of Ne-
gro Education (29; Sum.,
1960), pp. 252-59.   DHU
Thrall, Homer S. A Brief His-
tory of Methodism in Texas.
Nashville: Publishing House of
the M.E. Church, South, 1894.
                          IEG
   pp. 278, A.M.E. and C.M.
E. Church.
Thrift, Charles T. On the Trial
of the Florida Circuit Rider.
Lakeland, Fla.: Florida Col-
lege Press, 1944.   ISAR
   See section on St. John's
River Conference.
Tieuel, Robert C. The Story of
Methodism among Negroes in
the U.S. Copyright... by
Robert C.D. Tieuel, Jr. De-
signed by Portia Elaine Harris
Tieuel... Hutchinson, Kan.:
1945.   DLC
   Negro author.
   Reproduced from typewrit-
ten copy. "Catalogues of edu-
cational and reports of denom-
inational philanthropic institu-
tions."
Tucker, Frank C. The Method-

ist Church in Missouri, 1798-
1839. Joint Committee on the
Historical Societies of the Mis-
souri East and Missouri West
Annual Conference, 1966. IEG
   Negro Methodist included.
Turner, Wallace. The Mormon
Establishment. Boston:
Houghton Mifflin, 1966.
                        NN/Sch
   "The anti-Negro doctrine:"
p. (218)-245. "Will the Negro
doctrine change?" pp. 246-66.
Vernon. Walter H. Methodism
Moves Across North Texas.
Nashville: Parthenon, 1967.
                          IEG
   Negro members and preach-
ers in the Conference.
Wakely, Joseph B. Lost Chap-
ters Recovered from the Early
History of American Method-
ism. New York: Pr. by the
Author, 1858.
            DHU/MO; NN/Sch
   "Colored People in New
York City in the Infancy of
American Methodism." Biog-
raphy of Peter Williams, Ne-
gro minister.
Walker, George G. "What the
Methodist Church is Doing for
the Negro." World Outlook
(5:31, Oct. 1919).
               IEG; DLC; CtY
West, Anson. A History of
Methodism in Alabama. Nash-
ville: Publishing House, Meth-
odist Episcopal Church, South,
1893.   ISAR
   Chapters 27 and 35.
White, William S. The African
Preacher: An Authentic Nar-
rative. Philadelphia: Presby-
terian Board of Publications,
1849. Rare Book Room.
                     TxW; NcD
-- William S. White, D.D. and
His Times... An Autobiogra-
phy by his Son. Richmond:
Presbyterian Committee of
Publication, 1891. NcD; VC
Whitehead, C.L. Negro Bishop

Agitation of the Methodist
Episcopal Church and Colored
Members in Convention at
Nashville, Tennessee, October
22-23, 1914. n.p., 1914.
        TNMph
Wogaman, J. Philip. Methodism's
Challenge in Race Relations;

a Study of Strategy. Washington: Public Affairs Press,
1960. NN/Sch; CtY-D;
        DHU/MO
Wright, Nathan. The Riddle of
Life, & Other Sermons. Boston: Bruce Humphries, 1952.
        DHU/MO
    Negro author.

B. FOREIGN MISSIONS--THE AMERICAS
(EXCLUDING U.S.)

An Appeal to the Churches in
Behalf of the West Indian Mis-
sion. n.p., n.d. DHU/MO
Carneiro, Edison. ...Religioes
Negras; Notas de Etnografia
Religiosa... Rio de Janeiro:
Civilizacao Brasileira s.a.,
1936.   NcD
    Biblioteca de divulgacao
scientifica, dirigida pelo prof.
dr. Arthur Ramos. Vol. VII.
Religion of Negroes of Brazil.
Castillo de Aza, Zenón. Trujillo,
Benefactor de la Iglesia. (En
el Primer Aniversario del
Concordato). Ciudad Trujillo:
Editora del Caribe, 1955.
        NN/Sch
    Church and state during
life of Trujillo.
Dean, David M. "The Domestic
and Foreign Missionary Papers.
The Haiti Papers: 1855-1934."
Historical Magazine of the
Protestant Episcopal Church
(39:1, Mr., 1970), pp. 94-95.
        DHU/R
    Article describes papers.
Deren, Maya. Divine Horse-
men: The Living Gods of
Haiti. London: Longmans,
1953.   DHU/MO
Detweiler, Charles Samuel. The
Waiting Isles; Baptist Missions
in the Caribbean. Edited by
the Department of Missionary
Education, Board of Education
of the Northern Baptist Con-

vention... Boston: The Jud-
son Press, 1930.   NN/Sch
Dunningan, A. "Century of Chris-
tian Faith." Sepia (10; Nov.,
1961), pp. 56-61. DHU/MO
    "Protestant Episcopal
Church in Haiti."
Goncalves Fernandes, Albino.
...Xangos Do Wordeste; In-
vestigações Sobre os Cultos
Negro-Fetichistas do Recife
... Rio de Janeiro: Civilza-
ção Brasiléira, 1937.
        DHU/MO; NcD
    Religion of Negro race in
Brazil.
Granier de Cassagnac, Bernard
Adolphe. Voyage aux Antilles,
Françaises, Anglaises Dano-
laes, Espagnoles: à Saint-
Domingus et aux Etats-Unis
d'Amérique... Paris: Au
Comptoir des Imprimeurs-
Unis, 1843-1844. NN/Sch
    Slavery and the church in
the French West Indies.
Gray, Arthur Romeyn. That
Freedom; A Study of Democ-
racy in the Americas. New
York: The National Council,
1925.   NN/Sch
Grose, Howard Benjamin. Ad-
vance in the Antilles; the New
Era in Cuba and Porto Rico.
New York: Literature Dept.,
Presbyterian Home Missions,
1910.
    (Forward mission study

(Grose, H. B. cont.)
courses...)
"Haiti." Christian Union (1:5,
My., 1850), pp. 230-32.
Hurston, Zora Neale. Voodoo
Gods: An Inquiry into Native
Myths and Magic in Jamaica
and Haiti... London: J. M.
Dent & Sons, 1939.   A&M
Interchurch World Movement of
North America. Survey Depart-
ment. World Survey Conference:
Atlantic City, January 7 to 10,
Prepared by Survey Depart-
ment - Home Missions Divi-
sion. New York: 1920.
            NN/Sch; DHU/MO
International Missionary Council.
Dept. of Social and Economic Re-
search and Council. The Church
in the New Jamaica; a Study
of the Economic and Social
Basis of the Evangelical Church
in Jamaica, J. Merle Davis,
Director. New York: Dept.
of Social and Economic Re-
search & Counsel, Internation-
al Missionary Council, 1942.
                        NN/Sch
Jan, Jean Marie. Les Congrega-
tions Religieuses à Saint-
Dominique, 1681-1793. Port-
au-Prince: n.p., n.d.
                        NN/Sch
Jesuits. Letters from Missions.
Missions de l'Amérique. Paris:
La Society Catholique des
Bons Livres, 1827. NN/Sch
-- Letters from Missions. Mis-
sion de Cayenne et de la
Guyane Française. Avec une
carte géographique. Paris:
Julien, Lanier, Cosnard et
oe., 1857.   NN/Sch
Knapp, M. Diary Letters; a
Missionary, (sic), Trip Through
the West Indies and to South
America. Cincinnati: God
Revivalist Office, 1918.
                        NN/Sch
King, William Francis Henry.
Addington Venables Bishop of
Nassau. A Sketch of His Life

and Labours for the Church of
God. London: W. W. Gardner,
1878.   NN/Sch
Knox, John P. A Historical Account of St. Thomas, W. I.,
with its Rise and Progress in
Commerce; Missions and
Churches; Climate and its Adaptation to Invalids;... New
York: C. Scribner, 1852.
                        DHU/MO
Landes, Ruth. The City of Wom-
en. New York: Macmillan,
1947.   NcD
"The material for this book
about Brazil was gathered during an anthropological field
trip in Bahia and Rio de Janeiro in 1938 and 1939... It...
describes the life of Brazili-
ans of the Negro race."
Larsen, Jens Peter Mouritz.
Virgin Islands Story; a History
of the Lutheran State Church,
Other Churches, Slavery, Education, and Culture of the Danish West Indies, Now the Virgin Islands. Philadelphia:
Muhlenberg Press, 1950.
                        NN/Sch
Lawaetz, Herman. ... Brodre-
menighedens Mission i Dansk-
Vestindien, 1769-1848; Bidrag
Til en Charakteristik af Brod-
rekirken og dens Gerning og
af den Farvede Races Stil
ling til Christendommen. Kob-
enhaven: O. B. Wroblewski,
1902.   NN/Sch
Missions, Virgin Islands.
Levo, John Ernest. Black and
White in the West Indies. London: Society for the Propagation of the Gospel in Foreign
Parts, 1930.   CtY-D
Marrat, Jabez. In the Tropics;
or, Scenes and Incidents of
West Indian Life. London:
Wesleyan Conference Office,
1876.   NN/Sch
Mead, Frank Spencer. On Our
Door Step. New York: Friendship Press, 1948. NN/Sch

Missions in the Virgin Islands.

Moister, William. Memorials of Missionary Labours in Africa and the West Indies: with Historical and Descriptive Observations. New York: Lane & Scott, 1851.   NN/Sch

Morgan, Carol McAfee. Rim of the Caribbean. New York: Friendship Press, 1942.
NN/Sch
Missions in the West Indies and Central America.

Pilkington, Frederick. Daybreak in Jamaica. London: Epworth Press, 1950.   NN/Sch

Pinnington, John. "Factors in the Development of the Catholic Movement in the Anglican Church in British Guiana." Historical Magazine (37:4, December, 1968), pp. 355-69.
DHU/R

Price, Ernest. Bananaland; Pages from the Chronicle of an English Minister in Jamaica. London: Carey Press, 1930.
NN/Sch

Pressoir, Catts. Le Protestantisme Baftien... (Port-au-Prince) Impe. de la Société Biblique et des Livres Religieux d'Hafri, 1945. NN/Sch (v. 1, pt. 2)

Religious Persecution in Jamaica. Report of the Speeches of the Rev. Peter Duncan, Wesleyan Missionary and the Rev. W. Knibb, Baptist Missionary at a Public Meeting of the Friend of Christian Missions, Held at Exeter-Hall, August 15, 1832. London: S. Bagster, 1832.
DHU/MO

Reminiscences of the West India Islands. By a Methodist Preacher... Edited by D. P. Kiddler. New York: Pub. by Land & Scott for the Sunday School Union of the Methodist Episcopal Church, 1849.
NN/Sch

A Short Account of the Late Hurricane in the West Indies, as Far as Relates to the Missions of the Brethren in the Islands of St. Croix and St. Christopher. London: n. p., 1785.
NN/Sch

Staehelin, Felix, (ed.). Die Mission der Brüdergemeine in Suriname und Berbice im Achtzehnten Jahrhundert; Eine Missionsgeschichte Hauptachlich in Briefen und Originalberichten. Herrnhut: Verein fur Brudergeschichte in Kommission der Unitatsbuchhandlung in Gnadau, 1912.   NN/Sch

---

C. CHURCH AND NATIONAL RELIGIOUS ORGANIZATIONS RACE RELATIONS (INCLUDING HOME MISSIONS)

1. Churches

a. General

Albert, Aristides E. "The Church in the South." Methodist Review (74; Mr., 1892), pp. 229-40.   DHU/R
    "Colored Denominations," pp. 237-40.

The Asheville Conference. "A Conference of Christian Workers." Asheville, N. C.: n. p., 1898.   DHU/MO

Bakke, N. J. Illustrated Historical Sketch of Our Colored Missions. St. Louis: n. p., 1914.   DLC; NB

Betts, John R. "The Negro and the New England Conscience in the Days of John Boyle O'Reilly." Journal of Negro

(Betts, J. R. cont.)
History (51:4, Oct., 1966), pp.
246-61.   DHU
Brace, Charles Loring. Gesta
Christi: or History of Hu-
mane Progress Under Chris-
tianity... 4th ed., with new
preface and supplementary
chapter. New York: A. C.
Armstrong & Son, 1888.
                            DHU/MO
Bryson, Lyman. Approaches to
Group Understanding. Sixth
Symposium of the Conference
on Science, Philosophy and
Religion. New York: Harper
& Bros., 1947.   DHU/R
Catchings, L. Maynard. "Inter-
racial Activities in Southern
Churches." Phylon (13; Mr.,
1952), pp. 54-6.   DHU/MO
"Christians, White and Black."
Opportunity (7:10, Oct., 1929),
p. 303.   DHU/MO
Coogan, John E. "Christian Un-
touchables?" Review for Reli-
gious Research (5; 1946), pp.
107-13.   DCU/TH
Cotes, Sarah Jeannette. Pro-
gressive Missions in the South,
and Addresses. Atlanta:
Franklin Print. & Pub. Co.,
1906.   NcD
Councill, William Hooper. Syn-
opsis of Three Addresses Delivered at the Waterloo, Iowa,
July 10, 14, 15; Chautauqua
Assembly at Spirit Lake, Iowa,
July 11-12; and at State Normal School of Iowa at Cedar
Falls, July 15, 1900. n. p.,
1900.   NN/Sch
    Negro author.
Drake, St. Clair. Black Metropolis; a Study of Negro Life in
a Northern City. By St. Clair
Drake and Horace R. Cayton,
with an introduction by Richard
Wright. New York: Harcourt,
Brace & Co., 1945.
            DHU/MO; CtY-D
    Chapter 15, Power of the
    Pulpit.

"Evangelize the Negroes." The
Church at Home and Abroad
(2; Jl., 1887), pp. 61-4.
                            DHU/R
Felton, Ralph Almon. "Negro
Pastors Go to Rural Colleges."
Christian Century (61:1, Jan.
5, 1944), pp. 22+.   DHU/R
Forsyth, David D. Christian
Democracy for America. Cin-
cinnati: The Methodist Book
Concern, 1918.   NN/Sch
Glock, C. Y. and B. B. Ringer.
"Church Policy and the Atti-
tudes of Ministers and Parish-
ioners, on Social Issues."
American Sociological Review
(21; Apr., 1956), pp. 148-56.
                              DHU
-- "The Political Role of the
Church as Defined by its Pa-
rishioners." Public Opinion
Quarterly (18; Wint., 1954-
55), pp. 337-47.   DHU
Haynes, George Edmund. "The
Church and Negro Progress."
Annals of the American Acad-
emy of Political and Social
Sciences (130:229, Nov., 1928),
pp. 264-71.   DHU/R
    Negro author.
-- "The Unfinished Interracial
Task of the Churches." Jour-
nal of Religious Thought (2:1,
Aut. -Wint., 1945), pp. 53-59.
                            DHU/R
Heckman, Oliver S. "Northern
Church Penetration into the
South, 1860-1880." Doctoral
dissertation, Duke University,
1939.
Holloway, Vernon H. "Christian
Faith and Race Relations."
Religion in Life (14:2, Spr.,
1945), pp. 340-50.   DHU/R
Jack, Homer A. "The Emer-
gence of the Interracial Church."
Social Action (13; Ja. 1947),
pp. 31-37.   DHU/R
Johnson, Richard Hanson. "A
Critical Study of Religious
Work Among Negroes of St.
Mary's County, Maryland since

1865, with Special Reference to the Catholic, Episcopal and Methodist Churches." Master's thesis, Howard University, 1948.
Jones, Jerome W. "The Established Virginia Church and the Conversion of Negroes and Indians 1620-1760." Journal of Negro History (46:1, Ja., 1961), pp. 12-23. DHU
Kelly, Gerald, S.J. "Notes on Moral Theology, 1946." Theological Studies (8; 1947), pp. 97-117. DHU/R
Kitagawa, Daisuke. "Christianity and Race." World Christian Handbook (London: Dominion Press, 1962), pp. 5-9. DHU/R
Kramer, Alfred S. "Patterns of a Racial Inclusion Among Selected Congregations of Three Protestant Denominations: An Analysis of the Processes Through Which Congregations of Protestant Denominations Have Included Persons of Racial and Cultural Minority Groups." Doctoral dissertation, New York University, 1955. DLC
Abstract, Phylon (16; Sum., 1955), pp. 283-97. DHU/MO
Lee, Frank F. Negro and White in a Connecticut Town. New York: Bookman Associates, 1961. CtY-D
"Based upon the writer's unpublished Doctoral dissertation... Yale University, 1953."
Little, John. "City Mission For Colored People." Arcadius S. Trawick, (ed.). The New Voice in Race Adjustments (New York: Student Volunteer Movement, 1914), pp. 132-39. DHU/R
Loescher, Frank S. "The Protestant Church and the Negro: Recent Pronouncement." Social Force (26; Dec., 1947),

pp. 197-201. DAU; DCU/SW
Manschreck, Clyde L. "Religion in the South: Problem and Promise." Francis B. Simkins, (ed.). The South in Perspective, Institute of Southern Culture Lectures at Longwood College, 1958. Farmville, Va.: Longwood College, 1959. DLC
Massiah, J. Bowden. The General Convention and the Negro Problem; a Review of the Controversy over Missionary Districts for Negroes of the Church with Comments. Chicago: The Convention, 1913. TNF
Mays, Benjamin Elijah. "Obligation of Negro Christians in Relation to an Interracial Program." Journal of Religious Thought (2:1, Aut.-Wint., 1945), pp. 42-52. DHU/R
Article also in, Wm. S. Nelson, (ed.), The Christian Way in Race Relations (New York: Harper & Bros., Publishers, 1948), pp. 209-25. Negro author
McAfee, Joseph Ernest. "Church and Race Relations." Opportunity (7:2, Feb., 1929), pp. 39-41. DHU/MO
McCulloh, James E. "Cooperation of White and Negro Ministers for Social Service." Arcadius S. Trawick, (ed.). The New Voice in Race Adjustments (New York: Student Volunteer Movement, 1914), pp. 188-94. DHU/R
McKeon, Richard M. "Social Attitudes and the Negro." St. Augustine's Messenger (31:7, Sept. 1954), pp. 222-25, 236+. DHU/R
Miller, Robert Moats. American Protestantism and Social Issues, 1919-1934. Chapel Hill: University of North Carolina Press, 1958. DHU/R;INU;NN/Sch

Oniki, S. Garry. "Interracial Churches in American Protestantism." Social Action (16; Ja., 1950), pp. 4-22. DHU/R

Parker, J. Kenton. "Christian Relations Among Races." Southern Presbyterian Journal (10; Ag. 22, 1951), p. 7.
DLC; KyLXCB

Powell, Adam Clayton, Sr. "The Church in Social Work." Opportunity (1; Ja., 1923), pp. 15+. Negro author. DHU/MO

Poynter, W. T. "The Church and the Black Man." Methodist Review (20; Mr.-Apr., 1896), p. 79.   DLC; CtY-D

Quon, Jessica. Man's Inhumanity to Man. Alhambra, Calif.: n.p., 1947.   DLC

Reed, Richard Clark. "A Sketch of the Religious History of the Negroes in the South." Papers of the American Society of Church History, 2nd Series (New York: G.P. Putnam's Sons, 1914), v. 4, pp. 177-204. CtY-D; DHU/R; DLC
Account of White Missionary activities to Negroes in the South from the Colonial Period to circa 1900.

Robertson, William J. The Changing South. New York: Boni and Liveright, 1927.
DLC

Roy, Ralph Carl. "Roman Catholicism, Protestantism, and the Negro." Religion in Life (33; Aut., 1964), pp. 577+.
DHU/R; DAU/W; DGW

Shannon, Alexander Harvey. The Racial Integrity of the American Negro. Washington, D.C.: Public Affairs Press, 1953.
NN/Sch

Silver, Abba Hillel. "America's Minority Groups in War and Peace." Social Action (9:1, Ja. 15, 1943), pp. 30-6.
Pam. File; DHU/R

Silver, James W. Confederate Morale and Church Propa-

ganda. Tuscaloosa: Confederate Publishing Co., 1957.
DHU/MO
"An attempt to show what part religion played in bringing on secession and in promoting the War Between the States."

Smith, Lillian. "The White Christian and His Conscience." Presbyterian Outlook (127; Jl. 23, 1945), pp. 5-6.
NN/Sch; DLC; NcD; DHU/MO
Reprinted in South Today.

Taylor, Edward B. Calls to Christians of the New South, in Duty of Extending Help to the Weaker Race by Promoting the Education in Morals and Manners of its Members. n.p., n.d.   DHU/MO

Thomas, George Finger. Christian Ethics and Moral Philosophy. New York: Scribner, 1955.   NN/Sch

Tindley, Charles A. "Church That Welcomes 10,000 Strangers." World Outlook (5; Oct., 1919), pp. 5-6.
DLC; CtY-D; DHU/MO
Negro author.

Vail, T. H. "Missionary Bishops for Negroes." Church Review (41; 1883), p. 301.   DLC

Weatherford, Willis Duke. Present Forces in Negro Progress. New York: Association Press, 1912. NN/Sch; CtY-D;
DHU/MO
Missions to Negroes, pp. 145-65.

Weaver, Galen R. "Church Experiments in Community Action." Social Action (16:1, Ja. 15, 1950), p. 3. DHU/R
"What Can the Church Do?" Social Action (9:1, Ja. 15, 1943), pp. 44-45.   DHU/R

World Council of Churches. Ecumenical Statements on Race Relations; Development of Ecumenical Thought on Race Relations, 1937-1964. Geneva:

n. p. , 1965.
DLC; NcD; CtY-D

b. Roman Catholic

Bernard, Raymond. "Some Anthropological Implications of the Racial Admission Policy of the U.S. Sisterhoods." American Catholic Sociological Review (19; Je. , 1958), pp. 124-33. DCU/SW
"Birth of a Bishop: West Indian Priest Becomes First Named Prelate in U.S." Ebony (8; Ag. , 1953), pp. 25-28. DHU/MO
Brunini, J. G. "Negro Mission Jubilee; Church of St. Benedict the Moor." Commonweal (19; Dec. 8, 1933), pp. 158-9. DHU/R
Butsch, Joseph. "Catholics and the Negro." Journal of Negro History (2; Oct. , 1917), pp. 393-410. DHU/MO
Calvez, Jean Yves and Jacques Perrin. The Church and Social Justice: The Social Teaching of the Popes from Leo XIII to Pius XII, 1878-1958. London: Burns and Oates, 1961. INU
Campbell, Robert, (ed.). Spectrum of Catholic Attitudes. Milwaukee: Bruce Publishing Co. , 1969. DHU/R
Views on racial integration and anti-semitism, pp. 121-33.
Cantwell, Daniel M. "Race Relations--As Seen by a Catholic." The American Catholic Sociological Review, (7; Dec. , 1946), pp. 242+. DHU
Casey, John. "Mission Work Among the Negroes." St. Meinrad Historical Essays (1; 1932), pp. 216-23. DCU/ST
"The Catholic Church and Negroes: A Correspondence." Crisis (30; Jl. , 1925), pp. 120-24. DHU/MO
"Catholic Church and the Negro

Priest." Crisis (19; Ja. , 1920), pp. 122-23. DHU/MO
*Catholic Church in the United States. Commission for Catholic Missions Among the Colored People and the Indians. Our Negro and Indian Missions. Annual Report of the Secretary. NN/Sch; DHU/MO; DCU; DLC (1892, 1893, 1917, 1918, DHU/R, 1927-62.)
Title varies: Mission work among the Negroes and the Indians.
-- Appeal in Behalf of the Negro and Indian Missions in the United States. Clayton, Del. : Pr. at St. Joseph's Industrial School for Colored Boys, 1902. DLC
The Catholic Digest. Catholic Digest Reader; Selected by the Editors. Garden City, N. Y. : Doubleday, 1952. NN/Sch
Catholic Interracial Council. Sermons on Interracial Justice; Compiled by the Catholic Interracial Council of New York City, Under the Direction of the Reverend John La Farge. n. p. , 1957. NN/Sch
"Catholicism and the Negro." Jubilee (Sept. , 1955). NN/Sch; DGU; DCU/HU
Special issue.
Code, Joseph B. "Negro Sisterhood in the United States." America (58; 1938), pp. 318-19. DGU
Congar, Marie Joseph. The Catholic Church and the Race Question. Paris: UNESCO, 1953. CtY-D; DHU/R; NN/Sch; DLC
Cooley, Leo P. "Bishop England's Solution of the Negro Problem." Master's thesis, St. John's University, 1940.
Dedeaux, Mary Liberata (Sister). "The Influence of Saint Frances Academy on Negro Catholic Education in the Nineteenth

(Dedeaux, M. L. cont.)
Century." Master's thesis,
Villanova University, 1944.
DeHueck, Catherine. Friendship
House. New York: Sheed
and Ward, 1946.   NN/Sch
Doherty, Joseph F. Moral Prob-
lems of Interracial Marriage.
Washington, D. C. : The Cath-
olic University of America
Press, 1949. DCU; NN/Sch
Dunne, William. "Roman Catho-
lic Church: The Rationale
and Policies Underlying the
Maintenance of Higher Institu-
tions for Negroes." Journal of
Negro Education (29; Sum. ,
1960), pp. 307-14.   DHU
Emerick, A. J. "The Colored
Mission of Our Lady of the
Blessed Sacrament." Wood-
stock Letters (42; 1913), pp. 69-
82, 175-88, 352-62; (43; 1914),
pp. 10-23, 181-94.   DGU
The Epistle. The Conversion of
the Negro. New York: Saint
Paul Guild, 1945.   NN/Sch
    Issue of the Epistle, v. 11,
no. 2, Spr., 1945.
Farnum, Mable. The Street of
the Half-Moon. The Story of
Saint Peter Claver, Apostle of
the Negroes... Milwaukee:
Bruce Publishing Co. , 1940.
                       DHU/MO
Fegin, Joe R. Black Catholics in
the United States: An Explora-
tory Analysis. Hart M. Nelson
& Raytha L. Yokley. The Black
Church in America (New York:
Basic Books, 1971), pp. 246-
54.   DHU/R
    Also in his Slavery in the
Cities in the South, 1820-1860.
                        DHU/R
Fey, H. E. "Catholicism and the
Negro." Christian Century (61:
Dec. 20, 1944), pp. 1476-1479.
                        DHU/R
Fichter, Joseph H. "The Catho-
lic South and Race." Religious
Education (59:1, Ja. -Feb. ,
1964), pp. 30-33.   DHU/R

-- The Catholic Viewpoint on Race
Relations. Chicago: Univer-
sity of Chicago Press, 1954.
                        DCU
Foley, Albert S. "The Catholic
Church and the Washington Ne-
gro." Doctoral dissertation,
University of North Carolina,
1950.
-- "St. Elizabeth's Full Circle."
Interracial Review (24; 1951),
pp. 120-22.   DGU
Gillard, John Thomas. The
Catholic Church and the Amer-
ican Negro; Being an Investi-
gation of the Past and Present
Activities of the Catholic
Church in Behalf of the
12,000,000 Negroes in the
U.S., With an Examination of
the Difficulties which Affect
the Work of the Colored Mis-
sions. Baltimore: St. Joseph's
Society Press, 1929.
                        DHU/MO
-- "Catholicism and the Negro."
Interracial Review (12; Je. ,
1939), pp. 89-91. DHU/MO
-- Colored Catholics in the United
States, an Investigation of
Catholic Activity in Behalf of
the Negroes in the United
States and a Survey of the
Present Condition of the Col-
ored Missions. Baltimore:
The Josephite Press, 1941.
                 DHU/R; CtY-D
-- The Negro American; a Mis-
sion Investigation. Rev. by the
Josephite Fathers. Cincinnati:
Catholic Students' Mission Cru-
sade, 1935.
         NN/Sch; CtY-D; DHU/MO
-- "Negro Looks to Rome." Com-
monweal (21; Dec. 14, 1934),
pp. 193-5.   DHU/R
Granger, Lester B. "Catholic Ne-
gro Relations. " Opportunity
(25:3, Sum. , 1947), pp. 136-
49.   DHU/MO
Harte, Thomas J. "Catholic Organizations Promoting Negro-
White Race Relations in the

The American Negro and Religion 273

United States." Doctoral dissertation. Catholic University of America, 1944.
DCU; DHU/MO; NN/Sch
Catholic University of America: Studies in Sociology, Vol. 20.
Also published by Catholic University Press, 1947.
DHU/MO
Heithaus, C. H. "Jim Crow Catholicism." Time (55: Feb. 20, 1950), pp. 58-9. DHU/R
Herr, Dan. Realities, Significant Writing from the Catholic Press. Edited and with Introduction by Dan Herr and Clem Lane. Milwaukee: Bruce Publishing Co., 1958. DHU/MO
Herz, S. "Racism: Catholics Should Fight False Dogmas of Race Superiority." Commonweal (28; Jl. 8, 1938), pp. 296-7. DHU
Hogan, John A. "Church Work Among the Negroes: Letter dated Galveston, Texas, Aug. 3, 1901." Woodstock Letters (30; 1901), pp. 223-30. DGU
Huggins, Willis Nathaniel. "The Contribution of the Catholic Church to the Progress of the Negro in the United States." Doctoral dissertation, Fordham University, 1932. NN/Sch
Hunton, George K. All of Which I Saw, Part of Which I Was; the Autobiography of George K. Hunton as Told to Gary MacEoin. Garden City, N. Y.: Doubleday, 1967. INU; NcD
Hyland, Philip. "The Field of Social Justice." The Thomist (1; 1939), pp. 295-330.
DCU/TH
Janssens, Francis. "The Negro Problem and the Catholic Church." Catholic World (44; Mr., 1887), pp. 721-26.
DCU/HU; DHU/R
Kelly, Gerald, S. J. ...Guidance

for Religion. Westminster, Md.: Newman Press, 1956.
NN/Sch
"How to think and act about the race problem," pp. 303-16.
Kelly, Laurence J. "Negro Missions in Maryland." Woodstock Letters (38; 1909), pp. 239-44. DGU
LaFarge, John. "Caste in the Church: The Roman Catholic Experience." Survey Graphic (36; Ja., 1947), pp. 61+.
DHU
-- A Catholic Interracial Program. New York: The American Press, 1939. DHU/MO
-- The Catholic Viewpoint on Race Relations. Garden City, N. Y.: Hanover House, 1960. DHU/MO; INU; CtY-D; DLC
-- "Development of Cooperative Acceptance of Racial Integration." Journal of Negro Education (21; Sum., 1952), pp. 430-33. DHU
-- Interracial Justice: A Study of the Catholic Doctrine of Race Relations. New York: America Press, 1937. DHU/R
-- A John LaFarge Reader; Selected and Edited by Thurston N. Davis and Joseph Small. New York: America Press, 1956. NN/Sch
-- The Manner is Ordinary. New York: Harcourt, Brace, 1954. NN/Sch
-- No Postponement; U. S. Moral Leadership and the Problem of Racial Minorities. New York: Longmans Green, 1950. NN/Sch; INU
-- The Race Question and The Negro. New York: Longmans, Green & Co., 1945.
DHU/R; CtY-D
Catholic Doctrine on interracial justice...
-- ...The Religious Education of the American Negro... Brussels: International Centre for

(LaFarge, J. cont.)
Studies in Religious Educa-
tion, 1947.   NN/Sch
-- (ed.). Sermons on Interracial
Justice. New York: Catholic
Interracial Council, 1957.
                      NN/Sch
-- "The Survival of the Catholic
Faith in Southern Maryland."
The Catholic Historical Re-
view (21:1, Apr., 1935), pp.
1-20.   DHU/R
-- "Translating into Action."
Interracial Review (35; Apr.,
1962), pp. 92-5.   DCU/SW
Leonard, Joseph T. Theology
and Race Relations. Milwaukee:
Bruce Pub. Co., 1963.
        DHU/R; NN/Sch; CtY-D
Markoe, William M. "Catholic
Aid for the Negro." America
(26; Feb. 18, 1922), pp. 417-
18.
-- "Catholics, the Negro, a Na-
tive Clergy." America (25;
Sept. 24, 1921), pp. 535-37.
                        DLC
-- "Negro and Catholicism."
America (30; Feb. 23, 1924),
pp. 449-50.   DLC
McAvoy, Thomas Timothy, (ed.).
Roman Catholicism and the
American Way of Life. Notre
Dame, Ind.: University of
Notre Dame, 1960.   INU
pp. 156-63. Catholic
church and race relations.
McCorry, V.P. "Word; Catho-
lic Position on Racial Dis-
crimination." America (100;
Nov. 8, 1958), pp. 175-6.
                        DHU
McGroarty, Joseph G. "Census
Findings in a Negro Parish."
Catholic World (156:933, Dec.,
1942), pp. 325-29. DHU/R
McKay, Claude. Right Turn to
Catholicism. n.p., 1946.
                      NN/Sch
Negro author.
Meehan, Thomas Francis. "Mis-
sion Work Among Colored
Catholics." Catholic Mind (20;

Apr. 22, 1922), pp. 141-52.
                        DLC
Also in Catholic Historical
Society, Historical Records
and Studies. New York: n.p.,
1915. vol. 8, pp. 116-28.
                      NN/Sch
Merwick, Donna. "The Broken
Fragments of Afro-American
History: A Study of Catholic
Boston, 1850-1890." McCor-
mick Quarterly (22:4, My.,
1969), pp. 239-52. DHU/R
"Missionary in Alabama; Catho-
lic Priest Builds Schools and
Churches for Negroes, Cajans
Deep in Southern Backwoods."
Ebony (7; Ja., 1952), pp. 65-
70.   DHU/MO
Moody, Joseph N. "Slavation by
Cooperation in the Maryland
Counties." America (70; Ja.
22, 1944).   DHU
Moroney, T.B. "The Condition
of the Catholic Colored Mis-
sion in the United States."
American Ecclesiastical Re-
view (61; 1919), pp. 640-48.
                        DGU
Murphy, Edward F. Yankee
Priest, an Autobiographical
Journey, with Certain Detours,
from Salem to New Orleans.
Garden City, N.Y.: Double-
day, 1952.   NN/Sch
Murphy, John Clarence. "An
Analysis of the Attitudes of
American Catholics Toward
the Immigrant and the Negro,
1825-1925." Doctoral disser-
tation, Catholic University,
1940.   DHU/MO
Murphy, Miriam T. "Catholic
Missionary Work Among the
Colored People of the United
States, 1766-1866." American
Catholic Historical Society of
Philadelphia Records (35;
1924), pp. 101-36.   DGU
"Negro and the Roman Catholic
Church." Crisis (20; My.,
1970), pp. 17-22. DHU/MO
"Negro Catholics Looking and

Listening." Crisis (65:4, Apr.,
1958), pp. 216-23. DHU/MO
"Negroes and the Roman Catho-
lic Church." Catholic World
(27; 1883), pp. 374+.
DCU/HU
O'Connel, Jeremiah Joseph. Ca-
tholicity in the Carolinas and
Georgia. New York: Sadler
& Co., 1879. DLC; ICN
O'Hanlon, Mary Ellen (Sister).
The Heresey of Race. River
Forest: Rosary College, 1950.
NN/Sch
O'Reilly, Charles T. "Race
Prejudice Among Catholic
College Students in the United
States and Italy; a Compara-
tive Study of the Role of Re-
ligion and Personality in Inter-
Group Relations." Doctoral
dissertation, Notre Dame Uni-
versity, 1954.
Osborne, William Audley. "The
Race Problem in the Catholic
Church in the United States."
Doctoral dissertation, Teach-
ers College, Columbia Univer-
sity, 1954. DLC
Ostheimer, Anthony Leo. Chris-
tian Principles and National
Problems. New York: Sadler,
1945. NN/Sch
Penetar, Michael Palmo. "The
Social Thought of the Catholic
Worker on the Negro." Doc-
toral dissertation, Catholic
University, 1952.
Preher, Leo Marie, (Sister).
"The Social Implications in the
Work of Blessed Martin De
Porres"... Doctoral disserta-
tion, Catholic University, 1941.
DCU
"Racialism and Missions: The
Papal Injunction." East and
West Review (5:2, Apr., 1939),
pp. 161-65. DHU/R
Reemer, Theodore (Fr.). The
Catholic Church in the United
States. St. Louis: Herder,
1950. NN/Sch
Reynolds, Edward D. Jesuits for

the Negro. New York:
America Press, 1949.
DHU/R; NcD; CtY-D; NN/Sch
Riley, Helen (Caldwell). Color,
Ebony (New York: Sheed &
Ward, 1951. NN/Sch
Negro author.
Romero, Emanuel A. "The Ne-
gro in the New York Archdio-
cese." Catholic World (172:
1,030, Ja., 1951), pp. 6-12.
DHU/R
Rouse, Michael Francis. A
Study of the Development of
Negro Education under Catho-
lic Auspices in Maryland and
the District of Columbia. The
John Hopkins University Stud-
ies in Education, No. 22.
Baltimore: The John Hopkins
Press, 1935. DHU/MO
Sesser, Robert. Primer on In-
terracial Justice. Baltimore:
Helicon Press, 1932. NN/Sch
Sherwood, Grace H. The Oblates'
Hundred and One Years. New
York: The Macmillan Co.,
1931. DHU/MO
The Founding of the Col-
ored Order of the Oblate Sis-
ters of Providence in Balti-
more, Md., 1829.
Slattery, John Richard. The
Catholic Church and the Col-
ored Race. Baltimore, Md.:
Press of St. Joseph's Semi-
nary for the Colored Mission,
189-. NN/Sch
-- "The Catholic Church and the
Negro Race." J. H. Barrows,
(ed.). The World's Parliament
of Religions. Vol. II. (Chica-
go: Parliament Publishing Co.,
1893), pp. 1104-06. DHU/R
--"Josephites and Their Work for
the Negroes." Catholic World
(5; Ap., 1890), pp. 101-11.
DCU/HU
-- "Native Clergy." Catholic
World (52; Mr. 1891), pp.
882-93. DCU/HU
Staab, Giles J., The Dignity of
Man in Modern Papal Doc-

(Staab, G. J. cont.)
trine; Leo XIII to Pius XII,
1878-1955. Washington, D. C. :
The Catholic University of
America Press, 1957.   DCU
Tarry, Ellen. "Why is Not the
Negro Catholic?" Catholic
World (150:899, Feb. , 1940),
pp. 542-46.   DHU/R
Theobald, Stephen L. "Catholic
Missionary Work Among the
Colored People of the United
States (1776-1876)," American
Catholic Historical Society of
Philadelphia Records (35; 1924),
pp. 324-44.   DGU
Thomas, John Lawrence. The
American Catholic Family.
Englewood Cliffs, N. J. :
Prentice-Hall, 1956.
                    DLC; CtY-D
United States. Congress. Senate.
Discussion by the Senate on
the Position of the Roman
Catholic Church on Race Re-
lations. 71st Cong. , 2nd Ses. ,
Feb. 7, 1930. Congressional
Record, 3237.   DHU/L
Washington, Curtis. "Miami
Mission." St. Augustine's
Messenger (Ja. , 1946), pp. 1-
2.   DHU/MO
Williams, Alberta. "White
Priest Among Negroes." Sur-
vey Graphic (My. , 1944).
                         DHU
Wojniak, Edward J. Atomic
Apostle, Thomas M. Morgan,
S. V. D. Techny, Ill. : Divine
Word Publications, 1957.
                         NN/Sch
   Missions - Negroes, p.
212-52.
Woods, Frances Jerome (Sister)
"The Pope on Minority Rights."
Social Order (8; 1958), pp.
465-72.   DGU; DCU/SW

c. Congregational (United Church
   of Christ)

Catching, L. Maynard. "The
Participation of Racial and

Nationally Minority People in
Congregational Churches."
Journal of Negro Education
(15; Fall, 1946), pp. 681-84.
                         DHU/MO
Congregational Christian
Churches; General Council.
"Resolutions on Race Rela-
tions." Voted Without Dissent,
Je. 25, 1952, Claremont,
Calif.   Pam. File; DHU/R
-- "Resolution of the General
Council of the Congregational
Christian Church." Cleveland,
O. , Je. 22-26, 1950.
       Pam. File; DHU/R
Hammond, Lilly Hardy. In the
Vanguard of a Race. New
York: Council of Women for
Home Missions, 1922.
                    DHU/R; CtY-D
Hotchkiss, Wesley A. "Congre-
gationalists and Negro Educa-
tion." Journal of Negro Educa-
tion (45; Sum. , 1960) Reprint.
       Pam. File; DHU/R
Rankin, Jeremiah Eames. God's
Guarantee About Children. A
Sermon in the First Congrega-
tional Church, Washington,
D. C. April 30, 1832. Washing-
ton, D. C. : Pilgrim Press
Assoc. , 1882.   DHU/MO
Shinn, Roger L. The Education-
al Mission of Our Church.
Boston: United Church Herald,
1962.   DHU/R
Weaver, Galen R. "A Denomina-
tional Emphasis on Race Rela-
tions." Social Action (13:1,
Ja. , 1947), pp. 25-30.
                         DHU/R
   Efforts of Congregational
Christian denomination in race
relations.

d. Disciples of Christ (Christian
   Churches)

Fiers, A. Dale. "Race Relation
in Global Perspective." World
Call (39:6, Je. 1957), pp. 21-
22.   DHU/R

Smythe Lewis, (ed.). Southern
Churches and Race Relations.
Report of the Fourth Interra-
cial Consultation held at The
College of the Bible, July 16-
20, 1962. Lexington, Ky., The
College of the Bible, 1963.
Pam. File; DHU/R
Taylor, Marilyn. "Third Chris-
tian is Beautiful." World Call
(52:2, Feb., 1970), pp. 24+.
DHU/R
A Disciple of Christ Church
of Philadelphia and its interra-
cial church and its social ac-
tion program.

e. Friends--Quakers

The African's Friend. For the
Promotion of Religion and
Morality. No. 1-149; 1886-98.
Philadelphia, 1886-98. NN/Sch
"Religious tracts and writings, selected and published by
certain members of the Yearly
meeting of the Friends of
Philadelphia, appointed trus-
tees under the will of Charles
L. Willits, deceased, to se-
lect, print and distribute such
writings among the colored
people of the southern states
and Liberia." Title varies:
no. 1, 1886, The Willits jour-
nal... no. 2-149, 1886-98, The
African's friend. No more
published.
Chace, Elizabeth (Buffum). Two
Quaker Sisters. From the
Original Diaries of Elizabeth
B. Lovell, with an Introduction
by Malcolm R. Lovell, fore-
word by Rufus Jones. New
York: Liveright Publishing
Corp., 1937.
DHU/MO; CtY-D
DuBois, William Edward Burg-
hardt. "How Negroes Have Taken
Advantage of Educational Op-
portunities Offered by Friends,"
Journal of Negro Education, (6:1,
January, 1938), pp. 124-

131. DHU/MO
Negro author.
Dunlap, William Cook. Quaker
Education in Baltimore and
Virginia Yearly Meetings, with
an Account of Certain Meet-
ings of Delaware and the East-
ern Shore Affiliated with Phil-
adelphia. Based on the manu-
script sources. Philadelphia:
Science Press Printing Co.,
1936. NN/Sch
Issued also as thesis (Ph.D.)
University of Pennsylvania.
Friends, Society of American
Friends Service Committee.
Race and Conscience in Amer-
ica. Norman: University of
Oklahoma Press, 1959.
DLC; DHU/MO; NN/Sch
Friends, Society of. American
Friends Service Committee.
Some Quaker Approaches to
the Race Problem. Philadel-
phia: American Friends Serv-
ice Committee, 1946.
DLC; NN/Sch; DHU/MO
Pharr, Julia Marietta. "The Ac-
tivities of the Society of
Friends in Behalf of Negro
Education." Master's thesis,
Howard University, 1937.

f. Methodist Episcopal (United
Methodist)

"Are the Methodist Being
Tricked?" Christian Century
(54; Oct. 27, 1937), p. 1318.
DHU/R
Atkins, D. "The Unification of
the Methodist Episcopal
Church and the Methodist Epis-
copal Church, South." Meth-
odist Review Quarterly (73:2,
Apr., 1924), pp. 276-99.
DHU/R
Beach, Waldo. "Methodist Gen-
eral Conference: A Second
Glance." Christianity and
Crisis (16; Je. 11, 1956), pp.
73-4. DHU/R
"Bishop Kern Reassures Southern
Methodists." Christian Century

(Bishop Kern... cont.)
(54:45, Nov. 10, 1937), p.
1380.   DHU/R
"Bishops' Mission Brings Race
Together in Tennessee." To-
gether (8; Feb., 1964), p. 6.
                         DAU/W
"Bishops Seek to Bolster Council
Stand on Race." Christian
Advocate (8; Apr. 23, 1964),
p. 21.   DHU/R; DAU/W
Bowen, John Wesley Edward, (ed.)
An Appeal for Negro Bishops
but No Separation. New York:
Eaton and Marns, 1912.
NN/Sch; DHU/MO; DLC
Negro author.
    An appeal in the Methodist
    Episcopal Church for Negro
    bishops.
Butler, O.G. "Should Negroes
Leave the Methodist Church?"
Christian Century (53; Mr. 11,
1936), p. 403.   DHU/R
Caldwell, John, (bp.). "Negroes
and Methodist Episcopal
Church." Southern Methodist
Quarterly Review (26; 1866),
pp. 418+.   DLC; NcD
-- "Relations of the Colored
People to the Methodist Epis-
copal Church, South." Method-
ist Quarterly Review (48;
1866), pp. 418-43. DLC; CtY-D
Cameron, Richard M. Method-
ism and Society in Historical
Perspective. New York: Abing-
don Press, 1961.   DHU/R
    See chapter IV for Slavery;
    chapter V for Civil War and
    Reconstruction and chapter VII
    for Race Relations.
Carrington, Charles L. "The
Problem of the Negro in the
Methodist Church." Christian
Advocate (137; Ag. 15, 1962),
pp. 2+. Pam. File; DHU/R
Carter, Paul A. "The Negro
and Methodist Union." Church
History (21:1, Mr., 1952), pp.
55-69.   DHU/R
Clark, Elmer T., (ed.). The
Journal and Letters of Francis

Asbury. London: Epworth,
1958.   DLC
    Bishops views on slavery
    in America.
Commission on Inter-Racial Co-
operation, Inc. Cooperation in
Southern Communities; Sug-
gested Activities for Country
and City Inter-Racial Commit-
tees, Ed. by T.J. Woofter,
Jr. and Isaac Fisher. Atlanta,
Ga.: Commission on Inter-
Racial Cooperation, 1921.
              NN/Sch; DHU/MO
-- "Repairers of the Breach;" A
Story of Interracial Coopera-
tion between Southern Women,
1935-1940... Prepared by
Jessie Daniel Ames, and Ber-
tha Payne Newell (Mrs. W.A.
Newell), Atlanta: n.p., 1940.
                       NN/Sch
Convention for Bible Missions.
Proceedings of the Convention
for Bible Missions. n.p., n.d.
                     DHU/MO
Cranston, Earl. Breaking Down
the Walls. New York: Meth-
odist Book Concern, 1915.
                       DHU/R
    Chapter VIII, the role of
    the Negro in the unification of
    the Methodist Church.
"Decisions Confronting the Methodists." Christian Century
(53; Ja. 1, 1936), pp. 147,
195.   DHU/R
Deems, Charles Force. Annals
of Southern Methodism...
New York: J.A. Gray's Printing Office, 1865.   NN/Sch
    V. 2, pp. 190-209, Negroes
    and missions.
Diffendorfer, Ralph E., (ed.).
The World Service of the Methodist Episcopal Church. Coun-
cil of Boards of Benevolence.
Committee on Conservation and
Advance. Chicago: n.p., 1923.
                       DHU/R
    Part II, Board of Educa-
    tion for Negroes.
Downey, David George, (ed.).

Militant Methodism; the Story of the First National Convention of Methodist Men, Held at Indianapolis, Indiana, October Twenty-Eight to Thirty-One, Nineteen Hundred and Thirteen... New York: The Methodist Book Concern, 1913.
NN/Sch
Durham, E. C. "A Friendly Consideration of the Negro." Methodist Review (69:4, Oct., 1920), p. 682.   DHU/R
Edwards, John E. "Petersburg, Virginia, and Its Negro Population." Methodist Quarterly Review (64; Apr., 1882), pp. 320-37.   DLC; CtY-D
Emerson, Harriet E. Annals of a Harvester, Reviewing Forty Years of Home Missionary Work in Southern States. East Andover, N. H.: A. W. Emerson, Sons & Co, 1915.   NcD
Farish, Hunter D. The Circuit Rider Dismounts: A Social History of Southern Methodism 1865-1900. Richmond: Dietz Press, 1938.   DHU/MO
A Southern Methodist attitude toward Negro Methodists.
Felton, Ralph Almon. The Ministry of the Central Jurisdiction of the Methodist Church... Madison, N. J.: n. p., 1954.
NcD
Forsyth, David D. Christian Democracy for America. Cincinnati: The Methodist Book Concern, 1918.   NN/Sch
Fox, Henry J. "Our Work in the South." Methodist Review (Ja., 1874), pp. 31-2.   DHU/R
Gravely, William B. "The Afro-American Methodist Tradition: A Review of Sources in Reprint." Methodist History (9: 3, Apr., 1971), p. 214.
DHU/R
Hagood, Lewis Marshall. The Colored Man in the Methodist Episcopal Church. New York: Hunt & Eaton, 1890.

DHU/R; NN/Sch
Negro author.
Harmon, J. A. "The Negro: Our Duty and Relation to Him." Methodist Review Quarterly (75:1, Ja., 1926), pp. 56-66.
DHU/R
Hartzell, Joseph C., (bp.). "Methodism and the Negro in the United States." Journal of Negro History (8:3, Jl., 1923), pp. 301-15.   DHU/MO
Haygood, Atticus G. Our Brother in Black: His Freedom and His Future. Nashville: Southern Methodist Publishing Co., 1881.   DHU/MO
Jamison, Monroe F. Autobiography and Work of Bishop Monroe F. Jamison... Nashville: Pr. for the Author, 1912.
DHU/MO
Negro author.
Jenkins, Warren M. Steps Along the Way; the Origin and Development of the South Carolina Conference of the Central Jurisdiction of the Methodist Church. Columbia, S. C.: Socamead Press, 1967. NcD
Negro author.
Johnson, Henry M. "The Methodist Episcopal Church and the Education of the Southern Negroes, 1862-1900." Doctoral dissertation, Yale University, 1939.
Joint Commission on Unification of the Methodist Episcopal Church and the Methodist Episcopal Church, South. Proceedings. New York: Methodist Book Concern, 1918-24.   DLC
Kaufer, Sonya F. You Hold the Key to Human Rights. Cincinnati: Woman's Division of Christian Service, Board of Missions and Church Extension, Methodist Church, 1953.
NN/Sch
Kennedy, Gerald Hamilton. The Methodist Way of Life. Englewood Cliffs, N. J.: Prentice-

(Kennedy, G. H. cont.)
Hall, 1958.   NN/Sch
Kent, Juanita Ray. Our Negro
Neighbors; a World Friend-
ship Unit for Primary Chil-
dren. Nashville, Tenn.:
Cokesbury Press, 1936.
                               NN/Sch
Kirkland, H. Burnham. "The
Methodist Church and the Ne-
gro." B. D. thesis, Union
Theological Seminary, 1944.
Luccock, Halford E. and Paul
Hutchinson. The Story of Meth-
odism. New York: Abingdon-
Cokesbury Press, 1949.
                               DHU/R
     Chapter 23, Methodism and
the Negro.
Lyon, Ernest. Autonomy. n. p.:
Afro-American Co., n. d.
                               DHU/MO
     Negro author.
-- The Negro's View of Organic
Union. New York: Methodist
Book Concern, 1915.
             DHU/R; NN/Sch
     "The question of organic
union of the Methodist Episco-
pal Church, and the Methodist
Church, South."
Madron, Thomas W. "John Wes-
ley on Race: A Christian
View of Equality." Methodist
History (2; Jl., 1964), pp. 24-
34.   DHU/R
Mann, Harold W. Atticus Greene
Haygood: Methodist Bishop,
Editor and Educator. Athens:
University of Georgia Press,
1965.   DHU/MO
     Chapter XI, an account of
the Bishop's views on Negroes
in the Methodist Church and
higher education.
Matlock, Lucius C. "The Meth-
odist Episcopal Church in the
Southern States." Methodist
Review (Ja., 1872), pp. 103-
26.   DHU/MO
McMillan, William Asbury. "The
Evolution of Curriculum Pat-
terns in Six Senior Negro Col-

leges of the Methodist Church."
Doctoral dissertation, Univer-
sity of Michigan, 1957.
*Methodist Episcopal Church.
Freedmen's Aid Society. An-
nual Reports...   NcD-D;
DHU/MO; NN/Sch; OO; GAU
"Methodist Episcopal Negro Bish-
ops." Voice of the Negro (1:
7, Jl., 1904), pp. 270+.
                               DHU/MO
"Methodists and Race." News-
week (54; Sept. 14, 1959), p.
70.   DHU
"Methodists and Segregation."
Time (75; My. 9, 1960), p.
53.   DHU
"Methodists: Proposed Merger
Called Segregation of Ne-
groes." Newsweek (9; Feb. 13,
1937), p. 21.   DHU; DLC
Moore, John M. The Long Road
to Methodist Union. New
York: Abingdon-Cokesbury
Press, 1943.   DHU/R
     A history of unification by
a Southern Methodist Bishop
who played a prominent part
in the movement.
Mount Zion M. E. Church. His-
tory of Mount Zion M. E.
Church, 1816-96 and Official
Program of the 80th Anniver-
sary, Oct. 11-18, 1896. Wash-
ington, D. C.: Press of R. L.
Pendleton, n. d.   DHU/MO
Mudge, James. Historical
Sketch of the Missions of the
Methodist Episcopal Church.
n. p.: American Methodist Mis-
sion Press, 1877.   OWibfU
"Negro Methodists Consider Un-
ion." Christian Century (56;
Jl. 12, 1939), p. 867.
                               DHU/R
Perez, Joseph A. "Some Effects
of the Central Jurisdiction Up-
on the Movement to Make the
Methodist Church an Inclusive
Church. Doctoral dissertation,
Boston University, Graduate
School, 1964.
Prestwood, Charles M. "Social

Ideas of Methodist Ministers in Alabama Since Unification." Doctoral dissertation, Boston University, Graduate School, 1960.

Reed, John Hamilton. Racial Adjustments in the Methodist Episcopal Church. New York: The Neale Publishing Co., 1914.
DHU/MO; TNF; NcD; DHU/MO

Ridout, D. L. "Study Methodist Racial Attitudes." Christian Century (74; Ja., 30, 1957), pp. 147-8.   DHU/R

Rogers, Henry Wade. "The Status of the Negro." Methodist Review Quarterly (67:4, Oct., 1918), pp. 657-69.
DHU/R

Rumbough, Constance. Negro Americans; a World Friendship Unit for Junior Girls and Boys. Nashville, Tenn.: Cokesbury Press, 1936.
NN/Sch

Rust, Richard Sutton. The Freedmen's Aid Society of the Methodist Episcopal Church. New York: Tract Department, 1880.   DLC

Shaw, Daniel Webster. Should the Negroes of the Methodist Episcopal Church be Set Apart in a Church by Themselves. New York: Eaton & Mains, 1912.   DHU/MO
Negro author.

Soper, Edmund D. Racism: A World Issue. New York: Abingdon-Cokesbury Press, 1947.   DHU/R
United Methodist Church and race relations.

Southall, Eugene P. "The Attitude of the Methodist Episcopal Church, South, Toward the Negro from 1844 to 1870." The Journal of Negro History (16; Oct. 1931), pp. 359-70.
DHU/MO

Stotts, Herbert E. and Paul Deats. Methodism and Society:

Guidelines for Strategy. New York: Abingdon Press, 1962.
DHU/R
Pp. 316, statistics in Negroes in the Methodist Church.

Stowell, Jay S. J. W. Thinks Black... New York: The Methodist Book Concern, 1922.
FSU; DHU/R
The work of the Methodist Episcopal Church among American Negroes.

-- Methodist Adventures in Negro Education. New York: The Methodist Book Concern, 1922.
DHU/R; A&M; FSU

Sweet, William Warren. "Methodist Church Influence in Southern Politics." Mississippi Valley Historical Review (1:4, Mr. 1915), pp. 546-60. DHU

Thirkield, Wilbur Patterson. The Negro and the Organic Union of Methodism... An Address before the Working Conference on the Organic Union of Methodist Held at Northwestern University, 1916, Under the Auspices of the John Richard Lindgun Foundation. n. p., 1916.   DHU/MO

Thomas, Isaac Lemuel. Methodism and the Negro. New York: Eaton & Maine, 1910.
DHU/R; DLC
Negro author.

"Unification." Opportunity (2; 1924), p. 217.   DHU/MO
Concerns the Negro question and its implications on unification of the Methodist Church, South, with the Methodist Church.

United Methodist Church. Arizona District. Southern California-Arizona Conference. Human Relations Seminar. Central Methodist Church, Phoenix, Arizona, January 12-13, 1958.
Pam. File; DHU/R

-- Board of Christian Social Relations. Interracial Leadership Conference. Reports of

(U. M. Church cont.)
... Conferences at Columbus,
Ohio, 1957-59; Austin, Texas,
1957; Detroit, Mich. , 1957;
Florida, 1959; Indianapolis,
1957; Milwaukee, Wisconsin,
1958; Pittsburgh, Pa. , 1957;
St. Louis, Mo. , 1957; Atlan-
ta, Ga. , 1957. Mim.
            Pam. File; DHU/R
-- General Board of Social Eco-
nomic Relations. Methodist
Youth Interracial Conference.
Living and Working Together.
Detroit, Mich. , Apr. 18-20,
1958. Mim. Pam. File; DHU/R
Washington University. Social
Science Institute. Background
for St. Louis Race Relations
Conference of the Methodist
Church, May 9-10, 1957.
            Mim. DHU/R
Negro population, work and
housing.
Waters, James O. "A Planned
Program for the Junior High
Class of Shiloh Community
Methodist Church, Newburg,
Maryland." B. D. paper,
School of Religion, Howard
University, 1966.
Negro author.
"What the Methodist Church is
Doing for the Negro." World
Outlook (5; Oct. , 1919), p. 31.
            DLC; CtY-D
Wilson, W. W. "The Methodist
Episcopal Church in Her Re-
lations to the Negro in the
South." Methodist Review (75;
Sept. -Oct. , 1941), pp. 713-23.
            DLC; CtY-D
Wingeier, Douglas E. "The
Treatment of Negro-White Re-
lations in the Curriculum Ma-
terials of the Methodist Church
for Intermediate Youth, 1941-
1960." Boston University,
Graduate School, 1962.
Winton, G. B. Sketch of Bishop
Atticus G. Haygood, 1915.
            DHU/MO
Wogaman, J. Philip. "A Strat-

egy for Racial Desegregation
in the Methodist Church." Doctoral dissertation, Boston University, Graduate School, 1960.

g. Presbyterian

Anderson, John F. "A Time to
Heal: A Southern Church Deal
With Racism." International
Review of Mission (59:235, Jl. ,
1970), pp. 304-10. DHU/R
Presbyterian Church in the
United States and its racial
policy.
Anderson, Matthew. Presbyteri-
anism: Its Relation to the Ne-
gro. Illustrated by the Berean
Presbyterian Church, Phila-
delphia, with a Sketch of the
Church and Autobiography of
the Author. With Introduction
by F. J. Grimke and John M.
White. Philadelphia: John M.
White, Publisher, 1897.
DHU/MO; CtY-D; DHU/MO
Bell, John L. "The Presbyteri-
an Church and the Negro in
North Carolina." North Caro-
lina Historical Review (40; Ja. ,
1963), pp. 15-36.   DHU
Fisher, Samuel Jackson. The
American Negro. Pittsburgh,
Pa.: n. p., n. d.   NN/Sch
-- The Negro: an American As-
set. Pittsburgh, Pa. : Board
of Missions for Freedmen of
the Presbyterian Church in the
U. S. A. , 1918.
    NN/Sch; CtY-D; DHU/MO
Flickinger, Robert Elliott. The
Chocktaw Freedmen and the
Story of Oak Hill Industrial
Academy... Pittsburgh, Pa. :
Under the Auspices of the
Presbyterian Board of Mis-
sions for Freedmen, 1914.
        DHU/MO; DHU/R
Chapters, IV and VI, The
American Negro.
Flow, J. E. "The Federal Coun-
cil and Race Segregation."
Southern Presbyterian Journal

(5; My. 15, 1946; 10, Oct. 17, 1951), pp. 10, 17.
DLC; KyLxCB
Halloway, Harriette R. Suggestions to Leaders of Mission Study Classes Using "An African Trail." New York: Board of Foreign Missions and Woman's Boards of Foreign Missions of the Presbyterian Church in the U.S.A., 1917.   NN/Sch
Halsey, Abram W. A Visit to the West Africa Mission of the Presbyterian Church, in the U.S.A. New York: Board of Foreign Missions of the Presbyterian Church in the U.S.A., 1905.   NN/Sch
Little, John. "Lessons from Experience; Presbyterian Colored Missions, Louisville, Ky." Missionary Review (59; Je., 1936), pp. 312-15.
DHU/R
-- "Work of Southern Presbyterian Church for Negroes." Southern Workman (33; Ag., 1904), pp. 439+. DHU/MO
Love, H. Lawrence. "The Church and Human Rights." Southern Presbyterian Journal (11; Oct. 8, 1952), p. 9.
DLC; KyLxCB
Mallard, Robert. Plantation Life Before Emancipation. Richmond, Va.: Whittet & Shepperson, 1892.   NN/Sch
Mosley, B.W. "The Evangelization of the Colored People." Southern Presbyterian Review (25; Apr., 1874), pp. 230-33.
DLC; KyLxCB
Mounger, Dwyn. "Racial Attitudes in the Presbyterian Church in the United States, 1944-54." Journal of Presbyterian History (48:1, Spr., 1970), pp. 38-68.   DHU/R
Nelson, Hart M. and Raytha L. Yokely. "Presbyterians Civil Rights and Church Prouncements." Review of Religious

Research (12:1, Fall, 1970), pp. 43-50.   DHU/R
Results of a questionnaire to 3221 elders distributed in 1967.
Presbyterian Church Confederate States of America. Minutes of the General Assembly. Augusta, Ga.: Steam Power Press Chronicle & Sentinel, 1861. Vol. 1.   DHU/R
Reports of the Executive Committee on Domestic Missions including work with Negroes.
Randall, Virginia Ray. Shadows and Lights; the American Negro, also Program Material... New York: Board of National Missions of the Presbyterian Church in the United States of America, 1941.   NN/Sch
Rice, Joseph S. "The Challenge of the Negro to the Southern Presbyterian Church." Master's thesis, Princeton Seminary, 1946.
Seville, Janet Elizabeth. Like a Spreading Tree; the Presbyterian Church and the Negro. New York: Board of National Missions, Presbyterian Church in the U.S.A., 1936. NN/Sch
Snedecor, James G. "Ministers in Cooperation," Arcadius S. Trawick, (ed.). The New Voice in Race Adjustments. (New York: Student Volunteer Movement, 1914), pp. 178-83.
DHU/R
"Southern Presbyterians Take Racial Lead." Christian Century (67; Jl. 12, 1950), p. 836.
DHU/R
Spurlock, Frank. "New Jobs, New Understanding." Presbyterian Life (23:19, Oct. 1, 1970), pp. 22-24.   DHU/R
White Presbyterian Church opens a training center for blacks in Kansas City, Mo.
Steele, Algernon Odell. "Shifts in the Religious Beliefs and

284   Afro-American Religious Studies

(Steele, A. O. cont.)
Attitudes of Students in two
Presbyterian Colleges." Doc-
toral dissertation, University
of Chicago, 1942.   DLC
   Negro author.
Thompkins, Robert Edwin. "A
History of Religious Educa-
tion Among Negroes in the
Presbyterian Church in the
United States of America."
Doctoral dissertation, Univer-
sity of Pittsburgh, 1950.
Thompson, Ernest Thice. "Chris-
tian Relations Among Races."
Presbyterian Outlook (134; Je.
30, 1952).
        DLC; NN/Sch; NcD
United Presbyterian Church of
North America. Historical
Sketch of the Freedmen's Mis-
sions of the United Presbyter-
ian Church, 1862-1904. Knox-
ville, Tenn.: Printing Dept.,
Knoxville College, 1904.
                        NN/Sch
Walker, James Garfield. Presby-
terians and the Negro...
Greensboro, N. C., n. p., n. d.
                        DHU/MO

h. Protestant Episcopal

Bragg, George Freeman. "The
Church's Early Work for the
Colored Race." Living Church
(65; Jl. 16, 1921), pp. 351-
54.   DLC; CtY
Bratton, Theodore DuBose. "The
Christian South and Negro Ed-
ucation." Sewanee Review (16;
Jl., 1908), pp. 290-97. DHU
Demby, Edward Thomas. The
Mission of the Episcopal
Church Among the Negroes of
the Diocese of Arkansas.
Little Rock, Ark.: n. p.
190-?   NN/Sch
   Negro author.
"Episcopal Church in the South
Officially Inclusive (as to
Race). Its Witness has been
Stifled by Culturally-Condi-

tioned Laymen." Christianity
and Crisis (18; Mr. 3, 1958),
pp. 18-20.   DHU/R
"Episcopal Convention and the
Negroes." Independent (63;
Sept. 19, 1907), pp. 703-04.
                          DHU
Fairly, John S. The Negro in
His Relations to the Church...
Charleston, S. C.: Walker,
Evans & Cogswell Co., Print-
ers, 1889.   NN/Sch
Industrial Mission School Society,
Charleston, S. C. Prospectus
and Appeal of the Industrial
Mission School Society, Char-
tered, Charleston, S. C., Sep-
tember 22, 1887, for the Pur-
pose of Endeavoring to Im-
prove the Mental, Moral, So-
cial and Religious Condition of
the Negroes in the Diocese of
South Carolina. Charleston,
S. C.: Walker, Evans & Cogs-
well Co., Print., 1888.
                        NN/Sch
"Integrating Methodism; Elimina-
tion of Central Jurisdiction."
Christian Century 83; Jan. 5,
1966), pp. 3-4.   DHU/R
Johnson, John Howard. Harlem,
the War and Other Addresses.
New York: W. Malliet & Co.,
1942.   DHU/MO; NN/Sch
   Negro author.
Jones, Absalom. A Thanksgiving
Sermon. Preached January 1,
1808 in St. Thomas's, or the
African Episcopal Church,
Philadelphia, on Account of the
Abolition of the African Slave
Trade on that Day, by the Con-
gress of the U. S. By Absalom
Jones... Philadelphia: Pr. for
the Use of the Congregation,
Fry and Kammerer, Printers,
1808.   NN/Sch; NcD
Kershaw, J. "Negro Clergy,
Rights of in Protestant Epis-
copal Convention of South Car-
olina." Church Review (46;
1885), p. 466.   DLC
Miller, George Frazier. A Re-

ply to "The Political Plea" of
Bishop Cleland K. Nelson and
Bishop Thomas F. Gailor, at
the Cathedral of St. John the
Divine in the City of New
York, Sunday Evening, October
19, 1913. A Sermon by Rev.
George Frazier Miller, Rector
of St. Augustine's Church,
Brooklyn, Sunday Morning Oc-
tober 26, 1913. Brooklyn:
Interboro Press, 1913. NN/Sch
Negro author.
National Council of the Episcopal
Church. Just, Right & Necessary.
New York: The National Coun-
cil, 1955.   DHU/R
A study of reactions to the
Supreme Court decision on
segregation.
Newton, John B. The Commis-
sion on Work Among the Col-
ored People, its Work and
Prospects. Alexandria, Va.:
Hill Print, 1888.   NN/Sch
Protestant Episcopal Church
in the U.S.A. Detached from
the Virginia Seminary Maga-
zine, v. 1, no. 2. January, 1888.
"Open Church to Negroes: Epis-
copal Council Says All Equal
in Worship and Work of Church."--
Christian Century (60:9 Mr. 3,
1943), p. 276.   DHU/R
Protestant Episcopal Church in
the U.S.A. Church Congress,
Chicago, 1933. Chicago Papers, ...Spencer, Mass.: The
Heffernan Press, 1933. DLC
"How far should national
and racial distinctions be fos-
tered in the church?"
-- Church Congress San Francisco, 1927. Christ in the World
of To-day... New York: C.
Scribner's Sons, 1927.   DLC
Chapter entitled, "How can
the Church Satisfy the Religious
Needs of All Races?
-- Convention, 62d, New York City.
Journal of the Proceedings of
the Sixty-Second Convention of
the Protestant Episcopal Church

in the Diocese of New York,
Held in St. John's Chapel in
the City of New York, Wednes-
day, Sept. 12 to Saturday, Oc-
tober 3, inclusive, A.D. 1846.
New York: Henry M. Onder-
donk & Co., 1846.
(In: The Negro and the
Church, v.3.)
-- Liberia (Missionary District)
Annual Report to the Board of
Missions.   NN/Sch
-- -- Souvenir of the Twenty-
Fifth Anniversary Celebration
of the Consecration of the Rt.
Rev. Samuel David Ferguson
(June 24th, 1885 to June 26th,
1910) as Observed in Trinity
Parish, Monrovia, Sunday,
June 26th, 1910. Cape Palms,
Liberia: P. E. Mission Printing
Office, 1910.   NN/Sch
-- Liturgy and Ritual. Book of
Common Prayer. Evening Pray-
er. ... Centennial Service of
the New York African Society
for Mutual Relief, St. Philip's
Church, Whit-Sunday Evening,
June Seventh, Nineteen Hundred
and Eight. New York: n.p.,
1903.   NN/Sch
-- National Council. The Chris-
tian Fellowship in Action ...
New York: The National Coun-
cil, Protestant Episcopal
Church, 1945.   NN/Sch
-- -- Dept. of Missions and
Church Extension. ...Liberia...
New York: The National Coun-
cil of the Protestant Episcopal
Church, Dept. of Missions,
1924.   NN/Sch
Handbook of the Missions of
the Episcopal Church.
Roberts, Elizabeth Hill. Hand-
Book. Colored Work in Dioceses
of the South. For Practical Pur-
poses. Philadelphia: For sale,
Jacobs' Book Store, 1915.
                      NN/Sch
Protestant Episcopal Church
in the U.S.A. National Council.
Woman's Auxiliary. Pennsyl-

(Roberts, E. H. cont.)
vania Branch. Colored Committee.
Stringfellow, William. "Idolatry in Our Churches." Together (8; Sept. 1964), pp. 14+.
DAU/W
Written by an Episcopalian layman.
Tucker, Joseph Louis. The Relations of the Church to the Colored Race. Speech of the Rev. J. L. Tucker Before the Church Congress, Held in Richmond, Va., on the 24-27 Oct., 1882. Jackson, Miss.: C. Winkley, Steam Book and Job Print., 1882.
DHU/MO; NN/Sch
Weston, M. Moran. Social Policy of the Episcopal Church in the Twentieth Century. New York: Seabury Press, 1964.
DHU/R
Also Ph. D. thesis, Columbia Univ., 1954.
Whipple, Henry Benjamin, (bp.). Sermon Preached Before the Society for the Promotion of Church Work Among the Colored People. Bishop of Minnesota, at their Annual Meeting Held at St. John's Church, Washington, D. C., Sept. 27, 1877. Pub. by the Society. Baltimore: F. A. Hanzsche, 1877.   NN/Sch
Wilson, Arthur. Thy Will be Done; the Autobiography of an Episcopal Minister. New York: Dial Press, 1960.   NN/Sch
Missions in Cincinnati.
Wogaman, J. Philip. "Focus on Central Jurisdiction." Christian Century (80; Oct. 23, 1963), pp. 1296-98.   DHU/R
Former Negro division of the Methodist Church.
Woodward, Joseph Herbert. The Negro Bishop Movement in the Episcopal Diocese of South Carolina. McPhersonville, S. C.: H. Woodward, 1916.

NcD; NN/Sch

i. Lutheran

Cooper, J. C. "Lutheran Church and the Unchurched Negro." Lutheran Quarterly (11; Ag., 1959), pp. 274-51.   DHU/R
Cromer, Voigt R. Christian Action in Human Relations. New York: The United Lutheran Church in America. The Board of Social Missions, n. d.
Pam. File; DHU/R
Kampschmidt, William H. "Why the Evangelical Lutheran Church Established and Maintains a College for Negroes." Journal of Negro Education (29; Sum., 1960), pp. 299-306.   DHU
Krebs, Ervin E. The Lutheran Church and the American Negro. Columbus, O.: Board of American Missions, 1950.
DHU/MO
Ritchie, M. A. F. "Churches and Community Relations." Lutheran Quarterly (9; My., 1957), pp. 110-24.   DHU/R
Sease, Rosalyn Summer. Adult Guide on Christ, the Church, and Race. New York: Friendship Press, 1957.   NN/Sch
-- What About Race Relations? Six Forum Programs. Philadelphia: Women's Missionary Society, United Lutheran Church in America, Education Division, 1949.   NN/Sch
Witt, Raymond H. It Ain't Been Easy, Charlie. New York: Pageant Press, 1965.
DHU/MO; DLC
Church and race problems, Chicago.

j. Seventh Day Adventist

Bethmann, Erich W. Bridge to Islam; A Study of the Religious Forces of Islam and Christianity in the Near East. Nash-

ville: Southern Pub. Association, 1950.   DHU/R
Edwards, Josephine C. "From Africa to America." The Message Magazine (24:3, My. - Je., 1963), pp. 12+. DHU/R
Seventh Day Adventist Missions in Africa.
Simons, Norman G. "Origin of the Negro." Message Magazine (35:4, Jl., 1969), pp. 12+.   DHU/R

k. Baptist

American Baptist Home Mission Society. Forty Years' Work for the Negroes. New York: American Baptist Home Mission Society, 1901. DHU/MO
Carver, William O. The Furtherance of the Gospel. Nashville, Tenn.: The Sunday School Board of the Southern Baptist Convention, 1935.   NcD
Chaplin, Jeremiah. Duncan Dunbar; the Record of an Earnest Ministry. A Sketch of the Life of the Late Pastor of the McDougal St. Baptist Church, New York... 4th ed. New York: U.D. Ward, 1878.
                                 DHU/MO
   Chapters 3, 5 & 15 contain accounts of the minister's association with and feelings about the Negro.
Coward, Donald B. "The Vanishing Color Line in American Life." Missions: An International Baptist Magazine (148:2, Feb., 1950), pp. 83-5.   Pam. File; DHU/R
Eighmy, John Lee. "The Social Conscience of Southern Baptists from 1900 to the Present as Reflected in Their Organized Life." Doctoral dissertation, University of Missouri, 1959.
Ferris, George H. What is the Bible? Sermon Preached by Rev. George H. Ferris, D.D., in the First Baptist Church on

Sunday Morning, October 13, 1907. Printed by Request.
n.p., n.d.   DHU/MO
Foss, A.T. and E. Matthews. ...Facts for Baptist Churches. Collected, Arranged and Reviewed... Utica: Pub. by the American Baptist Free Mission Society, 1850. DHU/MO
Foy, Valentine. "A Historical Study of Southern Baptists and Race Relations, 1917-1947." Doctoral dissertation, Southwestern Baptist Theological Seminary, 1950.
Freeman, Edward A. The Epoch of Negro Baptists and the Foreign Mission Board. Kansas Central Seminary Press, 1953.
            DHU/MO; CtY-D
Hayne, Coe Smith. Race Grit; Adventures on the Borderland of Liberty. Ed. by the Dept. of Missionary Education, Board of Education of the Northern Baptist Convention... Philadelphia: The Judson Press, 1922.   CtY-D
Hill, Davis C. "Southern Baptist Thought and Action in Race Relations." Ph.D. thesis, Southern Baptist Theological Seminary, 1952.
Hill, Samuel S. Baptists North and South. Valley Forge: Judson Press, 1964.   NcD
Hughley, J.D. "Baptists and Religious Freedom." Baptist Quarterly (17; Apr., 1958), pp. 249-55.   DHU/R
Ide, George B. The Freedmen of War; a Discourse Delivered at the Annual Meeting of the American Baptist Home Mission Society, Phila., May 1863... Philadelphia: American Baptist Publishing Society, 1864.   DHU/MO
Kolb, Ernest C. "Four Major Efforts to Change the Polity of the Southern Baptist Convention, 1900-1919." Master's thesis, Duke University,

(Kolb, E. C. cont.)
1929.   NcD
Magruder, Edith C. A Histori-
cal Study of the Educational
Agencies of the Southern Bap-
tist Convention, 1845-1945.
New York: Bureau of Publi-
cations, Teachers College,
Columbia University, 1951.
No. 974.   NcD
Martin, Theodore. The Admin-
istration of Instruction in
Southern Baptist Colleges and
Universities. Nashville:
Bureau of Publications, George
Peabody College for Teachers,
1949.   NcD
Northern Baptist Convention.
Board of Education. Department
of Missionary Education. The
Road to Brotherhood... New
York: n. p., 1924.   CtY-D
Posey, Walter Brownlow. The
Baptist Church in the Lower
Mississippi Valley, 1776-1845.
Lexington: University of Ken-
tucky Press, 1957. NN/Sch
Riley, Benjamin Franklin. Me-
morial History of the Baptists
of Alabama; Being an Account
of the Struggles and Achieve-
ments of the Denomination
from 1808 to 1923. Philadel-
phia: American Baptist Pub.
Society (Judson Press), 1923.
                         DLC
Work among Negroes.
Rutledge, Arthur B. Mission to
America, A Quarter Century
of Southern Baptist Home Mis-
sions. Nashville, Tenn.:
Broadman Press, 1969.
                         DHU/R
Work with Negroes, pp.
133-42.
Shurden, Walter B. "The What
About the Blacks Controversy."
The Student: The Changing
Church. (50:3, Dec. 1970), pp.
42-4.   DHU/R
Southern Baptist Convention
and the black revolution.
"Southern Baptists Open Semi-

naries to Negroes." Christian
Century (68; Apr., 1951), pp.
452+.   DHU/R
Spain, Rufus B. At Ease in Zion, Social History of Southern
Baptists 1865-1900. Nash-
ville: Vanderbilt Press, 1961.
    DHU/R; INU; NcD
Chapter 2, Segregation in
the churches.
Starr, Edward C. A Baptist
Bibliography. Rochester,
N. Y.: American Baptist His-
torical Society, 1947-. DHU/R
Being compiled by the cura-
tor of the Samuel Colgate Bap-
tist Historical Collection. Vol-
umes are issued by alphabeti-
cal letters of surname of au-
thors.
Stripling, Paul Wayne. "The
Negro Excision from Baptist
Churches in Texas: 1861-
1870." Doctoral dissertation,
Southwestern Baptist Theologi-
cal Seminary, 1967.
Tupper, H. A. The Foreign Missions of the Southern Baptist
Convention. Philadelphia:
American Baptist Publ. Society.   DHU/MO
Whipple, Phila M. Negro Neigh-
bors, Bond and Free. Les-
sons in History and Humanity.
Boston: Woman's American
Baptist Home Mission Society,
1907.   NN/Sch; CtY-D
White, Charles Lincoln. The
Retaining of a Race; An Ad-
dress Delivered at Des Moines,
Iowa, May 24th, 1912, Com-
memorating the 50th Anniver-
sary of the Work of the Amer-
ican Baptist Home Mission So-
ciety Among the Negroes.
New York: American Baptist
Home Mission Society, 1912.
                         DLC
Woman's American Baptist Home
Mission Society, Chicago. Thirty-
Six Years' Work Among Ne-
groes, 1877-1911. Chicago,
Ill.: Woman's American Bap-

tist Home Mission Society,
1913. CtY-D
-- Twenty-Nine Years' Work
Among Negroes. Chicago:
Women's Baptist Home Mission
Society, 1906. NN/Sch

l. Judaism

Abrams, Charles. "Civil Rights
in 1956." Commentary (22:2,
Ag., 1956), pp. 101-09.
DHU/R
Berger, Morroe. "Desegregation, Law, and Social Science."
Commentary (23:5, My., 1957),
pp. 471-77. DHU/R
Bettelheim, Bruno. "Sputnik
and Segregation." Commentary
26:4, Oct., 1958), pp. 332-39.
DHU/R
An experienced psycholo-
gist and educator examines
this two-fold problem and sug-
gests that there may be a tendency to replace the color-line
by a new kind of social discrimination.
Bickel, Alexander M. "The Civil Rights Act of 1964." Commentary (48:2, Ag., 1964),
pp. 33-39. DHU/R
Burns, Haywood. "The Rule of
Law in the South." Commentary (40:3, Sept., 1965), pp.
80+. DHU/R
Danzig, David. "The Meaning of
Negro Strategy." Commentary
(37:2, Feb. 1964), pp. 41-46.
DHU/R
Glazer, Nathan. "Is 'Integration' Possible in the New
York Schools?" Commentary
(30:3 Sept., 1960), pp. 185-93.
DHU/R
Goodman, Paul. "The Children
of Birmingham." Commentary
(36:3, Sept., 1963), pp. 242-
44. DHU/R
Handlin, Oscar. "Civil Rights
After Little Rock." Commentary (24:5, Nov., 1957), pp.
392-96. DHU/R

Isaacs, Harold R. "Integration
and the Negro Mood." Com-
mentary (6:34, Dec., 1962),
pp. 487-97. DHU/R
Knoll, Erwin. "Washington:
Showcase of Integration."
Commentary (27:3, Mr., 1959),
pp. 194-202. DHU/R
Korey, William and Charlotte
Lubin. "Arlington--Another Lit-
tle Rock?" School Integration
Fight on Washington's Door-
step." Commentary (26:3,
Sept., 1958), pp. 201-09.
DHU/R
Kyle, Keith. "Desegregation
and the Negro Right to Vote."
Commentary (24:1, Jl., 1957),
pp. 15-19. DHU/R
"Liberalism and the Negro. A
Round-Table Discussion."
Commentary (37:3, Mr., 1964),
pp. 25-42. DHU/R
Participants: James Bald-
win, Nathan Glazer, Sidney
Hook and Gunnar Myrdal.
Lubell, Samuel. "The Negro
and the Democratic Coalition."
Commentary (38:2, Ag., 1964),
pp. 19-27. DHU/R
Majdalany, Gebran. "Reflections
on Racism, Anti-Semitism,
and Zionism." Liberation
(14:8, Nov., 1968), pp. 36-
40. DHU/R
Malev, William S. "The Jew of
the South in the Conflict on
Segregation." Conservative
Judaism (13; Fall, 1958), pp.
35-46. DLC
Mantinband, Charles. "From the
Diary of a Mississippi Rabbi."
American Judaism (13; Fall,
1958), pp. 35-46. DLC
Pierce, David H. "Is the Jew
a Friend of the Negro?"
Crisis (30; Jl., 1925), pp.
184-86. DHU/MO
Podhoretz, Norman. "My Negro
Problem--and Ours." Com-
mentary (35:2, Feb., 1963),
pp. 93-101. DHU/R
Editorial opinion.

Rorty, James. "Desegregation: Prince Edward County, Va." Commentary (21:11, My. 1956), pp. 431-38.   DHU/R
-- "Desegregation Along the Mason-Dixon Line." Commentary (18:6, Dec. 1954), pp. 493-503.   DHU/R
Rustin, Bayard and Tom Kahn. "Civil Rights." Commentary (39:6, Je., 1965), pp. 43-46.
                                DHU/R

Woodward, C. Vann. "The Great Civil Rights Debate." Commentary (24:4, Oct., 1957), pp. 283-91.   DHU/R

m. Eastern Orthodox

Florovsky, Georges. "Social Problem in the Eastern Orthodox Church." Journal of Religious Thought (8:1, Aut. -Wint. 1950-51), pp. 41-51. DHU/R

2. Organizations

a. General

African Mission School Association, New York. A Mission School Among the Colored People of New York. New York: n. p., 1868. NN/Sch
American Church Institute for Negroes. Annual Report for 1927 of the American Church Institute for Negroes. New York: Church Missions House, 1928.   DHU/MO
-- Down Where the Need is Greatest. A Record in the Field of Negro Education Through Divinity School, College, Junior Colleges, Industrial High and Normal Schools, Training School for Nurses, Summer Schools and Farmers' Conferences. New York: n. p., 1937?   NN/Sch; CtY-D
-- Our Church Industrial High School for Negroes. The Bishop Payne Divinity School, the Junior College, Under the Supervision of the American Church Institute for Negroes, the Accredited Auxiliary to the National Council of the Protestant Episcopal Church. New York: Abbott Press, 1925.
                                NN/Sch
"American Church Institute for Negroes." Spirit of Missions

(74:6, Je., 1909), p. 485.
                                DHU/R
American Moral Reform Society, Philadelphia. The Minutes and Proceedings of the 1st Annual Meeting of the American Moral Reform Society. Held at Philadelphia in the Presbyterian Church in 7th St., below Shippen, from the 14th to 19th of August, 1897. Philadelphia: Merrihew & Gunn, 1937.   DHU/MO
Archibald, Helen Allen, (ed.). Negro History and Culture; Selections for Use with Children. Chicago: Dept. of Curriculum Development, Chicago City Missionary Society, 1964.
                                CtY-D
Arthur, George R. Life on the Negro Frontier. New York: Associated Press, 1934.
                                DHU/MO
   Work of the Young Men's Christian Association.
Baker, Paul Earnest. Negro-White Adjustment; An Investigation and Analysis of Methods in the Interracial Movement in the United States; the History, Philosophy, Program, and Techniques of Ten National Interracial Agencies. Methods Discovered Through a Study of Cases, Situations, and Pro-

jects in Race Relations...
New York: Association Press,
1934.
DHU/R; CtY-D; DHU/MO
Issued also as thesis (Ph.
D.) Columbia University.
"Catholic Students' Mission Cru-
sade." Apostolate to Negro
America, by John T. Gillard,
and John La Farge... (and
others). Cincinnati: n.p.,
1959.   NN/Sch
" 'Christian Guide' to Race Atti-
tudes." New South (13:5, My.,
1958), pp. 3-7.   DHU/MO
Text of Guide adopted by
Gainesville-Hall County Min-
isterial Association, Georgia.
Committee on Negro Churches.
Report of Commission on
Christian Education, Commis-
sion on Evangelism, Commis-
sion on the Church and Social
Service, Commission on the
Church and Country Life.
Committee on Negro Churches,
Commission on Temperance.
New York: n.p., n.d.
                            DHU/MO
Conference of College Religious
Workers. Report of Conference
of College Religious Workers,
Held at Fisk University, Nash-
ville, Tenn. March 7-10, 1929.
n.p., n.d.   DHU/MO
"The Congregational National
Council." Voice of the Negro
(2:1, Jan., 1905), p. 661.
                            DHU/MO
Council of Christian Associations.
Christian Principles and Race
Relations: a Discussion Course
for College Groups Council of
Christian Associations, Student
Council, Y.W.C.A. ...Student
Department, Y.M.C.A. ...
New York: Association Press,
1926.   NN/Sch
Davis, Allison. The Negro
Church and Association in the
Lower South; a Research
Memorandum... The Negro
Church and Associations in

Chicago; a Research Memor-
andum Prepared by J.G. St.
Clair Drake... New York:
n.p., 1940. (Carnegie Myrdal
Study), the Negro in America.
                            NN/Sch
Negro authors.
Derrick, W.B. "The Work of
Evangelization Among the Ne-
groes." Elias B. Sanford,
(ed.), Church Federation: In-
ter-Church Conference of Fed-
eration, New York, November
15-21, 1905. (New York:
Fleming H. Revell Co., 1906),
pp. 520-24.   DHU/R
Negro author.
Drake, St. Clair. Churches and
Voluntary Associations in the
Chicago Negro Community.
Report of Official Project 465-
54-3-386 Conducted under the
Auspices of the Work Projects
Administration. Horace R.
Cayton, Superintendent...
Chicago: n.p., 1940.
                            DHU/MO
Harlow, Harold C. "Racial In-
tegration of the YMCA: A
Study of the Closing of Cer-
tain Negro YMCA's With Spe-
cial Reference to the Role of
Religious Factors. Doctoral
dissertation, Hartford Semi-
nary Foundation, 1961.
Haskin, Sara Estelle. The Up-
ward Climb. A Course in Ne-
gro Achievement. Missionary
Education Movement of the
U.S. and Canada. New York:
n.p., 1927.   DHU/R
Hayne, Coe Smith. For a New
America. New York: Council
of Women for Home Missions
and Missionary Education
Movement of the United States
and Canada. 1923.   CtY-D
Haynes, George Edmund. The
Trend of the Races. New
York: Council of Women for
Home Missions and Missonary
Education Movement of the
United States and Canada, 1922.

(Haynes, G. E. cont.)
DHU/R; CtY-D
Negro author.
Hefley, J. Theodore. "Freedom
Upheld: The Civil Liberties
Stance of the Christian Cen-
tury Between the Wars."
Church History (37:2, Je.,
1968), pp. 174-94.   DHU/R
An examination of the atti-
tude of the liberal publication
which has been described as
"Protestantism's most vigor-
ous voice," towards civil
rights issues that confronted
the nation between the two
World Wars.
Helm, Mary. The Upward Path:
The Evolution of a Race. New
York: Young People's Mis-
sionary Movement of the
United States and Canada,
1909. DHU/MO; DLC; NN/Sch;
CtY-D; DHU/R
Revised edition of "From
Darkness to Light."
Hickok, Laurens P. A Nation
Saved from its Prosperity On-
ly by the Gospel. A Dis-
course in Behalf of the Amer-
ican Home Missionary Society,
Preached in the Cities of New
York and Brooklyn... New
York: American Home Mis-
sionary Society, 1853.
DHU/MO
Hill, Timothy Arnold. "The
Church and Industry." Oppor-
tunity (9:1, Ja., 1931), pp.
18-19.   DHU/MO
Negro author.
Home Missions Council. Annual
Meeting of the Home Mission
Council. 1920, 1922.
DHU/MO
Hope, John. Relations Between
the Black and White Races in
America. New York: Inter-
national Missionary Council,
1928.   CtY-D
Negro author.
At the Jerusalem meeting
of the International Missionary

Council, March 24-April 8,
1928. IV. The Christian Mis-
sion in the light of race con-
flict.
International Missionary Council.
Assembly, Accra, 1957-1958.
The Ghana Assembly of the
International Missionary Coun-
cil, 28th December, 1957 to
8th January, 1958. Selected
papers, with an Essay on the
Role of the I. M. C. Edited by
Ronald K. Orchard. New
York: Friendship Press, 1958.
NN/Sch
"Encounter between Chris-
tian and non-Christian," by
Jesué Danho, pp. 41-6.
Kincheloe, Samuel C. "The
American City and Its Church."
New York: Friendship Press,
1940.   Pam. File; DHU
See Chapters IV, "What
Cities do to Churches;" V,
"What Churches do for Ci-
ties."
Kuhns, Frederick Irving. The
American Home Missionary
Society in Relation to the Anti-
Slavery Controversy in the
Old Northwest. Billings,
Mont.: n. p., 1959. CtY-D
Lee, Carleton L. "Patterns of
Leadership in Race Relations:
a Study of Leadership Among
Negro Americans." Doctoral
dissertation, University of
Chicago, 1951.
Lincoln, Charles Eric. "The
American Protest Movement
for Negro Rights." John P.
Davis, (ed.). The American
Negro Reference Book (Engle-
wood-Cliffs, N. J.: Prentice-
Hall, Inc., 1966), pp. 458-83.
DHU/R
Negro author.
Lockwood, Lewis. Mary S.
Peake, the Colored Teacher
at Fortress Monroe. Boston:
American Tract Society, 186-?
NN/Sch

Lott Carey. Baptist Foreign Mission Society of the United States. Annual Report of the Corresponding Secretary, 1925-1926. DHU/MO

-- Baptist Home and Foreign Mission Convention. Proceedings of the Fifth Annual Session of the Lott Cary Home and Foreign Mission Convention of the United States and of the Woman's Auxiliary Convention held with the Liberty Baptist Church. Washington, D. C., Sept. 10-14, 1902. n. p., n. d. DHU/MO

Markoe, William M. "Claver Clubs for Colored People." America (29; Ag. 4, 1923), pp. 268-69. DLC

McCulloch, Margaret C. "Educational Programs for the Improvement of Race Relations: Seven Religious Agencies." Journal of Negro Education (13:4, Sum., 1944), pp. 305-15. DHU/MO

McCulloh, James E., (ed.) Battling for Social Betterment, Southern Sociological Congress ... 1914. Nashville: Southern Sociological Congress, 1914. DHU/MO

"Ministers' Conference at Bettis." Southern Workman (50; Sept., 1921), p. 392. DHU/MO

Moore, George W. The Redemptive Work for the Negro. NN/Sch
Negro author.
In Lend a Hand (1896, v. 7, no. 5), pp. 355-61.

Moorland, Jesse E. "The Young Men's Christian Association Among Negroes." Journal of Negro History (9:2, Apr., 1924), pp. 127-38. DHU
Negro author.

National Conference of Colored Men of the United States, Nashville, Tenn., 1879. Proceedings of the National Conference of Colored Men of the United States, Held in the State Capitol at Nashville, Tenn. May 6, 7, 8 and 9, 1879. Washington, D. C. : R. H. Darby, Printer, 1879. NN/Sch

National Conference on Race and Religion. Race: Challenge to ' Religion, Original Essays and An Appeal to the Conscience. Chicago: H. Regnery Co., 1963. DHU/R; INU; DLC

National Conference on Religion in Independent Education. 7th Colordado Springs, 1962. Education for Decision. By Jas. Robinson. Editors: Frank R. Gaebelein... and others. New York: Seabury Press, 1963. NN/Sch

National Conference on the Christian Way of Life, New York. And Who is My Neighbor? An Outline for the Study of Race Relations in America... New York: Association Press, 1924. DHU/MO

"Negro Churches to Form Own Federal Council." Christian Century (51; Ja., 31, 1934), p. 139. DHU/R

Negro Young Peoples' Christian and Educational Congress. 1st. Atlanta, 1902. The United Negro: His Problems and His Progress... Held August 6-11, 1902. Atlanta, Ga.: D. E. Luther Pub. Co., 1902. NN/Sch
Religion, pp. 382-88.

The Negro Young People's Christian and Educational Congress. Souvenir Official Program and Music of the Young People's Christian and Educational Congress. Held July 31 to August 5, 1906. Convention Hall, Washington, D. C. Edited by Corresponding Secretary, I. Garland Penn. n. p., n. d. DHU/MO

New York Colored Mission. Annual Report. 1st, 1869. New York: n. p., 1869. NN/Sch

Penn, Irvine Garland, (ed.). The
United Negro: His Problems
and His Progress, Containing
the Addresses and Proceedings
the Negro Young People's
Christian and Education Con-
gress, Held August 6-11, 1902;
Introduction by Bishop W. J.
Gaines... edited by Prof. I.
Garland Penn... Prof. J. W. E.
Bowen... Atlanta, Ga.: D. E.
Luther Publishing Co., 1902.
DHU/R; DHU/MO; DLC
Negro author.
Protestant Council of the City of
New York. Dept. of Church Plan-
ning and Research. Profiles of
Nassau County Communities;
a Summary of Social, Econom-
ic and Housing Characteristics
of 94 Nassau Counties, 1960...
(Prepared for the Committee
of Church Planning and Re-
search, Nassau County Council
of Churches.) New York:
n. p., 1964.   NN/Sch
-- -- Upper Manhattan: a Com-
munity Study of Washington
Heights. Robert Lee, Study
Director; Clara Orr, Asst. to
the Director. New York: n. p.,
1954.   NN/Sch
Racial Relations and the Christian
Ideal; a Discussion Course for
College Students. New York:
Young Women's Christian Association, Young Men's Christian Association, 1923.
DHU/MO; CtY-D; NN/Sch
Religious Education Association.
Education and National Charac-
ter by Henry Churchill, Francis
Greenwood Peabody, Lyman
Abbott, Washington Gladden,
and others. Chicago: Reli-
gious Education Association,
1908.   DHU/MO
Southern Society for the Promo-
tion of the Study of Race Condi-
tions and Problems in the South.
Race Problems of the South;
Report of the Proceedings of
the First Annual Conference

Held under the Auspices of the
Southern Society for the Promoting of the Study of Race
Conditions and Problems in the
South, at Montgomery, Ala-
bama, May 8, 9, 10, A. D.
1900. Richmond, Va.: B. F.
Johnson Pub. Co., 1900.
NN/Sch; DHU/MO
Southern Sociological Congress.
2d Atlanta, 1913. The Challenge
of Social Service. Edited by
James E. McCulloch. Nash-
ville: Southern Sociological
Congress, 1913.   NN/Sch
The social problems of the
church by Walter Rauschen-
bush.
-- -- The South Mobilizing for Social Service. Addresses Delivered at the Southern Sociological Congress, Atlanta,
Georgia, April 25-29, 1913.
Edited by James E. McCulloch.
Nashville: Southern Sociological Congress, 1913. NN/Sch
-- 3d, Memphis, 1914. Battling
for Social Betterment. Southern Sociological Congress,
Memphis, Tennessee, May 6-
10, 1914. Edited by James
E. McCulloch. Nashville:
Southern Sociological Congress,
1914.   NN/Sch
"The Southern Sociological
Congress as a factor for social welfare by Booker T.
Washington," pp. 154-59.
-- 5th-7th, 1916-1918. Democracy in Earnest. Southern Sociological Congress, 1916-
1918. Edited by James E.
McCulloch. Washington, D. C.:
Southern Sociological Congress,
n. d.   NN/Sch
Church and race problems.
-- 8th, Knoxville, Tenn., 1919.
"Distinguished Service" Citizenship. Southern Sociological Congress, Knoxville, Tennessee. Edited by J. E. Mc-
Culloch. Washington, D. C.:
Southern Sociological Congress,

1919.   NN/Sch
    Chapter 8, The Church con-
    serving life.
Speer, Robert Elliott. Of One
    Blood, a Short Study of the
    Race Problem. New York:
    Council of Women for Home
    Missions and Missionary Edu-
    cation Movement of the United
    States and Canada, 1924.
                    CtY-D; DHU/M
    p. 147, race and religion.
-- Race and Race Relations: a
    Christian View of Human Con-
    tacts. New York: Revell,
    1924.   CtY-D
    "An abbreviated edition of
    this book was issued in the
    spring as a mission study text
    book by the Missionary Educa-
    tion Movement and the Coun-
    cil of Women for Home Mis-
    sions."   CtY-D
Stuntz, Hugh Clark. The United
    Nations Challenge to the
    Church. Nashville: Abing-
    don-Cokesbury Press, 1948.
                          NN/Sch
Sutherland, Robert L. Color
    Class and Personality. Pre-
    pared for the American Youth
    Commission. Washington,
    D.C.: American Council on
    Education, 1942.
                  DHU/MO; CtY-D
Thomas, Mary S. "The Ordeal
    of Koinonia Farm." Progres-
    sive (21; Ja. 1957), pp. 23-5:
                            DLC
    An account of the attacks
    on a Georgia religious and
    interracial camp and commu-
    nity.
Watson, Andrew Polk. "Primi-
    tive Religion Among Negroes
    in Tennessee." Master's thes-
    is, Fisk University, 1932.
Watson, J.J. "Churches and
    Religious Organizations." The
    Annals of the American Acad-
    emy of Political and Social
    Science (49; Sept., 1913), pp.
    120-28.   DHU

Weatherford, Willis Duke. "A
    Social Work Worth While."
    Southern Workman (43; Dec.,
    1914), pp. 665+.   DHU/MO
Wilkerson, Yolanda Barnett.
    Interracial Programs of Stu-
    dent YWCA's; an Inquiry Under
    Auspices of the National Stu-
    dent Young Women's Christian
    Association. New York:
    Woman's Press, 1948. CtY-D

b. Federal Council of Churches

Federal Council of the Churches
    of Christ in America. Annual
    Report, 1919, "Committee on
    Negro Churches: Report," pp.
    155-58.   DHU/R
-- Annual Report, 1921, "The
    Church and Race Relations,"
    pp. 79-82.   DHU/R
-- Annual Report, 1922, "United
    Work for Better Race Rela-
    tions," pp. 49-52.   DHU/R
-- Annual Report, 1923, "The
    Church and Race Relations,"
    pp. 59-66.   DHU/R
-- Annual Report, 1925, "The
    Church and Race Relations,"
    pp. 32-39.   DHU/R
-- The Church and Race Rela-
    tions: An Official Statement
    Approved at a Special Meeting,
    Columbus, Ohio, March 5-7,
    1946. New York: Federal
    Council of the Churches of
    Christ in America, Dept. of
    Race Relations, 1946.
                      NN/Sch; DLC
-- Biennial Report, 1934. "De-
    partment of Race Relations:
    Report," pp. 58-62.
                          DHU/R
    Also, pp. 75-79.
-- Biennial Report, 1936, "De-
    partment of Race Relations:
    Report," pp. 45-50. DHU/R
-- Biennial Report, 1940, "De-
    partment of Race Relations,"
    pp. 41-46.   DHU/R
    Also pp. 95-100.
-- Biennial Report, 1942, "De-

(Fed. Council of Churches of
Christ... cont.)
partment of Race Relations:
Report," pp. 102-06. DHU/R
-- Biennial Report, 1944, "De-
partment of Race Relations:
Report," pp. 86-90. DHU/R
-- Commission on the Church
and Minority Peoples. Negro
Churchmen Speak to White
Churchmen. New York: n.p.,
1944. DHU/R
-- Commission on the Church
and Race Relations. What Was
Said and Done at the First
National Interracial Confer-
ence. Cincinnati: Pub. by
the Commission, 1926.
DHU/R
-- Dept. of Race Relations...
Along the Interracial Front,
by George Edmund Haynes,
Executive Secretary, Dept. of
Race Relations. New York:
n.p., 1945. DHU/R; NN/Sch
*-- -- Annual Report. DHU/R;
1919, 1921, 1923, 1925.
NN/Sch; DLC.
*-- -- Biennial Report. DHU/R;
1934, 1936, 1940, 1942, 1944.
NN/Sch
-- -- Glimpses of Negro Ameri-
cans. New York: n.p.,
1936. DHU/R; NN/Sch
-- Official Handbook for Biennial
Meeting, 1934, "Department
of Race Relations," pp. 35-40.
DHU/R
-- Official Handbook for the
Quadrennial Meeting, 1932,
"Recommended by the Commis-
sion on Race Relations," pp.
68-71. DHU/R
-- Official Handbook for the Quad-
rennial Meeting, 1933, "Rec-
ommended by the Commission
on Race Relations," pp. 68-
71. DHU/R
-- Report to the Biennial Meet-
ing, 1942, "Department of
Race Relations," pp. 58-62.
DHU/R
-- Reports Submitted to the An-

nual Meeting of the Executive
Committee, 1930. "Race Re-
lations," pp. 30-33. DHU/R
-- Reports Submitted to the An-
nual Meeting of the Executive
Committee, 1931, "Race Re-
lations," pp. 24-28. DHU/R
-- Twenty Years of Church Fed-
eration: Report of the Federal Council of the Churches
of Christ in America, 1924-
1928. "The Church and Race
Relations," pp. 107-19.
DHU/R
-- Washington. Committee on
Race Relations. Report of the
Conference on the Betterment
of Race Relations in Washing-
ton, D.C. ...n.p., 1935.
DHU/MO
Haynes, George Edmund. To-
ward Interracial Peace: a
Description of the Movement
in the Federal Council of the
Churches of Christ in Amer-
ica, to Discover Methods and
Techniques for Applying Jus-
tice and Goodwill in Race Re-
lations Through the Evangeli-
cal Churches of the United
States. New York: n.p.,
1940. NN/Sch
    Negro author.
Reddis, Jacob L. The Negro
Seeks Economic Security
Through Cooperation. An Ad-
dress Delivered before the
National Seminar Consumer's
Cooperation of the Federal
Council of Churches of Christ
in America, Indianapolis, Ind.,
Jan. 1, 1936. Chicago, Ill.:
Pub. by Central States Co-
operative League, 1936.
DHU/MO

c. National Council of Churches
of Christ in the U.S.A.

Jacquet, Constant H. Man
Amidst Change; A Consulta-
tion Held at Airlie House,
Warrenton, Virginia, May 3-

6, 1962. New York: National
Council of the Churches of
Christ in the U. S. A. , 1963.
                    DHU/R
"NCC Takes Race Action." Chris-
tian Advocate (8; Apr. 23,
1964), pp. 23+.
          DAU/W; DHU/R
"National Council of Churches
Plans for Work in Poverty,
Narcotics, Race." Methodist
Story (9; Mr. , 1965), p. 46.
                    DAU/W
"National Council of Churches
Unit Asks Us Jurisdiction in
Civil Rights Slayings." Con-
cern (7; Oct. 15, 1965), pp.
16+.   DAU/W
National Council of the Churches
of Christ in the United States of
America. Churches and Social
Welfare. New York: n. p. ,
1955.   DHU/R
-- Growing Together; A Manual
for Councils of Churches.
New York: n. p. , 1955.
                    DHU/R
-- A Pronouncement, a Policy
Statement: Religious and Civil
Liberties in the U. S. A.
Adopted by the General Board,
Oct. 5, 1955.
          Pam. File; DHU/R
*-- Commission on Religion and
Race. Reports... v. 1- 1965-
                NcD; CtY-D
-- Dept. of Racial and Cultural
Relations. About Racially Inclu-
sive Churches. Partial Statis-
tical Survey of a Cross Sec-
tion of Racially Inclusive
Churches in the United States
(1950). Mim. Pam. File; DHU/R
-- -- Denominational Statements
with Reference to a Racially
Inclusive Fellowship. (Feb. ,
1955). Pam. File; DHU
-- -- Statements Adopted by Re-
ligious Groups (re) Segregation in the Public Schools.
(Interracial Publication, no.
84, Oct. , 1954).
          Pam. File; DHU/R

"Gives resolutions on race
adopted by various denominations."
-- Dept. of Youth Ministry. Rac-
ism in American Society.
White Plight? Youth Week
Resource Youth Organization,
Youth Ministry, Natl. Counc.
of Churches. Pam. File;
                    DHU/R
Ecumenical ways in which
youth and adults can work to-
gether in the struggle against
racism. "A pamphlet: Youth
Against Racism."
-- Division of Foreign Missions.
The Christian Mission for To-
day. New York: n. p. , 1958?
                    DHU/R
-- -- Study of the Common Chris-
tian Responsibility Toward the
Areas of Rapid Social Change.
1959.   DHU/R
-- Division of Home Missions.
Every Tribe and Tongue...
New York: Friendship Press,
1960.   DHU/R
"National Council of Churches
Steps Up Race Protest Moves."
Christian Advocate (7; Jl. 18,
1963), p. 24.
          DAU/W; DHU/R

d. World Council of Churches

Duff, Edward. The Social
Thought of the World Council
of Churches. New York:
Association Press, 1956.
                    DHU/R
Kraemer, Hendrik. World Cul-
tures and World Religions;
The Coming Dialogue. London:
Lutterworth Press, 1960.
                    DHU/R
Vries, Egbert de. Man in Com-
munity; Christian Concern for
the Human in Changing Society.
New York: Association Press,
1966.   DHU/R
World Council of Churches. Com-
mission on World Mission and
Evangelism. The Christian Min-

(World Counc. of Churches cont.)
istry in Latin America and the
Caribbean; Report of a Survey
of Theological Education in the
Evangelical Churches, Under-
taken Feb.-May, 1961, on Behalf of the International Missionary Council (now the Commission on World Mission and
Evangelism of the World Council of Churches). New York:
n.p., 1962.   DHU/R
-- Dept. on Studies in Evangelism. Planning for Mission;
Working Papers on the New
Quest for Missionary Communities. New York: U.S. Conference for the World Council
of Churches, 1966. DHU/R
-- Secretariat on Racial and
Ethnic Relations. "Race Relations in Ecumenical Perspective." No. 3 Geneva, Switzerland, Sept.-Nov., 1963.
            Pam. File; DHU/R

e. United Nations and Agencies

Bennett, John Coleman. Chris-
tian Social Ethics in a Chang-
ing World; An Ecumenical
Theological Inquiry. New
York: Association Press,
1966.   DHU/R
Cruise O'Brien, Conor. To
Katanga and Back: A UN
Case History. New York:
Grosset & Dunlap, 1966.
                     DHU/R
A Study by U.N. at Ka-
tanga, Congo (Province).
Nixon, Justin Wroe. The United
Nations and Our Religious
Heritage. New York: Church
Peace Union, 1953. DHU/R
Stuber, Stanley Irving. Human
Rights and Fundamental Free-
doms in Your Community.
New York: Association Press,
1968.   DHU/R
Stuntz, Hugh Clark. The United
Nations Challenge to the
Church. Nashville: Abing-

don-Cokesbury Press, 1948.
                     DHU/R
United Nations Educational, Sci-
entific and Cultural Organization.
Human Rights, Comments and
Interpretations; A Symposium.
London: A. Wingate, 1949.
                     DHU/R
-- Dept. of Mass Communication.
What is Race? Evidence from
Scientists. Based on Race
and Biology. Paris, 1952.
                     DHU/R

f. American Missionary Association.

American Missionary Associa-
tion. Annual Report. DHU/MO
(1922, 27, 28, 32, 33) DLC,*
NcD," CtY-D. *
-- The Eighty-Sixth Annual Re-
port... and the Proceedings of
the Annual Meeting Held at the
First Congregational Church,
Oak Park, Ill., Nov. 1, 2, 3,
1932. New York: American
Missionary Assoc., 1932.
                     DHU/MO
-- Forty Years of Missionary
Work. The Past and Present,
by Secretary Strieby. New
York: n.p., 1886. CtY-D
(Its Pamphlet no. 10)
-- History of the American Mis-
sionary Association: Its
Churches and Educational In-
stitutions Among the Freed-
men, Indians and Chinese,
with Illustrative Facts and
Anecdotes. New York: S.W.
Green, 1874. DHU/MO; DLC
-- The Nation Still in Danger;
or, Ten Years After the War.
A Plea by the American Mis-
sionary Association, with Con-
firmatory Articles by Rev. T.
D. Woolsey... Hon. Frederick
Douglass, Rev. Washington
Gladden, Gov. D.H. Chamber-
lain, and Hon. J.P. Hawley.
New York: Amer. Missionary
Assoc., 1875.   DLC

-- Ninety Years After. New
York: The American Missionary Assoc., n.d.   DHU/MO
Bailey, Flavius Josephus. "Policies of the American Missionary Association in Negro Education." Master's thesis,
Howard University, 1933.
                              DHU/MO
Beard, August Field. A Crusade
of Brotherhood. A History
of the American Missionary
Association. New York: Pilgrim Press, 1909.   DHU/MO
-- What the North is Doing for
the Christian Development of
the Southern Negro. The Great
Christian Denominational Agencies at Work in the South.
New York: n.p., 190-.   DLC
    Also, Missionary Review
    (27; Sept., 1904), pp. 660-66.
                         DHU/R; CtY-D
Blanchard, F.Q. "A Quarter
Century in the American Missionary Association." Journal
of Negro Education (6:2, Apr.,
1937), pp. 152-56.
                     DHU/R; DHU/MO
Brownlee, Frederick L. "Heri-
tage and Opportunity: The Ne-
gro Church Related College:
A Critical Summary." Journal
of Negro Education (29; Sum.,
1960), pp. 401-7.   DHU
-- Heritage of Freedom, A Centenary Story of Ten Schools
Offering Education in Freedom.
Philadelphia: United Church
Press, 1963.   DHU/R
    American Missionary As-
    sociation and Negro education.
-- New Day Ascending. Boston:
The Pilgrim Press, 1946.
                           CtY-D
    American Missionary As-
    sociation.
Cable, George Washington. What
the Negro Must Learn. Ad-
dress of Geo. W. Cable at the
Annual Meeting of the Ameri-
can Missionary Association,
held in Northhampton, Oct. 21-

23, 1890. New York: Ameri-
can Missionary Association,
1890.   NN/Sch
Drake, Richard Bryant. "The
American Missionary Associa-
tion and the Southern Negro,
1881-1888." Master's thesis,
Emory University, 1957.
Fairchild, Edward Henry. God's
Designs for and Through the
Negro Race. New York:
American Missionary Associa-
tion, 1882.   CtY-D
    (American Missionary As-
    sociation Pamphlet no. 7)
Hubbard, Henry W. American
Missionary Association. Work
Among the Colored People of
the South. New York: Congre-
gational Rooms, n.d.
                          DHU/MO
Johnson, Charles S. "American
Missionary Association Insti-
tute of Race Relations." Jour-
nal of Negro Education (13;
Fall, 1944), pp. 568-74. DHU
    Negro author.
-- Into the Main Stream, A Sur-
vey of Best Practices in Race
Relations in the South. Chapel
Hill: The University of North
Carolina Press, 1947.
    DHU/R; NN/Sch; CtY-D
    Survey conducted by the
    Race Relations Div., Ameri-
    can Missionary Association.
-- "Race Relations Program of
the American Missionary As-
sociation." Journal of Negro
Education (13:2, Spr., 1944),
pp. 248-52.   DHU
Johnson, Clifton Herman. Amer-
ican Missionary Association
Archives as a Source for the
Study of American History.
New York: n.p., 1965.
                          CtY-D
Lawrence, John B. History of
the Home Mission Board.
Nashville: Broadman Press,
1958.   NcD
Patterson, Joseph Norenzo. "A
Study of the History of the

(Patterson, J. N. cont.)
Contribution of the American
Missionary Association to the
Higher Education of the Negro,
with Special Reference to Five
Selected Colleges Founded by
the Association, 1805-1900."
Doctoral dissertation, Cornell
University, 1956.
Richardson, Joe M. "Christian
Abolitionism: The American
Missionary Association and the

Florida Negro." Journal of Negro Education (40:1, Wint.,
1971), pp. 35-44.   DHU
Storrs, Richard Salter. Our Nation's Work for the Colored
People. A Discourse Delivered in the Church of the Pilgrims, Brooklyn, N. Y., in
Behalf of the American Missionary Association. New York:
Holt Bros., 1890. DHU/MO;
NN/Sch

D. PREJUDICE AND SEGREGATION IN RELIGION AND
HIGHER EDUCATION

Ahmann, Mathew, (ed.) Race:
Challenge to Religion. Chi-
cago: Regnery, 1963.
    Speeches from a meeting of
the National Conference on
Religion and Race. DHU/R
Alexander, Will W. Racial Seg-
regation in the American Prot-
estant Church. New York:
Friendship Press, 1946.
                        DHU/MO
Allport, Gordon W. "Prejudice:
Is it Societal or Personal."
Journal of Social Issues (18),
pp. 130-32.   DHU
    Also in, Religious Educa-
tion (59:1, Ja. -Feb., 1964),
pp. 20-29.   DHU/R
-- "Religion and Prejudice."
Crane Review (2; 1959), pp. 1-
10.   DAU/W
-- "The Religious Context of
Prejudice." Journal for the
Scientific Study of Religion,
(5:3, Fall, 1966), pp. 447-57.
                    DHU/R
Argyle, M. Religious Behaviour.
Glencoe, Ill.: Free Press,
1955.   DHU/R
    Racial prejudice, pp. 55-
83.
Armistead, W. S. The Negro is
A Man, A Reply to Professor
Charles Caroll's Book "The
Negro is a Beast or in the

Image of God." Atlanta, Ga.:
Mutual Publishing Co., 1904.
    DHU/R; GEU; NcD
Ashley-Montagu, Montague Fran-
cis. Man's Most Dangerous
Myth: The Fallacy of Race.
New York: Columbia Univer-
sity Press, 1942.   DHU/R
Augusta, Marie (Sister). "Meth-
ods of Education in Race Re-
lations." Religious Education
(59:1, Ja. -Feb., 1964), pp.
43-46.   DHU/R
Baez-Carmargo, Gonzalo.
"Christianity and the Race
Problem." Henry C. Wallace,
(ed.). Christian Bases of
World Order. (New York:
Abingdon-Cokesbury Press,
1943), pp. 101-24.
        DHU/R; CtY-D
    Merrick lectures for 1943.
Bailey, Hugh C. Edgar Gardner
Murphy: Gentle Progressive.
Coral Gables, Fla.: University of Miami Press, 1968.
                    DHU/R
    Biography of an early 20th
century leader and pioneer in
race relations, on the national
level.
Barbee, J. M. "Pastor Faces
Racial Change." Christian Ad-
vocate (5:2, 1961), pp. 7+.
        DAU/W; DHU/R

Beach, Waldo. "Ecclesiology
and Race: In the Churches
of Southern Protestantism."
Union Seminary Quarterly Review (14; Ja., 1959), pp. 19-
25.   DHU/R
-- "Racial Crisis and the Prophet." New Christian Advocate
(1:11, Ag., 1957), pp. 28-32.
Bede, (Brother). A Study of
the Development of Negro Education under Catholic Auspices
in Maryland and the District
of Columbia. Baltimore: Johns
Hopkins University Press,
1935.   DLC; DCU
Bell, L. Nelson. "Racial Tensions." Southern Presbyterian
Journal (5; Feb. 15, 1947),
pp. 2-3.   DLC; KyLxCB
Benedict, Ruth. Race: Science
and Politics. New York:
Modern Age Books, 1940.
                      DHU/MO
pp. 158+ racism and Christianity.
Bennett, M. (Sister). "A Negro
University and a Nun." Community (25; Mr., 1966), pp.
10-12.   DHU/MO
Bennett, Richard K. "Segrega-
tion and World Peace." Friends
Intelligencer (109:22, My. 31,
1952), pp. 306-7.   DHU/R
"Bishop Jeanmard and the Erath
La. Case." St. Augustine's
Messenger (33:1, Jan., 1956),
24-7.   DHU/R
"Decree issued to the pa-
rishioners on violence to Ne-
groes in parish by Bishop of
Lafayette."
Bishop, Samuel H. "The Church
and the Negroes." Spirit of
Missions (74:3, Mr., 1909;
74:11, Nov., 1909), pp. 207-
209; 931-33.   DHU/R
Blackburn, George Andrew. The
Life Work of John L. Girar-
dean, D.D. ... Columbia,
S.C.: State Co., 1916. DLC
Professor, Prebyterian
Theological Seminary, Colum-

bia, S.C. and his view on
race, pp. 82-4.
Booker, Merrel D. and Auburn,
Carr. "White and Black Ex-
changed Parsonages and Pul-
pits." Missions: An Interna-
tional Baptist Magazine (148:
2, Feb., 1950), pp. 82-4.
Pam. File; DHU/R
Booth, Newell Snow. Youth
Guides on Races and Reconcil-
iation. New York: Friendship
Press, 19-?   NN/Sch
Detailed plans for using
these materials with youth
groups in the local church,
community, and in summer
conferences.
Bowen, John Wesley Edward.
"An Apology for the Higher
Education of the Negro." The
Methodist Review (79; Sept.,
1897), pp. 723-42.
DHU/R; DLC; CtY-D
Braceland, Francis J. and Mi-
chael Stock. "The Deep Roots of
Prejudice." Catholic World
(198:1, 184, Nov., 1963), pp.
109-14.   DHU/R
Brashares, Charles W. "Racism
and the Methodist Church."
Social Question Bulletin (37;
Feb., 1947), p. 20.
CtY-D; DLC
Favors "permissive legisla-
tion" to make possible more
unsegregated Methodist work in
the North.
Brennecke, Gerhard. "Inter-
Group Relations--The Church
Amid Racial and Ethnic Ten-
sions." Ecumenical Review (7:
1, Oct., 1954), pp. 49-55.
DHU/R
Brown, Robert Raymond (bp.).
"Little Rock and the Churches."
Union Seminary Quarterly Re-
view (13:2, Ja., 1958), pp.
19-27.   DHU/R
Discusses the Church's role
in the crisis over integration.
Brown, Sarah D. Launching Be-
yond the Color Line... Chi-

(Brown, S. D. cont.)
cago: National Purity Association, 1905.   NN/Sch
Brown, William M. The Crucial
Race Question, or Where &
How Shall the Color Line Be
Drawn. Little Rock: Arkan-
sas Churchman's Pub. Co.,
1907.   DHU/MO
Bucke, Emory S. "Will Method-
ism Continue Segregation."
Zions Herald (124; Mr. 13,
1946), p. 247.   DLC
Burnham, Kenneth E. "Racial
Prejudice in Relation to Edu-
cation, Sex, and Religion."
Journal for the Scientific Study
of Religion (8:2, Fall, 1969),
p. 318.
Burns, Aubrey. "Segregation
and the Church." Reprinted
from the Spring 1949 issue of
Southwest Review, Pub. by
University Press in Dallas.
Southern Methodist University,
Dallas, Texas.   DHU/R
Buster, William. "Jap and Ne-
gro: A Similarity of Social
Problem." Methodist Review
(Bimonthly)(87; Jl., 1905),
pp. 576-81.   DHU/R
Calhoun, D. "Human Freedom:
Religion is the Enemy." Lib-
eration (2; Jl.-Ag., 1957),
24-5.   DHU/R
Campbell, Charles Grimshaw.
Race and Religion. London:
Nevill, 1953.   INU
Campbell, Ernest Q. "Moral
Discomfort and Racial Segre-
gation--An Examination of the
Myrdal Hypothesis." Social
Forces (Mr., 1961), p. 229.
                        DHU
Campbell, Will D. Race and the
Renewal of the Church. Phila-
delphia: Westminster Press,
1962.   DHU/R; CtY-D
Carhart, C. L. "Churches and
Race Lines." Christian Cen-
tury (50:26, Je. 28, 1933),
pp. 849-50.   DHU/R
Dr. Kelly Miller quoted on

the church and race prejudice.
Carroll, Charles. The Negro a
Beast or In the Image of God.
St. Louis: American Book &
Bible House, 1900.   DLC
Cartwright, C.C. "Church,
Race and the Arts of Govern-
ment." Christianity and Crisis
(19; Feb. 16, 1959), pp. 12-
14.   DHU/R
Cartwright, Colbert S. "The
Southern Minister and the Race
Question." New South (13;
Mr. 1952), pp. 54-6. DAU/W
Catchings, L. Maynard. The
Church Can Eliminate Dis-
crimination and Segregation.
n.p., n.d.   DHU/MO
Negro author.
Reprint. American Unity
(v. 4 & 5, Jan. 1947).
"Church and Race: Letter to the
Editor." Christian Century
(80; Ag. 21, 1963), p. 1032.
                        DHU/R
Clinchy, Everett Ross. All in
the Name of God. Introd. by
Newton D. Baker. New York:
Day, 1934.   NN/Sch
Cohen, Henry. "Prejudice Re-
duction in Religious Educa-
tion." Religious Education (59:
2, Mr.-Apr., 1964), pp. 386-
91.   DHU/R
Cokes, George Louis. The
Eagle and the Cross; the Ra-
cial Problem in Perspective.
New York: Exposition Press,
1966.   DHU/MO; NN/Sch
"Comparison of Some Ethnic and
Religious Attitudes of Negro
and White College Students in
the Deep South." Social
Forces (30; My., 1952), pp.
426-28.   DHU
"Condemn Segregation." Zions
Herald (129; Feb. 14, 1951),
p. 157.   DLC
Cooper, Harold L. "Priests,
Prejudice, and Race." Catho-
lic Mind (57; 1959), pp. 499-
505.   DLC
-- "Questions and Answers on

Segregation." Social Order
(6; 1956), pp. 432-33.
                    DCU/SW
Culver, Dwight W. Negro Seg-
regation in the Methodist
Church. New Haven: Yale
University Press, 1953.
DHU/R; INF; INU; NN/Sch
Also issued as a thesis at
Yale University.
-- "Segregation in the Methodist
Church." Christian Century
(65; Apr. 14, 1948), pp. 325-
6.
Curry, Jabez Lamar Monroe.
... Education of the Negroes
Since 1860. Baltimore: n.p.,
1894.   NN/Sch
Dabbs, J. M. "Is a Christian
Community Possible?" Chris-
tian Century (57; Jl. 10, 1940),
pp. 874-6.   DHU/R
Dabney, Robert Lewis. Ecclesi-
astical Relation of Negroes.
Speech... in the Synods of
Virginia, Nov. 9, 1867,
Against the Ecclesiastical
Equality of Negro Preachers
in our Church and their Right
to Rule over White Christians.
Richmond: Pr. at the Office
of the Boys and Girls' Monthly,
1868.   NcD
Davidson, G. W. "Modern Missionaries and the Race Question; Condemned by NAACP."
Christian Century (82; Sept.
29, 1965), pp. 1183-6.
                    DHU/R
Davis, Allison. Children of
Bondage; the Personality Development of Negro Youth in
the Urban South. Prepared for
the American Youth Commission. Washington, D. C.:
American Council on Education, 1940.   CtY-D
Dean, John P. and Alex Rosen.
A Manual on Intergroup Relations. Chicago: University
of Chicago Press, 1955.
                    DHU/R
Denham, John. "A Christian

Educator's Involvement in the
Race Crisis." Religious Edu-
cation (59:1, Ja.-Feb., 1964),
pp. 95-7.   DHU/R
Dewey, H. P. Race Problems
and Their Christian Solution.
Sermon Delivered at the Annual Meeting of the American
Missionary Association, Held
in Des Moines, Iowa, Oct. 16,
1904. New York: American
Missionary Association, 1904.
                    DHU/MO
Didas, James F. "Negro Chal-
lenge to the Church." Catholic
Mind (50; 1952), pp. 257-62.
Dorey, Frank David. "The
Church and Segregation in
Washington, D. C., and Chi-
cago, Illinois: A Prolegom-
enon to the Sociological Analy-
sis of the Segregated Church."
Doctoral dissertation, Univer-
sity of Chicago, 1950.
                    DHU/R
Douglass, Frederick. "The
Church and Prejudice." The
Life and Writing of Frederick
Douglass. Vol. I. Ed. Philip
S. Foner. (New York: Inter-
national Publishers, 1950),
pp. 103-05.   DHU/R
  Negro author.
  A speech given at the Ply-
mouth Church Anti-Slavery So-
ciety, December, 1841 and
printed in the National Anti-
Slavery Standard, December
23, 1841.
-- Narrative of the Life of Fred-
erick Douglass an American
Slave. Benjamin Quarles,
(ed.). Cambridge: Harvard
University Press, 1967.
                    DHU/R; DHU/MO
  In the appendix Douglass
explains his position on Christianity and the hypocritical
nature of its dealings with
blacks.
Dowd, Jerome. The Negro in
American Life. New York:
The Century Co., 1926.

(Dowd, J. cont.)
                NcD; DHU/MO
Church and race.
Doyle, Bertram Wilbur. The
Etiquette of Race Relations in
the South. Chicago: Univer-
sity of Chicago Press, 1937.
                DHU/R
Chapter IV, Etiquette in
the Church.
DuBois, William Edward Burg-
hardt. The Revelation of Saint
Orgne, the Damned. Nash-
ville: Hemphill Co., 1939.
                DHU/MO
Negro author.
Commencement Address
Delivered at Fisk University,
1938. Indictment Against
America for segregated
churches.
Dunn, James J. "Priests and
Prejudice." Pastoral Life
(6; Mr.-Apr., 1958), pp. 29-
31.   DCU/ST
Eakin, Mildred Olivia (Moody).
Sunday School Fights Preju-
dice, by Mildred Moody Eakin
and Frank Eakin. New York:
Macmillan, 1953.
                DHU/R; NN/Sch
Edwards, Lyford P. "Religious
Sectarianism and Race Preju-
dice." American Journal of
Sociology (41:2, Sept., 1935),
pp. 167-79.   DHU
Edwards, Vetress Bon. Go
South--With Christ; a Study in
Race Relations. New York:
Exposition Press, 1959.
                DHU/MO; DLC
Negro author.
Emil, Mary (Sister). "Race Re-
lations and Higher Education."
Religious Education (59:1, Ja.-
Feb., 1964), pp. 107-11.
                DHU/R
Faulkner, L. E. "Reasons Why
the Presbyterian Church (U.S.)
Should Withdraw from the Fed-
eral Council of the Churches
of Christ in America." South-
ern Presbyterian Journal (Ag.

15, 1947).   DLC
"Favor the Admission of Negro
Students." Zions Herald (129;
Mr. 21, 1951), p. 227.
                DLC; CtY-D
Feagin, Joe R. "Prejudice and
Religious Types: A Focused
Study of Southern Fundamen-
talists." Journal for the Sci-
entific Study of Religion (4:1,
Fall, 1964), pp. 3-13.
                DHU/R
Federal Council of the Churches
of Christ in America. Dept. of
Research and Education. "The
Race Issue in Methodist Uni-
fication." Information Service
(16; Apr. 3, 1937), pp. 1-4.
                DHU/R
Fey, Harold. "Does the Catho-
lic Church Fear Too Many
Negro Converts?" (Affirma-
tive answer; with Rev. John
LaFarge giving negative.)
Christian Century (Dec. 20,
1944), condensed in Negro
Digest, Apr., 1945, pp. 29-
34.   DHU/R
Floyd, R. W. "Role of the
Church in 'de facto' Segrega-
tion." Christian Advocate (8;
Dec. 3, 1964), p. 7.
                DHU/R; DAU/W
Foley, Albert S. "Negro and
Catholic Higher Education."
Crisis (64; Ag.-Sept., 1957),
pp. 413-19.   DHU/MO
Frazer, William H. "Why I
Favor Preserving the Southern
Church." Southern Presbyter-
ian Journal (11; Jl. 23, 1952),
                DLC; KyLXCB
Friedel, Lawrence M. "Is the
Curse of Ham on the Negro
Race?" American Ecclesiasti-
cal Review (106; 1942), pp.
447-53.   DHU/R
Friedrichs, Robert. "Decline in
Prejudice among Church-Go-
ers Following Clergy-Led
Open-Housing Campaign."
Journal for the Scientific Study
of Religion (10:2 Sum., 1971),

pp. 152-56. DHU/R
Gallagher, Buell G. "Christian-
ity and Color." Conference
on Science, Philosophy and Re-
ligion, A Symposium, Vol. 6.
New York: Harper, 1944.
DHU/R
-- Color and Conscience: The
Irrepressible Conflict. New
York: Harper, 1946.
DHU/R; NN/Sch
Christian integrationist
position.
-- and Dwight Bradley. "The
Question of Race: Interpreted
by Science and Religion;" in
"Bibliography on the Ameri-
can Negro." Bulletin. (Bos-
ton: General Theological Li-
brary, 36:1, Oct., 1943), pp.
5-9. MBU
-- Portrait of a Pilgrim: A
Search for the Christian Way
in Race Relations. New York:
Friendship Press, 1946.
DHU/MO; CtY-D
Galloway, Charles B. The
South and the Negro. New
York: Southern Education
Board, 1904. DHU/MO
George Peabody College for
Teachers, Nashville. Division
of Surveys and Field Studies.
Negro Colleges and Schools
Related to the Methodist
Church; A Survey Report...
Nashville: Div. of Surveys
and Field Studies, George
Peabody College for Teachers,
1943. NN/Sch
"Report on the Survey of
Negro Colleges and Schools
Related to the Board of Edu-
cation and the Woman's Divi-
sion of Christian Service of
the Methodist Church."
Gillard, John Thomas. "Negro
Challenges Christianity."
Commonweal (16; Je. 1, 1932),
pp. 129-31. DHU
Gillespie, G. T. A Christian
View on Segregation. Green-
wood, Miss.: Citizens' Coun-

cil, 1957. DHU/MO
Gilligan, Francis James. The
Morality of the Color Line.
An Examination of the Right
and the Wrong of the Discrim-
ination Against the Negro in
the United States. Washington,
D.C.: Catholic University of
America, 1928. NN/Sch
Gleason, Robert W. "The Im-
morality of Segregation."
Thought (35; Aut., 1960), pp.
349-64. DCU/HU
Gordes, Robert. Race and the
Religious Tradition. New
York: Anti Defamation
League, 1962. DHU/R
Reprint from The Root and
the Branch by Robert Gordes,
University of Chicago Press,
1962.
Gordon, Milton. Assimilation in
American Life: The Role of
Race and Religion and Nation-
al Life. New York: Oxford
University Press, 1964.
DHU/R
Gossett, Thomas F. Race: The
History of an Idea in America.
New York: Schocken Books,
1965. DHU/R
Chapter 8, "The Social Gos-
pel and Race" Clergyman and
their refusal to attack racism
in the church in the latter
part of the nineteenth century
and early twentieth century.
Grant, George A. "Race Con-
flict." Methodist Review (Bi-
monthly) (92; My., 1910), pp.
423-30. DHU/R
Grimke, Francis James. The
Afro-American Pulpit in Re-
lation to Race Elevation.
Washington, D.C.: n.p., n.d.
DHU/MO; DHU/R; DLC;
NN/Sch
Also in Woodson, Carter G.
Francis James Grimke, Washington, D.C.: Association
Press, 1942.
-- The American Bible Society
and Colorphobia. Washington,

(Grimke, F. J. cont.)
D. C.: n. p., 1916.   DHU/MO
Negro author.
-- The Atlanta Riot. A Dis-
course Delivered... Oct. 7,
1906.   DHU/MO
-- The Birth of a Nation. Washington, D. C.: n. p., 1915.
                       DHU/MO
-- The Brotherhood of Man, the
Christian Church and the Race
Problem in the United States
of America. A Discourse delivered in the Fifteenth Street
Presbyterian Church, Washing-
ton, D. C., March 20, 1921.
                       DHU/MO
-- Character, the True Standard
by Which to Estimate Individuals and Races and by Which
They Should Estimate Themselves and Others... Washing-
ton, D. C.: Pr. by R. L. Pen-
delton, n. d.   DHU/MO
-- Christianity and Race Preju-
dice. Two Discourses Deliv-
ered in the Fifteenth Street
Church, Washington, D. C.
Washington, D. C.: n. p.,
1910.   NN/Sch
Also in Woodson, Carter
G., Francis James Grimke.
Washington, D. C., Associa-
tion Press, 1942.
-- Conditions Necessary to Per-
manent World Peace. A Dis-
course Delivered by the Rev.
Francis J. Grimke in the Fif-
teenth Street Presbyterian
Church, Washington, D. C.,
Nov. 3, 1935. Washington,
D. C.: n. p., 1935.   DHU/MO
-- Equality of Rights for All
Citizens: Black and White
Alike. A Discourse Delivered
in the Fifteenth Street Presby-
terian Church, Washington,
D. C., Sunday, Mar. 7, 1909.
Washington, D. C.: n. p.,
1909.   DHU/R; DHU/MO
Also in Woodson, Carter G.
Francis James Grimke, Wash-
ington, D. C.: Assoc. Press,

1942.
-- Evangelism and Institutes on
Evangelism. Washington,
D. C.: n. p., 1918.
             DHU/MO; DHU/R
-- Excerpts from a Thanksgiving
Sermon. Delivered Nov. 26,
1914 and Two Letters Ad-
dressed to Hon. Woodrow Wil-
son, President of the United
States. Washington, D. C.:
R. L. Pendelton, 1914.
                        DHU/R
Also in Woodson, Carter
G. Francis James Grimke.
Washington, D. C., Associated
Press, 1942.
-- Gideon Bands for Work With-
in the Race and for Work
Without the United States. A
Discourse in the Fifteenth
Street Presbyterian Church,
Washington, D. C., Sunday,
Mar. 2, 1913. Washington,
D. C.: R. L. Pendelton, 1913.
                       DHU/MO
-- God and the Race Problem.
Delivered in the Fifteenth
Street Presbyterian Church,
Washington, D. C. May 3, 1903,
on the Day Set Apart as a
Day of Fasting, Prayer, and
Humiliation for the Colored
People. Throughout the United
States. n. p., 1903.
Also in Woodson, Carter G.
Francis James Grimke. Wash-
ington, D. C.: Association
Press, 1942.
-- Great Preaching. Washington,
D. C.: n. p., n. d. DHU/MO
-- The Inheritance Which All
Parents May and Ought to
Leave to Their Children. De-
livered in the Fifteenth Street
Presbyterian Church, Washing-
ton, D. C. Washington, D. C.:
n. p., n. d.   DHU/MO
-- Jim Crow Christianity and the
Negro. Washington, D. C.:
n. p., n. d.   DHU/MO
-- A Message to the Race...
Delivered in the Fifteenth

Street Presbyterian Church, Washington, D. C., Mar. 1, 1925. Washington, D. C.: n. p., 1925.   DHU/MO

-- My Farewell Quadrennial Message to the Race. Delivered in the Fifteenth Street Presbyterian Church, Washington, D. C., Mar. 5, 1933. Subject: The Three Most Important Agencies in the Uplift of the Race. Washington, D. C., n. p., 1933.   DHU/MO

-- The Negro: His Rights and Wrongs, the Forces for Him and Against Him. Washington, D. C.: n. p., 1898.   DHU/MO
"Sermons...delivered in the Fifteenth Street Presbyterian Church, Washington, D. C., Nov. 20 and 27, and Dec. 4 and 11, 1898."

-- The New Year. A Discourse Delivered in the 15th Street Presbyterian Church, by the Pastor. Washington, D. C.: n. p., n. d.   DHU/MO

-- The Next Step in Racial Cooperation. A Discourse Delivered in the Fifteenth Street Presbyterian Church. Washington, D. C., Nov. 20, 1921. Washington, D. C.: n. p., 1921.   DHU/MO; NN/Sch

-- Our Young People: How to Deal With Them. Washington, D. C.: n. p., n. d.   DHU/MO

-- The Paramount Importance of Right Living...Delivered in the Fifteenth Street Presbyterian Church, Washington, D. C. ...on Men's Day, May 16, 1926, Under the Auspices of Men's Progressive Club of the Church. Washington, D. C.: Pub. by the Club, 1926.   DHU/MO

-- A Phase of the Race Problem, Looked at from Within the Race Itself. ...Delivered in the Fifteenth Street Presbyterian Church, Washington, D. C., Mr. 6, 1921. Washington,

D. C.: n. p., 1921.
          DHU/MO; NN/Sch

-- The Progress and Development of the Colored People of Our Nation. An Address Delivered Before the American Missionary Association, Wednesday...Oct. 21, 1908, at Galesburg, Illinois. n. p., 1908.   DHU/MO

-- Quadrennial Message to the Race... Introductory Remarks by Dr. G. Lake Imes. Washington, D. C.: n. p., n. d.   DHU/MO

-- The Race Problem as It Respects the Colored People and the Christian Church, in the Light of the Developments of the Last Year. A Discourse Delivered at a Union Thanksgiving Service Held at the Plymouth Congregational Church, Nov. 17, 1919. Washington, D. C.: n. p., 1919.   NN/Sch; DHU/MO
Also in Woodson, Carter G. and Francis James Grimke, Washington, D. C.: Associated Press, 1942.

-- The Race Problem... Two Suggestions as to its Solution. Washington, D. C.: n. p., 1919.   DHU/MO; DLC; DHU/R
Also in Woodson, Carter G. and Francis James Grimke, Washington, D. C.: Associated Press, 1942.

-- A Resemblance and a Contrast Between the American Negro and the Children of Israel; or, The Duty of the Negro to Contend Earnestly for his Rights Guaranteed under the Constitution ... Delivered in Fifteenth St. Presbyterian Church, Oct. 12, 1902 in Connection with the Encampment of the Grand Army of the Republic, in the City of Washington. n. p., 1902.   DHU/MO; DHU/R
Also in Woodson, Carter

(Grimke, F. J. cont.)
G., Francis James Grimke,
Washington, D. C.: Associ-
ated Press.
-- Rev. "Billy" Sunday's Cam-
paign in Washington, D. C.
January 6-March 3, 1918...
n. p., 1918.   DHU/MO
Also in Woodson, Carter G.,
Francis James Grimke. Wash-
ington, D. C., Associated
Press, 1942.
-- Some Lessons from the As-
sociation of President William
McKinley. Delivered Sept. 22,
1901. Washington, D. C.: n. p.,
1901.   DHU/MO
-- The Supreme Court's Decision
in Regard to the Scottsboro
Case. Washington, D. C.:
n. p., n. d.   DHU/MO
-- Theodore Roosevelt. An Ad-
dress delivered in the Fif-
teenth Street Presbyterian
Church, Washington, D. C.,
Feb. 9, 1919.
          DHU/MO; DHU/R
Also in the Woodson, Carter
G., Francis James Grimke,
Washington, D. C., Associated
Press, 1942.
-- The Things of Paramount Im-
portance in the Negro Race.
Delivered in the Fifteenth
Street Presbyterian Church.
Washington, D. C., Mar. 29,
1903. Washington, D. C.:
n. p., 1903.
          DHU/MO; DHU/R
Also in, Woodson, Carter
G., Francis James Grimke.
Washington, D. C.: Associated
Press, 1942.
-- Two Letters Addressed to Rev.
Sol. C. Dickey, General Sec-
retary of the Winona Assembly
and Bible Conference, Winona
Lake, Indiana, and Rev.
Charles Everest Granger, Pas-
tor of Gunton Temple Memori-
al Presbyterian Church. Wash-
ington, D. C.: n. p., 1916.
                        NN/Sch

-- Three Letters Addressed to the
New York Independent, Winston
Churchill (and) "Billy" Sunday,
by Rev. Francis J. Grimke.
Washington, D. C.: Press of
R. W. Pendleton, 1915.
          NN/Sch; DHU/MO
-- "Victory for the Allies and the
United States a Ground of Re-
joicing, of Thanksgiving."
Carter G. Woodson, Negro
Orators and Their Orations.
New York: Russell & Russell,
1969, pp. 690-708.
Also in Woodson, Carter
G., Francis James Grimke
Washington, D. C.: Associ-
ated Press, 1942. Sermon de-
livered at 15th St. Presbyteri-
an Church, Washington, D. C.,
Dec. 24, 1968.
          DHU/MO; DHU/R
-- A Vision of World Wide Peace.
A Talk Given to his Weekly
Prayer Meeting. Washington,
D. C.: n. p., n. d.   DHU/MO
-- A Word of Warning to the
Race. Washington, D. C.:
n. p., 1927.   DHU/MO
Hagood, Lewis Marahall. "The
Southern Problem." The
Methodist Review (Bimonthly)
(7; My., 1891), pp. 428-34.
                          DHU/R
Hammond, Lilly Hardy. "Hu-
man Races and the Race of
Man." Methodist Review
(Quarterly) (73:4, Oct., 1924),
pp. 623-33.   DHU/R
Hardy, Arthur W. "Political
Forces and the Christian Way."
The Christian Way in Race Re-
lations, William S. Nelson,
(ed.). (New York: Harper &
Bros. Publishers, 1948), pp.
77-96.   DHU/R
Haselden, Kyle Emerson. Man-
date for White Christians.
Richmond: John Knox Press,
1966.
     DHU/R; CtY-D; INU; DLC
-- The Racial Problem in Chris-
tian Perspective. New York:

Harper, 1959.
DHU/R; INU; NN/Sch
Holmes, Dwight O. W. The Evo-
lution of the Negro College.
New York: Teachers College,
Columbia University, 1934.
DHU/MO
Negro author.
Holmes, Thomas Joseph. Ashes
for Breakfast. In collabora-
tion with Gainer E. Bryan, Jr.
Valley Forge, Pa.: Judson
Press, 1969. CtY-D; DLC
Holsey, Lucius H. (bp.) "Race
Segregation." Washington Con-
ference on the Race Problem
in the United States. National
Sociological Society. How to
Solve the Race Problem.
(Washington, D. C.: Bersford,
Printer, 1904), pp. 40-66.
DHU/R
Negro author.
Bishop of the A. M. E.
Church. Contains reaction by
race leaders to the paper.
Houser, George M. "Racism
Sits in the Pews." Fellow-
ship (13; Feb. , 1947), pp. 26+.
DGW
Howard University, Washington,
D. C. School of Religion. ...The
Thirty-Fourth Annual Convoca-
tion, November 14-18, 1950.
Theme: The Church, the
State and Human Welfare...
Washington, D. C.: n. p.,
1951.   NN/Sch; DHU/R
Huntley, Thomas Elliott. As I
Saw it, not Communism but
Commonism; a Prophetic Ap-
praisal of the Status Quo, a
Message for All Times, for
America and for All Nations.
New York: Comet Press
Books, 1955.
DHU/MO; DLC; NN/Sch
Negro author.
Imes, William Lloyd. The Black
Pastures; An American Pil-
grimage in two Centuries; Es-
says and Sermons. Nashville:
Tenn.: Hemphill Press, 1957.

NN/Sch
Negro author.
Institute for Religious Studies,
Jewish Theological Seminary of
America. ...Civilization and
Group Relationships, a Series
of Addresses and Discussions,
Edited by R. M. MacIver. New
York: Institute for Religious
Studies, Distributed by Harper
& Bros. , 1945.
DHU/R; CtY-D
Religion and group tensions
by John LaFarge.
Institute for Religious and Social
Studies. Jewish Theological Semi-
nary of America. Discrimina-
tion and National Welfare. ...
Edited by R. M. MacIver. New
York: Institute for Religious
and Social Studies, 1949.
NN/Sch
How the church suffers by
John LaFarge.
Interracial Consultation. 2d. Col-
lege of the Bible, Lexington, Ky. ,
1960. Southern Churches and
Race Relations; Report of the
Second Interracial Consultation
Held at the College of the
Bible, July 18-22, 1960. Ed-
ited by Lewis S. C. Smythe.
Lexington, Ky.: College of the
Bible, 1960.   CtY-D
Ivy, A. C. and Irwin Ross. Re-
ligion and Race: Barriers to
College. New York: Anti-
Defamation League of B'nai
B'rith, 1949. (Public Affairs
Pamphlet no. 153).
Pam. File; DHU/R
Jacks, M. L. God in Education.
London: Rich & Cowan, 1939.
DLC
Jackson, Olive Scott. God in the
Flesh. Questions and An-
swers About Women Jews, Ne-
groes, and the Church. New
York: William-Frederick
Press, 1958.   NN/Sch
"Jim Crows Last Stand. " Crisis
(57; Je. , 1950), pp. 349-51.
DHU/MO

Johnson, Charles S. Background
to Patterns of Negro Segrega-
tion. New York: Thomas Y.
Crowell Co., 1970.   DHU/R
Negro author.
Church segregation, pp.
198, 276.
-- "Race Against Humanity." So-
cial Action (9:1, Ja. 15, 1943),
pp. 7-19.   DHU/R
Jones, David D. "Democracy,
Race, and the Church Related
College." Zions Herald (118;
Feb. 7, 1940), p. 125.
                DLC; CtY-D
Kaplan, Harry. "Race Relations
in College." Religious Educa-
tion (59:1, Ja.-Feb., 1964),
pp. 111-13.   DHU/R
Kastler, Norman M. "The
Church and the Color Line."
Opportunity (10:1, Ja., 1932),
pp. 8-11.   DHU/MO
Kennedy, Louise V. The Negro
Peasant Turns Cityward: Ef-
fects of Recent Migrations to
Northern Centers. New York:
Columbia University Press,
1930.   DHU/R
The church and the mi-
grant, pp. 202-06.
Knox, Ellis O. "The Trend of
Progress in the Light of New
Educational Concepts in a
Group of American Colleges
Dominated by Religious Influ-
ences." Doctoral dissertation,
University of Southern Cali-
fornia, 1931.
Kyles, Josephine H. "Is There
a Place for Church Supported
School in the Life of the Ne-
gro?" The Negro Journal of
Religion (4:6, Jl., 1938; 4:7,
Aug., 1938), pp. 9; 5. DHU/R
Negro author.
La Farge, John. "How the
Churches Suffer." R.M. Mac-
Iver, (ed.). Discrimination
and National Welfare: A Se-
ries of Addresses and Discus-
sions. Port Washington, N.Y.:
Kennikat Press, 1969, pp. 77-

81.   DHU/R
Lambert, Rollin E. "Race Re-
lations on the Campus." Re-
ligious Education (59:1, Ja.-
Feb., 1964), pp. 114-16.
                    DHU/R
Leavell, Ullin Whitney. Philan-
thropy in Negro Education.
Nashville, Tenn.: George
Peabody College for Teachers,
1930.   NN/Sch
Church and education.
Lee, Davis. "A Negro Looks at
Racial Issues." Southern Pres-
byterian Journal (8; Oct. 15,
1948), p. 5. DLC; KyLxCB
Leftwich, W.M. "The Race
Problem in the South." Quar-
terly Review (Methodist Epis-
copal Church, South), (6; Apr.
1889), p. 94. DLC; CtY-D
Leiffer, Murray H. "Segrega-
tion in Churches." Central
Christian Advocate (131:8,
Apr. 15, 1956), pp. 6-8.
                    DHU/R
Leiper, Henry. Blind Spots, Ex-
periments in the Self-Cure of
Race Prejudice. New York:
Friendship Press, 1929.
                    DHU/R
See Chapter VI, "Getting
the Golden Rule Angle" writ-
ten by an officer of The Am-
erican Missionary Association.
Loescher, Frank S. The Prot-
estant Church and the Negro:
A Pattern of Segregation.
New York: Association Press,
1948. DHU/R; INU; CtY-D
Logan, Rayford. What the Ne-
gro Wants. Chapel Hill: The
University of North Carolina
Press, 1944.   DHU/R
Chapters on the church and
race relations.
Lord, Samuel Ebenezer Church-
stone. God in a Troubled World.
Amherst, Nova Scotia: News
Sentinel Press, 1948. NN/Sch
Negro author.
-- The Negro and Organized Re-
ligion, an Attempt at Interpre-

tation. Kingston, Jamaica:
n. p. , 1935.   DLC
Macklin, John M. Democracy
and Race Friction. A Study
in Social Ethics. New York:
The Macmillan Co. , 1914.
                    DHU/MO
Pp. 41-43 Religious prejudice.
Maffett, Robert Lee. The King-
dom Within, A Study of the
American Race Problem and
its Solution. New York: Exposition Press, 1955. NN/Sch
Negro author.
Maritain, Jacques. "The Menace
of Racialism." Interracial Re-
view (10; 1937), pp. 70-71.
                    DCU/SW
Markoe, John P. "A Moral Ap-
praisal of the Color Line."
Homiletic and Pastoral Review
(48; 1948), pp. 828-36. DGU
Martin, J. G. and F. W. Westie.
"The Tolerant Personality."
American Sociological Review
(24; 1959), pp. 521-28. DHU
Attempts to prove there is
no relationship between re-
ligiosity and prejudice.
Maston, Thomas Bufford. Seg-
regation and Desegregation: a
Christian Approach. New York:
Macmillan, 1959.   CtY-D
Mayo, Amory D. The Work of
Certain Northern Churches in
the Education of the Freedman,
1862-1900. Washington: Goot
Printing Office, 1903.
          DHU/MO; NN/Sch
Mays, Benjamin Elijah. "Am-
sterdam on the Church and
Race Relation." Religion in
Life (9:1, Wint. , 1940), pp.
95-104.   DHU/R
Negro author.
World Council of churches
held in Amsterdam, Holland.
-- "A Centennial Commencement
Address: Higher Education
and the American Negro."
Journal of Religious Thought
(24:2, Aut. -Wint. , 1967-68),

pp. 4-12.   DHU/R
-- "The Church and Racial Ten-
sions." Christian Century (71:
36, Sept. , 1954), pp. 1068-
69.   DHU/R
-- "Realities in Race Relations."
Christian Century (48:12, Mr. ,
1931), pp. 404-06. DHU/R
-- "Second Assembly of the World
Council of Churches." Journal
of Religious Thought (10:2,
Spr. -Sum. , 1953), pp. 144-
48.   DHU/R
-- "The South's Racial Policy."
Presbyterian Outlook (132;
Nov. 6, 1950), p. 5.
            NN/Sch; DLC; NcD
-- "World Aspects of Race and
Culture." Missions (147:2, Feb.
1949), pp. 83-7.
          Pam. File; DHU/R
McDowell, Edward Allison.
Southern Churches and the Ne-
groes. n. p. , 194-? CtY-D
McGinnis, Frederick A. The
Education of Negroes in Ohio.
Wilberforce, O. : n. p. , 1962.
                    DHU/MO
Pp. 15-29, sec. The Atti-
tudes of religious denomina-
tions, p. 26-29.
McGrath, Oswin, OP. "The
Theology of Racial Segrega-
tion." Catholic Mind (55;
1957), pp. 483-86. DCU/TH
McIlvane, D. W. "Racial Balance
in Catholic Schools." Com-
munity (25; My. , 1966), p. 7.
                    DHU/MO
McKinney, Richard Ishmael. Re-
ligion in Higher Education
Among Negroes. New Haven:
Yale University Press, 1945.
          DHU/R; DLC
Negro author.
McNeill, Robert B. God Wills
Us Free: the Ordeal of a
Southern Minister. Intro. by
Ralph McGill. New York:
Hill and Wang, 1965.
          DLC; INU; DHU/MO
Story of a white minister dis-
missed from his pulpit because

(McNeill, R. B. cont.)
of his stand on segregation.
Meyer, A.C. "Integration in
Church Schools." Integrated
Education (2; Je.-Jl., 1964),
pp. 45-46.   DHU/MO
Miller, Kelly. Religion and Race.
(Reprinted from the "Student
World.") Geneva: n.p., 1926.
                      DHU/MO
  Negro author.
Miller, Robert Moats. "The At-
titudes of American Protes-
tantism Toward the Negro."
Journal of Negro History (41:
3, Jl., 1956), pp. 215-40.
                      DHU/MO
-- "The Protestant Churches and
Lynching." Journal of Negro
History (42:2, Apr., 1957), pp.
18-31.   DHU/MO
Moton, Robert Russa. What the
Negro Thinks. Garden City,
N.Y.: Doubleday, Doran and
Co., 1930.   CtY-D
  Negro author.
Moxom, Philip Stafford. Our
Problem with the Negro in
America; Sermon by Rev.
Philip S. Moxom, Delivered
at the Fifty-Seventh Annual
Meeting of the American Mis-
sionary Association, held in
Cleveland, Ohio, October 20,
1903. New York: C. Holt,
Printer, 1903.   NN/Sch
Murphy, Edgar Gardiner. The
Basis of Ascendency. New
York: Longmans Green & Co.,
1909.   DHU/MO
  A Christian approach to the
  race problem.
Muste, Abraham John. What the
Bible Teaches About Freedom;
a Message to the Negro
Churches. New York: Fel-
lowship of Reconciliation, 1943.
                      CtY-D
Myer, Gustavus. History of
Bigotry in the United States.
New York: Random House,
1943.   CtY-D
National Educational Assembly,

Ocean Grove, N. J. Christian
Educators in Council. Sixty
Addresses by American Edu-
cators; with Historical Notes
Upon the National Education
Assembly held at Ocean Grove,
N. J., August 9-12, 1883. Al-
so Illiteracy and Education
Tables from Census of 1880.
Compiled and Edited by Rev.
J. C. Hartzell, D. D. New
York: Phillips & Hunt; Cin-
cinnati: Cranston & Stowe,
1883.   NN/Sch
"Negro Christians Face a Grave
Decision." Christian Century
(52; Sept. 11, 1935), pp.
1134-5.   DHU/R
"Negro-White Church Union
Brings Melee." Washington
Post (je. 1, 1953).
    Pam. File; DHU/R
Nelson, William Stuart. "Reli-
gion and Racial Tension in
America Today." Conference
on Science, Philosophy, and
Religion. (New York: Harper,
1945).   DHU/R
  Negro author.
  Also in, Journal of Reli-
gious Thought (2:2, Spr.-
Sum., 1945), pp. 164-78.
                      DHU/R
Nicholson, Alfred William.
Brief Sketch of the Life and
Labors of Rev. Alexander Bet-
tis; Also an Account of the
Founding and Development of
the Bettis Academy. Trenton,
S. C.: The Author, 1913.
                      DHU/MO
  Negro author.
Oldham, Joseph Houldsworth.
Christianity and the Race
Problem. New York: Doran,
1925.   DHU/R; NN/Sch
Olson, Bernard E. Faith and
Prejudice. Intergroup Prob-
lems in Protestant Churches.
New Haven: Yale University
Press, 1963.   DHU/R
  Review, Commentary (35;
My., 1963), pp. 455-60. DHU

Reply: Olson, B. E. Commentary (36; Sept. , 1963), pp. 197-9.					DHU
O'Neill, Joseph Eugene. A Catholic Case Against Segregation. New York: Macmillan, 1961. DHU/R; CtY-D; DLC
Osborne, William Audley. The Segregated Covenant; Race Relations and American Catholics. New York: Herder & Herder, 1967.
DHU/MO; DLC; NcD; CtY-D
"Outlaw Color Segregation." Christian Century (63; Ag. 21, 1946), pp. 1010-11. DHU/R
Parsons, Talcott. "Racial and Religious Differences as Factors in Group Tensions." Conference on Science, Philosophy and Religion, A Symposium (New York: Harper, 1945, vol. 5). DHU/R
Paton, Alan. "The Person in Community." Edmund Fuller, (ed.). The Christian Idea (New Haven: Yale University Press, 1957), pp. 101-24. DHU/R; CtY-D
Payne, Enoch George. An Estimate of Our Negro Schools. New York: The American Church Institute for Negroes, 1943. DHU/MO; NN/Sch
Pearne, Thomas H. "The Race Problem--The Situation." Methodist Quarterly Review (71; Sept. -Oct. , 1890), pp. 690-705. DLC; CtY-D
Peterson, Frank L. The Hope of the Race. Nashville, Tenn. : Southern Publishing Association, 1934. DHU/MO
Pettigrew, Thomas F. A Profile of the Negro American. New York: D. Van Nostrand Co. , Inc. , 1964. DHU/MO Religion, pp. 47-8.
Pickens, William. "Christianity as a Basis of Common Citizenship. Arcadius Trawick, (ed.) The New Voice in Race Adjustments. (New York: Stu-

dent Volunteer Movement, 1914), pp. 34-40. DHU/R Negro author.
Pike, Esther, (ed.). Who is My Neighbor? Greenwich, Conn. : Seabury Press, 1960. NN/Sch "The Subjugated, by Michael Scott, pp. 215-30.
Pope, Liston. "Caste in the Church: The Protestant Experience." Survey Graphics (36; Ja. , 1947), pp. 59+. DHU
Powell, Adam Clayton, Jr. Marching Blacks. New York: Dial Press, 1945.
DHU/MO
Negro author.
Powell, Raphael Philemon. The Prayer for Freedom; a Memorial of the Prayer Pilgrimage, May 17, 1957. New York: n. p. , 1957. DHU/MO Negro author.
Prothro, E. Terry and John A. Jensen. "Comparison of Some Ethnic and Religious Attitudes of Negro and White College Students in the Deep South." Social Forces (30:4, My. , 1952), pp. 426-28. DHU
-- and M. O. King. "A Comparison of Ethnic Attitudes of College Students and Middle Class Adults from the Same State." Journal of Social Psychology (36; 1952), pp. 53-58. DHU
Finds no relationship between religiosity and prejudice.
"Race Relations and Religious Education." Religious Education (59:1, Ja. -Feb. , 1964), p. 2. DHU/R
"Racial Christianity." Time (48; Dec. 9, 1946), p. 73. DHU
"Racism Seen as Emerging from Planned Effect; Denounced by Protestant Leaders." Interchurch News (1; Feb. , 1960), p. 3. DLC
Randolph, A. Philip. "The Negro in American Democracy."

(Randolph, A. P. cont.)
Social Action (9:1, Ja. 15,
1943), pp. 22-29.   DHU/R
Discusses among other top-
ics the "Un-Christian Prac-
tices" of the White church.
Negro author.
Read, Margaret. "Inter-Group
Relations--The Church Amid
Racial and Ethnic Tensions."
Ecumenical Review (6:1, Oct.,
1953), pp. 40-7.   DHU/R
Reid, Ira D. A. "The Church
and Education for Negroes."
Trevor Bowen. Divine White
Right. A Study of Race Seg-
regation and Interracial Coop-
eration in Religious Organiza-
tions and Institutions. New
York: Harper & Bros., 1934.
                          DHU/MO
Negro author.
Reimers, David Morgan. "Ne-
gro Bishops and Diocesan Seg-
regation in the Protestant
Episcopal Church, 1870-1954."
Historical Magazine (31:3,
Sept., 1962), pp. 231-42.
                          DHU/R
Religious Drawings, Inc., Waco,
Tex. Race... Waco, Tex.,
1955. 27 Drawings on the
Subject of Race Relations,
Each Signed: Jack Hamm.
                          NN/Sch
Ridout, Lionel U. "The Church,
the Chinese and the Negroes
in California, 1849-1892."
Historical Magazine (28:2, Je.,
1959), pp. 115-38.   DHU/R
Roberts, James Deotis. "The
Christian Conscience and Le-
gal Discrimination." The
Journal of Religious Thought
(19:2, 1962-63), pp. 157-61.
                          DHU/R
"A careful examination of the
nature of the "Christian conscience" both in life and thought."
Robinson, James Herman. "Social Practices and the Christian Way." William S. Nelson,
(ed.). The Christian Way in

Race Relations. (New York:
Harper & Bros., Publishers,
1948), pp. 97-108.
            DHU/R; DHU/MO
Negro author.
Rokeach, Milton. "Political and
Religious Dogmatism: An Al-
ternate to the Authritarian Personality." Psychological Monographs (70:18, 1956), pp. 1-
43.   DHU
Roman, Charles Victor. "Racial
Self-Respect and Racial An-
tagonism." Methodist Review
(Quarterly) (62:4, Oct., 1913),
pp. 768-77.   DHU/R
Negro author.
-- Science and Christian Ethic.
Part I. Statement of Principles. Part II. Religion a Necessity to Man; Defense of a
Creed. Part III. Racial An-
tagonism; Principles Applied
to the Solution of a Socio-
ethico-economic Condition. n. p.
1943.   DHU/MO; NN/Sch
Roosevelt, Eleanor. "Race, Re-
ligion and Prejudice." New
Republic (106; My., 1942), pp.
630+.   DHU
Rose, Arnold M. The Negro's
Morale. St. Paul: Univer-
sity of Minnesota Press, 1949.
                          DHU/R
Rosenblum, A. L. "Ethnic Prejudice as Related to Social Class
and Religiosity." Sociology and
Social Research (43; 1958), pp.
272-75.   DHU
Salten, David G. "Education in
Race Relations." Religious
Education (59:1, Ja.-Feb.,
1964), pp. 37-43.   DHU/R
Sanford, Elias B., (ed.). Church
Federation. Inter-Church Con-
ference on Federation. New
York: Fleming H. Revell Co.,
1906.   DAU/R
Bishop W. B. Derrick, Ne-
gro made a plea for White
sympathy for the Negro, pp.
520-24.
Scarlett, William, (bp.), Toward

a Better World. Philadelphia:
Winston, 1946.   NN/Sch
The Negro problem, pp.
43-52.

Schulze, Andrew. My Neighbor
of Another Color. A Treatise
on Race Relations in the
Church. St. Louis, Mo. : A.
Schulze, 1941.
        NN/Sch; NcD; DLC

Schuyler, G. S. "Black America
Begins to Doubt." American
Mercury (25; Apr. , 1932), pp.
423-30.   DHU

Sellers, James E. The South
and Christian Ethics. New
York: Association Press,
1962. DHU/R; INU; CtY-D

Shaffer, Helen B. "Segregation
in Churches." Brief of Report Issued Sept. 3, 1954.
Editorial Research Reports (2:
11, Sept. 3, 1954).
        Pam. File, DHU/R

Shaw, Alexander P. Christianizing Race Relation as a Negro Sees It. Los Angeles:
Wetzer Pub. Co. , 1928.
                    DHU/MO
Negro author.

Sheerin, John B. "Is Segregation
at the End of Its Rope?" Catholic World (183; Apr. , 1956),
pp. 1-5.   DHU/R

Sheild, R. N. "A Southern View
of the Race Question." (Quarterly Review (Methodist Episcopal Church, South) (8; Jl. ,
1890), p. 335.   DLC; CtY-D

Sherman, Anthony C. "A Virginian's Shame." Religious
Education (59:1, Ja. -Feb. ,
1964), pp. 97-100.   DHU/R
A critique on the Church's
silence in the face of segregation in Virginia.

Simms, James. "The Union of
White Methodism." Crisis
(20; My. , 1920), pp. 14-17.
                    DHU/MO

Simpson, George Eaton and J.
Milton Yinger. Racial and Cultural Minorities, An Analysis

of Prejudice and Discrimination. New York: The Mac-
millan Co. , 1944.   DHU/R
Chapter 18, Minorities and
religion.

Simpson, J. David. "Non-Seg-
regation Means Eventual Inter-
Marriage." Southern Presbyterian Journal (6; Mr. 15,
1948).   DLC

Smith, Lillian. "Humans in
Bondage." Social Action (10:2,
Feb. 15, 1944), pp. 6-29.
                    DHU/R
A discussion of effects of
prejudice. Includes a section,
"The Church must dream a
new dream."

-- There Are Things to Do.
Clayton, Ga. , n. p. , 1943, 16
pp. Reprinted from South Today, Wint. , 1943-43.
                    DHU/MO
Religion and race.

Smith, Robert Edwin. Christianity and the Race Problem.
New York: Fleming H. Re-
vell Co. , 1922.
        DHU/MO; CtY-D

Sperry, Willard Learoyd. Reli-
gion and our Racial Tensions;
One of a Series of Volumes on
Religion in the Post-War
World. By Clyde Kluckhohn,
Everett R. Clincy, Edwin R.
Embree and Others ... Cam-
bridge: Harvard University
Press, 1945. DHU/R; CtY-D

Stevens, Francis B. "A Sign of
Change in Mississippi Methodism." Concern (7:15, Sept. 1,
1965), pp. 8-9, 14. DHU/R

Stoutemeyer, John Howard. "Re-
ligion and Race Education."
Doctoral dissertation, Clark
University, 1910.

Tanenbaum, Marc H. "The
American Negro: Myths and
Realities." Religious Education (59:1, Ja. -Feb. , 1964),
pp. 33-36.   DHU/R

Tarplee, Cornelius C. "Education and the Challenge of

(Tarplee, C. C. cont.)
Prejudice." Religious Education (59:1, Ja. -Feb., 1964),
pp. 47-9.   DHU/R
Taylor, Paul Lawrence. "An
Analysis of Religious Counseling Practices of Nine Selected
Negro Colleges." Doctoral dissertation, Indiana University,
1958.
"Teens Talk About Race, Religion and Prejudice." Negro
Digest (11; Jan., 1962), pp.
71-81.   DHU/MO
Thering, M. Rose Albert (Sister).
"Religious Education in Race
Relations: A Catholic Viewpoint." Religious Education (59:
1, Ja. -Feb., 1964), pp. 50-
55.   DHU/R
Thompson, Charles H. "The
Present Status of the Negro
and Church Related Colleges."
Journal of Negro Education (29:
4, Sum., 1960), pp. 236-44.
                         DHU/MO
Thurman, Howard. The Luminous Darkness; a Personal Interpretation of the Anatomy of
Segregation and the Ground of
Hope. New York: Harper &
Row, 1965.
DHU/R; DLC; INU; CtY-D
Negro author.
Tottress, Richard E. Heaven's
Entrance Requirements for
Races. New York: Comet
Press Books, 1957. DHU/R
Negro author.
Travers-Ball, I. "India and the
Negro Question; Here's How
Birmingham and Montgomery
Look to People Around the
World." America (109; Jl. 13,
1963), pp. 44-5.   DHU
Trawick, M. "The Good and
Bad of Race Prejudice." Methodist Quarterly Review (74:2,
Apr., 1925), pp. 243+.
                         DHU/R
Triandis, Harry C. and Leigh
M. Triandis. "Race, Social
Class, Religion, and National-

ity as Determinants of Social
Distance." Journal of Abnormal
and Social Psychology (Jl.;
1960), pp. 110-18.   DHU
Tuhl, Curtis G. "The American
Church and the Negro Problem."
Master's thesis, Graduate Seminary, Phillips University,
1946.
Van Deusen, John George. The
Black Man in White America.
Washington, D. C. Associated
Publishers, 1938.   NN/Sch
Waldraven, Robert U. "Racial
Friction in America." Methodist Review (Quarterly), (70:1,
Ja., 1921), pp. 31-43.
                         DHU/R
Wamble, G. Hugh. "Negroes and
Missouri Protestant Churches,"
Missouri Historical Review
(Apr., 1967).   DCU/SW
A study of the relation of
Negroes to Protestant churches
in Missouri based on the congregational records of thirty-
five churches including Grace
Episcopal Church, Jefferson
City.
Warner, W. Lloyd and B. H.
Junker. Color and Human Nature:
Negro Personality Development
in a Northern City. Washington, D. C.: American Council
on Education, 1941. DHU/MO
Warren, Robert Penn. Segregation. New York: Random
House, 1956.   DHU/MO
Washington Conference on the
Race Problem in the United States.
National Sociological Society. How
to Solve the Race Problem.
The Proceedings of the...
Held at the Lincoln Temple
Congregational Church; Nineteenth Street Baptist Church
and Metropolitan A. M. E.
Church. Washington, D. C.;
Nov. 9-12, 1903. Washington,
D. C.: Beresford, Printer,
1904.   DHU/R
Weatherford, Willis Duke. Race
Relations; Adjustment of

Whites and Negroes in the United States. Boston; New York: D. C. Heath & Co., 1934. CtY-D
Moral condition of Negroes.

Weaver, Robert C. "Community Action Against Segregation." Social Action (13:1, Ja., 1947), pp. 4-24. DHU/R
Includes discussion of Church action in Chicago. Negro author.

Wentzcl, Fred De Hart. Epistle to White Christians. Philadelphia: Christian Education Press, 1948.
CtY-D; NN/Sch; DHU/R

Whalen, William Joseph. The Latter-Day Saints in Modern World; an Account of Contemporary Mormonism. New York: John Day Co., 1964.
NN/Sch
"Mormonism and the Negro," pp. 245-57.

White, Frank L. "The Integration of Negro Chaplains in the Armed Forces." M. Div. Paper, School of Religion, Howard University, 1968.
Negro author.

White, P. J. "Jim Crow's Last Stand." Crisis (57; Je., 1950), pp. 349-51. DHU/MO

Whitsett, Dan C. "A Deep South Pastor Looks at Segregation." New Christian Advocate (2:2, Feb., 1958), pp. 8-11.
DHU/R
Steps a church can take to break segregation.

"Will the Church Remove the Color Line?" Christian Century (49; Dec. 9, 1931), pp. 1554-56. DHU/R

Williams, Alice Elizabeth. "An Analysis of the Ethical Theory and Social Thought of Buell Gallagher as Foundation Principles for Religious Education in Race Relations." Master's thesis, Howard University, 1964.

Williams, Robin Murphy. The Reduction of Inter-group Tensions: A Survey of Research on Problems of Ethnic, Racial, and Religious Group Relations. Prepared Under the Direction of the Committee on Techniques for Reducing Group Hostility. New York: n. p., 1947.
CtY-D

Wilson, Cody. "Extrinsic Religious Values and Prejudice." Journal of Abnormal and Social Psychology (Mr., 1960), pp. 286-91. DHU

Wilson, Frank T. "The Present Status of Race Relations in the United States." Journal of Religious Thought. (2:1, Aut. - Wint., 1945), pp. 30-41.
DHU/R
Negro author.

Woodson, Carter Goodwin. The Education of the Negro Prior to 1861. Washington, D. C.: The Associated Publishers, 1919. DHU/R
"Chapters II and VIII role of churches in educating Negroes."
Negro author.

-- (ed.). The Works of Francis J. Grimke. Washington, D. C.: Associated Publishers, 1942. DHU/R; DHU/MO

Woodward, C. Vann. "The Southern Ethic in a Puritan World." William and Mary Quarterly (Jl., 1968). DAU
Professor Woodward undertakes a fresh examination of the venerable dispute regarding Southern myths and their relation to the Southern ethic.

Yale Divinity School Seminar. Whither the Negro Church? Seminar held at Yale Divinity School, New Haven, Conn., April 13-15, 1931. New Haven: City Printing Co., Inc., 1932.
DHU/MO; CtY-D; NN/Sch

Yard, James M. "Color Tests the Church." Christian Cen-

(Yard, J. M. cont.)
tury (60; Sept. 29, 1943), pp.
1100+.   DHU/R
Young, Andrew J. "The Church
and Citizenship: Education of
the Negro in the South." Lewis

S. C. Smythe, (ed.). Southern
Churches and Race Relations.
(Lexington, Ky., The College of
the Bible, 1963), pp. 64-81.
        Pam. File, DHU/R
Negro author.

E. BIBLE AND RACE RELATIONS

Anthropology for the People; a
Refutation of the Theory of
the Adamic Origin of All
Races. By Caucasian (pseud.).
Richmond, Va.: Everett Wod-
dey Co., 1891.   TNF
Ariel, Buckner H. Payne. The
Negro: What is His Ethnologi-
cal Status? Is He the Progeny
of Ham? Is He a Descendant
of Adam and Eve--What is His
Relation to the White Race?
Cincinnati: n.p., 1867.
                       DHU/MO
Beach, Waldo. "A Theological
Analysis of Race Relations."
Paul Ramsey, (ed.). The The-
ology of H. Richard Niebuhr.
New York: Harper & Bros.,
1957, pp. 205-24.
Brown, James Russell. "An Ex-
amination of the Thesis that
Christianity in its Genesis was
a Technique of Survival for an
Underprivileged Minority"...
B.D. Paper, School of Religion,
Howard University, 1935.
"Christian Morality and Race
Issues." Life (56; Mar. 27,
1964), p. 4.   DHU
"Christian Preaching and Race Re-
lations." Interracial Review (37;
Je., 1964), pp. 115-17.DHU
Clark, H. B. "Basic Sources of
Race Relations Literature."
Union Seminary Quarterly Re-
view (20:3, Mr., 1965), p.
348.   DHU/R
Clarke, William Francis. The
Folly of Bigotry; an Analysis
of Intolerance. Chicago: Non-
Sectarian League for Ameri-

canism, 1940.   NN/Sch
Dean, Henry Talmadge. "Chris-
tian Implications in the Pro-
gram of the National Associa-
tion for the Advancement of
Colored People." Master's
thesis, Howard University,
1939.
Derricks, Cleavant. Crumbs
From the Master's Table.
New York: Pageant Press,
1955.   DHU/R
Negro author.
Farmer, James. "The Relation
Between Religion and Racism
with a Special Reference to
Christianity and the American
Scene." Master's thesis, How-
ard University, 1941.
Flow, J. E. "Is Segregation Un-
Christian?" Southern Presby-
terian Journal (10; Ag. 29,
1951).   DLC; KyLxCB
Gallagher, Buell G. "Conscience
and Caste: Racism in the
Light of the Christian Ethic."
Journal of Religious Thought
(2:1, Aut.-Wint., 1945), pp.
20-29.   DHU/R
Gilbert, Arthur. "The Bible
Speaks on Segregation." Chris-
tian Friends Bulletin (14:2, Apr.
1957), pp. 3-6.   DLC
Gillis, James M. "The Crime
of Cain." Opportunity (12:6,
Je., 1934), pp. 175, 185.
                     DHU/MO
Hershberger, Guy Franklin. The
Way of the Cross in Human
Relations. Scottdale, Pa.:
Herald Pr., 1958.   INU
Church and Race Problems,

pp. 333-41.
Kitagawa, Daisuke. "The Church
and Race Relations in Bibli-
cal Perspective." Religious
Education (59:1, Ja. -Feb.,
1964), pp. 7-10.   DHU/R
Little, Sara. Youth Guide on
Race Relations. New York:
Friendship Press, 1957.
                    NN/Sch; DLC
Lupton, D. E. Does the "Bible
Support Segregation?" Negro
Digest (11; Jl., 1962), pp. 77-
81.   DHU/MO
MacArthur, Kathleen W. The
Bible and Human Rights. New
York: Woman's Press, 1949.
                    DHU/R
Chapter, The Biblical bases
of human rights.
Maston, Thomas Bufford. The
Bible and Race. Nashville:
Boardman Press, 1959.
                DHU/R; CtY-D
-- "Biblical Teachings and Race
Relations," (reprint of ex-
cerpt). Review and Expositor
(56; Jl., 1959), pp. 233-43.
                    DLC; CtY-D
Mayer, M. "The Jim Crow
Christ." Negro Digest (13;
Feb. 1964), pp. 28-31.
                    DHU/MO
McColl, C. W. The Holy Ghost
in the Church and in the
Hearts of Believers. German-
town, Philadelphia: Press of
the Germantown Telegraph Co.,
1903.   DHU/MO
Miller, George Frazier. A Dis-
cussion: Is Religion Reason-
able? Mr. Clarence Darrow
Says Not to the Blackman...
Bishop Jones Says Yes...
Brooklyn: The Henne Press,
n. d.   DHU/MO
Negro author.
Morrisey, Richard A. Colored
People in Bible History. Ham-
mond, Ind.: Pr. for the Author by W. B. Conkey Co.,
1925.   DHU/MO
Moses, William Henry. Five

Commandments of Jesus, Mat-
thew 5:21-48... n. p., n. d.
                    DHU/MO
Negro author.
Nelson, John O. "New Testament
Power for Social Change."
Journal of Religious Thought
(15:1, Aut. -Wint., 1957-58),
pp. 5-14.   DHU/R
Nelson, William Stuart. "Our
Racial Situation in the Light of
the Judeo-Christian Tradition."
Repr. of Religious Education
(Mr. -Apr., 1944), pp. 74-77.
Pam. File, DHU/R
Negro author.
Orton, Hazel V. The American
Negro: A Series of Worship
Services to be Used in the
Junior Department of the
Church. New York: Methodist
Book Concern, 1929. NN/Sch
Payne, Buckner H. The Negro:
What is His Ethnological Stat-
us? Is He the Progeny of
Ham? Is He a Descendant of
Adam and Eve? ...What Is His
Relation to the White Race?
Enl., With A Review of His
Reviewers, Exhibiting the
Learning of "The Learned."
By Ariel, Pseud... Cincinnati:
Pub. for the Proprietor, 1872.
                    DHU/MO
Plecker, W. A. "Interracial
Brotherhood Movement, Is It
Scriptural?" Southern Presby-
terian Journal (5; Ja. 1, 1947),
pp. 9-10.   DLC; KyLxCB
Poinsett, Alex. "What the Bible
Really Says About Segrega-
tion." Ebony (17; Jl., 1962),
pp. 73-6.   DHU/MO
"Report on the Special Seminar
on: The Spiritual Implications
of Race and Culture." Social
Action (9:1, Ja. 15, 1943), pp.
37-43.   DHU/R
Richards, James McDowell. "The
Golden Rule and Racial Relationship." Presbyterian Outlook
(129; Apr. 21, 1947), pp. 5-6.
                NN/Sch; NcD; DLC

Robinson, William C. "Christ
Our Peace in Race Relations."
Southern Presbyterian Journal
(4; Jl., 1945). DLC; KyLxCB
Rooks, Charles Shelby. "The
Bible and Citizenship." So-
cial Action (25:2, Oct., 1958),
pp. 13-21. Pam. File, DHU/R
Rose, Stephen C. "Religion and
Race." Christianity and Crisis
(23; Feb. 4, 1963), pp. 39-43.
                                    DHU/R
"The Spiritual Implication of
Race and Culture in Our De-
mocracy." Social Action (9:1,
Ja. 15, 1943), pp. 20-21.
                                    DHU/R
Findings of a meeting in
Cleveland, Ohio, Dec. 8-9,
1942, sponsored by "Eight Co-
operating Interdenominational
Bodies."
Steele, Algernon Odell. The
Bible and the Human Guest.
New York: Philosophical Li-
brary, 1956.   NN/Sch
Negro author.
Sullivan, Kathryn (Mother).
"Sacred Scripture and Race."
Religious Education (59:1, Ja. -
Feb., 1964), pp. 10-13.
                                    DHU/R
Thompson, Ernest Trice. "Jesus
Among People of Other Races."
Presbyterian Outlook (131;
Mr. 21, 1949), pp. 13-14.
                    NN/Sch; DLC; NcD
Thompson, John Harry. "The

Negro Problem in Light of
New Testament Teachings."
B.D. Thesis, Graduate Semi-
nary, Phillips University,
1932.
Thurman, Howard. "God and the
Race Problem." Rufus M.
Jones. Together (Nashville:
Abingdon-Cokesbury Press,
1946), pp. 118-20.
            DHU/R; DHU/MO
Negro author.
-- Jesus and the Disinherited.
New York: Abingdon-Cokes-
bury Press, 1949.   DHU/R
-- Judgement and Hope in the
Christian Message." William
S. Nelson, (ed.). The Chris-
tian Way in Race Relations.
(New York: Harper & Bros.,
1948), pp. 229-35.   DHU/R
Tilson, Everett. Segregation
and the Bible. New York:
Abingdon Press, 1958. INU;
DHU/R; DHU/MO; CtY-D
Weimer, G. Cecil. "Christian-
ity and the Negro Problem."
Journal of Negro History (16:
1, Ja., 1931), pp. 67-78.
                            DHU/MO
West, Robert Frederick.
Preaching on Race. St. Louis:
Bethany Press, 1962.
                            NN/Sch
Zaugg, E. H. "The Present
Race Problem." Reformed
Church Review (3:3, Jl.,
1924), pp. 281-307. DHU/R

IV.   The Civil Rights Movement, c. 1954-1967

A.   THE CHURCH, SYNAGOGUE, AND INTEGRATION

1. General

Adkins, Rufus. "The Role of the Minister in the Civil Rights Movement of Little Rock Arkansas." B.D. Paper, School of Religion, Howard University, 1966.

Assenheimer, R. C. "Doing is the Difference; Student Interracial Ministry Reply. America (112; Apr. 17, 1965), pp. 560-1.   DHU

"Atlanta Manifesto," Theology Today (15:2, Jl., 1958), pp. 165-6.   DHU/R
    Statement by clergymen in Georgia on racial integration.

Baitzell, E. Digby. The Protestant Establishment: Aristocracy and Caste in America. New York: Random House, 1964.   DHU/R

Banner, William Augustus. "An Ethical Basis for Racial Understanding." Religious Education (59:1, Ja. -Feb., 1964), pp. 17-19.   DHU/R

Bernard, Raymond. "Protestant Work in Race Relations." Interracial Review (27; Ja., 1954), pp. 7-8.   DHU/MO

"Biracial Membership Exchange Scores Hit!" Pittsburgh Courier (Jl. 24; 1965).
    Pam. File, DHU/R

"Bishop Deplores Worshipers Shut-Out." World Outlook (24; Ja., 1964), p. 49.
    DHU/R; DAU/W

Blake, E. C. "Should Churches Speak Out on Race Problems

Here and Abroad?" Excerpts from Address, April 18, 1960. U. S. News & World Report (48; My. 2, 1960), pp. 100-03.   DHU

Blanchard, E. D. "National Council in Mississippi, Special Report." Christian Advocate (8; Aug., 13, 1964), p. 3.
    DAU/W; DHU/R

Bland, T. A. "Role of the Local Church In Human Relations." Review and Expositor (56; Jl., 1959), pp. 271-79.
    DLC; CtY-D

Boggs, Marion. "The Crucial Test of Christian Citizenship." New South (12; Jl. -Ag., 1957), pp. 7-8.   DHU/W
    Little Rock minister denounces legal hindrance toward solving the problem in America.

Boud, S. "Apartheid and the Church." Commonweal (72; Je. 3, 1960), pp. 250-3.
    DHU

Boyd, Malcolm. The Hunger, the Questions of Students and Young Adults. New York: Morehouse-Barlow, 1946.
    NN/Sch

Boyle, Sarah Patton and John Howard Griffin. "The Racial Crisis: An Exchange of Letters." Christian Century (May 22, 1968), pp. 679-83.
    DHU/R

Bryant, F. "On Integration in the Churches." Review and

(Bryant, F. cont.)
Expositor (53; Apr. , 1956),
pp. 200-06. DLC; CtY-D
Buchanan, H. A. "Church and
Desegregation (Sermon)."
Review and Expositor (52;
Oct. , 1955), pp. 475-82.
DLC; CtY-D
-- and B. W. Brown. "Integra-
tion: Great Dilemma of the
Church." Ebony (21; Je. ,
1966), pp. 163-4+. DHU
Burt, C. B. "From Grenda, Mis-
sissippi, a Minister Warns
Christians: Stand up or Get
Out!" Look (30; Dec. 27,
1966), pp. 34+. DHU
Campbell, Ernest Q. Christians
in Racial Crisis; a Study of
Little Rock's Ministry, by
Ernest Q. Campbell and Thos.
F. Pettigrew. Including
Statements on Desegregation
and Race Relation by the Lead-
ing Religious Denominations of
the United States. Washington:
Public Affairs Press, 1959.
DHU/R; CtY-D
-- and Thomas F. Pettigrew.
"Racial and Moral Crisis; The
Role of Little Rock Ministers."
American Journal of Sociology
(64; Mr. , 1959), pp. 509-16.
DHU
"Chicago Churches Try Integra-
tion." Christian Century (73;
Sept. 19, 1956), pp. 1080-81.
DHU
"Christian Views of Civil Rights."
America (115; Ag. 20, 1966),
p. 167. DHU
"Church and Civil Rights." Amer-
ica (111; Ag. 8, 1964), p.
122. DHU
"Church and Segregation." Life
(41; Oct. 1, 1956), pp. 46+.
DHU
"Church Elements in the Segre-
gation Struggle." Christian
Century (72; Je. 1, 1955), pp.
644+. DHU
"A Church Looks at Civil Rights
in North Carolina." New

South (18; Apr. , 1963), pp.
13-5. DHU/R
"Churches Teaching on Race."
America (115; Dec. 3, 1966),
p. 730. DHU
Churchill, A. A. "Church
Wavers in the South." Chris-
tian Century (73; Apr. 18,
1956), pp. 493+. DHU/R
"Churchmen and the Albany
Movement." Christianity Today
(6; Sept. 28, 1962), pp. 41-2.
DHU/R; DLC
"Civil Rights and Religion."
America (111; Jl. 25, 1964),
p. 79. DHU
Clark, Henry. "Churchmen and
Residential Desegregation."
Review of Religious Research
(5:3, Spr. , 1964), pp. 157-64.
DHU/R
Clark, Mary Twibill. Discrimi-
nation Today; Guidelines for
Civic Action. New York:
Hobbs, Dorman, 1966.
DHU/MO
"Clubs, Pistols and Rifles Block
Prayer Meet at Alabama Capi-
tol." Journal and Guide (Mr.
12, 1961), Pam. File, DHU/R
Cobb, Charles Earl. "Now More
Than Ever: the Church is
Challenged." Social Action (33:
4, Dec. , 1966), pp. 12-22.
DHU/R
    Negro author.
Cogley, John. "The Clergy Heeds
a New Call." New York Times
Magazine (My. 2, 1965). DHU
    Selma, Ala. , march and
church leaders involvement in
the civil rights movement.
Cole, Stewart Grant. Minorities
and the American Promise: the
Conflict of Principle and Practice. By Stewart G. Cole and
Mildred Wiese Cole; with a
foreword by William Heard Kil-
patrick. New York: Harper,
1954. (Bureau for intercultural
education publication series.
Problems of race and culture
in American education).

DHU/R; DHU/Sch
Church and Race Relations,
pp. 192-200.
Cox, Harvey. "Letter from Williamston." Christian Century
(80:49, Dec. 4, 1963), pp.
1516-18. DHU/R
North Carolina and protest.
Creger, Ralph and Erwin McDonald. A Look Down the Lonesome Road. Garden City,
N.Y.: Doubleday, 1964.
DHU/R
Fundamentalist Baptist minister offers a solution to the
"moral problem of integration."
Davies, Everett F. S. "The Negro Protest Movement: The
Religious Way." Journal of
Religious Thought (24:2, Aut. -
Wint., 1967-68), pp. 13-25.
DHU/R
Davis, Lloyd. "The Religious
Dimension of Interracial Justice." Interracial Review (35;
Feb., 1962), pp. 46-8.
DHU/R
"Dealing with Racial and Ethnic
Tensions." Christian Action
(19; Feb., 1964), pp. 6+.
ICU
"Delta Ministry." World Outlook
(24; Ag., 1964), pp. 14+.
DAU/W
DeMille, D. "All Race Church."
Sepia (7; Ag., 1959), pp. 68-
70. NN/Sch
Dinwoodie, W. "Missions' Council Considers Issue: Desegregation of Churches." Christian Century (72; Feb. 9,
1955), pp. 190+. DHU/R
Dollen, Charles, (ed.). Civil
Rights; a Source Book. Boston: St. Paul Editions, 1964.
NN/Sch
A compilation of excerpts
from writing of modern
Popes, statements from American Bishops, and quotations
from the New Testament dealing with the subject of civil

rights.
"Don't Come Unto Me: Negro
Admissions Cause Clergy
Sacking in Macon, Ga." New
Republic (155; Nov. 12, 1966),
pp. 9-10. DLC
"Drive on Discrimination Shows
Ecumenical Approach." Central Christian Advocate (139;
Feb. 15, 1964).
DHU/R; DAU/W
Eddy, Elizabeth M. "Student
Perspectives on the Southern
Church." Phylon (25:4, Wint.,
1964), pp. 369-81. DHU/MO
Eutsler, Frederick B. "A Theological Analysis of the Concept of Equality in American
Race Relations." Journal of
Religious Thought (17; Wint. -
Spr., 1960), pp. 3-14.
DHU/R
Also, Doctoral dissertation,
Yale University, 1957.
"Faith and Prejudice in Georgia;
Lovett Schools Whites-Only
Admission Policy." Time (82;
Nov. 15, 1963), p. 94. DHU
Fey, H. H. "Churches Meet Racial Crisis; with Test of Statement to Churches." Christian
Century (80; Dec. 18, 1963),
pp. 1572-3. DHU/R
Fey, Harold. "For Brotherhood
and Union." Christian Century
(76:24, Je. 16, 1954), pp.
726-28. DHU/R
Fichter, Joseph H. "American
Religion and the Negro." Daedalus: Journal of the American Academy of Arts and Sciences. (94:4, Fall, 1965), pp.
1085-1106. DHU/R; INU
"Role of organized religion
in the current Negro freedom
movement."
-- and George L. Maddox. "Religion in the South, Old and
New." John McKenney and Edgar Thompson, (eds.). The
South in Continuity and Change.
Durham, N.C.: Duke University Press, 1965. NcD

Foot, S. H. "On Reconciling
Races and Nations." World
Outlook (22; Mr., 1962), pp.
30+.   DAU/W
Frady, M. "God and Man in the
South; Church's Indifference
to Civil Rights Movement."
Atlantic Monthly (219; Ja.,
1967), pp. 37-42.   DHU
Frakes, Margaret. "Two
Churches Unafraid." Repr.
from the Christian Century
(Apr. 11, 1956), 4 pp.
Pam. File; DHU/R
Two all-white churches in
Chicago become interracial.
Franklin, John Hope and Isidore
Starr. The Negro in the 20th
Century; A Reader on the
Struggle for Civil Rights. New
York: Vintage Books, 1967.
DHU/R
Pp. 203-07, religious lead-
ers and civil rights. Also
Martin Luther King and S. C.
L. C.
Negro author.
Fraser, T. P. "Desegregation
and the Church." Union Semi-
nary Quarterly Review (11:3,
Mr. 1956), pp. 37-9. DHU/R
Friedrichs, R. W. "Christians
and Residential Exclusion."
Journal of Social Issues (15;
1959), pp. 14-23.   DHU/R
Fry, H. W. "On Race Relations."
Christian Century (81; Sept. 9,
1964), pp. 1121-2.   DHU/R
Gardner, E. C. "Justice and
Love." Theology Today (14:2,
Jl., 1957), pp. 212-22.
DHU/R
"Glorious Opportunity; Establish-
ment of Emergency Commis-
sion on Religion and Race."
Newsweek (62; Jl. 8, 1963),
p. 55.   DHU
Goodman, D. "Churches and Civ-
il Rights." Central Christian
Advocate (140; Oct. 15, 1965),
pp. 5+.   DAU/W; DHU/R
Graham, Billy. "Why Don't Our
Churches Practice the Brother-

hood They Preach?" Reader's
Digest (77; Ag. 1960), pp. 52-
6.   DHU
Gremley, W. "Negroes in Your
Parish." America (107; Sept.
1962), pp. 817-19. Reply.
Ahmann, M. (107; Apr. 14,
1962), p. 35.   DHU
Hadden, Jeffrey K. "Clergy In-
volvement in Civil Rights."
Annals of the American Acad-
emy of Political & Social Sci-
ence (387; Ja., 1970), pp.
118-27.   DHU
Hanish, Joseph J. "Catholics,
Protestants and the American
Negro." Nuntius Aulae (43;
1961), pp. 98-115.
Pam. File; DHU
Harper, L. Alexander. "School
Integration--Search for a Chris-
tian Context." Social Action
(32:1, Sept., 1965), pp. 31-
37.   DHU/R
Haselden, Kyle Emerson. "11
a. m. Sunday is Our Most Seg-
regated Hour." NY Times
Magazine (Ag. 2, 1964), p. 9+.
DHU
Hays, Brooks. A Southern Mod-
erate Speaks. Chapel Hill:
University of North Carolina
Press, 1959.   NN/Sch
Church and Race Relations,
pp. 195-215.
Hazzard, Walter R. "Why Ne-
groes Want Integration." Cen-
tral Christian Advocate (131:
12, Je. 15, 1956), pp. 4-6.
DHU/R
Henderlite, R. "Christian Way in
Race Relations." Theology To-
day (14; Jl., 1957), pp. 195-
211.   DHU/R
Hill, Samuel S. Southern Church-
es in Crisis. New York:
Holt, Rinehart and Winston,
1969.   DLC; DHU/R
Negro church, pp. 92+.
--"Southern Protestantism and
Racial Integration." Religion
in Life (33:3, Sum., 1964),
pp. 421-29.   DHU/R

"Historic Pulpit Swap; Negro and White Pastors Exchange Homes, Too." Ebony (12:12, Oct. 1957), pp. 69-70+. DHU/MO

"Hollow Gesture or Omens of Unity? Election of Negroes to Highest Honorary Posts in White-Dominated Protestant Churches." Christian Century (82; Jl. 14, 1965), p. 884. DHU/R

Horchler, Richard. "The Layman's Role in the Changing Community." Interracial Review (35; Ja., 1962), pp. 12-13. DHU/R

Hughley, Judge Neal. "The Church, the Ministry, and the Negro Revolt." Journal of Religious Thought (22:2, 1965-66), pp. 121-40. DHU/R
Negro author.

-- "Integration in the Church." Theology Today (14:2, Jl., 1957), pp. 223-28. DHU/R

Hurley, Phillip S. "Role of the Churches in Integration." Journal of Intergroup Relations (1; Sum., 1960), pp. 41-6. DLC

"Integration Hits the Churches." Ebony (13; My., 1958), pp. 43-4. DHU/MO

"Integration Lacks in Northern Churches." Christian Century (72; Oct. 12, 1955), pp. 1165+. DHU/R

Jordan, Clarence. "Christian Community in the South." Journal of Religious Thought (14:1, Aut. -Wint., 1956-57), pp. 27-36. DHU/R

Keedy, T. C. "Anomic and Religious Orthodoxy." Sociology and Social Research (43; 1958), pp. 34-7. DHU

Kelsey, George D. "Churches and Freedom." Journal of Religious Thought (14:1, Aut. -Wint., 1956-57), pp. 17-26. DHU/R
Negro author.

-- "The Ethico-Cultural Revolu-

tion in American Race Relations." Religion in Life (26:3, Sum., 1957), pp. 335-44. DHU/R

King, C. H. "Negro Ministers Have Not Failed. Have Sociologists?" Negro Digest (13; Nov., 1963), pp. 43-4. DHU/MO

Kitagawa, Daisuke. "The Pastor and the Race Issue." Motive (26; Oct., 1965), pp. 54+. DHU/R; DAU/W
Book review.

-- "Theological and Non-Theological Factors in Race Relations." Ecumenical Review (13:3, Apr., 1961), pp. 335-41. DHU/R

Kramer, Alfred S. "The Churches and Race Relations." News Service (34; Ja. -Feb., 1963), pp. 4-5. NN/Sch; CtY

Kruuse, Elsa. "The Churches Act on Integration." National Council Outlook (7; Mr., 1957), pp. 6-8. DHU/R

Lawrence, N. "Racially Inclusive Churches." National Council Outlook (4; Dec., 1954), pp. 10-12. DHU/R

Lee, J. Oscar. "Churches and Race Relations." Christianity and Crisis (17; Feb. 4, 1957), pp. 4-7. DAU/W

-- "The Freedom Movement and the Ecumenical Movement." The Ecumenical Review (17:1, Ja., 1965), pp. 18-28. DHU/R

-- "The Status of the Racial Integration in Religious Institutions." Repr. from The Journal of Negro Education, 1954, pp. 231-41.
Pam. File; DHU/R

Lincoln, Charles Eric. "Weep for the Living Dead." Christian Century (85:18, My. 1, 1968), p. 578. DHU/R
Negro author.

Long, Herman H. "Beyond Tokenism." Social Action (30:1,

(Long, H. H. cont.)
Sept. , 1963), pp. 5-13.
DHU/R
Negro author.
"Looking and Listening." Crisis
(65; Apr. , 1958), pp. 222-23.
DHU/MO
"Looking at the Other Side of
Church Inclusiveness." Cen-
tral Christian Advocate (140;
Jl. 1, 1965), p. 3.
DAU/W; DHU/R
"Many Methodists March." Cen-
tral Christian Advocate (138;
Oct. 15, 1963), p. 14.
DHU/R; DAU/W
Marcis, C. L. "Next Steps for
Churches in Race Relations."
Social Action (26; Sept. , 1959),
pp. 24-27.   DHU/R
Marx, Gray T. "Religion: Opi-
ate or Inspiration of Civil
Rights Militancy." Hart M.
Nelsen & Raytha L. Yokley,
et al. The Black Church in
America. (New York: Basic
Books, 1971), pp. 150-60.
DHU/R
Mather, P. B. "Religion and
Race; Local Efforts." Chris-
tian Century (80; Mar. 27,
1963), pp. 412-14.   DHU/R
Mays, Benjamin Elijah. "Church
Will be Challenged at Evan-
ston." Christianity and Crisis
(14:14, 1954), pp. 106-08.
DHU/R
Negro author.
--"Churches Will Follow."
Christian Century (81; Apr.
22, 1964), pp. 513-14.
DHU/R
McCoy, C. "Way Toward Inte-
gration." Christian Century
(75; Feb. 12, 1958), pp. 195-
7.   DHU
McGill, Ralph. "The Agony of
the Southern Minister." New
York Times Magazine (Sept.
27, 1959).   DHU
McMillan, G. "Silent White Min-
isters of the South." N. Y.
Times Magazine (Apr. 5,

1964), pp, 22+.   DHU
Merton, Thomas. "The Hot Summer of Sixty-Seven." Katallagete (Wint. , 1967-68), pp.
28-34.   DHU/R
A Catholic's criticism of
black militancy and a call for
the return to Dr. King's philosophy of non-violence.
"Methodist Bishops Evade Big
Issues." Christian Century
(73; My. 9, 1956), pp. 573+.
DHU/R
Meyers, R. N. "Christian Service Corp." Christianity Today
(8; Jl. 17, 1964), pp. 11-13.
DHU/R
"Militant Clergy; Critics Fire
Back." U. S. News (63; Nov.
27, 1967), pp. 66-8.   DHU
Miller, F. P. "Southern Protes-
tants and Desegregation."
New Republic (141; Nov. 2,
1959), pp. 17-18.   DGU
Miller, William Robert. Nonvio-
lence; A Christian Interpreta-
tion. New York: Association
Press, 1964.   DHU/R
Minear, L. "Hattiesburg: To-
ward Reconciliation; Hatties-
burg Ministers Project."
Christian Century (81; Mar.
11, 1964), pp. 340-1.
DHU/R
"Ministers' Statement of Convic-
tion on Race." New South (12;
Apr. , 1957), pp. 3-6.
DAU/W
Ministers Association of
Richmond, Va.
"Miracle in Kentucky; In Blue
Grass State Black and White
Work, Pray, Eat and Sleep
Together." Our World (8; Ag.
1953), pp. 20-26+.
DLC; DHU/MO
Mitchell, Henry H. "Toward a
New Integration." Christian
Century (85; Je. 12, 1968),
pp. 780-2.   DHU/R
Negro author.
Moellering, Ralph Luther. Chris-
tian Conscience and Negro

Emancipation. Philadelphia:
Fortress Press, 1965. NcD;
CtY-D; NN/Sch; DLC; A&M
"Negro Kneel-ins in White
Churches in Savannah, Ga."
New South (20; Jl. -Aug., 1965),
pp. 2, 8, 12.   DHU/R
Nelson, J. Robert. "Race and
Denomination--One Issue."
Christian Century (78; Dec.
27, 1961), pp. 1554-55.
                       DHU/R
"New Commitments of Religions
in Civil Rights; John LaFarge
Institute Report." America
(114; Feb. 26, 1966), pp. 292-
3.   DHU
Nichols, L. and L. Cassels.
"Churches Repent." Harper's
(211; Oct., 1955), pp. 53-7.
                        DLC
"No Panacea (Editorial)." Christian Century (82:34, Ag. 25,
1965), pp. 1027-28.
    Comments on the civil dis-
turbances in Watts and the
possible inadequacies of the
Civil Rights Act of 1964 and
the Voting Rights Act of 1965.
Northwood, Lawrence K. "Eco-
logical and Attitudinal Factors
in Church Desegregation."
Social Problems (6; Fall,
1958), pp. 150-63.   DAU
"183 Churches: No Color Bar."
Christian Advocate (6; Mr.
15, 1962), pp. 23+.
            DHU/R; DAU/W
Osborne, William. "The Church
and Negro: A Crisis in Leadership." Cross Currents (15;
Wint., 1965), pp. 129-50.
                       DHU/R
"The Other Mississippi." New
South (18; Mr., 1963), pp. 1+.
                       DHU/R
    Whole issue. Including
statements by groups of the
state's ministers.
Paton, Alan. "Church Amid Racial Tensions. Issue Con-
fronting the 1954 World Council Assembly." Christian

Century (71; Mr., 31, 1954),
pp. 393-4.   DHU/R
Pettigrew, Thomas F. "Where
in the Church has Failed in
Race." Religious Education
(59:1, Ja. -Feb., 1964), pp.
64-75.
    DAU/W; DCU/TH; DHU/R
Pope, Liston. "A Check of Procedures for Racial Integration." Social Action (13:1, Ja.
1947), pp. 38-43.   DHU/R
    Discusses what churches
can do to aid integration.
Porteous, A. C. "Seminary and
the Racial Crisis; Consulta-
tion on the Church and the
Racial Crisis." Christian Cen-
tury (81; Jan. 29, 1964), pp.
147-8.   DHU/R
"Prayers on Steps of Harlem
Hospital." Amsterdam News
(Ag. 4, 1956).   DHU/MO
"Preaching on Civil Rights."
America (111; Oct. 31, 1964),
p. 506.   DHU
"President Calls Chruchmen on
Race." Christian Advocate (7;
Jl. 4, 1963), p. 24. DAU/W
Prestwood, Charles M. "Dilem-
mas of the Deep South Clergy."
Christianity Today (5; Ja.,
1961), pp. 8-9.   DLC
"Protestant-Jewish-Roman Cath-
olic Conversation on the Sit-
Ins." Presbyterian Outlook
(142; Mr. 20, 1960), pp. 3-7.
                       NNUT
"Protestantism Speaks on Justice
and Integration." Christian
Century (75; Feb. 5, 1958),
pp. 164-6.   DHU/R
"Race and Religion." Common-
weal (64; Je. 22, 1956), pp.
290+.   DHU/R
-- Nation (197; Dec. 7, 1963), p.
378.   DHU
"Race Held Major Challenge to
U. S. Protestantism." Concern
(7; Mr. 15, 1965), p. 15.
                       DAU/W
"Racial Integration in the
Churches." Social Action (22;

("Racial Integration... cont.)
Dec. , 1955), p. 27.   DHU/R
"Racism; the Nation's False
Religion." Christian Century
(80; Feb. 6, 1963), p. 166.
                        DHU/R
"Reconciliation Through Anger:
Delta Ministry." Time (86;
Jl. 2, 1965), pp. 70-1. DHU
"Reformed Churches Take Strong
Stand on Race." Christian
Century (81; Sept. 2, 1964),
p. 1077.   DHU/R
"Religious Leaders Demand Civil
Rights Bill." Christian Cen-
tury (81; My. 13, 1964), p.
631.   DHU/R
"Religious Leaders Give Thanks
For Civil Rights Bill Pas-
sage." Concern (6:14, Jl. ,
1964).   DAU/W
"Report of a Housing Project Un-
dertaken by the Monthly Meet-
ing of the Religious Society of
Friends in Syracuse, New
York, 1954-55."
            Pam. File; DHU/R
"One Quaker Group's Ef-
forts to Integrate and Make
Available Better Housing for
Negroes."
Reston, James. "The Churches,
the Synagogues, and the March
on Washington." Religious
Education (59:1, Ja. -Feb. ,
1964), pp. 5+.
    DHU/R; DAU/W; DCU/TH
Reuter, George Sylvester. One
Blood; the Christian Approach
to the Civil Rights. New
York: Exposition Press, 1964.
DHU/MO; CtY-D; DLC; INU
"Rich Long Island's Church."
Color (11; Apr. , 1957), pp.
42-3.   TNF
"The Roots of Immorality in Race
Relations." Religious Educa-
tion (58; Mr. -Apr. , 1963), pp.
91-6.   DHU/R
Rose, Peter Isaac. They and We,
Racial and Ethnic Relations in
the United States. New York:
Random House, 1964. DHU/R

Religious groups in the
United States, pp. 64-6.
Rose, Stephen C. "Epitaph for
an Era." Christianity and
Crisis (23:10, Je. 10, 1963),
pp. 103-10.   DHU/R
Rountree, Malachi D. "The Ecumenical Movement and the Racial Problem in the Greater
Washington Area." B.D. Pa-
per, School of Religion, Howard University, 1964.
Negro author.
Rowland, Stanley J. "Jim Crow
in Church." Nation (182; My.
19, 1956), pp. 426-8. DHU
Roy, Ralph Lord. "Church Race
Policies Compared." The
Christian Century (73:22, My.
30, 1956), pp. 664-5. DHU/R
Ruark, G. "Carolinians See Racial Progress." Christian Century (71; Dec. 1, 1954), pp.
1472+.   DHU/R
Schneider, Louis, (ed.). Reli-
gion, Culture and Society.
New York: Wiley, 1964.
                        DHU/R
Negro ministers and the
civil struggle.
Schomer, H. "Race and Religion
in Albany." Christian Century
(79; Sept. 26, 1962), pp. 1155-
6.   DHU
Schulz, Larold K. "The Delta
Ministry." Social Action (31:
3, Nov. , 1964), pp. 30-34.
                        DHU/R
Schuyler, Joseph B. Northern
Parish. A Sociological and
Pastoral Study. Chicago:
Loyola University Press, 1961.
                         DCU
Survey of a Bronx parish,
showed majority favoring ra-
cial equality.
"Segregation and the Churches."
Time (65; Je. 30, 1955), pp.
54+.   DHU
"Selma, Civil Rights and the
Church Militant." Newsweek
(65; Mar. 29, 1965), pp. 75-
6.   DHU

"Seven Protestant Denominations Join Forces in Seattle Through CURE." Concern (6; Feb. 15, 1964), p. 15.   DAU/W

Seymour, R. "Interracial Ministry in North Carolina; What it was Like for a Southern White Church to have a Negro Assistant on its Staff." Christian Century (80; Sept. 15, 1962), p. 109.   DHU

Shepherd, Wilhelmina. "A Simple, Easy Way to Improve Racial Understanding." Religious Education (59:1, Ja. -Feb., 1964), pp. 84-5.   DHU/R

Smith, Elwyn A. "Stalemate in Selma." Christian Century (82: 34, Ag. 25, 1965), pp. 1031-33.   Pam. File; DHU/R
A perceptive analysis of the frustration which followed the marches in Selma, Alabama.

Southard, S. "Are Southern Churches Silent." Christian Century (80; Nov. 20, 1963), pp. 1429-32.   DHU/R

"Southern Desegregation; Protestant Churches." Time (84; Dec. 4, 1964), p. 94+.   DHU

"Southern Ministers Stand Up to Mobs." Christian Century (73; Oct. 10, 1956), pp. 1155+.   DHU/R

Spike, Robert W. "Civil Rights Involvement, Model for Mission: A Message to Churchmen." Detroit Industrial Society (No. 9, Nov., 1965).
          Pam. File; DHU/R
A series of occasional papers on Christian Faith and Industrial Society.

-- "Fissures in the Civil Rights Movement." Christianity and Crisis (26:2, Feb. 21, 1966), p. 21.   DHU/R

-- The Freedom Revolution and the Churches. New York: Association Press, 1965.
          DHU/R; INU; NcD; DLC

-- "Mississippi: an Ecumenical Ministry." Social Action (31:3, Nov., 1964), pp. 16-18.   DHU/R

Spivey, R. A. "Integration and the South: the South as a Cultural Unit." Union Seminary Quarterly Review (11; Mr., 1956), pp. 33-36.   DHU/R

Stagg, Paul Leonard. "A Minister's Involvement in the Racial Crisis." The Journal of Religious Thought (16:2, Sum. - Aut., 1959), pp. 77-94.
          DHU/R

"Stand and be Counted; Roman Catholics, Jews and Protestants Support Civil Rights Bill." Newsweek (63; My. 11, 1964), p. 90.   DHU

Stepp, Diane. "Ministers to Picket Food Chain." Atlanta Journal (Nov. 2, 1968),
          Pam. File; DHU/R

Stirewalt, M. L. "Observations on the Church and Segregation." Lutheran Quarterly (9; Ag., 1957), pp. 254-59.   DHU/R

Stringfellow, William. "Race Religion and Revenge; Negroes in New York's Harlem." Christian Century (79; Feb. 14, 1962), pp. 192-4.   DHU/R

Student Interracial Ministry Committee. Statement of Purpose. New York, Union Theological Seminary, n.d. "Racial Crisis: Complacency or Concern."
          Pam. File; DHU/R

"Student Perspectives on the Southern Church." Phylon (25; Wint., 1964), pp. 369-81.
          DHU/MO

"Summit Conference on Race, Religion." Ebony (18; Apr., 1963), pp. 43-4.   DHU/MO

Sweeney, Odile. "Sit Ins: American Students Seek Freedom from Indignity." Social Action (27:5, Ja., 1961), pp. 5-13.
          DHU/R

Taft, A. A. "Miami Spurns Integration." Christian Century (72; Oct. 19, 1955), pp. 1220+.
          DHU/R

Taves, I. "He Sees Competence, Not Color." Christian Herald (Oct., 1968), p. 29. DHU/R

"Texas Baptist for Racial Justice." Christian Century (73; Sept. 26, 1956), pp. 1091+. DHU/R

Thielicke, Helmut. Between Heaven and Earth Conversations with American Christians. New York: Harper & Row, 1965. DHU/R
Chapter VII, "Racial Integration and the Christian."

Tilson, Everett. "A Christian Brief for Integration." Journal of Religious Thought (18: 2, 1961-62), pp. 149-66. DHU/R

Towne, Anthony. "Revolution and the Marks of Baptism." Katallegete (Sum., 1967), pp. 2-13. DHU/R

Valentine, F. "The Court, The Church, and the Community." Review and Expositor (53; Oct., 1956), pp. 536-50. DLC; CtY-D

Warder, V. G. "Bounce Away From Church Integration." Music Ministry (5; Apr., 1964), pp. 12+. DAU/W; DHU/R

Weaver, Galen R. "Racial Integration in the Churches." Social Action (22:4, Dec., 1955), pp. 6-19. DHU/R

-- "There is Something You Can do For Human Relations in Your Church, in Your Community." New York Dept. of Race Relations, n.d. Pam. File; DHU/R

Webb, Maurice. "Race Tensions: Is a New Approach Possible?" Ecumenical Review (8:4, Jl., 1956), pp. 458-61. DHU/R

Westin, Alan R. Freedom Now! The Civil Rights Struggle in America. New York: Basic Books, 1964. INU
Pp. 297-306, the church and civil rights.

"When U.S. Churches Face Up to Integration." U.S. News & World Report (48; My. 16, 1960), pp. 61-3. DHU

White, W. L. "Los Angeles Aftermath Churches Respond to Racial Riots." Christian Advocate (9; Sept. 9, 1965), pp. 24+. DHU/R; DAU/W

Whitman, A. "How the Civil Right Struggle Challenges Our Churches." Redbook (125; Ag. 1965), pp. 55-7+. DLC
Also, Redbook (125; Sept. 1965), pp. 65+.

Wicklein, John. "The Church in the South and Segregation." New York Times (Jl. 5-8, 1959). DHU/R

Winter, Gibson. "Theology of Demonstration; Interrelation Between Freedom Movement and Christianity." Christian Century (82; Oct. 13, 1965), pp. 1249-52. DHU/R

Wofford, H. "Non-violence and the Law; the Law Needs Help." Journal of Religious Thought (15:1, Aut.-Wint., 1957-58), pp. 25-36. DHU/R
Churches role in non-violence.

"Wolf or Shepherd? Church Segregation in Alabama." Newsweek (65; Apr. 12, 1965), pp. 66-7. DHU

Zietlow, Carl P. "Race, Students, and Non-Violence." Religious Education (59:1, Ja.-Feb., 1964), pp. 116-20. DHU/R

2. Roman Catholic

Abbott, Walter M. "The Bible
Abused." Interracial Review
(36; Feb. 1963), pp. 26+.
DCU/SW
White Catholics who re-
sisted school desegregation.
Ahmann, Mathew. "Catholics
and Race." Commonweal (73;
Dec. 2, 1960), pp. 247-50.
DHU
Reply, W. V. D'Antonio
(73; Ja. 6, 1961), pp. 390-1.
--"Catholics and Racism in the
North." Catholic World (195;
Ag. 1962), pp. 266-74.
DHU/R
"Apostolic Delegate on Race."
America (105; Je. 3, 1961), p.
387.   DHU
Ball, William B. "New Frontiers
of Catholic Community Ac-
tion." Interracial Review (35;
Feb., 1962), pp. 49-51.
DCU/SW
Barrett, P. "Nuns in the Inner
City; Force for Freedom and
Creativity." Christian Century
(83; Ag. 31, 1966), pp. 1050-
3.   DHU/R
Bernard, Raymond. "The Negro
Prospect." Social Order (7;
Mr., 1957), pp. 135-6. Re-
view of The Negro Potential
by Eli Genzberg, and state-
ment of the responsibility of
Southern Catholics.
"Bishops Condemn Racial Injus-
tice." America (100; Nov. 29,
1958), p. 264.   DHU
"Bishops on Race." Commonweal
(69; Nov. 28, 1958), p. 219.
DHU
"Bishops on Racism." America
(109; Ag. 10, 1963), p. 127.
DHU
Canavan, Francis P. "Civil
Rights: Are They Moral
Rights, Too?" Catholic
World (187:1, 119, Je., 1958),

pp. 166-72.   DHU/R
"Cardinal in Harlem." America
(109; Jl. 17, 1963), p. 86.
DHU
"Cardinal McIntyre: A Ramparts
Special Report." Ramparts (3;
Nov., 1964), pp. 35-44.
DHU
Effect of Cardinal McIntyre's
refusal to support racial equal-
ity in Southern California.
"The Catholic Church in the Mod-
ern World. Statement Against
Racism." Interracial Review
(37; Dec., 1964), pp. 226.
DHU/MO
"Catholic Know-Nothings; Integra-
tionists and the Churches Ra-
cial Crisis in Chicago." News-
week (68; Ag. 29, 1966), pp.
641+.   DHU
"Catholic Sisters Have a Unique
Opportunity as Teachers to
Help Solve the Racial Prob-
lem." Interracial Review (29;
Je. 1960), p. 161. DHU/MO
"Catholic View on Segregation;
Tablet of London Editorial."
U. S. News (43; Oct. 4, 1957),
p. 124.   DHU
Reply. R. J. L'Hoste and
A. J. Pilie (43; Nov. 8, 1957),
p. 135.
"Catholics and Negroes." Amer-
ica (106; Dec. 9, 1961), p.
354.   DHU
"Catholics and Race." America
(109; Jl. 13, 1963; 110; Feb.
29, 1964), p. 33; pp. 276-7.
DHU
"Catholics and Racial Bias."
America (108; Mar. 16, 1963),
p. 351.   DHU
"Caution on Civil Rights; Opposi-
tion to Clerical Involvement."
Times (88; Ag. 26, 1966), p.
58.   DHU
"A Christian Approach, Social
Antipathies and the Christian

332   Afro-American Religious Studies

(A Christian Approach... cont.)
Remedy." Interracial Review
(34; My. 1961), pp. 281-82.
                       DHU/MO
  About South Africa.
"Church and Changing Urban Par-
  ish: Five Vignettes; Symposi-
  um." Catholic World (208; Dec.
  1968), pp. 117-28.   DHU/R
"Civil Rights Mass." America
  (104; Nov. 19, 1960), p. 253.
                           DHU
Clark, D. "City Catholics and
  Segregation." America (107;
  May 19, 1962), pp. 269-71.
  Reply: Baroni, G. C. (107; Je.
  30, 1962), p. 431.   DHU
-- "Philadelphia, Still Closed;
  Catholic Attitudes Toward Ra-
  cial Changes." Commonweal
  (80; My. 1, 1964).   DHU
"Cody All Alone." Christian
  Century (84; 10, Mr. , 1967),
  p. 302.   DHU/R
  Withdrawal of support from
  the Catholic interracial Coun-
  cil of Chicago by Archbishop
  Cody.
Cronin, J. F. "Interracial Justice:
  The Catholic Record." Social
  Order (11; Oct. , 1961), pp.
  345-55.   DHU
"Discrimination and the Christian
  Conscience." Journal of Negro
  Education (28:1, Wint. , 1959),
  pp. 66-9.   DHU/R
  Position of Catholic bishops
  in the United States.
"Doing is the Difference; Student
  Interracial Ministry." Amer-
  ica (112; Jan. 9, 1965), p. 33.
                           DHU
"Episcopal Leadership, Cardinal
  Cushing on Religious and Mor-
  al Responsibility of Catholics."
  America (111; Sept. 12, 1964),
  p. 249.   DHU
"Evasive Answers About Racial
  Change Given by Local Catho-
  lic Leaders." Interracial Re-
  view (Feb. , 1960), pp. 34-7.
                       DHU/MO
"For West Bishops on Race."

America (111; Sept. 12, 1964),
  p. 244.   DHU
"The Full Catholic Teaching in
  Racial Justice." Interracial
  Review (35; Oct. , 1962), pp.
  224-5.   DCU/SW
  Syllabus prepared by the Di-
  ocesan Department of Educa-
  tion, Charleston, S. C.
Gasnick, Roy M. "Franciscan
  Pledge to Interracial Justice."
  Social Order (12; Apr. , 1962),
  pp. 173-77.   DHU
-- "The Pope Speaks on Racism."
  The Homiletic and Pastoral Re-
  view (59; Je. , 1959), pp. 827-
  31.   DGU
Germillion, Joseph B. The Jour-
  nal of a Southern Pastor.
  Chicago: Fides Publishers As-
  sociation, 1957.   NN/Sch
Gibbons, R. W. "Blacklash and
  the Catholic Vote; Miller's
  Catholicism." Christian Cen-
  tury (81; Oct. 21, 1964), pp.
  1303-5.   DHU/R
Gillies, J. "Justice, Southern
  Style; Ashton Jones vs. Atlan-
  tas First Baptist Church."
  (Discussion) Christian Century
  (81; Feb. 26, 1964. 82; Je. 9,
  1965), pp. 270-2, 732.
                       DHU/R
Greeley, Andrew M. "White
  Parish--Refuge on Resource."
  Interracial Review (35; Jl. ,
  1962), pp. 168-9.   DHU/R
Gusweller, J. A. "Church and
  Community Action, Church of
  St. Timothy and St. Matthew,
  New York." Christian Century
  (76; Jl. 15, 1959), pp. 824-5.
                           DHU
Harbutt, Charles. "The Church
  and Integration." Jubilee (6;
  Feb. , 1959), pp. 6-15. DGU
Hartnett, Robert C. "The Divine
  Doctrine of Brotherhood."
  Interracial Review (35; Apr. ,
  1962), pp. 96-7.   DHU/R
"Heart of the Matter; Pastoral
  Letter Officially Banning Ra-
  cial Discrimination." Nation

(196; Mr. 16, 1963), p. 218.
DHU
Hellwig, M. "Crash Attack on
Prejudice, Suggestions for a
Parish Effort During Lent."
America (120; Feb. 15, 1969),
pp. 193-4. DHU
Holden, Anna. "A Call to Cath-
olics." Interracial Review (35;
Je., 1962), pp. 140-43. DHU
To participate in nonviolent
direct action movement.
"How Catholic Groups Should
Work to Integrate the Negro."
Interracial Review (38; Apr.,
1965), pp. 74+. DHU/MO
"How do Churches Get Involved?"
Christian Century (80; Apr.
3, 1963), p. 420. DHU/R
Hurley, Denis E. "Second, Vati-
can and Racism." Interracial
Review (36; Dec., 1963), p.
11. DHU/R
"Indicative Concession." Chris-
tian Century (84; 22 My.,
1967), p. 709. DHU/R
Unfavorable treatment given
Catholic Interracial Council by
Chicago Roman Catholic Arch-
diocese.
"Integration and the Christian
Conscience." Catholic Mind
(57; Oct., 1959), p. 469. DLC
"Interracial Council; Request for
Amendment Specify that It is
Un-Christian to Discriminate
on Grounds of Race." Amer-
ica (109; Nov. 9, 1963), p.
544. DHU
"Interracial Franciscans; Third
Order of St. Francis." Amer-
ica (105; Apr. 29, 1961), p.
206. DHU
"Interracial Justice." Catholic
International Outlook (17;
1956), pp. 21-22. DCU/ST
"Is Segregation at the End of Its
Rope?" Catholic World (183;
Apr., 1956), pp. 2-3.
DHU/R
La Farge, John. "American
Catholics and the Negro."
Social Order (12; Apr. 1962),

pp. 153-61. DHU
-- "Direct Action." Interracial
Review (36; Sept., 1963), pp.
159f. DCU/SW
Appeal to Catholic employ-
ers of labor.
-- "Pope John on Racism." Inter-
racial Review (36; Je., 1963),
pp. 110+. DCU/SW
-- "Why Say 'Interracial'?" In-
terracial Review (35; Feb.,
1962), pp. 44-45. DCU/SW
Mattingly, T. "Gwynn Oak; Nine
Catholic Priests Startled Bal-
timore by Joining with the
Pickets to Protest Segregation
at an Amusement Park."
America (109; Ag. 10, 1963),
pp. 136-7. Reply Gallagher,
F. K. (109; Sept. 14, 1963),
p. 249. DHU
McLees, A. V. "Catholic and
the NAACP." Crisis (63;
Je.-Jl., 1956), pp. 325-27+.
DHU/MO
McManus, Eugene P. Studies in
Race Relations. Baltimore:
Josephite, 1961. DHU/MO
An appeal for Christian
principles in race relations.
DLC
Mehan, Joseph. "Catholic Per-
spectives on Interracialism."
Interracial Review (35; Oct.,
1962), pp. 222-23. DCU/SW
"Mockery of Tokenism; Meeting
of Catholic Negroes and Whites
in Memphis." America (112;
Apr. 3, 1965), p. 444. DHU
"Moral Miracle; Cardinal Cush-
ing's Plea for Change of Atti-
tude Toward Negroes." Amer-
ica (110; Je. 6, 1964), p.
785. DHU
"National Catholic Conference for
Interracial Justice Commit-
ment." (Jl.-Ag., 1969).
Pam. File; DHU/R
"The National Catholic Confer-
ence for Interracial Justice
Launches a New Project to
Use Church Buying Power to
Fight Bias in Employment

(The Natl. Catholic Conference
cont.)
Against Negroes, Jews and
Other Minorities. Interracial
Review (37; Oct., 1964), pp.
178.   DHU/MO
National Catholic Conference for
Interracial Justice. "Statement
and Resolutions Adopted by
Council Delegates in Confer-
ence, November 17, 1963 at
Washington, D. C." Interracial
Review (37; Ja. 1964), pp. 1+.
              DCU/SW
"Negro Dilemma: The Catholic
Parish." Interracial Review
(36; Sept., 1963), pp. 167-69+.
              DHU/MO
"No Postponement; Concerning
Jesuit Letter on the Race
Question." America (109; Dec.
14, 1963), pp. 762-3.   DHU
"Nuns at Selma Sister Thomas
Marguerite." America (112;
Apr. 3, 1965), pp. 454-6.
              DHU
O'Connor, John J. "Catholic In-
terracial Movement." Social
Order (10; Sept., 1960), pp.
290-95.   DCU/SW
Palms, Charles L. "A Harlem
Priest Reports on Salem."
Catholic World (201:1, 203, Je.,
1965), pp. 171-76.   DHU/R
An interview with Fr. Ed-
ward T. Dugan.
Pohlhaus, J. Francis. "Catholic
Involvement in Civil Rights
Legislation." Interracial Re-
view (36; Oct., 1963), pp.
192-95.   DCU/SW
"Priestly Witness; Protest
Against Failure of the Arch-
diocese to Take Leadership on
Civil Rights Issues." America
(112; Jan. 16, 1965), pp. 66+.
              DHU
"Priests in Protest." America
(109; Jl. 27, 1963), p. 91.
              DHU
"Priests' Pledge on Race."
America (109; Oct., 1963), p.
376.   DHU

"Priests' Protest." Time (85;
Jan. 8, 1965), p. 38. DHU
"Racial Agenda for Catholics."
Christianity Today (12; My.
24, 1968), p. 39.   DHU/R
"Racial Polls; Attitude of Catho-
lics." America (111; Nov. 7,
1964), p. 541.   DHU
"Religion and Race." America
(110; My. 16, 1964), p. 662.
              DHU
"Religion and Race; Moves of
Protestant Communions to Fos-
ter Racial Unity." America
(110; Je. 6, 1964), p. 785.
              DHU
"Rev. William L. Lane Made
History When He Was Named
the First Negro Priest to
Serve a Racially Mixed Congre-
gation." Sepia (14; My., 1965),
p. 35.   DHU/MO
Schuyler, Joseph B. "Apostolic
Opportunity." Interracial Re-
view (35; Ja., 1962), pp. 20-
21.   DCU/SW
Senser, Robert. Primer on In-
terracial Justice. Baltimore:
Helicon, 1962.   DHU/MO
Catholic viewpoint.
Sheerin, John B. "Catholic Involvement in Civil Rights."
Catholic World (201:1, 201,
Apr., 1965), pp. 93-96.
              DHU/R
Split-Level Lives; American Nuns
Speak on Race, edited by Sis-
ter Mary Peter Traxler.
Techny, Ill.: Divine Word
Publications, 1967. DHU/MO
Essays developed from lec-
tures, experiences, and semi-
nars by members of traveling
workshop teams sponsored by
the National Catholic Confer-
ence for Interracial Justice.
Thomas, Howard E. Organizing
for Human Rights; a Handbook
for Teachers and Students, by
Howard E. Thomas and Sister
Mary Peter. Dayton, O.: G.
A. Pflaum, 1966.   DLC
Thorman, Donald J. "Catholic

Approach to the Race Problem." America (95; My. 5,
1956), pp. 133-34.   DHU
"Toward Open Hiring; Anti-Dis-

crimination Pleges in Church
Contracts." Commonweal (81;
Ja. 15, 1965), p. 500. DHU

3. Congregational (United Church of Christ)

Artopoeus, Otto F. "Nonviolence-
Struggle Without Hate."
United Church Herald (6:8,
Apr. 18, 1963), pp. 16-17.
                        DHU/R
Barber, Carroll G. "Human
Rights and Public Interest."
United Church Herald (5:21,
Nov. 15, 1962), pp. 14+.
                        DHU/R
    Account of the Annual Race
Relations Institute held under
auspices of United Church of
Christ and the A.M.A.
"Clergy and Nuns March; No
Outsiders." America (112;
Mr. 27, 1965), p. 411. DHU
Congregational Christian Churches;
Council for Social Action. "Chris-
tian Social Action in the Con-
gregational Christian Churches,
1955-56." Pam. File; DHU/R
Gibbons, R. and H. F. Flemme.
"For Such a Time as This
Prospectus for Social Action
in the United Church of
Christ." Social Action (23; Je.
1957), pp. 12-22.   DHU/R
Hackett, Allen. "Let Us Wor-
ship Him Together." Social
Action (25:5, Ja., 1959), pp.
12-15.   DHU/R
    "A Reflection on Herman
Long's report: Racial Inclu-
siveness in Congregational
Christian Churches."
Maddocks, Lewis I. "Civil

Rights--1966." United Church
Herald (9:2, Ja. 15, 1966),
pp. 33+.   DHU/R
    Written by Washington sec-
retary for the U.C.C. Council
for Social Action.
"March on With Might." United
Church Herald (8:9, My. 1,
1965), pp. 2-3.   DHU/R
Parker, E. C. "United Church
of Christ General Synod."
Christian Century (84; Ag. 9,
1967), pp. 1026-8. DHU/R
"Recommendations by U.C.C.
Ministers for Racial and So-
cial Justice." Social Action
(34:1, Sept., 1967), pp. 36-
39.   DHU/R
Schulz, Larold K. "The United
Church of Christ Responds."
Social Action (31:3, Nov.,
1964), pp. 23-29.   DHU/R
    Discusses denomination's
response to Mississippi Sum-
mer, 1964.
United Church of Christ. Council
for Christian Social Action.
"Call to Christian Action in
Society." Social Action (26;
Sept., 1959), pp. 5-10.
                        DHU/R
    Section II Social Action (27;
Oct., 1960), pp. 22-3.
Weaver, Galen R. "Racial Prac-
tices in Congregational Chris-
tian Churches." Social Action
(25:5, Ja., 1959), pp. 3-11.
                        DHU/R

4. Disciples of Christ (Christian Churches)

Bingham, Walter. "Black Men Discover Themselves." World Call (51:6, Je., 1969), pp. 22-23.   DHU/R
Negro author.

Cartwright, Colbert S. "Christian Churches (Disciples of Christ) as Racial Ferment (in the South) accelerates Pastors and Congregations take Divided Stand on Issue." Christianity and Crisis (18; Mr. 3, 1958), pp. 18-20.   DHU/R

-- "Band Together for Genuine Unity." New South (16; Ja., 1961), pp. 6-10.   DAU/W
Little Rock minister's speech at Conference on Community Action.

"The 'Christian Churches' Become a 'Church'." Christianity Today (13:1, Oct. 11, 1968), pp. 40-41.   DHU/R
Disciples of Christ. Church's urban crisis program.

Fey, H. E. "Disciples on Civil Rights; International Convention of Christian Churches." Christian Century (80; Nov. 27, 1963), pp. 1326-7. DHU/R

Wallace, David M. "Beyond Boycotts." World Call (50:1, Ja., 1968), pp. 16-18.   DHU/R
Author, program director of Operation Breadbasket in Chicago, is a Disciple of Christ minister.

5. Friends--Quakers

Apsey, Lawrence S. and Elinore Atlee. "Defusers of Violence." Friends Journal (13:13, Jl. 1, 1967), pp. 351-52.   DHU/R

Bradley, Sam. "Martin Luther King and Freedom." Friends Journal (7:18, Sept. 15, 1961), pp. 370+.   DHU/R

Burton, John W. Nonalignment. New York: J. H. Heineman, 1966.   DHU/MO
Papers from a series of discussions held by the Friends of Peace and International Relations Committee in London, 1963.

"The First Civil Rights Act: Letter from the Past--228." The Friends Journal (13:8, Apr. 15, 1967), pp. 188-89.   DHU/R

Forbush, Bliss. "Integration in Baltimore Friends School." Friends Intelligencer (112:1, Ja. 1, 1955), pp. 7-8. DHU/R

Friends, Society of. American Friends Service Committee. Community Relations Program. The Public School System of Washington, D. C. Prepared by Irene Osborne Community Relations Program, American Friends Service Committee. September, 1953. Washington, D. C.: n. p., 1954.   NN/Sch

-- -- -- Toward the Elimination of Segregation in the Nation's Capitol; The Report of an AFSC Community Relations Project with Public Schools and Recreation Areas, 1951-1955. Philadelphia: American Friends Service Committee, Community Relations Program, 1955.   NN/Sch

-- -- Fair Housing Handbook; A Practical Manual for Those Who Are Working to Create and Maintain Inclusive Communities. Philadelphia: n. p.,

1964.   DHU/MO
-- Peace Committee. Philadelphia. "A Perspective on Nonviolence." Friends Journal (3:
14, Apr. 6, 1957), pp. 220-
29.   DHU/R
    "A practical study and an
inquiry into nonviolence, now
in America." Suggested for
First-day School classes and
study groups.
Hatch, Margaret L. D. "Selma
Still Has Problems." Friends
Journal (12:7, Apr. 1, 1966),
pp. 171-72.   DHU/R
Hearn, Winifred and Betty Stone.
"Course in Nonviolence."
Friends Journal (10:21, Nov.
1, 1964), pp. 500-01.
                        DHU/R
Hortenstine, Virgie B. "Message
from a Tennessee Prison."
Friends Journal (8:10, My. 15,
1962), pp. 209-10. DHU/R
-- "Work, Violence, and Faith in
Fayette County." Friends
Journal (9:22, Nov. 15, 1963),
pp. 484-86.   DHU/R
Loescher, Frank S. "A Reli-
gious Approach to Discrimina-
tion." Friends Journal (1:23,

Dec. 3, 1955), p. 364.
                        DHU/R
National Conference of Friends
on Race Relations, Black Moun-
tains, N. C., July 6-9. "Power:
Black, White, Shared."
Friends Journal (13:16, Ag. 15,
1967), p. 439.   DHU/R
Pemberton, John De J. "The Civ-
il Rights Revolution." Friends
Journal (10:11, Je. 1, 1964),
pp. 246-48.   DHU/R
Taylor, Richard K. "Religion and
Race." Friends Journal (9:4,
Feb. 15, 1963), pp, 81-2.
                        DHU/R
Tolles, Frederick B. "Friends
and Racial Discrimination."
Friends Journal (3:33, Ag. 17,
1957), pp. 533-34. DHU/R
Wixom, Robert L. "Letter from
Little Rock." Friends Journal
(4:19, My. 10, 1958), pp. 298-
300.   DHU/R
    Also, (4:20, My. 17, 1958),
pp. 313-15 and (4:18, My. 3,
1958), pp. 282-3.   DHU/R
Yungblut, John. "Triple Revolu-
tion in Atlanta." Friends
Journal (10:13, Jl. 1, 1964),
pp. 293-4.   DHU/R

6. Methodist Episcopal (United Methodist)

"Action Now: Integration Pro-
posal to be Debate at General
Conference." Together (7;
Nov. 1963), pp. 3-6.
            DAU/W; DHU/R
"Adopt Race Statement." Meth-
odist Layman (24; My., 1964),
p. 24.   DAU/W
"Adopt Strong Race Stand to
Study Church State." Christian
Advocate (8; My. 21, 1964),
p. 4+.   DAU/W; DHU/R
"Aid to Race Workers." Chris-
tian Advocate (8; Sept. 24,
1964), p. 24. DAU/W; DHU/R
"Alabama Bishop Calls for Re-
sponsibility and Patience."

Concern (7; Apr. 1, 1965), p.
14.   DAU/W
"All Persons May Attend Method-
ist Service." Concern (7; My.,
15, 1965), p. 15.   DAU/W
"Atlanta Ministers Ask Racial
Calm." Christian Century (74;
Nov. 13, 1957), p. 1340.
                          DHU
"Attempt to Integrate Churches
Result in Arrest." Together
(7; Dec., 1963), p. 8.
            DAU/W; DHU/R
Bagby, Grover C. "Methodism's
Fears of Racial Merger." Cen-
tral Christian Advocate (142:1,
Ja. 1, 1967), pp. 9+.

(Bagby, G. C. cont.)
        Pam. File; DHU/R
"Beyond Lip Service: Methodist Church's General Conference." Time (83; My. 15,
1964), p. 53.   DHU
Bibbons, J. C. "Analysis of Cur-
rent Nonviolence Movements."
Central Christian Advocate
(138; Sept. 15, 1963), pp. 4+.
                 DAU/W; DHU/R
"Bi-racial Church Council Re-
organized." Concern (4; Jl.
1, 1962), p. 17.   DAU/W
"Bishop Asks Methodists to Help
Ease Tension." Christian Advocate (8; Jl. 16, 1964), p.
22.   DHU/R; DAU/W
"Bishop Calls for Phalanx of
Freedom Riders." Central
Christian Advocate (136; Sept.
15, 1961), p. 7.
                 DAU/W; DHU/R
Campbell, Will D. "Starting
Place is Christian Race Relations." Motive (22; My, 1962),
p. 31+.   DHU/R
"Christian Social Concerns Up-
hold 'Right of Protest' In Discipline." Central Christian Advocate (139; Apr. 15, 1964),
p. 14.   DHU/R; DAU/W
"Church Segregation Denounced
by Bishops." Central Christian Advocate (139; Ja. 1,
1964), p. 3. DHU/R; DAU/W
"Churches Pledge to Welcome
All." Concern (4; My. 1,
1962), p. 17.   DAU/W
"Clergyman Counsels Students on
Integration." Central Christian Advocate (136; Feb. 1,
1961), p. 15.   DAU/W
Collins, D. E. "Christian Race
Relations." Central Christian
Advocate (139; My. 15, 1964),
p. 6.   DAU/W
"Conference Adopts Statements
on Race." Central Christian
Advocate (139; Ja. 1, 1964),
pp. 22+.   DAU/W; DHU/R
Crum, Jack. "Why I Favor Inte-
gration." New Christian Advo-

cate (1:5, Feb., 1957), pp.
34-6.   DHU/R
"Demonstration Defused by Meth-
odist Bishops." Christian Cen-
tury (80; Dec. 4, 1963), pp.
1498-1501).   DHU/R
Dennis, Joseph J. "Need for
Brotherhood." Central Christian Advocate (133:23, Dec. 1,
1958), pp. 4-6.   DHU/R
Dennison, Doris. "Prophets in
Action." Wesley Quarterly (20;
Jl. -Sept., 1961), pp. 8+.
                      DHU/R
Dunbar, L. W. "That They May
Be Free." (Reprint) Concern
(5; Sept. 1, 1963), pp. 9+.
                      DAU/W
Gordh, G. "Conversion and the
Southern Conscience." Concern (7; Ag. 1-15, 1965), pp.
4+.   DAU/W
Gordon, Mamye. "Christianity
and the Race Problem." Cen-
tral Christian Advocate (133:
20, Oct. 15, 1958), pp. 5-6.
                      DHU/R
Haywood, J. W. "Watching De-
segregation at Work." Cen-
tral Christian Advocate (132:
19, Oct. 1, 1957), pp. 6-7.
                      DHU/R
"Hold Thanksgiving Service After
Passage of Civil Rights Bill."
Central Christian Advocate
(13; Ag. 15, 1964), pp. 12+.
                 DAU/W; DHU/R
Howard, Tillman J. "The Ra-
cial Issue Before Methodism."
Christian Advocate (139; Feb.
15, 1964), pp. 5+.
        Pam. File; DHU/R
"Jackson Chruch Bishop Breaks
Color Bar." Christian Advo-
cate (9; Nov. 18, 1965), pp.
21+.   DAU/W; DGW
Jackson, J. H. "Christ, the
Church and Race." Central
Christian Advocate (136:8,
Apr. 15, 1961), pp. 4+.
                 DHU/R; DAU/W
King, J. T. "Challenge to Chris-
tian Leadership." Central

Christian Advocate (136; Feb. 1, 1961), pp. 7+.
DHU/R; DAU/W
--"Christianity and Social Justice." Central Christian Advocate (136; Nov. 1, 1961), p. 5. DHU/R; DAU/W

Kitly, H. "Where Were Methodists at the March?" Concern (5; Oct. 15, 1963), p. 12.
DAU/W

"Kneel Ins." Concern (5; Nov. 1, 1963), p. 12. DAU/W

Mathews, J. K. "Bishops Speak on Race." Church Advocate (8; Ja. 2, 1964), pp. 7+.
DHU/R; DAU/W
--"Easter in Jackson; Methodist Bishops Barred from Galloway Memorial Methodist Church." Christian Century (81; Apr. 15, 1964), pp. 478-80. DHU/R

"McComb Methodists Aid Negro Rights." Christian Advocate (8; Dec. 3, 1964), p. 24.
DHU/R; DAU/W

McDermott, Wm. F. "A Lincoln in Ebony." New Christian Advocate (1:2, Nov., 1956), pp. 97-102. DHU/R

"Methodist Affirm Civil Disobedience as Citizen's Right." New York Times (My. 4, 1968).
Pam. File; DHU/R

Methodist Church, Department of Research and Survey. The Church and the Racially Changing Community, by Robert L. Wilson and James H. Davis, Jr. New York: Abingdon Pr., 1966. INU; NcD; DLC; NN/Sch

"Methodist, Others Rally to Aid in Birmingham." Christian Advocate (7; Oct. 10, 1963), p. 24. DAU/W; DHU/R

"Methodist Racial Unit Defines Goals." Christian Century (79; My. 9, 1962), pp. 592-3.
DHU/R

"Methodist React to California Riots." Central Christian Advocate (140; Oct. 15, 1965), p. 11. DHU/R; DAU/W

"Methodists Relax Law View." The Washington Post (My. 4, 1968). Pam. File; DHU/R

"Methodist Students Helped Ease Tensions at University of Georgia." Christian Advocate (5; Feb. 2, 1961), p. 24.
DAU/W; DHU/R

"Methodist Study Race Relations." Afro American (Nov. 15, 1960), Pam. File; DHU/R

"Methodists Vote Four-Year Integration." Christian Century (81; My. 13, 1964), p. 630.
DHU/R

"Ministers Endorse Maryland Sit-Ins." Concern (3; Dec. 15, 1961), p. 4. DAU/W

"Ministers Endorse Sit-in Demonstrations." Central Christian Advocate (137; Ja. 15, 1962), p. 15. DHU/R; DAU/W

"Mississippi Church Admits Negroes." Concern (7; Nov. 15, 1965), p. 16. DAU/W

"Mississippians Repudiate Religious Freedom, Capital Street Methodist Church in Jackson, Miss." Christian Century (80; Nov. 20, 1963), pp. 1425-6. DHU/R

Mitchell, E. O. "Interpretation: Action for Brotherhood." Concern (6:11, Dec. 1, 1964).
DAU/W

Mooth, V. "True Brotherhood is Found in Christ." Church Advocate (Ag., 1968), p. 11.
DHU/R

"Plan Strategy on Race." Christian Advocate (7; Dec. 19, 1963), pp. 21+.
DHU/R; DAU/W

"Press Fair-Housing Drive After Amendment of Law." Christian Advocate (8; Dec. 17, 1964), pp. 23+. DHU/R; DAU/W

"Race Lines Must Fade in Churches." Journal and Guide (My. 12, 1956).
Pam. File; DHU/R

"Methodists abolish All Negro Central Conference."

"Racists Challenge Methodists;
Methodist Bishop Barred from
Galloway Church, Jackson,
Miss." Christian Century (81;
Apr. 8, 1964), p. 454.
                    DHU/R
Ragan, Roger. "Methodist and
Residential Segregation of the
Negro." Concern (5; Jl. 15,
1963), pp. 4+.   DAU/W
"Religion and Race, Advocate
Special Report." Christian
Advocate (7; Feb. 28, 1963),
p. 7.   DAU/W; DHU/R
Roy, Ralph Lord. "Methodists:
Crisis of Conscience." Nation
(198; Mar. 16, 1964), pp. 262-
5.   DHU
Schooler, R. "Missionary's Wit-
ness and Civil Rights." Cen-
tral Christian Advocate (139;
Nov. 15, 1964), pp. 12+.
                    DAU/W; DHU/R
"Segregated Worship Hit." Concern (7; Sept. 15, 1965), p.
15.   DAU/W
"Segregation To Be Out After
Merger With EUB." Central
Christian Advocate (140; Oct.
1, 1965), p. 14.
                    DAU/W; DHU/R
Seller, J. E. "Christian and Human Relations." Roundtable
(12; Feb., 1964), p. 31.
        DAU; DCU/ST; DGW; DGU
"6 Methodist Churches Sign Wel-
coming Statement." Central
Advocate (37; My. 1, 1962),
pp. 15+.   DHU/R; DAU/W
"Southern Methodists Would Re-
tain Race Divisions." Christian Century (72; Feb. 23,
1955), pp. 229+.   DHU/R
Thompson, T. "Another Pilgrimage to Jackson; Seven Ministers Barred from Capitol
Street Methodist Church."
Christian Century (81; Apr.
22, 1964), pp. 511-12.
                    DHU/R

"To Picket Segregated Churches
in Oklahoma City." Central
Christian Advocate (136; Sept.
15, 1961), pp. 16+.
                    DHU/R; DAU/W
"Trinity Church in Orangeburg
Movement." Central Chris-
tian Advocate (139; Feb. 15,
1964), pp. 18+.
                    DHU/R; DAU/W
"12 Jailed in Mississippi for
Appearance at Church and
Sunday School." Concern (5;
Nov. 1, 1963), p. 15.
                    DAU/W
"Urges Some Rightists Investi-
gated, Lauds Poise of Reli-
gious Demonstrators." Cen-
tral Christian Advocate (139;
Nov. 1, 1964), pp. 9+.
                    DHU/R; DAU/W
Waid, W. L. Interpretation:
Conversion and the Southern
Conscience (reply to Conver-
sion and the Southern Con-
science, by G. Gordh). Con-
cern (7; Oct. 15, 1965), pp.
10+.   DAU/W
Walker, E. J. "Methodist Urban
Convocation." Christian Cen-
tury (75; Mr. 12, 1958), pp.
319-20.   DHU/R
Warnock, Henry Y. "Southern
Methodists, the Negro, and
Unification: The First
Phase." Journal of Negro
History (52:4, Oct., 1967),
pp. 287-304.   DHU
"White Parish's Negro Rector
Cites High Morale, Support."
Central Christian Advocate
(140; Jl. 15, 1965), pp. 10+.
                    DHU/R; DAU/W
Wilkins, R. "Church Renewal
and Race by Interracial Coun-
cil of Methodist." Concern
(5; Sept. 1, 1963), pp. 9+
                    DAU/W

7. Presbyterian

Calhoun, M. P. "Presbyterian Church, U. S., after Division and Silence, Its Ministers are again Speaking Against Racism." Christianity and Crisis (18; Mr. 3, 1958), pp. 24-6. DHU/R

"The Church and Race: A Promising First Step." Presbyterian Life (12:10, My. 15, 1959), pp. 26-28. DHU/R

Civil Rights: The Backlash That Wasn't There. Presbyterian Life (17:12, Je. 15, 1964), pp. 19-22. DHU/R Report of the 176th General Assembly of the Presbyterian Church.

"Concern V. Concerned; Presbyterian Group Fear Church's Increasing Involvement in Social Issues." Time (90; Oct. 13, 1967), p. 50. DHU

"Death in the Sunday School." Presbyterian Life (Editorial) (16:19, Oct. 15, 1963), pp. 4+. DHU/R Opinion on the shooting of six black children at the Sixteenth Street Baptist Church in Birmingham, Alabama.

Gittings, James A. "Clergymen Demonstrate in Hattiesburg, Mississippi." Presbyterian Life (17:4, Feb. 15, 1964), pp. 30-3. DHU/R

Ikeler, Bernard. "Troubleshooters of the Racial Crisis." Presbyterian Life (15:11, Je. 1, 1962), pp. 21-23. DHU/R

Michie, Doyne E. "Hattiesburg: Trial and Debate." Presbyterian Life (17:7, Apr. 1, 1964), pp. 28-29. DHU/R

"No Private Domain; Racism at Home Viewed from the Churches' Mission Posts Abroad; Statements of the Presbyterian Board of World

Missions." Christian Century (81; Feb. 5, 1964), p. 184. DHU/R

Nygren, Malcolm. "The Church and Political Action." Christianity Today (13:12, Mr. 14, 1969), pp. 9-12. DHU/R

"Presbyterian Vote $100,000 for Fund to Aid Poor People." New York Times (My. 21, 1968). Pam. File; DHU/R

"Presbyterians Hold Line on School Prayers; Racial Justice." Christian Century (80; Dec. 11, 1963), p. 1538. DHU/R

"Race Relations: Churchmen Take the Lead." Presbyterian Life (10:3, Feb. 2, 1957), p. 18. DHU/R

Reimers, David Morgan. "The Race and Presbyterian Union." Church History (31:2, Je., 1962), pp. 203-15. DHU/R

Sissel, H. B. "Civil Rights Legislation." Presbyterian Life (16:21, Nov. 1, 1963), pp. 27-28. DHU/R

-- "Days of Preparation." Presbyterian Life (17:9, My. 1, 1964), pp. 7-8. DHU/R Predicts a new era in civil rights lies just ahead.

-- "Segregation in Sumter, South Carolina." Presbyterian Life (10:1, Ja. 5, 1957), pp. 6+. DHU/R

Smylie, James H. "Conflict of Concerns; Tensions Affecting Souther Presbyterians." Christian Century (82:52, Dec. 29, 1965), pp. 1602-06. DHU/R

"Southern Presbyterians Strengthen Race Stand." Presbyterian Life (17:11, Je. 1, 1964), pp. 31-2. DHU/R

Wright, Paul S. "Desegregating Human Hearts." Presbyterian Life (17:9, My. 1, 1964), pp. 19+. DHU/R

8. Protestant Episcopal

"Bells in the Delta; Episcopal
Civil Rights Activists." Time
(85; Feb. 26, 1965), p. 71.
                              DHU
"Church and Race." Christian
Social Relations Bulletin (2:7,
Je., 1965).
     Whole issue deals with race
and the Protestant Episcopal
Church. Pam. File; DHU/R
"Churches Challenged; National
Council of Churches and South-
ern Presbyterians." America
(112; Ja. 2, 1965), p. 4. DHU
Osgood, Charles and Willie
Charles. "When Blacks Join
Whites." The Episcopalian

(135:5, My., 1970), pp. 24+.
                              DHU/R
     Case study of Grace Prot-
estant Episcopal Church, Syracuse, New York.
Protestant Episcopal Church in
the U.S. National Council.
"Bridge Building in Race Relations: What the Episcopal
Church Has Said and Done."
     Pam. File; DHU/R
"To Right a Wrong; Call for
Episcopalians to Respond Cre-
atively to Racial Riots."
Newsweek (70; Sept. 25, 1967),
p. 116.   DHU

9. Lutheran

Ferrer, J. M. "N.E.T.'s A
Time for Burning: Involve-
ment of the Augustana Luther-
an Church, Omaha, with Civil
Rights." Life (62; Feb. 10,
1967), p. 12.   DHU
Lutheran View of Race Crisis."
America (118; Feb. 3, 1968),
p. 139.   DHU
"Lutherans Seek Negroes for the
Ministry." Atlanta World (Mr.

27, 1968). Pam. File; DHU/R
"New Lutheran Spirit; Pledge to
Support Agencies Promoting
Integrated Housing." Newsweek
(70; Jl. 24, 1967), pp. 70-1.
"Two-Edged Sword; a Time for
Burning, Film on Racial Pat-
terns in a Lutheran Parish."
America (115; Nov. 19, 1966),
pp. 643-4.   DHU

10. Seventh Day Adventist

Education: "A Perennial Priority
(Editorial)." Message Magazine (29:7, Oct., 1963), pp.
5-6.   DHU/R
     "Equal opportunity for each
individual to obtain a sound
and suitable education."
Ford, Leighton. "Evangelism in
a Day of Revolution." The
Message Magazine (36:4, Jl.,
1970), pp. 4-7.

     Pam. File; DHU/R
"What the position of a
Church should be in an age of
revolution."
Keidel, Levi O. "Where America's Racial Troubles Began."
Message Magazine (35:4, Jl.,
1969), pp. 22+.   DHU/R
Motley, Constance B. "Progress
in Race Relations." The Message Magazine (31:4, Jl.,

1965), pp. 7+.   DHU/R   Come Back in Disguise?" The
Negro author.   Message Magazine (29:5, Ag.,
Smith, Norma J. "Will Slavery   1963), pp. 13+.   DHU/R

11. Baptist

Barnette, H. H. "What can South-   President of the National
ern Baptists do About the Ra-   Baptist Convention, U.S.A.,
cial Issue?" Christianity To-   Inc. gives his views on the
day (1; Je. 24, 1957), pp. 14-   civil rights struggle.
16.   DHU/R   Negro author.
Bryant, Baxton. "Where We   "Negro Baptist May Go Political."
Are in Civil Rights." Baptist   Atlanta Constitution (Ag. 14,
Student (47:5, Feb., 1968), pp.   1968). Pam. File; DHU/R
21-23.   DHU/R   Nichols, S. "Richmond Church
Davis, William P. "Race Issue: Suit Dismissed; Admission of
Where Are We?" Baptist Stu-   Negroes to Membership in
dent (47:9, Je., 1968), pp.   First Baptist Church." Chris-
11-15.   DHU/R   tian Century (83; Mr. 30,
"In a Spirit of Repentance: Ad-   1966), pp. 411-12.   DHU/R
mission of Sin Regarding Ra-   "Southern Baptists Break Silence."
cial Issues by Southern Baptist   Christian Century (81; Jl. 22,
Convention." Time (85; Je. 11,   1964), p. 925.   DHU/R
1965), p. 68.   DHU   Steele, Henry M. "The Time Is
Jackson, Joseph Harrison. Un-   Now." Baptist Leader (32:1,
holy Shadows and Freedom's   Apr., 1970), pp. 2. DHU/R
Holy Light. Nashville: Tow-   Baptists Conv. to serve as
send Press, 1967.   DHU/R   catalyst to help churches.

12. Judaism

Bernards, Solomon S. "Race Re-   ington Afro-American (Apr.
lations in the Jewish School   13, 1968).
Curriculum." Religious Edu-   Pam. File; DHU/R
cation (59:1, Ja.-Feb., 1964),   Rinder, Irwin D. "Jewish Identi-
pp. 60-63.   DHU/R   fication and the Race Relations
Brickner, Balfour. "Projects   Cycle." Doctoral dissertation,
Under Synagogue Auspices."   University of Chicago, 1953.
Religious Education (59:1, Ja.-   Rubenstein, Richard L. "The
Feb., 1964), pp. 76-80.   Rabbi and Social Conflict."
                       DHU/R   Religious Education (59:1, Ja.-
Discusses Jewish projects   Feb., 1964), pp. 100-06.
for racial justice.   DHU/R
Pilch, Judah. "Civil Rights and   Ungar, Andre. "To Birmingham
Jewish Institutions." Religious   and Back." Conservative Juda-
Education (59:1, Ja.-Feb.,   ism (18; Fall, 1963), pp. 1-
1964), pp. 86-89.   DHU/R   17.   DLC
"Rabbi Says Civil Rights Move-   Story of 19 Rabbis' trip to
ment Belongs to All." Wash-   Birmingham.

Vorspan, Albert. "Segregation   can Judaism (7; Ja. , 1958),
and Social Justice." Ameri-   pp. 10-11.   DLC

13. Church of the Brethren

Crouse, M. "Integration in the   Gardner, R. B. "Evangelical
Church of the Brethren."   Christianity and Racial Ten-
Brethren Life and Thought (4;   sions." Brethren Life and
Spr. , 1959), pp. 41-51.   Thought (4; Aut. , 1959), pp.
                       DAU/W   47-51.   DAU/W

14. Unitarian Universalist Association

Atkins, James. "New Voice in   "How 'Open' is the Unitarian
Birmingham." Unitarian Reg-   Door?" Christian Register
ister and the Universalist   (Apr. , 1954), Repr. DHU/R
Leader (141:3, Mr. , 1962),   Howlett, Duncan. "A Lover of
pp. 5-7.   DHU/R   His Fellow Man: Two Trib-
Blanshard, Mary H. "The Out-   utes to James J. Reeb." Reg-
look for Equal Rights." Uni-   ister-Leader (147:5, My. ,
tarian Universalist Register   1965), p. 5.   DHU/R
Leader (141:3, Mr. , 1962),   Tribute to Associate Minis-
pp. 13-15.   DHU/R   ter of All Souls Church, Wash-
Cheetham, Henry H. Unitarian-   ington, D. C. who was shot in
ism and Universalism. An   Selma, Alabama participating
Illustrated History. Boston: in a freedom march.
Beacon Press, 1962. DHU/R   MacLean, Angus H. The Wind
Unitarianism and social   in Both Ears. Boston: Beacon
justice.   Press, 1965.   DHU/R
Harrington, Donald. "Black and   Unitarian Universalist min-
White Action." Now: The   ister discusses religious lib-
Magazine of the Unitarian Uni-   erals.
versalist Association (50:15,   Merrill, Charles. "Negro Pres-
Aut. , 1969), p. 4.   sure and White Liberals."
Hemstreet, Robert. "We Shall   Register-Leader (149:6, Je.
Overcome." Unitarian Univer-   1967), pp. 3-6.   DHU/R
salist Register Leader (145:9,   Mitchell, Henry H. "The Cold,
Nov. , 1963), pp. 4-6. DHU/R   White Church." Register-
Unitarian and Universalists   Leader (148:7, Mid-Sum. ,
join Washington March for   1966), pp. 14-15.   DHU/R
jobs and freedom.   Repr. from Christian Cen-
Hoffman, Clifton G. "On Trial   tury (Mr. 30, 1966). DHU/R
in Mississippi." Unitarian   Negro author.
Register and the Universalist   Newman, Richard A. "Black
Leader (140:7, Mid-Sum. ,   Power and White Liberals."
1961), pp. 3-5.   Unitarian Universalist Register-
Report of trial shows basis   Leader (148:9, Nov. 1966), pp.
for sentencing of twenty-seven   7-8.   DHU/R
Freedom Riders.

Ulman, Joseph N. "Two Days
in Alabama--1965." Unitarian

Universalist Register-Leader
(147:5, My. , 1965), pp. 6-9
DHU/R

B. SOUTHERN CHRISTIAN LEADERSHIP CONFERENCE
    AND MARTIN LUTHER KING, JR.

Abernathy, Ralph David. "My
Last Letter to Martin."
Ebony (23:9, Jl. , 1968), pp.
58-61.   DHU/MO
"Acceptance Speech of Martin
Luther King, Jr. of the Nobel
Peace Prize on December 10,
1964." Negro History Bulle-
tin (31; My. , 1968), pp. 20-
21.   DHU/MO
"Accused Killer, a Clumsy Man
with Closed Eyes." Life (64;
Apr. 26, 1968), p. 42B. DHU
Adams, S. J. "Measuring Up the
Catholic Press and Rev. Dr.
Martin Luther King, Jr."
America (118; My. 4, 1968),
p. 624.
   Discussion. (118; Je. 22,
1968), p. 781.   DHU
"Aim: Registration; Promoting
Desegregation in Selma,
Ala." Time (85; Jan. 29,
1965), pp. 20-1.   DHU
Alexander, Mithrapuram K.
Martin Luther King: Martyr
for Freedom. New Delhi:
New Light Publishers, 1968.
                        NcD
"American Dream: Address,
June 6, 1961." Negro Histor-
ical Bulletin (31; May, 1968),
pp. 10-15.   DHU/MO
"As 150,000 Said Farewell to
Dr. King." U.S. News (64;
Apr. 22, 1968), pp. 38-9.
                        DHU
"Assassination According to
Capote." Time (91; My. 10,
1968), p. 65.   DHU
"Assassins: Who Did It, and
Why? Ray: Ninety-Nine
Years and a Victory." News-
week (73; Mr. 24, 1969), pp.

28-32.   DHU
Baldwin, James. "Dangerous
Road Before Martin Luther
King." Harper (222; Feb. ,
1961), pp. 33-42.   DHU
Balk, A. "What Memorial to
Martin Luther King? Ways
of Rectifying Injustices." Sat-
urday Review of Literature
(51; My. 4, 1968), p. 18.
                        DHU
"Beauty for Ashes; Committee of
Concern Organized to Rebuild
Negro Churches Bombed and
Burned in Mississippi." Time
(85; Feb. 5, 1965), p. 61.
                        DHU
Bedau, Hugo Adam. Civil Dis-
obedience Theory and Prac-
tice. New York: Pegasus,
1969.   DHU/R
Bennett, John C. "Martin Luther
King, Jr. 1929-1968." Chris-
tianity and Crisis (28:6, Apr.
15, 1968), pp. 69-70.
                      DHU/R
Bennett, Lerone. "Martyrdom of
Martin Luther King, Jr."
Ebony (23; My. , 1968), pp.
174-81.   DHU/MO
--What Manner of Man: A Bi-
ography of Martin Luther
King, Jr. Chicago: Johnson
Publishing Co. , 1964.
            INU; DHU/R
"Big Man is Martin Luther King,
Jr." Newsweek (62; Jl. 29,
1963), pp. 30-2.   DHU
Booker, Simeon. "50,000 March
on Montgomery." Ebony (20;
My. 1965), pp. 46-8+.
                    DHU/MO
"Boycotts Will Be Used: Inter-
view with Martin Luther King."

("Boycotts... cont.)
U.S. News and World Report
(56; Feb. 24, 1964), pp. 59-
61.   DLC
Brennecke, H. E. "Memorial to
Dr. King." Negro History
Bulletin (31; My., 1968), p. 8.
                        DHU/MO
Buckley, William F. "Memorial
for Dr. King." National Re-
view (21; Oct. 21, 1969), p.
1078.   DGU
-- "On Bugging Martin Luther
King." National Review (21;
Jl. 15, 1969), p. 714. DGU
Cameron, J. M. "British View
on Martin Luther King." Com-
monweal (88; Apr. 26, 1968),
p. 164.   DHU/R
Campbell, Will D. "The Sit-Ins:
Passive Resistance or Civil
Disobedience." Social Action
(27:5, Ja., 1961), pp. 14-18.
                         DHU/R
Chandler, Russell. "King in the
Capital." Christianity Today
(12; Ja. 5, 1968), pp. 44-6.
                         DHU/R
"Children's Tribute to Dr. Mar-
tin Luther King, Jr." Negro
History Bulletin (31; My.,
1968), p. 2.   DHU/MO
"Churchmen Defend Sit-in Stu-
dent." Christian Century (80;
Je. 26, 1963), p. 821. Dis-
cussion (80; Sept. 11, Oct. 9,
1963), pp. 1239, 1. DHU/R
Clarke, J. W. and J. W. Soule.
"How Southern Children Felt
About King's Death." Trans-
Action (5; Oct., 1968), pp.
34-5.   DCU/SW
Clayton, Edward Taylor. Martin
Luther King: The Peaceful
Warrior. Englewood Cliffs,
N.J.: Prentice-Hall, Inc.,
1968.   INU; DHU/R
Cleghorn, R. "Martin Luther
King Jr., Apostle of Crisis."
Saturday Evening Post (236;
Je. 15, 1963), pp. 15-19.
                           DHU
"Conner and King." Newsweek

(61; Apr. 22, 1963), p. 28+.
                           DHU
Cook, Bruce. "King in Chicago."
Commonweal (84:6, Apr. 29,
1966), pp. 175-77. DHU/R
Cook, Samuel DuBois. "Is Mar-
tin Luther King, Jr. Irrele-
vant?" New South (26:2, Spr.,
1971), pp. 2-14.   DHU/R
-- "King, Martin Luther." Jour-
nal of Negro History (53:4,
Oct., 1968), pp. 348-54. DHU
"Dispute Between Hoover and
King: The FBI's Answer to
Criticisms; FBI Analysis of
Telegram." U.S. News (57;
Dec. 6, 1967), pp. 46+. DHU
"Doctor King: A Year Later;
California Senate Refuses to
Honor Dr. King's Memory."
Nation (208; Apr. 14, 1969),
p. 453.
"Doctor King and the Paris Press
(Editorial)." America (2;
Nov. 13, 1965), p. 560. DLC
"Doctor King Carries Fight to
Northern Slums." Ebony (21;
Apr. 1966), pp. 94-6+.
                        DHU/MO
"Doctor King: in Tribute; Ex-
cerpts From his Writings."
Christian Century (85; Apr. 17,
1968), p. 503.   DHU/R
"Doctor King's Case for Nonvio-
lence." America (115; Nov.
12, 1966), p. 578.   DHU
"Doctor King's Closed Session
Set the Strategy." Life (58;
Mr. 19, 1965), p. 35+. DHU
"Doctor King's Disservice to His
Cause." Life (62:16, Apr. 21,
1967), p. 4.   DHU/R
"Doctor King's Murder: Nagging
Questions Remain." U.S.
News (66; Mr. 24, 1969), p.
13.   DHU
"Doctor King's Nobel Prize."
America (111; Oct. 31, 1964),
p. 503.   DHU
Douglas, Carlyle C. "Ralph Ab-
ernathy." Ebony (25:3, Ja.,
1970), pp. 40-50.
                  Pam. File; DHU/R

A Negro Baptist Minister fights to keep Martin Luther King's dream alive. "Dream Still Unfulfilled." Newsweek (73; Apr. 14, 1969), pp. 34-5. DHU

Dugan, George. Abernathy Asks Presbyterians to Give $10 Million for the Poor." New York Times (My. 18, 1968). Pam. File; DHU/R

Dunbar, E. "Visit With Martin Luther King." Look (27; Feb. 12, 1963), pp. 92-6. DHU

"Endorse Dr. King for Nobel Prize." Christian Century (81; Ag. 12, 1964), p. 1308. DHU

"Equality is Not Negotiable." Christian Century (80; Sept. 4, 1963), p. 1069. DHU/R

Evtushenko, E. A. "In Memory of Dr. Martin Luther King." Negro History Bulletin (31; My., 1968). p. 14. DHU/MO

"Execution of Dr. King." Ramparts Magazine (6; My., 1968), pp. 46-7. DHU/R

Fager, C. E. "Dilemma for Dr. King." Christian Century (83; Mr. 16, 1966), pp. 331-2. DHU

"Four Poets on Martin Luther King." Nation (206; Je. 24, 1968), p. 831. DHU

Franklin, Ben A. "Mourning for Dr. King Ended; Abernathy Now Man in Charge." New York Times, Sunday, Ag. 17, 1969. Pam. File; DHU/R

"From the Birmingham Jail; Excerpt from Letter." Negro History Bulletin (31; My., 1968), p. 19. DHU/MO

Galphin, Bruce M. "Does Martin Luther King Have a Future in Politics." Negro Digest (20; Ja., 1962), pp. 41-7. SCBHC; DHU/MO

Galphin, Bruce M. "Political Future of Dr. King." The Nation (Sept. 23, 1961). DLC

Garland, Phyl. "I've Been to the Mountaintop." Ebony (23:

7, My., 1968), pp. 124, 126-42. DHU/R

"Georgia Imprisons Martin Luther King, Jr." Christian Century (77; Nov. 9, 1960), p. 1300. DHU

"Georgia Justice." Nation (191; Nov. 5, 1960), pp. 338-9. DHU

"Georgia Whodunit." Newsweek (60; Jl. 23, 1962), pp. 18-19. DHU

Gerasimov, G. Fire Bell in the Night. By G. Gerasimov, G. Kuznetsov and V. Morev. Moscow: Novosti Press Agency Pub. House, 1968. NcD

Gessell, J. M. "Memphis in Holy Week." Christian Century (85; My. 8, 1968), pp. 19-20. DHU/R

"Gift of Love." McCall's Magazine (94; Dec., 1966), pp. 146-7. DLC

Good, P. "Chicago Summer: Bossism, Racism and Dr. King." Nation (203; Sept. 19, 1966), pp. 237-42. DHU

Goodman, G. "Doctor King, One Year After: He Lives, Man!" Look (33; Apr. 15, 1969), pp. 29-31.

"Graham and King as Ghetto-mates." Christian Century (83; Ag. 10, 1966), p. 976. DHU

Halberstam, M. "Are You Guilty of Murdering Martin Luther King?" New York Times Magazine (Je. 9, 1968), pp. 27-9+. DHU

Halberstam, David. "Notes from the Bottom of the Mountain. Harper's (236; Je. 1968), pp. 40-2. DHU

"Hammer of Civil Rights." Nation (198; Mr. 9, 1964), pp. 230-4. DHU

"Hanh, Nhat. "A Letter to Martin Luther King from a Buddhist Monk." Liberation (10: 9, Dec., 1965), pp. 18-19. DHU/R

Hare, Alexander P. Nonviolent
Direct Action, American
Cases: Social-Psychological
Analyses. Washington, D. C. :
Corpus Books, 1968. DHU/R
Includes protests led by
Martin Luther King.
Hendrick, George. "Dr. King's
Pilgrimage to Nonviolence."
Gandhi Magazine (3; Ja. , 1959),
pp. 63-5.   DHU
--"Gandhi and Dr. Martin Lu-
ther King." Gandhi Magazine
(3; Ja. , 1959), pp. 18-22.
                             DHU
Hentoff, Nat. "Peaceful Army."
Commonweal (72; Je. 10,
1960), pp. 275-8   DHU
"Hoover-King Meeting." News-
week (64; Dec. 14, 1964), p.
22+.   DHU
Houck, J. B. "Nonviolence and
Christian Tradition." Commu-
nity (27; Dec. , 1967), p. 4.
                         DHU/MO
"How Martin Luther King Won
the Nobel Peace Prize." U. S.
News (58; Feb. 8, 1965), pp.
76-7.   DHU
"How Some Clergymen Who Cam-
paigned in '65 See Poor
People's March." National Ob-
server (My. 27, 1968).
                Pam. File; DHU/R
Howard, R. "Requiem to Dr.
Martin Luther King, Jr." Ne-
gro History Bulletin (32; Apr.
1969), p. 17.   DHU/MO
Huie, W. B. "Story of James
Earl Ray and the Plot to As-
sassinate Martin Luther King."
Look (32; Nov. 12; Nov. 26,
1968), pp. 90-7+, pp. 86-7+.
                         DHU
--and A. C. Hanes; P. Foreman.
"Why James Earl Ray Mur-
dered Doctor King." Look (33;
Apr. 15, 1969), pp. 102-4+
                         DHU
Hunt, James D. "Gandhi and the
Black Revolution." Christian
Century (86:40, Oct. 1, 1969),
pp. 1242-44.   DHU/R

A comparison between Mar-
tin Luther King and Gandhi.
"Johnson, King and Ho Chi Minh."
Christianity Today (12; Jan. 5,
1968), pp. 24-5.   DHU/R
Jones, J. "Priests, Sisters, and
Martin Luther King." Commu-
nity (25; Sept. 1965), pp. 4-
6.
"Kennedy to Mrs. King: Did a
Phone Call Elect Kennedy
President?" Negro Digest
(11; Nov. , 1961), pp. 45-9.
                         DHU/MO
Kiely, H. C. "Judgement and
Grace in Selma." Concern (7;
Apr. 1, 1965), pp. 6+.
                         DAU/W
"King." New Yorker (41; My. 1,
1965), pp. 35-7.   DLC
"King Acts for Peace." Christian
Century (82; Sept. 29, 1965),
pp. 1180+.   DHU/R
"King Comes to Chicago." Chris-
tian Century (82; Ag. 11,
1965), pp. 974+.   DHU/R
King, Coretta. "How Many Men
Must Die?" Life (64:16, Apr.
19, 1968), pp. 34-5.
                Pam. File; DHU/R
--"The Legacy of Martin Luther
King, Jr." Theology Today
(27:2, Jl. , 1970), pp. 129-39.
                         DHU/R
"King Is the Man, Oh Lord."
Newsweek (71; Apr. 15, 1968),
pp. 34-8.   DHU
King, Martin Luther. "Bold De-
sign for a New South." Na-
tion (196; Mr. 30, 1963), pp.
259-62.   DAU
--"The Burning Truth in the
South." Progressive (24; My. ,
1960), pp. 8-10.   DGU
--"Case Against Tokenism."
New York Times Magazine (Ag.
5, 1962), p. 11+.   DHU
--"The Current Crisis in Race
Relations." New South (13;
Mr. , 1958), pp. 8-12.
                DAU/W; DHU/MO
Negro author.
--"Dreams of Brighter Tomor-

rows." Ebony (20; Mr. 1965),
pp. 35-6; 38, 40, 42, 44, 46.
                    DHU/MO
-- "Facing the Challenge of a
New Age." Phylon (18; Spr.,
1957), pp. 25-34.   DHU/MO
-- "Freedom's Crisis; Last Steep
Ascent." Nation (202; Mr. 14,
1966), pp. 288-92.   DHU
-- "Fumbling on the New Fron-
tier." Nation (194; Mr. 3,
1962), pp. 190-3.   DHU
-- "Hate is Always Tragic; Ex-
cerpts from Address." Time
(80; Ag. 3, 1962), p. 13.
                         DHU
-- "I Have a Dream." John Hope
Franklin and Isidore Starr.
The Negro in the 20th Century
(New York: Vintage Books,
1967), pp. 143-47.   DHU/R
-- "A Legacy of Creative Pro-
test." Jules Chametzky and S.
Kaplan. Black and White in
American Culture. An Anthol-
ogy from the Massachusetts
Review. (The University of
Massachusetts Press, 1969.)
                       DHU/R
-- "Let Justice Roll Down."
Nation (200; Mr. 15, 1965), pp.
269-73.   DHU
-- Letter from Birmingham City
Jail. Philadelphia: American
Friends Service Committee,
1963.   CtY-D; DHU/R
     Addressed to Bishop C. C. J.
Carpenter and seven other
clergymen.
-- "Love, Law and Civil Disobedi-
ence." New South (16; Dec.,
1961), pp. 3-11.   DAU/W
-- "Love Your Enemies. A Ser-
mon Delivered by Dr. Martin
Luther King, Jr. ... in the
Andrew Ranking Memorial
Chapel, Howard University,
Washington, D. C. on Sunday,
Morning, Nov. 10, 1957." Jour-
nal of Religious Thought (27:2,
Sum. Suppl, 1970), pp. 31-41.
                       DHU/R
-- "The Luminous Promise."

Progressive (26; Dec., 1962),
pp. 34-7.   DGU
-- A Martin Luther King Treas-
ury. Yonkers: Educational
Heritage, 1964.
          DHU/MO; NN/Sch
-- The Measure of a Man. Phil-
adelphia: Pilgrim Press, 1968.
                       DHU/R
-- "Memorial Issue to Martin Lu-
ther King." Negro History
Bulletin (31:5, My., 1968).
                    DHU/MO
-- "The Montgomery Bus Boy-
cott." Bradford Chalmers.
Chronicles of Black Protest
(New York: The New Ameri-
can Library, 1968), pp. 177-
87.
     Includes also "I Have a
Dream."
-- "Religious Commitment for Ra-
cial Equality." United Church
Herald (6; Mr. 7, 1963), pp.
8-10.   DHU/R
-- Strength to Love. New York:
Harper & Row, 1963.
          DHU/R; DLC; INU
-- Stride Toward Freedom; the
Montgomery Story. New York:
Harper, 1958. CtY-D; DHU/R
-- "Time for Freedom Has
Come." New York Times Mag-
azine (Sept. 10, 1961), pp.
25+.   DHU
-- The Trumpet of Conscience.
New York: Harper & Row,
1968.   CtY-D; DHU/R
-- "We Are Still Walking." Lib-
eration (1; Dec., 1956), pp.
6-9.   DHU/R
-- Where Do We Go From Here:
Chaos or Community? New
York: Harper & Row, 1967.
                       DHU/R
-- "Who is Their God?" Nation
(195; Oct. 13, 1962), pp. 209-
10.   DHU
-- Why We Can't Wait. New
York: Harper & Row, 1964.
              CtY-D; DHU/R
"King Moves North." Time (85;
Apr. 30, 1965), pp. 32-3. DHU

"King Proposed for Peace Prize."
Christian Century (81; Feb. 12,
1964), p. 198.   DHU/R
"King Receives Nobel Prize."
Christian Century (81; Oct. 28,
1964), p. 1324.   DHU/R
"King Speaks for Peace." Chris-
tian Century (84; Apr. 19,
1967), pp. 492-93.   DHU/R
"King Wants White Demonstra-
tors." Christian Century (81;
Je. 3, 1964), pp. 724-5.
                        DHU/R
"King's Last March." Time (91;
Apr. 19, 1968), pp. 18-19.
                        DHU
"King's Last March: We Lost
Somebody." Newsweek (71;
Apr. 22, 1968), pp. 26-31.
                        DHU
"King's Last Tape: Excerpts."
Newsweek (72; Dec. 18, 1968),
pp. 34+.   DHU
"King's Targets." Newsweek (63;
Je. 22, 1964), pp. 26+. DHU
"The Legacy of Martin Luther
King." Life (64:19, Apr.,
1968), pp. 28-33.   DHU
"Letter from Birmingham Jail."
Christian Century (80; Je. 12,
1963), pp. 763-73; Excerpts.
Ebony (18; Ag., 1963), pp.
23-6+; Time (83; Ja. 3, 1964),
p. 15. Same. Negro History
Bulletin (27; Mr. 1964), p.
156.   DHU
Lewis, Claude. "Reverend Jesse
Jackson: Passage to Prog-
ress." Tuesday (Jl., 1968),
pp. 6-8; 26.
          Pam. File; DHU/R
Lincoln, Charles Eric. "Five
Fears for Integration." Cen-
tral Christian Advocate (132:
17, Sept. 1, 1957), pp. 4-7.
Negro author.
--Martin Luther King, Jr., A
Profile. New York: Hill &
Wang, 1970.   DHU/R
Lokos, Lionel. House Divided;
the Life and Legacy of Martin
Luther King. New Rochelle,
N.Y.: Arlington House,

1968.   DHU/MO; NcD
Lorew, Joseph. "I've Been to
the Mountaintop." Life (64:12,
Apr., 1968), pp. 74-84. DHU
"Love Shall Overcome." Presby-
terian Survey (58:6, Je.,
1968), entire issue.
          Pam. File; DHU/R
"What the white Christian
must know to deal with white
racism."
Maguire, John David. "Martin
Luther King and Vietnam."
Christianity and Crisis (27:7,
My. 1, 1967), pp. 89-90.
                        DHU/R
--"Martin Luther King, Jr.,
1929-1968." Christianity and
Crisis (28:6, Apr. 15, 1968),
pp. 69-70.   DHU/R
"Man of Conflict Wins a Peace
Prize." U.S. News (57; Oct.
26, 1964), p. 24.   DHU
"Man of the Year." Time (83;
Jan. 3, 1964), pp. 13-16+.
Reply. Nation (198; Jan. 13,
1964), pp. 41-2.   DHU
"March on Washington: What to
Expect." U.S. News (64; Mr.
18, 1968), pp. 44+. DHU/R
"Martin Luther King, Jr. and
Mahatma Gandhi." Negro
History Bulletin (31; My.,
1968), pp. 4-5.   DHU/MO
"Martin Luther King and the
Right to Know." America
(120; Mr. 22, 1969), p. 323.
                        DHU
"Martin Luther King, Jr.: Man
of 1963." Negro History Bulle-
tin (27; Mr., 1964), pp. 136-
7.   DHU/MO
Martin Luther King. "Mourns
Death of Martin Luther King."
(editorial) Life (64:5, Apr. 12,
1968), p. 4.   DHU
--Nation (200; Apr. 15, 1968),
p. 490.   DHU/R
--Reporter (Apr. 18, 1968).
                        DLC
"Martin Luther King. Who he
is... What he Believes." U.S.
News (58; Apr. 5, 1965),

pp. 18+.   DHU
"Martin Luther King's Reaction:
A Statement and a Disagree-
ment." U.S. News (57; Nov.
30, 1964), p. 58.   DHU
"Martyrdom Comes to America's
Moral Leader." Christian
Century (85; Apr. 17, 1968),
p. 475.   DHU/R
McDermott, J. A. "Chicago Cath-
olic Asks: Where Does My
Church Stand on Racial Jus-
tice?" Look (30; Nov. 1,
1966), pp. 82+.   DHU
Meltzer, Milton, (ed.). In Their
Own Words: A History of the
American Negro 1916-1966.
New York: Thomas Y. Cro-
well Co., 1967.   DHU/R
Martin Luther King speaks
on Bus Boycott, 1954 and de-
mands of "March on Washing-
ton."
"Memo to Martin Luther King."
National Review (19:49, Dec.
12, 1967), pp. 1368-69.
DGU; DGW
"Memphis March Leads to Riot."
Senior Scholar (92; Apr. 11,
1968), pp. 22-3.   DHU/R
"Men Behind Martin Luther
King." Ebony (20; Je., 1965),
pp. 104-06.   DHU/MO
Miller, Perry. "The Mind and
Faith of Martin Luther King."
The Reporter (Oct. 30, 1958).
DLC
Miller, William Robert. Martin
Luther King, Jr.: His Life,
Martyrdom and Meaning for
the World. New York: Wey-
bright and Talley, 1968.
DHU/MO
Narcisse, Louis H. "His Grace
King; the West Coast's Most
Colorful Religious Leader."
Sepia (9; Feb., 1961), pp. 42-
7.   DHU/MO
"No False Moves for King."
Christian Century (80; Je. 17,
1963), p. 919.   DHU
"No Peace For Winner of Peace
Prize." U.S. News (58; Feb.

1, 1965), pp. 19+.   DHU
"Nobelman King." Newsweek (64;
Oct. 26, 1964), p. 77. DHU
Nonviolence After Gandhi; A
Study of Martin Luther King,
Jr. Edited by G. Ramachand-
ran and T. K. Mahadevan.
New Delhi: Gandhi Peace
Foundation, 1968.   NcD
"Now Dr. King's Marchers Turn
North." U.S. News (58; My.
3, 1965), pp. 8+.   DHU
Nuby, C. "He Had a Dream."
Negro History Bulletin (31;
My., 1968), p. 21. DHU/MO
O'Dell, J. H. "Charleston's Leg-
acy to the Poor Peoples Cam-
paign." Freedomways (9:3,
Sum., 1969), pp. 197-211.
DHU/R
Southern Christian Leader-
ship Conference Role in
Charleston, S. C.
"Off Hoover's Chest: With Ex-
cerpts from Press Confer-
ence." Newsweek (64; Nov.
30, 1964), p. 30.   DHU
"On to Montgomery." Newsweek
(65; Mr. 29, 1965), pp. 21-
2.   DHU
Osborne, J. "Doctor Kings Me-
morial." New Republic (161;
Oct. 11, 1969), pp. 9-10.
DHU
Patterson, Lillie. Martin Luther
King, Jr., Man of Peace.
Champaign, Ill.: Garrard
Pub. Co., 1969. DHU/R; NcD
"Peace Prize Causes Contro-
versy: Reactions in Atlanta."
Christian Century (82; Ja. 13,
1965), p. 39.   DHU/R
"Peace With Justice." Common-
weal (78; My. 31, 1963), p.
268.   DGU
"Peaceful Kingdom." National
Review (16; Dec. 29, 1964),
p. 1135.   DAU
"Pertinent Memorials." Chris-
tian Century (86; Apr. 2,
1969), p. 459.   DHU/R
Peters, W. "Man Who Fights
Hate With Love." Redbook

352

Afro-American Religious Studies

(Peters, W. cont.)
(117; Sept., 1961), pp. 36-7.
DLC
"Pilgrimage to Non-Violence."
Christian Century (77; Apr.
13, 1960), pp. 439-41. DHU
Pilpel, H. F. "Copyright Case
Material; unauthorized Record-
ing of Speech by M. L. King."
Publisher's Weekly (185; Apr.
6, 1964), p. 28. DHU
Pitcher, Alvin. "Martin Luther
King Memorial." Criterion
(7:2, Wint., 1968). DLC
-- and David Wallace (et al).
"The Breadbasket Story."
Church in Metropolis (No. 16,
Spr., 1968), pp. 3-5; 10.
DHU/R
"Posthumous Pillory." Time
(96:7, Ag. 17, 1970), pp. 12-
13. DHU/R
Commentary on the book,
The King God Didn't Save, by
John Williams (New York:
Coward-McCann, 1970).
"Prince of Peace Is Dead."
Ebony (23; My. 1968), p. 172.
DHU/MO
"Prophetic Ministry?" Newsweek
(60; Ag. 20, 1962), pp. 78-9.
DHU
Quarles, Benjamin. "Martin Lu-
ther King in History." Ne-
gro History Bulletin (31; My.
1968), p. 9. DHU/MO
Ramsey, Paul. Christian Ethics
and the Sit-In. New York:
Association Pr., 1961.
CtY-D; DHU/R; INU
Ray, J. E. "Deepening Mystery
of Dr. King's Assassination."
U. S. News (64; My. 27, 1968),
p. 10. DHU
"Reactions to the Slaying of Mar-
tin Luther King: Symposium."
America (118; Apr. 20, 1968),
pp. 534-6. DHU
Reddick, Lawrence D. Crusader
Without Violence: A Biogra-
phy of Martin Luther King, Jr.
New York: Harper and Row,
1959. DHU/R

Negro author.
"Revolt Without Violence: the
Negroes New Strategy; Interview." U. S. News (48; Mr.
21, 1960), pp. 76-8. DHU
Richardson, W. H. "Martin Luther King, Unsung Theologian." Commonweal (88; My.
3, 1968), pp. 201-3. DHU
Rogers, Cornish. "SCLC:
Rhetoric or Strategy?" Christian Century (87:35, Sept. 2,
1970), p. 1032. DHU/R
Rohler, J. "Life and Death of
Martin Luther King." Christianity Today (12; Apr. 26,
1968), pp. 37-40. DHU/R
Romero, P. W. "Martin Luther
King and his Challenge to
White America." Negro His-
tory Bulletin (31; My. 1968),
pp. 6-8. DHU/MO
"Roundup: Foreign Tribute to
Dr. King." Christian Century
(85; My. 8, 1968), pp. 629-
30. DHU/R
Rowan Carl T. "Heart of a Pas-
sionate Dilemma." Saturday
Review (42; Ag. 1, 1959), pp.
20-1. DHU
--"Martin Luther King's Tragic
Decision." Reader's Digest
(91:545, Sept., 1967), pp. 37-
42. DHU
Schrag, P. "Uses of Martyr-
dom." Saturday Review of
Literature (51; Apr. 20, 1968),
pp. 28-29. DHU
Schulz, W. "Martin Luther
King's March on Washington."
Reader's Digest (92; Apr.,
1968), pp. 65-9. DHU
Scott, Robert L. The Rhetoric
of Black Power. New York:
Harper & Row, 1969. DHU/R
Negro author.
Chapter 3, Martin Luther
King, Jr. writes about the
birth of the black power slo-
gan.
"Shades of Bull Conner; Attacked
in Selma, Alabama Hotel."
(65; Feb. 1, 1965),

pp. 21-2. DHU
Sharma, Mohan Lal. "Martin
Luther King: Modern Amer-
ica's Greatest Theologican of
Social Action." Journal of Negro History (53:3, Jl., 1968),
pp. 259-63. DHU/MO
Shaw, Rodney. "On the Freedom Road." Concern (7:7, Apr.
15, 1965), pp. 6-8. DHU/R
"Reflections on the Salem
to Montgomery March from
one who walked the fifty
miles."
"Showdown for Non-Violence."
Look (32; Apr. 16, 1968), pp.
23-5.
Sitton, C. "Doctor King, Sym-
bol of the Segregation Strug-
gle." New York Times Maga-
zine (Ja., 1962), pp. 10+.
DHU
Slack, Kenneth. Martin Luther
King. London: S. C. M. Press,
1970. DHU/R
Smylie, James H. "On Jesus,
Pharoahs, and the Chosen
People. Martin Luther King
as Biblical Interpreter and Hu-
manist." Interpretation (24:1,
Ja. 1970), pp. 74+. DHU/R
Thomas, C. W. "Nobel Peace
Prize Goes to Martin Luther
King." Negro History Bulletin
(28; Nov. 1964), p. 35.
DHU/MO
"Tribute to the Rev. Martin Lu-
ther King, Jr." Ebony (16;
Apr., 1961), pp. 91-2+.
DHU/MO
Turner, W. W. "Some Disturb-
ing Parallels; Assassinations
of M. L. King and J. F. Ken-
nedy." Ramparts Magazine (6;
Je. 29, 1968), pp. 33-6.
DHU/R
"Two Perspectives, One Goal;
Accepts Peace Prize." Time
(84; Dec. 18, 1964), p. 21.
DHU
"Un-Christian Christian." Ebony
(20; Ag. 1965), pp. 76-80.
DHU/MO

Wainwright, L. "Martyr of the
Sit-Ins." Life (49; Nov. 7,
1960), pp. 123-4+. DHU
Also in Negro History Bul-
letin (24; Apr., 1961), pp.
147-51+. DHU
"Waiting for Miracles." Time
(80; Ag. 3, 1962), pp. 12-13.
DHU
Weaver, Galen R. "Rebuke to
Dr. King? Negro Official
Speaks Out; Excerpts from Ad-
dress, Aug. 19, 1965." U. S.
News and World Report (59;
Ag. 30, 1965), pp. 16+.
DHU
"When Dr. King Went to Jail
Again." U. S. News and World
Report (53; Jl. 23, 1962), p.
10. DHU
"Why They Follow King." Chris-
tian Advocate (9; Apr. 8,
1965), pp. 2+.
DHU/R; DAU/W
"Will This Prophet Be Heard?"
America (118; Apr. 20, 1968),
p. 532. DHU
Williams, Jim. "King: A Filmed
Record Montgomery to Mem-
phis." Freedomways (10:3,
Third Quarter, 1970), pp. 226-
36.
An evaluation of the film
on activities of Martin Luther
King, Jr. DHU/R
Williams, John A. The King God
Didn't Save. Coward McCann,
1970. DHU/R
"Reflections on the life and
death of Martin Luther King."
Wills, G. "Martin Luther King
is Still on the Case." Esquire
(70; Ag. 1968), pp. 98-104+.
DLC
"Year of Homage to Martin Lu-
ther King." Ebony (24; Apr.
1969), pp. 31-4+. DHU/MO
"Year Later: Honors for Dr.
King; Violence Too." U. S.
News and World Report (66;
Apr. 14, 1969), p. 8. DHU
Young, Andrew J. "Demonstra-
tions: A Twentieth Century

Christian Witness." Social Action (30; My., 1964), pp. 5-
12.   DHU/R
Negro author.
-- "Hope in the Quest for Economic Justice." Tempo (1:25,
Oct. 15, 1969), pp. 5+.
                           DHU/R

-- "Results of Frustration."
Tempo (1:3, Dec. 1, 1968).
                           DHU/R
Young, Peter. "Who Killed Rev.
King? An Interview with
Rev. Bevel." Liberator (9:3,
Mr., 1969), pp. 4-5.
                           DHU/R

C. SOCIAL ACTION--GENERAL

Abrecht, Paul. The Churches
and Rapid Social Change. Gar-
den City, N.Y.: Doubleday,
1961.   DHU/R
Bibliography: p. (208)-216.
"The Church and the Conflict
of Nationalism and Colonial-
ism:" p. (95)-112.
Adams, J. L. "Theological Bases
of Social Action." Journal of
Religious Thought (8:1, Aut.-
Wint., 1950-51), pp. 6-21.
                           DHU/R
Alexander, Raymond P. "The
Church: A Symbol of Commit-
ment." Negro History Bulletin
(28; Ja., 1965), pp. 77-8+.
                           DHU/MO
Alford, Neal B. The Invisible
Road to Peace. Boston: Mead-
or Pub. Co., 1957.
                           DHU/MO
Negro author.
Allan, A. K. "Community Church
of New York City." Crisis (64;
Oct., 1957), pp. 473-77.
                           DHU/MO
"Argument Returns to Dynamite;
Koinonia Farm." Christian
Century (74; Je. 26, 1957), p.
780.   DHU
Austin, Anne. "The Crisis Par-
ish of East Harlem." Social
Action (16:1, Ja. 15, 1950),
pp. 23-33.   DHU/R
Bates, Daisy. The Long Shadow
of Little Rock: A Memoir.
New York: David McKay Co.,
1962.   DHU/R
Negro author.

"Minister action in the
tragedy that placed Little Rock
on the world stage." pp. 156-
60.
"Blacklash Hits the Churches."
Christian Century (81; Ag. 12,
1964), pp. 1004-5.   DHU/R
Brazier, Arthur M. Black Self-
Determination: The Story of
the Woodlawn Organization.
Grand Rapids, Mich.: William
B. Eerdmans Pub. Co., 1969.
                       DHU/R; DLC
Negro author.
Burney, H. L. "Drop-Out Prob-
lem and the Churches." Cen-
tral Christian Advocate (140;
Dec. 15, 1964), p. 4.
                       DHU/R; DAU/W
Bush, J. B. "Is America Chris-
tian?" Negro History Bulle-
tin (27; Apr. 1964), p. 173+.
                       DHU/MO
Campbell, H. W. "Communica-
tion: The Pastor in Social
Unrest." Christian Advocate
(9; Nov. 4, 1965), pp. 15+.
                       DAU/W; DHU/R
Campbell, Will D. "The Role of
Religion in Segregation Crises."
New South (15:1, Ja., 1960),
pp. 3-11.   DHU/MO
Cater, D. G. "Church and the
Reliefers; Urban Negro Slum
Dwellers." Christian Century
(82; Feb. 24, 1965), pp. 232-
5.   DHU/R
"Church Council Speaks on Afri-
can Issues." Christian Cen-
tury (77; Apr. 27, 1960),

p. 500.   DHU
Clark, Mary T. Discrimination
Today; Guidelines for Civic
Action. Foreword by John J.
Wright. New York: Hobbs,
Dorman, 1966.
            DHU/M; INU; DLC
"Company Capitulates to De-
mands of Clergy." Central
Christian Advocate (137; My.
1, 1962), p. 19.
            DAU/W; DHU/R
"Court Cases Brought by Chris-
tian Movement for Human
Rights Against Commissioner
of Public Safety in Birming-
ham." Race Relations Law
Reporter (5; Win., 1960), pp.
1150-52.   DHU/L
Crawford, Evans E. "Some So-
ciological Perspectives of So-
cial Change in the Negro Re-
ligious Community and its
Leadership." Journal of Re-
ligious Thought (18:1, 1961),
pp. 67-77.   DHU/R
    Negro author.
Cuninggim, Merrimon. "The
Southern Temper." New
South (13; Jl. -Ag., 1958), pp.
7-8.   DHU/R
"Division to 'Do-Sponsor' U.N.
Seminar on World View of
Race Relations." Concern (4;
Dec. 15, 1962), p. 12.
                            DAU/W
Dodds, Elizabeth D. Voices of
Protest and Hope. New York:
Friendship Press, 1965.
                            DHU/R
    Chapter 7, The Church,
voice of hope.
Duff, E. "Boston's St. Joseph
Retreat League." Social Order
(8; Je., 1958), pp. 265-68.
                            DCU/SW; DGU
--"Social Action in the American
Environment." Social Order (9;
Sept., 1959), pp. 297-308.
                            DCU/SW; DGU
Egerton, John. "Lucius Pitts and
U. W. Clemon." New South
(25:3, Sum., 1970), pp. 9-20.

                            DHU/R
    The role Miles College
president and students played
in the civil rights struggle in
Birmingham, Alabama.
Ellison, Virginia H. "It Hap-
pened in Shippensburg!" Religious Education (59:1, Ja. -
Feb., 1964), pp. 80-83.
                            DHU/R
    An incident of segregation
in Pennsylvania and the subsequent action of churchmen is
discussed.
Fichter, Joseph H. Social Relations in the Urban Parish.
Chicago: University Press,
1954.   DHU/R
Fiske, Edward B. "Social Action
for the Parish." New York
Times (Oct. 13, 1968).
            Pam. File; DHU/R
Garman, Harold W. "A Theory
of Responsible Action for Bos-
ton Clergymen in Relation to
the 1963 March on Washington." Doctoral dissertation,
Boston University Graduate
School, 1965.
Gehres, M. "Cleveland's Project
Friendship." Presbyterian
Life (21; Ag. 1, 1968), p. 5.
                            DAU/W
Gilliam, W. A. "Prepare Chris-
tians for Revolution." United
Evangelical Action (24; Dec.,
1965), pp. 9-11.   KyLOS
Graham, Billy. "Billy Graham
Makes Plea for an End to In-
tolerance." Life (41; Oct. 1,
1956), pp. 138+.   DHU
Halberstam, David. "The Sec-
ond Coming of Martin Luther
King." Harper's (235:1407,
Ag., 1967), pp. 39-51. DAW
Hamblin, Dora Jane. "Crunch in
the Church." Life (Oct. 4,
1968), pp. 79-87.
            Pam. File; DHU/R
    Protestant ministers and so-
cial action.
Harmon, John J. "Towards a
Style for the White Church."

(Harmon, J. J. cont.)
Church in Metropolis (17;
Sum., 1968), pp. 1-3. DHU/R
Harriman, New York. Discrimi-
nation, What Can Churches
Do? A Handbook and Report
on the Religious Leadership
Conference of Equality of Op-
portunity. Harriman House,
N. Y. Arden House. Apr. 28-
29, 1958.   DHU/MO
Hedgeman, Anna A. The Trum-
pet Sounds. A Memoir of Ne-
gro Leadership. New York:
Rinehart and Winston, 1964.
Negro author.
Height, Dorothy Irene. The
Christian Citizen and Civil
Rights; a Guide to Study and
Action. By Dorothy L. Height
and J. Oscar Lee... New
York: Woman's Press, 1949.
(Public Affiars News Service,
v. 12, no. 4).   NN/Sch
Negro author.
Hickey, Neil. Adam Clayton
Powell and the Politics of
Race. New York: Fleet,
1965.   DHU/R
Humphrey, Hubert Horatio. Inte-
gration vs. Segregation. New
York: Crowell, 1964.
                           DHU/MO
Keenan, C. "Church Leaders on
School Segregation." America
(11; Jl. 10, 1954), pp. 378-
9.   DHU
Kenealy, William J. "Racism
Desecrates Liberty, Perverts
Justice and Love." Social
Order (13; My., 1963), pp. 5-
20.   DHU
    By a professor of law,
Loyola University, Chicago.
Kirk, W. Astor. "Responsible
Use of Social Power by the
Church in Race Relations."
Central Christian Advocate
(138; Ag. 15, 1963), pp. 4+.
                        DAU/W; DHU/R
Negro author.
Kretzschmer, R. "Church in Dis-
advantaged Communities."

World Outlook (25; Dec., 1964),
pp. 11+.   DAU/W
Leo, J. "Black Anti-Semitism."
Commonweal (89:19, Feb. 14,
1969), pp. 618-20.   DHU/R
Lester, Julius. Revolutionary
Notes. New York: Richard
W. Baron, 1969.   DHU/R
Negro author.
"Martin Luther King, Jr.,"
pp. 82-90. "The Poor People's
Campaign and Radicals," pp.
124-27.
"Jewish Racism and Black
Anti-Semitism," pp. 181-84.
Lindsey, A. J. "Church and So-
cial Action." United Evangel-
ical Action (17; Jl. 15, 1958),
pp. 227-30.   KyLS
Martin, W. C. "Shepherds vs.
Flocks; Church Involvement
in Fight Assault on Kodak."
Atlantic Monthly (220; Dec.,
1967), pp. 53-9.   DHU
Meier, August and Elliot Rud-
wick. The Making of Black
America. New York: Athen-
eum Press, 1969.   DHU/R
"Negro Churches Lead Mass 'Get
Out the Vote' Drive." At-
lanta World (Oct. 24, 1968).
        Pam. File; DHU/R
Nelson, William Stuart. "Thor-
eau and American Nonviolent
Resistance." Jules Chamezky,
and S. Kaplan, (eds.). Black
and White in American Cul-
ture. An Anthology from the
Massachusetts Review. (n. p.,
The University of Massachu-
setts Press, 1969), pp. 106-
10.   DHU/R
Negro author.
Nerberg, Well. "Religion in a
Secularized Society." Review
of Religious Research (3:4,
Spr., 1962), pp. 145-58.
                           DHU/R
Niebuhr, Reinhold. "The Negro
Minority and its Fate in a
Self-Righteous Nation." Mc-
Cormick Quarterly (22:4, My.,
1969), pp. 201-10. DHU/R

Article makes a plea for
the church to engage in full
struggle for justice.
Also in, Social Action (35:
2, Oct., 1968), pp. 53-64.
DHU/R
"Nonviolence: The Only Road to
Freedom." Ebony (21; Oct.
1966), pp. 27-30. DHU/MO
Parsonage, R. R. "Blacklash
and Christian Faith." Chris-
tian Century (81; Oct. 21,
1964), pp. 1300-2. DHU/R
Pope, Liston. "Organized Re-
ligion and Pressure Groups."
Conference on Science, Phi-
losophy and Religion. A Sym-
posium. New York: Harper,
1945. Chapter 25. DHU/R
Proctor, Samuel D. The Young
Negro in America, 1960-1980.
New York: Association Press,
1966. DHU/R
Negro author.
"Progress in Little Rock."
Christian Century (80; My. 8,
1963), p. 606. DHU/R
Purnell, J. M. In his Pavilions.
Reflections Upon Religion and
Modern Society. New York:
Exposition Press, 1959.
DHU/MO
Negro author.
Reyburn, William D. "Christian
Responsibility Toward Social
Change." Practical Anthro-
pology (7; My., 1960), pp.
124-31. DHU/R
Root, Robert. Struggle of De-
cency: Religion and Race in
Modern America. New York:
Friendship Press, 1965.
CtY-D; DHU/MO; NN/Sch;
DHU/R; NcD
Rose, Arnold M. The Negro
Protest. Philadelphia: The
American Academy of Political
and Social Science, 1965.
(Annals of... January, 1965).
DHU/R
Ross, Harry. Souls Don't Have
Color. Detroit, Mich.: Pub.
and distributed by UAW-CIO

Fair Practices and Anti-Dis-
crimination Department, 1953.
NcD
Ruoss, Meryl. Citizen Power
and Social Change. The Challenges to Churches. New York:
The Seabury Press, 1968.
DHU/R
"School Integration is Proceed-
ing: Churches Face Many
Problems on Desegregation."
Christian Century (71; Oct. 6,
1954), pp. 1195+. DHU/R
See, Ruth D. What Can We Do?
New York: Friendship Press,
1965. DHU/R
"Directed to Christian youth
within the church who are
looking for solutions to the
perplexing questions of race
prejudice and suspicion that
are consistent with their faith."
Smith, Earnest A. "The Church
and the 1967 Civil Rights
Bill." Concern (9:11, Je. 15,
1967), pp. 4-6. DHU/R
Stevick, Daniel B. Civil Diso-
bedience and the Christian.
New York: Seabury Press,
1969. DHU/R
" '3rd Society' Held Forgotten in
Racial Tension." New York
Times (Nov. 18, 1968).
Pam. File; DHU/R
Ullman, V. "In Darkest America: Delta Ministry Programs
in Mississippi." Nation (205;
Sept. 4, 1967), pp. 177-80.
DHU
Wallace, Helen K. Keys in Our
Hands. Valley Forge: The
Judson Press, 1967. DHU/R
Dedicated to Dr. Leon H.
Sullivan, Negro minister, and
the work of the Opportunities
Industrialization Center, found-
ed by him.
Weaver, Galen R. "Racial Change
and Relevant Religious Faith
and Action." Religious Educa-
tion (59:1, Ja.-Feb., 1964),
pp. 91-4. DHU/R
Wine, S. T. "Humanistic Re-

(Wine, S. T. cont.)
ligious Humanism (Sum.,
1968), p. 124.   DHU/R
Wood, Violet. In the Direction
of Dreams. Stories, N.Y.:
Friendship Press, 1949.

NN/Sch
Church and race relations,
pp. 65-93.
Zeuner, R. W. "Pastor and Social Action." Christian Advocate (9; Ag. 26, 1965), pp.
9+.   DAU/W; DHU/R

D. ORGANIZATIONS

"Council Rescinds Restrictions;
Clergymen's Participation in
Racial Justice Projects."
Christian Century (82; Mar.
10, 1965), p. 293.   DHU/R
Fey, H. E. "N. C. C. Acts on Ra-
cial Crisis." Christian Century
(80; Je. 19, 1963), pp. 797-8.
                       DHU/R
"Fresh Look at Black America;
Conference of the National
Council of Churches." Chris-
tian Century (84; Oct. 25,
1967), pp. 1340-1.   DHU
"Interchurch Social Mission;
Forming Interreligious Com-
mittee Against Poverty."
America (114; Feb. 19, 1966),
p. 246.   DHU
"Michigan Council Releases Poli-
cy Statement on Civil Rights,
1960." Interchurch News (1;
Ag., 1960), p. 4.   DLC
"A Missionary Presence in Mis-
sissippi 1964." Social Action
(31; Nov., 1964), pp. 1-48.
                       DHU/R
     The National Council of
Churches and the Mississippi
Summer Project.
"National Council Churches
Launches Interfaith Movement
in Race Crisis." Christian
Advocate (7; Jl. 4, 1963), p.
22.   DHU/R; DAU/W
"Racism and the Council." Amer-
ica (109; Nov. 2, 1963), p.
507.   DHU
"The Role of the National Council
of Churches in the Mississippi
Summer Project." Social Ac-

tion (31:3, Nov., 1964), pp.
10-15.   DHU/R
Rose, Stephen C. "N. C. C. Vis-
its Clarksdale." Christian
Century (80; Sept. 11, 1963),
pp. 1104-6.   DHU/R
Satterwhite, John H. "For Au-
thentic Freedom; COCU and
Black Churches." Christian
Century (87; Feb. 25, 1970),
p. 236.   DHU/R
     Negro author.
Saunders, F. Brooks. "The
Church and Communication
with the Urban Society." David
McKenna, (ed.). The Urban
Crisis (Grand Rapids, Mich.:
Zondervan, 1969), pp. 61-76.
                       DHU/R
Shriver, Donald W. "Southern
Churches in Transition." New
South (25:1, Wint., 1970), pp.
40-47.   DHU/R
"Support for Mississippi Volun-
teers Reaffirmed by National
Council of Churches." Con-
cern (6; Jl. 15, 1964), pp.
14+.   DAU/W
Survey by Protestant Council of
the City, of New York of Inter-
racial Aspects of the City's
Protestant Churches. New
York Times (Feb. 10, 1957).
                       DLC; DHU
"Toward Integration; Christian
Life Commission." Time (86;
Nov. 26, 1965), p. 68. DHU
Visser't Hooft, Willem Adolph.
The Ecumenical Movement and
the Racial Problem. Paris:
UNESCO, 1954.

DHU/R; NN/Sch; CtY-D
Zinn, Howard. SNCC, The New
Abolitionists. Boston: Beacon
Press, 1964.   DHU/R

A study of the members of
the Student Nonviolent Coordi-
nating Committee in action and
a suggestion as to their contribution to American civilization.

V. The Contemporary Religious Scene

A. CHURCH AND THE URBAN CRISIS

Adams, John P. "The Church Must Read the Riot Act." Concern (9:6, Oct. 1, 1967), pp. 7-13, 19-21. DHU/R
-- "A Letter from the Milwaukee Ghetto: Put it Down in Black and White." Concern (9:17, Oct. 15, 1967), pp. 4-11. DHU/R
-- "A Report from Milwaukee." Concern (9:19, Nov. 15, 1967), pp. 4-5, 11, 13-15. DHU/R
-- "Thoughts on a Bombing." Concern (10:1, Ja. 1-15, 1968), pp. 6-9. DHU/R
"After South Bend, A Sampling of Comments on the Main Issue." The Episcopalian (134: 11, Nov. 1969), pp. 33+. DHU/R
Ahmann, Mathew. "Church and the Urban Negro." America (118; Feb. 10, 1968), pp. 181-5. Discussion (118; Apr. 13, 1968), p. 456. DHU
Bartlett, Bob. The Soul Patrol. Plainfield: Logos International, 1970. DHU
Youth group of Philadelphia that goes into city areas to help people discover the real power of the Christian religion."
Beach, Waldo. Christian Community and American Society. Philadelphia: Westminster Press, 1969. CtY-D
"Bearers of Christ. Address on the Role of the Catholic Church and Other Churches in the Struggle for Racial Improvement in Our Society." New

South (20; Sept., 1965), pp. 13-15. DHU/R
Bervine, J. W. "Christian Concern and Black Business." United Evangelical Action (28; Fall, 1969), pp. 31-3. NcMjHi
Beukema, George G. "Inner City Shared Ministry." The Reformed Review (23:1, Fall, 1969), pp. 51-55. DHU/R
Breeden, Jim. "Church, Racism and Boston." Tempo (1:5, Dec. 15, 1968), p. 8. DHU/R
An interview.
Breen, Jay. "Parish in Hades." Negro Digest (9:6, Apr., 1951), pp. 75-8. DHU/MO
Work of three Protestant ministers in East Harlem, New York City.
Brockway, Allan R. "Riotous Judgement of God." Concern (7:15, Sept. 1, 1965), pp. 12-13. DHU/R; DAU/W
-- "The Urban Riots, the Church and the Future." Concern (9: 16, Oct. 1, 1967), p. 4. DHU/R
Brown, R. "The Christian and the Riot Report." Pulpit Feb., 1969), p. 11. DAU/W
Byrd, Cameron Wells. "Black Power, Black Youth, City's Rebellion. Implication for Youth Ministry." An address, the Pastor of Christ United Church of Christ. Detroit: n. p., n. d. Pam. File; DHU/R
Campbell, James. "Black Community Developers' Search for

360

Roles." Christian Advocate (13:23, Nov. 27, 1969), p. 28. DAU/W

Carling, Francis. "Move Over," Students, Politics, Religion. New York: Sheed & Ward, 1969.   DHU/R
Chapter IV, Religion and Rebellion.

Castle, Robert W. Prayers for the Burned-Out City. New York: Shee & Ward, 1968. DHU/R; DLC

"Catholics and Urban Problems." America (115; Ag. 20, 1966), p. 168.   DHU

Charland, William A. "Contracts and Covenants: A Model for Interracial Social Action." Pastoral Psychology (21:204, My., 1970), pp. 39+. DHU/R

Chatman, Jacob L. "A Black Pastor Speaks to the Issues of His Community." Baptist Leader (31:12, Mr., 1970), pp. 6+.   DHU/R

The Church and the Urban Racial Crisis, edited by Matthew Ahmann and Margaret Roach. Techny, Ill.: Divine Word Publications, 1967. DLC; DHU/R
"The major addresses and background papers prepared for the August, 1967, convention of the National Catholic Conference for Interracial Justice held at Rockhurst College in Kansas City, Missouri."

"Church and Violence in the Nation." The Progressive Nabi (1:1, Apr., 1969), pp. 1-9. Pam. File; DHU/R

"Church Money for the Slums." America (119; Nov. 9, 1968), p. 425.   DHU

"Churches Confront Urban Crisis." Christianity Today (12; Je. 21, 1968), pp. 26-8. DHU/R

Clark, Henry. The Church and Residential Desegregation: a Case Study of an Open Hous-

ing Covenant Campaign. New Haven, Conn.: College & University Press, 1965. DHU/R; INU; NN/Sch

Clark, Kenneth Bancroft. Dark Ghetto; Dilemmas of Social Power. New York: Harper & Row, 1965.   DHU/R
Negro author.
Negro church, pp. 174-83.

Coleman, C.D. "The Crisis in the Nation: Study Guide and Outline for Church and Community Use." Pam. File; DHU/R
Written by secretary of Christian Methodist Episcopal Church, Bd. of Christian Education.

Coles, Robert. "The Lord of the Ghettos. The God Who Asked People to Cross Rivers and Deserts." Commonweal (92:7, Nov. 13, 1970), pp. 167-74.   DHU/R

Conant, Ralph E. "Black Control: A White Dilemma." Perspective (10:1, Spr., 1969), pp. 9-21.

Cully, Kendig B. and F. Nile Harper. Will the Church Lose the City? New York: The World Publishing Co., 1969. DHU/R
Chapter 10, The Black Church in search of a new theology.

Di Gangi, Mariano. "The Church and the Inner City," David McKenna, (ed.). The Urban Crisis (Grand Rapids, Mich.: Zondervan, 1969), pp. 108-20. DHU/R

Drummond, Elanor. "Lady Dynamo in Los Angeles." Presbyterian Life (23:8, Apr., 15, 1970), pp. 14+.   DHU/R
Work of Mrs. Francis L. Hollis, Synod of Southern California Committee on Urban & Specialized Ministries.

Dugan, George. "Interfaith Group to Aid Urban Negroes." New

(Dugan, G. cont.)
York Times (My. 15, 1968).
Pam. File; DHU/R
-- "Presbyterians Define Role in
Welfare Program." New York
Times (My. 20, 1968).
Pam. File; DHU/R
Duncan, W. J. "Non-Prophet Or-
ganization; Church in the Inner
City." Commonweal (89; Dec.
20, 1968), pp. 400-02. DHU/R

The Edge of the Ghetto; a Study
of Church Involvement in
Community Organization. By
John Fish and others. New
York: Seabury Press, 1968.
DLC
Elder, Frederick. Crisis in
Eden: A Religious Study of
Man and Environment. Nash-
ville: Abingdon, 1970.
DHU/R
Ellison, John Malcus. They
Sang Through the Crisis.
Chicago: Judson Press, 1961.
DHU/MO; DLC
Negro author.
Ellul, Jacques. Violence; Re-
flections from a Christian
Perspective. New York:
The Seabury Press, 1969.
DHU/R
Fry, John R. Fire and Black-
stone. Philadelphia: J. B.
Lippincott Co., 1969. DHU/R
The Woodlawn Organization
of the First Church, Presby-
terian, Southside Chicago and
the "Blackstone Rangers."
Gandy, Samuel L. "Youth Es-
tablishments and Protest."
Theology Today (23:2, Jl.,
1966), pp. 316-23.
Pam. File; DHU/R
The younger generation and
its relation to religious organ-
izations.
Negro author.
Greeley, Andrew M. "Changing
City." Catholic World (188;
Mr., 1959), pp. 481-7. DHU
-- "City Life and the Churches."

America (103; Ag. 27, 1960),
pp. 573-4.   DHU
Hargraves, J. Archie. Stop
Pussyfooting Through a Revo-
lution: Some Churches That
Did. New York: United
Church Board for Homeland
Ministries, n.d.
Pam. File; DHU/R
Examples of churches that
got involved in urban problems.
Harrod, Howard L. "The Culture of Poverty." Concern
(7:8, My. 1, 1965), pp. 13-
15.   DHU/R
-- The Ghetto, the Churches and
Social Change: An Evaluation
of the Community Service Project, Washington, D.C., Au-
gust, 1965. Mim. DHU/R
Report on the Howard Uni-
versity Community Service
Project, begun in 1961 in co-
operation with some local ministers of the Washington, D.C.
area.
Herberg, Will. Protestant, Catholic, Jew. Garden City, N.Y.:
Doubleday, 1955.   DHU/R
Chapter on the Negro problem in Protestant city churches.
Hilton, Bruce. The Delta Ministry. New York: Macmillan,
1969.   CtY-D; DHU/R; DLC
Hobson, Sheila. "The New Black
Church; Genesis, Acts and
Revelations." Contact: The
Magazine of Black Involvement (2:9, Nov. 1970), pp.
9-11.   Pam. File; DHU/R
Negro author.
Hook, H. Phillip. "Biblical Mandate for an Inner City Minis-
try." Bibliotheca Sacra (127:
506, Apr.-Je., 1970), pp.
140+.   DHU/R
"How to Carry Out a Conviction;
Episcopal Church Poverty
Programs for Urban Ghettos."
Time (90; Sept. 29, 1967), pp.
53-4.   DHU

James, G. M. "Seminar in the Slums." Christian Life (29; Je., 1967), pp. 34+. DHU/R

Johnson, Benton. "Ascetic Protestantism and Political Preference in the Deep South." American Journal of Sociology (69; Ja., 1964), pp. 359-66.   DHU
        Tie between Republicans and fundamentalist.

Johnson, Philip A. Call Me Neighbor, Call Me Friend: the Case History of the Integration of a Neighborhood on Chicago's South Side. Garden City, N. Y.: Doubleday, 1965.
        INU; DHU/R; DLC; CtY-D

Jones, Madison. "On the Neighborhood Level." Interracial Review (35; Ja., 1962), pp. 1262-3.   DHU/R
        Relationships between Negroes and Catholics.

Karsch, Carl G. "The Meaningful Minority." Presbyterian Life (23:4, Feb. 15, 1970), pp. 8+.   DHU/R
        In suburban Washington, D. C. several denominations organized programs for social action.

Kenrick, Bruce. Come Out the Wilderness; the Story of East Harlem Protestant Parish. Drawing by Joseph Papin. New York: Harper, 1962.
        INU; DHU/R; NN/Sch; CtY-D

King, C. H. "Growing Rebellion in the Negro Church." Negro Digest (12; Mr., 1963), pp. 38-45.   DHU/MO; DLC

Kirk, W. Astor. "Poverty, Powerlessness, the Church." Concern (7:8, My. 1, 1965), pp. 10-12.   DHU/R
        Negro author.

Kramer, Alfred S. "For Those Who Inherit." Religious Education (59:1, Ja. -Feb., 1964), pp. 56-59.   DHU/R
        The religious educator's responsibility in dealing with ra-

cial prejudice.

Kuehn, B. H. "Inner City: An Evangelical Eye-Opener." Christianity Today (13; Ja. 3, 1969), pp. 31-2.   DHU/R

Lambert, Herbert H. "Two Days in the Inner City." World Call (52:2, Feb., 1970), pp. 23+.   DHU/R

Lambert, I. C. "Businessmen Churches and the Ghetto." Christian Century (85; Fcb. 7, 1968), pp. 181-2.   DHU/R

Lee, Robert, (ed.). Cities and Churches: Readings on the Urban Church. Philadelphia: Westminster, 1962. DHU/R

Liu, William T. "The Community Reference System, Religiosity, and Race Attitudes." Social Forces (39; My., 1961), pp. 324-28.   DHU

Lowe, J. R. "Power of Your Purse; Project Equality: Encourager of Fair Employment Practices." McCall's Magazine (95; Apr., 1968), p. 7.

Maddocks, Lewis J. "Panthers vs. Police. Challenge to the Christian. The Nature of the Conflict." Social Action (37: 3, Nov., 1970), pp. 17-29.
                DHU/R

Marshall, Kenneth E. "White Boom-Black Depression." Social Action (36:6, Feb., 1970), pp. 7-17.   DHU/R

Mathe, Judy. "A City Only Needs One Riot." The Episcopalian (133:8, Ag., 1968), pp. 12-14. Pam. File; DHU/R
        A discussion of Northcott Neighborhood House in Milwaukee and its problems and achievements.

McCord, William and John Howard. Life Styles in the Black Ghetto. New York: W. W. Norton & Co., Inc. 1969,   DHU/R
        Pp. 107-17, religion.

McKenna, David L. The Urban Crisis: A Symposium on the

(McKenna, D. L. cont.)
Racial Problem in the Inner
City. Grand Rapids, Mich.:
Zondervan Pub. House, 1970.
DHU/R
Chapter 1, The church and
communication within the ur-
ban society.
McLaurin, Dunbar S. "The Ghe-
diplan: An Approach to
Ghetto Economic Development."
Social Action (36:6, Feb.,
1970), pp. 27-31.   DHU/R
Practical guidelines of how
the churches can help in at-
taining overall economic de-
velopment.
McManus, Michael J. "Barn
Raising in the Ghetto." Christian Herald (93:4, Apr., 1970),
pp. 21-8.   DHU/R
McPeak, William. "Social Prob-
lems are Human Problems."
Interracial Review (35; Nov.,
1962), pp. 253-4.
DCU/SW; DCU
McPeak, Francis W. "The
Churches and Public Housing
in Washington." Social Action
(10:9, Nov. 15, 1944), pp.
4-26.   DHU/R
Mearns, John G. "Changes in
the Black Ghetto--II: Cleve-
land." Saturday Review (53:
31, Aug. 1, 1970), pp. 13-15.
DHU/R
Merton, Thomas. Seeds of De-
struction. New York: Mac-
millan, 1967.   NcD;
DHU/MO; INU; DLC; NN/Sch
"The Black Revolution."
Middeke, Raphael. "Black and
Poor in Cairo." Common-
weal (90:17, Jl. 25, 1969),
pp. 453-54.
Pam. File; DHU/R
Millea, Thomas V. Ghetto Fever.
Milwaukee: Bruce Pub. Co.,
1968.   DLC; NcD
"Minister Defends Aid to Slum
Gangs." New York Times (Je.
25, 1968).
Pam. File; DHU/R

Moberg, David O. "The Church
and the Urban Crisis." David
McKenna, (ed.). The Urban
Crisis (Grand Rapids, Mich.:
Zondervan, 1969), pp. 32-47.
DHU/R
Murray, Michael H. "Holy Week
in Kansas City." Church in
Metropolis (No. 17, Sum.,
1968), pp. 4-7, 11-13.
DHU/R
--"MICA, Kansas City." Church
in Metropolis (No. 17, Sum.,
1968), pp. 8-10.   DHU/R
National Council of Churches.
Dept. of Social Justice. "The
Church and the Urban Crisis."
Mim. Includes Declaration
of Black Churchmen, Declara-
tion of White Churchmen in
response. Resolution on the
Crisis in the Nation by Gen-
eral Board.
Pam. File; DHU/R
Norman, Clarence. "A Study of
How the East Harlem Protes-
tant Is Trying to Solve Some
of the Social and Religious
Problems of an Inner City
Parish." B.D. Paper, School
of Religion, Howard Univer-
sity, 1964.
Odell, Brian N. "Ghetto Ethnic."
Catholic World 210:1, 259,
Feb. 1970), pp. 213-15.
DHU/R
Paul, Joan. "The Bishop Who
Speaks for the Poor." The
Lamp, A Christian Unity Mag-
azine (69:4, Apr., 1971), pp.
16-25.   DHU/R
About Bishop Michael R.
Dempsey, Auxiliary Bishop of
Chicago.
Payne, Ethel L. "Father Groppi,
A Latter Day John Brown."
Chicago Daily Defender (Sept.
30-Oct. 6, 1967).
Pam. File; DHU/R
Payton, Benjamin F. "Civil
Rights and the Future of
American Cities." Social Ac-
tion (33:4, Dec., 1966), pp.

6-11.   DHU/R
    Negro author.
Powell, Don. "We Stayed in the
Inner City." HIS (30:2, Nov.,
1969), pp. 18-19.
    Pam. File; DHU/R
"Project Equality in New York."
America (119; Jl. 20, 1968),
pp. 27-28.   DHU
Protestant Episcopal Church in
the U.S.A. Executive Council.
Showdown at Seattle. New
York: Seabury Press, 1968.
                        DHU/R
    Prepared under the aus-
pices of Executive Council of
the Episcopal Church, an account of the women of the
Church to Presiding Bishop
John Hines plea to the people
gathered at the Triennial Con-
vention to deal with the urban
problems in America.
Putney, Snell and Russell Middle-
ton. "Rebellion, Conformity,
and Parental Religious Ideol-
ogies." Sociometry (24; Je.,
1961), pp. 125-36.   DHU
Rainwater, Lee and William L.
Yancey. The Moynihan Report
and the Politics of Contro-
versy. Cambridge: M.I.T.
Press, 1967.   DHU/MO
Rashford, N.J. "Parishes in the
Central City." America (117;
Oct. 7, 1967), pp. 381-3.
                        DHU
Rhodes, Rhoda. "Accent Local
Church: Taking a Giant Step
into the Business World."
United Church Herald (14:5,
May 1971), pp. 14-7. DHU/R
Richardson, Lincoln. "Rochester's
White Activists." Presbyter-
ian Life (Ag. 1, 1968), p. 12.
                        DAU/W
"The Riot Report and the
Churches." Christian Century
(85:13, Mr. 27, 1968), pp.
379-80.   DHU/R
"Riot Report and the 'Hit'
Churches." Christianity To-
day (12; Feb. 2, 1968), p.

44.   DHU/R
Roberts, Harriet C. "Root Out
Racial Malpractice." Christian Century (89:2, Feb.,
1971), pp. 72-3.   DHU/R
Rooks, Charles Shelby. "New
Ministers for the New City."
Christian Ministry (1:2, Ja.,
1970), pp. 12-17.
    Pam. File; DHU/R
    Negro author.
-- "The Rebirth of Hope." National Elmentary Principal
(48:1, Sept., 1968), pp. 44-
50.   Pam. File; DHU/R
    Negro minister in keynote
speech at Princeton, N.J.,
for parents, teachers and
community on race relations.
-- "Response to a Speech of
George Cabot Lodge." Anglican Theological Review (50:1,
Ja., 1968), pp. 47-51.
                        DHU/R
"Roundup. Religious Agencies
and the Urban Crisis." Christian Century (86; Feb. 12,
1969), pp. 223-4+. DHU/R
Salley, Columbus & Ronald Behm.
Your God is Too White.
Downers Grove, Ill.: Inter-
Varsity Press, 1970. DHU/R
    Racial Crisis in America
written by two evangelicals,
one black and the other white.
Schaller, Lyle E. Planning for
Protestantism in Urban Amer-
ica. New York: Abingdon
Press, 1965.   DHU/R
"Second Chance for Suburbia."
Christian Century (85; Oct.
16, 1968), p. 1296. DHU/R
Senn, Milton. "Race, Religion
and Suburbia." Journal of In-
tergroup Relations (3; Spr.,
1962), pp. 159-70.   DLC
Shipley, David O. Neither Black
Nor White, The Whole Church
for a Broken World. Waco,
Tex.: Word Books, 1971.
                        DHU/R
    Outlines a dynamic pro-
gram for a church related

(Shipley, D. O. cont.)
ministry designed to serve the
individual, black or white.
Simms, David M. "Ethnic Ten-
sions in the Inner-City Church."
Journal of Negro Education.
(31; Fall, 1962), pp. 448-54.
DHU/MO
Simon, A. "Gospel and the Urban
Crisis." Concordia Theologi-
cal Monthly (40; Je., 1969),
pp. 493-500.   DHU/R
Stromberg, Jerome. "The
Church and the Urban Family."
David McKenna, (ed.). The
Urban Crisis (Grand Rapids,
Mich.: Zondervan, 1969), pp.
96-107.   DHU/R
Sullivan, Leon H. Build Brother
Build. Chicago: Ebony Book-
shop, 1970.   DHU/R
Opportunities Industrializa-
tion Center, founder explains
program.
Negro minister of Philadel-
phia.
--"Conquering Poverty Through
Self-Help." Christian Econ-
omics (21:18, Sept. 30, 1969),
DHU/R
Clergyman-educator shares
his tested formula for an ef-
fective answer to poverty.
Tillman, James A. Not by
Prayer Alone; a Report on the
Greater Minneapolis Interfaith
Fair Housing Program. Phila-
delphia: United Church Press,
1964. DHU/R; DLC; CtY-D
Turner, Franklin D. "St. George's
Episcopal Church; An Inner City
Church, Washington, D. C."
Faith and Form (3; Apr., 1970),
pp. 16-19.   DHU/R
Negro author.
"Un-Ghettoing Suburbia." Tempo
(Nov. 15, 1968).
Pam. File; DHU/R
United Presbyterian Church in
the United States. Education in
the City Church. Philadelphia:
The United Presbyterian Church,
U. S. A. Bd. of Christian Edu-

cation, 1967.   DHU/R
Project in the inner-city
churches of Chicago, its purpose for a possibility of a
truly evangelical impact on the
people of the city.
Van Ness, Paul. "An Experi-
mental Church Related Counseling Program for the Inner
City." Pastoral Psychology
(20:198, Nov. 1, 1969), pp.
15+.   DHU/R
Walker, Lucius. "Church Renewal in Rural and Urban
America." International Review
of Mission (58:230, Apr.,
1969), pp. 158-64.   DHU/R
--"Mass Based Organization: A
Style for Christian Mission."
Church in Metropolis (No. 17,
Sum., 1968), pp. 21-6.
DHU/R
Washington, Betty. "Milwaukee
Struggle Nears Crisis." Chi-
cago Daily Defender (Sept. 23-
29, 1967), Pam. File; DHU/R
About a white priest, Fr.
James E. Groppi, leader of
open housing demonstrations
in Milwaukee.
Waterman, Kenneth S. "The
Church in the Ghetto." Church
in Metropolis (No. 15, Wint.,
1967), pp. 23-7.   DHU/R
Willie, Charles V. Church Ac-
tion in the World: Studies in
Sociology and Religion. New
York: Morehouse-Barlow Co.,
1969.   DHU
"Crisis in American cities
--a call for church action,"
pp. 119-38.
Wilson, Robert L. and James H.
Davis. The Church and the Ra-
cially Changing Community.
Nashville: Abingdon Press,
1966.   DHU/MO
Winter, Gibson. The Suburban
Captivity of the Churches.
Garden City, N. Y.: Doubleday
& Co., 1961.   DHU/R; TNU
Negro churches, pp. 112-18.
Wright, Nathan. Ready to Riot.

New York: Holt, Rinehart &
Winston, 1968.			DHU/R
Account of the factors that
led to the riots in Newark,
N. J. , by a former Protestant

Episcopal priest.
Younger, G. D. "Church and Urban Renewal." Review. Commonweal (82; Jl. 23, 1965), p.
540.				DHU

B. BLACK SEPARATISM

1. Black Theology, Black Power, and Black Religion

Adams, Charles G. "The Burden
of the Black Religion." Tempo
(2:5; 6, Dec. 15-Ja. 1, 1970),
p. 15.				DHU/R
Allen, Blanche T. "An Analysis
and Interpretation of Thirty-
One Poems of James Weldon
Johnson Implications for Black
Religious Experience." M.
Div. Paper, School of Religion,
Howard University, 1971.
Negro author.
"Artists Portray a Black Christ."
Ebony (26:6, Apr. , 1971), pp.
177-80.			DHU/R
Bailey, Leroy. "A Comparative
Analysis of The Negro Church
in America, by E. Franklin
Frazier and Black Religion,
by Joseph R. Washington, Jr."
M. Div. Paper, School of Re-
ligion, Howard University,
1971.
Negro author.
"Baldwin Excoriates Church for
Hypocritical Race Stance."
Afro-American (Jl. 16, 1968).
		Pam. File; DHU/R
Banks, Walter R. "Two Impos-
sible Revolutions? Black Pow-
er and Church Power." Jour-
nal for the Scientific Study of
Religion (8:2, Fall, 1969), pp.
263+.				DHU/R
Barbour, Floyd B. , (ed.). The
Black Power Revolt: A Col-
lection of Writings on "Black
Power." Boston: Extending
Horizons Books, 1968. DHU/R
Contains articles by black

theologians.
Barndt, Joseph R. Why Black
Power. New York: Friend-
ship Press, 1968.	DHU/R
Chapter 6, Freedom, Pow-
er and the Church."
Becker, William H. "Black Pow-
er in Christological Perspec-
tive." Religion in Life (38:3,
Aut. , 1969), pp. 404-14.
				DHU/R
Bennett, Robert A. "Black Ex-
perience and the Bible." The-
ology Today (27:4, Ja. , 1971),
pp. 422-33.			DHU/R
Berry, Benjamin D. "Soul Broth-
ers, Unite: Comments on the
Black Church." Katallagete
(2:2, Fall, 1969), pp. 30-33.
				DHU/R
"Black Baptist Demands Met."
Journal and Guide (Je. 8,
1968).	Pam. File; DHU/R
"Demands of the delegates
to the American Baptist Con-
vention for more representa-
tion."
"The Black Church." Journal of
Negro Education of the A. M.
E. Church. (30:3, Mr. -My.
1970), pp. 2, 16.	DHU/R
Editorial on Contributions
of traditional "Negro Church."
Black Church/Black Theology.
Summation of Lectures Given
in Washington, D. C. , Spring
1969 at Georgetown Univer-
sity. J. Deotis Roberts,
Walter Yates, Joseph R.
Washington and Preston Wil-

(Black Church... cont.)
liams.
Mim. Pam. File; DHU/R
Negro author.
Black Militancy and the University; Report of a Conference for Campus Clergy, November 29-December 1, 1968 at Shaw University, Raleigh, N. C. Washington, D. C.: National Newman Apostolate, 1969.
DLC; Pam. File; DHU/R
"Racism and its theological implications."
Black Power in the Pulpit." Time (90; Nov. 17, 1967), p. 87.   DHU
"Black Power Moves on Churches." U. S. News & World Report (Ag. 26, 1968).
Pam. File; DHU/R
"Black Power Restated by United States Presbyterians." Chicago Daily Defender. (Ag. 13-19, 1966). Pam. File; DHU/R
"The Black Religious Experience and Theological Education for the Seventies: A Report of the Special AATS Committee. Theological Education (6:3, Spr., 1970), suppl. DHU/R
Bone, Richard. "A Black Man's Quarrel with the Christian God." New York Times Book Review (Sept. 11, 1966). DHU
Brown, Clifton F. Black Religion, 1968. Hart M. Nelson & Raytha L. Yokley, et. al. The Black Church in America (New York: Basic Books, 1971). Negro author. DHU/R
Brown, Clifton F. "Black Religion--1968." Patricia Romero, (ed.). In Black America (Washington, D. C.: United Publishing Co., 1969), pp. 345-53.   DHU/R
Brown, Harold O. J. "Evolution, Revolution or Victory." Christianity Today (14:14, Apr. 10, 1970), pp. 10-15.
DHU/R

"Written by a Negro Evangelist taken from his address on Evangelism to the U. S. Congress of Evangelism."
Browne, Robert S. "The Case for Black Separatism." Cross Currents (18:4, Fall, 1968), pp. 471-82.   DHU/R
Cassels, Louis. "Black Power Becoming Force in Religious Life." Chicago Daily Defender (Nov. 1, 1968).
Pam. File; DHU/R
Chandler, Russell. "Church Militants Fashion a New Black Theology." The Evening Star (Nov. 2, 1968).
Pam. File; DHU/R
Cleage, Albert. Black Messiah New York: Sheed & Ward, 1968.   DHU/R; DLC
--"The Black Messiah." (New York: Sheed & Ward, 1968) Review by Robert Batchelder. Encounter (31:1, Wint., 1970), p. 79.   DHU/R
--"Interview: Al Cleage on Black Power." Repr. from United Church Herald, Feb., 1968. Pam. File; DHU/R
"Clergy Meet Shows Black Power Growth." Afro-American (Oct. 29, 1968). Pam. File; DHU/R
Coggins, Ross. "On the Street Where You Live." Baptist Student (49:8, My., 1970), pp. 26+.   DHU/R
Article deals with Christians on fair housing.
Coleman, C. D. "Agenda for the Black Church." Religious Education (64:6, Nov. -Dec., 1969), pp. 441-46. DHU/R
"Color God Black." New York Times (Nov. 10, 1968).
Pam. File; DHU/R
Committee on Theological Prospectus, National Committee of Black Churchmen. "Black Theology: A Statement of the National Committee of Black Churchmen." Christian Century (86:42, Oct. 15, 1969),

p. 1310.   DHU/R
Cone, James H. "Black Con-
sciousness and the Black
Church." Christianity and
Crisis (30:18, Nov. 2 & 16,
1970), pp. 244-50.   DHU/R
Negro author.
--"Black Consciousness and the
Black Church: A Historical-
Theological Interpretation."
The Annals of the American
Academy of Political and So-
cial Science (37; Ja., 1970),
pp. 49-55.   DHU/R
--"Black Power, Black Theol-
ogy, and the Study of Theol-
ogy and Ethics." Theological
Education (6:3, Spr., 1970),
pp. 202-15.   DHU/R
-- Black Theology and Black Pow-
er. New York: Seabury
Press, 1969. DHU/R; DLC
--"Black Theology and Black
Power." Christian Century
(86:51, Dec. 17, 1969), pp.
1619+.   DHU/R
A review.
--"Black Theology and Violence."
The Tower, Alumni Magazine,
Union Theological Seminary
(Spr., 1969).   NNUT
-- A Black Theology of Libera-
tion. Philadelphia: Y. B.
Lippincott & Co., 1970.
                      DHU/R
--"Failure of the Black Church."
Liberator (9:5, My., 1969),
pp. 14-17; 22+.   DHU/R
--"Toward a Black Theology."
Ebony (25:10, Ag., 1970), pp.
113-16.   DHU/R
Copher, Charles B. "Perspec-
tive and Questions: The Black
Religious Experience and Bib-
lical Studies." Theological
Education (6:3, Spr., 1970),
pp. 181-88.   DHU/R
Culverhouse, Patricia. "Black
Religion: Folk or Christian.
Foundation: A Baptist Journal
of History and Theology. (13:
4, Oct. -Dec., 1970), pp. 295-
315.   DHU/R

Curry, Norris S. "When the Subject is the Negro Church,"
(Guest editorial). The Christian Index (103:9, Apr. 30,
1970), pp. 3-4.   DHU/R
Daniels, Joseph. "The Psycho-
dynamics of Racism." Chris-
tianity Today. (15:1, Oct. 9,
1970), pp. 12-14.   DHU/R
Davis, Emory G. "Religion and
Black Power." Chicago Daily
Defender (Sept. 9-15, 1967),
Pam. File; DHU/R
Dickinson, Richard. "Black The-
ology and Black Power." En-
counter (3:4, Aut., 1970), pp.
387-92).   DHU/R
"Review of James Cone's
Black Theology and Black Pow-
er (New York: Seabury Press,
1969)."
"Dr. Benjamin Mays Gives Black
Power's Definition." Journal
and Guide (My. 11, 1968).
Pam. File; DHU/R
Dole, Kenneth. "Pastor Sees
'Black Theology' in Militants."
Washington Post (Dec. 14,
1968), Pam. File; DHU/R
Fiske, Edward B. "The Black-
White Power Struggle in the
Church." Tempo (22:1, Sept.
1, 1969), pp. 3; 11. DHU/R
--"The Messiah is Black."
Tempo (1:4, Dec. 1, 1968),
p. 5.   DHU/R
--"Now a Challenge to the
Church From the Blacks."
Mim. 2 pp.
Pam. File; DHU/R
Flournoy, Ray. Black Christian
Studies. Denver, Colo.: The
Church of the Black Cross,
1971. vol. 1.
Pam. File; DHU/R
Foster, Isaac & Leon Howell.
"On Growing Up Black in Mis-
sissippi." Tempo (1:22, Sept.
1, 1969), pp. 6-7. DHU/R
Memories of Isaac Foster,
founder and administrator of
"Freedom City."
Fry, John R. "Soul." McCor-

(Fry, J. R. cont.)
mick Quarterly (23:2, Ja.,
1970), pp. 123-29.   DHU/R
Theological implications of
the usage of the word "Soul"
by Blacks.
Gardiner, James J. and J. Deotis Roberis. Quest for a Black
Theology. Philadelphia: Pilgrim Press, 1971.   DHU/R
Georgetown University, Washington, D. C. Black Church/Black
Theology. Summation of Lectures given by James D. Ro-
berts, Walter L. Yates,
Joseph R. Washington, Jr.,
and Preston Williams at a Institute sponsored by the Gray-
moor Ecumenical Institute and
the Georgetown University,
Department of Theology. Feb.
1970. Mim.
          Pam. File; DHU/R
Gray, Ocam J. "An Analysis of
Revivalism in America With
Special Reference to Charles
G. Finney and the Black Re-
ligious Perspective." M. Div.
Paper, School of Religion,
Howard University, 1971.
Negro author.
Gregory, Dick. "Knowing the
Truth." The Episcopalian
(133:4, Apr., 1968), pp. 14-
15.   Pam. File; DHU/R
Groves, Richard. "Black Power
in the Church." The Student:
The Changing Church (50:3,
Dec. 1970), pp. 45-7. DHU/R
Hanson, Geddes. "Black Theol-
ogy and Protestant Thought."
Social Progress (Sept. -Oct.
1969), pp. 5-12.   DLC
"Happening at St. Louis." (Edi-
torial). Tempo (1:4, Dec. 1,
1968).   DHU/R
Harding, Vincent. "The Afro-
American Past." Motive (28:
7, Apr., 1968), pp. 6-11.
                     DHU/R
Negro author.
--"Black Power and the Amer-
ican Christ." Floyd Barbour,

(ed.). The Black Power Re-
volt (Boston: Extending Hori-
zon Books, 1968), pp. 85-93.
                     DHU/R
--"The Gift of Blackness."
Repr. New York: Dept. of
Publication Services, 1967.
     Pam. File; DHU/R
Also in Katallagete (Sum.,
1967), pp. 17-22.   DHU/R
--"Reflections and Meditations
on the Training of Religious
Leaders for the New Black
Generation." Theological Edu-
cation (6:3, Spr., 1970), pp.
189-201.   DHU/R
--"The Religion of Black Power."
Donald R. Cutler, (ed.). The
Religious Situation, 1968.
(Boston: Beacon Press, 1969),
pp. 3-37.   DHU/R
--"The Uses of the Afro-Amer-
ican Past." Donald R. Cutler,
(ed.). The Religious Situation,
1969. (Boston: Beacon Press,
1969), pp. 829-40. DHU/R
Hargraves, J. Archie. "Blacken-
ing Theological Education."
Christianity and Crisis (29;
Apr. 14, 1969), pp. 93-8.
                     DHU/R
Harrington, M. "Religion and
Revolution." Commonweal
(91; Nov. 14, 1969), pp. 203-
4.   DHU/R
Haughley, J. "Black Theology."
America (120:20, My. 17,
1969), p. 583.   DHU
Henry, Hayward. "Toward a Religion of Revolution," The
Black Scholar (2:4, Dec.,
1970), pp. 27-31.   DHU
Negro author.
Herzog, Frederick. "The Politi-
cal Gospel," Christian Cen-
tury (87:46, Nov. 18, 1970),
pp. 1380-83.   DHU/R
Professor of Systematic
Theology at Duke University
asks what has gone wrong with
white theology.
--"Theology of Liberation."
Continuum (7:4, Wint., 1970),

pp. 515-24. DHU/R
Hickman, Garrison M. "A Critique of Black Theology." M. Div. Paper, School of Religion, Howard University, 1971. Negro author.
Hill, Bob. "The Dilemma of the Black Christian." Moody Monthly (69:11, Sept., 1969), pp. 34-37. DHU/R
Responses to Article (70:4, Dec., 1969), pp. 30-31.
Hill, Edward V. "White Liberals Behind Black Militancy." Christian Economics (23:3, Feb. 11, 1970), pp. 2+. DHU/R
Article by Negro minister of Watts, California. Negro author.
Hobbs, Helen. "Who Speaks for America's Blacks?" Christian Herald (92:8, Ag., 1969), pp. 16-21. DHU/R
Hodges, William H. "Not by White Might Nor by Black Power." Christianity Today (15:1, Oct. 9, 1970), pp. 5-10. DHU/R
Horton, Frank L. "Teaching Black History in the Local Church." Christian Advocate (14:3, Feb. 5, 1970), pp. 11+. DHU/R
Hough, Joseph C. Black Power and White Protestants; a Christian Response to the New Negro Pluralism. New York: Oxford University Press, 1968. DHU/R; INU
"In Search of a Black Christianity." Time (94:1, Jl. 4, 1969), pp. 57-8. Pam. File; DHU/R
Jackson, Jesse L. "Black Power and White Churches." Church in Metropolis (16; Spr., 1968), pp. 6-9. DHU/R
Negro author.
Johnson, Joseph A. (bp.). "The Legitimacy of Black Theology." Christian Index (103:7, Apr. 9, 1970), pp. 3-4. DHU/R

Negro author.
-- "Jesus: the Liberator." Andover Newton Quarterly (10: 3, Ja., 1970), pp. 58-96. DHU/R
"Quest for the Black Jesus and the limitations of White Theology."
-- The Soul of the Black Preacher. Philadelphia: United Church Press, 1971. DHU/R
Johnson, William R. "A Black Prayer and Litany." Theology Today (26:3, Oct., 1969), pp. 262-65. DHU/R
Jones, Lawrence N. "Black Churches in Historical Perspective." Christianity and Crisis (30:18, Nov. 2 & 16, 1970), pp. 226-28. DHU/R
Author is acting President and Professor of Afro-American Church History at Union Theological Seminary, New York.
Negro author.
-- "They Sought a City: The Black Church and Churchmen in the Nineteenth Century." Union Seminary Quarterly Review (26:3, Spr., 1971), pp. 253-72. DHU/R
Jones, Major J. "Black Awareness: Theological Implications of the Concept." Religion in Life (38:3, Aut., 1969), pp. 389-403. DHU/R
Negro author.
-- Black Awareness: A Theology of Hope. Nashville: Abingdon Press, 1971. DHU/R
Kennedy, Robert F. "Suppose God is Black." Look (Ag. 23, 1966), pp. 45-7.
Pam. File; DHU/R
Kennedy, William T. "The Genius of Black Preaching." A. M. E. Zion Quarterly Review (83:2, Sum., 1971), pp. 100-8. DHU/R
Kilgore, Thomas. "The Black Church." Ebony (25:10, Ag. 1970), pp. 106-10. DHU/MO

King, Martin Luther. "Black
Power." Ross & Barker. The
Afro-American Readings. New
York: Van Nostrand, Rein-
hold Co., 1970, pp. 389-403.
                      DHU/MO
    Negro author.
Ledit, Joseph H. "Dark Madon-
nas." The Chronicle: Official
Organ of the Federated Colored Catholics (5:1, Ja., 1932),
pp. 2-4.   DHU/MO; DHU/R
Lincoln, Charles Eric. Black Na-
tionalism and Christian Con-
science." Concern (5; Sept.
15, 1963), pp. 5+. DAU/W
    Negro author.
Lippincott, H. H. "Still Jimcrow
Churches?" Christian Century
(72; Feb. 9, 1955), pp. 172+.
                      DHU/R
Long, Charles H. "The Black
Reality: Toward a Theology
of Freedom." Criterion (8:2,
1969), pp. 2-7.
         Pam. File; DHU/R
Response to above article
by Nathan A. Scott, pp. 8-11.
         Pam. File; DHU/R
    Negro author.
Longcope, Kay. "Toward a New
Black Church." Tempo (1:4,
Dec. 1, 1968), p. 3. DHU/R
"The Magic of..."Black Nativity."
Sepia (14; Je., 1965), pp. 36-
41.   DHU/MO
Marshall, Calvin B. "The Black
Church--Its Mission is Liber-
ation." The Black Scholar (2:
4, Dec., 1970), pp. 13-19.
                      DHU/R
    Negro author.
Mason, William. "Hermeneutics
and the Black Experience."
Reformed Review (23:4, Sum.,
1970), 217+.   DHU/R
McCall, Emmanuel L. "The
Black Struggle, How Can You
Help?" The Baptist Student
(49:2, Nov., 1969), pp. 19+.
                      DHU/R
McClain, William B. "The Gen-
ius of the Black Church."

Christianity and Crisis (30:8,
Nov. 2 & 16, 1970), pp. 250-
2.   DHU/R
"Miracle in Atlanta --A Black
Christ." Ebony (24:2, Dec.,
1968), pp. 33-40.
         Pam. File; DHU/R
Mitchell, Henry H. "Black Chris-
tianity in the Post-Christian
Era., U.S.A." The Black
Scholar (2:4, Dec., 1970), pp.
43-9.   DHU
    Negro author.
--"Black Power and the Chris-
tian Church." 8 pp. Mim.
         Pam. File; DHU/R
"Written by the pastor of
Calvary Baptist Church, Santa
Monica, Calif. for seminary
students at American Baptist
related theological schools."
--"Issues and Perspectives: The
Practical Field and its Rela-
tionship to the Black Man's
Practice of the Christian
Faith." Theological Education
(6:3, Spr., 1970), pp. 216-23.
                      DHU/R
Moltmann, Jürgen. "Toward a
Political Hermeneutics of the
Gospel." Union Seminary Quar-
terly Review (23:4, 1968), pp.
303-23.   DHU/R
Moss, James A. "The Negro
Church and Black Power."
An Address. Journal of Human
Relations (2: Spr., 1964), pp.
152-61.   DAU; DCU/SW
Moss, Leonard W. and Stepen C.
Cappannari. "The Black Madon-
na: An Example of Culture
Borrowing." Scientific Monthly
(76:6, Je., 1953), pp. 319-24.
         Pam. File; DHU/R
Based on a paper presented
to the Anthropology Section of
the American Association for
the Advancement of Science,
December 28, 1952, St. Louis,
Missouri.
Murray, Michael H. "White
Churches and Black Power."
Church in Metropolis (no. 16,

Spr. , 1968), pp. 1-3. DHU/R
Nelsen, Hart M. and Raytha Yok-
ley, (eds.). The Black Church
in America. New York: Basic
Books, Inc. , 1971. DHU/R
Collection of writings pre-
viously published by social sci-
entists and journalists selected
to reveal the complex nature
of the black church.
Nelson, J. Robert. "The World
Council and Race: Give the
Black Man his Own Turf."
Catholic World (209:1254,
Sept. 1, 1969), pp. 256-61.
DHU/R
Newman, Richard. "Black Power,
Black Nationalism, Black Re-
bellion." Concern (9:16, Oct.
1, 1967), pp. 5-6. DHU/R
Newman, Richard A. "Black
Power." Concern (8:15, Sept.
1, 1966), p. 4.
Pam. File; DHU/R
Niebuhr, Richard R. "Theologi-
ans Comments on the Negro
in America." Reporter (15;
Nov. 29, 1956), pp. 24-5.
Discussion (15; Dec. 27,
1956), p. 3. DHU/R
Norman, Clarence. "A Construc-
tive Study of the Concept of
Liberation in Contemporary
' Black Religion ' With Special
Preference to the Thought of
James Cone, Vincent Harding
and James Deotis Roberts."
Doctor of Religion Paper,
School of Religion, Howard
University, 1971.
Negro author.
Norton, W. "Black Power Gos-
pel." Christian Life (Oct. ,
1968), pp. 39+. DHU/R
Ntlabati, Gladstone. "The Two
Apartheids: White Man's
Heaven--Black Man's Hell."
Social Action (34:8, Apr. ,
1968), pp. 26-34. DHU/R
Obatala, J. K. "Islam and Black
Liberation." Liberator (10:6,
Je. , 1970), pp. 4-10. DHU/R
Oliver, C. Herbert. "Black

Power; What Does it Mean?"
Journal of the American Scien-
tific Affiliation (22:2, Je. ,
1970), pp. 44-5. DHU/R
Deals with the political, so-
cial and religious ramification
of Black Power.
Payne, Ethel L. "Survey Shows
Role of Black in Church."
Chicago Daily Defender (Ja.
16, 1969). Pam. File; DHU/R
Poinsett, Alex. "The Black Re-
volt in White Churches."
Ebony (23:11, Sept. , 1968),
pp. 63-8. Pam. File; DHU/R
--"The Quest for a Black
Christ." Ebony (24:3, Mr. ,
1969), pp. 170-8. DHU/MO
Powell, Adam Clayton, Jr.
"Black Power in the Church."
The Black Scholar (2:4, Dec. ,
1970), pp. 32-4. DHU/R
Negro author.
Price, Jo-Ann. "Churches Have
'Betrayed' Negroes, James
Baldwin Tells World Assem-
bly." Washington Post (Jl. 8,
1968). Pam. File; DHU/R
Rashke, Richard. "Black Theol-
ogy: A Gospel of Confronta-
tion." The Lamp/A Christian
Unity Magazine (68:5, My. ,
1971), pp. 2-4. DHU/R
The White Administrator of
the International Research and
Self-Study team of the Divine
Word Missionaries.
"Regarding the Race Crisis (Tom
Skinner Cites Need for Negro
Christian Responsibility).
Wesleyan Advocate (Feb. 10,
1969), p. 6. DAU/W
"Religion; The Black Church;
Three Views." Time (95:14,
Apr. 6, 1970), pp. 71+.
Pam. File; DHU/R
Relyea, Harold C. "The Theol-
ogy of Black Power." Religion
in Life (38:3, Aut. , 1969), pp.
415-20. DHU/R
Rice, Willa Mae. "Black Separa-
tists Preaching 'KKK Gospel'
J. H. J. Warns." Pittsburgh

(Rice, W. M. cont.)
Courier (Sept. 21, 1968).
    Pam. File; DHU/R
Roberts, James Deotis. "Folk-
lore and Religion: The Black
Experience." Journal of Re-
ligious Thought (27:2, Sum.
Suppl., 1970), pp. 5-15.
                        DHU/R
    Negro author.
Rogers, Jefferson P. "The
Church in Crisis." Church
and Society (55:5, My. -Je.,
1970), pp. 24-28.   DHU/R
    "In the true church there
can be no basic divisions be-
tween the black church and
the white church."
Rooks, Charles Shelby. "The
Black Church and Theological
Education." Nexus (12:3, Spr.,
1969), pp. 13-16+.
    Pam. File; DHU/R
    Negro author.
-- "The Black Church Looks
Ahead."
    Mim. Pam. File; DHU/R
    Sermon preached at Lin-
coln Memorial Temple United
Church of Christ, Nov. 30,
1969, Washington, D. C.
-- "Crisis in Church Negro Lead-
ership." Theology Today (22:
3, Oct., 1965), pp. 323-35.
    Pam. File; DHU/R
-- "From Genesis to Revelation:
Black Identity in the Church."
Shawensis (Sum., 1969), pp.
30-34. Pam. File; DHU/R
-- "God's Grace and New Begin-
nings." Dimension; Theology
in Church and World (6:1,
Fall, 1968), pp. 34-40.
    Pam. File; DHU/R
-- "Implications of the Black
Church for Theological Education." Voice (61:1, Ja.,
1969), pp. 3-5+.
    Pam. File; DHU/R
-- "Theological Education and the
Black Church," Christian Cen-
tury (8:7, Feb. 12, 1969), pp.
212-16.   DHU/R

-- "Why a Conference on the
Black Religious Experience."
Theological Education (6:3,
Spr., 1970), pp. 173-80.
                        DHU/R
Ruether, Rosemary. "Black The-
ology and Black Church." The
Journal of Religious Thought
(26:2, Sum. Suppl., 1969), pp.
26-33.   DHU/R
-- "Black Theology and Black
Church." Religious Education
(64:5, Sept. -Oct., 1969), pp.
347-51.   DHU/R
Rutenber, C. G. "American Bap-
tists Respond to Black Power
Challenge." Christian Century
(85:27, Jl. 3, 1968), pp. 878-
80.   DHU/R
Satterwhite, John H. Will the
Black Experience Make Meth-
odists One People? Repr.
    Pam. File; DHU/R
    Speech made at Annual
Meeting of Commission on Ec-
umenical Affairs, Western
N. C. Conference, United Meth-
odist Church, Duke University,
Graduate Center, Wednesday,
October 28, 1970.
    Negro author.
Schackern, Harold. "Toward a
New Black Theology." Tempo
(Dec. 1, 1968).
    Pam. File; DHU/R
"A Separate Black Church Ahead?"
Christianity Today (8:4, Nov.
22, 1968), pp. 40-42.
    Pam. File; DHU/R
Sheares, Reuben A. "Beyond
White Theology." Christianity
and Crisis (30:18, Nov. 2 &
16, 1970), pp. 229-35.
                        DHU/R
    "The role in status of
Blacks in relation to the gos-
pel in white theology was that
of an outsider."
Skinner, Tom. How Black is the
Gospel? Philadelphia: J. B.
Lippincott Co., 1970.
                        DHU/R
    Negro author.

-- Words of Revolution. Grand
Rapids, Mich.: Zondervan
Pub. House, 1970.   DHU/R
Sleeper, Charles Freeman.
Black Power and Christian Re-
sponsibility; Some Biblical
Foundations for Social Ethics.
Nashville: Abingdon Press,
1969.   DHU/R; CtY-D
"SNCC Position Paper on Black
Power. "Who Is the Real Vil-
lain--Uncle Tom or Simon Le-
gree?" Thomas Wagstaff,
(ed.). Black Power: The Radical Response to White America (Beverly Hills: Glencoe
Press, 1969), pp. 11-118.
              DHU/R
Soulen, Richard N. "Black Worship and Hermeneutic." Christian Century (87:6, Feb. 11,
1970), pp. 168+.   DHU/R
Starr, Paul. "Black Panthers
and White Radicals." Com-
monweal (92:12, Je. 12, 1970),
pp. 294-97.   DHU/R
Stepp, Diane. "Baptist Deny
Failing to Act on Social Ills."
Atlanta Constitution (Sept. 5,
1968). Pam. File; DHU/R
-- "Decatur Baptist Become Relevant." Atlanta Constitution (Ag.
31, 1968).
            Pam. File; DHU/R
Stiles, B. J. "Where Have All
the Negroes Gone?" Motive
(28:4, Ja., 1968), pp. 4-5.
              DHU/R
"Theological Education and the
Black Church." Information
Service (48; Mr. 8, 1969), p.
6.   CtY; DLC
Thomas, Harold A. "The Ideol-
ogy of Black Power." Dimen-
sion: Theology in Church and
World (6:1, Fall, 1968), pp.
47-60. Pam. File; DHU/R
Thomas, Neil. "White Church
and Black Business." Com-
monweal (90:19, Ag. 22,
1969), pp. 503-04. DHU/R
Thompson, J. Earl. "Black
Studies and White American-

ism." Andover Newton Quarterly Review (62:2, Nov.,
1969), pp. 56-65.
            Pam. File; DHU/R
Thurman, Howard. "Mysticism
and Ethics." Journal of Religious Thought (27:2, Sum.
Suppl., 1970), pp. 23-30.
              DHU/R
    Negro author.
Trueblood, Roy W. "Union Nego-
tiations Between Black Methodists in America." Methodist
History (8:4, Jl., 1970), pp.
18-29.   DHU/R
United Methodist Church. Board
of Missions. "Youth Black Coalition Trigger Missions Debate."
Christian Advocate (13:22, Nov.
13, 1969), pp. 24+. DHU/R
Vincent, John. "A Renaissance
for Theology Through Rac-
ism." Christian Advocate (14:
9, Apr. 30, 1970), pp. 7-8.
              DHU/R
Vivian, C. T. Black Power and
the American Myth. Philadel-
phia: Fortress Press, 1970.
              DHU/R
    Chapter 4, "Christian love
and Christian hate."
    Negro author.
Wallace, W. J. L. "The Black
Church: Past and Present."
The A. M. E. Zion Quarterly
Review (82:2, Sum., 1970),
pp. 63-72.   DHU/R
-- "The Mission of the Black
Church." The A. M. E. Zion
Quarterly Review (82:2, Sum.,
1970), pp. 73-76. DHU/R
Ward, Hiley H. Prophet of the
Black Nation. Philadelphia:
Pilgrim Press, 1969. DHU/R
    Chapters on black God,
black gospel and strife at the
shrine.   DHU/R
Washington, Joseph R. Black
and White Power Subreption.
Boston: Beacon Press, 1969.
              DHU/R
    Negro author.
-- Black Religion; the Negro and

(Washington, J. R. cont.)
Christianity in the United
States. Boston: Beacon Press,
1964. DHU/R; DHU/Sp; INU;
OWibfU; DLC
-- The Politics of God. Boston:
Beacon Press, 1967.
DHU/R; DLC; NcD
Part II, Chapter VI, "Ir-
rational Color Prejudice:
America's Preconscious White
Folk Religion."
-- "Revolution Not Resuscitation."
Religious Education (59:2, Mr. -
Apr., 1964), pp. 171-73.
DHU/R
Future role of Black
Church.
Watkin, E. "Black Power in the
Church in Harlem." U. S.
Catholic (Mr., 1969), pp. 30+.
DCU
Wheeler, Lillian. "Rev. Eaton
Gives Views on Religion's
Role in Black University."
The Hilltop (Nov. 22, 1968).
Pam. File; DHU/R
Negro author.
Williams, A. Cecil. "Blacks
Are Not for Sale." Black
Scholar (2:4, Dec., 1970), pp.
35-42.   DHU/R
Minister employs jazz
rhythm and blues and African
dance in his church services
in San Francisco.
Negro author.
Williams, Preston N. "The At-
lanta Document: An Interpre-
tation." Christian Century
(86:42, Oct. 15, 1969), pp.
1311-12.   DHU/R
A reaction to the statement
on Black Theology by National
Committee of Black Church-
men.
Negro author.
-- "Black Church, Origin, His-
tory and Present Dilemma."
McCormick Quarterly (22:4,
My., 1969), pp. 223-37.
DHU/R
-- "The Black Experience and

Black Religion." Theology To-
day (26:3, Oct., 1969), pp.
246-61.   DHU/R
-- "Black Theology: A Statement
of the National Committee of
Black Churchmen." Christian
Century (86:42, Oct. 15, 1969,
p. 1310.   DHU/R
-- "The Ethical Aspects of the
Black Theology Phenomenon,"
Journal of Religious Thought
(26:2, Sum. Suppl., 1969), pp.
34-45.   DHU/R
-- "Ethics and Ethos in the Black
Experience." Christianity and
Crisis, (31:9, May 1971), pp.
104-09.   DHU/R
"Victimization and the
search for Black identity."
Williamson, Joseph C. "Theol-
ogy and Revolution." Andover
Newton Quarterly (10:2, Nov.,
2, Nov., 1969).
Pam. File; DHU/R
Wilmore, Gayraud S. "The Case
for a New Black Church Style."
Hart M. Nelsen & Raytha L.
Yokley, et al. The Black
Church in America (New York:
Basic Books, 1971), pp. 324-
34.   DHU/R
Also in Church in Metrop-
olis (18; Fall, 1968), pp. 18-
22.
Negro author.
-- "White Church and the Search
for Black Power." Social
Progress (Mr. -Apr., 1967).
ICMcC
Wilson, Frank T. "The Black
Revolution: Is There a Black
Theology?" The Journal of
Religious Thought (26:2, Sum.
Suppl., 1969), pp. 5-14.
DHU/R
Negro author.
Witheridge, D. "Why Neglect the
Negro Churches?" Christian
Century (85:42, Oct. 16,
1968), p. 1303.   DHU/R
Woodruff, James E. P. "Black
Power Vis-à-Vis "The King-
dom of God'." Malcolm Boyd,

(ed.). The Underground Church (New York: Sheed & Ward, 1968), pp. 84-101. DHU/R

Wren, Christopher S. "Black Power Shakes the White Church." Look (Ja. 7, 1969), Pam. File; DHU/R

Wright, Leon E. "Black Theology or Black Experience?" Journal of Religious Thought (26:2, Sum. Suppl., 1969), pp. 46-56. DHU/R
Negro author.

Wright, Nathan. "Black Power: A Creative Necessity." Catholic World (204:1,219, Oct., 1966), pp. 46-51. DHU/R

Negro author.
-- Black Power and Urban Unrest; Creative Possibilities. New York: Hawthorn Books, 1967. DHU/R; CtY-D
"Negro ministers: Statement on Black power.
-- "Black Power What? Why? How? Social Action (34:5, Ja., 1968), pp. 23-31. DHU/R
-- "Power and Reconciliation." Concern (9:16, Oct. 1, 1967), pp. 14-16. DHU/R
-- "Why Black Power?" The Christian Science Monitor (Sept. 18, 1967). Pam. File; DHU/R

2. Black Caucuses

"Angela and the Presbyterians." Christian Century, Editorial. (88:27, Je. 7, 1971), p. 823. DHU/R
Synod of United Presbyterian Church contributes to Angela Davis defense fund.

"Black Catholic Pastor: A 'Cool' Priest." The Lamp (68:2, Feb. 1970), pp. 16-19. DHU/R
Discusses Fr. Salmon, deputy vicar of Harlem and first black pastor in Archdiocese of New York.

"The Black Catholics." Newsweek (Ja. 27, 1969), p. 55. Pam. File; DHU/R

"Black Caucus Speakers at All Souls." Afro-American (Ja. 18, 1969). Pam. File; DHU/R

"Black Churchmen Achieve Recognition." The United Church Herald (12:8, Ag., 1969), pp. 12-13. DHU/R

"Black Methodists for Church Renewal: Black Churchmen Build Unity." Together (14:1, Ja., 1969), pp. 10+. DHU/R

Christmas, Faith C. "Appoint Black Pastor, Priests Urge Cody." Chicago Daily Defender (Dec. 12, 1968). Pam. File; DHU/R

Gopaul, P. "A Black Priest Looks at His Racist Church." U.S. Catholic, Jl. '69, p. 13. DCU

Grey, M. (Sister Martin de Porres). "The Church Revolution and Black Catholics." The Black Scholar (2:4, Dec., 1970), pp. 20-4. DHU/R
Negro author.

Griffin, John Howard. "The Position of the Catholic Church in the Black Community." The Church and the Black Man (Dayton, O.: Pflaum Press, 1969), pp. 118-32. DHU/R
Position paper of Catholic Black Caucus, January 1969.

Henry, Hayward. "Black Affairs Council." Now: The Magaof the Unitarian Universalist Association (50:15, Aut., 1969), pp. 12-15. DHU/R
Negro author.

Kiely, P. "A Cry for the Black Nun Power." Commonweal (88:22, Sept. 27, 1968), p. 650. DHU/R

Nannes, Caspar. "Black Cleric
Demand Baptists Elect Negro."
Evening Star (My. 30, 1968).
          Pam. File; DHU/R
"On Dow and Calico, (Editorial)."
Christian Century (86:50, Dec.
10, 1969), pp. 1571+.
          Pam. File; DHU/R
United Methodist Church and
the Black Churchmen.
Ostling, Richard N. "Racial
Chic Goes to Church." Chris-
tian Herald (94:7, Jl., 1971),
pp. 14-20.   DHU/R
Protestant Episcopal Church
and its role in current social
issues.
Perry, David B. "Black Men and
the Quaker Bag." Friends Journal (16:1, Ja. 1, 1970), pp.
6-7.   DHU/R
Presbyterian Church in the
United States. General Assembly.
"Race, Racism and Repres-
sion." Church and Society (61:
1, Sept.-Oct. 1970), pp. 12-
20.   Pam. File; DHU/R
"Rashke, Richard. "Trust for
Black Catholics." Common-
weal (92:2, Mr. 20, 1970), p.
25.   DHU/R
Roberts, James Deotis. "The
Black Caucus and the Failure
of Christian Theology." The
Journal of Religious Thought
(26:2, Sum. Suppl., 1969), pp.
15-25.   DHU/R
Negro author.
Rollins, J. Metz. "Black Churchmen Meet in Atlanta." Presbyterian Life (24:2, Ja., 1971),
pp. 30-31.   DHU/R
Rooks, Charles Shelby. "The
Black Church: Its Implications
for Lutheran Theological Edu-

cation." Repr. from Concord-
ia Theological Monthly (40:10,
Nov. 1969).   DHU/R
Negro author.
"School Ouster Charged by Black
Priests." Chicago Daily De-
fender (Je. 1-7, 1968).
          Pam. File; DHU/R
"Seven Negro Priests Criticize
Church." New York Times
(Feb. 18, 1968).
          Pam. File; DHU/R
Stepp, Diane. "Methodist Tag
$46,000 for Negro Church
Aid." Constitution (Oct. 31,
1968). Pam. File; DHU/R
Tinney, James S. "Many Whites
Attend Black Congress."
Christianity Today (15:1, Oct.
9, 1970), pp. 43-4. DHU/MO
Black Congress on Evangel-
ism called by black pastors.
Walker, Lucius. "Opportunities
for Minority Development."
Church and Society (41:3, Ja.-
Feb., 1971), pp. 22-26. DHU/R
Presbyterians' role in church
and race.
Negro author.
"The White Liberal and the Black
Rebellion: A Study in Anguish."
Respond (1:3, Fall, 1967).
          Pam. File; DHU/R
"This issue discusses Uni-
tarianism and the 'Black Cau-
cus'."
Wilmore, Gayraud S. "From Pro-
test to Self-Development?"
Church and Society (41:3, Ja.-
Feb., 1971), pp. 6-13. DHU/R
Chairman of United Presby-
terian Division of Church and
Race analyzes some of the fac-
tors that are basic to racial jus-
tice.

3. Reparations

Abernathy, Ralph David. "A
Black Preacher Looks at the
Black Manifesto." Christian

Century (86:33, Ag. 13, 1969),
pp. 1064-65.   DHU/R
Atkins, Anselna. "Christians!

James Forman Wants Your
Shirt." The Lamp (67:9, Sept.
1969), pp. 21-23; 30. DHU/R
Belford, Lee A. "Questions
About the Black Manifesto."
The Churchman (183:9, Nov.,
1969), pp. 6-7. DHU/R
"The Black Manifesto." Tempo
(1:16, Je. 1, 1969), pp. 4,
15. DHU/R
The complete text as adopt-
ed by National Black Econom-
ic Development Conference.
"The Black Manifesto and Its
Aftermath." Tempo (1:16, Je.
1, 1969), pp. 3+.
Pam. File, DHU/R
"Black Manifesto Declares War
On Churches," Christianity
Today (My. 23, 1969), p. 29.
DHU/R
"Black Over White." Common-
weal (90:11, My. 30, 1969),
pp. 308-09. DHU/R
A critique of the "Black
Manifesto."
Campbell, Ernest T. "The Case
for Reparations." Theology
Today (26:3, Oct., 1969), pp.
266-83. DHU/R
"Church and State in the Black
Manifesto." Church and State
(21:10, Nov., 1969), pp. 11+.
DHU/R
"Did We Endorse the Black Man-
ifesto?" (Editorial). Christian
Century (86:27, Jl. 2, 1969),
p. 894. DHU/R
Dowey, Edward A., Jr. "The
Black Manifesto: Revolution,
Reparation and Separation."
Theology Today (26:3, Oct.,
1969), pp. 288-93. DHU/R
Edwards, John. "Jesuits Pay
Bonds for Exploited Blacks."
Modern Society (13:1, Ja. -
Feb., 1970), pp. 7+.
Pam. File; DHU/R
"Episcopalians Hold Special Con-
vention: Historic Session."
Christian Century (86:40, Oct.
1, 1969), pp. 1262-63.
DHU/R

Reparation payment made by
this denomination.
Foley, Judy Mathe. "Dealing with
a Manifesto." Episcopalian
(134:7, Jl., 1969), pp. 11-12.
DHU/R
Goetz, Ronald. "Black Manifesto:
The Great White Hope."
Christian Century (86:25, Je.
18, 1969), pp. 832-33.
DHU/R
Green, Mark. "Reparations for
Blacks." Commonweal (90:13,
Je., 1969), pp. 359-62.
DHU/R
Holland, Darrell W. "Massachu-
setts Conference Commits $1
Million to Black Churchmen."
United Church Herald (13:1,
Ja. 1, 1970), pp. 36-7.
DHU/R
"How to Rob a Church." Pres-
byterian Journal (Je. 18,
1969), pp. 12+. DLC
"Reparations."
Howell, Leonard and Robert S.
Lecky. "Reparation Now?"
Christianity and Crisis (29:9,
My. 26, 1969), p. 141.
DHU/R
Lecky, Robert S. Black Mani-
festo, Religion Racism and
Reparations. New York:
Sheed & Ward, 1969.
DHU/R; CtY-D
Lovelace, John A. "The Black
Manifesto." Christian Advo-
cate (13:14, Jl. 10, 1969),
pp. 3, 21-22. DHU/R
"Manifesto (of National Black
Economic Development Con-
ference) Information Service
(48; My. 17, 1969), p. 1.
DLC; CtY
"Methodists Vow New Priorities.
Funding Still Uncertain."
Christianity Today (15:17, My.
22, 1970), pp. 763+. DHU/R
Morsell, John A. "The NAACP
and Reparations." The Crisis
(77:3, Mr., 1970), pp. 96-
101. DHU/R

"National Council of Churches'
General Board Responds to the
Black Manifesto." Tempo (1:
24, Oct. 1, 1969), pp. 4; 11.
DHU/R
"The NCC and the Black Mani-
festo." Tempo (1:19, Jl. 15,
1969), pp. 3-5.
Pam. File; DHU/R
"Negro Church Rejects Plan."
Denver Post (Aug. 8, 1969).
Pam. File, DHU/R
A. M. E. Church rejects the
plan of James Forman for
"reparations."
Nelson, J. Robert. "Preparation
for Separation and Reparation;
the Churches Response to Rac-
ism?" Demands on the World
Council of Churches. Chris-
tian Century (86; Feb. 14,
1969), pp. 862-5.   DHU/R
Rensenbrink, Dorothy. "Two
Crowded Days in Indianapolis."
Tempo (1:24, Oct. 1, 1969),
pp. 3; 11.   DHU/R
"Reparations, Tactics and the
Churches: Some Comments."
Tempo (1:16, Je. 1, 1969),
pp. 6-7.   DHU/R
"The Requests Were Severe But
the Tone was Gentle." Christian Advocate (14:9, Apr. 30,
1970), p. 6.   DHU/R
"Riverside Replys." Information
Service (48; My. 17, 1969),
p. 7.   CtY
(Relates to Black Mani-
festo demands.)
Roddy, Sherman S. "Black Mani-
festo--A Reappraisal." Church
and Society (55:5, My. -Je.,
1970), pp. 39-50.   DHU/R
"A white Presbyterian pastor states black demands upon
white people is a necessity at
the present time."
Rose, Stephen C. "The Manifesto
and Renewal." Christianity and
Crisis (29:9, My. 26, 1969),
pp. 142-43.   DHU/R
-- "Suggested Soulful Responses
to the Black Manifesto: Repa-

ration Now!" 2 pp. Mim.
Pam. File; DHU/R
-- "Wake-ing Up the Church."
Christian Century (87; Ja. 14,
1970), p. 50.
General Assembly Meeting,
1969 Black Manifesto.
Sayre, Charles A. "A Cross-
roads--Nonviolence or Black
Manifesto." Christian Advo-
cate (14:5, Mr. 5, 1970), pp.
18+.   DHU/R; DAU/W
Schomer, H. "The Manifesto and
the Magnificat." Christian
Century (86:26, Je. 25, 1969),
pp. 866-67.   DHU/R
Schuchter, Arnold. Reparations:
The Black Manifesto and its
Challenge to White America.
Philadelphia: J. B. Lippincott
Co., 1970.   DHU/R
"Some Comments on the Black
Manifesto." Church Herald (Jl.
11, 1969), p. 6.   DHU/R
Stackhouse, Max L. "Repara-
tions: A Call to Repentance."
Colloquy (3:2, Feb., 1970),
pp. 18-26.   DHU/R
"Synagogue Council Responds to
Manifesto." Information Serv-
ice (48; My. 17, 1969), p. 8.
CtY; DLC
"Text of Demands Made to River-
side Church (relates to Black
Manifesto demands)." Infor-
mation Service (48; My. 17,
1969), p. 6.   CtY; DLC
"Unitarians Approve Negro-Led
Council; Allocate $1 Million."
New York Times (My. 28,
1968). Pam. File; DHU/R
United Church of Christ. Office
of the President. "A Report
from the Seventh General Syn-
od, 1969." Pam. File; DHU/R
"Resolutions taken on so-
cial change. A letter addressed
to James Forman in reply to
the request for 'reparation.'"
United Methodist Church. Board
of Health and Welfare Ministries.
"One Million Dollars for Black
Health Welfare." Christian

Advocate (13:22, Nov. 13, 1969), pp. 23+. DHU/R

Vorspan, Albert. "How James Forman Lost His Cool But Saved Religion in 1969: A Modern Bible Story." Christian Century (86:32, Ag. 6, 1969), p. 1042. DHU/R

Wells, Charles A. "Black Reparations How and To Whom." Friends Journal (16:3, Feb. 1, 1970), pp. 69+. DHU/R

White, Andrew. "The Role and Future of the Negro Church." (Editorial) Journal of Religious Education of the African Methodist Episcopal Church (29:4, Je. -Ag., 1969), pp. 2-5.
Editor discussed Black Manifesto.
Negro author.
-- Way the Church Should Evan-

gelize Black Youth." Religious Education (64:6, Nov. -Dec., 1969), pp. 446-50. DHU/R

Whiten, Bennie E. "Reparations and the Contribution of the Church." Social Action (36:6 Feb., 1970), pp. 18-26. DHU/R
Negro author.

"Will the Black Manifesto Help Blacks?" Christian Century (86:21 My. 21, 1969), p. 701. DHU/R

Wilmore, Gayraud S. "Reparations: Don't Hang Up On the Word." Theology Today (26: 3, Oct., 1969), pp. 284-87. DHU/R

Wogaman, J. Philip. "Testing the Rhetoric of the Black Manifesto." Christian Advocate (8:17, Sept. 4, 1969, pp. 9-10. DHU/R

4. National Committee of Black Churchmen--Local Groups

"Black Power: Statement by National Committee of Negro Churchmen." Concern (8:15, Sept. 1, 1966), pp. 5-7. DHU/R

Boynton, Ernest. "Christianity's Black Power." Church in Metropolis (no. 19; Wint., 1968), pp. 20-24. DHU/R
A discussion of the Black Caucus Movement as reflected at the second annual convocation of the National Committee of Black Churchmen in St. Louis, 1968.

"Chicago's Black Churchmen: How Their New Executive Sees Their Role." Christian Century (87:18, My. 6, 1970), pp. 578-80. DHU/R

"A Message to the Churches from Oakland." Tempo (2:4, Dec. 1, 1969), pp. 10-14. DHU/R

"National Committee of the Black Churchmen." Constitution 6 pp. Mim.

Pam. File; DHU/R
--"Reflections on Some Documents... Renewal (10:7, Oct. - Nov., 1970). DHU/R
Complete issue devoted to NCBC.
-- Third Annual Convocation. Nov. 11-14, 1969. Oakland, Calif. Pam. File; DHU/R

Shockley, Grant S. "Ultimatum and Hope: The Black Churchmen's Convocation; An Interpretation." Christian Century (8:71, Feb. 12, 1969), pp. 217-19. Pam. File; DHU/R

Stone, M. "Chicago Black Churchman: How Their New Executive Sees Their Role." Christian Century (87; My. 6, 1970), pp. 578-80. DHU/R

Watts, Leon W. "The National Committee of Black Churchmen." Christianity and Crisis (30:18, Nov. 2 & 16, 1970), pp. 237-43. DHU/R

Wilmore, Gayraud S. "National

(Wilmore, G. S. cont.)
Committee of Black Churchmen. Africa and Afro-Americans; Report of Conversations
Between N. C. B. C. Official and

Members of the All Africa
Conference of Churches."
Christian Century (87; July 3,
1970), pp. 686+.   DHU/R

C. THE JEW AND THE NEGRO

"Advice to Jews." Chicago Daily
Defender (Nov. 15, 1968.
   Pam. File; DHU/R
Rabbi Bernard Weinberger
makes a plea for better rela-
tions between Jews and
blacks.
"American Jewish Congress
Names Urban-Affair Aide."
New York Times (Dec. 8,
1968). Pam. File; DHU/R
   "Will guide programs aimed
at reducing community ten-
sions."
Becker, William H. "Black and
Jew: Ambivalence and Affini-
ties." Soundings (53:4, Wint.,
1970), pp. 413-39.   DHU/R
Berson, Lenora A. The Negroes
and the Jews. New York:
Random House, 1971. DHU/R
Review, City Magazine of
Urban Life and Environment.
(Jl. -Ag., 1971), by Clifton F.
Brown.
"Blacks, Jews, and Violence."
Jewish Spectator (Je., 1969),
pp. 2+.   NN
"Boycott by Negro Churches."
Together (6:5, My., 1962), p.
73.   DHU/R; DAU/W
   Boycott of some 200 Negro
Churches in Baltimore, Md. of
businesses practicing discrim-
ination in employment.
Brotz, Howard M. "Negro 'Jews'
in the United States." Hart M.
Nelsen & Raytha L. Yokley,
et al. The Black Church in
in America (New York: Basic
Books, 1971), pp. 194-209.
                          DHU/R
   Also in Phylon (13; Dec.,

1952), pp. 324-37.
Cohen, Henry. Justice, Justice:
A Jewish View of the Black
Revolution. New York: Union
of American Hebrew Congrega-
tions 1969.   DHU/R
Conference on Negro-Jewish Re-
lations in the U. S., New York,
1964. Negro-Jewish Relations
in the United States; Papers
and Proceedings. New York:
Citadel Press, 1966.   INU
Dugan, George. "Negroes and
Jews Seek an Accord." New
York Times (Dec. 7, 1968).
   Pam. File; DHU/R
"Forward Together; Protestant-
Catholic-Jewish Cooperation."
Commonweal (76; Jl. 13, 1962),
p. 389.   DHU
Glazer, N. "Blacks, Jews and
the Intellectuals," Commen-
tary (47:4, Apr., 1969), p.
33.   DHU/R
Graham, Alfredo. "White Jews,
Black Jews Not Kosher."
Pittsburgh Courier (Jl. 16,
1960). Pam. File; DHU/R
Halpern, Ben. Jews and Blacks:
The Classic American Minori-
ties. New York: Herder &
Herder, 1971.   DHU/R
Hentoff, Nat. Black Anti-Semi-
tism and Jewish Racism.
New York: Richard W. Baron,
1970.   DHU/R
"Jewish and Negro Clergy Meet
on School Tensions." New
York Times (Nov. 13, 1968).
   Pam. File; DHU/R
"Jewish Congress to Press Sup-
port of Aid to Negroes." New
York Times (Dec. 16, 1968).

Pam. File; DHU/R
"Jews are Advised to Ease Tensions." New York Times (Oct. 27, 1968).
Pam. File; DHU/R
"Rabbi Weinberger advises Jewish people to give up explosive businesses in ghetto areas."
Kovach, Bill. "Facist and Anti-Semite Strain Old Negro-Jewish Ties." New York Times (Sept. 23, 1968).
Pam. File; DHU/R
Negro and Jew: an Encounter in America. New York: Macmillan, 1967. INU; FSU
"Negro Leaders Here Urged to Reject Anti-Jew Leaflet." New York Times (Dec. 13, 1968).
Pam. File; DHU/R
Raab, Earl. "The Black Revolution and the Jewish Question." Commentary (47:1, Ja., 1969), pp. 23-33. Pam. File; DHU/R
"Rights Expert Tells Jewish Congress Liberals Fail Negro." New York Times (My. 17, 1968). Pam. File; DHU/R
Sengstacke, John H. "Negroes and Jews." (Editorial) Chicago Daily Defender (Dec. 19, 1968). Pam. File; DHU/R
Negro author.
Spiegel, Irving. "B'nai B'rith Head Scores Militants." New York Times (Sept. 8, 1968).
Pam. File; DHU/R
-- "Jewish Unit Sets a Negro Aid Drive." New York Times (Apr. 3, 1968).

Pam. File; DHU/R
-- "Jews in Suburbia Scored as Racist." New York Times (My. 25, 1968).
Pam. File; DHU/R
-- "Jews Told Aid is 'Imperative' in Negroes Fight for Equality." New York Times (Oct. 28, 1968). Pam. File; DHU/R
-- "Rabbis Here Urge Rights for Negro." New York Times Apr. 9, 1968).
Pam. File; DHU/R
-- "Rabbis Score School Decentralization." New York Times (Feb. 1, 1968).
Pam. File; DHU/R
-- "Zionist Deplores Black Extremists." New York Times (Sept. 13, 1968).
Pam. File; DHU/R
Stringfellow, William. "Negro Anti-Semitism." World Call (49:1, Ja., 1967), p. 29.
DHU/R
"Tension Between Blacks, Jews Deplored." Chicago Daily Defender (Dec. 14, 1968).
Pam. File; DHU/R
"Unity Group Deplores Negro Bias, Reaction." Washington Post (Nov. 15, 1968).
Pam. File; DHU/R
"President of National Conference of Christians and Jews warns against rising passions of Negro anti-semitism."
Vorspan, Albert. "The Negro Victory and the Jewish Failure." American Judaism (13: 1, Fall, 1963).
DLC; Pam. File; DHU/R

D.   General

Baptists Are Urged to Study Carefully Before Casting Vote." Atlanta Constitution (Sept. 7, 1968). Pam. File; DHU/R
Bennink, Richard John. "The Minister and His Role." The Reformed Review (23:1, Fall,

1969), pp. 56+. DHU/R
Bloy, Myron. "Culture and Counter-Culture." Religious Education (64:5, Sept. -Oct., 1969), pp. 357-62. DHU/R
Caldwell, Gilbert H. "Black Folk in White Churches." Christian

(Caldwell, G. H. cont.)
Century (86:7, Feb. 12, 1967),
pp. 209-11.   DHU/R
Campbell, Will D. "A Conversa-
tion With Will Campbell:
Prophet Poet, Preacher-at-
Large." The Student (50:3,
Dec. 1970), pp. 291. DHU/R
A conversation with the di-
rector of the Committee of
Southern Churchmen on the fu-
ture of the black church.
Carr, Oscar C. "The Church,
Mission, Race and Me." The
Lamp (68:3, Mr., 1970), pp.
20+.   DHU/R
"Church Heads Urged to Promote
Education of Black Youngsters."
Chicago Daily Defender (Ja.
14, 1969). Pam. File; DHU/R
"Convention Opened by Negro
Baptists." The New York
Times (Sept. 5, 1968).
            Pam. File; DHU/R
Davis, John L. "National Baptist
Confab Starts 88th Session To-
day." Atlanta (Sept. 4, 1968).
            Pam. File; DHU/R
Dole, Kenneth. "Reason Urged on
Racial Unit." Washington
Post (Feb. 24, 1968).
            Pam. File; DHU/R
Dugan, George. "Billions for
Poor Urged by Leaders of
Four Religions." New York
Times (Apr. 29, 1968).
            Pam. File; DHU/R
Eckhardt, Kenneth W. "Relgiosity
and Civil Rights Militancy."
Review of Religious Research
(2:3, Spr., 1970), pp. 197-
203.   DHU/R
Edwards, David L. "Religion
and Change." Theology To-
day (26:3, Oct., 1969), pp.
353+.   DHU/R
Ehrenhalt, Alan. "Chicago
Priest Fights for White Neigh-
borhood." Chicago Daily De-
fender (Dec. 29, 1968).
            Pam. File; DHU/R
Fiske, Edward B. "Rites, Echo,
War and Racial Strife." New

York Times (Apr. 13, 1968).
(Apr. 13, 1968).
            Pam. File; DHU/R
Foley, Judy Mathe. "Modeste
in Motion." The Episcopal-
ian (134:11, Nov., 1969), pp.
24+.   DHU/R
Leon E. Modeste, Direc-
tor, General Convention Spe-
cial Program of Protestant
Episcopal Church (minority
self-help).
Friberg, H. "Reformation...
Then and Now." Christian-
ity Today (Oct. 25, 1968),
p. 3.   DHU/R
Hare, Nathan. "Emptiness of
Negro Middle Class Church
Life." Negro Digest (14; Ag.,
1965), pp. 34-9.   DHU/MO
Negro author.
Harper, F. Nile. "Social Pow-
er and the Limitation of
Church Education." Reli-
gious Education (64:5, Sept.-
Oct., 1969), pp. 390-98.
                       DHU/R
Hitchcock, James. "The Chris-
tian and Change." Christian
Century (87:1, Ja. 7, 1970),
pp. 7-11.   DHU/R
Hofmann, Paul. "Clergymen
Meeting Strong; Resistance to
Involvement in Secular
Causes." New York Times
(Apr. 12, 1968).
            Pam. File; DHU/R
Hoover, Theressa. "Keepers of
the Faith and Changing So-
ciety." The Church Woman
(35:9, Nov., 1969), pp. 25-
28.   Pam. File; DHU/R
"How Many Men Must Die."
Life (64:19, Apr. 1968), pp.
34-5.   DHU
Jefferson, Frederick D. "Faith
and Reconciliation in Black
and White." McCormick
Quarterly (22:4, My., 1969),
pp. 253-62.   DHU/R
Johnson, Thomas A. "McKis-
sick Says Talk was Barred."
New York Times (Dec. 12,

1968). Pam. File; DHU/R
Korby, Kenneth F. "Different
Ministries, Different Means,
One God: A Theological Opin-
ion on the Racial Issue." Con-
cordia Theological Monthly (41:
2, Feb., 1970), pp. 86+.
                    DHU/R
Leas, Speed B. "The Missionary
and the Black Man." Malcolm
Boyd, (ed.). The Underground
Church (New York: Sheed &
Ward, 1968), pp. 159-76.
                    DHU/R
Lee, Robert and Ralph L. Roy.
"The Negro Church," Chris-
tian Century (74:44, Oct. 30,
1957), pp. 1285-87.   DHU/R
Marr, Warren, II. "Which Way
to Equality?" United Church
Herald (13:3, Mr. 1, 1970),
p. 13.   DHU/R
Present racial program of
American Missionary History
Association.
Martin, Douglas L. "The White
Protestant Church and Black
Freedom." Foundations, a
Baptist Journal of History and
Theology (13:2, Apr. -Je.,
1970), pp. 159-74.   DHU/R
Mulder, John M. "The Church
as a Financial Institution, or
Forgive Us Our Debts." The-
ology Today (26:3, Oct., 1969),
pp. 294-98.   DHU/R
Nelson, William Stuart. "Mo-
handas K. Gandhi: The Non-
Violent Answers." Friends
Journal (15:18, Oct. 1, 1969),
pp. 548+.   DHU/R
Negro author.
Perez, Joseph A. "Social Action
Means Confronting Institutions."
Christian Advocate (14:6, Mr.
19, 1970).   DHU/R
"Presbyterians Aid Negro Busi-

ness." New York Times (Apr.
27, 1968). Pam. File; DHU/R
"Progressive National Baptists
Elect Dr. E. R. Searcy, Presi-
dent." Atlanta World (Sept.
10, 1968).
        Pam. File; DHU/R
"Race Rift Grows, Lindsay As-
serts." New York Times
(Apr. 23, 1968).
        Pam. File; DHU/R
Governor's Speech to Inter-
Faith Group."
"Religions Join in War on Job
Discrimination." Pittsburgh
Courier (Sept. 21, 1968).
        Pam. File; DHU/R
"Rev. Helen Archibald a Congre-
gationalist Minister Runs a
One-Woman Show in the
Brownsville Section of Brook-
lyn, N. Y." The Lamp (167:1,
Ja., 1969), pp. 15+. DHU/R
Rooks, Charles Shelby. "Crisis
in Theological Education."
City of God (3:1, Ag., 1970),
pp. 7-17. Pam. File; DHU/R
Negro author.
Ruether, Rosemary. "The Messi-
anic Core." Commonweal (91:
15: Ja. 16, 1970), pp. 423+.
                    DHU/R
The left tradition in church
and society.
--"The Search for Soul Power in
the White Community." Chris-
tianity and Crisis (30:7, Apr.
27, 1970), pp. 83-5. DHU/R
Trudgian, Raymond. "Religious
Education for a Multi-Racial
Society." Learning for Living
(9:1, Sept., 1969), pp. 19+.
                    DHU/R
White, Woodie W. "Black and
White Merger at Any Cost."
Christian Advocate (13:20,
Oct. 16, 1969), p. 9.
                    DHU/R

E. RACISM AND CONTEMPORARY CHURCH

Bailey, Kenneth K. Southern
White Protestantism in the
Twentieth Century. New York:
Harper, 1964. DHU/R; INU
Baldwin, James. "Our Divided
Society: A Challenge to Reli-
geious Education." Religious
Education (64:5, Sept. -Oct.,
1969), pp. 342-46.   DHU/R
-- "White Racism or World Community?" Religious Education
(64:5, Sept. -Oct., 1969), pp.
342+.   DHU/R
Barbour, Russell B. Black and
White Together; Plain Talk for
White Christians. Philadelphia: United Church Press,
1967. DHU/R; CtY-D; NcD;
                          DLC
Basen, Carol. Showdown at Seattle. New York: Seabury
Press, 1968. DLC; NcD
    Prepared under the aus-
pices of the Executive Council
of the Episcopal Church.
    Reports, including excerpts
from the proceedings, of the
meeting of the women of the
church during the National Convention of the Protestant Episcopal Church in the U.S.A.,
Seattle, September 1967.
Bastide, Roger. "Color, Racism
and Christianity." John Hope
Franklin, (ed.). Color and
Race (Boston: Beacon Press,
1968), pp. 34+.   DHU/R
Beckmann, Klaus-Marten. "Ger-
man Churches and Missions
Face the Race Question." International Review of Mission
(59:235, Jl., 1970), pp. 311-
15.   DHU/R
Beckwith, John Q. The Race
Problem and the South; Five
Lectures, January-February
1958. Washington, D.C.: Organizing Committee, Christianity and Modern Man Lectures,

1958.   CtY-D
    (A Christianity and modern
man publication, 26.)
Berrigan, Philip. No More
Strangers. New York: Mac-
millan, 1965.
    DHU/R; INU; NcD
    Racial patterns and the
Christian.
-- A Punishment for Peace. New
York: Macmillan, 1969.
                      CtY-D
    Chapter IV, Racial patterns
and the Christians.
"Bishop Shaw Urges New Direc-
tion for Churchmen." Afro-
American (Nov. 12, 1968).
    Pam. File; DHU/R
    "Speech when elected presi-
dent of the National Committee
of Black Churchmen."
Blau, Joseph L. "Religion and
the Two Faces of America."
Roger L. Shinn. Search for
Identity Essays on the Ameri-
can Character. (New York:
Harper & Row, 1964), pp. 29-
38.   DHU/R
Boyd, Bob. "Breaking Down the
Wall of Fear." Tempo (2:8,
Feb. 1, 1970), pp. 3+.
                      DHU/R
    Young Lutheran group and
Black Youth Unlimited visit
the Delta Ministry in Missis-
sippi.
Boyd, Malcolm, (ed.). On the
Battle Lines. New York:
Morehouse-Barlow, 1964.
                      NN/Sch
-- (ed.). The Underground
Church. New York: Sheed &
Ward, 1968.   DHU/R
    Contains chapters on Race
and Church.
Brewer, David Leslie. Utah
Elites and Utah Racial Norms.
Salt Lake City, Univ. of Utah,
1966.   INU; DLC

Brink, William. Black and White: A Study of United States Racial Attitudes Today. New York: Simon Press, 1967. DHU/R
-- and Louis Harris. The Negro Revolution in America. New York: Simon & Schuster, 1963. DHU/R; INU; CtY-D
Chapter 6, "The Role of the Negro Church," pp. 96-110.

Brown, John Pairman. The Liberated Zone. A Guide to Christian Resistance. Richmond, Va.: John Knox Press, 1969. DHU/R

Brown, Robert Raymond, (bp.). Bigger Than Little Rock. Greenwich, Conn.: Seabury Press, 1958. DLC; DHU/R; NYP/Sch; CtY-D
Section 6 "Religion and Segregation."

"Churches Must Play Key Role in Quest for Racial Justice." Afro-American (Apr. 6, 1968). Pam. File; DHU/R

Churchill, Rhona. White Man's God. New York: Morrow, 1962. DLC

"Confronting the Racial Crisis." (Editorial). Christianity Today (12:10, Feb. 16, 1968), pp. 26-28. DHU/R

Davies, Alfred T., (ed.). The Pulpit Speaks on Race. New York: Abingdon Press, 1965. DHU/R; DHU/MO; DLC; CtY-D

Davies, Lawrence E. "Wide Bias Found in Church People." The New York Times (Mr. 26, 1968). Pam. File; DHU/R

Deschner, John. "Ecclesiological Aspects of the Race Problem." International Review of Missions (59:235, Jl., 1970), pp. 285-95. DHU/R

"Dr. Taylor Addresses World Meet, Liberia, Hits Racism." Pittsburgh Courier (Ag. 24, 1968), Pam. File; DHU/R
President of the Progressive National Baptist Conven-
tion delivered an address on "Racial Justice."

Dodson, Gordon. Race and Immigration: A Christian's Viewpoint. London: Church Pastoral-Aid Society, 1968. DLC

Dole, Kenneth. "Baptist Image on Equality Disturbs Cleric." The Washington Post (Apr. 27, 1968). Pam. File

Doty, Robert C. "Pope Asks Vietnam Peace; Calls for an End of Racism." New York Times (Apr. 15, 1968). Pam. File; DHU/R

Dugan, George. "18 Negro Priests in Antibias Move." New York Times (Jl. 28, 1968). Pam. File; DHU/R

Dumond, Dwight Lowell. "Democracy and Christian Ethics." Journal of Negro History (46: 1, Ja., 1961), pp. 1-11. DHU

Early, Tracy. "All Africa Church Conference Steps Up Campaign on Racism." World Call (53:6, Je., 1971), pp. 22-23. DHU/R

Edwards, Herbert O. "Racism and Christian Ethics in America." Katallagete (Wint., 1971), pp. 15-24. DHU/R
Negro author.

Epps, B. Crandell. "Church can Heal Racial Injustice." Christian Science Journal (88:5, My., 1970), pp. 252-54. DHU/R

Ezell, Humphrey K. The Christian Problem of Segregation. New York: Greenwich Book Publishers, 1959. NN/Sch; CtY-D

Grier, William and Price Cobbs. The Jesus Bag. New York: McGraw-Hill Book Co., 1971. DHU/R
Chapter on Religion and the American Black Man. Negro author.

Grimes, Alan P. Equality in America; Religion, Race and the Urban Majority. New

(Grimes, A. P. cont.)
York: Oxford University Press,
1964.   INU
Groppi, James E. "The Church
and Civil Rights." Malcolm
Boyd, ed. The Underground
Church (New York: Sheed &
Ward, 1968), pp. 70-83.
                         DHU/R
Hackett, Allen. For the Open
Door. Philadelphia: United
Church Press, 1964.   DLC
Hadden, Jeffrey K. The Gather-
ing Storm in the Churches.
Garden City, N. Y.: Double-
day, 1969.   DHU/R
Halvorson, Lawrence W. The
Church in a Diverse Society.
Minneapolis: Augsburg Pub.
House, 1964.   CtY-D
Harding, Vincent. Must Walls
Divide? New York: Friend-
ship Press, 1965.
           DHU/MO; DHU/R
Negro author.
Hessel, Dieter T. Reconciliation
and Conflict: Church Contro-
versy Over Social Involvement.
Philadelphia: The Westminster
Press, 1969.   DHU/R
Church's mandate to con-
cern itself with race as well
as other social problems in
the world.
Hill, Clifford. S. Race: A Chris-
tian Symposium; Edited by Clif-
ford S. Hill & David Mathews.
London: Gollancz, 1968. DLC
Holtrop, Donald. Notes on Chris-
tian Racism. Grand Rapids,
Mich: Wm. B. Eerdmans Pub.
Co., 1969.   DHU/R
Jackson, Giovanna R. "Afro-
American Religion and Church
and Race Relations." Indiana
University Libraries and Focus,
(Sum., 1969). Mim. bibl.
           Pam. File; DHU/R
Jackson, Jesse. "Christianity,
the Church, and Racism." Re-
ligious Education (65:2, Mr. -
Apr., 1970), pp. 90-98.
                         DHU/R

Negro author.
Jeffers, Robert A. "The 'Poor
of God' and the Black Christian in America." Catholic
World (213:1, 275, Je., 1971),
pp. 126-29.   DHU/R
Jones, Howard O. Shall We Overcome? A Challenge to Negro
and White Christians. Westwood, N. J.: F. F. Revell Co.,
1966.   DLC;
NN/Sch; DHU/R; DHU/MO
Jurji, E. "Religious Convergence
and the Course of Prejudice."
Journal of the American Acad-
emy of Religion (37:2, Je.,
1969), pp. 119+.   DHU
Kelsey, George D. "The Chris-
tian Way in Race Relations."
Wm. S. Nelson, (ed.). The
Christian Way in Race Rela-
tions (New York: Harper &
Bros., 1948), pp. 29-48.
                         DHU/R
Negro author.
-- Racism and the Christian Un-
derstanding of Man. New
York: Scribner, 1965. NcD;
     DHU/R; NN/Sch; CtY-D
Killian, Lewis M. and Charles
Grigg. Racial Crisis in America:
Leadership in Conflict. Engle-
wood Cliffs, N. J.: Prentice
Hall, 1964.   DHU/R
Kitagawa, Daisuke. The Pastor
and the Race Issue. New
York: Seabury Press, 1965.
DHU/R; INU; DLC; NN/Sch;
                         CtY-D
-- Race Relations and Christian
Mission. New York: Friend-
ship Press, 1964.   DLC;
DHU/R; DHU/MO; NN/Sch
Krebs, A. V. "Prejudice in the
Pews; Sociologists Report."
America (118; Je. 15, 1968),
pp. 715-6.   DHU
Lecky, Robert S. and H. Elliott
Wright. Can These Bones Live?
New York: Sheed & Ward,
1969.   DHU/R
Pp. 142-159, "Black Man -
White Church."

Lee, Robert, (ed.). Religion and Social Conflict. New York: Oxford Univ. Press, 1964. INU Pp. 37-54, race and church.

Legg, Sam. "Black Mistrust and White Justice." Friends Journal (15:23, Dec. 15, 1969), pp. 714-15.   DHU/R

Lincoln, Charles Eric. "How Now America?" Christianity and Crisis (28:4, Apr. 1, 1968), pp. 56-59.   DHU/R Negro author. "Racism: the mother of crime."

-- Is Anybody Listening to Black America. New York: Seabury Press, 1968.   DHU/MO

Littell, Franklin H. Wild Tongues, A Handbook of Social Pathology. London: The Macmillan Co., 1969.   DHU/R Suggestions as to how the church can fight racism.

Lucas, Lawrence. Black Priest, White Church; Catholics and Racism. New York: Random House, 1970.   DHU/R

Lutze, Karl E. To Mend the Broken; the Christian Response to the Challenge of Human Relations Problems. St. Louis: Concordia Pub. House, 1966.   NcD; DLC

MacKaye, William R. "Tolerated Segregation Charged to Adventists." Washington Post (Feb. 24, 1968). Pam. File; DHU/R

Marrow, Alfred J. Changing Patterns of Prejudice. A New Look at To-Day's Racial Religious and Cultural Tensions. Philadelphia: Chilton, 1962.   DHU/R

Mason, Philip. Christianity and Race. New York: St. Martin's Press, 1957. DHU/R; DLC

Mays, Benjamin Elijah. Disturbed About Man. Richmond, Va.: John Knox Press, 1969.   DHU/R Last chapter, "The Church Amidst Ethnic and Racial Ten-

sions." Negro author.

McDermott, Patrick P. "A New Encyclical on Social Justice." Christian Century (88:24, Je., 16, 1971), pp. 748-51.   DHU/R Includes statement on "Institutional Racism."

"Missionaries Urged to Include Race Problems, Objectors in Program." Chicago Daily Defender (Dec. 21, 1968). Pam. File; DHU/R

Moberg, David O. The Church as a Social Institution; The Sociology of American Religion. Englewood Cliffs, N.Y.: Prentice-Hall, 1962. "The Church and social problems," pp. 445-80.   NN/Sch

Mol, J. Religion and Race in New Zealand. A critical review of the policies and practices of the churches in New Zealand relevant to racial integration, with historical appendices by Rev. J.T. Holland and Rev. G.L. Laurenson. Christchurch: National Council of Churches, 1966.   DLC

Morrison, George. "St. Louis Militants Tell Aims." Washington Post (Je. 2, 1969). Pam. File, DHU/R Demonstrate to show "Racism in Churches."

Mueller, Samuel A. and Joyce A. Swean. "Omnis America in Partes Tres Dursa Est." Christian Century (86:43, Oct. 22, 1969), pp. 342+.   DHU/R "The nation is not divided into white and black camps; there is an important, if rather small middle camp, the white non-Christian."

"Negro Priest Assails Catholic Church as Racist." New York Times (Apr. 19, 1968). Pam. File; DHU/R

Norris, Hoke, (ed.). We Dissent.

(Norris, H. cont.)
New York: St. Martin's Pr.,
1963.   INU
Oliver, C. Herbert. No Flesh
Shall Glory. Nutley, N. J.:
Presbyterian and Reformed
Pub. Co., 1959.   CtY-D
Orchard, R. F. "Christian Re-
sponsibility in a Plural So-
ciety." International Review
of Mission (59:235, Jl., 1970),
pp. 316-23.   DHU/R
Pannell, William E. My Friend,
the Enemy. Waco, Tex.:
Word Books, 1968.   DLC
Paton, Alan. The Christian Ap-
proach to Racial Problems in
the Modern World. London:
Christian Action, 1959?
                      NN/Sch
   "One of the Christian Ac-
tion Stafford Cripps Memorial
Lectures entitled 'The Chris-
tian and This World,' which
were delivered in St. Paul's
Cathedral, in the autumn of
1959, before the St. Paul's
Lecture Society."
Paton, William. The White Man's
Burden... London: Epworth
Press, 1939.   NN/Sch
Pitcher, Alvin. "White Racism
and Black Development." Re-
ligious Education (65:2, Mr.-
Apr., 1970), pp. 84-89.
                      DHU/R
Pope, Liston. The Kingdom Be-
yond Caste. New York:
Friendship Press, 1957.
           DHU/R; CtY-D
   P. 81 - Church, race and
democracy.
"Precious in His Sight." News-
week (76:6, Ag. 10, 1970),
pp. 69-70.   DHU/R
   Segregation in a Birming-
ham Baptist Church.
Quaintance, Charles W. "Race
Evolution and Mormonism."
Christian Century (88:19, My.
12, 1971), pp. 586-89.
                      DHU/R
"The Racial Crisis." Social Ac-

tion (36:1, Sept. 1, 1969),
pp. 23-29.   DHU/R
Racism and White Christian; a
Resource Study, by Students
at the Chicago Theological
Seminary. Chicago: Chicago
Theological Seminary, 1968.
                       DLC
Reimers, David Morgan. White
Protestantism and the Negro.
New York: Oxford University
Press, 1965.
   DHU/R; DLC; CtY-D; NN/Sch
Religious Leadership Conference
on Equality of Opportunity. Har-
riman, New York. Discrimina-
tion. What Can Churches Do?
A Handbook and Report on the
Religious Leadership Confer-
ence...Arden House. Aug.
28-29, 1958. New York:
Commission Against Discrimi-
nation, 1958.   DHU/MO
Rice, Gene. "God in the
Storm." The Journal of Re-
ligious Thought (26:2, Sum.
Suppl., 1969), pp. 70-74.
   A comparison of psalm 29
and present race relations in
America.
Robinson, James Herman. ...
Love of This Land. Illustrated
by Elton C. Fax. Philadelphia:
Christian Education Press,
1956.   DHU/R
   Church and race relations.
Negro author.
Rogers, Cornish. "White Eth-
nics and Black Empowerment."
Christian Century (87:46, Nov.
18, 1970), pp. 1380-81.
                      DHU/R
Root, Robert. Progress Against
Prejudice; the Church Con-
fronts the Race Problem.
New York: Friendship Press,
1957. DHU/R; DLC; NN/Sch
Rose, Benjamin Lacy. Racial
Segregation in the Church.
Richmond, Va.: Outlook
Pub., 1957.   CtY-D
Ross, James Robert. The War
Within. New York: Sheed &

Ward, 1971.   DHU/R
"Black Theology."
Negro author.
Rowland, Stanley J. Land in
Search of God. New York:
Random House, 1958. NN/Sch
Roy, Ralph Lord. Apostles of
Discord; a Study of Organized
Bigotry and Disruption on the
Fringes of Protestantism. Bos-
ton: Beacon Press, 1953.
                        DLC
Beacon studies in church
and state. "Originally...the
author's thesis."
Russell, Jean. God's Lost
Cause: A Study of the Church
and the Racial Problem. Lon-
don: S.C.M. Press, 1968.
DHU/R; DLC; CtY-D; NcD
Schulze, Andrew. Fire From the
Throne: Race Relations in
the Church. St. Louis: Con-
cordia Pub. House, 1968.
                    NcD; DLC
Seiler, J. E. "The Church-Rac-
ist or Christian." Church
Management (46:5, Feb., 1970),
pp. 22+.   DHU/R
Sessions, R. P. "Are Southern
Ministers Failing the South?"
Saturday Evening Post (234;
My. 13, 1961), p. 37. DHU
Setiloane, Gabriel M. "A Per-
sonal Encounter With Racism."
International Review of Mission
(59:235, Jl. 1970), pp. 324-32.
                        DHU/R
African minister discusses
racism and church in England.
Shepherd, George W., Jr. "Con-
troversy Over the WCC Pro-
gram to Combat Racism."
IDOC International North Amer-
ican Edition (Apr. 24, 1971),
pp. 71-78.   DHU/R
Shockley, Donald G. "First Bap-
tist, Birmingham; A Case
Study of Wineskins Bursting."
Christian Century (87:48, Dec.
2, 1970), pp. 1462-3. DHU/R
White minister resigns because church membership re-

fuses to adopt open member-
ship.
Shriver, Donald W. The Unsilent
South: Prophetic Preaching in
Racial Crisis. Richmond:
John Knox Press, 1965. INU;
DHU/R; CtY-D; NN/Sch; DLC
Smith, Frances S. "World Coun-
cil Struggles with Racism."
United Church Herald (12:11,
Nov., 1969), pp. 46-47.
                        DHU/R
Spear, Allan H. Black Chicago:
The Making of a Negro Ghet-
to, 1890-1920. Chicago: The
University Press, 1967.
                        DHU/R
For a treatment of the
Black Church in Chicago as an
aspect of the Institutional Ghet-
to, see pp. 91-97; and the ef-
fect of Negro migration from
the South on ghetto churches
in Chicago, pp. 174-79.
"Special Fund to Combat Racism:
World Council of Churches."
IDOC, International (Dec. 12,
1970), pp. 7-28.   DHU/R
Stegall, W. "Baptism, Race and
the East Bay." Pulpit (Feb.
1969), p. 4.   DAU/W
Stewart, John J. Mormonism and
the Negro; an Explanation and
Defense of the Doctrine of the
Church of Jesus Christ of Lat-
ter-Day Saints in Regard to
Negroes and Others of Negroid
Blood. With a Historical Sup-
plement, The Church and the
Negroid People, by Wm. E.
Berrett. Orem, Utah: Book-
mark Division, Community
Press, Pub. Co., 1963.
DHU/MO; CtY-D; NN/Sch
Stringfellow, William. "Harlem
Rebellion and Resurrection."
Christian Century (87:45, Nov.
11, 1970), pp. 1345-48.
                        DHU/R
Fourteenth article in a se-
ries, How My Mind Has
Changed.
-- My People is the Enemy: An

(Stringfellow, W. cont.)
Autobiographical Polemic.
New York: Holt, 1964.
          DHU/R; CtY-D
An indictment of the Chris-
tian response to racial crisis.
Vivian, C. T. America's Joseph.
Philadelphia: Fortress Press,
1971.   DHU/R
Parallels the social and re-
ligious situation today with the
O. T. account of Joseph and his
brothers.
Negro author.
Watson, Bill. "Digging at the
Roots of White Racism."
Friends Journal (16:6, Sept.
15, 1970), p. 500.
Formation of Society of
Friends new race relations
committee, Friends for Human
Justice.

"What the Churches Are Doing
on the Crisis Front." Journal
of Religious Education (29:4,
Je. -Ag., 1969), p. 13.
                         DHU/R
Whitman, Frederick L. "Subdi-
mensions of Religiosity and
Race Prejudice." Review of
Religious Research (3; Spr.,
1962), pp. 166-74.   DHU/R
World Council of Churches, Sec-
retariat for Migration. Division
of Inter-Church Aid, Refugee and
World Service. "An Ecumenical
Programme to Combat Rac-
ism." Migration Today (13;
Aut., 1969), pp. 54-59.
             Pam. File; DHU/R
Wright, Nathan. Let's Face
Racism. Camden, N. J.:
Thomas Nelson, 1970.
                         DHU/R
Negro author.

Appendix I: Periodicals and Serials.

The Abyssinian. v. 1, no. 1-
Feb. 9, 1964- . New York:
Abyssinian Baptist Church.
(Frequency varies.) NN/Sch
Africa. v. 1- Jan., 1938- .
Metuchen, N. J. ("Edited and
published... with ecclesiasti-
cal approbation by the Mis-
sionary Sisters of Our Lady
of Africa...")
Africa Report. v. 1- 1955- .
Washington, D. C.   DCU
Africa Today. v. 1- 1953- .
New York.   DCU
African Advance. v. 1- Jl.,
1916- . Old Umtali, Rho-
desia: Rhodesia Mission Con-
ference of the Methodist Epis-
copal Church.   CtY
African Ecclesiastical Review.
v. 1- 1959-. Masaha, Ugan-
da.   DCU
The African Listener. Lusaka,
Northern Rhodesia: (Maga-
zine of the Central African
Broadcasting Station, Lusaka.)
                         NN/Sch
African Methodist Episcopal
Church Magazine. v. 1, nos.
1-12; Sept., 1841-May, 1844.
Brooklyn, N. Y.: Piercy and
Reed, Printers.   TNF
The A. M. E. Church Review. v.
1- Jl., 1884- . Philadelphia:
Publishing House of African
M. E. Church. DHU/R; DLC;
CtY-D; TNF; NN/Sch; GAU
The A. M. E. Zion Church Quar-
terly. See The A. M. E. Zion
Quarterly Review.

The A. M. E. Zion Quarterly
Review. v. 1, no. 1- Jan., 1888-
Charlotte, N. C. (Title va-

ries: The A. M. E. Zion
Church Quarterly.) DHU/R
NN/Sch; DLC; NcD
African Mission of the White
Fathers. v. 1- 1927- . Bristol,
England.   NN/Sch
The African Missionary. v. 1-
1914- . (Cork) S. M. A.: The
Society of African Missions.
                         NN/Sch
The African News. v. 1-2, v. 3,
nos. 1-4; Jan., 1889-Apr.,
1891. Vineland, N. J.: T. B.
Welch and Son.   NN/Sch
African Repository. v. 1-68,
Mr., 1825-Ja., 1892. Wash-
ington, D. C.: American Col-
onization Society. (Title va-
ries: v. 1-25 as African Re-
pository and Colonial Journal.)
                          DLC
The African Spokesman, 1859.
A. M. E. Z. Church.
African's Friend for the Promotion of Religion and Morality.
no. 1-149, 1886-98. Philadelphia.   InRE
Africa's Golden Harvest. Johannesburg: South Africa
Compounds Mission.   CtY
Afro-American Presbyterian.

Almanach de Notre Dame du
Sacré-Coeur. 1-, 1895-.
Borgehout-Anvers: Les Mis-
sionaires du Sacré-Coeur.
                         NN/Sch
American and Foreign Anti-
Slavery Society. Report. 1st-
1839/40- . New York.
                         CtY-D
American Baptist. v. 1-28,
1845-72. New York. ICU; OO

393

American Baptist Memorial, A
Statistical Biographical and Historical Magazine. v. 1-15, 1842-
56. New York. (Title va-
ries: 1842-Sept., 1844 as
Baptist Memorial and Monthly
Chronicle; Oct., 1844-Dec.,
1851, Baptist Memorial and
Monthly Record.)
       DLC; SCBHC; CtY
American Church Institute for
Negroes. Report. 1st- .
1906/07-. New York. (An-
nual, 1906/07-19; irregular,
1934- . Title varies: 1906/
07- Annual Report; 19- .
Report. Reports for 1930,
1940/42 have also distinctive
titles.)   NN/Sch
American Missionary. v. 1-10,
1846-56; 2nd ser., v. 1-20,
1856-76; new ser., v. 1- ,
1877- . New York: Ameri-
can Missionary Association.
           CtY; DLC
The American Missionary. v.
-82; -Dec. 1928. New York:
American Missionary Association, and, Apr. 1909-1928, by
the Congregational Home Missionary Society and other Congregational Societies.
        DHU/R; NN/Sch
American Missionary Register.
v. 1- 1820- . New York.
           DHU/R
The Anti-Slavery Examiner. v.
1-14, 1836-45. New York:
American Anti-Slavery Society.
       DLC; CtY; CU
Anti-Slavery Tracts. n. 1-20.
1855-56, new series n. 1-
1860- . New York: Ameri-
can Anti-Slavery Society.
          DLC; NNC
The (Atlanta) Methodist Advocate.
M. E. Church.
Baptist Leader. v. 1- 1883- .
Birmingham, Ala.   NHC
Baptist Student Union Bulletin.
v. 1- 1956- . Nashville,
Tenn.: National Baptist Stu-
dent Union Headquarters.

Baptist Training Union Leader.
v. 1, 1958-. Nashville: Na-
tional Baptist Training Union
Board of the National Baptist
Convention, U. S. A.   SCBHC
Baptist World. v. 1-23, 1897-
Aug. 1919. Louisville, Ky.
           DLC; NN
Birmingham Era. A. M. E.
Church. Formerly Christian
Era.
Le Bulletin des Missions. t. 1-
1899- . Bruges: Abbaye de
Saint-André-loz-Bruges.
(Title varies.)   NN/Sch
Capitol City Defender. 1960-
1964. C. M. E. Church.
Catholic Missions. v. 1- ,1924- .
New York.   NN/Sch
The Cavalla Messenger. 1843-
1863? Cavalla, West Africa:
(Protestant Episcopal Church
in the U. S. A. Missionary Dis-
trict of Liberia.)   NN/Sch
Central Africa: A Monthly Rec-
ord of the Work of the Univer-
sities' Mission to Central Af-
rica. no. 1- , 1863- . Lon-
don.   NN/Sch
Central Christian Advocate. v.
1- , 1852- . Kansas City,
Kan.   DLC
Charlotte Messenger. 1882-1890
(?). North Carolina (?)
A. M. E. Z. Church.
Christian Educator: A Quarterly
Magazine of Facts Relating to
Christian Education in the South.
v. 1- , 1889- . Cincinnati:
Freedmen's Aid and Southern
Education Society, Methodist
Episcopal Church.   DLC
The Christian Index. v. 1- ,
1867- . Jackson, Tenn.:
C. M. E. Church Publishing
House, ("Official Organ of the
Christian Methodist Episcopal
Church.")   DHU/R
The Christian Leader. v. 29- ,
1926- . Boston: Universal-
ist Publishing House. DLC;
           DHU
Formerly Universalist Leader.

Christian Plea. v. 1- , 1899-.
Columbus, O.: Negro Dis-
ciples of Christ.
Christian Recorder.   v. 1- ,
1852- . Philadelphia: Moth-
er Bethel A. M. E. Church.
The Church Advocate. v. 1-23,
-1913? Baltimore, Md. NNG
Church and Race. v. 1, no. 1-,
July 8, 1963- . Lebanon, Pa.
(Frequency varies. Issued by
the National Council of the
Protestant Episcopal Church
in the U. S. A. , Department of
Christian Social Relations, Di-
vision of Christian Citizen-
ship.)   DLC; NN/Sch
Church and Race Memo.   New
York: Division of Church and
Race, United Presbyterian
Church. (Issued periodically.)
Pam. File; DHU/R
The Church Herald.   v. 1- ,
1913- .   Charleston, S. C.
NNG
Church in Metropolis. v. 1- ,
1964- . Lebanon, Pa. : Na-
tional Council of Episcopal
Church.   DHU/R
Church Life. v. 1- , 1887- .
Cleveland: Department of Pub-
licity of Diocesan Council.
NNG; DHU/MO
The Church Magnet. v. 1, no.
1- . Dec. 14, 1930- . New
York: Church Magnet Pub-
lishing Co. ("Endorsed by the
Interdenominational Preachers
Meeting and the Baptist
Preachers' Conference of New
York and Vicinity. ") NN/Sch
The Church School Herald-Jour-
nal. Charlotte, N. C. : A. M. E.
Zion Pub. House. DHU/MO
Claver Almanac for the African
Missions. St. Louis: Sodality
of St. Peter Claver. NN/Sch
Colored American Magazine. v.
1-17, My. 1900-Nov. 1909.
Boston, Mass.   DLC
Colored Citizen. 1866. Missis-
sippi. M. E. Church.
Community (formerly Catholic

Interracialist). v. 1- , Mr. ,
1941- . Chicago. (Title va-
ries: Harlem Friendship
House News, Mr. , 1941-Jl. /
Ag. , 1948; Catholic Interra-
cialist, 1948-Jl. /Ag. , 1955).
NN/Sch
Congo Mission News. Nouvelles
Missionaires du Congo. Estab-
lished 1912. Leopoldville,
Belgian Congo.   NN/Sch
Congo Missionary Messenger.
Berne, Ind. ; Chicago: Congo
Inland Mission Board. NN/Sch
Crisis: A Record of the Darker
Races.   v. 1- , Nov. , 1910- .
New York: National Associa-
tion for the Advancement of
Colored People.   DHU/R
The Danville Quarterly Review...
v. 1-4, Mr. 1861-Dec. 1864.
Danville, Ky. : Association of
Ministers.
DHU/MO; DLC; CtY
Dini Na Mila. v. 1- , 1965- .
Uganda, East Africa: Make-
rere College.   DHU/R
The Drum Call. v. 1- , Jan. ,
1922- . Elat, Cameroun:
("Official Quarterly of the
West African Mission of the
Presbyterian Church in the
U. S. A. ")   NN/Sch
East and West. Nov. 1899-Oct.
1900. New York. DLC; NN
Eastern Index. 1902. Pittsbow,
N. C. C. M. E. Church.
Ecumenical Press Service. v. 1,
1934. Geneva, Switzerland;
World Council of Churches.
DHU/R
Ecumenical Review. v. 1- ,
1948- . Geneva: World Coun-
cil of Churches. Formerly
Christendom.   DHU/R
Evangelishes Missions-Magazin.
v. 1-41, 1816-56; ns. v. 1,
1857- . Basel, Switzerland.
CtY; DLC; NN/Sch
L'Évangile en Afrique. Léopold-
ville, Congo Belge. NN/Sch
Faith. Washington, D. C.
DHU/MO

Fayetteville Educator. North
Carolina (?). A. M. E. Z.
Church.
Fellowship. v. 1-, 1935-.
New York: Fellowship of
Reconciliation.   DHU/R
Florida African Methodist. Love
Oak, Fla.: Edward Waters
College. A. M. E. Church.
The Foreign Missionary. v. 1-,
1880- . Philadelphia: Board
of Foreign Missions, United
Lutheran Church in America.
DHU/MO; CtY-D
The Foundation. Atlanta, Ga.:
Gammon Theological Semi-
nary.   DHU/MO; GAU
The Friend of Africa. v. 1-3
(no. 1-28); Jan. 1, 1841-Feb.,
1843. London: By the com-
mittee of the Society for the
Extinction of the Slave Trade,
and for the Civilization of Af-
rica.   DLC
Gammon Theological Seminary
Bulletin. Atlanta, Ga.   GAU

Georgia African Methodist. At-
lanta, Ga.: Morris Brown
College. A. M. E. Church.
The Ghana Bulletin of Theology.
v. 1-, 1965-. Legon, Ghana;
University of Ghana, Depart-
ment for the Study of Reli-
gions.   DHU/R
The Goal. Wilberforce, O.
A. M. E. Church.
Gospel Trumpet. C. M. E.
Church.
Grand Old Christian. Virginia
Conference of A. M. E. Church.
Herald of Truth. 1885-1887.
Waco, Tex. College Journal
of Paul Quinn College.
Hibbert Journal. v. 1-, 1902-.
Boston: L. Phillips. DHU/R
The Hinterland. v. 1-, Sept.,
1922-. West Park, N. Y.:
(Published bi-monthly in the
interests of the Holy Cross
Liberian Mission.)   NN/Sch
Home and Foreign Fields. v. 1-
21, 1916-1937. Nashville:

Southern Baptist Convention.
CtY-D; DHU/MO
The Home Mission College Re-
view. v. 1-3, 4, no. 1, My.
1927-My. 1930. Raleigh,
N. C.: Shaw University.
The Home Mission Monthly. v.
1-38, no. 1-4; Nov., 1886-
Feb., 1924. New York:
(Vols. 1-10 published by the
Woman's Executive Committee
of Home Missions of the Pres-
byterian Church; v. 11-38 by
the Woman's Board of Home
Missions of the Presbyterian
Church.)   DHU/R; NN/Sch
IDOC: International Documenta-
tion on the Contemporary Church.
North American Edition. V. 1-,
1970-.   DHU/R
The Informer. v. 1-, Jl., 1956-.
Indianapolis, Ind.: ("Official
Organ of the Seventh Episco-
pal District of the Christian
Methodist Episcopal Church.")
DHU/MO
International Review of Missions.
v. 1-, 1912-. Edinburgh,
Scotland.   DHU/R; DCU
Interracial News Service: A Di-
gest of Trends and Developments
in Human Relations. v. 1-,
1930-. New York: Depart-
ment of Race Relations, Fed-
eral Council of Churches.
NN/Sch; CtY
Interracial Review: A Journal
for Christian Democracy. v. 1,
Mr., 1928- . New York:
Catholic Interracial Council.
(Title varies.)
DCU; NN/Sch; NcD
The Josephite Harvest. v. 1-
1922-. Baltimore: Society of
Saint Joseph of the Sacred
Heart.   NN/Sch
Formerly, The Colored
Harvest.
Journal of Human Relations. v.
1-, 1952-. Wilberforce, O.
DCU
Journal of Intergroup Relations.
v. 1-, My., 1958- . New

York: ("A publication of the National Association of Intergroup Relations Officials.")
NN/Sch
Journal of Negro Education. v. 1-, 1932-. Washington, D.C.
DHU/R
Journal of Negro History. v. 1-1916- . Lancaster, Pa.
DHU; DAU; DCU; DLC; NN/Sch
The Journal of Religion in Africa. v. 1-, Leiden, Belgium: J. Brill.   DHU/R
Journal of Religious Education of the African Methodist Episcopal Church. Nashville, Tenn.: Division of Christian Education of the African Methodist Episcopal Church.   DHU/R
Journal of Religious Thought. v. 1-, 1943- . Washington, D.C.: School of Religion, Howard University.
DHU/R; DAU
The Juvenile Missionary Magazine and Annual. London: Directors of the London Missionary Society.   NN/Sch
Katallagete. v. 1-, June 1965-. Nashville, Tenn.: The Committee of Southern Churchmen.   DHU/R
The Layman. New York: ("Official Organ of the Lay Leaders Council, representing Epworth, Metropolitan, Mt. Calvary, Salem, St. Mark's and Trinity Methodist Churches.") NN/Sch
Liberia. Bulletin no. 1-34; Nov., 1892-Feb., 1909. Washington, D.C.: American Colonization Society.   CtY-D
Lott Carey Herald. v. 1-, 1913?-. Richmond, Va.: Lott Carey Foreign Mission Society.   KyLS; TxSS
The Message Magazine. v. 1-, 1935- . Nashville: Southern Pub. Association. DLC; CtY
The Messenger; World's Greatest Negro Monthly. v. 1-, 1917. New York.   DLC; NN
Subtitle varies.

Methodist Banner. Washington Conference. M.E. Church.
Methodist Overseas Missions: Gazeteer and Statistics. v. 1-, 1946- . New York: Division of World Missions and Woman's Division of Christian Service of the Board of Missions of the Methodist Church.
NN/Sch
Methodist Quarterly Review. v. 1-79, no. 4, Ja. 1847-1930. Louisville.   DLC; CtY-D
Title varies: Quarterly Review of the Methodist Episcopal Church; Methodist Review.
Methodist Review. v. 1-114, no. 3, 1818-1931. New York.
DLC; CtY-D
Title varies: Methodist Magazine, Methodist Magazine and Quarterly Review.
The Metropolitan Witness. v. 1-, Sum., 1957-. New York: Metropolitan Community Methodist Church.   NN/Sch
Minister's Wives' Herald. Richmond: National Association of Ministers' Wives.   DHU/R
Mission Fields at Home. v. 1-6, no. 10/11, Oct., 1928-Jl./Ag., 1934. Cornwells Heights, Pa.: ("Published by the Sisters of the Blessed Sacrament.")   NN/Sch
The Missionary Herald at Home and Abroad. v. 1-147, no. 13, Je., 1805-Mr., 1951. Worcester, Mass.: American Board of Commissioners for Foreign Missions, Je., 1805-Ag., 1939; Missions Council of the Congregational Church and Christian Churches, Sept. 1939-Mr., 1951. (Title varies.)
DHU/R; NN/Sch
The Missionary Magazine. Jacksonville, Fla.: Women's Missionary Society, A.M.E. Church.   DHU/MO
The Missionary Messenger. 1940. Philadelphia: Woman's Mis-

(The Missionary Messenger cont.)
sionary Council, C. M. E.
Church.
Missionary Record. 1868. A.
M. E. Church. Formerly,
Charleston Leader.
The Missionary Recorder. Tulsa,
Okla. : Woman's Missionary
Society, A. M. E. Church.
                     DHU/MO
Missionary Review of the World.
v. 1-, 1878- . New York.
                     DHU/R; DAU
The Missionary Seer. v. 1-,
1900- . Washington, D. C.
                     DHU/R
Le Missioni del Comboni: Peri-
odico Monsile Illustrato di Propa-
ganda per la Redenzione dell'
Africa. Brescia: Instituto Mis-
sionario "Daniele Comboni."
                     NN/Sch
Missions, an International Bap-
tist Magazine. v. 1-38, 1910-
47. Boston: Northern Bap-
tist Convention.
          DLC; DHU/MO; CtY-D
Muslim World. v. 1-, 1911- .
Hartford: Hartford Seminary
Foundation. CtY; DLC; NN
Title varies: 1911-. Oct.
1947, The Moslem World.
The National Baptist Extension
Advocate. Los Angeles: Na-
tional Baptist Extension Board
of America.   DHU/MO
The National Baptist Magazine.
v. 1-7, no. 8, 1894-Dec.
1900. Washington, D. C. :
American National Baptist
Convention. DLC; DHU/MO
National Baptist Student Union
Echo. Nashville.   DHU/MO

National Baptist Union-Review.
v. 1, 1899. Nashville, Tenn. :
National Baptist Pub. Board,
                     NN; DLC
National Council Outlook. v. 1-,
1951-. New York: National
Council of the Churches of
Christ in the U. S. A. DHU/R
1918-1950 as Federal Coun-

cil Bulletin.
Near East. v. 1-, 1908- . Lon-
don.   DLC
The Negro Churchman. New
York: "Published ... by the
Consistory in the Interest of
the African Orthodox Church."
                     NN/Sch
The Negro Journal of Religion:
An Interdenominational Review.
Wilberforce, O.   NN/Sch
Negro Trends. v. 1, no. 1-.
Dec. 10, 1951- . Washington,
D. C.   NN/Sch
The New Day. v. 1-, 1937- .
New York: New Day Publ.
Co.   MB; NN
Father Divine's cult.
New Light. 1886-? M. E.
Church.
New South. v. 1-, 1946- .
Atlanta, Ga. DHU/R; DAU
New York Missionary Research
Library. Occasional Bulletin.
v. 1- , 1960- . New York.
          DHU/R; NN/Sch; DCU
Opportunity; a Journal of Negro
Life. v. 1-, 1923- . New
York: National Urban League
for Social Service Among Ne-
groes. CtY; DLC; NN
Orita: Ibadan Journal of Reli-
gious Studies. v. 1-, 1967-.
Nigeria: Ibadan University
Press.   DHU/R
The Orthodox Messenger. Mi-
ami, Fla. : Southern Juris-
diction of the African Ortho-
dox Church.   DHU/MO
Our Colored Missions. v. 1-,
1907- . New York: Catholic
Board for Mission Work Among
the Colored People.
                     DHU/R; NN/Sch
The Parish Bulletin. v. 1-,
1931/32. New York: "Publ.
Monthly in the interest of the
Church of the Crucifixion...
New York City..." NN/Sch
Phylon. v. 1-, 1940-. Atlanta,
Ga.   DHU/MO; DCU; DAU
Plain Dealer. C. M. E. Church.

The Progressive Nabi. v. 1,
no. 1, Apr. 1969. Atlanta:
Interdenominational Theological Center.   GAU
Prophetic Religion. v. 1-,
1940- . Chapel Hill, N. C.:
Fellowship of Southern Church-
men.   NcU
Race Relations: A Monthly Sum-
mary of Events and Trends. v.
1-5, Ag., 1943-Je./Dec.,
1948. Nashville: Social Sci-
ence Institute, Fisk Univer-
sity.   CtY-D
Religion and Society. v. 1-,
1968- . Stillwater, Minn.:
Religion and Society, Inc.
                       DHU/R
Religious Herald. v. 1-, 1828-.
Richmond, Va.   DLC
Repository of Religion and Lit-
erature. 1858-60. Philadelphia.
A. M. E. Church.
St. Augustine's Messenger. Bay
St. Louis, Miss.: Divine
Word Society.
                 DHU/R; NN/Sch
St. Augustine's Parish Review.
v. 1- , 1932- . Washington,
D. C.: Parishioner's of St.
Augustine's Church.
Second Baptist Advocate. De-
troit: Second Baptist Church.
                       DHU/MO
The Seminarian. v. 1-, 1943-.
Nashville: American Baptist
Theological Seminary.
Signs of Soul: National Black
Sisters Conference Newsletter.
1969- . Pittsburgh, Pa.
                       DHU/R
Social Action. v. 1-, Mr.
1935- . Boston: The Pilgrim
Press.   DHU/R
Soul Force. Atlanta: Southern
Christian Leadership Confer-
ence.
South African Outlook: A Jour-
nal Dealing with Missionary and
Racial Affairs. v. 1-, 1870- .
Lovedale, C. P. South Africa:
Lovedale Press.   NN/Sch

Southern Christian Advocate.
v. 1-, 1837- . Columbia,
S. C.: Methodist Episcopal
Church, South.   DLC
Southern Christian Leadership
Conference Newsletter. v. 1-,
My. 1961. Atlanta. SCLC
Southern Christian Recorder.
v. 1-, 1889- . Nashville.
                 IEG; NjMD
Southwestern Christian Advocate.
v. 1- , 1878- . New Orleans.
                       DLC
Standard. v. 1-67. 1853-1920.
Chicago.
The Star of Zion. The Official
Organ of the African Methodist
Episcopal Zion Church. Char-
lotte, N. C.: A. M. E. Zion
Publication House.
                 DLC; NN/Sch
The Sunday School Worker. v.
1-7, 1918-24. Philadelphia.
                 CtY; DLC
Target. no. 1-, Dec., 1963- .
Nairobi: East African Ven-
ture Co.   DHU/R
Texas Methodist. A. M. E.
Church.
Torchlight Appeal. 1888. A. M.
E. Church.
The Vanguard: The Church in
Human Relations. v. 1-, Jan./
Feb., 1954- . Valparaiso,
Ind.: Lutheran Human Rela-
tions Association of America.
                       DHU/MO
Vindicator. 1888- . Birming-
ham, Ala. A. M. E. Church.
Formerly Methodist Vindi-
cation.
Vivante Afrique; Revue General
des Mission D'Afrique. Namur,
Belgium.   DLC
The Voice: A Journal of Catho-
lic Negro Opinion. v. 1-, Jan.
1934-. Philadelphia: Feder-
ated Colored Catholics of the
United States.   DHU/MO
The Voice of Antioch. v. 1-,
1931- . Boley, Okla.: Antioch Baptist Church.
                       DHU/MO

Voice of Missions. v. 1-, 1892-.
New York: Missionary Depart-
ment, African Methodist Epis-
copal Church.   DHU/MO;
DHU/R; NN/Sch; CtY-D
Voice of the People.   A. M. E.
Church.
Washington Conference Journal.
1886-? M. E. Church.
Watchman-Examiner. v. 1-,
1819-.   DLC; CtY-D
The Wesleyan Missionary
Notices. v. 1-, 1816-. Lon-
don: Wesleyan Mission Home.
DHU/MO; DLC; CtY-D; EtY
Western Christian Recorder.
1892-1899? Kansas City,
Kan.: ("Organ of the Fifth
Episcopal District of the
A. M. E. Church.") NN/Sch
The Western Friend. 1870-?
St. Louis: M. E. Church.
Western Index. 1908. A. M. E.
Church.
Western Trumpet. Topeka, Kans.:
A. M. E. Church.
White Fathers' Missions. v. 1-
35, 1895-Je., 1943; new ser.
v. 1-, Sept., 1943-.

Montreal: "White Fathers,
Missionaries of Africa."
NN/Sch
Women and Missions. v. 1-23,
no. 9, Apr., 1924-Dec.,
1946. New York: Woman's
Committees of the Board of
National Missions, and the
Board of Foreign Missions of
the Presbyterian Church in the
U. S. A.   NN/Sch
Women's Christian Recorder.
A. M. E. Church.
Women's Missionary Recorder.
Nashville: Women's Mite Mis-
sionary Society.   DHU/MO
The Worker. Washington, D. C.:
Women's Convention of Nation-
al Baptist Convention, Inc.
DHU/MO
Yale Review. v. 1-19, My.,
1892-Feb., 1911; new series
v. 1-Oct., 1911-. New Haven,
Conn.   CtY; DLC
Formerly New Englander
and Yale Review.
Zion's Standard Weekly Review.
1867. A. M. E. Z. Church.

African Methodist Episcopal Zion Church. Unpublished materials.
NcSalL
Allen, Richard and Absolom Jones. To the People of Colour. Mms. NN
American Home Missionary Society Archives. Issues of Slavery and the Civil War in Northern Churches. Amistad Research Center, Dillard Univ., New Orleans, La.
American Missionary Association Archives. Letters, Evangelical Abolitionism, Free Presbyterian Church. Amistad Research Center, Dillard Univ., New Orleans, La.
American Negro Historical Society. Records, 1790-1901. Ca. 3000 items. (Includes material on the First and Second African Presbyterian Churches of Philadelphia.)
Penna. Hist. Society.
Anti-Slavery Materials. Mms. Letters, diaries. Tract Repository (24-issues, 1893-1895) Issued at Philadelphia to furnish Freedmen with reading material. INRE
Benjamin W. Arnett Papers.
OWibfU
Includes mms. by Henry McNeal Turner and Daniel A. Payne.
E. W. Blyden See George L. Ruffin Papers.

Edward Blyden. Various Letters, Manuscripts.
NN/Sch; DLC; NjP
Rhodes House Library, Oxford University College; London

School of Economics; Salisbury Court London ECI; Public Records Office, England; University of Ibadan, Nigeria.
John E. Bruce Papers. NN/Sch
(John E. Bruce was an A. M. E. Zion layman.)
Thomas Clarkson Papers, 1760-1846. (English philanthropist and abolitionists.) 50 items.
DHU/MO
210 Items, Henry E. Huntington Library (San Marino, Calif.).
Daniel Coker Journal. (Journal kept on the West Coast of Africa, Apr. 21-Sept. 21, 1821)
DLC
Levi Jenkins Coppin Papers.
OWibfU
Alexander Crummell Papers.
NN/Sch
John Miller Dickey Papers. (Presbyterian minister; founder of Lincoln University, Chester, Pa.) PLU
Paul Lawrence Dunbar Papers. Letter to Alexander Crummel, 9 September 1894. 2 pp., ms.
NN/Sch
John G. Fee Papers. (Presbyterian clergyman, Founder of Berea College, Berea, Kentucky). KyBB
Friends, Society of. Association of Friends for the Free Instruction of Adult Colored Persons. Minutes, 1789-1822; 1878-91. PFL
-- Beehive School for Colored Children. Managers Minutes, 1865-1888. PFL
-- Indiana Yearly Meeting. Records, 1821-1920. (Includes

(Friends, Society of, cont.)
minutes of the Committee on
the Concerns of the People of
Colour).   INRE
-- Institute for Colored Youth.
First Minute Book, 1837-59.
Original draft of Minutes,
1850-58.
Minutes of Board of In-
struction, 1868-97.   PFL
-- Minutes of the Society (of
Women Friends) for the Free
Instruction of African Females.
1795-1845.   PFL
-- Papers on Educational Work
Among Negroes. Friends
Freedmen's Association, 1863-
1935.   PFL
-- Quaker protest literature on
the importation of slaves.
(1698).   PFL
-- New England Yearly Meeting.
Abolition Society Book. In-
cludes petitions and other pa-
pers relating to slavery; an
account of the African School
and Meeting House in Providence (printed). Covers
years 1798-1830.   RPB
-- Baltimore Society for the
Protection of Free People of
Color. Minutes, with Constitution and By-Laws. 1827-29.
MFL
David Ethan Frierson Papers.
1839-96. 272 items. (Includes a catechism for Negroes.)   ScU
Henry Highland Garnet Speeches.
NN/Sch
Frances Grimke Papers and Sermons.   DHU/MO
Cornelius Mack Hall Correspondence and Records of Mil-
waukee's Inner City Develop-
ment Project, 1965-66. 25 ft.
microfilm, 530 items, 16 mm.
Milwaukee County Historical
Society.
Lemuel Haynes Papers. NN/Sch

James A. Healy. 2 diary mms.,
1849, 1891; Sermons and

lectures. Holy Cross College
Archives.
Charles Leander Hill Papers.
Ca. 2000 items.   OWibfU
Mildred J. Hill. See Avery
Robinson Papers.

James Theodore Holly Letters
and Papers.   NN/Sch
Lilly Family Papers. 1924-60.
(Correspondence, sermons
and other materials relating
to Presbyterian Church and
the Negro.) Hist. Foundation
of the Presbyterian and Reformed Churches (Montreat,
N. C.).
C. Eric Lincoln Papers. GAU

Methodism. Extensive collection mms., books and pamphlets.   IEG
Methodist Episcopal Church.
Border States. Conference
Reports.   DLC
-- Freedmen's Aid Society. Papers, 1865-1877. GAU; Amistad Research Center, Dillard Univ., New Orleans, La.
Milwaukee's Inner City Development Project. Records. See
Cornelius Mack Hall Correspondence.

Thomas Montgomery Letters.
1841-1907. 149 items. (In-
cludes information on religious
activities of Negro soldiers.)
Minn. Hist. Society
Robert Hamill Nassau Papers.
(Presbyterian Missionary to
Africa.)   PLU
Theodore Parker Papers. (Mass.
Unitarian Minister, Abolition-
ist.)   DLC; MB
Daniel A. Payne. See Benjamin
W. Arnett Papers.

Daniel A. Payne Papers.
OWibfU; NN/Sch
Presbyterian Church. Synod of
New York and New Jersey.
Extract from Minutes of the

Directors of the African School
established by this group.
                              NjPT
Presbyterian Church in the U.S.
Synods. Minutes, 1788-1956.
(Includes minutes of the Afro-
American Synod, 1916.)
   Hist. Foundation of the
Presbyterian and Reformed
Churches (Montreat, N. C.).
                              PPPrHi
Protestant Episcopal Church in
the U.S.A. Provinces. North-
west. Records, 1914-42.
Minn. Hist. Soc.
Reverdy Cassius Ranson Pa-
pers.   OWibfU
C. L. Remond. See George L.
Ruffin Papers.

Avery Robinson Papers. 1895-
1964. (Includes two note-
books of Negro hymns col-
lected and annotated by Mildred J. Hill.)   OrU
John S. Rock. See George L.
Ruffin Papers.

George L. Ruffin Papers. (Includes papers of E. W. Blyden,
C. L. Remond, John S. Rock
and George W. Williams.)
291 mms.   DHU/MO
William Sanders Scarborough
Papers. 936 mms.   OWibfU
Matthew Simpson Papers. Mss
include correspondence of
white abolitionists and missionaries to freedmen in post-
war South.   DLC

Slavery and Abolitionists' Pa-
pers.   OO
Slavery and Abolitionists' Pa-
pers (1792-1865).   DHU/MO
Slavery Papers.   PLU
Edward F. Stratton Papers.
1750-1961. 207 mms. (In-
cludes Quaker documents, let-
ters and reports of Edward
Williams and wife, teachers
in schools for freedmen in
Mississippi and Texas.) PSW
Benjamin T. Tanner. See also
Carter G. Woodson Collection.

Lewis Tappan Papers.   DLC
Contains minister's corre-
spondence on abolition.
Henry McNeal Turner Papers.
42 mss. DHU/MO; NN/Sch
Henry McNeal Turner. See
Benjamin W. Arnett Papers.

Western Anti-Slavery Society Pa-
pers, 1834, 1835, 1837-46.
                              DLC
Edward Williams Correspondence.
See Edward F. Stratton Papers.

George W. Williams. See
George L. Ruffin Papers.

Carter G. Woodson Collection of
Negro Papers and Related
Documents.   DLC
Underground Railroad. Mms.
Miscellaneous file on Levi
Coffin and Underground Rail-
road.   INRE

Appendix III: Sources

African Bibliographic Center.
Special Bibliographic Series.
New York: Negro Universi-
ties Press, 1969- . 7 vols.
Allison, William H. Inventory
of Unpublished Material for
American Religious History in
Protestant Church Archives
and Other Repositories. Wash-
ington, D. C. : Carnegie Insti-
tution of Wash. , 1910.
American Friend. Richmond,
Ind. , American Friends Board
of Foreign Missions, 1924-38.
American Journal of Theology.
Chicago: University of Chi-
cago Press, 1897-1920.
American Missionary. New
York: American Missionary
Association, 1886; 1909-1928.
American Missionary Register.
New York: J. & J. Harper,
1820-1825.
American Presbyterian Review.
New York: C. Scribner,
1859-1870.
American Protestant Magazine.
New York: The American
Protestant Society, 1845.
American Quarterly Register.
Boston: Perkins Marvin,
1827-43.
American Society of Church His-
tory Papers. 2d. series ...
New York City, The Red Dia-
mond Press, 1908-1910.
American Theological Library
Association. Index to Religious
Periodical Literature. Chi-
cago: American Theological
Library Association, 1949-.
Andover Review: A Religious
and Theological Monthly. Boston:
Houghton, Mifflin and Co. ,

1884-1893.
Anglican Theological Review.
New York: Columbia Univer-
sity Press, 1918-1969.
Assembly's Magazine ... Phila-
delphia: General Assemblies
Missionary Magazine, Wm.
Farrand & Co. , 1805-1808.
Atlanta, Georgia. Interdenomi-
national Theological Center.
Library. A Select Bibliogra-
phy: The Black Experience.
Mim.
Barrow, John G. A Bibliogra-
phy of Bibliographies in Reli-
gion. Ann Arbor, Mich. :
Edwards Bros. , 1955.
The Biblical Repository and Clas-
sical Review. Andover, Mass. :
n. p. , 1831-1850.
The Biblical World. Chicago:
University of Chicago Press,
1893-1920.
The Bibliographic Index; A Cumu-
lative Bibliography of Bibliogra-
phies. New York: H. W. Wil-
son Co. , 1939.
A Bibliography of African and
Afro-American Religions.
Princeton, N. J. : The Fund
for Theological Education,
Inc. , 1970. Mim.
Bowen, J. W. E. , (ed.). Africa
and the American Negro: Ad-
dresses and Proceedings of
the Congress on Africa. Miami, Fla. : Mnemosyne Publ.
Inc. , 1969. Repr.
Brown, William Wells. The
Black Man, His Antecedents,
His Genius and His Achievements. Miami, Fla. : Mne-
msoyne Pub. Co. , 1969.
(Originally published in

404

1865 by Robert Wallcut, Boston.)

Campbell, Ernest Q. Christians in Racial Crisis. Washington, D.C.: Public Affairs Press, 1959.

Campbell, Will D. Race and the Renewal of the Church. Philadelphia: Westminster Press, 1962.

The Christian Index. Jackson, Tenn., C.M.E. Church, 1867-1970.

Christian Librarians' Fellowship. Christian Periodical Index; A Selected List. A Subject Index to Periodical Literature. Prepared by Librarians of the Christian Librarians' Fellowship, 1950-.

The Church at Home and Abroad. Philadelphia: Presbyterian Board of Publishers, 1887-1899.

Church History. Scottdale, Pa.: The American Society of Church History, 1932-.

The Church Militant. Boston: Board of Missions of the Diocese of Massachusetts, 1898-1906.

Church Missionary Review. London: Church Missionary Society, 1890-1927.

The Church Overseas; An Anglican Review of Missionary Thought and Work. London: Missionary Council of the Church Assembly Press, 1928-34.

The Church Quarterly Review. London: Spottiswoode & Co., 1876-1920.

The Churchman's Magazine. New Haven: Comstock Griswold & Co., 1804.

Conference on Science, Philosophy and Religion in Their Relation to the Democratic Way of Life. Papers of the Meetings. New York: Harper, 1940-.

The Congregational Quarterly.

Boston: 1859-1878.

The Congregationalist and Herald of Gospel Liberty. Boston: 1816-.

Daedalus. The Negro American. Boston: Houghton, Mifflin, 1966.
(Edited by Talcott Parsons and Kenneth Clark...) (Daedalus Library, v. 7) Also issued as vol. 94, no. 4 & vol. 95, no. 1, of Daedalus Magazine.

Davis, John P., (ed.). The American Negro Reference Book. Englewood Cliffs, N.J.: Prentice Hall, 1966.

Diehl, Katharine Smith. Religions, Mythologies, Folklores: An Annotated Bibliography. New Brunswick, N.J.: Scarecrow Press, 1956.

Dumond, Dwight L. A Bibliography of Anti-Slavery in America. Ann Arbor: University of Michigan Press, 1961.

Ebony. The Negro Handbook. Compiled by the Editors of Ebony. Chicago: Johnson Pub. Co., 1966.

Ebony. The White Problem in America. Chicago: Johnson Publishing Co., 1966.

Enid Oklahoma. Phillips University Graduate Seminary. Catalogue of Theses 1913-1965. Graduate Seminary, Phillips University, Enid, Oklahoma. Mim.

Federal Council Bulletin. New York: 1918-1950. Reports. Microf.

Ferry, Henry. The Negro Church. Course Bibliography, School of Religion, Howard University, 1969. Mim.

Fisk University. Nashville. Amistead Research Center. Author and Added Entry Catalog of the American Missionary Association Archives, With References to Schools and

(Fisk Univ., cont.)
  Mission Stations. Westport,
  Conn.: Greenwood Publishing Corp., 1970.
Florida. State University. Cata-
  log of the Negro Collections
  in Florida Agricultural Me-
  chanical University Library
  and the Florida State Univer-
  sity. n.p., 1969. Mim.
Gann, L. H. and P. Duignan,
  (eds.). Colonialism in Africa:
  1870-1960. Vol. I. New
  York: Cambridge University
  Press, 1969.
Gravely, William B. Log of
  Summer Travel to American
  Libraries for Research Ma-
  terials on Afro-American Re-
  ligious History. Typewritten.
Guide to Religious and Semi-
  Religious Periodicals. Flint,
  Mich.: National Library of
  Religious Periodicals, 1968-.
Hamer, Philip M., (ed.). A
  Guide to Archives and Manu-
  scripts in the United States.
  Compiled for the National
  Publications Commission. New
  Haven: Yale University Pr.,
  1961.
Hicks, Richard L. and Henry
  H. Mitchell, (comp.). An An-
  notated Bibliography for "The
  Black Experience in Amer-
  ica" and "Introduction to
  Black Church History." Sep-
  tember, 1970. Mim.
  "Prepared for classes in
  the Black Religious Experi-
  ence."
Indiana University. Afro-Ameri-
  can Religion and Race Rela-
  tions: A Bibliography ...
  Bloomingdale, Indiana Univer-
  sity.
  (Focus Black: American
  Bibliographic Series.) Mim.
International Review of Missions.
  Edinburgh, 1912-1970.
Journal of Presbyterian Histori-
  cal Society. Philadelphia:
  The Presbyterian Historical

Society, 1958-1970.
Journal of Religion in Africa.
  Leiden: E. J. Brill, 1967-.
Journal of Religious Thought.
  Washington, D. C.: Howard
  University, School of Religion,
  1943-.
Lewin, Evans L. Royal Empire
  Society. Bibliographies. An-
  notated Bibliography of Recent
  Publications on Africa, South
  of the Sahara with Special Ref-
  erence to Administrative Po-
  litical Economic & Sociological
  Problems. London: The
  Royal Empire Society, 1943.
Little, Lawrence C. A Bibliog-
  raphy of Doctoral Disserta-
  tions on Adults and Adult Ed-
  ucation. Pittsburgh: Univer-
  sity of Pittsburgh Press,
  1963. (rev. ed.)
Livingstone College. Salisbury,
  N. C. Carnegie Library. An In-
  dex to Biographical Sketches
  and Publications of the Bish-
  ops of the A. M. E. Zion
  Church. Compiled by Louise
  M. Rountree, Salisbury:
  1963. Mim.
Marshall, Albert P., (comp.).
  A Guide to Negro Periodical
  Literature. Jefferson, Mo.:
  Lincoln University, 1941-.
  Mim.
Martin, Thomas P. "Sources of
  Negro History in the Manu-
  script Division of the Library
  of Congress." Journal of Ne-
  gro History (19:1, Ja. 1934),
  pp. 72+.
McDonough, John. "Manuscript
  Resources for the Study of
  Negro Life and History."
  Quarterly Journal of the Li-
  brary of Congress, (26:3, Jl.,
  1969), pp. 126-48.
McEwan, P. J. M., (ed.). Af-
  rica from Early Times to
  1800. New York: Oxford
  University Press, 1968.
Melton, J. Gordon, (comp.).
  A Bibliography of Black

Methodism. Evanston, Ill.:
Institute for the Study of Amer-
ican Religion, 1970. (Biblio-
graphic monograph no. 1.)
Mim.
Methodist History. Lake Junal-
uska, N. C., Association of
Methodist Historical Societies,
1962-.
Methodist Periodical Index. An
Author and Subject Index to
Selected Methodist Periodicals. Edited by Elizabeth
Hughey, 1961-65.
The Methodist Review. New
York: J. Soule & T. Mason,
1818-1928.
Miller, Elizabeth W. The Negro
in America: A Bibliography.
Cambridge: Harvard Univer-
sity Press, 1966.
The Missionary Herald at Home
and Abroad. Boston: Amer-
ican Board of Commissioners
of Foreign Missions, 1805-
1951.
The Missionary Review of the
World. Princeton, N. J.: 1878;
1881; 1888-1939.
Muslim World; A Quarterly Re-
view of History, Culture, Re-
ligions and the Christian Mis-
sion in Islamdom. Hartford:
Hartford Seminary Foundation,
1911-1970.
National Council Outlook. New
York: National Council of the
Churches of Christ in the
U. S. A., 1951-1959.
The National Preacher and Village
Pulpit. New York: J & J.
Harper, 1826-1866.
The Negro Journal of Religion.
Wilberforce, O.: Wilberforce
University, 1938-1940.
The New-Church Review; a Quar-
terly Journal of the Christian
Thought and Life Set Forth
from the Scriptures by Eman-
uel Swedenbog. Boston: Mass.
New-Church Union, 1894-1901.
New South. Atlanta: Southern
Regional Council, 1962-1969.

New World, A Quarterly Review
of Religion, Ethics and Theology. Boston: Houghton, 1893;
1896-1900.
New York (City). Historical Records Survey Works Projects
Administration. Calendar of
the Manuscripts in the Schomburg Collection of Negro Literature... New York: And-
ronicus Pub. Co., Inc., n. d.
-- Missionary Research Library.
Africa South of the Sahara;
A Selected and Annotated Bibliography of Books in the Missionary Research Library on
Africa and African Countries
South of the Sahara. Com-
piled by Robert L. Lehman...
New York: n. p., 1959.
-- Public Library. Research Li-
braries. Dictionary Catalog of
the Manuscript Division. Bos-
ton: G. K. Hall & Co., 1962.
9 vols. Suppl. 2 vols, 1967.
-- Public Library. Schomburg
Collection. Dictionary Catalog of
the Schomburg Collection of
Negro Literature and History.
Boston: Hall, 1962. 12 vols.
Suppl. 2 vols., 1967.
The Oberlin Quarterly Review.
Oberlin, O.: Fitch., 1845-
1849.
Ohio. Central State College.
Wilberforce Library. Index to
Selected Periodicals. Boston:
G. K. Hall, 1950-.
Our Monthly: A Magazine of Re-
ligion and Literature. Phila-
delphia: A. Martien, 1870-
1874.
The Panoplist, and Missionary
Magazine United. Boston: E.
Cotton, Farr & Co., 1805-
1820.
Parker, Joseph I. Directory of
World Missions. New York:
International Missionary
Church, 1938.
Peel, John D. Y. Aladura. A
Religious Movement Among the
Yoruba. London: Pub. for

(Peel, J. D. Y. cont.)
the Institute by the Oxford
University Press, 1968.
Porter, Dorothy B., (comp.).
Howard University Master's
Theses ... 1918-1945. Washington, D. C.: The Graduate
School, Howard University,
1946. Mim.
-- "Library Sources for the
Study of Negro Life and His-
tory." Journal of Negro Ed-
ucation (5:2, Apr., 1936), pp.
232-44.
-- (ed.). Negro Protest Pamph-
lets. New York: Arno Press
and The New York Times,
1969. Wm. L. Katz, editor
of series.
Practical Anthropology. Tarry-
town, N. Y.: W. A. Smalley,
1953-1970.
Presbyterian Banner. Pittsburgh,
Pa.: Presbyterian Banner
Press, 1901-1937.
Presbyterian Church in the
United States. Board of Foreign
Missions. A Catalogue of the
Books and Maps Belonging to
the Library of the Board of
Foreign Missions of the Pres-
byterian Church. New York:
Mission House, 1847.
Presbyterian Home Missionary.
Cincinnati, O.: Elm Street
Printing Co., 1881-1886.
The Presbyterian Quarterly.
New York: Randolph, 1887-
1904.
Presbyterian Quarterly Review.
Philadelphia: Hazard, 1852-
1862.
The Presbyterian Review. New
York: Presbyterian Review
Assn., 1880-1889.
Presbyterian Review and Re-
ligious Journal. New York:
Presbyterian Colleagues,
1934-38.
Princeton Theological Review.
Philadelphia: James Kay,
1829-.
Ramsey, Paul, (ed.). Religion

Essays ... Englewood Cliffs,
N. J.: Prentice-Hall, 1964.
Reader's Guide to Periodical Lit-
erature. New York: H. W. Wil-
son, 1900-.
The Reformed Church Review.
Lancaster, Pa.: Reformed
Church, 1849-1926.
Religion in Life: A Christian
Quarterly. New York: The
Abingdon Press, 1932-.
Religious Intelligencer. New
Haven: Nathan Whiting, 1816-
1831.
Simmons, William J. Men of
Mark: Eminent, Progressive
and Rising... Cleveland, O.:
Geo. M. Rewell & Co., 1887.
Smith, James Ward. Religion
in American Life. Prince-
ton, N. J.: Princeton Univer-
sity, 1961. 3 vols.
Princeton studies in Amer-
ican civilization.
Southern Presbyterian Review.
Columbia, S. C.: 1851-1875.
The Spirit of Missions. New
York: The Domestic and For-
eign Missionary Society of the
Protestant Episcopal Church
in the U. S., 1839-1938.
Target. Nairobi: East African
Venture Co., 1963-1970.
Tempo, News and Opinion of the
Life of the Church in Society.
New York: National Council
of Churches, 1968-1970.
The Theological and Literary
Magazine. n. p., 1848-1855.

The Theological Review and General Repository of Religious
and Moral Information. Baltimore: John D. Toy, 1822.
Thompson, Edgar T. and Alma
M. Race and Region: A De-
scriptive Bibliography Compiled with Special Reference
to Relations Between White
and Negroes in the United
States. Chapel Hill: University of North Carolina Press,
1949.

Trawick, Arcadius M., (ed.).
The New Voice in Race Ad-
justments. New York: Stu-
dent Volunteer Movement,
1914.
    Addresses and reports pre-
sented at the Negro Christian
Student Conference, Atlanta,
Georgia, May 14-18, 1914.
View in Theology. New York:
n. p., 1824-1835.
Washington, D. C. Howard Uni-
versity. Moorland-Spingarn Col-
lection. The African Collection
in the Moorland Foundation:
1958. Mim.
West, Earle H., (comp.). A
Bibliography of Doctoral Re-
search on the Negro, 1933-
1966. University Micro-
films, 1969.
Women and Missions. New
York: Woman's Committee of
the Board of Missions of the
Presbyterian Church in the
U. S. A., 1924-1938.
Woodson, Carter Goodwin. The
African Background Outlined.
Washington, D. C.: Associa-
tion for the Study of Negro
Life and History, Inc., 1936.
-- Negro Orators and Their

Orations. New York: Rus-
sell & Russell, 1969.
-- (ed.). The Works of Francis
J. Grimke. Washington, D. C.:
The Associated Publisher,
Inc., 1942. 3 vols.
Work, Monroe N., (ed.). A
Bibliography of the Negro in
Africa and America. New
York: Octagon Books, 1965.
Reprint of 1928 ed.
-- (ed.). Negro Year Book, An
Annual Encyclopedia of the
Negro. Tuskegee, Ala.:
Tuskegee Institute, 1912-.
Wright, Richard Robert, (ed.).
Centennial Encyclopedia of
the African Methodist Episco-
pal Church... Philadelphia:
A. M. E. Book Concern, 1916.
Yale University. Divinity School
Day Missions Library. Cata-
logue of the Foreign Missions
Library of the Divinity School
of Yale University. New
Haven: Tuttle, Morehouse,
and Taylor, Printers, 1892.
Yearbook of Negro Churches.
With Statistics and Records
of Achievements of Negroes,
1935/36. Wilberforce, O.:
Pr. at Wilberforce University,
1936.

Index

The symbols following the names below are classification codes relating directly to the Table of Contents. "II-D 6," for example, refers to: "II. Christianity and Slavery in the New World; D. SLAVERY, NEGROES, AND THE CHURCH; 6. Methodist Episcopal --Methodist Episcopal, South." Looking this up in the Table of Contents, one finds that II-D 6 begins on p. 126 and authors within that section, of course, are arranged alphabetically.

Abbey, Richard.	II-D 6	Ahmann, Mathew.	III-D
Abbott, Ernest H.	III-A 3		IV-A 2
Abbott, Walter M.	IV-A 2		V-A
Abdul, M. O. A.	I-C	Aikaman, William.	II-D 7
Abernathy, Ralph David.	IV-B	Ajayi, J.	I-E 1 b
	V-B 3	Akeley, Delia J.	I-E 3 e
Abrahams, Wille.	I-C	Albert, Aristides E.	III-C 1 a
Abrams, Charles.	III-C 1 l	Aldrich, G. B.	III-A 3
Abrecht, Paul.	IV-C	Alexander, Ann.	II-D 5
Ackiss, Thelma D.	III-A 3	Alexander, Mithrapuram K.	
Adams, C.	II-D 6		IV-B
Adams, C. C.	III-A 1 a vi	Alexander, Raymond P.	IV-C
Adams, Charles G.	II-H	Alexander, Stella.	II-D 5
	IV-B 1	Alexander, Will W.	III-D
Adams, Donald Conrad.		Alexander, William T.	III-A 4
	III-A 1 a ii	Alexandre, Pierre.	I-C
Adams, Elizabeth Laura.	III-A 5	Alford, Neal B.	IV-C
Adams, Henry.	III-A 4	Allan, A. K.	IV-C
Adams, John G.	II-D 1	Alland, Alexander.	III-A 1 b iii
Adams, John Greenleaf.	II-D 1	Allard, Paul.	II-D 1
Adams, J. L.	IV-C	Allen, Blanche T.	V-B 1
Adams, John P.	V-A	Allen, Cuthbert Edward.	II-D 2
Adams, Revels A.	III-A 1 a i	Allen, George.	II-D 1
Adams, S. J.	IV-B		II-D 3
Adams, W. Y.	I-A	Allen, Isaac.	II-C
Adams, William.	II-D 1	Allen, Joseph Henry.	II-D 1
Addison, James T.	I-C	Allen, L. Scott.	III-A 5
Addison, James Thayer.	I-E 1 g	Allen, Richard.	III-A 4
	II-D 8	Allen, Roland.	I-C
Adger, John Bailey.	II-B	Allen, William F.	II-H
Adkins, Rufus.	IV-A 1	Allen, William G.	II-D 1
Agbebi, Mojola.	I-E 3 a	Allensworth, A. M.	III-A 3
Agutter, William.	II-F		

Alleyne, Cameron Chesterfield,   Ashanin, C. B.   III-A 1 a viii
  (bp.).   I-E 1 a   Asher, Jeremiah.   III-A 1 a vi
                                 III-A 4   III-A 4
Allport, Gordon W.   III-D   Ashley-Montagu, Montague
Alston, Leonard.   I-E 1 a   Francis.   III-D
Alstork, John Wesley, (bp.).   Ashmore, Harry S.   III-A 2 b
                                 III-A 4
Alves Correia, Manuel.   I-E 1 q   Assenheimer, R. C.   IV-A 1
Alvord, John Watson.   II-G   Atkins, Anselna.   V-B 3
Ambali, Augustine.   I-E 1 t   Atkins, D.   III-C 1 f
Amero, Constant.   I-B   Atkins, James.   IV-A 14
Anderson, August Magnus.   Atkins, Thomas.   II-D 1
                               I-E 1 g   Atlee, Elinore.   IV-A 5
Anderson, H. C.   III-A 1 a viii   Atterbury, Anson Phelps.   I-C
Anderson, James H. III-A 1 a ii   Atwood, Jesse H.   III-A 4
Anderson, John F.   III-C 1 g   Augusta, Marie (Sister). III-D
Anderson, J. N. D.   I-C   Austin, Anne.   IV-C
Anderson, Llewellyn Kennedy.   Austin, James Trecothick.
                               I-E 1 r   II-D 1
Anderson, Matthew. III-C 1 g   Ayandele, E. A.   I-C
Anderson, Robert.   III-A 1 a i   II-E 1 b
Anderson, Robert Earle. I-E 1 o   Azikiwe, Ben N.   I-C
Anderson, Susan.   I-E 1 b
Anderson, William T. I-E 1 r
Andersson, Efraim. I-E 3 d   Bach, Marcus.   III-A 1 b iv
Andre, Marie.   I-E 1 b   Bacon, Ephraim   I-E 1 n
Andrews, Rena M.   II-D 2   Bacon, Leonard.   II-D 1
Anet, Henri.   I-E 1 j   II-D 3
Anscombe, Francis Charles.   Bacon, Thomas.   II-C
                     II-G   II-B
Applegarth, Albert C. II-D 5   Bacote, Samuel Wm.   III-A 4
Apsey, Lawrence S.   IV-A 5   Badertscher, Jean.   I-E 1 c
Aptheker, Herbert.   II-D 5   Baeta, C. G.   I-C
Arce, Laurent d'.   I-B   I-E 3 a
Archibald, Helen Allen. III-C 2 a   I-E 3 e
Argyle, M.   III-D   Baetman, Joseph.   I-B
Ariel, Buckner H. Payne. III-E   Baez-Carmargo, Gonzala. III-D
Armistead, W. S.   III-D   Bagby, Grover C.   IV-A 6
Armistead, Wilson.   II-D 1   Bailey, Augustus Caesar.
Armstrong, George Dodd. II-C   III-A 1 a iii
                       II-D 7   Bailey, Flavius Josephus.
Armstrong, Mary F.   II-H   III-C 2 f
Arnett, Benjamin W. III-A 1 a i   Bailey, Hugh C.   III-D
                      III-A 3   Bailey, J. Martin.   I-E 3 e
                      III-A 4   Bailey, Kenneth K.   V-E
Arnold, Benjamin.   III-A 3   Bailey, Leroy.   V-B 1
Arnold, S. G.   II-G   Baird, James B.   I-E 1 r
Arnold, W. E.   III-A 5   Baird, Robert.   II-D 1
Arnot, Frederick Stanley. I-E 1 j   Baitzell, E. Digby.   IV-A 1
Arthur, George R.   III-C 2 a   Baker, George C.   II-D 6
Artopoeus, Otto F.   IV-A 3   Baker, Paul Ernest.   III-C 2 a
Asamoa, F. A.   I-E 3 e   Baker, Ray Stannard. III-A 3
Asbury, Francis.   II-D 6   Bakke, N. J.   III-C 1 a

Balandier, George.   I-C
Baldwin, James.   III-A 2 b
                            III-A 4
                              IV-B
                              V-B 1
                               V-E
Balk, A.   IV-B
Ball, William B.   IV-A 2
Balme, Joshua Rhodes.   II-D 1
Bane, Martin J.   I-E 1 o
                            I-E 1 s
Bangs, Nathan.   II-D 8
Banks, Arthur Leslie.   I-E 3 e
Banks, Walter R.   V-B 1
Banks, William L.   III-A 4
Banner, William Augustus.
                            IV-A 1
Barbee, J. M.   III-D
Barber, Carroll G.   IV-A 3
Barber, Jesse Belmont.   III-A 5
Barber, Mary Ann S.   I-E 1 b
Barber, Verle L.   II-D 7
Barbour, Floyd B.   V-B 1
Barbour, Russell B.   V-E
Barclay, Wade Crawford.
                           III-E 1 r
Bardolph, Richard.   III-A 3
Bare, Paul W.   III-A 1 a viii
Barmento, Alexandre.   I-E 1 q
Barndt, Joseph R.   V-B 1
Barnes, Albert.   II-C
                            II-D 1
                            II-D 7
Barnes, Bertram H.   I-E 1 t
Barnes, Gilbert H.   II-F
Barnes, Roswell P.   I-E 1 a
Barnes, William.   II-D 1
Barnette, H. H.   IV-A 11
Barrett, David B.   I-C
                             I-E 2
                            I-E 3 e
Barrett, P.   IV-A 2
Barrow, A. H.   I-E 1 p
Barrow, David.   II-F
Barrows, John Henry.
                          III-A 1 a i
Barsotti, Giulio.   I-E 1 k
Bartels, Frances L.   I-E 1 a
Bartlett, Bob.   V-A
Bartlett, S. C.   I-E 1 r
Bartlett, T. R.   II-C
Barton, John W.   III-A 2 c
Barton, William E.   II-H

Bascom, Henry B.   II-D 6
Basden, George T.   I-E 1 b
Basen, Carol.   V-E
Basker, Roosevelt.   II-D 7
Bassett, George W.   II-D 3
Bassett, John Spencer.   II-D 1
                            II-D 6
Bassett, William.   II-D 5
Bastide, Roger.   V-E
Bates, Daisy.   IV-C
Batten, J. Minton.   III-A 1 a i
Battle, Allen O.   III-A 1 b ii
Baugh, J. Gordon.   III-A 1 a vi
Baxter, Daniel Minort.
                          III-A 1 a i
Baxter, Richard.   II-D 1
Beach, Harlan Page.   I-E 1 r
Beach, Waldo   III-C 1 f
                            III-D
                            III-E
                             V-A
Beacham, C.   I-E 1 s
Beanland, Lillian L.   I-E 1 m
Beard, Augustus Field.
                          III-C 2 f
Beattie, John.   I-C
Beatty-Brown, Florence R.
                          III-A 3
Beaty, Leroy F.   II-D 6
Beaver, R. Pierce.   I-E 1 r
Beaver, Robert Pierce.   II-D 1
Becken, H. J.   I-E 2
Becker, William H.   V-B 1
                             V-C
Beckett, L. M.   III-A 4
Beckmann, Klaus-Marten.   V-E
Beckwith, John Q.   V-E
Bedau, Hugo Adam.   IV-B
Bede, (Brother).   III-D
Bedinger, Robert Dabney.
                            I-E 1 j
Bedwell, H. Kenneth.   I-E 1 g
Beecher, Charles.   II-C
                            II-D 1
Beecher, Henry Ward.   II-D 1
Beecher, Lyman.   II-D 1
Beeson, Lewis.   II-D 3
                            II-D 6
Beetham, Thomas.   I-E 3 e
Beiderbecke, Heinrich.   I-E 1 s
Belford, Lee A.   V-B 3
Bell, John.   I-E 1 j
Bell, John L.   III-C 1 g

Bell, L. Nelson.   III-D
Bell, W. B.   II-H
Bell, William Clark.   I-E 1 r
Bellamy, V. Nelle.   I-E 1 o
Belshaw, Harry.   I-E 3 a
Belts, Albert Deems.   III-A 5
Belts, John R.   III-C 1 a
Beman, Nathan S. S.   II-D 7
Bender, C.   I-C
Benedict, David.   III-A 1 a vi
Benedict Ruth.   III-D
Benezet, Anthony.   II-D 5
Benham, Marian S.   I-E 1 c
Ben-Jochannan, Yosef.   I-C
Bennett, Ambrose Allen.
                            III-A 1 a vi
Bennett, John C.   III-C 2 e
                            IV-C
                            IV-B
Bennett, J. Harry.   II-A
Bennett, Lerone.   IV-B
Bennett, M.   III-D
Bennett, Richard K.   III-D
Bennink, Richard John.   V-D
Bentley, D. S.   III-A 1 a i
Bentley, H. Margo.   I-E 1 j
Berdiaev, Nickolai A.   II-C
Bergama, Stuart.   I-E 1 k
Berger, Morroe.   I-C
                            III-A 2 b
                            III-C 1 l
Bernard, Raymond.   III-C 1 b
                            IV-A 1
                            IV-A 2
Bernardi, Bernardo.   I-E 1 r
Bernards, Solomon S.   IV-A 12
Berrigan, Philip.   V-E
Berrigan, P. F.   III-A 3
Berry, Benjamin D.   V-B 1
Berry, Lewellyn L.   III-A 1 a i
Berry, Philip.   II-D 1
Berson, Lenora A.   V-C
Berthoud, Paul.   I-E 1 q
Bertsche, James E.   I-E 2
Bervine, J. W.   V-A
Beslier, Genevieve G.   I-E 1 j
Bethmann, Erch W.   III-C 1 j
Betker, John P.   II-D 6
Bettelheim, Bruno.   III-C 1 l
Beukema, George G.   V-A
Bewes, Thomas Frances C.
                            I-E 1 d
Beynon, Erdmann D.   III-A 2 c

Bibb, Henry.   II-F
Bibbons, J. C.   IV-A 6
Bickel, Alexander M.   III-C 1 l
Bickersteth, E.   I-E 1 s
Bidlake, John.   II-D 1
Billings, R. A.   III-A 3
Billingsley, Andrew.   III-A 4
Billy, Ed. de.   I-E 1 s
Bingham, Rowland V.   I-E 1 e
Bingham, Walter D.   IV-A 4
Bird, Mark Baker.   II-A
Birkett, Mary.   II-D 5
Birney, Catherine H.   II-F
Birney, James Gillespie.   II-C
                            II-D 1
                            II-D 5
Birney, William.   II-D 8
Birnida, (Prince.)   I-C
Bishop, Samuel H.   III-D
Bishop, Shelton Hale.   III-A 4
Bittinger, Joseph B.   II-D 7
Blackburn, George Andrew.
                            III-D
Blacknall, O. W.   III-A 3
Blackson, Lorenzo D.   III-A 4
Blackwell, George L.   III-A 4
Blake, Charles C.   III-A 1 a i
Blake, E. C.   IV-A 1
Blakeslee, Helen V.   I-E 1 d
Blanchard, E. D.   IV-A 1
Blanchard, F. Q.   III-C 2 f
Blanchard, Jonathan.   II-D 7
Bland, T. A.   IV-A 1
Blanshard, Mary H.   IV-A 14
Blanton, Robert J.
                            III-A 1 a viii
Blau, Joseph L.   V-E
Bleeby, Henry.   II-A
Bleeker, Sonia.   I-C
Blied, Benjamin J.   II-D 2
Bliss, Edwin M.   I-E 1 r
Blodgett, C.   II-D 3
Blomjous, Joseph.   I-E 3 e
Bloy, Myron.   V-D
Blyden, Edward Wilmot.   I-C
                            I-E 1 r
                            III-A 4
Boatright, Mody Coggin. III-A 3
Boaz, R.   III-A 1 b iv
Boddie, Charles E.   III-A 4
Bodo, John R.   I-E 3 c
                            II-D 1
Boggs, Marion.   IV-A 1

Bokwe, John K.   I-E 1 c
Bolivar, William C.   III-A 5
Bolles, John R.   II-C
Bolton, S. C.   II-B
Bone, Richard.   V-B 1
Bond, T. E.   II-D 6
Bontemps, Arna W.   II-H
                              III-A 2 b
Booker, Merrel D.   III-D
Booker, Simeon.   IV-B
Boole, William H.   II-C
Boone, Clinton C.   I-E 1 j
Boone, Theodore S.   III-A 1 a vi
Booth, Abraham.   II-C
Booth, Joseph.   I-E 1 t
Booth, L. Venchael.   III-A 1 a vi
Booth, Newell Snow.   I-E 1 r
                              III-D
Boothe, Charles Octavius.
                              III-A 1 a vi
Bordeaux, Henry.   I-E 3 b
Borders, William Holmes.
                              III-A 1 a vi
                              III-A 4
Botkin, Benjamin Albert.   II-H
Boud, S.   IV-A 1
Bouey, Harrison N.   III-A 4
Boulden, Jesse Freeman.   III-A 4
Bourne, George.   II-C
                              II-D 7
Bourne, Henry Richard F.
                              I-E 1 r
Bousell, John.   II-D 5
Bowditch, William Ingersoll.
                              II-D 1
Bowen, Elias.   II-D 6
Bowen, John Wesley Edward.
                              I-E 3 e
                              II-F
                              III-A 1 a viii
                              III-A 4
                              III-A 5
                              III-C 1 f
                              III-D
Bowen, Thomas J.   III-A 4
Bowen, Trevor.   III-A 3
Bowley, Samuel.   II-F
Boyd, Archard H.   III-A 1 a vii
Boyd, Bob.   V-E
Boyd, Jesse Lansy.   II-D 12
Boyd, Malcolm.   IV-A 1
                              V-E
Boyd, Richard H.   III-A 1 a vi

Boyd, William E.   II-D 1
Boyer, Laura F.   III-A 3
Boyle, Sarah Patton.   II-G
                              IV-A 1
Boynton, Charles Brandon.
                              II-D 3
Boynton, Ernest.   V-B 4
Brace, Charles Loring.
                              III-C 1 a
Bracey, John M.   III-A 3
Bradburn, Samuel.   II-D 6
Braden, Charles Samuel.
                              III-A 1 b iv
Bradford, R.   II-H
Bradley, David Henry.
                              III-A 1 a ii
Bradley, Fulton C. III-A 1 a vii
Bradley, L. Richard.   III-A 3 i
Bradley, Sam.   IV-A 5
Bragg, George Freeman.
                              III-A 3
                              III-A 4
                              III-A 5
                              III-C 1 h
Brain, B.   I-E 1 r
Brainerd. M.   II-F
Branceland, Francis J.   III-D
Brashares, Charles W.   III-D
Brasio, Antonio Duarte. I-E 1 q
Bratton, Theodore DaBose.
                              III-C 1 h
Brawley, Benjamin Griffin.
                              II-F
                              III-A 3
                              III-A 4
Brawley, Edward M.
                              III-A 1 a vi
                              III-A 3
                              III-A 4
Braxton, P. H. A.   III-A 4
Brayshaw, E. Russell. I-E 3 c
Brayton, Patience.   II-F
Brazier, Arthur M.   IV-C
Brean, H.   III-A 1 b iv
Breathett, George.   II-A
Breeden, Jim.   V-A
Breen, Jay.   V-A
Breitman, George.   III-A 2 b
Brennecke, Gerhard.   III-D
Brennecke, H. E.   IV-B
Brewe, H. Peers.   II-G
Brewer, David Leslie.   V-E
Brewer, John Mason.   II-H

Brickner, Balfour.   IV-A 12
Bridgman, Frederick B. I-E 1 c
Briggs, J.   I-E 1 f
Brink, William.   V-E
Brisbane, Robert H.   III-A 3
Brisbane, William Henry.   II-C
Broadbent, Samuel.   I-E 1 s
Broadbent, T. David S.   I-E 1 b
Brockway, Allan R.   V-A
Brokhave, Joseph D.   II-D 2
Brooke, Samuel.   II-C
Brookes, Iveson L.   II-D 1
Brooks, Charles H.   III-A 1 a vi
Brooks, George S.   II-F
Brooks, Jerome.   III-A 5
Brooks, Phillips.   II-B 8
Brooks, Walter H.   III-A 1 a vi
                            III-A 3
                            III-A 4
Brooks, William E.   III-A 5

Broomfield, Gerald Webb.
                            I-E 3 d
                            II-C
Brotz, Howard.   III-A 2 a
                            III-A 3
                            V-C
Brown, Annie E.   III-A 4
Brown, Archer W.   III-A 3
Brown, Clifton F.   V-B 1

Brown, Ethelred.   III-A 5
Brown, Hallie Q.   III-A 4
Brown, Harold O. J.   V-B 1
Brown, Ina Corinne.   I-E 1 r
                            III-A 3
Brown, Isaac Van Arsdale. II-F
Brown, James.   II-D 1

Brown, James Russell.   III-E
Brown, John M.   III-A 4
Brown, John Mason.   II-H
Brown, John Pairman.   V-E
Brown, John Tom.   I-E 1 r
Brown, Kenneth I.   I-E 2
Brown, L. P.   III-A 2 b
Brown, Lorenzo Quincy.
                            III-A 1 a iii
Brown, M. R.   III-A 3
Brown, R.   V-A
Brown, Robert Raymond.   III-D
                            V-E
Brown, Sarah D.   III-D

Brown, Solyman.   II-D 1
Brown, William B.   II-D 1
Brown, William M.   III-D
Brown, William Wells.   III-A 3
Browne, George D.   I-E 1 o
Browne, Robert S.   V-B 1
Brownlee, Charles.   I-E 1 e
Brownlee, Frederick L.
                            III-C 2 f
Brownlee, Margaret.   I-E 1 c
Brownlow, William Gannaway.
                            II-D 6
Bruce, J. G.   II-D 6
Bruce, John Edward.   III-A 4
Bruce, Philip A.   II-G
Bruner, Clarence Vernon. II-B
Brunini, J. G.   II-C 1 b
Brunner, Edmund DeS.
                            III-A 1 viii
Brunner, John H.   II-D 1
Bryant, Baxton.   IV-A 11
Bryant, F.   IV-A 1
Brydon, G. McClaren.   III-A 5
Bryson, Lyman.   III-C
Buchanan, George.   II-F
Buchanan, H. A.   IV-A 1
Buchner, J.H.   II-A
Bucke, Emory S.   II-D 6
Buckingham, G.   II-C
Buckley, James M.   II-D 6
Buckley, William F.   IV-B
Buehrer, E. T.   III-A 3
Bulifant, Josephine Christiana.
                            I-E 1 b
Bulkley, Charles H. A.   II-D 3
Bullock, Ralph W.   III-A 4
Bunton, Henry C.   III-A 4
Burdette, Mary G.
                            III-A 1 a viii
Burgan, I. M.   III-A 4
Burgess, Lois F.   III-A 4
Burgess, Margaret E.
                            III-A 1 a viii
Burgess, Thomas.   II-F
Burham, Kenneth E.   III-D
Burleigh, Charles C.   II-D 1
                            II-F
Burlin, Natalie.   II-H
Burney, H. L.   IV-C
Burns, Aubrey.   III-D
Burns, W. Haywood. III-A 2 b
                            III-C 1 l

Burroughs, Nannie Helen.
                    III-A 4
Burt, C. B.   IV-A 1
Burt, Jairus.   II-D 1
Burton, E. D.   I-E 1 r
Burton, John W.   IV-A 5
Burton, William F.   I-E 1 j
Bury, Herbert.   II-A
Bush, J. B.   IV-C
Bushnell, Horace.   II-D 3
Buster, William.   III-D
Buswell, James Oliver. II-D 1
Butcher, Charles Simpson.
                    III-A 4
Butler, Alfred J.   I-C
Butler, Annie Robins. I-E 1 r
Butler, O. G.   III-C 1 f
Butler, William H. H. III-A 1 a i
Butsch, Joseph.   III-A 5
                    III-C 1 b
Butt, G. E.   I-E 1 l
Butt, Israel Lafay.   III-A 1 a i
Butterfield, Kenyon Leech.
                    I-E 1 c
Buxton, T. F. V.   I-E 1 j
Byers, Theodore F. III-A 1 a iii
Byrd, Cameron Wells.   V-A

Cable, George Washington.
                    III-C 2 f
Cadbury, Henry J.   III-A 5
Cadbury, N. H.   III-A 4
Cade, John B.   II-D 1
                    III-A 4
Caine, Richard Harvey. III-A 4
Cairns, Earle Edwin.   II-D 1
Caldwell, Gilbert H.   V-D
Caldwell, J. C.   III-A 1 a i
Caldwell, J. H.   II-D 6
                    III-C 1 f
Caldwell, Josiah S.   III-A 4
Calhoun, D.   III-D
Calhoun, M. P.   IV-A 7
Callaway, Godfrey.   I-E 1 c
Calloway, Henry.   I-C
Calverley, Edwin Elliott.
                    III-A 2 b
Calvez, Jean Yves.   III-C 1 b
Cameron, J. M.   IV-B
Cameron, Richard M.   III-C 1 f
Cameron, W. M.   I-E 2
Campbell, Belle M.   I-E 1 c

Campbell, Charles G.   III-D
Campbell, Ernest Q.   III-A 1
                    III-D
Campbell, Ernest T.   V-B 3
Campbell, H. W.   IV-C
Campbell, Israel.   III-A 4
Campbell, J. P.   III-A 4
Campbell, James.   V-A
Campbell, John.   I-E 1 c
Campbell, Matthew.   III-A 4
Campbell, Robert.   III-C 1 b
Campbell, Robert F.   II-B
Campbell, Will D.   III-D
                    IV-A 6
                    IV-C
                    V-D
Camphor, Alexander P.
                    II-E 1 o
Canavan, Francis P.   IV-A 2
Cancela, Luis L.   I-E 1 q
Candler, John.   II-D 5
Cannon, N. Calwell.   II-C
Cantril, Hadley.   III-A 1 b iv
Cantwell, Daniel M.   III-C 1 b
Canzoneri, Robert.   III-A 3
Capen, Nahum.   II-D 1
Capper, Joseph.   I-E 1 r
Carey, Lott.   I-E 1 r
                    III-A 4
Carey, Walter.   I-E 1 d
Carhart, C. L.   III-D
Carling, Francis.   V-A
Carman, Adam.   II-D 6
Carneiro, Edison.   III-B
Carpenter, George W.   I-E 1 r
Carr, Oscar C.   V-D
Carrington, Charles L.
                    III-C 1 f
Carrington, William E. III-A 3
Carrington, William Orlando.
                    III-A 5
Carrol, Daniel Lynn.   II-F
Carroll, Charles.   III-A 3
                    III-D
Carroll, H. K.   III-A 1 a viii
                    III-A 3
Carroll, J. M.   II-G
Carroll, Kenneth L.   II-F
Carsten, Kenneth N.   I-E 3 c
Carstens, Kenneth.   I-E 1 c
Carter, Cullen T.   II-D 6
Carter, Edward R. III-A 1 a iii
                    III-A 3

Carter, Eugene J.   III-A 1 a viii
Carter, Luther C.   III-A 4
Carter, Paul A.   III-C 1 f
Carter, Randall Albert.
                       III-A 1 a iii
                          III-A 3
                          III-A 4
Cartland, Fernando G.   II-D 5
Cartwright, Colbert S.   III-D
                          IV-A 4
Caruthers, Eli Washington.
                           II-D 7
                            II-F
Carver, William O.   III-C 1 k
Casey, John.   III-C 1 b
Cash, W. Wilson.   I-E 3 e
Cassels, Louis.   V-B 1
Castillo de Aza, Zenon.   III-B
Castle, Robert W.   V-A
Caswell, Henry.   II-A
Catchings, L. Maynard.   III-A 3
                        III-C 1 a
                        III-C 1 c
                          III-D
Cater, D. G.   IV-C
Cattell, Elizabeth.   III-A 4
Catto, William T.   III-A 5
Caution, Tollie L.   III-A 5
Cawood, Lesley.   I-E 3 c
Cayton, Horace.   III-A 3
Chace, Elizabeth (B.).   II-D 5
                        III-C 1 e
Chadwick, W.   I-E 1 r
Chalmers, John A.   I-E 1 c
Chamberlin, David.   I-E 1 c
Chambers, Herbert A.   II-H
Chandler, Elizabeth M.   II-F
                           II-D 5
Chandler, Russell.   III-A 1 a vi
                          IV-B
                          V-B 1
Channing, Edward.   II-D 1
Channing, William E.   II-D 10
Chaplin, David.   II-A
Chaplin, Jeremiah.   III-C 1 k
Chapman, Louis R.   II-E 1 g
Chapman, Maria W.   II-H
Chapman, William.   II-E 1 l
Charland, William A.   V-A
Charles-Picard, Gilbert.   I-C
Charlesworth, Maria L.   I-E 1 n
Charlton, Huey E.   III-A 4
Chatham, J. G.   III-A 5

Chatman, Jacob L.   V-A
Chautard, Leon.   II-C
Cheever, George B.   II-C
                           II-D 1
                           II-D 3
                           II-F
Cheever, Henry T.   II-D 3
Cheshire, Joseph B.   III-A 3
Child, Lydia M. F.   II-B
                           II-D 5
                           II-F
Chirgwin, A. M.   I-E 1 r
                           II-H
Chitty, Arthur B.   III-A 5
Chivers, W. R.   III-A 3
Christian, John.   II-D 1
Christensen, A. M. H.   II-H
Christiansen, Ruth.   I-E 1 m
Christmas, Faith C.   V-B 2
Christofersen, Arthur F.
                           I-E 1 c
Christol, Frank.   II-E 1 m
Christy, David.   II-C
                           II-D 1
                           I-E 1 o
Chritzberg, A. M.   III-A 5
Church, Roberta.   III-A 5
Churchill, A. A.   IV-A 1
Churchill, Rhona.   V-E
Clair, Mathew W.   III-A 5
Clanton, Solomon T., Jr.
                         III-A 4
                      III-A 1 a vii
Clark, Calvin M.   II-D 3
Clark, D.   IV-A 2
Clark, Davis W.   II-D 6
Clark, Elmer T.   II-B
                        III-A 1 b iv
Clark, H. B.   III-E
Clark, Henry.   IV-A 1
                           V-A
Clark, Kenneth B.   III-A 2 b
                           V-A
Clark, Mary T.   IV-A 1
                           IV-C
Clark, Michael.   III-A 2 b
Clark, Robert D.   II-D 6
Clark, Rufus W.   II-D 1
Clark, Samuel.   II-E 1 s
Clark, William A.   III-A 3
Clarke, J. W.   IV-B
Clarke, James F.   II-D 10
                           II-F

Clarke, Richard F.   II-D 2   V-B 1
Clarke, Walter.   II-D 1   Coleman, Charles C.   III-A 4
Clarke, William F.   III-E   Coleman, Clinton R.
Clarkson, Thomas.   II-D 5   III-A 1 a ii
                            II-F   Coleman, Elihu.   II-D 5
Clay, Cassius M.   II-D 1   Coleman, John W.
Clayton, Edward T.   IV-B   III-A 1 a viii
Cleage, Albert B.   V-B 1   Coleman, Lucretia H. N. III-A 4
Cleaveland, Elisha L.   II-D 3   Coles, George.   II-D 6
Cleaver, Eldridge.   III-A 3   Coles, Robert.   III-A 3
Cleghorn, R.   IV-B   V-A
Clement, George C. III-A 1 a ii   Coles, Samuel B.   II-E
                            III-A 4   Collier, Casa.   II-D 7
Clement Rufus E.   III-A 3   Collins, D. E.   IV-A 6
Clemes, W. W.   III-A 3   Collister, Peter.   I-E 1 d
Clendenen, Clarence C. I-E 1 r   Collyer, Isaac J. P.   II-D 6
Cleveland, Charles D.   II-D 7   Colver, Nathaniel.   II-C
Clifton, Denzil T.   II-D 8   II-D 1
Clinchy, Everett R.   III-D   Comhaire, J. L.   I-E 3 e
Cline, Catherine A.   I-E 3 d   Conant, Ralph E.   V-A
Clinton, George W. III-A 1 a vi   Cone, James H.   V-B 1
                            III-A 3   Congar, Marie Joseph.
                            III-A 4   III-C 1 b
Clough, Simon.   II-F   Connell, Francis J.   III-A 5
Clyde, Nathana L.   III-A 3   Connelly, Marcus C.   II-H
Coan, Josephus R.   I-E 1 g   Conner, James M.   III-A 4
                        III-A 1 a i   Conover, Helen F.   I-E 1 r
                            I-E 3 e   Considine, John J.   I-E 3 e
Cobb, Charles E.   IV-A 1   Constance, Marie, (Sister).
Cobb, Howell.   II-C   I-E 1 j
Cobern, Camden M.   I-C   Converse, John K.   II-F
Cockin, Frederic A.   III-A 3   Conway, Moncure D.   II-D 1
Code, Joseph B.   III-C 1 b   II-D 10
Coggeshall, Samuel W.   II-D 6   Coogan, John E.   III-C 1 a
Coggins, Ross.   V-B 1   Cook, Bruce.   IV-B
Cogley, John.   IV-A 1   Cook, Richard B. III-A 1 a viii
Cohen, Chapman.   II-D 1   Cook, Samuel D.   IV-B
Cohen, Henry.   III-D   Cooksey, Joseph J.   I-E 1 b
                            V-C   I-E 1 k
Cohen, Lily Y.   II-H   Cooley, John K.   I-E 1 r
Coke, Thomas.   II-A   Cooley, Leo P.   III-C 1 b
                            II-D 6   Cooley, Timothy M.   III-A 5
Coker, Daniel.   III-A 4   Cooper, Anna J. (H.).   III-A 4
Cokes, George L.   III-D   Cooper, Harold L.   III-D
Colclough, J. G.   III-A 1 a iii   Cooper, J. C.   III-C 1 i
Coldham, Geraldine E. I-E 1 r   Cooper, Joseph.   I-C
Cole, Arthur C.   II-D 1   Copher, Charles B.   V-B 1
Cole, Charles C.   II-F   Copley, Esther.   II-A
Cole, Henry.   II-E 1 f   Coppin, Levi J.   I-E 1 c
Cole, S. W. R.   III-A 1 a vi   Coppinger, William.   I-E 1 r
Cole, Stewart G.   IV-A 1   Corey, Charles H.
Coleman, C. D.   III-A 1 a iii   III-A 1 a viii
                            V-A   Corey, Stephen J.   I-E 1 j

Cornish, Samuel E.   II-F
Corrothers, James D.   III-A 4
Cotes, Sarah J.   III-C
Couch, Paul.   II-D 1
Councill, William H.   III-C
Courlander, Harold.   I-C
                             II-H
Cousins, Henry T.   I-E 1 c
Coward, Donald B.   III-C 1 k
Cox, Harvey.   IV-A 1
Cox, John H.   II-H
Cox, John Morris.   III-A 1 a i
Cox, Melville B.   I-E 1 o
Coxill, H. Wakelin.   I-E 3 d
Crabites, P.   III-A 2 b
Crain, James A.   II-D 4
Crane, Jonathan T.   II-D 6
Crane, William H.   I-E 2
Cranston, Earl.   III-A 5
                          III-C 1 f
Crapsey, Algernon S.   III-A 5
Crawford, Daniel.   I-E 1 r
Crawford, Evans E.   III-A 4
                           IV-C
Crawford, John R.   I-E 1 j
Creger, Ralph.   IV-A 1
Cripps, Arthur S.   I-E 1 r
Crite, Allan R.   III-A 4
Crogman, W. H.   III-A 4
Cromer, Voigt R.   III-C 1 i
Cromwell, John W.   II-E
                      III-A 1 a viii
                          III-A 3
Cronan, Edward P.   II-C
Cronin, J. F.   IV-A 2
Cronon, Edmund D.   III-A 4
Crook, Roger H.   III-A 3
Cross, Jasper W.   II-D 7
Crothers, Samuel.   II-D 1
Crouse, M.   IV-A 13
Crowther, E.   I-E 1 c
Cruise O'Brien, Conor.
                          III-C 2 e
Crum, Jack.   IV-A 6
Crum, Mason.   III-A 5
Crummell, Alexander.   II-D 8
                          I-E 1 o
                          III-A 4
                          III-A 5
Cuffel, Victoria.   II-D 1
Cully, K.   V-A
Culp, D. W.   III-A 4
Cultrera, Samuele.   I-E 1 j

Culver, Dwight W.   III-D
Culverhouse, Patricia.   V-B 1
Culwick, Arthur T.   I-E 1 r
Cummings, George D.   II-F
Cuninggim, Merrimon.   IV-C
Curran, Francis X.   III-A 3
Current, William C.   III-A 4
Curry, Daniel.   II-D 1
Curry Jabez, L. M.   III-D
Curry, Norris S.   V-B 1
Curtis, Anna L.   II-D 5
Curtis, George T.   II-D 1
Cushman, Mary F.   I-E 1 q
Cutting, Sewall S.   II-D 12
Cuvelier, Jean.   I-E 1 j

Dabbs, J. M.   III-D
Dabney, Robert L.   III-D
Daigre, Father.   I-E 1 s
Dale, Marcus.   III-A 4
Damboriena, Prudencio.   I-E 3 e
Dana, James.   II-D 1
Danforth, Mildred E.   II-D 5
Dangerfield, Abner W.   III-A 4
Daniel, Everard W.   III-A 5
Daniel, Robert P.
                      III-A 1 a viii
Daniel, Vattel E.   III-A 1 b iv
                          III-A 3
Daniel, W. Harrison.   II-D 12
Daniel, William A.
                      III-A 1 a viii
                          III-A 3
Daniels, Joseph.   V-B 1
Danquah, Joseph B.   I-C
Danzig, David.   III-C 1 1
Darrow, Clarence.   III-A 3
Davenport, F. M.   III-A 3
Davenport, William H.
                       III-A 1 a ii
Davidson, G. W.   III-D
Davidson, Hannah F.   I-E 1 1
Davidson, Robert.   II-D 7
Davie, Maurice R.   III-A 3
Davies, Alfred T.   V-E
Davies, Everett F. S.   IV-A 1
Davies, Horton.   I-E 1 c
Davies, Lawrence E.   V-E
Davies, Samuel.   II-D 1
Davis, Allison.   II-C 2 a
                           III-D
Davis, Arnor S.   III-A 1 a ii

Davis, David B.   II-D 1
Davis, Emory G.   V-B 1
Davis, Felix L.   III-A 1 a vi
Davis, Henderson S.   II-H
Davis, J. A.   III-A 4
Davis, J. T.   II-D 7
Davis, James A.   III-A 1 a i
Davis, John L.   V-D
Davis, John M.   I-E 1 r
Davis, John W.   III-A 1 a vi
Davis, Lloyd.   IV-A 1
Davis, Monroe H.   III-A 1 a i
Davis, Noah.   III-A 4
Davis, Owen.   II-D 1
Davis, William E.   I-E 1 j
Davis, William P.   IV-A 11
Day, Helen C.   III-A 4
Day, Norris.   II-C
Day, Richard E.   III-A 4
Dealtry, William.   I-E 1 r
Dean, Christopher.   I-E 1 r
Dean, David M.   III-B
Dean, Emmett S.   III-A 1 a viii
Dean, Henry T.   III-E
Dean, John P.   III-D
Dean, Paul.   II-D 10
De Baptiste, Richard D. D.
                           III-A 4
De Beer, Z. J.   I-E 3 c
De Bow, James D. B.   II-C
De Charms, Richard.   II-D 1
Decker, Vincent de.   II-D 2
Decleene, Arnold.   II-D 2
De Costa, Benjamin F.   III-A 5
Dedeaux, Mary L. (Sister).
                          III-C 1 b
Deems, Charles F.   III-C 1 f
Dehoney, Wayne.   III-A 1 a vi
Delano, Isaac O.   I-E 1 b
Delany, Martin R.   I-E 1 r
D'Elia, Donald J.   III-A 4
De Hueck, Catherine.   III-C 1 b
Demby, Edward T.   III-C 1 h
De Mille, D.   IV-A 1
Deming, D. D.   II-D 1
Dempsey, James.   I-E 1 r
Denham, John.   III-D
Denis, Leopold.   I-E 1 j
Denlinger, S.   III-A 1 b iv
Dennett, Richard E.   I-E 2
Dennis, Joseph J.   IV-A 6
Dennison, Doris.   IV-A 6
Deren, Maya.   III-B

Derrick, W. B.   III-A 4
                          III-C 2 a
Derricks, Cleavant.   III-E
Desai, Ram.   I-E 3 e
Deschamps, Hubert J.   I-C
Deschner, John.   V-E
Dett, Robert N.   II-H
Detweiler, Charles S.   III-B
Detweiler, Frederick G.
                          III-A 4
De Vinne, Daniel.   II-D 6
Devresse, L.   I-E 1 r
Dewey, H. P.   III-D
Dewey, Orville.   II-D 10
Dexter, Henry M.   II-F
Dickey, James H.   II-F
Dickinson, James T.   II-D 3
Dickinson, Noadiah S.   II-D 3
Dickinson, Richard.   V-B 1
Dickson, Andrew F.   II-B
Dickson, Kwesi.   I-C
Didas, James F.   III-D
Dieu, Leon.   I-E 1 j
Diffendorfer, Ralph E. III-C 1 f
Di Gangi, Mariano.   V-A
Diggs, James R.   III-A 3
Diggs, M. A.   III-A 5
Dillard, James A.   III-A 1 a vi
Dillon, Merton L.   II-D 5
Dinwoodie, W.   IV-A 1
Dixon, D. M.   I-B
Dixon, William T.   III-A 4
Dobbins, Frank S.   I-C
Dodds, Elizabeth D.   IV-C
Dodds, Fred W.   I-E 1 b
Dodson, Dan.   III-A 3
Dodson, Gordon.   V-E
Doering, Alma E.   I-E 1 j
Doherty, Joseph F.   III-C 1 b
Dole, Kenneth.   V-B 1
                            V-D
                            V-E
Dollar, George W.   II-D 1
Dollard, John.   III-A 3
Dollen, Charles.   IV-A 1
Donald, Henderson H.   III-A 3
Dorey, Frank D.   III-A 1 a viii
                            III-D
Dorough, Charles D.   II-D 1
Doty, Robert C.   V-E
Dougall, James W. C.   I-E 1 r
Douglas, Arthur J.   I-E 1 t
Douglas, Carlyle C.   IV-B

Douglass, Frederick.	II-D 1	Dundes, Alan.		II-H
	II-G	Dunham, Chester F.		II-F
	III-A 4	Dunham, Dows.		I-A
	III-D	Dunlap, William C.		III-C 1 e
Douglass, Harlan P.	II-G	Dunlop, John.		II-D 3
	III-A 1 a viii	Dunn, James.		III-D
Douglass, Robert L.	III-A 4	Dunne, William.		III-C 1 b
Douglass, William.	III-A 3	Dupee, George W.		III-A 4
	III-A 4	Du Plessis, Johannes.		I-E 1 c
Doulophilus.	II-C			I-E 1 r
Dovlo, C. K.	I-E 3 e	Du Preez, Andries B.		I-E 3 c
Dowd, Jerome.	III-A 3	Durden, Lewis M.	III-A 1 a vi
	III-D	Durham, E.C.		III-C 1 f
Dowey, Edward A., Jr.	V-B 3	Dussercle, Roger.		I-E 1 m
Downey, David G.	III-C 1 f	Du Toit, Stefanus.		I-E 1 c
Dowling, John.	III-A 1 a viii			I-E 3 c
Downs, Karl E.	III-A 5	Dye, Royal J.		I-E 1 g
Doyle, Bertram W.	III-D	Dye, William M.		I-C
Drake, Richard B.	III-C 2 f	Dyson, Walter.	III-A 1 a viii
Drake, St. Clair.	III-C 1 a			
	III-C 2 a			
Drake, Thomas E.	II-D 5	Eakin, Frank.		III-D
Dreves, Francis M.	I-E 1 j	Eakin, Mildred O.		III-D
Drew, Samuel.	II-A	Early, Sarah J.W.	III-A 1 a i
Drewes, Christopher F.	III-A 5	Early, Tracy.		V-E
Driberg, Jack H.	I-C	Earnest, Joseph B.		III-A 3
Drimmer, Melvin.	III-A 2 b	Eason, James H.		III-A 3
Drisler, H.	II-C	Easton, Hosea.		II-C
Drummond, Andrew L.	II-D 1			III-A 4
Drummond, Elanor.	V-A	Eby, Omar.		I-C
Drury, Clifford M.	II-D 7	Eckhardt, Kenneth W.		V-D
Dube, J. L.	I-E 1 c	Eddy, Ansel D.		III-A 3
Dubois, Henri M.	I-E 1 r	Eddy, Elizabeth M.		IV-A 1
Du Bois, William E. B.	I-C	Eddy, George N.	III-A 2 b
	III-A 3	Eddy, Norman G.	III-A 1 b v
	III-C 1 e	Edge, Frederick M.		II-D 1
	III-D	Edgerton, Walter.		II-D 5
Dudley, Miss Mary.	II-C	Edward, (Brother).		I-E 1 o
Duff, Edward.	III-C 2 d	Edwards, Bryan.		I-D
	IV-C	Edwards, David L.		V-D
Duffield, George.	II-D 1	Edwards, H.	III-A 2 b
Dugan, George.	IV-B	Edwards, Herbert O.		V-E
	V-A	Edwards, John.		V-B 3
	V-C	Edwards, John E.	III-C 1 f
	V-D	Edwards, Jonathan.		II-D 1
	V-E	Edwards, Josephine C.		
Dumond, Dwight L.	II-D 1			III-C 1 j
	V-E	Edwards, Lyford P.		III-D
Dunbar, E.	IV-B	Edwards, S. J. C.		III-A 5
Dunbar, L.W.	IV-A 6	Edwards, V. A.		III-A 3
Duncan, James.	II-C	Edwards, Vetress Bon.		III-D
Duncan, Sylvia.	I-E 1 j	Eekhof, Albert.		II-D 13
Duncan, W. J.	V-A	Egerton, John.		IV-C

Ehrenhalt, Alan.   V-D
Ehrman, Albert.   III-A 2 a
Eichelberger, James W.
                      III-A 1 a ii
Eighmy, John L.   III-C 1 k
Elaw, Zilpha.   III-A 4
Elder, Frederick.   V-A
Eleazer, Robert B.   III-A 3
Elkholy, Abdo A.   III-A 2 b
Ellerbee, A. W.   II-D 8
Elliott, Charles.   II-C
                            II-D 6
Ellis, Alfred B.   I-E 1 a
                          I-E 1 r
Ellis, James J.   I-E 1 j
Ellis, John T.   II-D 2
Ellis, William.   I-E 1 s
Ellison, John M.   II-D 1
                     III-A 1 a vi
                          III-A 3
                          III-A 4
                             V-A
Ellison, Virginia H.   IV-C
Ellul, Jacques.   V-A
Ely, Effie S.   III-A 3
Embree, Edwin R.   III-A 3
Embry, James C.   III-A 1 a i
Emerick, A. J.   III-C 1 b
Emerson, Harriet E.   III-C 1 f
Emery, E. B.   II-D 1
Emery, M. T.   I-E 1 o
Emil, Mary (Sister).   III-D
Endicott, Mary A.   I-E 1 i
England, John.   II-D 2
Entwistle, Mary.   I-C
Epega, David O.   I-C
Epps, Archie C.   II-C
Epps, B. C.   V-E
Essien-Udom, Essien V.
                          III-A 2 b
Eubanks, John B.   III-A 3
Eutsler, Frederick B.   IV-A 1
Evangelicus.   II-C
Evans, Joshua.   II-D 1
Evans, Luther.   I-C
Evans, Stanley G.   I-E 1 r
Evans, William.   II-D 5
Evans-Pritchard, Edward E.   I-C
Evtushenko, E. A.   IV-B
Ewart, David.   II-C
Ewell, John L.   III-A 4
Ezell, Humphrey K.   V-E

Faduma, Orishatukeh.   I-E 1 r
                          I-E 3 a
                          III-A 3
Fager, C. E.   IV-B
Fahey, Frank J.   III-A 5
Fahs, Charles Harvey.   I-E 1 r
Fahs, Sophia B.   I-E 1 s
Fairchild, Edward H.   III-C 2 f
Fairly, John S.   III-C 1 h
Fanon, Frantz.   I-E 3 e
Farish, Hunter D.   III-C 1 f
Farmer, James.   III-E
Farnum, Mable.   III-C 1 b
Farrow, S. S.   I-C
Faulk, John H.   III-A 4
Faulkner, L. E.   III-D
Faulkner, William J.   II-D 1
Faure, Jean.   I-E 1 s
Fauset, Arthur H.   III-A 1 b iv
Fave, Armand J.   II-D 2
Favre, Edouard.   I-E 1 c
Fawcett, Benjamin.   II-D 1
Feagin, Joe R.   III-D
Fee, John G.   II-C
Fegin, Joe R.   III-C 1 b
Fehderau, Harold W.   I-E 2
                          I-E 3 d
Felton, Ralph A.   III-A 3
                          III-A 4
                         III-C 1 a
                         III-C 1 f
Fenner, Thomas P.   II-H
Fenton, Thomas.   I-E 1 s
Ferguson, John.   I-C
Ferm, Vergilius T. A.   III-A 3
Fernandez, James W.   I-C
                          I-E 2
Ferrer, J. M.   IV-A 9
Ferrill, London.   III-A 4
Ferris, George H.   III-C 1 k
Ferry, Henry J.   III-A 4
Fey, H. E.   III-C 1 b
                          IV-A 4
Fey, H. H.   IV-A 1
Fey, Harold.   III-D
                          IV-A 1
Fichter, Joseph H.   II-H
                         III-C 1 b
                          IV-A 1
                           IV-C
Fickland, R. William.   III-A 3
Fickling, Susan M. M.   II-B
Fields, J. B.   III-A 4

Fiers, A. Dale.	III-C 1 d	Forbush, Bliss.	II-D 5
Fife, Robert O.	II-D 4		IV-A 5
Finley, James B.	III-A 4	Ford, C. E.	III-A 3
Finney, Charles G.	II-D 3	Ford, Leighton.	IV-A 14
Fintan, Father.	I-E 1 s	Ford, Theodore P.	II-C
Fish, Carl Russell.	II-D 1	Forde, H. A.	I-E 1 r
Fish, Henry Clay.	II-D 1	Forman, Jacob G.	II-D 1
Fishel, Leslie H.	III-A 4		II-D 3
Fisher, A. B.	I-E 1 r	Forrest, Edna M.	III-A 3
Fisher, George E.	II-D 1	Forsberg, Malcolm.	I-E 1 r
Fisher, Lena L.	I-E 1 r	Forster, Daniel.	II-D 3
Fisher, Miles M.	I-E 1 r	Forster, John.	II-D 5
	II-H	Forster, William.	II-D 5
	III-A 1 a vi	Forsyth, David D.	III-C 1 f
	III-A 1 a viii	Fortenbaugh, Robert.	II-D 9
	III-A 1 b iv	Fortes, Meyer.	I-C
	III-A 3	Foss, A. T.	III-C 1 k
	III-A 4	Foster, Daniel.	II-D 1
Fisher, Ruth B.	I-E 1 s	Foster, Eden B.	II-D 3
Fisher, Samuel J.	III-C 1 g	Foster, Gustavus L.	III-A 4
Fisher, William S.	I-E 1 s	Foster, Isaac.	V-B 1
Fiske, Edward B.	IV-C	Foster, Robert V.	II-D 7
	V-B 1	Foster, Stephen S.	II-D 1
	V-D		II-F
Fitton, James.	II-D 2	Fountain, William A.	
Fitzgerald, John.	II-D 1		III-A 1 a i
Fitzgerald, M. L.	I-C	Fouroadier, Etienne.	I-E 1 s
Fitzgerald, W. P. N.	II-C	Fowler, Andrew.	III-A 1 a vi
Fitzhugh, George.	II-D 1		III-A 3
Fleming, Walter L.	II-G	Fox, George.	II-D 1
Fletcher, John.	II-D 1	Fox, Henry J.	III-C 1 f
Fletcher, Thomas.	II-C	Fox, William.	I-E 1 r
Flickinger, Daniel K.	I-E 1 k	Fox, William K.	III-A 3
	I-E 1 s	Foy, Valentine.	III-C 1 k
Flickinger, Robert E.	III-C 1 g	Frady, M.	IV-A 1
Flora, George R.	I-E 1 o	Frakes, Margaret.	IV-A 1
Florovsky, Georges.	III-C 1 m	Frame, George.	I-E 1 c
Flournoy, Ray.	V-B 1	France, H.	I-C
Flow, J. E.	III-C 1 g	Franck, Louis.	I-E 1 j
	III-E	Franklin, Ben A.	IV-B
Floyd, Olive B.	I-E 1 r	Franklin, John H.	I-C
Floyd, R. W.	III-D		III-A 5
Floyd, Silas X.	III-A 4		IV-A 1
Flynn, R. O.	III-A 3	Fransioli, Joseph.	II-D 2
Foley, Albert S.	III-A 4	Fraser, Donald.	I-E 1 r
	III-A 5	Fraser, T. P.	IV-A 1
	III-C 1 b	Frazer, James G.	I-C
	III-D	Frazer, William H.	III-D
Foley, Judy M.	V-B 3	Frazier, Edward F.	III-A 3
	V-D		III-A 4
Foot, S. H.	IV-A 1	Frease, E. F.	I-C
Foote, Julia A. J.	III-A 4	Freeman, Edward A.	III-C 1 k
Forbes, Edgar A.	I-E 3 a	Freeman, Thomas B.	I-E 1 r

Friberg, H.	V-D	Gardner, R. B.	IV-A 13
Friedel, Lawrence M.	III-D	Garland, Phyl.	III-A 4
Friedricks, R. W.	IV-A 1		IV-B
	III-D	Garlick, Phyllis L.	I-E 1 j
Frost, Maria G.	II-C		II-D 1
Frosthingham, Frederick.	II-D 1	Garman, Harold W.	IV-C
Frothingham, Octavius B.		Garnet, Henry H.	III-A 3
	II-D 10		III-A 4
	II-F	Garnett, Thomas C.	II-H
Frucht, Richard.	III-A 3	Garrettson, Freeborn.	II-F
Fry, C. Luther.	III-A 3	Garrison, William L.	II-C
Fry, H. W.	IV-A 1	Gartlan, Jean.	I-C
Fry, John R.	V-A	Garvey, Marcus.	III-A 1 b iv
	V-B 1	Gasnick, Roy M.	IV-A 2
Fueter, Paul D.	I-E 3 e	Gaul, Harvey B.	II-H
Fuller, Edward J.	II-D 1	Gaustad, Edwin S.	II-D 1
Fuller, Erasmus T.	II-D 6	Gavan Duffy, Thomas.	I-E 1 r
Fuller, J. Latimer.	I-E 1 c	Gaynor, W. C.	III-A 5
Fuller, Richard.	II-D 12	Geddes, Michael.	I-B
Fuller, Thomas O.	III-A 3	Gehres, M.	IV-C
	III-A 1 a vi	Gelman, Martin.	III-A 3
Fullerton, William Y.	I-E 1 j	George, Poikail J.	I-E 1 r
Funk, Joseph.	II-H	George, Zelma W.	II-H
Furfey, Paul H.	II-D 1	Georges, Norbert.	III-A 5
Furlong, C. W.	I-E 1 r	Geppert, Dora H.	II-G
Furman, Richard.	II-D 12	Gerasimov, G.	IV-B
Furness, William H.	II-D 1	Germillion, Joseph B.	IV-A 2
	II-D 10	Geronim da Montesarchio, (Fr.).	
	II-F		I-E 1 j
Gaba, C. R.	I-C	Gessell, J. M.	IV-B
Gaddie, Daniel A.	III-A 4	Geyer, Franz X.	I-E 1 e
Gaines, Wesley J.	III-A 1 a i	Gibbons, James.	II-D 2
Gairdner, G. D. A.	I-C	Gibbons, R.	IV-A 3
Gairdner, W. H.	I-C	Gibbons, R.W.	IV-A 2
Galbreath, George.	III-A 4	Gibbs, Jonathan C.	II-D 7
Gale, Hubert P.	I-E 1 j	Gibson, A. B. B.	III-A 1 a i
Gale, William K.	I-E 1 s	Gibson, Bertha A.	II-F
Gallagher, Buell G.	III-D	Gibson, Edmund.	II-B
	III-E	Gibson, John W.	III-A 3
Gallaudet, Thomas H.	II-C	Gibson, Joseph K.	III-A 3
Galloway, Charles B.	III-D	Giddings, Joshua R.	II-C
Galphin, Bruce M.	IV-B	Giffen, John K.	I-E 1 e
Galphin, William.	II-D 1		I-E 1 s
Gandy, Samuel L.	III-A 3	Gilbert, Arthur.	III-E
	V-A	Gillard, John T.	III-A 3
Gannett, Ezra S.	II-D 1		III-A 5
	II-D 10		III-C 1 b
Gannett, William C.	II-D 10		III-D
Gannon, Michael V.	II-D 2	Gillespie, G. T.	III-D
Ganse, Hervey D.	II-C	Gillette, Francis.	II-D 3
Garber, Paul N.	II-D 6	Gilliam, W. A.	IV-C
Gardiner, James J.	V-B 1	Gillies, J.	IV-A 2
Gardner, E. C.	IV-A 1	Gilligan, Francis J.	III-D

Gilliland, James.   II-D 7
Gillis, James M.   III-E
Giltner, John H.   II-F
Gingyera-Pinciwa, A. G. G.
                                 I-E 1 r
Girardeau, J. L.   II-G
Gist, Grace.   III-A 1 a i
Gittings, James A.   IV-A 7
Glass, Victor T.   III-A 4
Glazer, N.   III-C 1 1
                                 V-D
Gleason, Robert W.   III-D
Glenn, Norval D.   III-A 3
Glennie, Alexander   II-B
Glock, C. Y.   III-C 1 a
Gloucester, Henry.   II-H
Gloucester, John.   III-A 5
Gobat, Samuel.   I-E 1 k
Gochet, Jean B.   II-D 2
Godwyn, Morgan.   II-D 1
Goens, Anna.   III-A 4
Goerner, H. C.   I-E 1 r
Goetz, Ronald.   V-B 3
Gogarty, Henry A.   I-E 1 d
Goin, Edward F.   III-A 5
Goncalves Fernandes, A.   III-B
Good, P.   IV-B
Goodell, William.   II-D 1
Goodman, D.   IV-A 1
Goodman, G.   IV-B
Goodman, Paul.   III-C 1 1
Goodwin, Daniel R.   II-D 1
Goodwin, Morgan.   II-B
                                 II-D 1
Gopaul, P.   V-B 2
Gordes, Robert.   III-D
Gordh, G.   IV-A 6
Gordon, Asa H.   III-A 3
Gordon, Buford F.   III-A 3
                                 III-A 4
Gordon, David M.   III-A 5
Gordon, Mamye.   IV-A 6
Gordon, Milton.   III-D
Gordja, Joseph.   I-E 1 s
Gossett, Thomas F.   III-D
Gouge, William.   II-D 1
Gouilly, Alphonse.   I-C
Gowan, Richard.   I-E 1 e
Goyau, Georges.   I-E 1 s
Graham, Alfredo.   V-C
Graham, Billy.   IV-A 1
                                 IV-C
Graham, John H.   III-A 5

Graham, Lorenz B.   I-C
Graham, Robert H. C.   I-E 1 j
Grahame, Nigel B. M.   I-E 1 r
Granderson, Elizabeth.   III-A 4
Grandy, Moses.   III-A 4
Granger, Arthur   II-C
Granger, Lester B.   III-C 1 b
Granier de Cassagnac, Bernard
   A.   III-B
Grant, George A.   III-D
Grant, John H.   III-A 4
Gravely, William B.   II-D 6
                                 III-C 1 f
Gray, Arthur R.   III-B
Gray, Henderson.   III-A 1 a viii
Gray, Oscam J.   V-B 1
Gray, Thomas.   II-F
Grayston, E. Alisan.   I-E 1 r
Grebert, F.   I-E 1 h
Greeley, Andrew M.   IV-A 2
                                 V-A
Green, A. R.   III-A 1 a i
Green, Ashbel.   I-E 1 o
Green, Beriah.   II-C
                                 II-D 1
                                 II-D 3
                                 II-D 5
                                 II-D 7
Green, Charles S.   I-E 1 b
Green, Constance M.   III-A 3
Green, David B.   III-A 3
Green, Fletcher M.   II-D 1
Green, Mark.   V-B 3
Greenberg, Joseph.   I-C
Greene, Lorenzo J.   II-D
Greene, Sherman L.
                                 III-A 1 a i
Greenfell, W. D.   I-E 1 q
Greenleaf, Jonathan.
                                 III-A 1 a viii
Greenslade, Stanley L.   II-D 1
Gregory, Dick.   V-B 1
Gregg, Howard D.   III-A 1 a i
Gremley, W.   IV-A 1
Greville, Robert K.   II-D 1
Grey, M. (Sister Martin de
   Porres)   V-B 2
Grier, William.   V-E
Griffin, Clifford S.   III-A 3
Griffin, Edward D.   II-D 7
Griffin, Eunice.   III-A 1 a i
Griffin, John H.   III-A 3
                                 V-B 2

Griffith, Francis L.   I-C
Griffith, T. L.   III-A 4
Griggs, Leverett S.   II-D 1
Grill, C. Frederick.   III-A 5
Grimes, Alan P.   V-E
Grimes, Leonard A.   II-D 1
Grimes, William W.   III-A 1 a i
Grimke, Angelina E.   II-D 1
                              II-F
Grimke, Francis J.   II-G
                             III-A 3
                             III-A 4
                             III-A 5
                             III-D
Grimke, Sarah M.   II-D 1
Grissom, Mary A.   III-A 3
Grissom, W. L.   III-A 5
Groffier, Valerien.   I-E 1 s
Groppi, James E.   V-E
Grose, Howard B.   III-B
Groselaude, Etienne   I-E 1 s
Gross, Alexander.   II-D 6
Grosvenor, Cyrus P.   II-D 1
Grout, L.   III-A 3
Groves, Charles P.   I-E 1 r
Groves, Richard.   V-B 1
Grubb, Norman P.   I-E 1 j
Gruber, Jacob.   II-E
Guebels, Leon.   I-E 1 j
Guice, John A.   II-D 6
Guilcher, Rene F.   I-E 1 i
                              I-E 1 s
Guinness, Fanny E.   I-E 1 s
Gullins, William R.   III-A 1 a i
Gulliver, J. P.   II-D 3
Gurley, Ralph R.   I-E 1 o
Gustafson, James M.   III-A 4
Gusweller, J. A.   IV-A 2
Guthrie, John.   II-F
Gwaltney, Grace.   III-A 3
Gwynne, L. H.   I-E 1 e

Hacher, Leroy C.   III-A 1 a vi
Hackett, Allen.   IV-A 3
                              V-E
Hadden, Jeffrey K.   IV-A 1
                              V - E
Hadfield, Percival.   I-C
Hagood, Lewis M.   III-C 1 f
                             III-D
Hague, William.   II-C
Hair, P. E. H.   I-D

Haitz, Linn.   I-C
Halberstam, David.   IV-B
                             IV-C
Halberstam, M.   IV-B
Haley, Alex.   III-A 2 b
Haley, James.   III-A 1 a viii
Haliburton, G. M.   I-E 2
Hall, A. L.   III-A 4
Hall, Barnes M.   II-C
Hall, Edward B.   II-D 10
Hall, Ernest N.   III-A 4
Hall, Frederick.   II-H
Hall, Nathaniel.   II-D 1
                              II-D 3
Hall, P. W.   II-D 1
Hallack, Cecily R.   I-E 1 r
Halloway, Harriette R.   II-C 1 g
Halpern, Ben.   V-C
Halsey, Abram W.   I-D
                              I-E 1 m
                             III-C 1 g
Halvorson, Lawrence W.   V-E
Hamblin, Dora J.   IV-C
Hamilton, Charles H.   III-A 3
Hamilton, Fayette M.
                          III-A 1 a iii
Hamilton, W. T.   II-C
Hamilton, William.   II-F
Hammon, Jupiter.   II-D 1
Hammond, E. W. S.   I-E 1 r
Hammond, J. D.   III-A 3
Hammond, Lilly H.   III-A 3
                             III-C 1 c
                             III-D
Hance, Gertrude R.   I-E 1 c
Handlin, Oscar.   III-C 1 l
Handy, James A.   III-A 1 a i
Handy, Robert T.   III-A 3
Hanen, Gilbert.   II-D 1
                              II-G
Hanh, Nhat.   IV-B
Hanish, Joseph J.   IV-A 1
Hansberry, William L.   I-B
                              I-C
Hanson, Geddes.   III-A 3
                              V-B 1
Hanson, V. W.   III-A 1 a i
Harbutt, Charles.   IV-A 2
Harding, Vincent.   III-A 3
                             III-A 4
                              V-B 1
                              V-E
Hardy, Arthur W.   III-D

Hardyman, J.   I-E 1 s   Harvey, M. L.   III-A 3
Hare, Alexander P.   IV-B   Harvey, W.   III-A 1 a viii
Hare, Maud C.   II-H   Haselden, Kyle E.   III-D
Hare, Nathan.   V-D   IV-A 1
Harford, Charles F.   I-E 1 j   Haskin, Sara E.   III-C 2 a
Hargett, Andrew H.   Hastings, Adrain.   I-E 3 b
                  III-A 1 a viii   Hatch, Margaret L. D.   IV-A 4
                  III-A 3   Hatch, Reuben.   II-C
Hargett, James H.   III-A 5   Hatcher, William E.   III-A 4
Hargraves, J. A.   V-A   Hatchett, John F.   III-A 2 b
                          V-B 1   Hatfield, Edwin F.   II-H
Harlan, Howard H.   III-A 4   Hattersley, Charles W. I-E 1 j
Harlow, Harold C.   III-C 2 a   Haughley, J.   V-B 1
Harlow, Ralph V.   II-D 1   Hawks, Francis L.   I-A
Harmon, J. A.   III-C 1 f   Hayford, Mark C.   I-E 1 s
Harmon, John J.   IV-C   Haygood, Atticus G.   III-A 3
Harnack, H.   I-E 1 r   III-A 4
Harper, F. N.   V-D   III-C 1 f
Harper, L. A.   IV-A 1   Hayne, Coe S.   III-C 1 k
Harr, Wilbur C.   I-E 1 r   III-C 2 a
Harrington, Donald.   IV-A 14   Hayne, J. E.   II-C
Harrington, M.   V-B 1   Haynes, George E.   I-E 1 r
Harris, Cicero R.   III-A 1 a ii   III-A 3
Harris, Eugene.   II-D 1   III-C 1 a
Harris, J. H.   I-E 1 r   III-C 2 a
Harris, John.   II-D 1   III-C 2 b
Harris, Marquis L.   III-A 5   Haynes, Lemuel.   II-D 1
Harris, R.   IV-A 1   II-D 3
Harris, Raymund.   II-C   III-A 4
Harris, Sara.   I-E 1 o   Haynes, Leonard L.   III-A 3
                  III-A 1 b iv   Haynes, Nathaniel S.   II-D 4
Harris, Solomon P. III-A 1 a vi   Hays, Brooks.   IV-A 1
Harris, William F.   Hayward, Victor E. W.   I-E 2
                  III-A 1 a viii   Haywood, Delores C.   I-E 1 o
Harris, William L.   II-D 6   Haywood, J. W.   IV-A 6
Harrison, Alexina (Mackay).   Hazzard, Walter R.   IV-A 1
                          I-E 1 j   Heard, William H.   I-E 1 r
Harrison, Ira E.   III-A 1 b v   III-A 1 a i
Harrison, Walter R.   III-A 3   Hearn, Winifred.   IV-A 4
Harrison, William P.   II-C   Heckman, Oliver S.   III-C 1 a
                          II-D 6   Hedgeman, Anna A.   IV-C
Harrod, Howard L.   V-A   Hedgley, David R.   III-A 3
Hart, Albert B.   II-D 1   Hefley, J. T.   III-C 2 a
Hart, Levi.   II-F   Height, Dorothy I.   IV-C
Harte, Thomas J.   III-C 1 b   Heithaus, C. H.   III-C 1 b
Hartland, F. S.   I-C   Helander, Gunnar.   I-E 1 g
Hartmann, M.   I-C   Hellwig, M.   IV-A 2
Hartnett, Robert C.   IV-A 2   Helm, Mary.   III-C 2 a
Hartshorn, William N.   III-A 3   Helm, T. G.   II-F
Hartzell, Joseph C.   I-E 1 r   Helper, Hinton R.   II-D 1
                          III-C 1 f   Helser, Albert D.   I-E 1 b
Harvey, Claire.   III-A 4   I-E 1 r
Harvey, H.   II-D 12   Hemmens, Harry L.   I-E 1 j

Hemptinne, Jean Felix de.
                                   I-E 1 j
Hemstreet, Robert.   IV-A 14
Henderlite, R.   IV-A 1
Henderson, George W.   III-A 4
Hendrick, George.   IV-B
Hening, E.   I-E 1 o
Henkle, Moses M.   II-D 6
Henning, C. G.   III-A 3
Henry, George W.   II-H
Henry, Hayward.   V-B 1
                           V-B 2
Henry, Romiche.   III-A 4
Hensey, Andrew F.   I-E 1 j
Henson, Herbert H.   II-D 1
Henson, Josiah.   III-A 4
Hentoff, Nat.   III-A 2 b
                           IV-B
                           V-C
Hepburn, D.   II-H
                           III-A 5
Hepburn, James D.   I-E 1 s
Herberg, Will.   V-A
Hernton, Calvin C.   III-A 2 b
Herr, Dan   III-C 1 b
Hersey, John.   II-D 1
Hershberger, Guy F.   III-E
Herskovits, Melville F.   I-C
                           I-E 3 e
                           II-H
Herz, S.   III-C 1 b
Herzog, Frederick.   V-B 1
Hess, Mahlon M.   I-E 3 e
Hessel, Dieter T.   V-E
Hester, William H. III-A 1 a vi
Hetherwick, Alexander.   I-C
                           I-E 3 d
Hewitt, Doris W.   III-A 3
Hewson, Leslie A.   I-C
Hickey, Neil.   IV-C
Hickman, Garrison M.   V-B 1
Hickman, Thomas L.   III-A 5
Hickok, C. T.   III-A 3
Hickok, Laurens P.   III-C 2 a
Hicks, Elias.   II-D 5
Hicks, William.   III-A 1 a vi
Higgins, Godfrey (Sir).   III-A 4
Higginson, Thomas W.   II-C
                           II-D 1
                           II-H
Hilford, M. R.   I-D
Hill, Andrew W.   III-A 1 a vi
Hill, Bob.   V-B 1

Hill, Charles L.   III-A 4
Hill, Clifford S.   II-A
                           V-E
Hill, Daniel G.   III-A 3
                           III-A 4
Hill, Davis C.   III-C 1 k
Hill, Edward V.   V-B 1
Hill, Hilley.   III-A 1 b
Hill, John L.   III-A 4
Hill, Richard H.   III-A 1 a vi
Hill, Samuel S.   III-C 1 k
                           IV-A 1
Hill, Timothy A.   III-C 2 a
Hillhouse, William.   II-D 1
Hilton, Bruce.   V-A
Hilty, Hiram H.   II-D 5
Hinderer, Anna (Martin).
                           I-E 1 e
Hirsch, Leo H.   III-A 1 a viii
Hitcher, B.   I-E 1 m
Hitchcock, James.   V-D
Hobbs, Helen   V-B 1
Hobley, Charles W.   I-E 1 d
Hobson, Shelia.   V-A
Hodges, Charles E.   II-D 1
Hodges, George W.
                    III-A 1 a viii
                           III-A 5
Hodges, Ruth H.   III-A 1 a i
Hodges, William H.   V-B 1
Hodgman, Stephen A.   II-C
Hodgson, E.   I-C
Hoff, John F.   II-B
Hoffman, Clifton G.   IV-A 14
Hoffman, Mamie G.   III-A 3
Hofmeyr, Jan H.   I-C
Hogan, John A.   III-C 1 b
Holcombe, William H.   II-D 1
Holden, Anna   IV-A 2
Holden, Edith.   I-E 1 r
Holland, Darrell W.   V-B 3
Holland, Frederic M.   II-G
Holland, Jerome H.   III-A 3
Holland, Timothy J.   II-D 2
Holley, Myron.   II-F
Holloman, John L. S.   III-A 4
Holloway, Vernon H. III-C 1 a
Holly, Alonzo P.   III-A 3
Holly, James T.   II-D 8
                           III-A 4
Holmes, Daniel.   II-C
Holmes, Dwight O. W.   III-D
Holmes, Edward A. III-A 1 a vi

Holmes, James H.	III-A 4	Hubbard, Henry W.	III-C 2 f
Holmes, John B.	I-E 1 r	Huckel, W.	I-E 1 r
Holmes, Thomas J.	III-D	Huddleston, Trevor.	I-C
Holsey, Lucius H.	III-A 1 a iii	Huggins, Willis N.	III-C 1 b
	III-D	Hughes, Langston.	III-A 4
Holtrop, Donald.	V-E	Hughes, W.	I-E 1 r
Holway, James D.	I-C		II-C
Hood, James W.	III-A 1 a ii	Hughley, J. D.	III-C 1 k
	III-A 4	Hughley, Judge Neal.	III-A 3
Hood, Solomon P.	III-A 1 a ii		IV-A 1
Hook, H. P.	V-A	Hughson, Shirley C.	I-E 1 n
Hoover, Theressa.	V-D	Huie, W. B.	IV-B
Hope, John.	III-C 2 a	Hulme, Kathryn C.	I-E 1 j
Hopes, W. K.	III-A 1 a i	Humphrey, Heman.	II-D 1
Hopkins, John H.	II-C		II-D 3
Hopkins, Josiah.	II-C	Humphrey, Hubert H.	IV-C
Hopkins, Samuel	II-D 12	Humphreys, Nicholas.	I-E 1 c
Hopmann, Paul.	V-D	Hunt, James D.	IV-B
Horchler, Richard.	IV-A 1	Huntley, Thomas E.	III-D
Hore, Edward G.	I-E 1 f	Hunton, George K.	III-C 1 b
Horner, Norman A.	I-E 1 m	Hurley, Denis E.	I-E 3 c
Hortenstine, Virgie B.	IV-A 4		IV-A 2
	IV-A 5	Hurley, Phillip S.	IV-A 1
Horton, Frank L.	V-B 1	Hurst, John H.	III-A 4
Horton, Joseph P.	II-D 6	Hurst, Leonard.	I-E 1 s
Hoshor, John.	III-A 1 b iv	Hurston, Zora N.	III-B
Hosmer, William.	II-C	Hutchinson, Bertram.	I-E 1 c
	II-D 1	Hyde, A. B.	II-F
Hoss, Elijah E.	III-A 5	Hyland, Philip.	III-C 1 b
Hotchkiss, Wesley A.	III-C 1 c		
Hotchkiss, Willis R.	I-E 1 r		
Houck, J. B.	IV-B	Ide, George B.	III-C 1 k
Hough, J.	II-D 1	Idowv, E. Bolaji.	I-C
Hough, John A.	II-F	Ikeler, Bernard.	IV-A 7
Hough, Joseph C.	V-B 1	Illo, John.	III-A 2 b
Houghton, James	II-C	Imbart de la Tour, Joseph H. B.	
Houser, George M.	III-D		II-D 2
Houston, David.	II-F	Imes, G. Lake.	III-A 3
Hovey, Sylvester.	II-A		III-A 4
How, Samuel B.	II-D 13	Imes, William L.	III-D
Howard, John R.	III-A 2 b	Ireland, William B.	I-E 1 h
Howard, R.	IV-B	Irish, David.	II-D 5
Howard, Tillman J.	IV-A 6	Irstam, Tor.	I-C
Howard, Victor B.	II-D 7	Isaac, Ephraim.	I-B
	II-F	Isaacs, Esther B.	III-A 1 a i
Howe, R.	II-H	Isaacs, Harold R.	III-C 1 l
Howell, C. V.	III-A 1 b iv	Ivimey, Joseph.	II-D 5
Howell, E. M.	I-E 3 a	Ivy, A. C.	III-D
Howell, Hazel W.	III-A 2 b	Iwarsson, J.	I-C
Howell, Leonard.	V-B 3		
Howitt, William	II-F		
Howlett, Duncan.	IV-A 14	Jack, Homer A.	III-C 1 a
Hubbard, Ethel D.	I-E 1 c	Jack, Thomas C.	II-D 7

Jackman, Stuart B.   I-E 3 c
Jacks, M. L.   III-D
Jackson, Algernon B.   III-A 3
Jackson, Andrew W.   III-A 4
Jackson, Benjamin F.
                    III-A 1 a vi
Jackson, Bruce H.   II-H
Jackson, Edward J.   III-A 1 a i
Jackson, George P.   II-H
Jackson, Giovanna R.   V-E
Jackson, J. H.   IV-A 6
Jackson, James C.   II-B
Jackson, Jesse.   V-E
Jackson, Jesse L.   V-B 1
Jackson, John H.   II-H
Jackson, Joseph H.   III-A 1 a vi
                          IV-A 11
Jackson, Joseph J.   III-A 1 a vi
Jackson, Luther P.   II-B
Jackson, Mahalia.   II-H
Jackson, Olive S.   III-D
Jackson, Samuel M.   I-E 1 r
Jacques, Oliver.   I-E 1 f
Jadot, Jean.   I-E 3 d
Jalla, Adolphe.   I-E 1 c
James, Cyril L. R.   I-E 1 r
James, G. M.   V-A
James, Horace   II-D 3
James, J. A.   I-E 1 r
James, Sydney V.   II-D 5
James, Willis L.   II-H
Jamison, Monroe F.   III-C 1 f
Jan, Jean M.   III-B
Janney, Samuel M.   II-D 5
Janssens, Francis.   III-C 1 b
Jaquet, Constant H.   III-C 2 c
Jason, William C.   III-A 5
Jasper, John J.   III-A 4
Jay, John   II-D 8
                          II-F
Jay, William   II-D 1
                          II-D 8
                          II-F
Jeffers, Robert A.   V-E
Jefferson, Frederick D.   V-D
Jeffrey, George.   II-D 1
Jenifer, John T.   III-A 1 a i
Jenkins, John J.   III-A 3
Jenkins, Warren M.   III-C 1 f
Jenkins, William S.   II-D 1
Jenness, Mary.   III-A 4
Jernagin, W. H.   III-A 3
Jernegan, Marcus W.   II-B

Jervey, Edward D.   II-G
Jessup, Lewis.   II-D 1
Jessye, Eva A.   II-H
Jeter, Henry N.   III-A 1 a viii
                          III-A 4
Jocelyn.   II-C
Jocelyn, Simeon S.   II-F
Johnson, Benton.   III-A 1 b ii
                          V-A
Johnson, Charles S.   III-A 3
                          III-C 2 f
                          III-D
Johnson, Clifton H.   II-C
                          III-C 2 f
Johnson, Edward A.   III-A 3
Johnson, Evan M.   II-D 1
Johnson, Frederick E.   III-A 3
Johnson, Guion.   III-A 3
Johnson, Hall.   II-H
Johnson, Harvey.   III-A 4
Johnson, Henry M.   III-C 1 f
Johnson, Henry T.   III-A 1 a i
                          III-A 3
                          III-A 4
Johnson, Herrick   II-D 7
Johnson, James H. A.
                    III-A 1 a i
Johnson, James W.   II-H
                          III-A 3
Johnson, John A.   III-A 1 a i
Johnson, John H.   III-A 4
                          III-C 1 h
Johnson, Joseph A.   III-A 4
                          V-B 1
Johnson, Mordecai W.   III-A 3
                          III-A 4
Johnson, Philip A.   V-A
Johnson, R. J.   III-A 1 a vi
Johnson, Robert R.
                    III-A 1 a viii
Johnson, Richard H.   III-C 1 a
Johnson, Samuel   I-E 1 r
Johnson, Thomas A.   V-D
Johnson, T. Broadwood.
                          I-E 1 j
Johnson, Thomas L.   I-E 1 m
Johnson, Thomas S.   I-E 3 e
Johnson, W. Bishop   III-D
Johnson, William A.
                    III-A 1 a vi
Johnson, William H.   III-A 4
                          I-C
Johnson, William R.   V-B 1

Johnson, William P.   I-E 1 t   Kamper, Pieter P.   I-E 3 b
Johnston, Henry H.   I-E 1 r   Kampschmidt, William H.
                           III-A 3   III-C 1 i
Johnston, Henry M.   III-C 1 f   Kanyua, Jesse N.   I-C
Johnston, James.   I-E 1 r   Kaplan, Harry.   III-D
Johnston, Robert.   II-D 6   Karefa-Smart, John.   I-E 3 e
Johnston, Ruby.   III-A 3   Karon, Bertram P.   III-A 3
Johnstone, Ronald L.   III-A 3   Karpas, Melvin R.   III-A 2 b
                           III-A 4   Karsch, Carl G.   V-A
Jones, Absalom.   II-D 1   Kastler, Norman M.   III-D
                          III-C 1 h   Kaufer, Sonya F.   III-C 1 f
Jones, Arthur G.   I-E 3 d   Kay, John.   II-D 7
Jones, Benjamin S.   II-F   Keable, Robert.   I-E 3 d
Jones, Charles C.   II-B   Kealing, H. T.   III-A 3
Jones, Daniel.   III-A 4   Kearns, H. C., O. P.   III-A 5
Jones, (Mrs.) David B.   I-E 1 c   Keedy, T. C.   IV-A 1
Jones, David D.   III-D   Keefer, Justus.   II-C
Jones, Herbert G.   I-E 1 j   Keenan, C.   IV-C
Jones, Howard O.   V-E   Keene, Calvin.   II-D 5
Jones, J.   IV-B   Keesee, Robert E.   II-H
Jones, Jerome W.   III-C 1 a   Keet, B.   I-E 3 c
Jones, John G.   III-A 5   Keidel, Levi O.   IV-A 10
Jones, John R.   II-D 1   Keith, George.   II-D 5
Jones, Lawrence.   V-B 1   Keller, Jean.   I-E 3 d
Jones, LeRoi.   II-H   Kellersberger, Julia L. I-E 1 j
Jones, Madison.   V-A   Kelley, H.   III-A 1 b iv
Jones, Major J.   V-B 1   Kelly, Gerald, S. J.   III-C 1 a
Jones, Raymond J.   III-A 1 b iv   III-C 1 b
Jones, Robert E.   III-A 4   Kelly, Laurence J.   III-C 1 b
                           III-A 5   Kelly, Edmund.   III-A 4
Jones, Rufus M.   II-D 5   Kelly, Raymond.   II-H
Jones, Singleton T.   III-A 1 a ii   Kelsey, George D.   IV-A 1
Jones, Summerfield F.   III-A 3   V-E
Jordan, Artishia.   III-A 1 a i   Kemble, Frances A.   II-D 1
Jordan, Casper L.   III-A 1 a i   Kemp, Dennis.   I-E 1 a
                           III-A 4   Kenealy, William J.   IV-C
Jordan, Clarence.   IV-A 1   Kennard, Richard.
Jordan, David M.   III-A 5   III-A 1 a viii
Jordan, John P.   I-E 1 b   Kennedy, Gerald H.   III-C 1 f
Jordan, Lewis G.   I-E 1 o   Kennedy, John H.   II-D 1
                       III-A 1 a vii Kennedy, Louise V.   III-D
Jordan, Richard.   II-D 5   Kennedy, P.   III-A 1 a viii
Jordan, Winthrop D.   III-A 3   Kennedy, Robert E.   II-H
Jorns, Auguste   II-D 5   Kennedy, Robert F.   V-B 1
Joseph, Gaston.   I-E 1 s   Kennedy, William T.   V-B 1
Jowers, Joseph B.   III-A 3   Kenrick, Bruce.   V-A
Jullan, George W.   II-D 1   Kent, Juanita R.   III-C 1 f
Jump, Chester J.   I-E 1 j   Ker, Leander.   II-D 1
Junkin, George.   II-D 1   Kerlin, Robert T.   II-H
Junod, Henri A.   I-C   Kershaw, J.   III-C 1 h
Jurji, E.   V-E   Kettell, George F.   II-D 1
                                      Kicherer, Johannes J. I-E 1 c
                                      Kidder, B. F.   I-C

Kiefl, Franz X.	II-D 1	Knox, Ellis O.		III-D
Kiely, H. C.	IV-B	Knox, John P.		III-B
Kiely, P.	V-B 2	Knox, William.		II-B
Kilgore, Thomas.	V-B 1	Koger, Azzie B.	III-A 1 a vi	
Kilham, Hannah.	I-E 1 s	Kolb, Ernest C.		III-C 1 k
Killian, Lewis M.	V-E	Kootz-Kretschmer, Elise.	I-E 1 f	
Kilson, Marion.	I-C	Korby, Kenneth F.		V-D
Kinch, Emily C.	I-E 1 s	Korey, William.		III-C 1 l
Kincheloe, Samuel C.	III-C 2 a	Kotze, Jacobus C. G.	I-E 3 c	
King, C. H.	IV-A 1	Kovach, Bill.		V-C
	V-A	Kraemer, Hendrik.		III-C 2 d
King, Coretta S.	IV-B	Kramer, Alfred S.		III-C 1 a
King, Dearine E.	II-H			IV-A 1
King, J. T.	IV-A 6			V-A
King, Martin L.	III-A 4	Krapf, Ludwig.		I-E 1 r
	IV-B	Krebs, A. V.		V-E
	V-B 1	Krebs, Ervin E.		III-C 1 i
King, Noel Q.	I-C	Krebs, John M.		II-D 1
King, William F. H.	III-B	Krehbiel, Henry E.		II-H
King, Willis J.	II-H	Kretzschmer, R.		IV-C
	III-A 5	Kritzeck, James.		I-C
Kingsford, Edward.	II-D 1	Krosney, Herbert.		III-A 2 b
Kingsley, Harold M.		Kruger, E. T.		II-H
	III-A 1 a viii	Kruuse, Elsa.		IV-A 1
Kingsnorth, John S.	I-E 3 b	Kuchn, B. H.		V-A
Kingston, Vera.	I-E 1 r	Kuhns, Frederick I.		III-C 2 a
Kirk, W. Astor.	IV-C	Kull, Irving S.		II-D 7
	V-A	Kumm, Herman K. W.	I-E 1 r	
Kirkland, H. Burnham.	III-C 1 f	Kumm, K.		I-E 1 e
Kirkpatrick, Lois.	I-E 1 r	Kyle, Keith.		III-C 1 l
Kirman, J. M.	III-A 2 b	Kyles, Josephine H.		III-D
Kirrane, John P.	III-A 5	Kyles, Lynwood W.		III-A 3
Kitagawa, Daisuke.	I-E 3 e	Lacey, Leslie.		III-A 2 b
	III-C 1 a	Lacy, Charles L.		II-D 1
	III-E	Lacy, Creighton.		I-E 1 s
	IV-A 1	LaFarge, John.		III-A 4
	V-E			III-A 5
Kitching, Arthur L.	I-E 1 j			III-C 1 b
Kitly, H.	IV-A 6			III-D
Kittler, Glenn D.	I-E 1 j			III-A 2
Kiwanicka, Joseph.	I-E 3 e	LaFaye, Jean Baptiste de.	II-D 2	
Klein, Herbert S.	II-D 1	Laffitte, J.		I-E 1 i
Kletzing, Henry F.	III-A 3	Lafon, Thomas.		II-D 1
Klingberg, Frank J.	II-D 1	Lagos, Frank M.		I-E 3 e
	II-D 8	Laing, George E. F.		I-C
	III-D	Laing, Samuel.		II-D 14
Knak, Siegfried.	I-E 1 r	Lamar, J. S.		III-A 3
Knapp, M.	III-B	Lambert, Herbert H.		V-A
Knappert, Jan.	I-C	Lambert, I. C.		V-A
Knibb, William.	IV-A 6	Lambert, R. E.		III-A 3
Knight, Edgar W.	II-B	Lambert, Rollin E.		III-D
Knight-Bruce, Geo. W. H.	I-E 1 s	Lamble, Thomas A.		I-E 1 k
Knoll, Erwin	III-C 1 l	Lander, Ernest M.		III-A 3

Landes, Ruth.   III-B
Landman, W. A.   I-E 3 c
Lane, Isaac.   III-A 1 a v
Larroque, Patrice.   II-D 1
Larsen, Jens P. M.   III-B
Lasbrey, Bertram.   I-E 3 a
                            I-E 3 d
Latimer, James.   II-A
Latourette, Kenneth S.   I-E 1 r
Laue, James E.   III-A 2 b
Laurence, Charles R.   III-A 3
Laurent de Lucques, (Fr.) I-D
La Vaissiere, Camille de. I-E 1 s
Lavanoux, Maurice.   I-E 3 e
Lavigerie, Charles M. A.   II-D 2
Law, William.   II-C
Lawaetz, Herman.   III-B
Lawrence, John.   II-C
Lawrence, John B.   III-C 2 f
Lawrence, N.   IV-A 1
Lawson, R. C.   III-A 4
Lawton, Samuel M.   III-A 3
Lawyer, Zelma W.   I-E 1 l
Lay, Benjamin.   II-D 1
Lazenby, Marion E.   III-A 5
Leach, William H.   III-A 1 a i
Leas, Speed B.   V-D
Leavell, Ullin W.   III-D
Leavell, Zachery T.   II-D 12
Lechler, Gotthard V.   II-D 1
Lecky, Robert S.   V-B 3
                            V-E
Lee, Benjamin F.   III-A 1 a i
                            III-A 4
Lee, Carleton L.   III-C 2 a
Lee, Davis.   III-D
Lee, Frank F.   III-C 1 a
Lee, J. Oscar.   III-A 1 a viii
                            III-A 3
                            IV-A 1
Lee, Jarena.   III-A 1 a i
Lee, John F.   III-A 4
Lee, Luther.   II-C
                            II-D 6
Lee, R. L.   III-A 3
Lee, Robert.   V-A
                            V-D
                            V-E
Lee, Umphrey.   II-D 6
Leeuwen, Arend T. V.   I-C
Leftwich, W. M.   III-D
Legg, Sam.   V-E
Lehman, H. C.   III-A 3

Leiffer, Murray H.   III-A 3
                            III-D
Leighton, Nathan.   II-C
Leiman, Melvin.   III-A 2 b
Leiper, Henry.   III-D
LeJau, Francis.   II-D 1
LeMone, Archie.   III-A 3
Lenski, Gerhard E.
                      III-A 1 a viii
Leo, J.   V-C
Leonard, Joseph T.   III-C 1 b
Leone, John S.   I-E 3 a
Lerner, Gerda.   II-D 5
LeRoy, Alexander.   II-C
Lerrigo, Peter H. J.   I-E 1 j
Lester, Julius.   IV-C
Levine, M. H.   III-A 3
Levine, Richard M.   IV-A 4
Levo, John E.   III-B
Levtzion, Nehemia.   I-C
Lewis, Archibald.   I-C
Lewis, Carlos A.   III-A 4
Lewis, Claude.   IV-B
Lewis, Evan.   II-D 1
Lewis, Hylan G.   III-A 3
Lewis, I. M.   I-C
Lewis, John H.   III-A 3
Lewis, John W.   III-A 4
Lewis, Thomas P.   III-A 1 a vi
Lhande, Pierre.   I-E 1 s
Licorish, David N.   III-A 3
                            III-A 4
Lienhardt, G.   I-C
Lighton, George.   I-C
Lillingston, Kathleen M. E.
                            I-E 1 j
Lincoln, Charles E.   III-A 2 b
                            III-C 2 a
                            IV-A 1
                            IV-B
                            V-B 1
                            V-E
Lindsey, A. J.   IV-C
Lines, Stiles B.   II-D 8
Lippincott, H. H.   IV-B 1
Lips, Julius.   III-A 1 b iv
Lipscombe, E. H.   III-A 4
Littell, Franklin H.   V-E
Little, John.   III-C 1 a
                            III-C 1 g
Little, Malcolm.   III-A 2 b
Little, Sara.   III-E
Litwack, Leon F.   II-G

Liu, William T.   V-A
Livingstone, David.   I-E 1 g
                               I-E 1 r
                               I-E 1 s
Livingstone, William P.   I-E 1 b
                               I-E 1 r
                               I-E 1 s
                               I-E 1 t
Lloyd, Albert B.   I-E 1 j
                               I-E 1 r
Lloyd, Arthur Y.   II-F
Lloyd, Thomas E.   I-E 1 r
Locke, Alain.   II-H
Locke, Mary S.   II-D 1
Lockley, Edith.   III-A 1 b iv
Lockwood, Lewis.   III-C 2 a
Loescher, Frank S.   III-C 1 a
                                  III-D
                               IV-A 5
Loewen, Jacob A.   I-C
Logan, Rayford.   III-D
Loguen, Jermain W.   II-D 1
                               III-A 3
Lokos, Lionel.   IV-B
Lomax, Alan.   II-H
Lomax, J. A.   II-H
Lomax, Louis E.   III-A 2 b
Long, Charles.   III-A 1 a i
Long, Charles H.   I-C
                               III-A 4
                                V-B 1
Long, Herman H.   IV-A 1
Long, John D.   II-D 1
Longcope, Kay.   V-B 1
Longstreet, Augustus B.   II-D 1
Loram, Charles T.   I-C
Lord, John C.   II-D 7
Lord, Nathan.   II-D 7
Lord, Samuel E. C.   III-D
Lorew, Joseph.   IV-B
Lory, Maris J.   I-E 1 j
Loth, Heinrich.   I-E 3 e
Lotz, Adolf.   II-D 1
Lounsbury, Thomas.   II-C
Love, Edgar.   III-A 3
Love, Emanuel K.   III-A 1 a vi
                               III-A 4
Love, H. Lawrence.   III-C 1 g
Love, Horace T.   II-D 1
Love, J. Robert.   III-A 5
Love, William D.   II-D 1
Lovejoy, Joseph C.   II-C
Lovejoy, Owen.   II-C

Lovelace, John A.   V-B 3
Lovewell, Lyman.   II-D 1
Lowe, J. R.   V-A
Lubell, Samuel   III-C 1 l
Lucas, George W.
                          III-A 1 a viii
Lucas, J. Olumide.   I-C
Lucas, Lawrence.   V-E
Lucatello, Enrico.   I-E 1 k
Luccock, Halford E.   III-C 1 f
Ludwig, Charles.   I-E 1 d
Lugira, A. M.   I-C
Luke, James.   I-E 1 r
Lundy, John P.   II-C
Lunn, Arnold H. M.   II-F
Lupton, D. E.   III-E
Lutze, Karl E.   V-E
Lynch, Hollis R.   III-A 4
Lyon, Ernest.   III-C 1 f
Lyon, James A.   II-D 7
Lyons, Adelaide A.   II-C

Mabie, Catharine.   I-E 1 j
MacArthur, Kathleen W.   III-E
Macbeth, James.   II-C
Macdonald, Allan J.   I-E 1 r
Macdonald, Duff.   I-E 1 t
Macdonald, Eugene M.   II-D 1
Macdonald, James.   I-C
Macdonnell, John de C. I-E 1 j
Macgregor, J. K.   I-E 1 r
Macgregor-Hastie, Roy.
                               I-E 1 r
MacKay, Alexander M.   I-E 1 j
MacKaye, William R.   V-E
MacKenzie, J.   I-D
MacKenzie, Jean K.   I-E 1 m
MacKenzie, John.   I-E 1 s
MacKenzie, William D. I-E 1 c
MacKerrow, P.   III-A 1 a viii
MacKintosh, Catharine W.
                               I-E 1 g
                               I-E 1 s
                               I-E 1 t
MacLean, Angus H.   IV-A 14
Maclean, Norman.   I-E 1 t
MacMaster, Richard K.   II-F
MacMillan, Margaret (Burnham).
                               II-D 6
Maddocks, Lewis J.   IV-A 3
                                  V-A
Maddry, Charles E.   I-E 1 b

Madron, Thomas W.   III-C 1 f
Maesen, William A.   III-A 2 b
Maffett, Robert L.   III-D
Magee, J. H.   III-A 1 a viii
Magruder, Edith C.   III-C 1 k
Maguire, John D.   IV-B
Main, John K.   I-E 1 c
Maio, Augusto.   I-E 1 g
Majdalany, Gebran.   III-C 1 l
Makunike, Ezekiel C.   I-E 3 e
Malcolm X See Little, Malcolm.
Malcolm, L. W. D.   I-C
Malev, William S.   III-C 1 l
Mallard, Robert.   III-C 1 g
Mañaricua, Andres E. de. II-D 2
Mann, Harold W.   III-C 1 f
Mannoni, O.   III-A 3
Manschreck, Clyde L.   III-C 1 a
Mantinband, Charles.   III-C 1 l
Marais, Barend J.   I-E 1 r
March, Daniel.   II-D 1
Marcis, C. L.   IV-A 1
Margolies, Edward.   III-A 3
Maritain, Jacques.   III-D
Markoe, John P.   III-D
Markoe, William M.   III-A 3
                         III-C 1 b
                         III-C 2 a
Marr, Warren I. I.   V-D
Marrat, Jabez.   III-B
Marriott, Charles.   II-D 5
Marrow, Alfred J.   V-E
Marrs, Elijah P.   III-A 1 a viii
                         III-A 4
Marsh, J. B. T.   II-H
Marsh, Leonard.   II-C
Marsh, William H.   II-F
Marshall, Calvin B.   V-B 1
Marshall, Kenneth E.   V-A
Martin, Denis.   I-E 3 e
Martin, Douglas L.   V-D
Martin, Isaac P.   III-A 5
Martin, J. G.   III-D
Martin, John H.   II-D 10
Martin, John S.   III-A 4
Martin, Theodore.   III-C 1 k
Martin, W. C.   IV-C
Martin, Walter R.   III-A 2 b
Marty, Martin E.   III-A 3
Marvin, Abijah P.   II-D 1
Marx, Gary.   III-A 3
                         IV-A 1
Mason, C. B.   II-D 6

Mason, Madison C. B.   I-E 1 r
Mason, Philip.   V-E
Mason, William.   V-B 1
Massaia, Guglielmo (Cardinal).
                         I-E 1 k
Massey, James E.   III-A 1 b i
                         III-A 4
Massiah, J. Bowden. III-C 1 a
Massie, James W.   II-D 1
Masters, Henry.   I-E 1 l
Maston, Thomas B.   III-D
                         III-E
Mathe, Judy.   V-A
Mather, Cotton.   II-D 1
Mather, P. B.   IV-A 1
Mathews, Basil J.   I-C
                         I-E 1 r
Mathews, Donald G.   II-D 6
Mathews, Edward.   II-D 12
Mathews, J. K.   IV-A 6
Mathews, Marcia M.
                    III-A 1 a i
Matlack, Lucius C.   II-D 6
                         III-C 1 f

Mattingly, T.   IV-A 2
Mattison, Hiram.   II-D 6
May, George.   II-D 1
May, Samuel J.   II-D 1
                         II-D 10
                         II-F
Mayard, Aurora.   III-A 4
Mayer, M.   III-E
Mayo, Amory D.   III-D
Mays, Benjamin E.
                    III-A 1 a viii
                         III-A 3
                         III-A 4
                         III-C 1 a
                         III-D
                         IV-A 1
                         V-E
Mazrui, Ali A.   I-C
Mbiti, John S.   I-C
                         I-E 1 r
McAfee, Joseph E.   III-C 1 a
McAfee, Sara J.   III-A 1 a iii
M'Caine, Alexander.   II-C
McAll, Samuel.   II-D 8
McAlpine, William H. III-A 4
M'Carter, J. Mayland.   II-D 6
McAvoy, Thomas T.   III-C 1 b

McCabe, Joseph.	II-D 1	McNeill, Robert B.	III-D
McCall, Daniel F.	I-C	McNeilly, James H.	II-B
McCall, Emmanuel L.	V-B 1	McPeak, William.	V-A
McClain, William B.	V-B 1	McPeek, Francis W.	V-A
McClellan, G. E.	III-A 4	McTyeire, H. N.	II-B
McColl, C. W.	III-E	McWright, A.	II-C
McCord, William.	V-A	Meachum, John B.	III-A 1 a vi
McCorry, V. P.	III-C 1 b	Meacham, Standish.	II-D 1
McCoy, C.	IV-A 1	Mead, Frank S.	III-A 1 a viii
McCulloch, Margaret C.			III-A 3
	III-C 2 a		III-B
McCulloh, James E.	III-C 1 a	Meade, William.	II-B
	III-C 2 a	Mearns, John G.	V-A
McDaniels, Geraldine.	III-A 4	Mears, William.	I-E 1 c
McDermott, J. A.	IV-B	Mechan, Thomas F.	III-C 1 b
McDermott, Patrick.	V-E	Mecklin, John M.	III-D
McDermott, William F.	IV-A 6	Medbery, Rebecca B.	I-E 1 n
McDowell, Edward A.	III-D	Medford, Hampton T.	
McDowell, Henry C.	III-A 4		III-A 1 a ii
McEwen, Able.	II-D 3		III-A 4
McFarlan, Donald M.	I-E 1 s	Meehan, Thomas F.	III-C 1 b
McFerrin, John B.	III-A 5	Mehan, Joseph.	IV-A 2
McGiffert, Arthur C.	II-F	Meier, August.	III-A 3
McGill, Alexander T.	II-D 7		IV-C
McGill, Ralph.	IV-A 1	Melish, William H.	II-D 8
McGinnis, Frederick A.	III-D	Meltzer, Milton.	IV-B
McGlotten, Mildred L.	III-A 4	Memminger, C. G.	II-D 7
McGrath, Oswin O. P.	III-D	Mencken, H. L.	III-A 3
McGroarty, Joseph G.	III-C 1 b	Mendelsohn, Jack.	I-C
McGuire, U. M.	III-A 1 a viii	Mercer, Samuel A. B.	I-A
McIlhenny, Edward A.	II-H	Meredith, Thomas.	II-C
McIlvane, D. W.	III-D	Meridith, Robert.	II-F
McKay, Claude.	III-C 1 b	Merrill, Charles.	IV-A 14
McKay, John.	III-A 4	Merrill, Stephen E.	II-D 6
Mckeen, Silas.	II-C	Merton, Thomas.	IV-A 1
McKeon, Richard M.	III-C 1 a		V-A
McKelvey, Blake.	II-G	Merwick, Donna.	III-C 1 b
McKenna, David L.	V-A	Mett, John R.	I-B
McKiever, Charles.	II-D 5	Meyer, A. C.	III-D
McKinney, Richard I.		Meyers, R. N.	IV-A 1
	III-A 1 a viii	Michie, Doyne E.	IV-A 7
	III-D	Middeke, Raphael.	V-A
McLanahan, Samuel.	I-E 1 s	Migeod, Frederick W. H.	I-C
McLaughlin, Wayman B.	II-H	Mileham, Geoffrey S.	II-C
McLaurin, Dunbar S.	V-A	Miles, Edward.	II-D 5
McLees, A. V.	IV-A 2	Milingo, Emmanuel.	I-E 3 c
McLeod, Alexander.	II-D 7	Millea, Thomas V.	V-A
McManus, Eugene P.	IV-A 2	Miller, Basil W.	I-E 1 r
McManus, Michael J.	V-A	Miller, Ernest J.	III-A 4
McMillan, G.	IV-A 1	Miller, F. P.	IV-A 1
Mcmillan, Margaret B.	II-D 6	Miller, George F.	III-A 4
McMillan, William A.	III-C 1 f		III-C 1 h
McNeil, Jesse J.	III-A 4		III-E

Miller, Harriet P.   III-A 4
Miller, John J.   III-A 1 a ii
Miller, Kelly.   III-A 3
                              III-D
Miller, Paul M.   I-E 3 b
Miller, Perry.   IV-B
Miller, Richard R.   II-D 2
Miller, Robert M.   III-C 1 a
                              III-D
Miller, Samuel.   II-D 7
                               II-F
Miller, Theodore D.   III-A 4
Miller, Walter R. S.   I-C
                            I-E 1 b
Miller, William R.   III-A 3
                            IV-A 1
                              IV-B
Milles, John H.   III-A 1 a ii
Milligan, Robert H.   I-C
                            I-E 1 e
Mills, Job S.   I-E 1 r
Mills, M. Gertrude.   III-A 5
Minear, L.   IV-A 1
Minor, Richard C.   III-A 4
Mitchell, Constance.   I-E 3 c
Mitchell, E. O.   IV-A 6
Mitchell, Henry H.   III-A 4
                            IV-A 1
                             V-B 1
Mitchell, Joseph.   II-D 6
                           III-A 4
Mitchell, Richard P.   I-C
Mitchell, Robert C.   I-E 2
Mitchell, Robert E.   I-E 3 2
Mixon, W. H.   III-A 1 a i
M'Keown, Robert L.   I-E 1 b
Moberg, David O.   V-A
                               V-E
Mobley, Harris.   I-E 1 a
Moellering, Ralph L.   IV-A 1
Moffat, Robert.   I-E 1 g
Moister, William.   III-B
Mol, J.   V-E
Montgomery, H. H.   I-E 3 e
Montgomery, Leroy J.   III-A 3
                           III-A 4
Moody, Joseph N.   III-C 1 b
Moon, Bertha L. H.   III-A 4
Moon, Henry L.   III-A 2 b
Moor, Vincent de.   I-E 1 e
Moore, Clark D.   I-E 3 e
Moore, Dale H.   I-B
Moore, Edmund A.   II-D 7

Moore, George W.   III-C 2 a
Moore, H. E.   II-D 1
Moore, John J.   III-A 1 a ii
Moore, John M.   III-C 1 f
Moore, Joseph G.   II-A
Moore, Wilbert E.   II-F
Moorland, Jesse E.   III-A 4
                          III-C 2 a
Mooth, V.   IV-A 6
Morant, John J.   III-A 4
Mordell, Albert.   II-D 5
Moret, Alexandre.   I-A
Morgan, Carol M.   III-B
Morgan, Joseph H.   III-A 1 a i
Moroney, T. B.   III-C 1 b
Morrill, Anson P.   II-D 1
Morris, Charles S. III-A 1 a vi
                      III-A 1 a viii
Morris, Colin M.   I-E 3 e
                            I-E 3 d
Morris, Madison C. B.   III-A 4
Morris, Robert.   II-C
Morris, Samuel S.   III-A 1 a i
Morrisey, Richard A.   III-E
Morrison, George.   V-E
Morrison, James H.   I-E 1 r
Morrow, Ralph E.   II-G
Morse, Jedidiah.   II-D 1
Morse, Samuel F. B.   II-C
Morse, Sidney E.   II-C
                            II-D 1
Morse, W. H.   III-A 4
Morsell, John A.   III-A 2 b
                             V-B 3
Morton, Lena B.   III-A 4
Morton, William P.   I-E 3 a
Moseley, B. W.   III-C 1 g
Moses, William H.
                      III-A 1 a vii
                             III-E
Moss, James A.   V-B 1
Moss, Leonard W.   V-B 1
Motley, Constance B.   IV-A 10
Moton, Robert R.   III-D
Mott, John R.   I-E 1 r
Mott, Lucretia (Coffin).   II-F
Mouezy, Henri.   I-E 1 r
Moulton, Phillips.   II-D 1
Mounger, Dwyn.   III-C 1 g
Moxom, Philip S.   III-D
Mudge, James.   III-C 1 f
Mudge, Zachariah A.   II-D 1
Muelder, Walter.   III-A 3

Mueller, John T.   I-E 1 r
Mueller, Samuel A.   V-E
Muhammad, Elijah.   See Poole,
   Elijah.
Mulder, John M.   V-D
Murdock, John N.   II-D 12
Murphy, Edgar G.   III-D
Murphy, Edward F.   III-C 1 b
Murphy, Jeannette R.   II-H
Murphy, John C.   III-C 1 b
Murphy, Miriam T.   III-C 1 b
Murray, Albert V.   I-E 1 r
Murray, Andrew E.   II-D 7
Murray, Florence. III-A 1 a viii
Murray,   Michael H.   V-A
                              V-B
Murray, William.   II-A
Muste, Abraham J.   III-D
Mutwa, Credo V. M.   I-C
Mveng, Elgelbert.   I-C
Myer, Gustavus.   III-D
Myers, John B.   I-E 1 h
Myrdal, Gunnar.   III-A 3

Nadel, Siegfried F.   I-E 1 b
Nail, Olin W.   III-A 5
Nanna, John C.   III-A 5
Nannes, Caspar.   V-B 2
Narcisse, Louis H.   IV-B
Nash, J. O.   I-E 3 c
Nassau, Robert H.   I-C
                              I-E 1 h
                              I-E 1 r
National Council of the Churches
   of Christ in the United States
   of America.   See National
   Council of Churches.
Nau, Henry.   I-E 1 b
Naylor, Wilson S.   I-E 1 r
N'Daye, Jean P.   III-A 2 b
Neill, Stephen C.   I-E 3 e
Nelsen, Hart M.   III-C 1 g
                              V-B 1
Nelson, Clarence T. R.   III-A 5
Nelson, Isaac.   II-D 1
Nelson, John O.   III-E
Nelson, J. Robert.   I-C
                              IV-A 1
                              V-B 1
                              V-B 3
Nelson, Robert G.   I-E 3 e
                              I-E 1 j

Nelson, William S.   II-C
                              III-A 3
                              III-D
                              III-E
                              IV-C
Nerberg, Well.   IV-C
Nevin, Edwin H.   II-D 7
Nevin, John W.   II-C
Nevin, Robert.   II-C
Nevinson, Henry W.   I-E 1 r
Newborn, Captolia D.
                    III-A 1 a iii
Newby, Idus.   III-A 3
Newcomb, Harvey.   II-D 1
Newhall, Fales H.   II-F
Newman, Albert H.
                    III-A 1 a viii
Newman, Louis C.   II-C
Newman, Richard.   IV-A 14
                              V-B 1
Newsome, Effie L.   III-A 1 a i
                              III-A 4
Newton, Alexander H.
                    III-A 1 a i
Newton, John B.   III-A 3
                              III-C 1 h
Newton, Percy J.   III-A 3
Nichol, Francis D.   II-D 11
Nichols, Decatur W.   III-A 4
Nichols, L.   IV-A 1
Nichols, S.   IV-A 11
Nicholson, Alfred W.   III-D
Niebuhr, Helmut R.
                    III-A 1 a viii
Niebuhr, Reinhold.   IV-C
Niebuhr, Richard R.   IV-B 1
Niles, A.   II-H
Niles, John M.   II-D 5
Nina Rodrigues, Raymundo. I-C
Nisbet, Richard.   II-B
Nixon, Justin Wroe.   III-C 2 e
Nketia, J. H.   I-C
                              I-E 3 e
Noble, Frederic P.   I-E 3 e
Noble, Walter J.   I-E 3 c
Norman, Clarence.   IV-B 1
                              V-A
Norris, John W.   III-A 1 a i
Norris, Hoke.   V-E
North, Eric M.   I-E 1 r
Northcott, C.   I-C
Northcott, William C.   I-C
Northwood, Lawrence K. IV-A 1

Norton, W.   V-B 1   Osborne, J.   IV-B
Norwood, John N.   II-D 6   Osborne, William.   II-G
Noshy, Ibrahim.   I-B   IV-A 1
Nott, Samuel.   II-D 3   Osborne, William A.   III-C 1 b
Ntlabati, Gladstone.   V-B 1   III-D
Nuby, C.   IV-B   Osgood, Charles.   IV-A 8
Nuermberger, Ruth A.   II-D 5   Osir, Clerah.   I-C
Nunns, Theodora.   I-E 1 c   Ostheimer, Anthony L. III-C 1 b
Nygren, Malcolm.   IV-A 7   Ostling, Richard.   IV-B 2
Nystrom, Gertrude E.   I-E 1 s   Ottley, Roi.   III-A 1 b iv
                                      Overs, Walter H.   I-E 1 r
                                      Owen, Anna K.   II-H
Obatala, J. K.   V-B 1   Owen, Robert D.   II-C
O'Connel, Jeremiah J. III-C 1 b   Owens, I. V.   III-A 5
O'Connor, John J.   IV-A 2
Odell, Brian N.   V-A   Padwick, C. E.   I-E 1 s
O'Dell, J. H.   IV-B   Page, Jesse.   I-E 1 b
Odum, Howard W.   II-H   Palfrey, John G.   II-D 10
                          III-A 3   Palmer, Benjamin M.   II-B
Offley, Greenburg W.   II-D 1   II-D 7
                          III-A 4   Palmer, F. B.   III-A 1 a viii
O'Hanlon, Mary E. (Sister).   Palmer, John M.   III-A 1 a i
                          III-C 1 b   Palms, Charles L.   IV-A 2
Ohsberg, Harry O.   III-A 1 a vi   Pannell, William E.   V-E
Okon, Gabriel.   I-E 1 b   Parenti, Michael.   III-A 2 b
Olcott, John W.   III-A 4   Parker, E. C.   IV-A 3
Oldendorp, Christian G. A. III-B   Parker, J. Kenton.   III-C 1 a
Oldham, Joseph H.   I-E 1 j   Parker, Joel.   II-D 1
                          I-E 1 r   Parker, Robert A. III-A 1 b iv
                          III-D   Parker, Theodore.   II-C
Olinton, Desmond K.   I-E 1 c   II-D 10
Oliver, C. Herbert.   V-B 1   II-F
                          V-E   Parks, H. B.   III-A 1 a i
Oliver, Pearleen.   III-A 1 a viii   Parks, William J.   II-D 6
Oliver, Roland.   I-E 1 s   Parr, Martin W.   I-E 3 d
Olmstead, Clifton E.   III-A 4   Parratt, J. K.   I-E 3 a
Olson, Bernard E.   III-D   Parrinder, Edward G.   I-C
Olson, Gilbert W.   I-E 1 n   I-E 1 b
O'Neil, Michael J.   III-A 4   Parrish, Charles H.
O'Neill, Joseph E.   III-D   III-A 1 a vi
Oniki, S. Garry.   III-C 1 a   Parrish, John.   II-F
Onwauchi, Patrick C.   Parsons, A.   III-A 1 b ii
                    III-A 1 b iv   Parsons, Ellen C.   I-E 1 r
Oosthuizer, Gerhardus C.   I-C   Parsons, M. E.   I-E 1 q
                          I-E 3 e   Parsons, Robert T.   I-C
Orchard, R. F.   V-E   I-E 1 a
Orchard, Ronald K.   I-E 1 c   Parsons, Talcott.   III-D
                          I-E 1 r   Parsons, Theophilus.   II-D 1
O'Reilly, Charles T.   III-C 1 b   Parsonage, R. R.   IV-C
Orjala, Paul.   III-B   Paton, Alan.   I-E 3 c
O'Rorke, M.   I-E 1 a   III-D
Orton, Hazel V.   III-E   IV-A 1
Osborn, Charles.   II-D 5   V-E

Paton, David M.   I-E 1 c
Paton, William.   V-E
Patten, William.   II-D 3
Patterson, Bernardin J.   III-A 4
Patterson, Caleb P.   II-D 1
Patterson, James.   II-D 1
Patterson, Joseph N.   III-C 2 f
Patterson, Lillie.   IV-B
Patterson, S. J.   III-A 4
Patton, C.   I-E 1 r
Patton, Cornelius H.   I-C
Patton, Robert W.   III-A 5
Patton, William W.   II-C
   II-D 1
   II-D 3
Paul, Austin.   I-E 1 j
Paul, Joan.   V-A
Paul, Nathaniel.   II-F
   III-A 4
Paulding, James K.   II-C
Pauw, Berthold B. A.   I-C
Pawelzik, Fritz.   I-E 3 e
Paxton, John D.   II-D 1
Payne, Buckner H.   III-E
Payne, Christopher.   III-A 4
Payne, Daniel A.   III-A 1 a i
   III-A 3
   III-A 4
Payne, Enoch G.   III-D
Payne, Ethel L.   V-A
   V-B 1
Payne, John.   I-E 1 o
Payton, Benjamin F.   V-A
p'Bitek, Okot.   I-E 1 r
Peabody, Andrew P.   II-D 10
Peabody, Charles.   II-H
Peabody, George B.   I-E 1 o
Peabody, William B.   II-D 1
   II-F
Peacock, Amjogollo E.   I-E 1 n
Pearce, Gordon J.   I-E 1 j
Pearne, Thomas H.   II-G
   III-D
Pearson, Colbert H.   III-A 1 viii
Peck, George.   II-D 6
Peck, H. W.   III-A 4
Peck, Nathaniel   II-F
Pederson, Pernie C.   I-E 1 c
Peel, John D. Y.   I-C
   I-E 3 a
Peckard, Peter.   II-F
Peeters, Paul.   I-E 1 j
Pegues, Albert W.   III-A 1 a vi

Pelt, Owen D.   III-A 1 a vi
Pemberton, John De J.   IV-A 4
Penetar, Michael P.   III-C 1 b
Penn, Irvine G.   III-A 3
   III-A 4
   III-C 2 a
Pennington, Edgar L.   II-B
Pennington, James W. C.   II-D 3
   III-A 4
Percy, Douglas C.   I-E 1 b
Perez, Joseph A.   III-C 1 f
   V-D
Perkins, A. E.   II-H
   III-A 4
Perkins, Haven P.   II-B
Perkins, Justin.   II-D 1
Perlo, Filippo.   I-E 1 d
Perry, Calbraith B.   III-A 5
Perry, David B.   V-B 2
Perry, Lewis.   II-C
Perry, Naomi.   III-A 1 a i
Perry, Nathaniel.   II-C
Perry, Rufus L.   II-C
   III-A 4
Persons, I. S.   III-A 1 vi
Peters, W.   IV-B
Peterson, Daniel H.   III-A 4
Peterson, Frank L.   III-A 5
   III-D
Petrie, William M.   I-A
Pettiford, William R.   III-A 4
Pettigrew, M. C.   III-A 1 a iii
Pettigrew, Thomas F.   III-D
   IV-A 1
Pharr, Julia M.   II-C 1 e
Phelan, Macum.   II-D 6
Phelps, Amos A.   II-C
Phillips, Charles H.
   III-A 1 a iii
Phillips, Henry L.   III-A 5
Phillips, J. E. Tracy.   I-C
Phillips, Ray E.   I-E 1 r
Pickens, Andrew L.   II-D 7
Pickett, Clarence E.   II-D 5
Piepkorn, Arthur C.
   III-A 1 a vi
Pierce, Alfred M.
   III-A 5
Pierce, David H.   III-C 1 1
Pierce, Paul S.   II-G
Pierenne, Jacques.   I-A
Pierpont, Ivan de.   I-E 1 j
Pierpont, John.   II-D 1

Pierre, C. E.   II-D 1
Pierson, Arthur T.   I-E 1 n
                             I-E 1 r
Pike, Esther.   III-D
Pike, G. D.   II-H
Pilch, Judah.   IV-A 12
Pilkington, F.   I-E 3 a
Pilkington, Frederick.   III-B
Pilkington, George.   II-D 2
Pillsbury, Parker.   II-D 1
                             II-F
Pilpel, H. F.   IV-B
Pineau, Henry.   I-E 1 t
Pinnington, John.   III-B
Pipes, William Harrison.   III-A 3
Pipkin, James J.   III-A 3
Pistorius, Philippus V.   I-E 3 c
Pitcher, Alvin.   IV-B
                             V-E
Pitman, Frank W.   II-A
                             II-B
Pitts, S. G.   I-E 3 c
Pius, N. H.   III-A 1 a vi
Pleasants, D. M.   III-A 3
Plecker, W. A.   III-E
Ploski, Harry A.   III-A 3
Plumer, William S.   II-B
Podhoretz, Norman.   III-C 1 l
Pohlhaus, J. Francis.   IV-A 2
Poindexter, James.   III-A 4
Poinsett, Alex.   III-A 3
                             III-E
                             V-B 1
Pollard, Myrtle E.   III-A 3
Ponton, M. M.   III-A 4
Pool, Frank K.   III-A 5
Poole, Elijah.   III-A 2 b
Pope, Liston.   III-A 3
                             III-D
                             IV-A 1
                             IV-C
                             V-E
Porteous, A. C.   IV-A 1
Porter, Dorothy.   II-D 1
Porter, Noah.   II-D 1
Posey, Walter B.   II-D 1
                             II-D 6
                             II-D 7
                             II-D 8
                             II-D 12
                             III-A 5
                             III-C 1 k
Poteat, Ervin M.   III-A 3

Potter, Alonzo.   II-D 1
Pottinger, John L.   III-A 1 a i
Poulard, Grady E.   III-A 2 b
Pound, Louise.   II-H
Powdermaker, Hortense.
                             III-A 3
Powell, Adam Clayton, (Jr.).
                             III-A 1 a viii
                             III-A 3
                             III-A 4
                             III-D
                             V-B 1
Powell, Adam Clayton, (Sr.).
                             III-A 3
                             III-A 4
                             III-C 1 a
Powell, Don.   V-A
Powell, Jacob W.   III-A 1 a ii
Powell, Raphael P.   III-D
Powell, Ruth M.   III-A 1 a viii
Poynter, W. T.   III-C 1 a
Pratt, S. A. J.   I-E 3 e
Pratt, Waldo S.   II-H
Preher, Leo Marie (Sister).
                             III-C 1 b
Pressoir, Catts.   III-B
Preston, J. T. L.   III-A 3
Prestwood, Charles M.
                             III-C 1 f
                             IV-A 1
Price, Ernest.   III-B
Price, Ira M.   I-A
Price, Jo-Ann.   V-B 1
Price, Joseph C.   III-A 4
Price, Thomas.   III-A 3
Priest, Josiah.   II-C
Priestly, Joseph.   II-F
Prindle, Cyrus.   II-C
Pritchard, James B.   I-A
Proctor, Henry H.   III-A 4
Proctor, Henry H.   II-H
Proctor, Samuel D.   IV-C
Prothro, E. Terry.   III-D
Puaux, Frank.   I-E 1 c
Puckett, Newbell N.   II-H
                             III-A 3
Pullen, Wm. H.   II-D 6
Puller, F. W.   I-E 2
Purce, Charles L.   III-A 4
Purnell, J. M.   IV-C
Purvis, John B.   I-E 1 j
Purvis, Robert.   II-D 1
Putnam, George.   II-D 1

Putnam, George (cont.). II-D 3
Putnam, Mary B. II-B 12
Putney, Snell. V-A

Quaintance, Charles W. V-E
Quarles, Benjamin. II-F
  III-A 1 a vi
  IV-B
Quatrefoges de Breau, A.
  I-E 1 r
Quayle, W. A. III-A 3
Quint, Alonzo Hall. II-D 3
Quinton, G. G. H. I-B
Quon, Jessica. III-C 1 a

Rabb, Earl III-A 2 b
  V-C
Radin, Paul. I-C
Ragan, Roger. IV-A 6
Rainwater, Lee. V-A
Ramos, Arthur. II-A
Ramsaur, William H. I-E 1 o
Ramsay, James. II-A
  II-C
Ramsey, Paul. IV-B
Ramseyer, Friedrick A. I-E a
Rand, Earl W. III-A 1 a viii
Randall, Virginia R. III-C 1 g
Randolph, A. Philip. III-D
Randolph, Edwin A. III-A 4
Rankin, Charles H. II-G
Rankin, Jeremiah E. III-C 1 c
Rankin, John. II-D 1
  II-F
Ransom, C. N. I-E 1 r
Ransom, Reverly C. III-A 1 a i
  III-A 3
  III-A 4
Ransome, William L.
  III-A 1 a vi
Raphall, Morris J. II-C
Rashford, N. J. V-A
Rashke, Richard. V-B 1
  V-B 2
Rasky, Frank. III-A 1 b iv
Rattray, Robert S. I-C
Rawson, David P. I-E 3 e
Ray, J. E. IV-B
Raymond, Charles A. II-B
Read, Margaret. III-D
Reading, Joseph H. I-E 1 s

Reapsome, J. W. III-A 1 b v
Reaves, A. I-E 3 c
Record, Wilson. III-A 2 b
Reddick, Lawrence C. IV-B
Reddis, Jacob L. III-C 2 b
Redford, A. H. II-D 6
Redi, Gaines S. III-A 1 a i
Reed, John H. III-C 1 f
Reed, John M. III-A 4
Reed, Richard C. III-C 1 a
Reemer, Theodore. III-C 1 b
Rees, A. Herbert. I-B
Reeves, Richard A. I-E 3 c
Reid, Barney F. III-A 1 a vi
Reid, Ira de A. III-A 1 a vi
  III-A 1 b v
  III-A 3
  III-D
Reid, Stevenson N. III-A 1 a vi
Reimers, David M. III-C
  III-D
  IV-A 7
  V-E
Reiss, Julian J. III-A 4
Relyea, Harold C. V-B 1
Renard, Alice. III-A 3
Resenbrink, Dorothy. V-B 3
Reston, James. IV-A 1
Reuter, Edward B. III-A 3
Reuter, George S. IV-A 1
Reyburn, William D. I-E 3 a
  I-E 3 e
Reynolds, Barries. I-C
Reynolds, Edward D. III-C 1 b
Reynolds, Elhanan W. II-D 1
Reynolds, Grant. II-D 1
Reynolds, Louis B. III-A 4
Reynolds, Mary C. III-A 1 vi
Rhodes, Rhoda. V-A
Rice, David. II-D 7
Rice, Edwin B. I-E 1 o
Rice, Esme R. I-E 1 k
Rice, Gene. V-E
Rice, Joseph S. III-C 1 g
Rice, Madeleine H. II-D 2
Rice, Willa M. V-B 1
Richards, Charles G. I-E 1 r
Rhoads, Samuel. II-D 5
Richards, James M. III-A 5
  III-E
Richardson, Harry V. III-A 3
Richardson, James. I-E 1 s
Richardson, Joe M. II-G

III-C 2 f   Rohler, J.   IV-B

Richardson, Lee.   III-A 3   Rohrer, John H.   III-A 1 a viii
Richardson, Lincoln.   I-E 2   Rokeach, Milton.   III-D
                            V-A   Rollins, J. Metz.   V-B 2
Richardson, W. H.   IV-B   Roman, Charles V.   I-E 1 j
Richie, Willis T.   III-A 3   III-A 1 a i
Richings, G. F.   III-A 3   III-A 3
Richmond, Legh.   II-B   III-D
                            II-D 1   Romero, Emanuel A.   III-C 1 b
Richmond, Thomas.   II-D 1   Romero, P. W.   IV-B
Ricks, George R.   II-H   Rooks, Charles S.   III-A 3
Riddell, William R.   II-D 12   III-A 4
Riddick, John H.   III-A 3   III-E
Ridgel, Alfred L.   III-A 5   V-A
Ridout, D. L.   III-C 1 f   V-B 2
Ridout, Lionel U.   III-D   Rookwood, George L.   II-F
Rigord.   II-D 2   Roome, William J. W.   I-C
Riley, Benjamin F.   III-C 1 k   I-E 1 j
Riley, Helen.   III-C 1 b   I-E 1 r
Riley, Walter H.   III-A 5   Roosevelt, Eleanor.   III-D
Riley, Willard D.   I-B   Root, David.   II-D 1
Rinder, Irwin D.   IV-A 12   II-D 3
Ring, Rodney E.   II-D 1   II-F
Ritchie, M. A. F.   III-C 1 i Root, Robert.   IV-C
Robert, Mattie A. III-A 1 a viii   V-E
Roberts, Andrew D.   I-E 2   Rorty, James.   III-C 1 l
Roberts, Elizabeth H. III-C 1 h   Roscoe, John.   I-C
Roberts, Harriet C.   V-A   Rose, Arnold M.   III-A 2 b
Roberts, James D.   III-A 3   III-D
                            III-D   IV-C
                            V-B 1   Rose, Benjamin L.   V-E
                            V-B 2   Rose, George H.   II-A
Ross, Brownlee J.   I-C   Rose, Ralph.   II-D 5
                            I-E 1 c   Rose, Peter I.   IV-A 1
Robertson, Archibald T.   II-H   Rose, Stephen C.   III-E
                            III-A 3   IV-A 1
Robertson, William J. III-C 1 a   IV-D
Robinson, James H.   I-E 1 r   V-B 3
                            III-A 4   Roseberry, Robert S.   I-E 1 r
                            III-D   Rosenberg, Bruce A.   III-A 4
                            V-E   Rosenblum, A. L.   III-D
Robinson, J. P.   III-A 4   Ross, Emory.   I-E 1 r
Robinson, John.   II-D 7   I-E 3 c
Robinson, Robert.   II-C   Ross, Frederick A.   II-D 1
Robinson, William C.   III-E   II-D 7
Roche, Richard J.   III-A 5   Ross, Harry.   IV-C
Roddy, Sherman S.   V-B 3   Ross, James R.   V-E
Rogers, Cornish.   III-A 3   Ross, William S.   II-D 1
                            IV-B   Rosten, Leo.   III-A 1 a viii
Rogers, Henry W.   III-C 1 f Roston, David W.   III-A 4
Rogers, Jefferson P.   V-B 1   Rotberg, Robert I.   I-E 3 e
Rogers, Tommy W.   II-D 7   Rothberg, Robert I.   I-E 1 l
Rogers, Walter C.   III-A 4   Rountree, Malachi D.   IV-A 1

Rouse, Michael F.   III-C 1 b
Rowan, Carl T.   IV-B
Rowland, Stanley J.   IV-A 1
                             V-E
Roy, Ralph C.   III-C 1 a
Roy, Ralph L.   IV-A 1
                             IV-A 6
                             V-E
Ruark, G.   IV-A 1
Rubenstein, Richard L.   IV-A 12
Ruchames, Louis.   II-F
Rudwick, Elliot M.   III-A 3
Ructher, Rosemary.   I-E 1 f
                             V-B 1
                             V-D
Ruggles, David.   II-F
Rumbough, Constance.   III-C 1 f
Ruoss, Meryl.   IV-C
Rush, Benjamin.   II-C
Rush, Christopher.   III-A 1 a i
                          III-A 4
Rusillon, Henry.   I-C
Rusling, G. W.   III-A 1 a viii
Russell, Charles L.   III-A 4
Russell, Daniel H.   III-A 1 a viii
Russell, James S.   III-A 3
Russell, Jean.   V-E
Russell, Michael.   I-A
Russo, Pasquale.   II-D 1
Rust, Richard S.   III-C 1 f
Rustin, Bayard.   III-C 1 l
Rutenber, C. G.   V-B 1
Rutherford, J.   I-E 1 r
Rutledge, A.   III-A 3
Rutledge, Arthur B.   III-C 1 k
Rutledge, D.   III-A 4
Ryland, Robert.   II-B

Sachs, Bernard.   I-E 3 c
Sackey, Isaac.   I-E 3 a
Sadler, George W.   I-E 1 b
Sailer, Thomas H. P.   I-E 1 r
St. John, B.   I-D
Sales, Jane.   I-E 2
Sales, Richard.   I-E 1 c
Salley, Columbus.   V-A
Salotti, Carlo.   I-E 1 j
Salten, David G.   III-D
Salter, William.   II-D 3
Salviac, Martial de.   I-E 1 k
Samarin, William J.   I-E 3 e
Sampson, John P.   III-A 1 a i

Samuels, Gertrude.   III-A 2 b
Sanders, William D.   II-D 3
Salisbury, W. Seward.   III-D 3
Sanford, Elias B.   III-D
Sangree, Walter H.   I-E 1 d
Sargent, Charles J.
                       III-A 1 a viii
Satterwhite, John H.   III-A 5
                             V-B 1
                             V-D
Saunders, F. Brooks.   V-D
Savage, Horace C.   III-A 4
Sawyer, Leicester A.   II-C
Sayre, Charles A.   V-B 3
Scarlett, William.   III-D
Schab, Fred.   III-A 3
Schackern, Harold.   V-B 1
Schaff, Philip.   II-C
                           II-D 1
Schaller, Lyle E.   III-A 2 b
                             V-A
Schaub, Friedrich.   II-D 1
Schauffler, A. F.   I-E 1 b
Scheiner, Seth M.   III-A 3
Schermerhorn, Richard A.
                       III-A 1 b v
Schneider, Louis.   IV-A 1
Schneider, T.   I-E 3 c
Schockley, G.   V-B 4
Schon, James F.   I-E 1 s
Schoener, Allon   III-A 4
Scholler, Clement.   I-E 1 j
Schomburg, Arthur A.   III-A 3
                          III-A 4
Schomer, H.   IV-A 1
                           V-B 2 e
                             V-B 3
Schooler, R.   IV-A 6
Schouler, James.   II-D 1
Schrag, P.   IV-B
Schreyer, George M.   II-D 6
Schuchter, Arnold.   V-B 3
Schulz, Larold K.   IV-A 1
                             IV-A 3
Schulz, W.   IV-B
Schulze, Andrew.   III-D
Schuyler, G. S.   III-D
Schuyler, Joseph B.   IV-A 1
                             IV-A 2
Scott, Allen L.   III-A 5
Scott, Anna M.   I-E 1 c
Scott, Michael.   II-D 1
Scott, Nathan A.   III-A 4

Scott, Orange.   II-D 6   Shepherd, Robert H. W. I-E 1 c
Scott, Osborne S.   III-A 4   I-E 3 c
Scott, Robert L.   IV-B   Shepherd, Wilhelmina.   IV-A 1
Seabury, Samuel.   II-D 8   Shepherd, William H.   I-E 1 j
Sears, Edmund H.   II-D 1   I-E 1 r
Sease, Rosalyn S.   III-C 1 i Shepperson, George.   I-E 1 t
See, Ruth D.   IV-C   Sherman, Anthony C.   III-D
Seebach, Margaret R.   I-E 1 o   Sherman, Richard B.   III-A 1 b
Seiler, J. E.   IV-A 6   Sherwin, Mark.   III-A 2 b
                          V-E   Sherwin, Oscar.   II-F
Sellers, James E.   III-D   Sherwood, Grace H.   III-C 1 b
Semple, Robert B.   III-A 1 a vi Shillito, Edward.   I-E 1 r
Sengstacke, John H.   V-C   III-A 4
Senior, Robert C.   II-D 3   Shinn, Roger L.   III-C 1 c
Senn, Milton.   V-A   Shipley, David O.   V-E
Senser, Robert.   IV-A 2   Shipp, Albert M.   III-A 5
Sesser, Robert.   III-C 1 b Shirmer, Charles F.   II-B
Sessions, R. P.   V-E   Shockley, Donald G.   III-A 3
Setiloane, Gabriel M.   I-E 3 c   V-B 4
                          V-E   V-E
Seville, Janet E.   III-C 1 g Shorter, Susie I.   III-A 1 a i
Sewall, Samuel.   II-D 1   Shriver, Donald W.   V-D
Sexton, Jessie E.   II-D 3   V-E
Seymour, R.   IV-A 1   Shurden, Walter B.   III-C 1 k
Shack, William S.   III-A 2 b Sibley, James L.   I-E 1 o
Shaffer, Helen B.   III-D   Siebert, Wilbur H.   II-D 5
Shanks, Caroline L.   II-C   Sibree, James.   I-E 1 s
Shannon, Alexander H.   I-C   Sideboard, Henry Y.
                          III-C 1 a   III-A 1 a iii
Sharma, Mohan L.   IV-B   Sihler, Wilhelm.   II-C
Sharp, Granville.   II-C   Silver, Abba H.   III-C 1 a
Sharp, W.   I-E 1 r   Silver, James W.   III-C 1 a
Sharrieff, Osman.   III-A 2 b Skinner, Tom.   III-A 4
Shaw, Alexander P.   III-A 4   Simmons, George F.   II-F
                          III-D   Simmons, William J.   III-A 4
Shaw, Benjamin G.   III-A 4   Simms, David M.   V-A
Shaw, Daniel W.   III-C 1 f Simms, James.   III-D
Shaw, George B.   III-A 4   Simms, James M.
Shaw, Herbert B.   III-A 4   III-A 1 a viii
Shaw, James B. F.   III-A 4   Simms, Joseph D.   III-A 4
                          III-A 5   Simon, A.   V-A
Shaw, Mabel.   I-E 1 l   Simon, Jean M.   I-E 1 r
Shaw, Rodney.   IV-B   Simons, Norman G.   III-C 1 j
Shaw, Trever.   I-E 1 b   Simpson, George E.   III-D
Shaw, William.   I-E 1 c   Simpson, J. David.   III-D
Sheares, Reuben A.   V-B 1   Simpson, Matthew.   II-D 6
Shedd, William G. T.   II-D 7   Sims, David.   III-A 1 a viii
Sheerin, John B.   I-E 3 c   Sinclair, Georges H.   III-A 3
                          III-D   Singleton, George A.   II-B
                          IV-A 2   III-A 1 a i
Sheild, R. N.   III-D   Sipkins, Henry.   II-D 1
Shelling, Richard I.   II-D 8   Sisk, Glenn N.   III-A 3
Shepherd, George W.   V-E   Sissel, H. B.   IV-A 7

Sitton, C.	IV-B	Smith, Timothy L.	II-D 1
	V-B 1	Smith, William A.	II-D 1
Sketon, D. E.	III-A 5	Smothers, Felton C.	III-A 4
Skinner, Tom.	III-A 4	Smucker, Orden C.	II-D 5
Skolaster, Hermann	I-D 1 m	Smylie, James.	II-D 7
Slack, Kenneth.	IV-B	Smylie, James H.	IV-A 7
Slattery, John R.	II-D 7		IV-B
	III-A 5	Smythe, Lewis.	III-C 1 d
	III-C 1 b	Snedecor, James G.	III-C 1 g
Sleeper, Charles F.	V-B 1	Snell, C. D.	I-E 1 c
Slicer, Henry.	II-D 6	Snowden, Frank M.	I-B
Sloane, James R. W.	II-D 7	Soper, Edmund D.	III-C 1 f
Small, John R.	II-D 1	Sottochiesa, Gino.	I-E 1 k
	III-A 4	Soulen, Richard N.	V-B 1
Smectymnuus, pseud.	II-D 1	Sourey, J. C.	I-C
Smedes, Susan D.	II-B	Southall, Eugene P.	III-C 1 f
Smit, M. T. R.	I-E 1 c	Southard, S.	IV-A 1
Smith, Allen H.	III-A 3	Southern, Arthur E.	I-E 1 a
Smith, Amanda.	III-A 4	Sowande, Fela.	I-C
Smith, Asa D.	II-D 7	Spain, Rufus B.	III-C 1 k
Smith, Charles S.	III-A 1 a i	Spalding, David.	III-A 5
Smith, David.	III-A 1 a i	Speaks, R. L.	III-A 3
Smith, E.	II-C	Spear, Allan H.	V-A
Smith, Earnest A.	IV-C	Spear, Samuel T.	II-D 1
Smith, Edwin W.	I-C	Spearman, Aurelia L. P.	
	I-E 1 c		III-A 4
	I-E 1 r	Spearman, Henry K.	III-A 4
	I-E 1 l	Speel, C. J.	I-C
Smith, Edward	II-D 7	Speer, Robert E.	I-E 1 r
Smith, Elwyn A.	IV-A 1		III-C 2 a
Smith, Frances S.	V-E	Speers, Wallace C.	III-A 4
Smith, George.	III-A 4	Spellman, A. B.	III-A 2 b
Smith, Gerrit.	II-D 7	Spence, Hartzell.	III-A 1 a viii
	II-F	Spencer, David.	III-A 1 a vi
Smith, Goldwin.	II-C	Spencer, Dwight.	III-A 1 a viii
Smith, H. H.	III-A 4	Spencer, Ichabod S.	II-D 7
Smith, H. Shelton.	II-D 7	Sperry, Willard L.	III-A 3
Smith, H. Sutton.	I-E 1 j		III-D
Smith, Henry.	II-D 1	Spiegel, Irving.	V-C
Smith, Herbert M.	I-E 1 f	Spike, Robert W.	IV-A 1
Smith, Hubert W.	III-A 4	Spivey, Charles S.	III-A 4
Smith, J. Allister.	I-E 1 c	Spivey, R. A.	IV-A 1
Smith, James H.	III-A 1 a i	Spring, Gardiner.	II-F
Smith, Jeremiah.	II-C	Springer, John M.	I-E 1 j
Smith, John W.	III-A 4		I-E 1 s
Smith, Lillian.	III-C 1 a	Springes, Helen E.	I-E 1 j
	III-D	Spurlock, Frank.	III-C 1 g
Smith, Lucius E.	I-E 1 o	Spywood, G. A.	III-A 4
Smith, Noel.	I-E 3	Staab, Giles J.	III-C 1 b
Smith, Norma J.	IV-A 10	Stackhouse, Max L.	V-B 3
Smith, Paul D.	III-A 4	Stackhouse, Perry J.	
Smith, Robert E.	III-D		III-A 1 a vi
Smith, Robert W.	II-A	Stacy, George W.	II-H

Staehelin, Felix.   III-B   Stock, Sarah G.   I-E 1 j
Stagg, Paul L.   IV-A 1   Stokes, A. Jackson.   III-A 4
Staiger, C. Bruce.   II-F   Stokes, James C.   II-D 6
Stakely, Charles A.   Stokes, Olivia P.   III-A 1 a vi
                       III-A 1 a viii   Stone, Betty.   IV-A 4
Stampp, Kenneth M.   II-D 1   Stone, M.   V-B 4
Stange, Douglas C.   III-A 4   Stone, Thomas T.   II-D 1
Stanley, M. W.   I-E 1 r   Storrs, Richard S.   II-D 3
Stanton, Henry B.   II-F   III-C 2 f
Stanton, Robert L.   II-D 1   Stotts, Herbert E.   III-C 1 f
Stanton, William R.   II-D 1   Stoutemeyer, John H.   III-D
Starkey, Marion L.   II-D 3   Stow, N.   I-C
Starr, Edward C.   III-C 1 k
Starr, Paul.   V-B 1   Stowe, David M.   I-E 1 d
Stauffer, Milton T.   I-E 1 r   Stowe, Harriet E.   II-C
Stearns, Oliver.   II-F   II-D 1
Steele, Algernon O.   III-C 1 g Stowe, Lyman B.   II-F
                             III-E   Stowell, Jay S.   III-C 1 f
Steele, Henry M.   III-A 1 a viii   Strange, Robert.   III-A 3
                             IV-A 11   Streeter, S. W.   II-C
Steele, J.   II-D 1   Streicher, Henri.   I-E 1 j
Stegall, W.   V-E   Stringfellow, Thornton.   II-C
Steinthal, S. Alfred.   II-D 10   Stringfellow, William. III-A 1 h
Stephenson, George M.   II-D 1   IV-A 1
Stephenson, Isaiah H.   III-A 4   V-C
Stephenson, John W.   III-A 4   V-E
Stepp, Diane.   IV-A 1   Stripling, Paul W.   III-C 1 k
                             V-B 1   Strom, Herbert E.   II-D 1
                             V-B 2   Stromberg, Jerome.   V-A
Sterrett, N. B.   III-A 1 a i   Stroyer, Jacob.   III-A 4
Stetson, Caleb.   II-D 3   Stuart, Charles.   II-C
Stevens, Abel.   II-D 6   II-F
                             III-A 4   Stuart-Watt, Eva.   I-E 1 f
Stevens, D. A.   I-E 3 e   Stuber, Stanley Irving.
Stevens, Francis B.   III-D   III-C 2 e
Stevens, George E.   III-A 3   Stuntz, Hugh Clark.   III-C 2 a
Stevenson, J. D.   III-A 1 a viii   III-C 2 e
Stevenson, J. W.   III-A 4   Sullivan, Kathryn.   III-E
Stevick, Daniel B.   IV-C   Sullivan, Leon H.   V-A
Steward, Theophilus G.   Summer, Charles.   II-D 1
                       III-A 1 a i   Sunderland, La Roy.   II-C
                             III-A 4   II-D 1
                             III-A 5   Sundkler, Bengt G. M.   I-C
Stewart, James.   I-E 1 r   I-E 3 c
Stewart, John J.   V-E   Sutherland, Robert L.   III-A 3
Stewart, Maria W.   III-A 1 a vi   III-C 2 a
                             III-A 4   Swaney, Charles B.   II-D 6
Stiles, B. J.   V-B 1   Sweeney, Odile.   IV-A 1
Stiles, Joseph C.   II-D 7   Sweet, William W.   II-D 12
Stinetorf, Louise A.   I-E 1 j   II-D 1
Stirewalt, M. L.   IV-A 1   II-D 6
Stirling, Leader.   I-E 1 f   II-G
Stock, Eugene.   I-E 3 e   II-H

Sweet, Wm. W. (cont.)
    III-A 1 a viii
    III-C 1 f
Swift, Job.   III-A 4
Sylvester, H.   III-A 5
Synder, John.   III-A 1 a vi

Taft, A. A.   IV-A 1
Talbert, Horace.   III-A 1 a viii
Talbot, Edith A.   II-H
Talbot, Percy.   I-E 1 r
Tanenbaum, Marc H.   III-D
Tallant, Robert.   III-A 1 b iv
Tankerson, Richard E.
    III-A 1 a viii
Tannenbaum, Frank.   II-D 1
Tanner, Benjamin T. III-A 1 a i
    III-A 4
Tanner, Carlton M. III-A 1 a i
Tanner, R. E. S.   I-E 3 e
    I-E 3 b
Tappan, Lewis.   II-D 1
    II-D 7
    II-F
Tarplee, Cornelius C.   III-D
Tarry, Ellen.   III-C 1 b
Tarter, Charles L.   III-A 3
Tatum, E. Ray.   III-A 4
Taves, I.   IV-A 1
Taylor, Alrutheus A.   II-G
Taylor, Bartlett.   III-A 4
Taylor, Edward B.   III-C 1 a
Taylor, George F.   III-C 1 a
Taylor, Howard E.   IV-A 2
Taylor, Hubert V.   II-D 7
Taylor, Isaac L.   III-A 3
    III-C 1 f
Taylor, James B.   III-A 4
Taylor, Joe G.   II-D 1
Taylor, John V.   I-C
    I-E 1 l
    I-C
Taylor, Marilyn.   III-C 1 d
Taylor, Marshall W.   II-H
    III-A 4
Taylor, Paul L.   III-D
Taylor, Preston.   III-A 4
Taylor, Richard K.   IV-A 5
Taylor, Stephen E.   I-E 1 r
Taylor, Thomas J.   II-D 6
Taylor, William.   I-E 1 c
    I-E 1 r

Teba, Wea.   III-A 5
Tegnaeus, Harry.   I-C
Tempcls, Placide.   I-C
Terry-Thompson, Arthur C.
    I-C
Thayer, William M.   II-D 1
Theobald, Stephen L. III-C 1 b
Thering, M. Rose.   III-D
Thielicke, Helmut.   IV-A 1
Thirkield, Mary H.   III-A 5
Thirkield, Wilbur P.
    III-A 1 a viii
    III-A 3
    III-A 5
    III-C 1 f
Thomas, Alfred A.   II-D 7
Thomas, Allen C.   II-D 5
Thomas, C. W.   IV-B
Thomas, Edgar G. III-A 1 a vi
Thomas, Harold A.   V-B 1
Thomas, James S.   III-A 3
    III-A 5
Thomas, George B.   I-E 2
Thomas, John L.   III-C 1 b
Thomas, Mary S.   III-C 2 a
Thomas, Neil.   V-B 1
Thomas, Thomas E.   II-B
    II-D 7
Thompkins, Roberta E.
    III-C 1 g
Thompson, Andrew.   II-D 1
Thompson, Charles H.   III-D
Thompson, Daniel C.   III-A 4
Thompson, Ernest T.   II-D 7
    III-C 1 g
    III-E
Thompson, George.   I-E 1 n
    II-D 1
    II-D 6
    II-D 7
    II-F
Thompson, J. Earl.   V-B 1
Thompson, John H.   III-E
Thompson, Joseph P.   II-C
    II-D 1
Thompson, L.   II-C
    II-D 3
Thompson, Patrick H.
    III-A 1 a vi
Thompson, R. Ward. I-E 1 r
Thompson, Robert E.   II-D 7
Thompson, T.   IV-A 6
Thompson, Thomas.   II-C

Thompson, Vincent B.   I-E 3 e
Thompson, W.   I-C
Thomson, Andrew M.   II-D 1
Thoonen, J. P.   I-E 1 j
Thorman, Donald J.   IV-A 2
Thorne, Richard.   III-A 2 b
Thornton, Douglas M.   I-E 1 r
Thornwell, James H.   II-B
Thrall, Homer S.   III-A 1 a iii
                          III-A 5
Thrift, Charles T.   III-A 5
Thurman, Howard.   II-H
                          III-A 4
                          III-D
                          III-E
                          V-B 1
Tieuel, Robert C.   III-A 5
Tildsley, Alfred.   I-E 1 s
Tillman, James A.   V-A
Tilmon, Levin.   III-A 4
Tilsley, George E.   I-E 1 j
Tilson, Everett.   III-E
                          IV-A 1
Tilton, Theodore.   II-D 3
Tindley, Charles A.   III-A 4
                          III-C 1 a
Tinker, E. L.   III-A 1 b iv
Tinker, Reuben.   II-D 7
Tinney, James S.   III-A 1 a v
                          V-B 2
Tobias, Channing H.   III-A 3
Tolbert, Horace.   III-A 1 a i
Tolles, Frederick B.   IV-A 5
Tolton, Augustus.   III-A 4
Toomer, Jean.   III-A 4
Tottress, Richard E.   III-D
Towne, Anthony.   IV-A 1
Townsend, Vince M.   III-A 1 a i
Tracy, Joseph.   II-F
Travers-Ball, I.   III-D
Trawick, Arcadius   III-A 3
Trawick, Arch.   III-A 3
Trawick, M.   III-D
Trent, William J.   III-A 1 a viii
Trew, J. M.   II-B
Triandis, Harry C.   III-D
Trimingham, John S.   I-C
                          I-E 1 e
                          I-E 1 k
Trobisch, Walter A.   I-E 3 e
Trollope, Frances.   III-A 3
Tross, Joseph S. N.   III-A 4
Troxler, George.   II-F

Trudgian, Raymond.   V-D
Trueblood, Roy W.   V-B 1
Truly, Mary E.   I-E 3 a
Truman, George.   II-A
Truss, Matthew B.   III-A 4
Tucker, Frank C.   III-A 5
Tucker, John T.   I-E 1 q
Tucker, Joseph L.   III-C 1 h
Tucker, Sarah.   I-E 1 b
Tuhl, Curtis G.   III-D
Tupper, H. A.   III-A 1 a viii
                          III-C 1 k
Turner, Franklin D.   V-A
Turner, Harold W.   I-E 2
Turner, Henry M.   I-C
                          III-A 1 a i
                          III-A 3
                          III-A 4
Turner, Harold W.   I-E 2
Turner, W. W.   IV-B
Turner, Wallace.   III-A 5
Tyler, Alice.   II-D 1
Tyler, Edward R.   II-C
Tyler, Josiah.   I-E 1 r
Tyms, James D.   I-C
                          III-A 1 a vi
                          III-A 1 b iv
                          III-A 3
Tyng, Stephen H.   I-E 1 n
Tyson, Bryan.   II-D 1

Uchendu, Victor C.   I-E 1 b
Ullendorff, Edward.   I-C
Ulman, Joseph N.   IV-A 14
Ullman, V.   IV-C
Umunna, V. N.   I-C
Ungar, Andre.   IV-A 12
Usher, Roland G.   I-C

Vail, Stephen M.   II-C
                          II-D 1
Vail, T. H.   III-C 1 a
Valentine, F.   IV-A 1
Van Catledge, John.
                          III-A 1 a ii
Van der Linde, Jan M.   II-D 1
Vander Velde, Lewis B. II-D 7
Van der Post, Laurens. I-E 2
Vandervall, Randall B. III-A 4
Van Deusen, John G.   III-D
Van Dyke, Henry J.   II-D 1

Van Dyke, Henry J. (cont.)   II-F
Van Ness, Paul.   V-A
Varick, James.   III-A 4
Varney, Peter D.   I-E 3 a
Vass, Samuel N.   III-A 1 a viii
Vassall, William F.   I-E 1 r
Vaughan, Edward T.   I-E 1 r
Vaughn, C. C.   III-A 4
Veal, Frank R.   II-D 1
Veenstra, Johanna.   I-E 1 b
Velde, H. T.   I-A
Verger, Pierre.   I-C
Vernier, Charles.   I-E 1 r
Vernon, B. J.   I-C
Vernon, Robert.   III-A 2 b
Vernon, Walter N.   III-A 5
Vibert, Faith.   II-B
Victor, Osmund.   I-E 1 s
Vincent, A. B.   III-A 1 a viii
Vincent, John.   V-B 1
Visser't Hooft, Willem A.   IV-D
Vivian, C. T.   V-B 1
                                 V-E
Von Hoffman, Carl.   I-E 1 l
Vorspan, Albert.   V-C
                                IV-A 12
                                 V-B 3
Vries, Egbert de.   III-C 2 d

Waddell, Hope M.   I-E 1 b
Wadlow, Rene.   I-E 3 e
Waid, W. L.   IV-A 6
Wainwright, L.   IV-B
Wakely, Joseph B.   III-A 5
Wakin, E.   V-B 1
Waldmeier, Theophilus.   I-E 1 k
Waldraven, Robert U.   III-D
Walker, Andre R.   I-C
Walker, C. T.   III-A 3
Walker, E. J.   IV-A 6
Walker, Frank D.   I-E 1 b
                             I-E 1 r
                                II-A
Walker, George G.   III-A 3
                             III-A 5
Walker, Harry J.   III-A 3
Walker, James G.   III-C 1 q
Walker, Lucius.   V-A
                                 V-B 2
Walker, R. H.   I-E 3 b
Walker, Samuel A.   I-E 1 r
Walker, T. C.   III-A 1 a viii

Wall, Martha.   I-E 1 r
Wallace, Archer.   I-E 1 r
Wallace, Cyrus W.   II-D 1
Wallace, David M.   IV-A 4
Wallace, Helen K.   IV-C
Wallace, Jesse T.   II-G
Wallace, S. B.   III-A 1 a iii
Wallace, W. J. L.   V-B 1
Wallbridge, Edwin A.   I-E 1 r
Wallis, John P. R.   I-E 1 l
Walls, A. F.   I-E 2
Walls, William J.   III-A 4
                           III-A 1 a ii
                             III-A 3
                             III-A 4
Walters, Alexander.   III-A 4
Walton, O. M.   III-A 1 a ii
Waltz, Alan K.   III-A 3
Wamble, G. Hugh.   III-D
Wambutda, Daniel N.   I-E 1 r
Warburton, Mabel C.   I-E 1 j
Ward, A.   I-E 1 r
Ward, Gertrude.   I-E 1 r
Ward, Henry D.   II-D 8
Ward, Hiley H.   V-B 1
Ward, James W.   II-C
Ward, Jonathan.   II-C
Ward, Samuel.   II-F
Ward, Samuel R.   III-A 4
Ward, Thomas P.   III-A 4
Ward, William J.   I-E 1 b
Warder, V. G.   IV-A 1
Warfield, B. B.   II-G
Warmelo, N. J.   I-C
Warner, Andrew J.   III-A 4
Warner, W. Lloyd.   III-D
Warnock, Henry Y.   IV-A 6
Warren, Ebenezer W.   II-C
Warren, Edwin R.   II-D 1
Warren, Robert P.   III-D
Wartgker, H.   III-A 2 a
Washington, Betty.   V-A
Washington, Booker T.   III-A 3
Washington, Curtis.   III-C 1 b
Washington, Joseph R.   III-A 3
                             III-A 4
                                 V-B 1
Washington, L. Barnwell.
                                II-D 1
Washington, R. Francis.
                           III-A 1 a i
Waterbury, Maria.   II-G
Waterman, Kenneth S.   V-A

Waters, James O.   III-C 1 f
Watkin, E.   V-B 1
Watkins, Richard H.   II-D 12
Watson, A.   I-C
Watson, Andrew P.   III-A 2 c
Watson, Bill.   V-E
Watson, Edgar B.   III-A 4
Watson, Frank D.   II-D 5
Watson, J. J.   III-A 3
                          III-C 2 a
Watson, James J.   III-A 3
Watson, Richard.   II-A
Watt, Rachel S.   I-E 1 r
Watts, Leon W.   V-B 4
Waugh, E.   II-H
Wayman, Alexander W.
                          III-A 1 a i
Weatherford, Allen E.   III-A 3
Weatherford, Willis D.
                          III-A 1 a viii
                          III-A 3
                          III-C 1 a
                          III-C 2 a
                          III-D
Weaver, Galen R.   III-C 1 a
                          III-C 1 c
                          IV-A 1
                          IV-A 3
Weaver, Robert C. III-A 1 a viii
                          III-D
Webb, James M.   II-C
Webb, Maurice.   IV-A 1
Webber, W.   III-A 3
Webster, Allan N.   I-E 1 r
Webster, Hutton.   I-C
Webster, James B.   I-E 1 b
Webster, Sherman N.
                          III-A 1 a viii
Weeks, Annie F.   I-E 1 b
Weeks, John H.   I-C
                          I-E 1 j
                          II-D 5
Weimer, G. Cecil.   III-E
Weisenburger, Francis P.
                          III-A 3
Weiss, H.   II-A
Weiss, John.   II-D 3
Weitfrecht, H. U.   I-E 1 r
Welbourn, Frederick B. I-E 1 d
                          I-E 2
Welch, F. G.   I-C
Welch, Galbraith.   I-C
Welch, James.   I-C

Weld, Theodore D.   II-C
Wells, Charles A.   V-B 3
Wells, Goldie R.   I-E 1 j
Welton, Michael R.   I-E 2
Welton, Michael.   I-C
Weman, Henry.   II-H
Wengatz, John C.   III-A 3
Wentzel, Fred D.   III-D
Wenzel, Tristen.   I-E 1 r
Wesley, Charles H.   II-H
                          III-A 1 a i
                          III-A 3
Wesley, John.   II-D 6
West, Anson.   III-A 5
West, C. S.   III-A 1 a viii
West, E. Courtenay. I-E 1 r
West, Robert F.   III-E
Westermann, Diedrich.   I-C
                          I-E 1 r
Westin, Alan R.   IV-A 1
Westink, D. E.   I-E 3 b
Weston, M. Moran. III-C 1 h
Whalen, William J.   III-D
Wharton, Vernon L.   III-A 3
Wheaton, N. S.   II-C
Wheeler, Benjamin F.
                          III-A 1 a ii
Wheeler, Lillian.   V-B 1
Whipple, Charles K.   II-D 1
                          II-D 3
                          II-D 6
                          II-F
Whipple, Henry B.   III-C 1 h
Whipple, Phila M.   III-C 1 k
Whitcomb, William C.   II-D 3
White, Amos J.   I-E 1 c
White, Andrew.   V-B 1
                          V-B 3
White, B.   II-C
White, Charles L.   III-C 1 k
White, Eugene W.
                          III-A 1 a viii
White, Frank.   III-D
White, Horace A.   III-A 3
White, J. T.   III-A 4
White, Newman.   II-H
White, Newman I.   II-A
                          II-H
White, P. J.   III-D
White, Paul H. H.   I-E 1 f
White, W. J.   III-A 4
White, W. L.   IV-A 1
White, William S.   II-C

White, Wm. S. (cont.)   II-D 7
                               III-A 5
White, William S.   III-A 4
White, Woodie W.   V-D
Whitehead, C. L.   III-A 5
Whiten, Bennie E.   V-B 3
Whiting, Albert N.   III-A 1 b iii
Whitman, A.   IV-A 1
Whitman, A. A.   III-A 4
Whitman, Frederick L.   V-E
Whitsett, Dan C.   III-D
Whitted, J.   III-A 1 a viii
Whittier, A. Gerald.   III-A 4
Whyte, Quintin.   I-E 1 c
Wicklein, John.   IV-A 1
Wigham, Eliza.   II-D 5
Wight, Willard E.   II-D 2
Wilberforce, Samuel.   II-D 8
Wilberforce, William.   II-A
Wilcox, W. D.   I-E 1 r
Wilder, George A.   I-E 1 c
Wiley, Bell I.   III-A 3
Wiley, Calvin H.   II-C
Wilkerson, James.   III-A 4
Wilkerson, Yolanda B.   II-C 2 a
Wilkins, R.   IV-A 6
Wilkinson, James G.   II-D 1
Wilkinson, James J. G.   II-D 1
Wilmore, Gayraud S.   V-B 1
                               V-B 2
Willey, Austin.   II-D 1
Williams, A. Cecil.   V-B 1
Williams, Alberta.   III-C 1 b
Williams, Alice E.   III-D
Williams, Chancellor.
                       III-A 1 b iv
                       III-A 1 b v
Williams, Daniel T.   III-A 2 b
Williams, Ethel L.   III-A 4
Williams, Florence D.   III-A 4
Williams, George W.   III-A 3
Williams, H. M.   III-A 4
Williams, Henry R.   III-A 4
Williams, Jim.   IV-B
Williams, John.   IV-B
Williams, John A.   IV-B
Williams, John G.   II-H
Williams, Joseph.   I-C
Williams, Kenny J.   III-A 3
Williams, Lacey K.   III-A 1 a vi
Williams, M. L.   II-H
                               III-B
Williams, Peter.   II-F

                               III-A 4
Williams, Preston N.   V-B 1
Williams, Robin M.   III-D
Williams, Thomas S.   II-D 1
Williams, W. B.   I-C
Williams, Thomas L.   II-D 6
Williams, Walter B.   I-E 1 o
Williamson, Jolt.   II-G
Williamson, Joseph C.   V-B 1
Willie, Charles V.   V-A
Willis, John J.   I-E 1 j
Williston, Seth.   II-C
Willoughby, W.   III-A 1 b v
Willoughby, William C.   I-C
Wills, G.   IV-B
Willson, Edmund B.   II-D 10
Wilmore, Gayraud S.   V-B 1
                               V-B 2 d
                               V-B 3
                               V-B 4
Wilson, Arthur.   III-C 1 h
Wilson, Christopher J. I-E 1 j
Wilson, Cody.   III-D
Wilson, Elizabeth L.   III-A 3
Wilson, Frank T.   I-E 1 r
                               III-D
                               V-B 1
Wilson, G. R.   II-B
Wilson, Jesse R.   I-E 1 j
Wilson, Monica.   I-C
Wilson, Robert L.   III-A 3
                               V-A
Wilson, Gold R.   III-A 3
Wilson, W. W.   III-C 1 f
Wiltgen, Ralph M.   I-E 1 a
Wine, S.   IV-C
Wingeier, Douglas E.   III-C 1 f
Winter, Gibson.   IV-A 1
                               V-A
Winton, G. B.   III-C 1 f
Wipper, Audrey.   I-C
Wise, Namon.   III-A 4
Wish, Harvey.   II-E
Wishlade, R. L.   I-E 1 t
Wisner, William C.   II-C
Witheridge, D.   V-B 1
Withington, Leonard.   II-D 3
Witt, Raymond H.   III-C 1 i
Wixom, Robert L.   IV-A 5
Wofford, H.   IV-A 1
Wogaman, H. Philip.   III-A 5
                               III-C 1 f
                               III-C 1 h

	V-B 3	Yates, Walter L.	III-A 3
Wojniak, Edward J.	III-C 1 b		III-A 4
Wolcott, Samuel T.	II-C	Yates, William.	III-A 4
	II-D 1	Yinger, J. Milton.	III-A 3
Wolfram, Walter A.	III-A 3	Yonker, Thomas W.	
Wood, John W.	III-A 4		III-A 1 a viii
Wood, Violet.	IV-C	Young, Andrew J.	III-D
Woodruff, James E. P.	V-B 1		IV-B
Woods, Frances J.	III-C 1 b	Young, John C.	II-C
Woodson, Carter G.	II-D 5	Young, Peter.	IV-B
	III-A 3	Young, Viola M.	III-A 3
	III-D	Younger, G. D.	V-A
Woodward, C. Vann.	III-C 1 l	Young-O'Brien, Albert H.	
	III-D		I-E 1 b
Woodward, Joseph H.	III-C 1 h	Yungblut, John.	IV-A 4
Woodworth, C.	I-E 1 r		
Woofter, Thomas J.	III-A 3		
Woolman, John.	II-C	Zanzibar, Frank.	I-E 3 e
	II-D 1	Zaugg, E. H.	III-E
	II-D 5	Zuener, R. W.	IV-C
Woolridge, Nancy B.	II-D 1	Zietlow, Carl P.	IV-A 1
Worksworth, J.	I-C	Zilversmit, Arthur.	II-D 5
Work, Frederick J.	II-H	Zinn, Howard.	IV-D
Work, Monroe N.	III-A 1 a viii	Zoa, Jean.	I-E 3 e
	III-A 3	Zulu, A. H.	I-E 3 c
Work, John W.	II-H	Zululand, Wilmot.	I-E 3 c
Wren, Christopher S.	V-B 1	Zwemer, Samuel M.	I-C
Wright, Charlotte.	I-E 1 c		I-E 1 r
Wright, Elizur.	II-G		
Wright, Henry C.	II-C		
	II-D 1		
Wright, James M.	III-A 3		
Wright, Jeremiah.	II-H		
Wright, Leon E.	V-B 1		
Wright, Nathan.	III-A 4		
	III-A 5		
	V-A		
	V-B 1		
	V-E		
Wright, Paul S.	IV-A 7		
Wright, Richard R.	III-A 1 a i		
	III-A 3		
	III-A 4		
Wright, Stephen J.	III-A 1 a viii		
Wrong, Margaret.	I-E 1 r		
Wyatt-Brown, Bertram.	III-D 3		
Wynn, Daniel W.	III-A 3		
	III-A 4		
Yahuda, Abraham S.	I-A		
Yancy, J.	III-A 1 a i		
Yard, James M.	III-D		